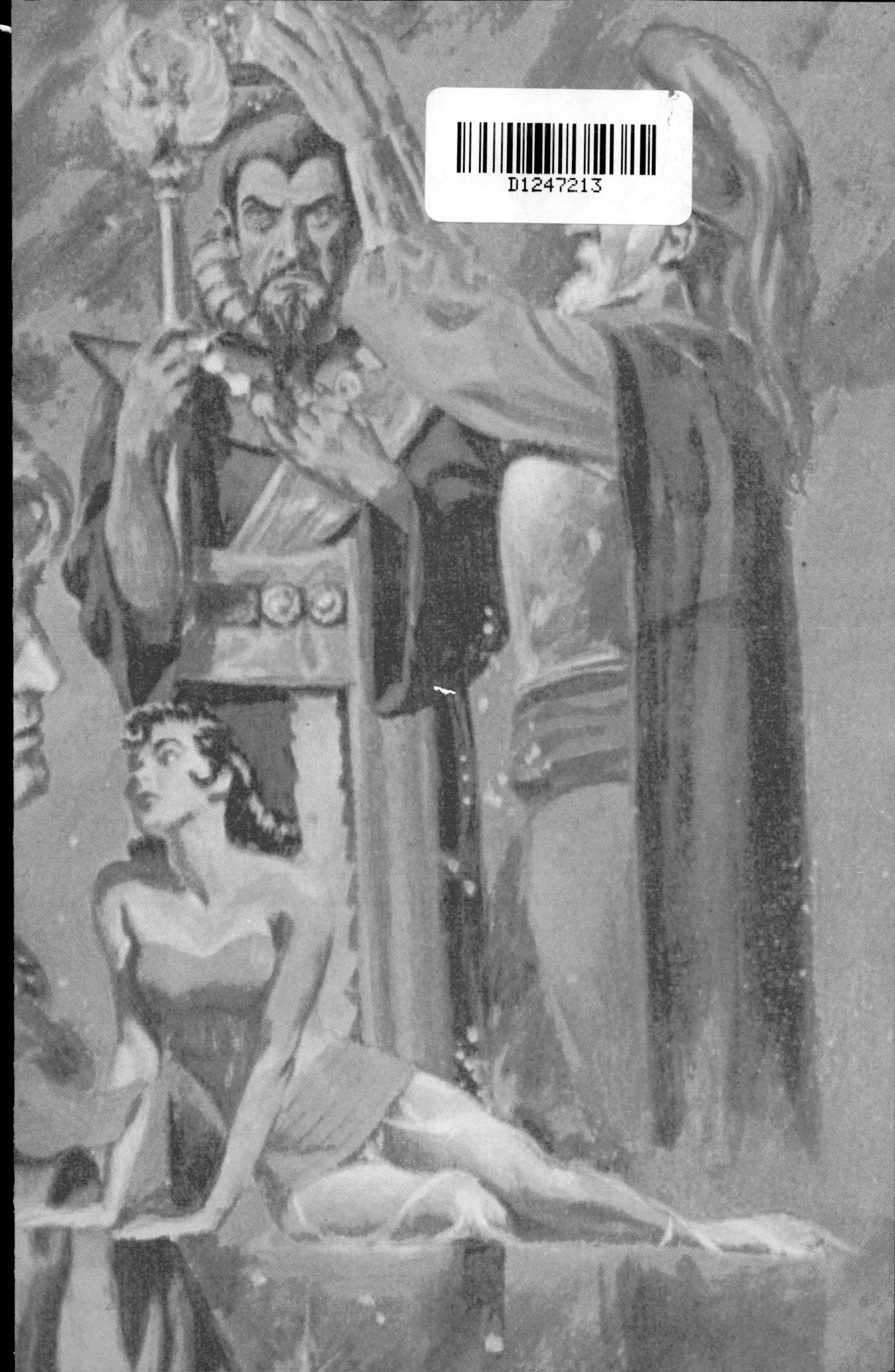

FLASH GORDON

FLASH GORDON

COMIC BOOK ARCHIVES

VOLUME 4

Written by

JOHN WARNER

and

GARY POOLE

Art by

CARLOS GARZÓN

and

FRANK BOLLE

Introduction by
ARTHUR LORTIE

DARK HORSE BOOKS®

Publisher – Mike Richardson
Collection Editor – [illegible]
Collection Designer – [illegible]
Art Director – Lia Ribacchi

Thanks to [illegible]

Published by Dark Horse Books
A division of Dark Horse Comics, Inc.
10956 SE Main Street
Milwaukie, OR 97222

DarkHorse.com

To find a comics shop in your area, call the Comic Shop Locator Service toll-free at (888) 266-4226

First edition: [illegible] 2011
ISBN 978-1-59582-717-3

1 3 5 7 9 10 8 6 4 2

This volume collects material from Flash Gordon [illegible], originally published from [illegible] by [illegible].

Printed by Midas Printing International, Ltd., [illegible] Province, China

Mike Richardson president and publisher · Neil Hankerson executive vice president · Tom Weddle chief financial officer · Randy Stradley vice president of publishing · Michael Martens vice president of book trade sales · Anita Nelson vice president of business affairs · Micha Hershman vice president of marketing · David Scroggy vice president of product development · Dale LaFountain vice president of information technology · Darlene Vogel senior director of print, design, and production · Ken Lizzi general counsel · Davey Estrada editorial director · Scott Allie senior managing editor · Chris Warner senior books editor · Diana Schutz executive editor · Cary Grazzini director of print and development · Lia Ribacchi art director · Cara Niece director of scheduling

TABLE OF CONTENTS

While all attempts have been made to restore proper attribution to the creators of these stories, we regret if any errors have been made. Please contact the publisher with any new information for correction in a subsequent volume.

These stories are a product of their time, and therefore certain elements may be out of step with present-day sensibilities. While such instances can be regrettable, the material presented here is unedited for historical accuracy.

A TRUE CREATIVE TEAM EFFORT:
FLASH GORDON CREATORS IN THE LATE 1970S

Though he was the single most important artist of the Flash Gordon projects, he was busy directing his talents at yet another Raymond creation, Secret Agent X-9 (retitled Secret Agent Corrigan), on the daily syndicated strip. So the writer/editors did the next best thing—they hired a Williamson assistant (and a fellow transplant from Bogotá) named Carlos Garzón, for the bulk of the Gold Key run.

Garzón would later team with Williamson on a comic-book adaptation of *Star Wars: Return of the Jedi* and other *Star Wars* projects. Though he had worked on *Secret Agent X-9* as early as 1966, he moved permanently to the US in 1974, finding work immediately on horror comics for Warren and with John Cullen Murphy on the syndicated strip *Big Ben Bolt*. At Gold Key, he first showed his versatility by working on the comic-book versions of Warner Bros. cartoon stars like Bugs Bunny and Daffy Duck.

Probably due to deadline issues, Gold Key staffer and illustrator Frank Bolle ably filled in for Garzón on the third and fourth issues of the Gold Key run. Bolle was a prolific artist, working on comic books during the early 1950s, when he drew stories for Magazine Enterprises. He was also ubiquitous, working on magazines, books, and comic strips as well. He even illustrated a number of science-fiction projects, including issue 23 of the *Flash Gordon* series in 1979 (ironically following Williamson's work there), and adaptations of John Christopher's *The Tripods* novels for the Boy Scouts of America magazine *Boys' Life*.

The importance of *Flash Gordon*—with scripts by Wood and others, art by Garzón and others—would continue after a transfer of the franchise and other Gold Key properties to its sister publisher, Whitman.

Arthur Lortie is a freelance researcher, specializing in science-fiction characters, themes, and creators. He was taught to read, at age three, from the daily Flash Gordon comic strip by his father, a fan of the character since its first appearance. He has assisted on Dark Horse's Mac Raboy's Flash Gordon books, a biography of Alex Raymond, writer Harry Harrison's bibliography, a collection of science-fiction curiosities, and much more.

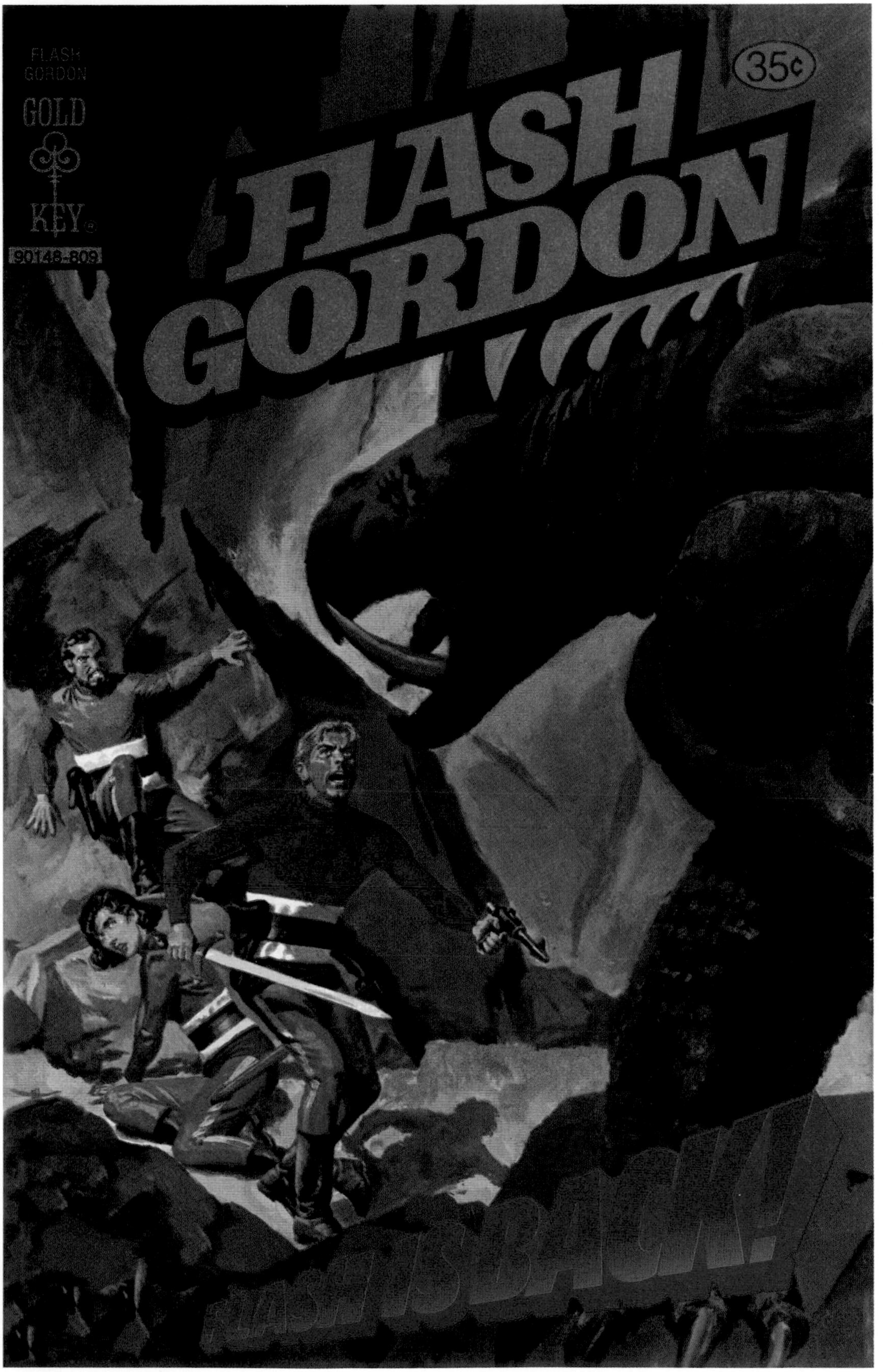
FLASH GORDON
GOLD KEY
90146-809
35¢
FLASH GORDON
FLASH IS BACK!

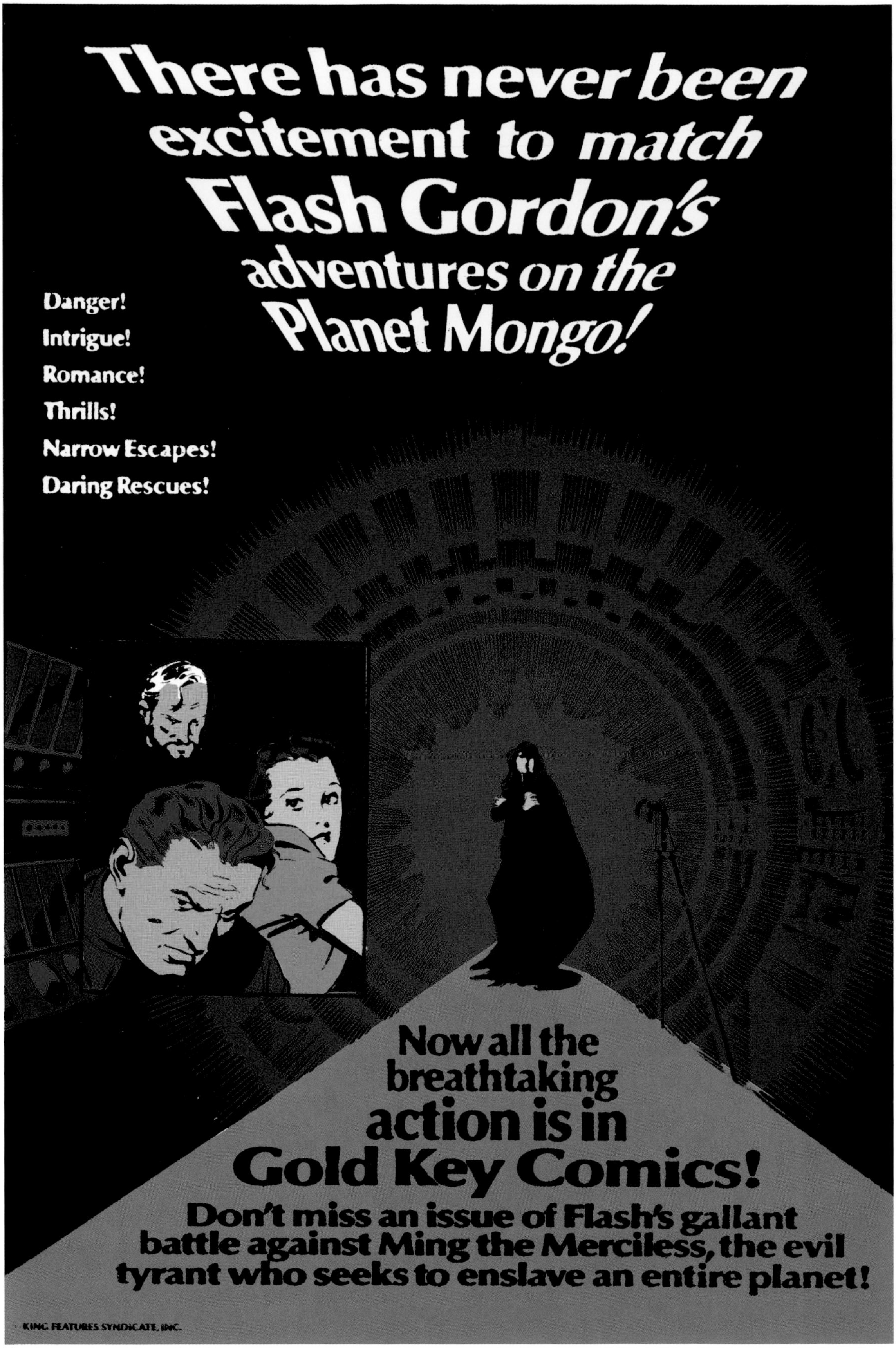
There has never been excitement to match Flash Gordon's adventures on the Planet Mongo!
Danger!
Intrigue!
Romance!
Thrills!
Narrow Escapes!
Daring Rescues!
Now all the breathtaking action is in Gold Key Comics!
Don't miss an issue of Flash's gallant battle against Ming the Merciless, the evil tyrant who seeks to enslave an entire planet!
KING FEATURES SYNDICATE, INC.

FLASH GORDON
RETURN TO MONGO

CREATED BY ALEX RAYMOND

SOMEWHERE IN OUR SOLAR SYSTEM, A SMALL STAR CRUISER ARCS GRACEFULLY INTO PLANET-FALL ON A WORLD CALLED MONGO!

ABOARD THE CRUISER ARE FLASH GORDON, DR. HANS ZARKOV AND DALE ARDEN! THREE YEARS BEFORE, THEY LEFT A MONGO UNITED IN PEACE!

THEY ARE ABOUT TO RETURN -- TO A NIGHTMARE!

WE SHOULD BE EXPECTED! I'VE BEEN BEAMING STRONG ELECTROMAGNETIC TRANS-MISSIONS FOR MOST OF OUR JOURNEY!

SEE IF KING BARIN HAS ANY COMMUNION CHANNELS OPEN, FLASH!

RIGHT!

TEXT: JOHN WARNER
ART. CARLOS GARZÓNR

90148 - B09
FLASH GORDON #19 - 787

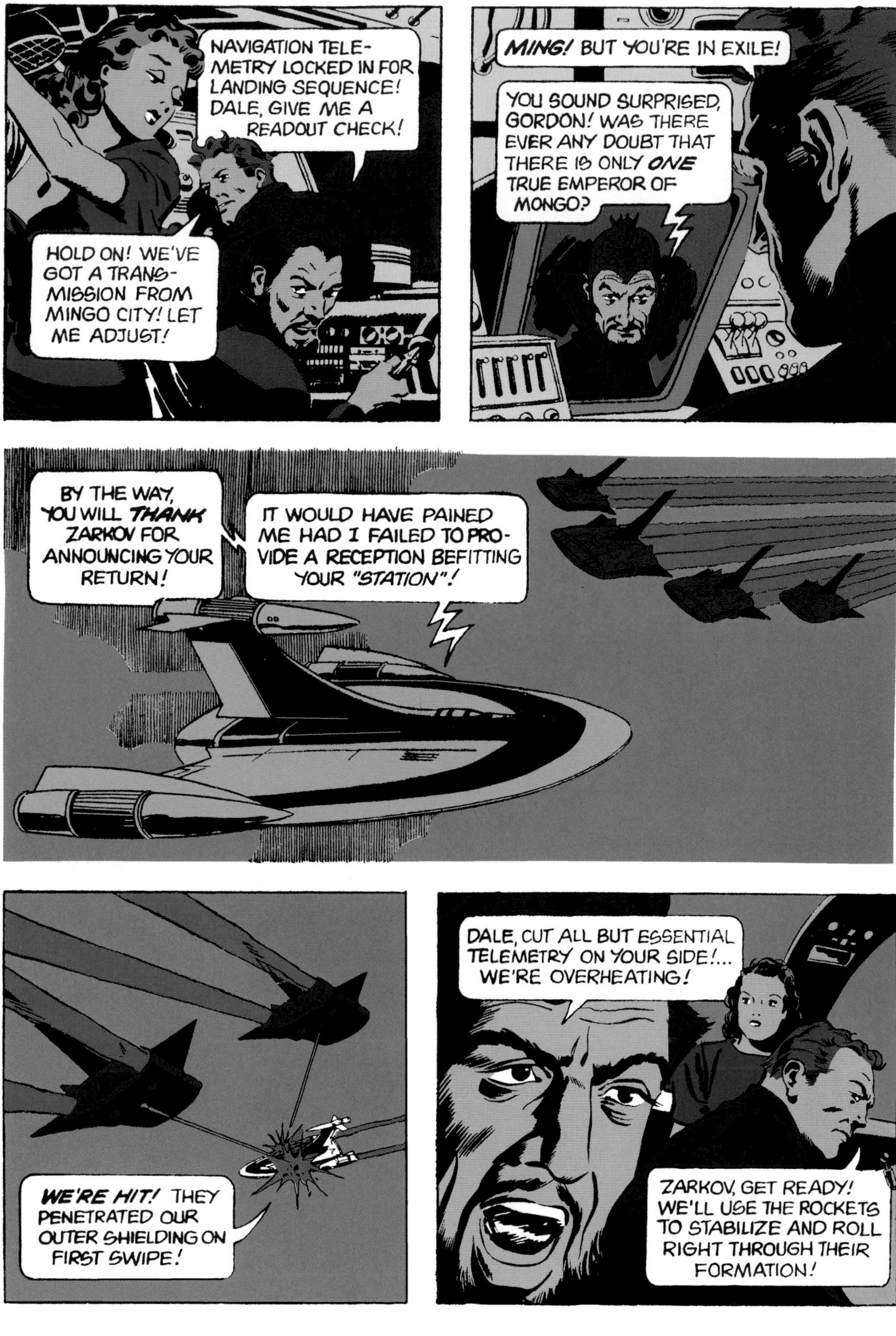
NAVIGATION TELEMETRY LOCKED IN FOR LANDING SEQUENCE! DALE, GIVE ME A READOUT CHECK!
HOLD ON! WE'VE GOT A TRANSMISSION FROM MINGO CITY! LET ME ADJUST!
MING! BUT YOU'RE IN EXILE!
YOU SOUND SURPRISED, GORDON! WAS THERE EVER ANY DOUBT THAT THERE IS ONLY ONE TRUE EMPEROR OF MONGO?
BY THE WAY, YOU WILL THANK ZARKOV FOR ANNOUNCING YOUR RETURN!
IT WOULD HAVE PAINED ME HAD I FAILED TO PROVIDE A RECEPTION BEFITTING YOUR "STATION"!
WE'RE HIT! THEY PENETRATED OUR OUTER SHIELDING ON FIRST SWIPE!
DALE, CUT ALL BUT ESSENTIAL TELEMETRY ON YOUR SIDE!... WE'RE OVERHEATING!
ZARKOV, GET READY! WE'LL USE THE ROCKETS TO STABILIZE AND ROLL RIGHT THROUGH THEIR FORMATION!

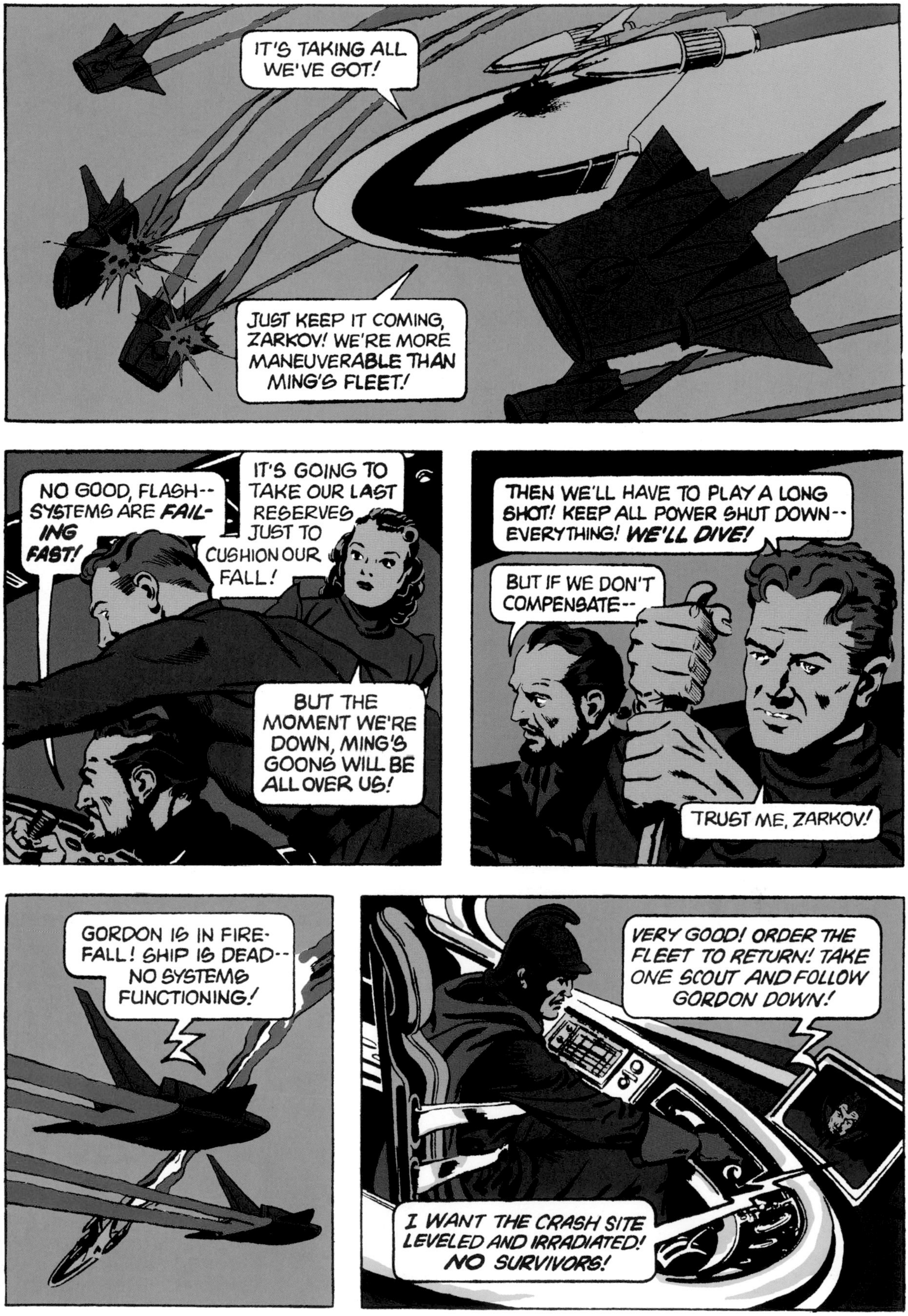
IT'S TAKING ALL WE'VE GOT!
JUST KEEP IT COMING, ZARKOV! WE'RE MORE MANEUVERABLE THAN MING'S FLEET!
NO GOOD, FLASH-- SYSTEMS ARE FAIL-ING FAST!
IT'S GOING TO TAKE OUR LAST RESERVES JUST TO CUSHION OUR FALL!
BUT THE MOMENT WE'RE DOWN, MING'S GOONS WILL BE ALL OVER US!
THEN WE'LL HAVE TO PLAY A LONG SHOT! KEEP ALL POWER SHUT DOWN-- EVERYTHING! WE'LL DIVE!
BUT IF WE DON'T COMPENSATE--
TRUST ME, ZARKOV!
GORDON IS IN FIRE-FALL! SHIP IS DEAD-- NO SYSTEMS FUNCTIONING!
VERY GOOD! ORDER THE FLEET TO RETURN! TAKE ONE SCOUT AND FOLLOW GORDON DOWN!
I WANT THE CRASH SITE LEVELED AND IRRADIATED! NO SURVIVORS!

YOU WERE RIGHT, FLASH! MING WAS TAKEN IN! HE'S LEFT ONLY TWO SCOUTS TO FOLLOW US DOWN!

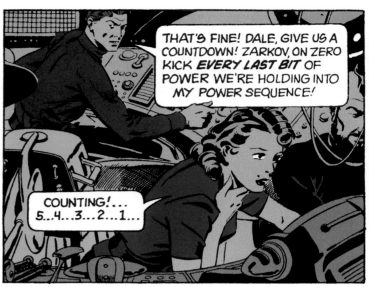

THAT'S FINE! DALE, GIVE US A COUNTDOWN! ZARKOV, ON ZERO KICK *EVERY LAST BIT* OF POWER WE'RE HOLDING INTO MY POWER SEQUENCE!

COUNTING!... 5...4...3...2...1...

...NOW!

YOU'VE GOT IT, FLASH-- BUT NOT MUCH! TWO MINUTES OF FUNCTION INTENSITY AT MOST!

IT'LL DO, ZARKOV-- AND MING'S GOING TO GET IT ALL!

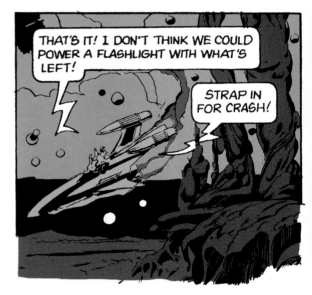

THAT'S IT! I DON'T THINK WE COULD POWER A FLASHLIGHT WITH WHAT'S LEFT!

STRAP IN FOR CRASH!

SHREEEEK!

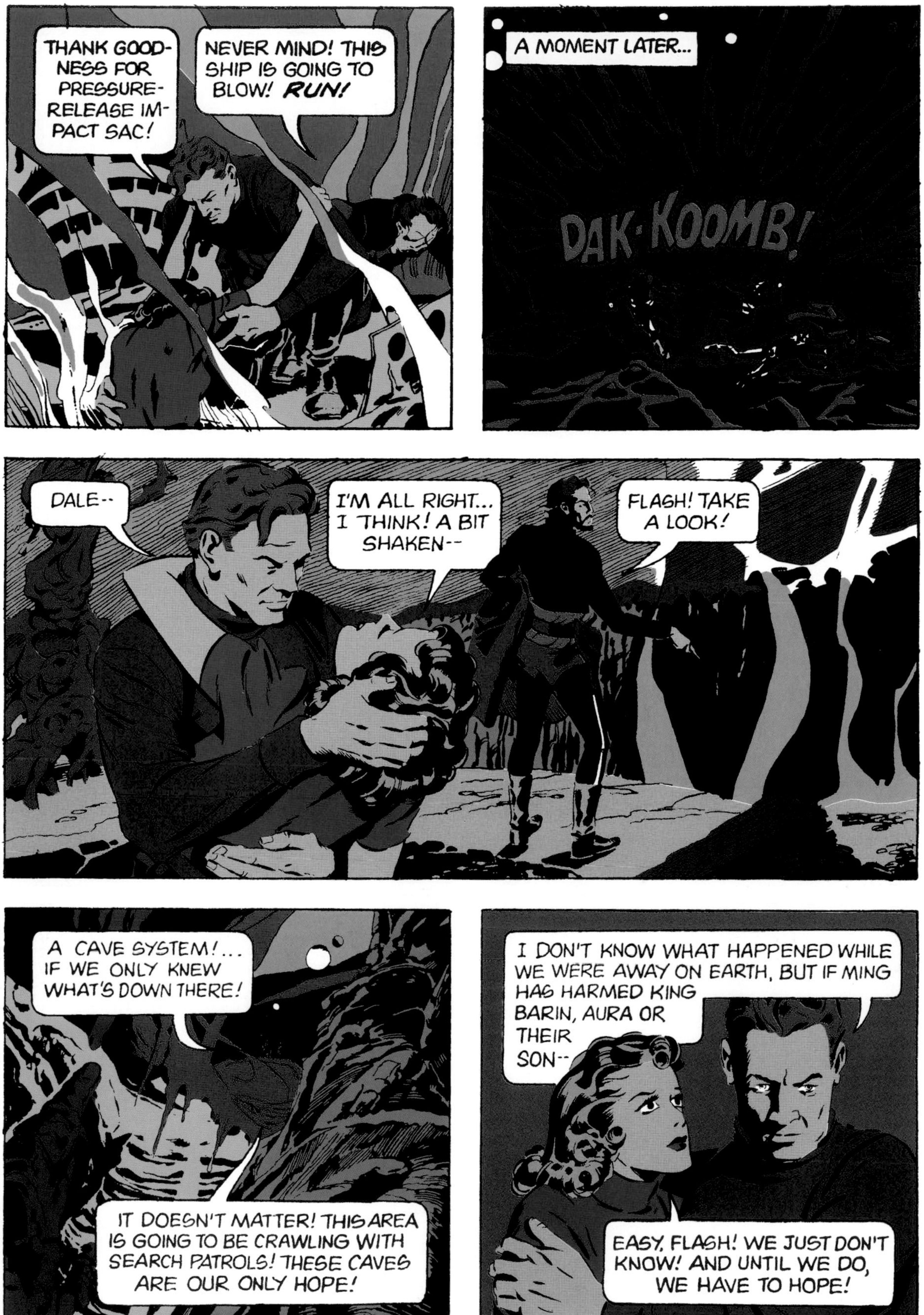
THANK GOODNESS FOR PRESSURE-RELEASE IMPACT SAC!
NEVER MIND! THIS SHIP IS GOING TO BLOW! RUN!
A MOMENT LATER...
DAK-KOOMB!
DALE--
I'M ALL RIGHT... I THINK! A BIT SHAKEN--
FLASH! TAKE A LOOK!
A CAVE SYSTEM!... IF WE ONLY KNEW WHAT'S DOWN THERE!
IT DOESN'T MATTER! THIS AREA IS GOING TO BE CRAWLING WITH SEARCH PATROLS! THESE CAVES ARE OUR ONLY HOPE!
I DON'T KNOW WHAT HAPPENED WHILE WE WERE AWAY ON EARTH, BUT IF MING HAS HARMED KING BARIN, AURA OR THEIR SON--
EASY, FLASH! WE JUST DON'T KNOW! AND UNTIL WE DO, WE HAVE TO HOPE!

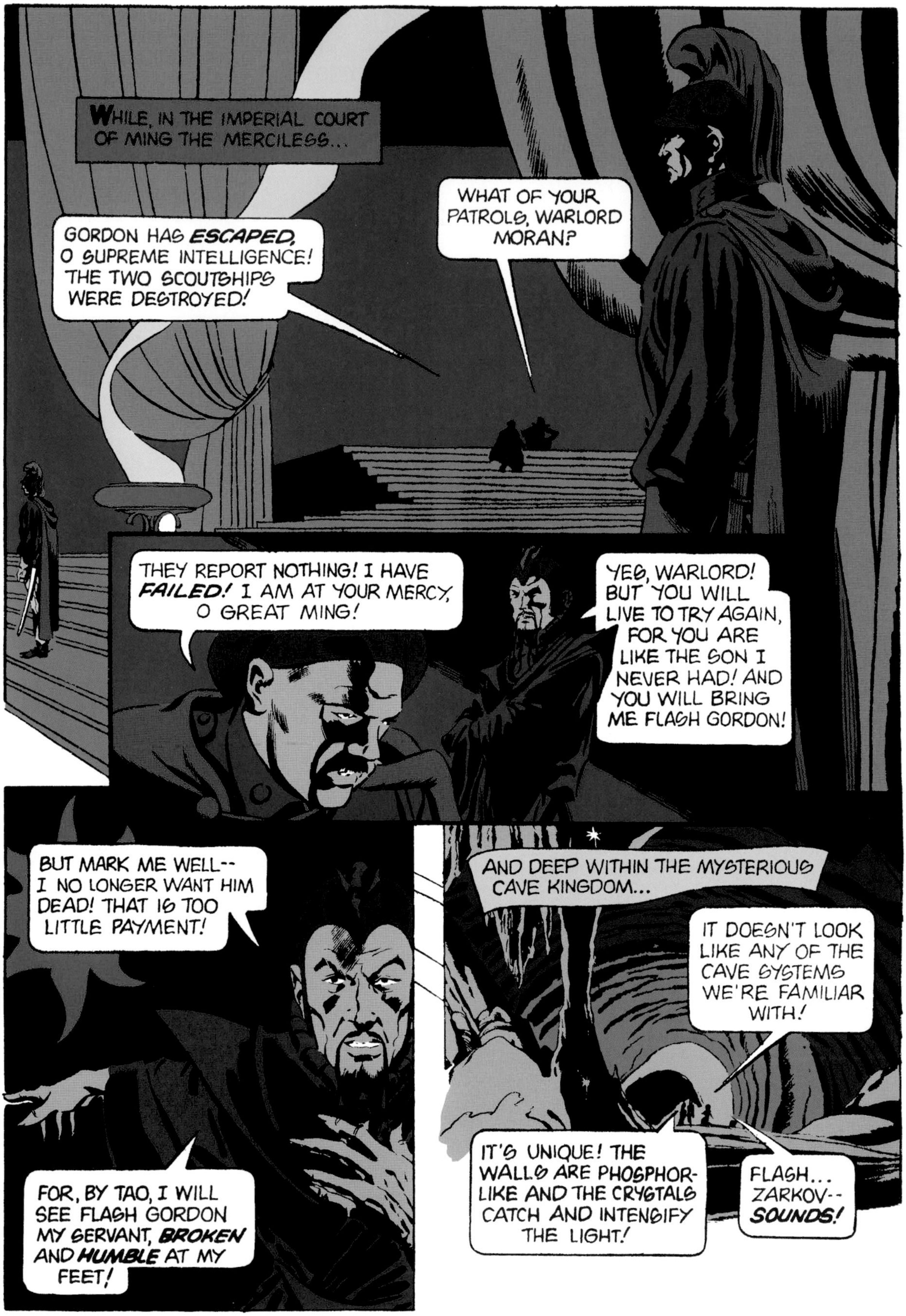
WHILE, IN THE IMPERIAL COURT OF MING THE MERCILESS...
GORDON HAS ESCAPED, O SUPREME INTELLIGENCE! THE TWO SCOUTSHIPS WERE DESTROYED!
WHAT OF YOUR PATROLS, WARLORD MORAN?
THEY REPORT NOTHING! I HAVE FAILED! I AM AT YOUR MERCY, O GREAT MING!
YES, WARLORD! BUT YOU WILL LIVE TO TRY AGAIN, FOR YOU ARE LIKE THE SON I NEVER HAD! AND YOU WILL BRING ME FLASH GORDON!
BUT MARK ME WELL-- I NO LONGER WANT HIM DEAD! THAT IS TOO LITTLE PAYMENT!
FOR, BY TAO, I WILL SEE FLASH GORDON MY SERVANT, BROKEN AND HUMBLE AT MY FEET!
AND DEEP WITHIN THE MYSTERIOUS CAVE KINGDOM...
IT DOESN'T LOOK LIKE ANY OF THE CAVE SYSTEMS WE'RE FAMILIAR WITH!
IT'S UNIQUE! THE WALLS ARE PHOSPHOR-LIKE AND THE CRYSTALS CATCH AND INTENSIFY THE LIGHT!
FLASH... ZARKOV-- SOUNDS!

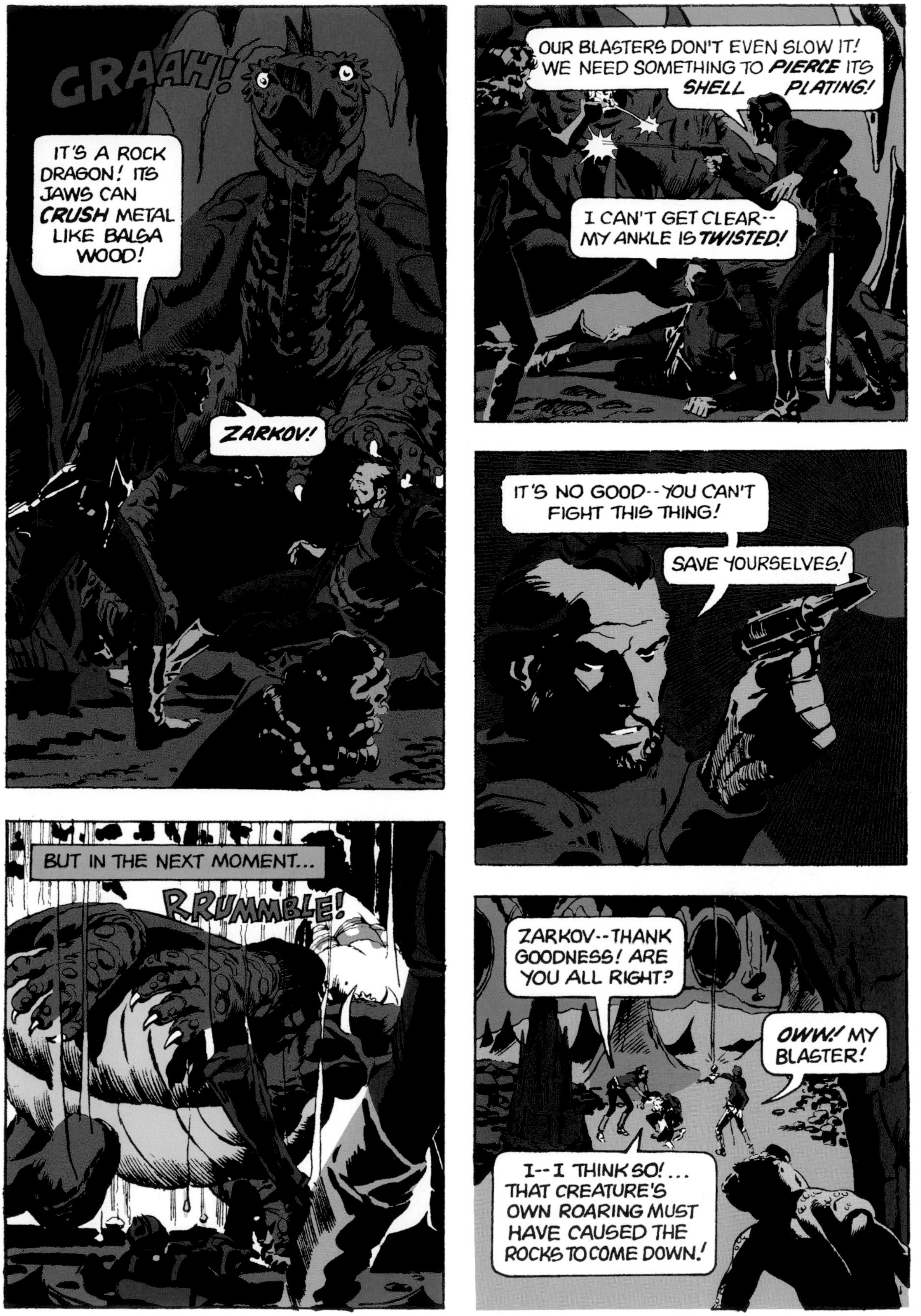

GRAAAH!
IT'S A ROCK DRAGON! ITS JAWS CAN CRUSH METAL LIKE BALSA WOOD!
ZARKOV!
OUR BLASTERS DON'T EVEN SLOW IT! WE NEED SOMETHING TO PIERCE ITS SHELL PLATING!
I CAN'T GET CLEAR-- MY ANKLE IS TWISTED!
IT'S NO GOOD--YOU CAN'T FIGHT THIS THING!
SAVE YOURSELVES!
BUT IN THE NEXT MOMENT...
RRUMMBLE!
ZARKOV--THANK GOODNESS! ARE YOU ALL RIGHT?
OWW! MY BLASTER!
I--I THINK SO!... THAT CREATURE'S OWN ROARING MUST HAVE CAUSED THE ROCKS TO COME DOWN!

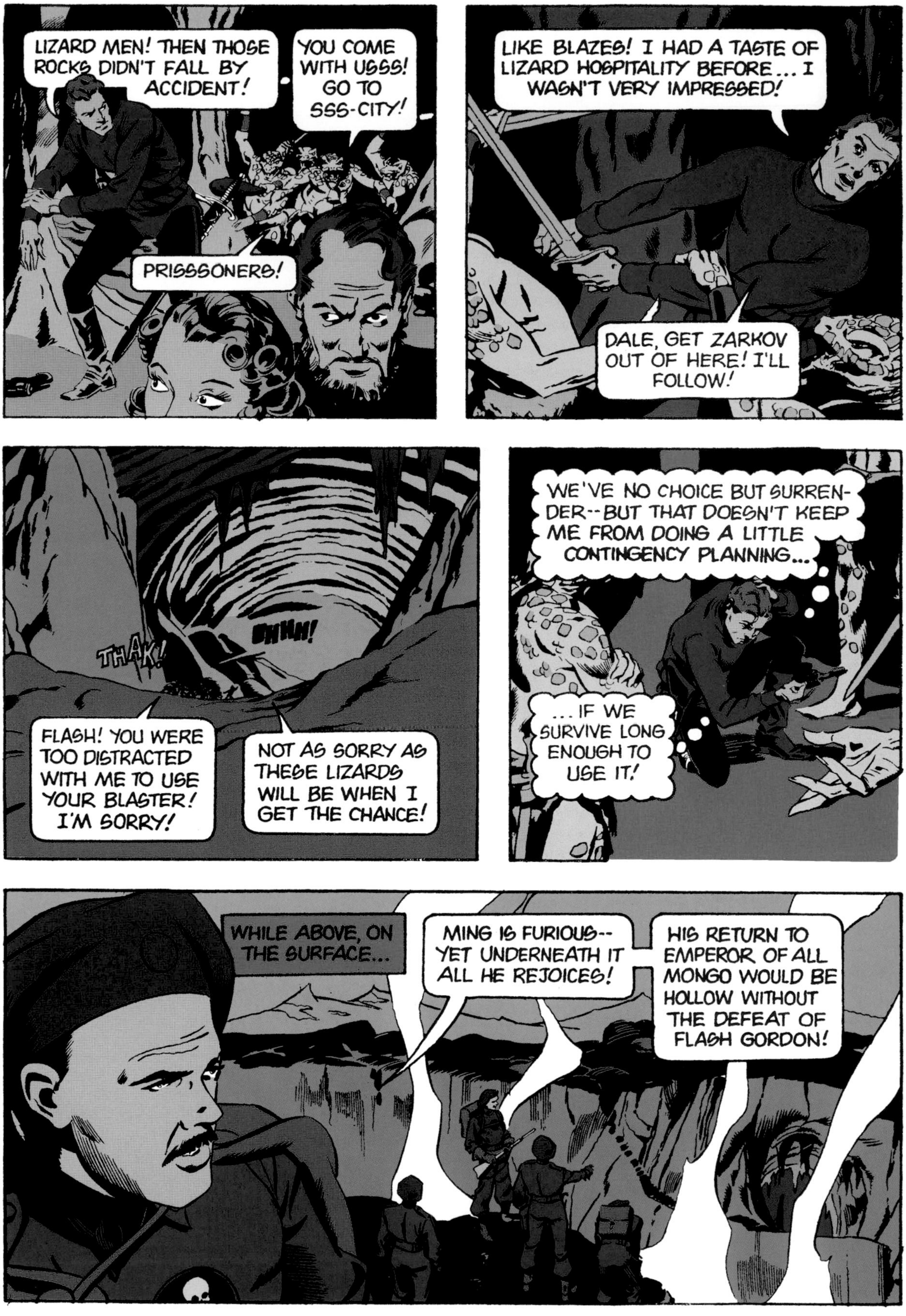
LIZARD MEN! THEN THOSE ROCKS DIDN'T FALL BY ACCIDENT!
YOU COME WITH USSS! GO TO SSS-CITY!
PRISSSONERS!
LIKE BLAZES! I HAD A TASTE OF LIZARD HOSPITALITY BEFORE... I WASN'T VERY IMPRESSED!
DALE, GET ZARKOV OUT OF HERE! I'LL FOLLOW!
THAK!
UHHH!
FLASH! YOU WERE TOO DISTRACTED WITH ME TO USE YOUR BLASTER! I'M SORRY!
NOT AS SORRY AS THESE LIZARDS WILL BE WHEN I GET THE CHANCE!
WE'VE NO CHOICE BUT SURRENDER--BUT THAT DOESN'T KEEP ME FROM DOING A LITTLE CONTINGENCY PLANNING...
...IF WE SURVIVE LONG ENOUGH TO USE IT!
WHILE ABOVE, ON THE SURFACE...
MING IS FURIOUS--YET UNDERNEATH IT ALL HE REJOICES!
HIS RETURN TO EMPEROR OF ALL MONGO WOULD BE HOLLOW WITHOUT THE DEFEAT OF FLASH GORDON!

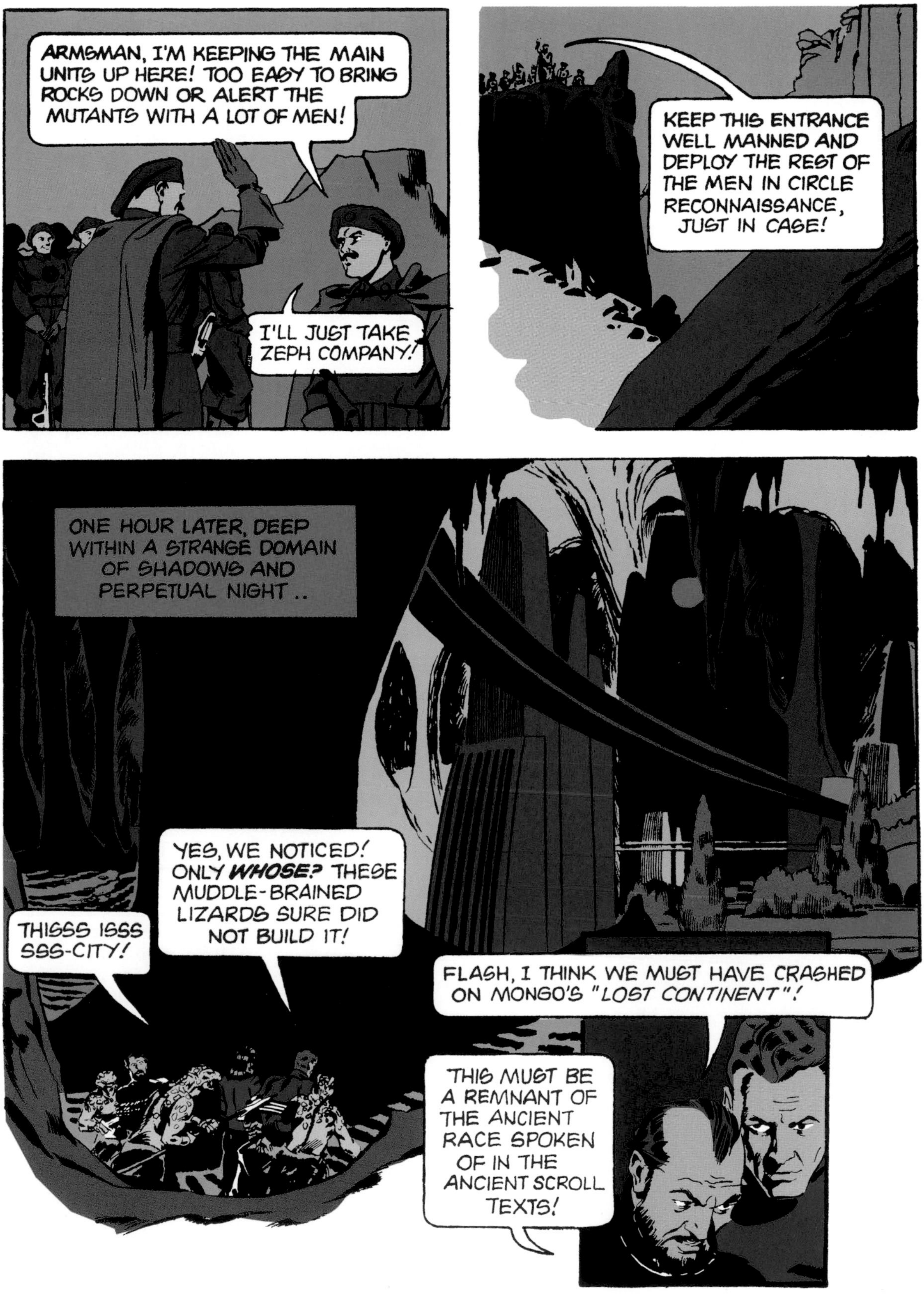
ARMSMAN, I'M KEEPING THE MAIN UNITS UP HERE! TOO EASY TO BRING ROCKS DOWN OR ALERT THE MUTANTS WITH A LOT OF MEN!
I'LL JUST TAKE ZEPH COMPANY!
KEEP THIS ENTRANCE WELL MANNED AND DEPLOY THE REST OF THE MEN IN CIRCLE RECONNAISSANCE, JUST IN CASE!
ONE HOUR LATER, DEEP WITHIN A STRANGE DOMAIN OF SHADOWS AND PERPETUAL NIGHT ..
THISSS ISSS SSS-CITY!
YES, WE NOTICED! ONLY *WHOSE?* THESE MUDDLE-BRAINED LIZARDS SURE DID NOT BUILD IT!
FLASH, I THINK WE MUST HAVE CRASHED ON MONGO'S "*LOST CONTINENT*"!
THIS MUST BE A REMNANT OF THE ANCIENT RACE SPOKEN OF IN THE ANCIENT SCROLL TEXTS!

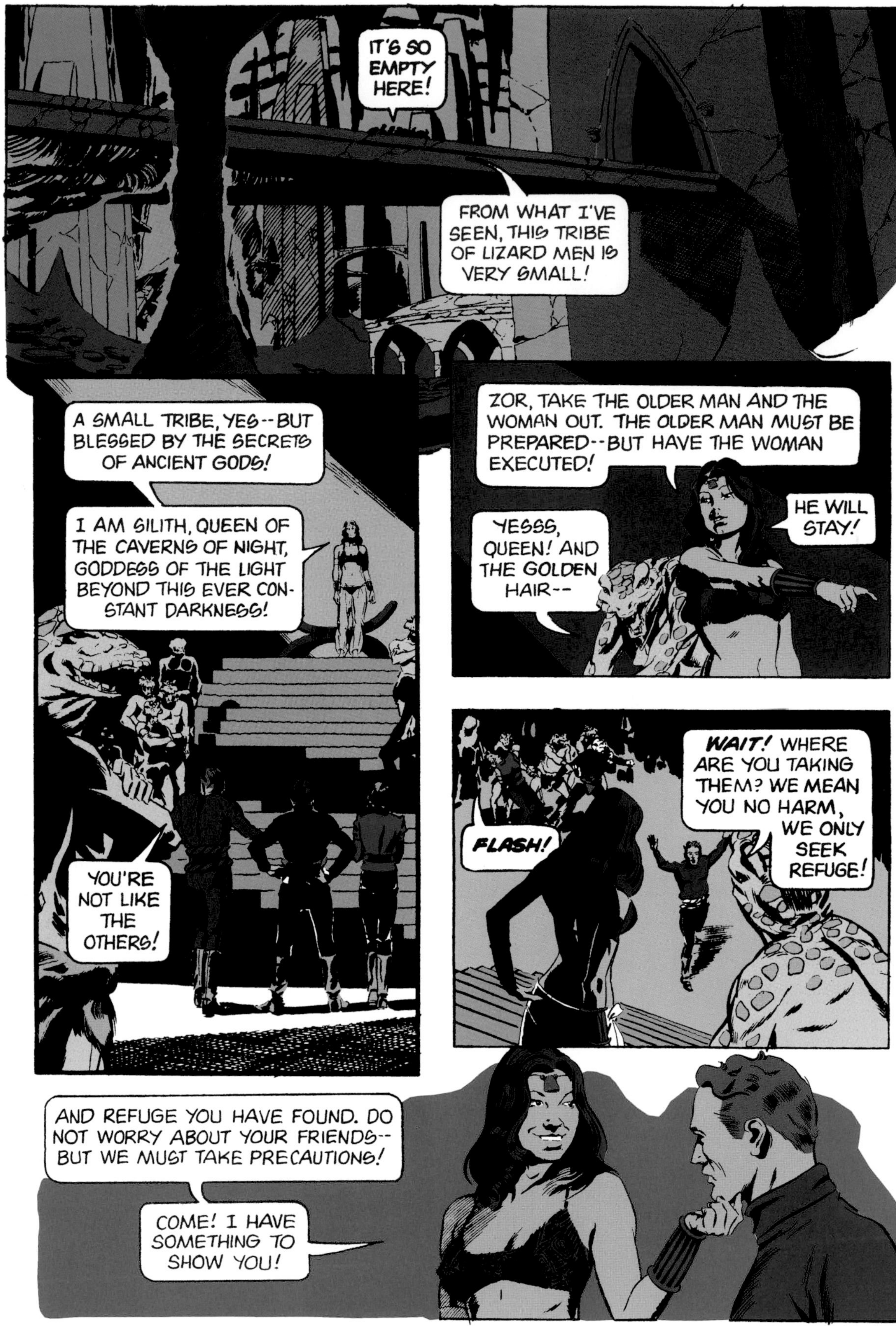
IT'S SO EMPTY HERE!
FROM WHAT I'VE SEEN, THIS TRIBE OF LIZARD MEN IS VERY SMALL!
A SMALL TRIBE, YES--BUT BLESSED BY THE SECRETS OF ANCIENT GODS!
I AM SILITH, QUEEN OF THE CAVERNS OF NIGHT, GODDESS OF THE LIGHT BEYOND THIS EVER CONSTANT DARKNESS!
YOU'RE NOT LIKE THE OTHERS!
ZOR, TAKE THE OLDER MAN AND THE WOMAN OUT. THE OLDER MAN MUST BE PREPARED--BUT HAVE THE WOMAN EXECUTED!
YESSS, QUEEN! AND THE GOLDEN HAIR--
HE WILL STAY!
FLASH!
WAIT! WHERE ARE YOU TAKING THEM? WE MEAN YOU NO HARM, WE ONLY SEEK REFUGE!
AND REFUGE YOU HAVE FOUND. DO NOT WORRY ABOUT YOUR FRIENDS--BUT WE MUST TAKE PRECAUTIONS!
COME! I HAVE SOMETHING TO SHOW YOU!

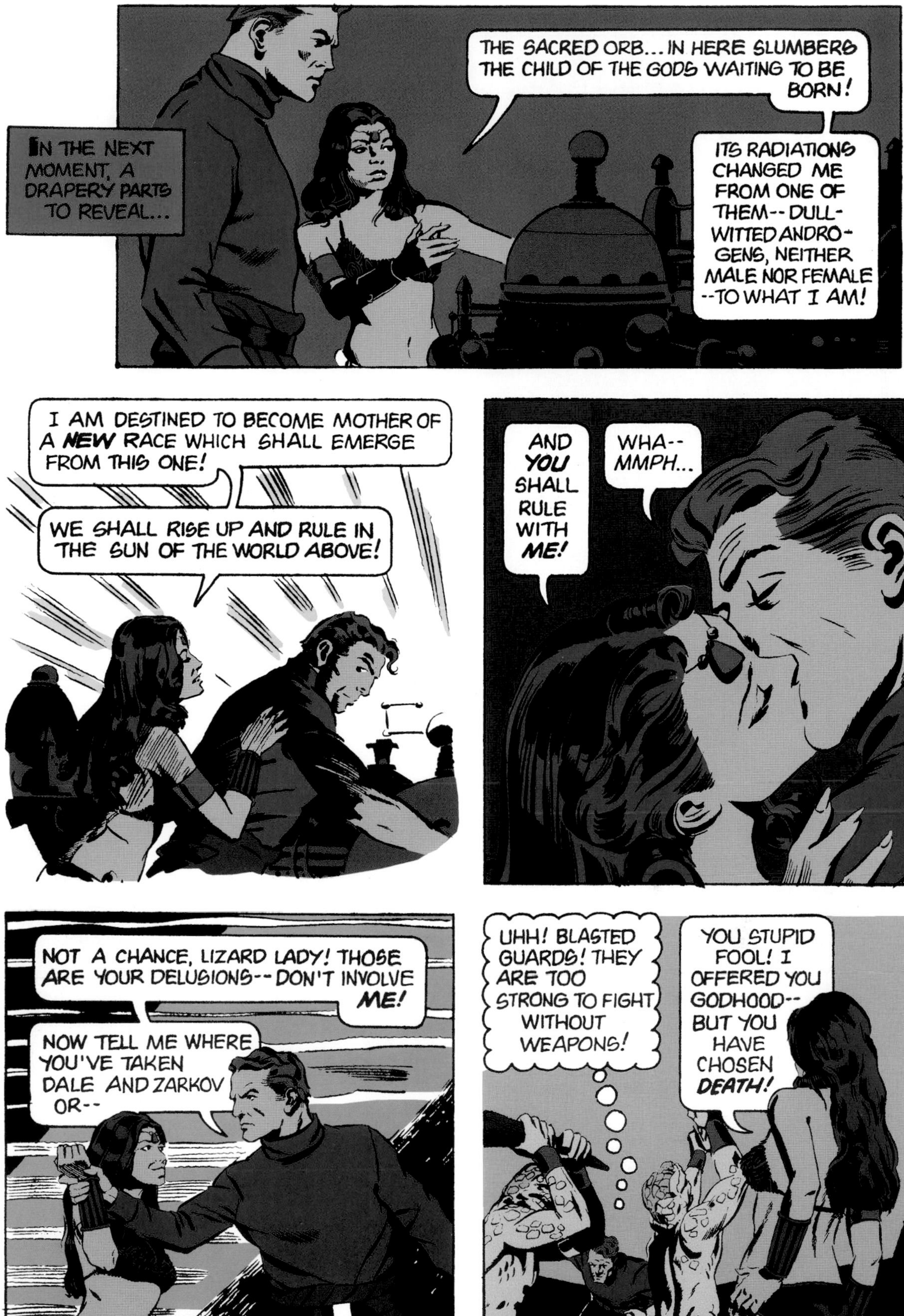
IN THE NEXT MOMENT, A DRAPERY PARTS TO REVEAL...
THE SACRED ORB... IN HERE SLUMBERS THE CHILD OF THE GODS WAITING TO BE BORN!
ITS RADIATIONS CHANGED ME FROM ONE OF THEM-- DULL-WITTED ANDRO-GENS, NEITHER MALE NOR FEMALE --TO WHAT I AM!
I AM DESTINED TO BECOME MOTHER OF A NEW RACE WHICH SHALL EMERGE FROM THIS ONE!
WE SHALL RISE UP AND RULE IN THE SUN OF THE WORLD ABOVE!
AND YOU SHALL RULE WITH ME!
WHA-- MMPH...
NOT A CHANCE, LIZARD LADY! THOSE ARE YOUR DELUSIONS-- DON'T INVOLVE ME!
NOW TELL ME WHERE YOU'VE TAKEN DALE AND ZARKOV OR--
UHH! BLASTED GUARDS! THEY ARE TOO STRONG TO FIGHT WITHOUT WEAPONS!
YOU STUPID FOOL! I OFFERED YOU GODHOOD-- BUT YOU HAVE CHOSEN DEATH!

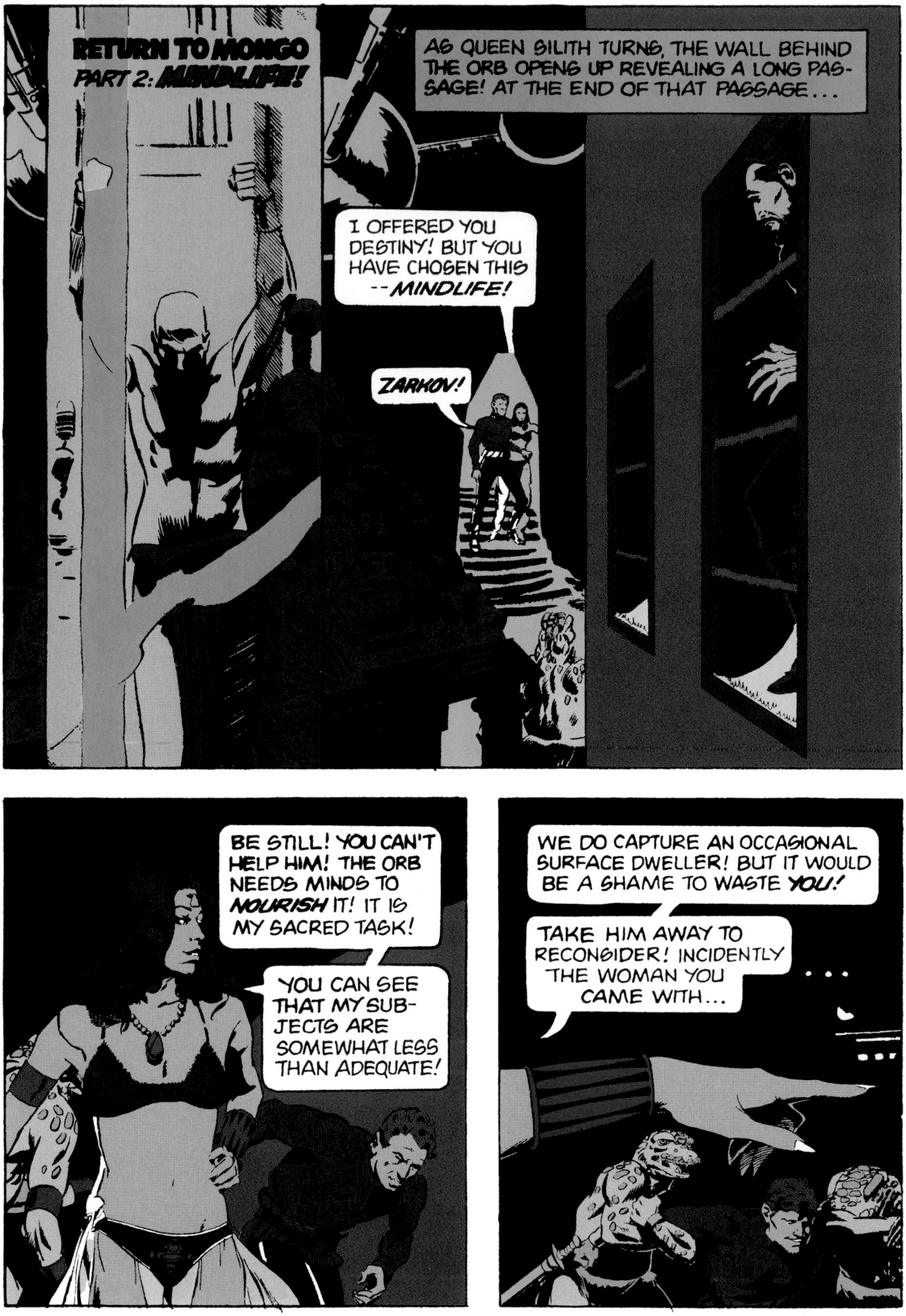
RETURN TO MONGO
PART 2: MINDLIFE!
AS QUEEN SILITH TURNS, THE WALL BEHIND THE ORB OPENS UP REVEALING A LONG PASSAGE! AT THE END OF THAT PASSAGE...
I OFFERED YOU DESTINY! BUT YOU HAVE CHOSEN THIS --MINDLIFE!
ZARKOV!
BE STILL! YOU CAN'T HELP HIM! THE ORB NEEDS MINDS TO NOURISH IT! IT IS MY SACRED TASK!
YOU CAN SEE THAT MY SUBJECTS ARE SOMEWHAT LESS THAN ADEQUATE!
WE DO CAPTURE AN OCCASIONAL SURFACE DWELLER! BUT IT WOULD BE A SHAME TO WASTE YOU!
TAKE HIM AWAY TO RECONSIDER! INCIDENTLY THE WOMAN YOU CAME WITH...

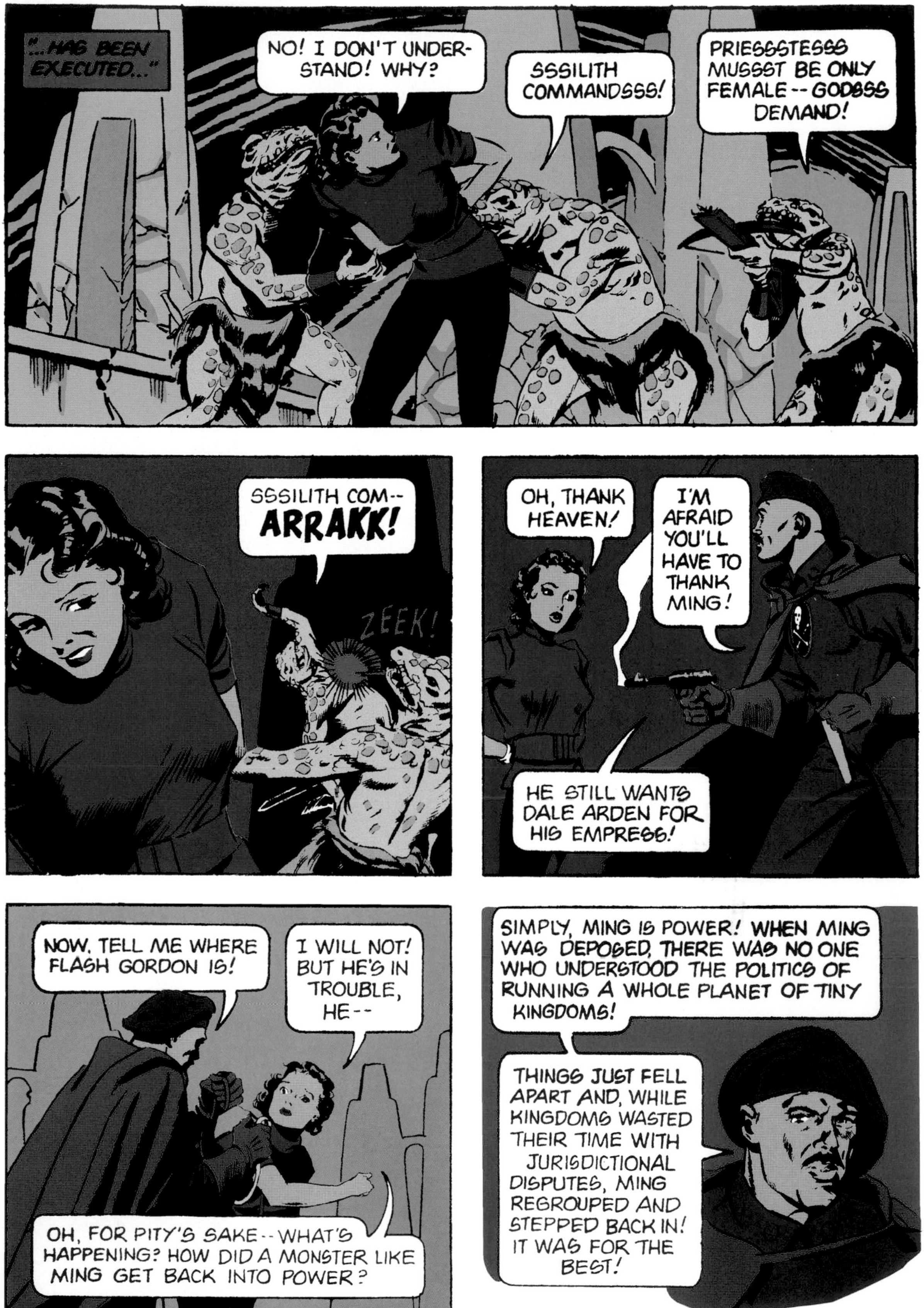
"...HAS BEEN EXECUTED..."
NO! I DON'T UNDER-STAND! WHY?
SSSILITH COMMANDSSS!
PRIESSSTESSS MUSSST BE ONLY FEMALE -- GODSSS DEMAND!
SSSILITH COM-- ARRAKK!
ZEEK!
OH, THANK HEAVEN!
I'M AFRAID YOU'LL HAVE TO THANK MING!
HE STILL WANTS DALE ARDEN FOR HIS EMPRESS!
NOW, TELL ME WHERE FLASH GORDON IS!
I WILL NOT! BUT HE'S IN TROUBLE, HE--
OH, FOR PITY'S SAKE--WHAT'S HAPPENING? HOW DID A MONSTER LIKE MING GET BACK INTO POWER?
SIMPLY, MING IS POWER! WHEN MING WAS DEPOSED, THERE WAS NO ONE WHO UNDERSTOOD THE POLITICS OF RUNNING A WHOLE PLANET OF TINY KINGDOMS!
THINGS JUST FELL APART AND, WHILE KINGDOMS WASTED THEIR TIME WITH JURISDICTIONAL DISPUTES, MING REGROUPED AND STEPPED BACK IN! IT WAS FOR THE BEST!

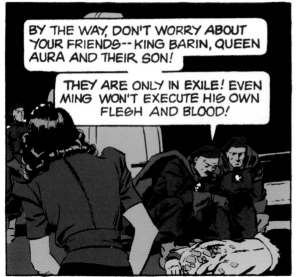

BY THE WAY, DON'T WORRY ABOUT YOUR FRIENDS--KING BARIN, QUEEN AURA AND THEIR SON!

THEY ARE ONLY IN EXILE! EVEN MING WON'T EXECUTE HIS OWN FLESH AND BLOOD!

BUT ENOUGH! YOU SAID GORDON WAS IN TROUBLE, WHICH I ASSUME TO MEAN WITH THESE SAME LIZARD MUTANTS!

LAR, KEEP WATCH ON HER! THE REST OF US WILL PRO-CEED SILENTLY!

WHILE ELSEWHERE, INSIDE THE CITY...

IF SILITH WASN'T BLUFFING AND DALE IS-- I WANT TO SCREAM...BUT I'VE GOT TO REMAIN CALM!

I'LL GET EVEN-- BELIEVE IT-- BUT FIRST I'VE GOT TO GET ZARKOV OUT OF HERE!

THIS OUGHT TO HELP!... IT'S THE POWER PACK TO MY BLASTER! I PALMED IT WHEN I SURRENDERED THE WEAPON!

NOW, IF I CAN JUST ACTIVATE...

...IT!

SKKRAAKK!

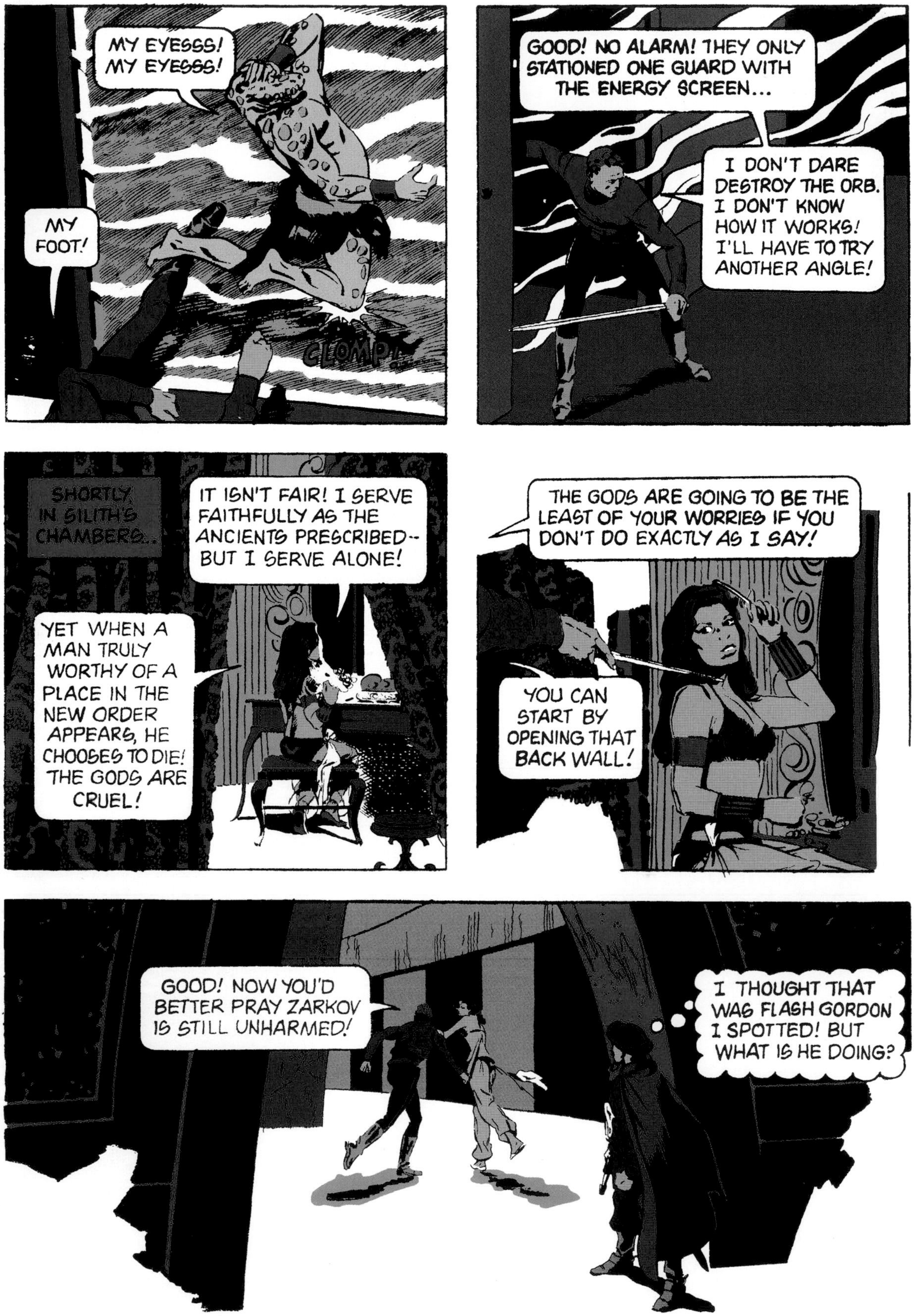
MY EYESSS! MY EYESSS!
MY FOOT!
CLOMP!
GOOD! NO ALARM! THEY ONLY STATIONED ONE GUARD WITH THE ENERGY SCREEN...
I DON'T DARE DESTROY THE ORB. I DON'T KNOW HOW IT WORKS! I'LL HAVE TO TRY ANOTHER ANGLE!
SHORTLY IN SILITH'S CHAMBERS...
IT ISN'T FAIR! I SERVE FAITHFULLY AS THE ANCIENTS PRESCRIBED-- BUT I SERVE ALONE!
YET WHEN A MAN TRULY WORTHY OF A PLACE IN THE NEW ORDER APPEARS, HE CHOOSES TO DIE! THE GODS ARE CRUEL!
THE GODS ARE GOING TO BE THE LEAST OF YOUR WORRIES IF YOU DON'T DO EXACTLY AS I SAY!
YOU CAN START BY OPENING THAT BACK WALL!
GOOD! NOW YOU'D BETTER PRAY ZARKOV IS STILL UNHARMED!
I THOUGHT THAT WAS FLASH GORDON I SPOTTED! BUT WHAT IS HE DOING?

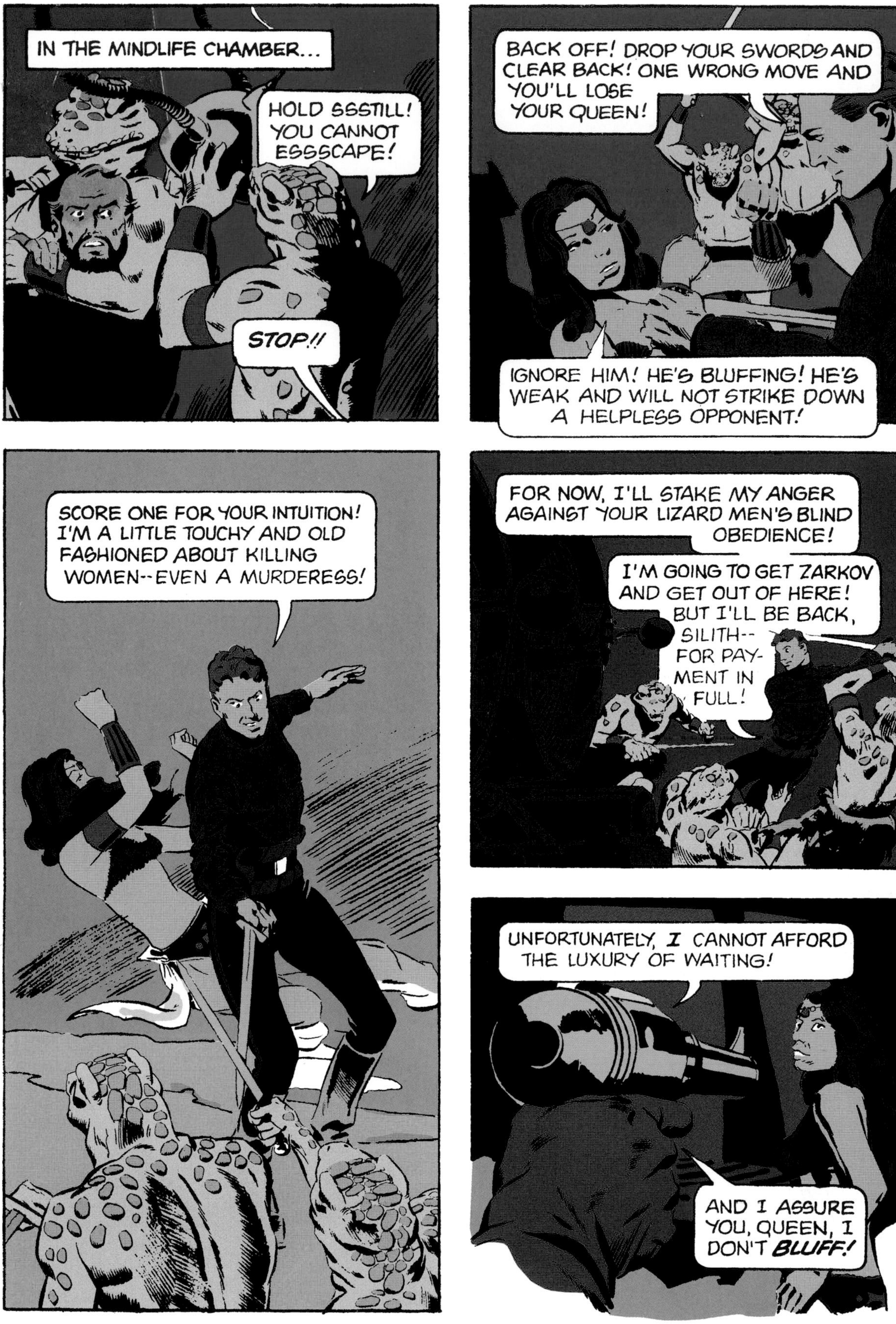
IN THE MINDLIFE CHAMBER...
HOLD SSSTILL! YOU CANNOT ESSSCAPE!
STOP!!
BACK OFF! DROP YOUR SWORDS AND CLEAR BACK! ONE WRONG MOVE AND YOU'LL LOSE YOUR QUEEN!
IGNORE HIM! HE'S BLUFFING! HE'S WEAK AND WILL NOT STRIKE DOWN A HELPLESS OPPONENT!
SCORE ONE FOR YOUR INTUITION! I'M A LITTLE TOUCHY AND OLD FASHIONED ABOUT KILLING WOMEN--EVEN A MURDERESS!
FOR NOW, I'LL STAKE MY ANGER AGAINST YOUR LIZARD MEN'S BLIND OBEDIENCE!
I'M GOING TO GET ZARKOV AND GET OUT OF HERE! BUT I'LL BE BACK, SILITH-- FOR PAYMENT IN FULL!
UNFORTUNATELY, I CANNOT AFFORD THE LUXURY OF WAITING!
AND I ASSURE YOU, QUEEN, I DON'T BLUFF!

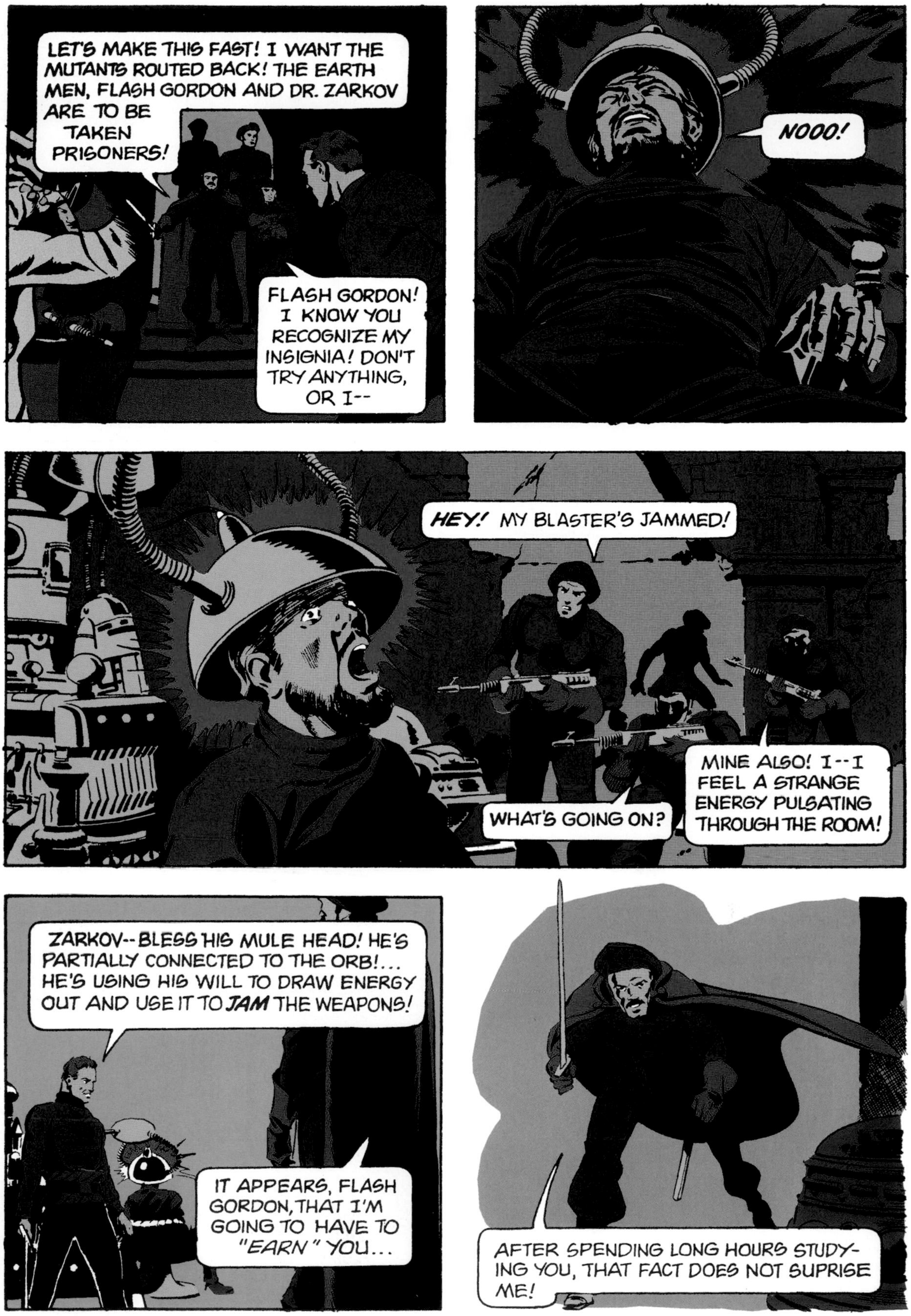
LET'S MAKE THIS FAST! I WANT THE MUTANTS ROUTED BACK! THE EARTH MEN, FLASH GORDON AND DR. ZARKOV ARE TO BE TAKEN PRISONERS!
FLASH GORDON! I KNOW YOU RECOGNIZE MY INSIGNIA! DON'T TRY ANYTHING, OR I--
NOOO!
HEY! MY BLASTER'S JAMMED!
WHAT'S GOING ON?
MINE ALSO! I--I FEEL A STRANGE ENERGY PULSATING THROUGH THE ROOM!
ZARKOV--BLESS HIS MULE HEAD! HE'S PARTIALLY CONNECTED TO THE ORB!... HE'S USING HIS WILL TO DRAW ENERGY OUT AND USE IT TO JAM THE WEAPONS!
IT APPEARS, FLASH GORDON, THAT I'M GOING TO HAVE TO "EARN" YOU...
AFTER SPENDING LONG HOURS STUDYING YOU, THAT FACT DOES NOT SUPRISE ME!

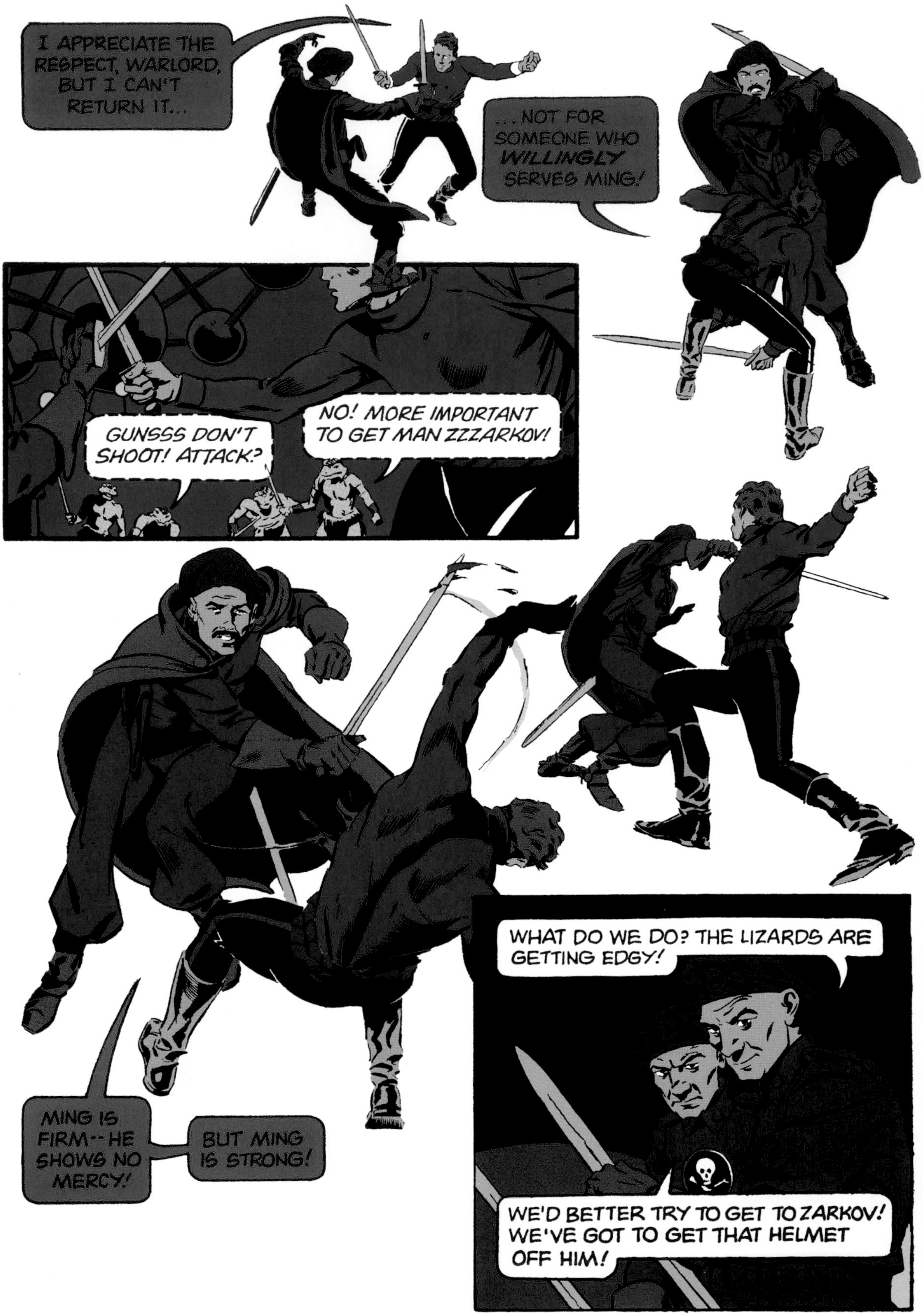
I APPRECIATE THE RESPECT, WARLORD, BUT I CAN'T RETURN IT...
...NOT FOR SOMEONE WHO WILLINGLY SERVES MING!
GUNSSS DON'T SHOOT! ATTACK?
NO! MORE IMPORTANT TO GET MAN ZZZARKOV!
MING IS FIRM--HE SHOWS NO MERCY!
BUT MING IS STRONG!
WHAT DO WE DO? THE LIZARDS ARE GETTING EDGY!
WE'D BETTER TRY TO GET TO ZARKOV! WE'VE GOT TO GET THAT HELMET OFF HIM!

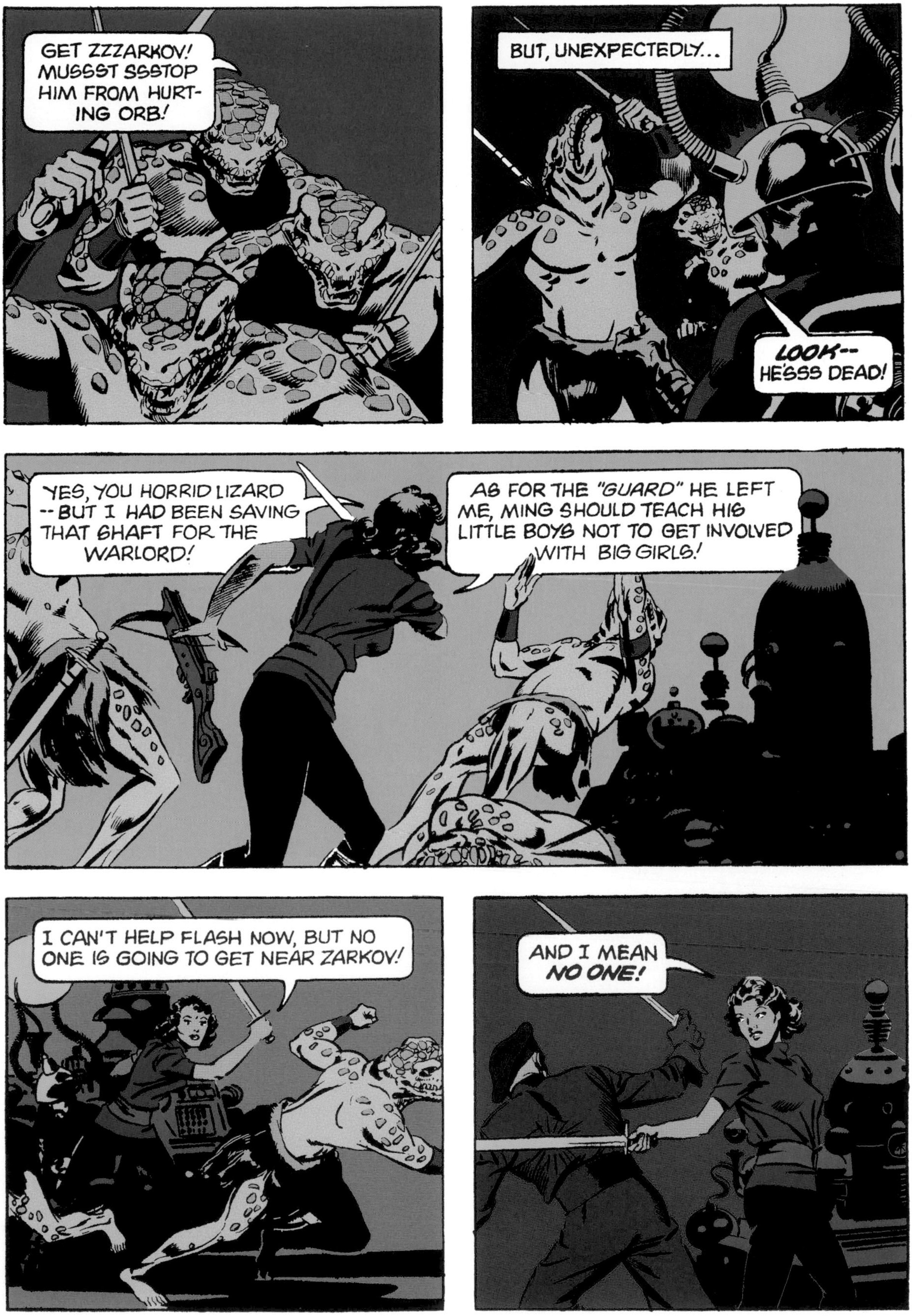
GET ZZZARKOV! MUSSST SSSTOP HIM FROM HURTING ORB!
BUT, UNEXPECTEDLY...
LOOK-- HE'SSS DEAD!
YES, YOU HORRID LIZARD --BUT I HAD BEEN SAVING THAT SHAFT FOR THE WARLORD!
AS FOR THE "GUARD" HE LEFT ME, MING SHOULD TEACH HIS LITTLE BOYS NOT TO GET INVOLVED WITH BIG GIRLS!
I CAN'T HELP FLASH NOW, BUT NO ONE IS GOING TO GET NEAR ZARKOV!
AND I MEAN NO ONE!

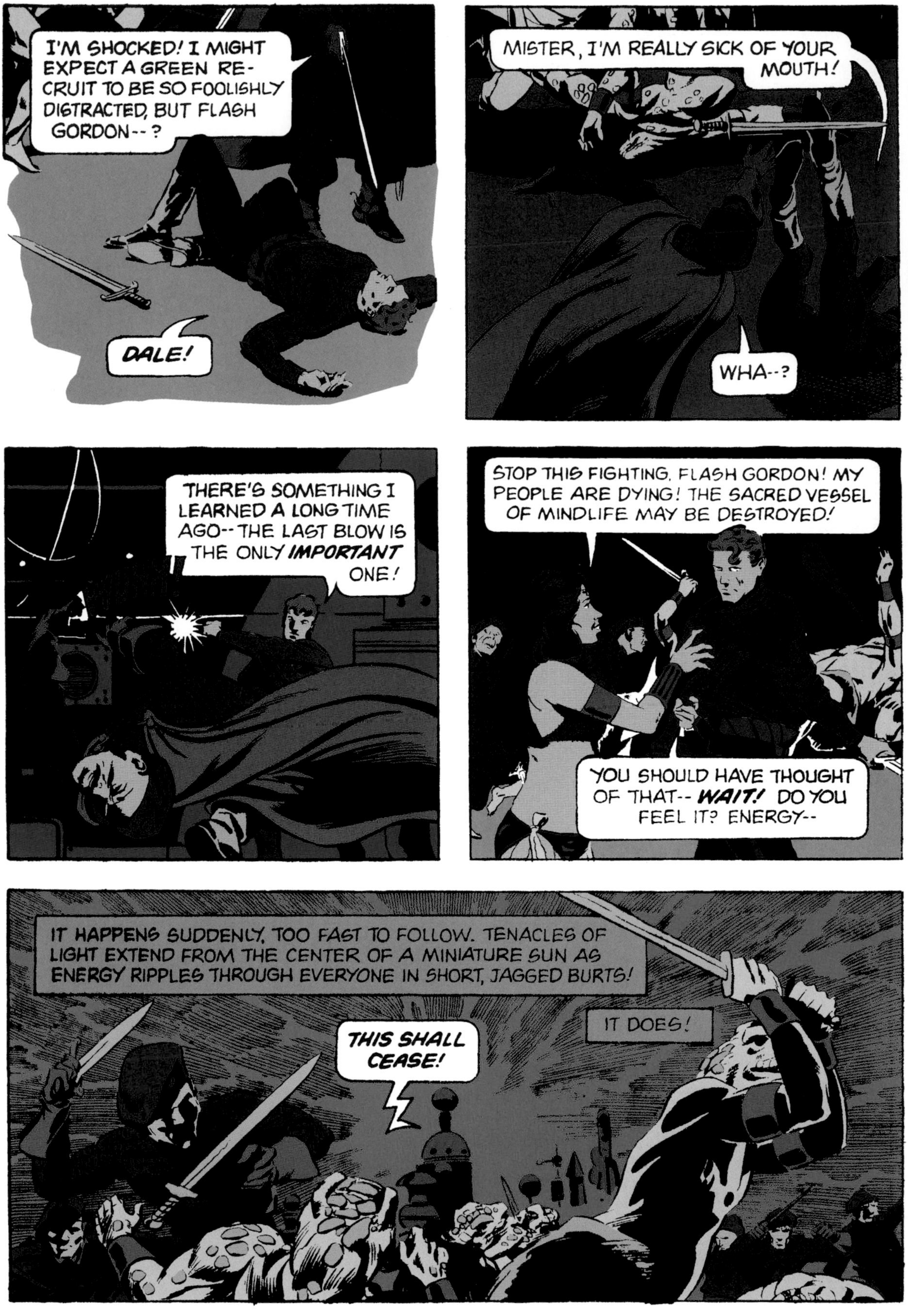
I'M SHOCKED! I MIGHT EXPECT A GREEN RE-CRUIT TO BE SO FOOLISHLY DISTRACTED, BUT FLASH GORDON-- ?
DALE!
MISTER, I'M REALLY SICK OF YOUR MOUTH!
WHA--?
THERE'S SOMETHING I LEARNED A LONG TIME AGO-- THE LAST BLOW IS THE ONLY IMPORTANT ONE!
STOP THIS FIGHTING, FLASH GORDON! MY PEOPLE ARE DYING! THE SACRED VESSEL OF MINDLIFE MAY BE DESTROYED!
YOU SHOULD HAVE THOUGHT OF THAT-- WAIT! DO YOU FEEL IT? ENERGY--
IT HAPPENS SUDDENLY, TOO FAST TO FOLLOW. TENACLES OF LIGHT EXTEND FROM THE CENTER OF A MINIATURE SUN AS ENERGY RIPPLES THROUGH EVERYONE IN SHORT, JAGGED BURTS!
THIS SHALL CEASE!
IT DOES!

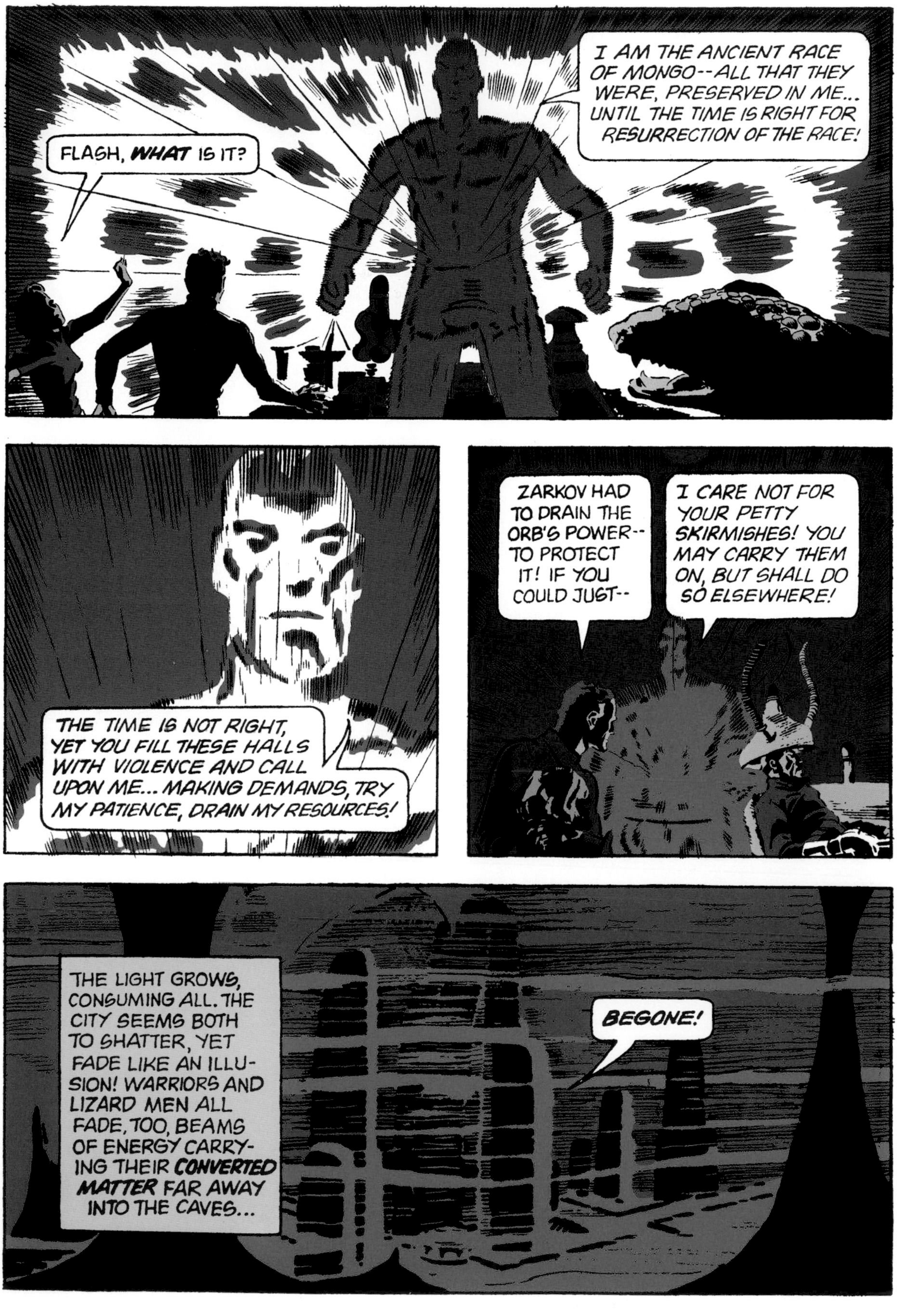

FLASH, WHAT IS IT?
I AM THE ANCIENT RACE OF MONGO--ALL THAT THEY WERE, PRESERVED IN ME... UNTIL THE TIME IS RIGHT FOR RESURRECTION OF THE RACE!
THE TIME IS NOT RIGHT, YET YOU FILL THESE HALLS WITH VIOLENCE AND CALL UPON ME... MAKING DEMANDS, TRY MY PATIENCE, DRAIN MY RESOURCES!
ZARKOV HAD TO DRAIN THE ORB'S POWER--TO PROTECT IT! IF YOU COULD JUST--
I CARE NOT FOR YOUR PETTY SKIRMISHES! YOU MAY CARRY THEM ON, BUT SHALL DO SO ELSEWHERE!
THE LIGHT GROWS, CONSUMING ALL. THE CITY SEEMS BOTH TO SHATTER, YET FADE LIKE AN ILLUSION! WARRIORS AND LIZARD MEN ALL FADE, TOO, BEAMS OF ENERGY CARRYING THEIR CONVERTED MATTER FAR AWAY INTO THE CAVES...
BEGONE!

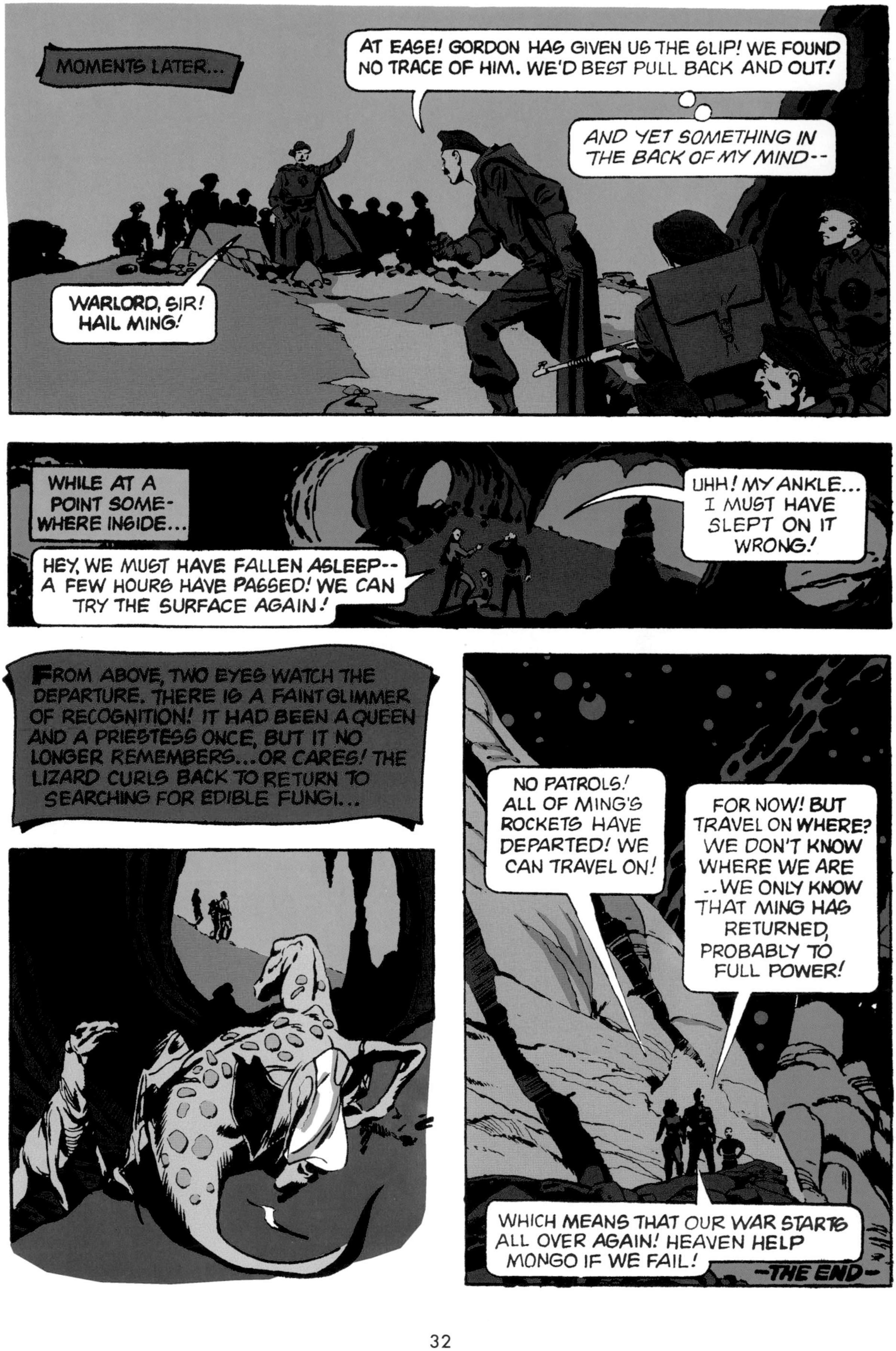
MOMENTS LATER...
AT EASE! GORDON HAS GIVEN US THE SLIP! WE FOUND NO TRACE OF HIM. WE'D BEST PULL BACK AND OUT!
AND YET SOMETHING IN THE BACK OF MY MIND--
WARLORD, SIR! HAIL MING!
WHILE AT A POINT SOMEWHERE INSIDE...
HEY, WE MUST HAVE FALLEN ASLEEP-- A FEW HOURS HAVE PASSED! WE CAN TRY THE SURFACE AGAIN!
UHH! MY ANKLE... I MUST HAVE SLEPT ON IT WRONG!
FROM ABOVE, TWO EYES WATCH THE DEPARTURE. THERE IS A FAINT GLIMMER OF RECOGNITION! IT HAD BEEN A QUEEN AND A PRIESTESS ONCE, BUT IT NO LONGER REMEMBERS...OR CARES! THE LIZARD CURLS BACK TO RETURN TO SEARCHING FOR EDIBLE FUNGI...
NO PATROLS! ALL OF MING'S ROCKETS HAVE DEPARTED! WE CAN TRAVEL ON!
FOR NOW! BUT TRAVEL ON WHERE? WE DON'T KNOW WHERE WE ARE ..WE ONLY KNOW THAT MING HAS RETURNED, PROBABLY TO FULL POWER!
WHICH MEANS THAT OUR WAR STARTS ALL OVER AGAIN! HEAVEN HELP MONGO IF WE FAIL!
-THE END-

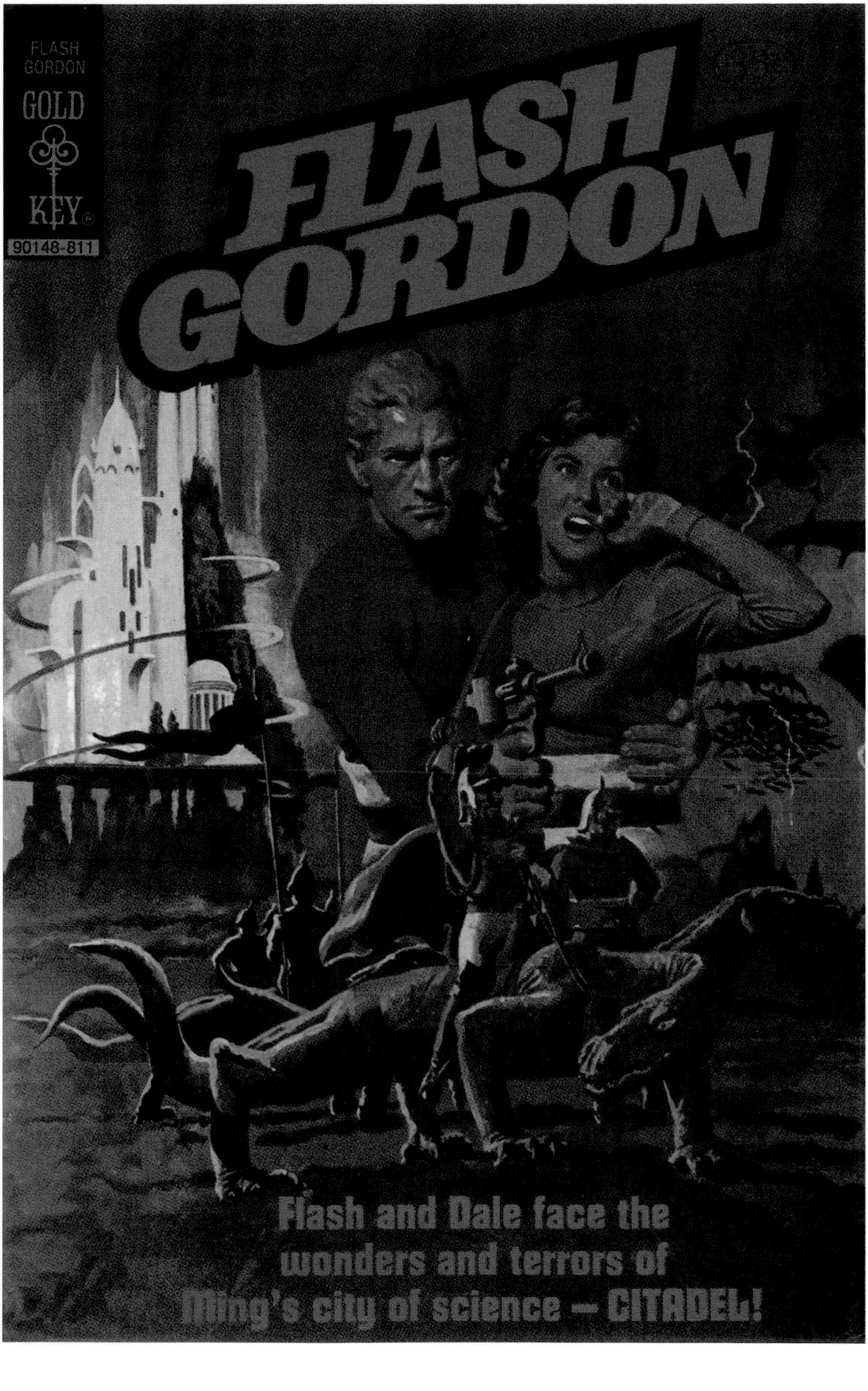
FLASH
GORDON
GOLD
KEY
90148-811
FLASH
GORDON
Flash and Dale face the
wonders and terrors of
Ming's city of science — CITADEL!

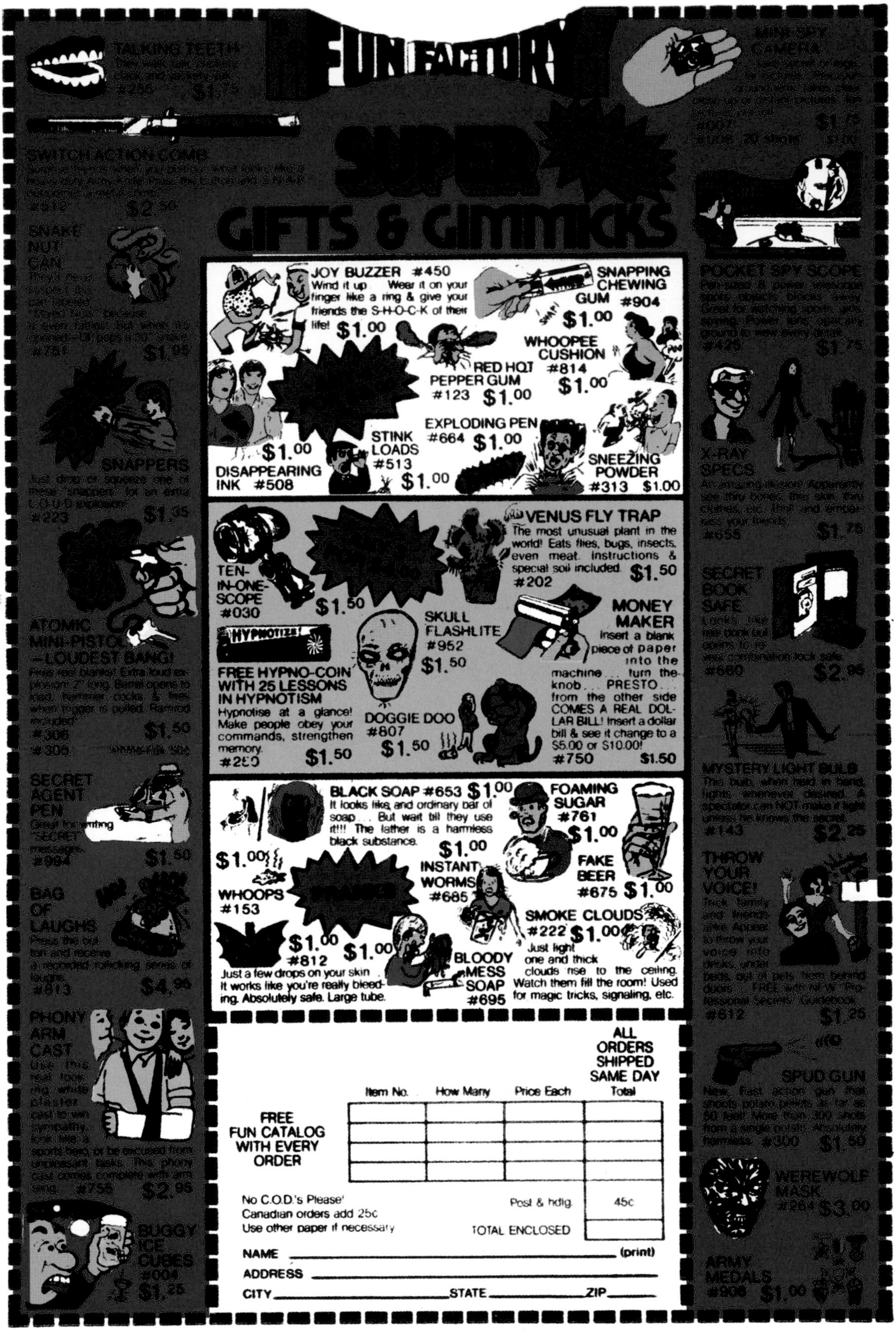

FUN FACTORY
SUPER GIFTS & GIMMICKS
TALKING TEETH
#255 $1.75
SWITCH ACTION COMB
#512 $2.50
SNAKE NUT CAN
#751 $1.95
SNAPPERS
#223 $1.35
ATOMIC MINI-PISTOL —LOUDEST BANG!
#306 $1.50
SECRET AGENT PEN
#994 $1.50
BAG OF LAUGHS
#613 $4.95
PHONY ARM CAST
#755 $2.95
BUGGY ICE CUBES
#004 $1.25
MINI SPY CAMERA
$1.75
POCKET SPY SCOPE
#425 $1.75
X-RAY SPECS
#655 $1.75
SECRET BOOK SAFE
#660 $2.95
MYSTERY LIGHT BULB
#143 $2.25
THROW YOUR VOICE!
#612 $1.25
SPUD GUN
#300 $1.50
WEREWOLF MASK
#264 $3.00
ARMY MEDALS
#908 $1.00
JOY BUZZER #450
Wind it up. Wear it on your finger like a ring & give your friends the S-H-O-C-K of their life! $1.00
SNAPPING CHEWING GUM #904
SNAP!
$1.00
WHOOPEE CUSHION #814 $1.00
RED HOT PEPPER GUM #123 $1.00
EXPLODING PEN #664 $1.00
STINK LOADS #513 $1.00
$1.00 DISAPPEARING INK #508
SNEEZING POWDER #313 $1.00
VENUS FLY TRAP
The most unusual plant in the world! Eats flies, bugs, insects, even meat. Instructions & special soil included. $1.50
#202
TEN-IN-ONE-SCOPE #030 $1.50
SKULL FLASHLITE #952 $1.50
MONEY MAKER
Insert a blank piece of paper into the machine... turn the knob... PRESTO... from the other side COMES A REAL DOLLAR BILL! Insert a dollar bill & see it change to a $5.00 or $10.00!
#750 $1.50
HYPNOTIZE!
FREE HYPNO-COIN WITH 25 LESSONS IN HYPNOTISM
Hypnotise at a glance! Make people obey your commands, strengthen memory.
#250 $1.50
DOGGIE DOO #807 $1.50
BLACK SOAP #653 $1.00
It looks like and ordinary bar of soap... But wait till they use it!!! The lather is a harmless black substance.
$1.00 INSTANT WORMS #685
FOAMING SUGAR #761 $1.00
FAKE BEER #675 $1.00
$1.00 WHOOPS #153
$1.00 #812 $1.00
Just a few drops on your skin. It works like you're really bleeding. Absolutely safe. Large tube.
BLOODY MESS SOAP #695
SMOKE CLOUDS #222 $1.00
Just light one and thick clouds rise to the ceiling. Watch them fill the room! Used for magic tricks, signaling, etc.
ALL ORDERS SHIPPED SAME DAY
FREE FUN CATALOG WITH EVERY ORDER
Item No. How Many Price Each Total
No C.O.D.'s Please!
Canadian orders add 25c
Use other paper if necessary
Post & hdlg. 45c
TOTAL ENCLOSED
NAME (print)
ADDRESS
CITY STATE ZIP

Stranded in an alien world, Flash Gordon, Dale Arden and Dr. Hans Zarkov struggle against the evil emperor, Ming the Merciless, who seeks to enslave an entire planet.....

FLASH GORDON on the PLANET MONGO

CITADEL PART ONE

STORY BY : JOHN WARNER
ART BY : CARLOS GARZON
CREATED BY : ALEX RAYMOND

PROLOGUE: SOMEWHERE ON THE PLANET MONGO...

HOLO-COMMUNICATION FROM HIS INFINITENESS, MING THE MERCILESS, ON PRIORITY SCRAMBLER CIRCUIT! STAND BY!

FLASH GORDON HAS RETURNED TO MONGO! HE IS SOMEWHERE ON THE **CONTINENT!**

SOONER OR LATER THEY WILL FIND CITADEL! OR--YOU WILL FIND **THEM!** I AM DISPATCHING A UNIT FROM MINGO CITY WHICH I WILL LEAD PERSONALLY!

I SEE! AN ENTIRE UNIT! ISN'T THAT EXCESSIVE?

"REALISTIC! THEY ARE VERY DANGEROUS..."

SURVEY-SCOUT TO CENTRAL--INTRUDER ALERT! DISPATCH SECURITY FOR INTERCEPT!

90148-811
FLASH G.#20-789

"YOU SAID 'THEY,' MING. THEN ZARKOV IS WITH HIM ALSO?"

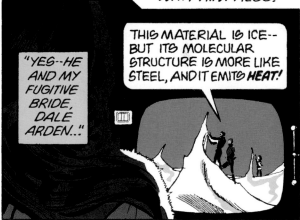

"YES--HE AND MY FUGITIVE BRIDE, DALE ARDEN..."

THIS MATERIAL IS ICE-- BUT ITS MOLECULAR STRUCTURE IS MORE LIKE STEEL, AND IT EMITS **HEAT!**

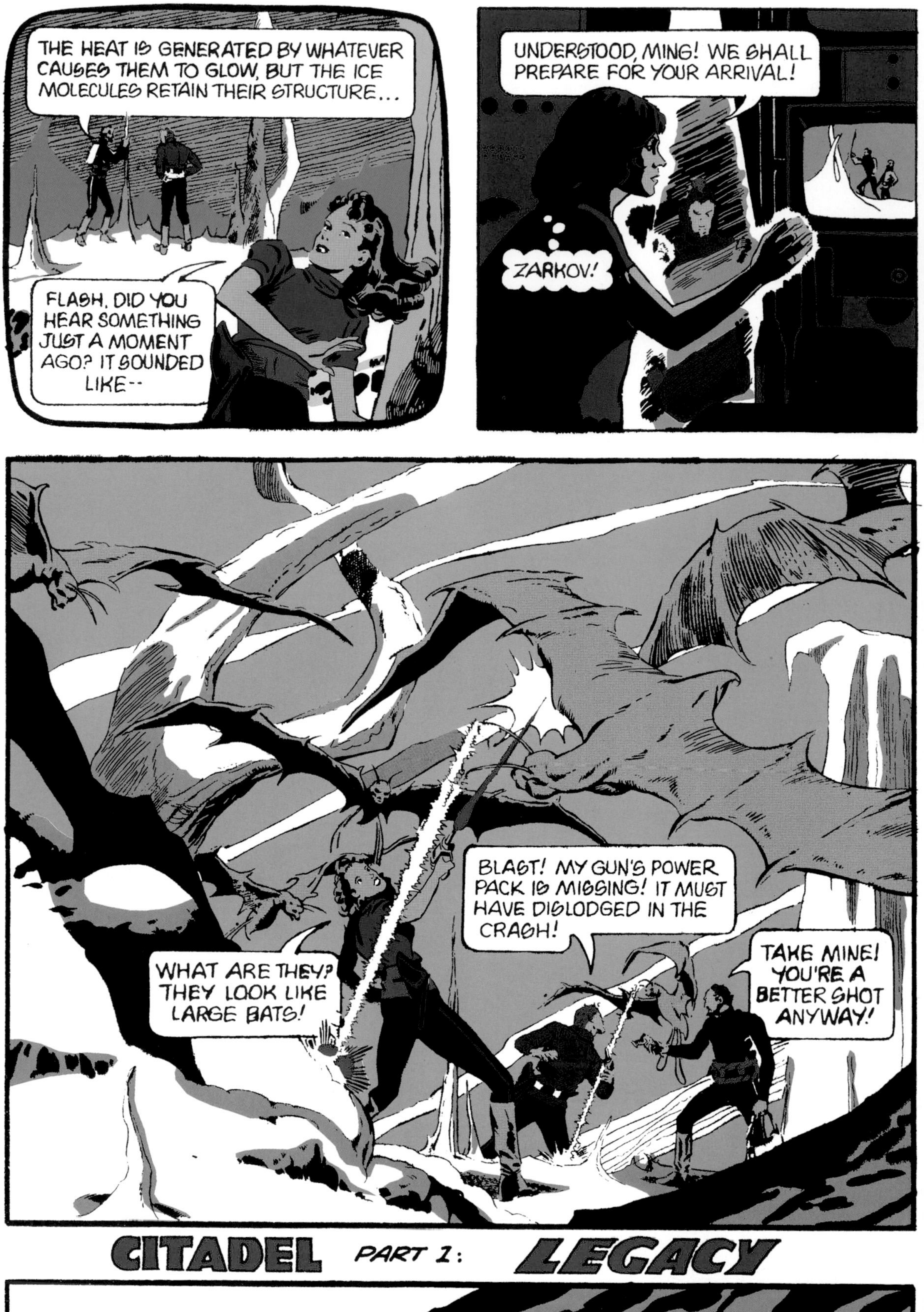
THE HEAT IS GENERATED BY WHATEVER CAUSES THEM TO GLOW, BUT THE ICE MOLECULES RETAIN THEIR STRUCTURE...
FLASH, DID YOU HEAR SOMETHING JUST A MOMENT AGO? IT SOUNDED LIKE--
UNDERSTOOD, MING! WE SHALL PREPARE FOR YOUR ARRIVAL!
ZARKOV!
WHAT ARE THEY? THEY LOOK LIKE LARGE BATS!
BLAST! MY GUN'S POWER PACK IS MISSING! IT MUST HAVE DISLODGED IN THE CRASH!
TAKE MINE! YOU'RE A BETTER SHOT ANYWAY!

CITADEL *PART 1:* LEGACY

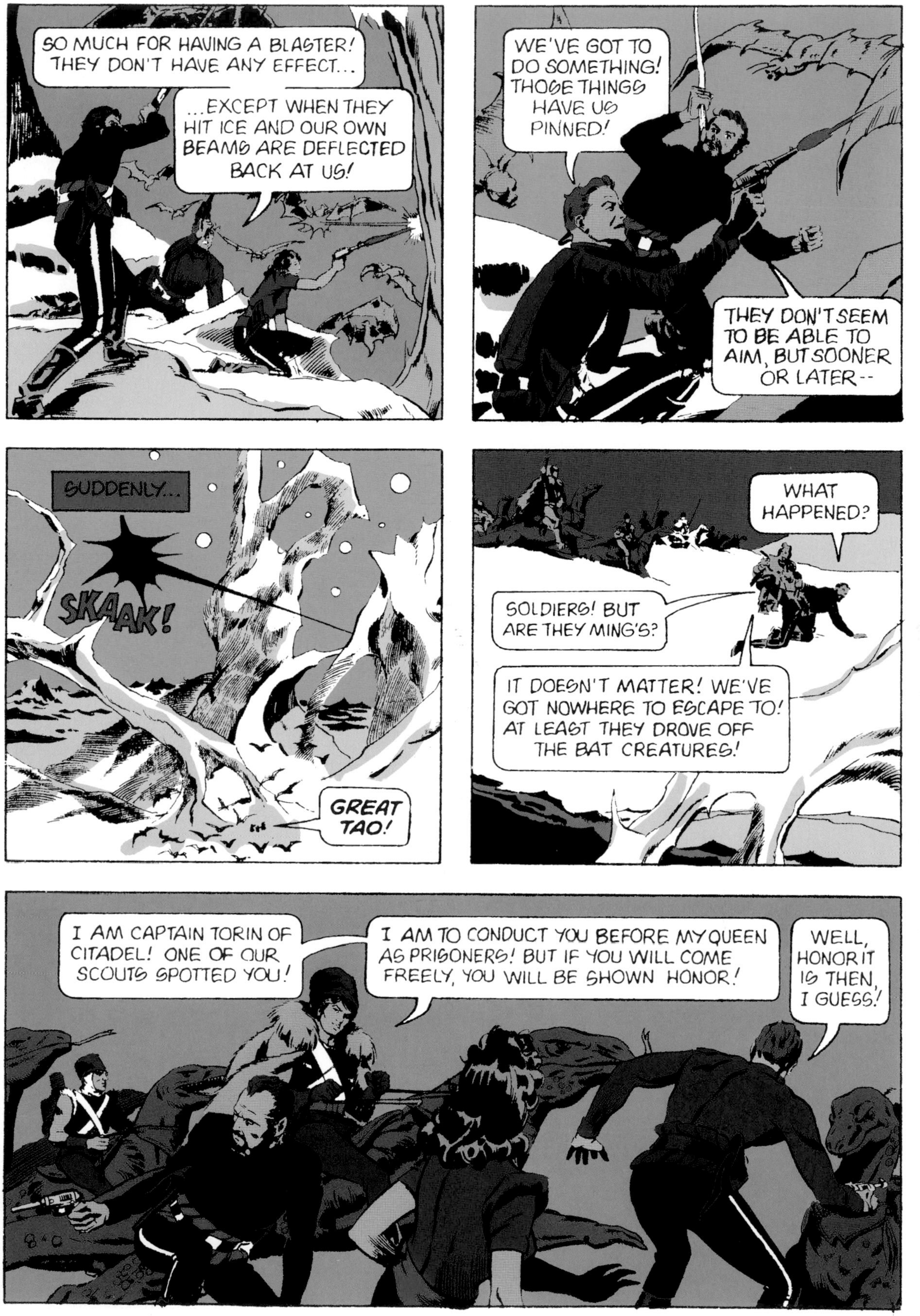
SO MUCH FOR HAVING A BLASTER! THEY DON'T HAVE ANY EFFECT...
...EXCEPT WHEN THEY HIT ICE AND OUR OWN BEAMS ARE DEFLECTED BACK AT US!
WE'VE GOT TO DO SOMETHING! THOSE THINGS HAVE US PINNED!
THEY DON'T SEEM TO BE ABLE TO AIM, BUT SOONER OR LATER--
SUDDENLY...
SKAAAK!
GREAT TAO!
WHAT HAPPENED?
SOLDIERS! BUT ARE THEY MING'S?
IT DOESN'T MATTER! WE'VE GOT NOWHERE TO ESCAPE TO! AT LEAST THEY DROVE OFF THE BAT CREATURES!
I AM CAPTAIN TORIN OF CITADEL! ONE OF OUR SCOUTS SPOTTED YOU!
I AM TO CONDUCT YOU BEFORE MY QUEEN AS PRISONERS! BUT IF YOU WILL COME FREELY, YOU WILL BE SHOWN HONOR!
WELL, HONOR IT IS THEN, I GUESS!

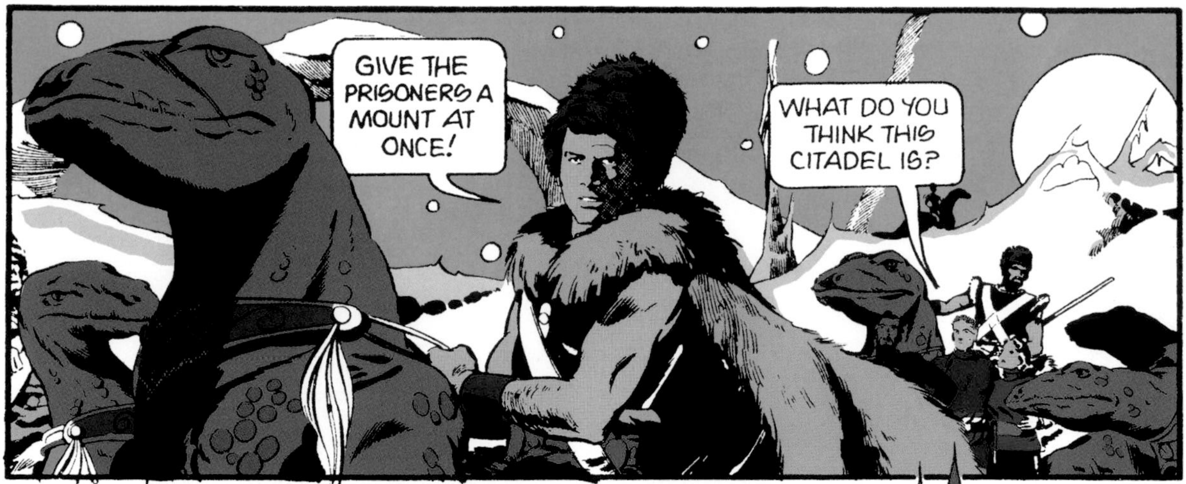
GIVE THE PRISONERS A MOUNT AT ONCE!
WHAT DO YOU THINK THIS CITADEL IS?

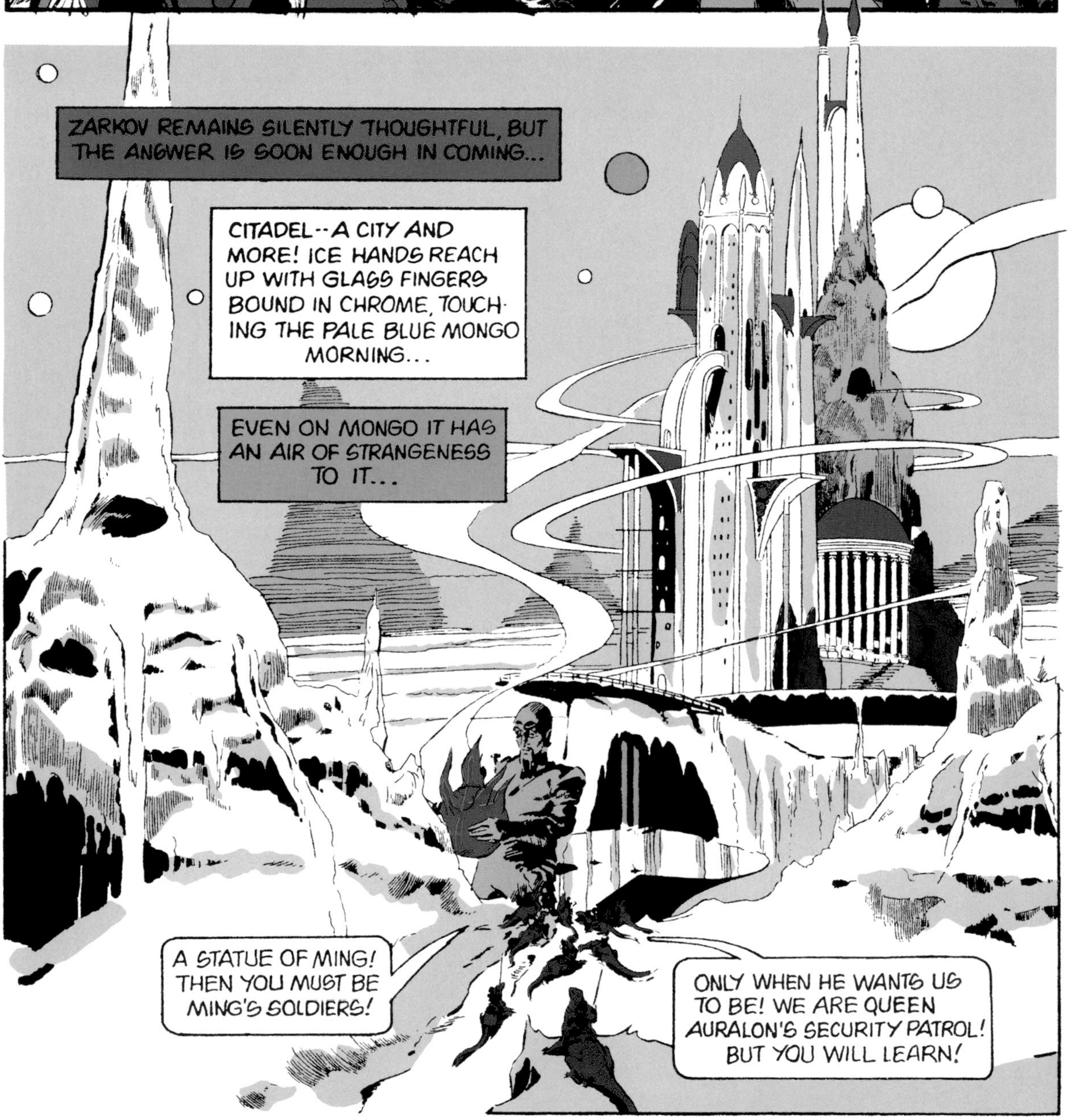
ZARKOV REMAINS SILENTLY THOUGHTFUL, BUT THE ANSWER IS SOON ENOUGH IN COMING...
CITADEL--A CITY AND MORE! ICE HANDS REACH UP WITH GLASS FINGERS BOUND IN CHROME, TOUCHING THE PALE BLUE MONGO MORNING...
EVEN ON MONGO IT HAS AN AIR OF STRANGENESS TO IT...
A STATUE OF MING! THEN YOU MUST BE MING'S SOLDIERS!
ONLY WHEN HE WANTS US TO BE! WE ARE QUEEN AURALON'S SECURITY PATROL! BUT YOU WILL LEARN!

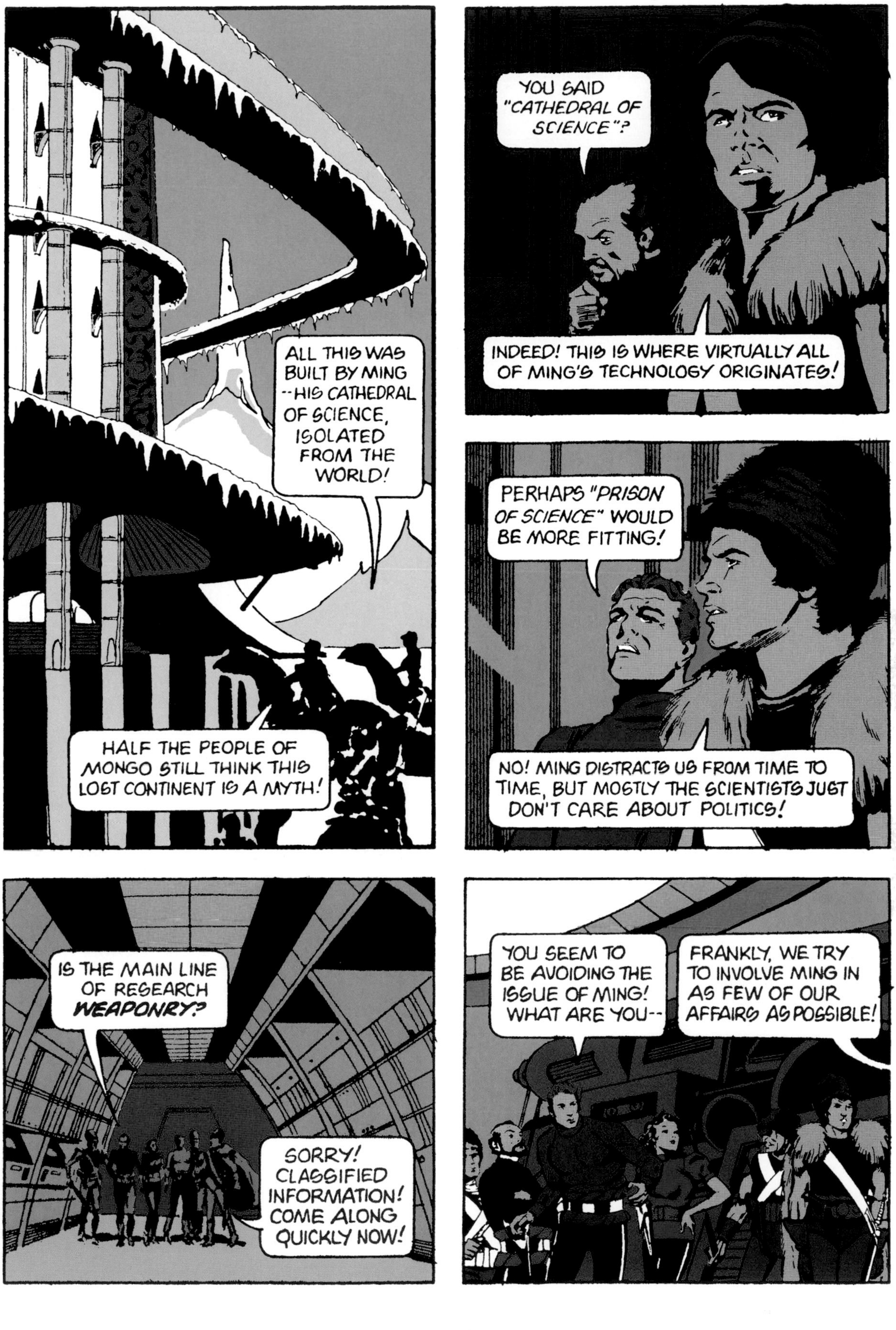
ALL THIS WAS BUILT BY MING --HIS CATHEDRAL OF SCIENCE, ISOLATED FROM THE WORLD!
HALF THE PEOPLE OF MONGO STILL THINK THIS LOST CONTINENT IS A MYTH!
YOU SAID "CATHEDRAL OF SCIENCE"?
INDEED! THIS IS WHERE VIRTUALLY ALL OF MING'S TECHNOLOGY ORIGINATES!
PERHAPS "PRISON OF SCIENCE" WOULD BE MORE FITTING!
NO! MING DISTRACTS US FROM TIME TO TIME, BUT MOSTLY THE SCIENTISTS JUST DON'T CARE ABOUT POLITICS!
IS THE MAIN LINE OF RESEARCH WEAPONRY?
SORRY! CLASSIFIED INFORMATION! COME ALONG QUICKLY NOW!
YOU SEEM TO BE AVOIDING THE ISSUE OF MING! WHAT ARE YOU--
FRANKLY, WE TRY TO INVOLVE MING IN AS FEW OF OUR AFFAIRS AS POSSIBLE!

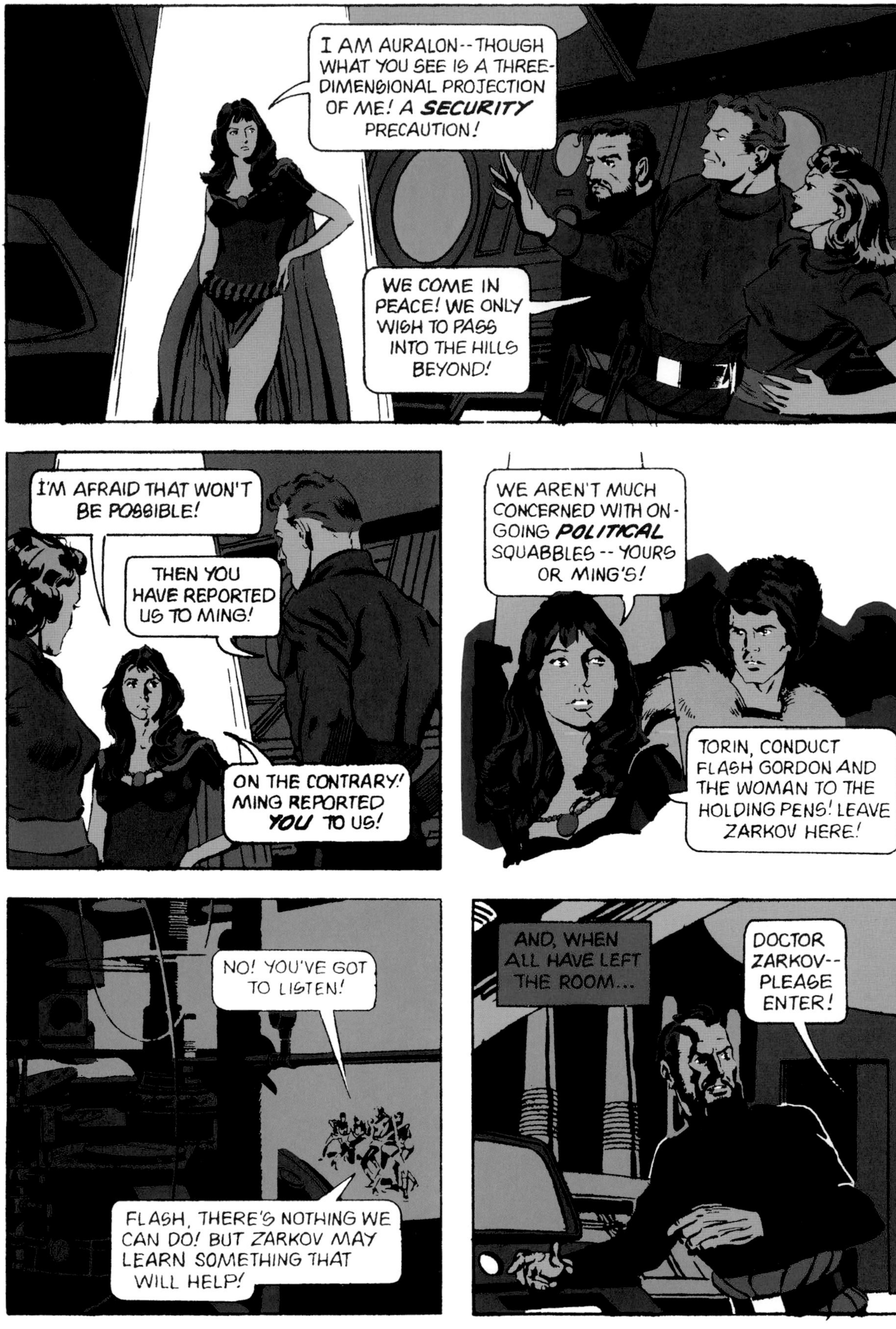
I AM AURALON--THOUGH WHAT YOU SEE IS A THREE-DIMENSIONAL PROJECTION OF ME! A SECURITY PRECAUTION!
WE COME IN PEACE! WE ONLY WISH TO PASS INTO THE HILLS BEYOND!
I'M AFRAID THAT WON'T BE POSSIBLE!
THEN YOU HAVE REPORTED US TO MING!
ON THE CONTRARY! MING REPORTED YOU TO US!
WE AREN'T MUCH CONCERNED WITH ON-GOING POLITICAL SQUABBLES -- YOURS OR MING'S!
TORIN, CONDUCT FLASH GORDON AND THE WOMAN TO THE HOLDING PENS! LEAVE ZARKOV HERE!
NO! YOU'VE GOT TO LISTEN!
FLASH, THERE'S NOTHING WE CAN DO! BUT ZARKOV MAY LEARN SOMETHING THAT WILL HELP!
AND, WHEN ALL HAVE LEFT THE ROOM...
DOCTOR ZARKOV--PLEASE ENTER!

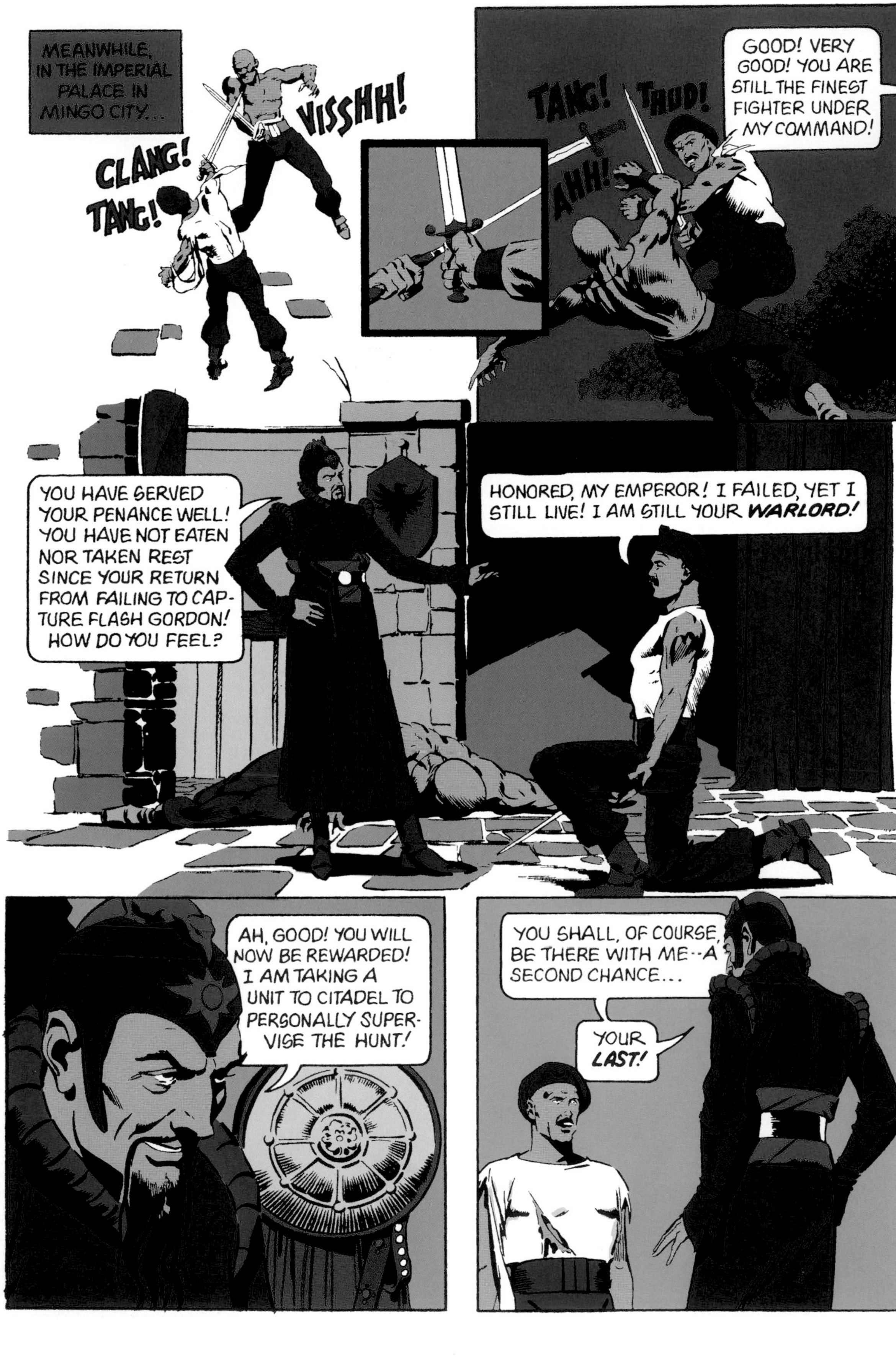
MEANWHILE, IN THE IMPERIAL PALACE IN MINGO CITY...
VISSHH!
CLANG!
TANG!
TANG!
THUD!
AHH!
GOOD! VERY GOOD! YOU ARE STILL THE FINEST FIGHTER UNDER MY COMMAND!
YOU HAVE SERVED YOUR PENANCE WELL! YOU HAVE NOT EATEN NOR TAKEN REST SINCE YOUR RETURN FROM FAILING TO CAPTURE FLASH GORDON! HOW DO YOU FEEL?
HONORED, MY EMPEROR! I FAILED, YET I STILL LIVE! I AM STILL YOUR WARLORD!
AH, GOOD! YOU WILL NOW BE REWARDED! I AM TAKING A UNIT TO CITADEL TO PERSONALLY SUPERVISE THE HUNT!
YOU SHALL, OF COURSE, BE THERE WITH ME--A SECOND CHANCE...
YOUR LAST!

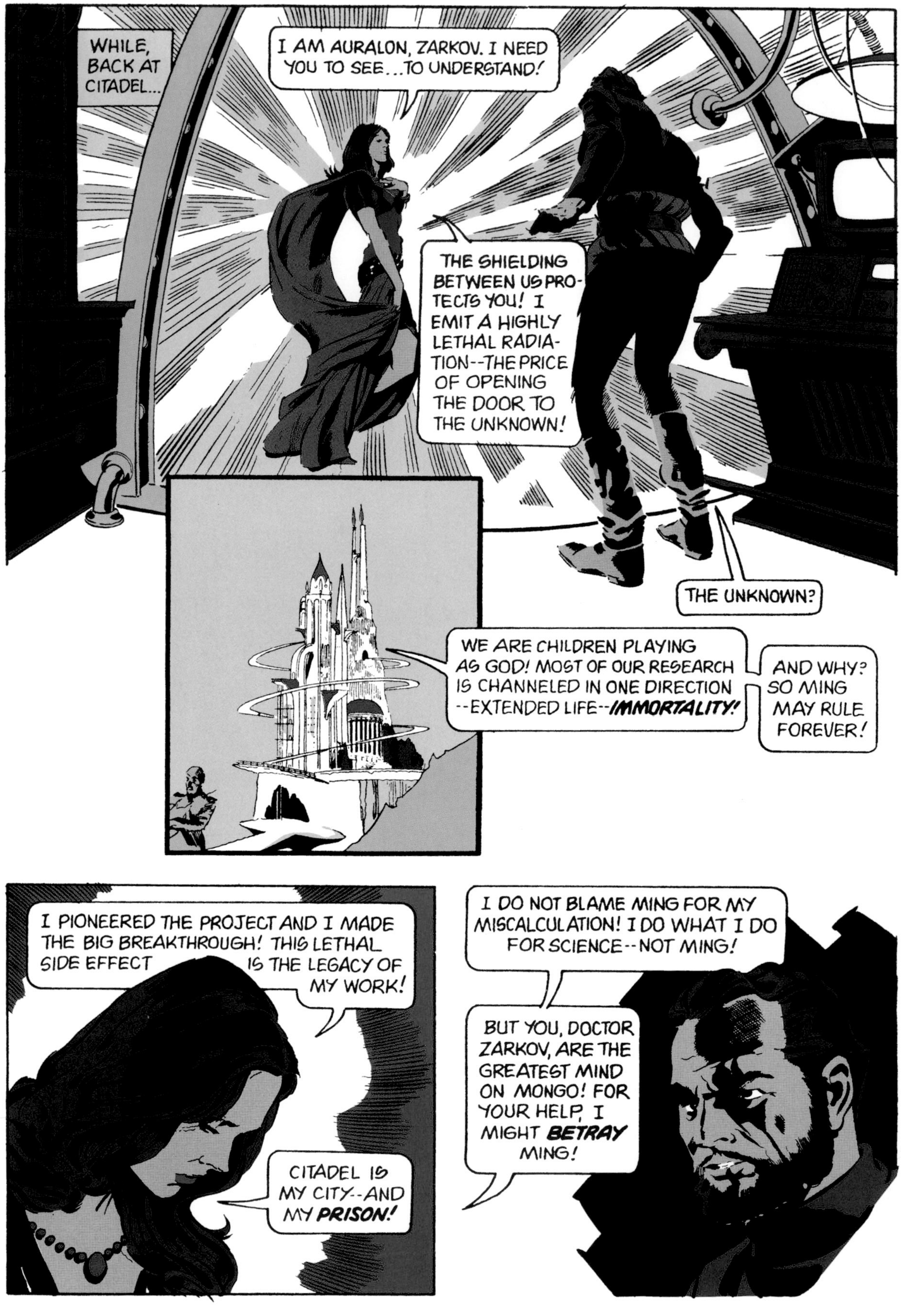
WHILE, BACK AT CITADEL...
I AM AURALON, ZARKOV. I NEED YOU TO SEE...TO UNDERSTAND!
THE SHIELDING BETWEEN US PROTECTS YOU! I EMIT A HIGHLY LETHAL RADIATION--THE PRICE OF OPENING THE DOOR TO THE UNKNOWN!
THE UNKNOWN?
WE ARE CHILDREN PLAYING AS GOD! MOST OF OUR RESEARCH IS CHANNELED IN ONE DIRECTION --EXTENDED LIFE--**IMMORTALITY!**
AND WHY? SO MING MAY RULE FOREVER!
I PIONEERED THE PROJECT AND I MADE THE BIG BREAKTHROUGH! THIS LETHAL SIDE EFFECT IS THE LEGACY OF MY WORK!
CITADEL IS MY CITY--AND MY **PRISON!**
I DO NOT BLAME MING FOR MY MISCALCULATION! I DO WHAT I DO FOR SCIENCE--NOT MING!
BUT YOU, DOCTOR ZARKOV, ARE THE GREATEST MIND ON MONGO! FOR YOUR HELP, I MIGHT **BETRAY** MING!

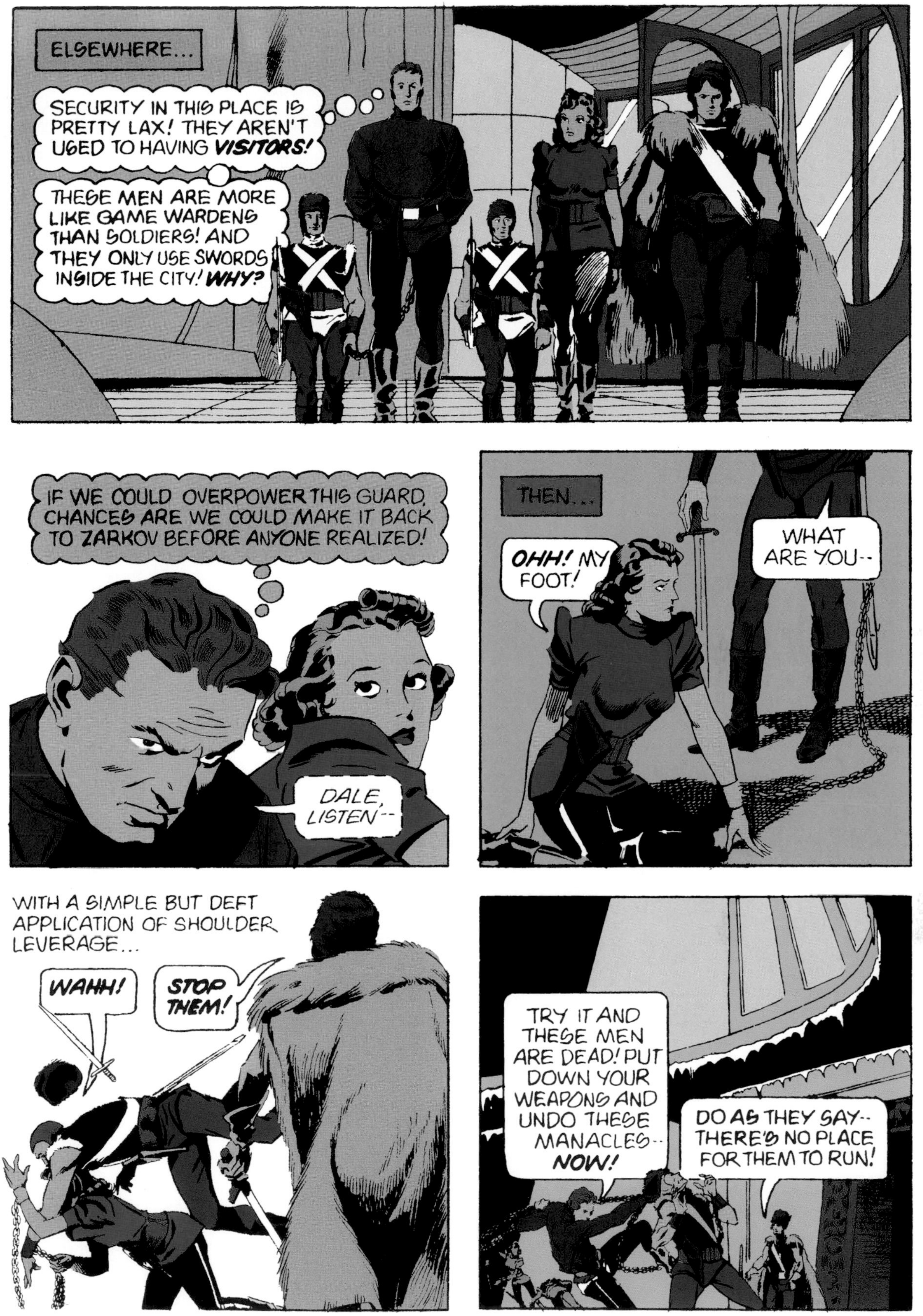
ELSEWHERE...
SECURITY IN THIS PLACE IS PRETTY LAX! THEY AREN'T USED TO HAVING VISITORS!
THESE MEN ARE MORE LIKE GAME WARDENS THAN SOLDIERS! AND THEY ONLY USE SWORDS INSIDE THE CITY! WHY?
IF WE COULD OVERPOWER THIS GUARD, CHANCES ARE WE COULD MAKE IT BACK TO ZARKOV BEFORE ANYONE REALIZED!
DALE, LISTEN--
THEN...
OHH! MY FOOT!
WHAT ARE YOU--
WITH A SIMPLE BUT DEFT APPLICATION OF SHOULDER LEVERAGE...
WAHH!
STOP THEM!
TRY IT AND THESE MEN ARE DEAD! PUT DOWN YOUR WEAPONS AND UNDO THESE MANACLES-- NOW!
DO AS THEY SAY-- THERE'S NO PLACE FOR THEM TO RUN!

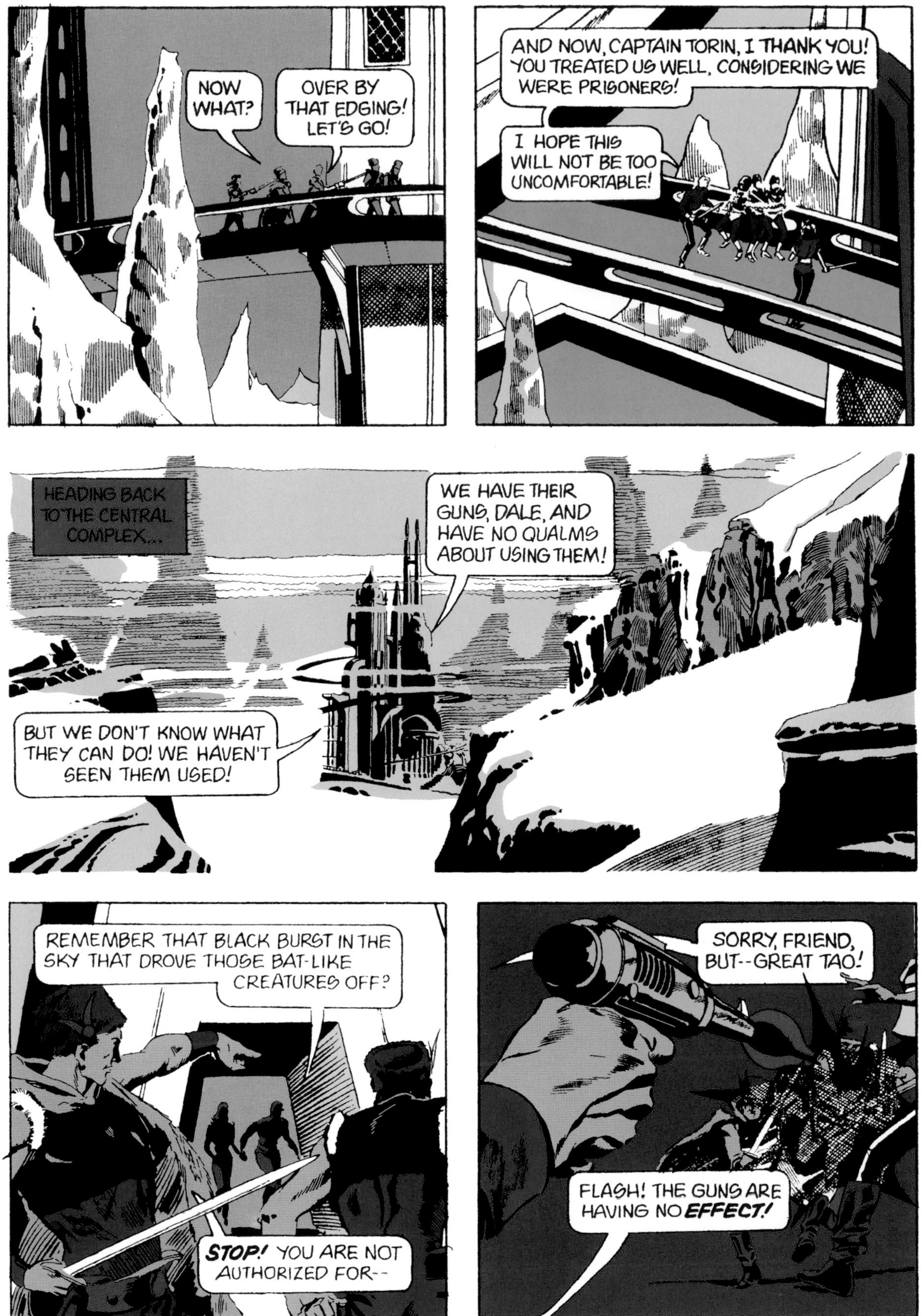
NOW WHAT?
OVER BY THAT EDGING! LET'S GO!
AND NOW, CAPTAIN TORIN, I THANK YOU! YOU TREATED US WELL, CONSIDERING WE WERE PRISONERS!
I HOPE THIS WILL NOT BE TOO UNCOMFORTABLE!
HEADING BACK TO THE CENTRAL COMPLEX...
WE HAVE THEIR GUNS, DALE, AND HAVE NO QUALMS ABOUT USING THEM!
BUT WE DON'T KNOW WHAT THEY CAN DO! WE HAVEN'T SEEN THEM USED!
REMEMBER THAT BLACK BURST IN THE SKY THAT DROVE THOSE BAT-LIKE CREATURES OFF?
STOP! YOU ARE NOT AUTHORIZED FOR--
SORRY, FRIEND, BUT--GREAT TAO!
FLASH! THE GUNS ARE HAVING NO EFFECT!

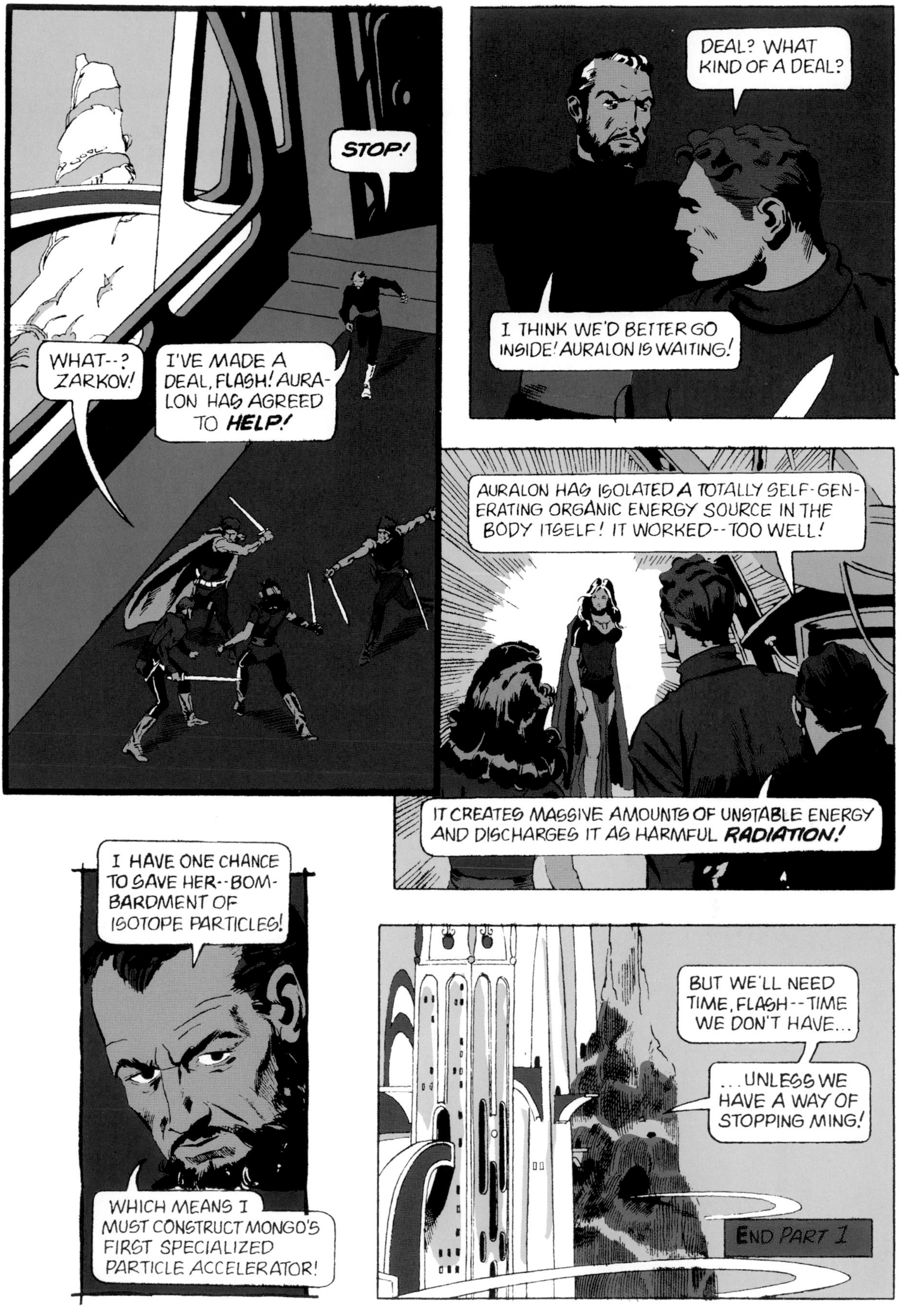
STOP!
WHAT--? ZARKOV!
I'VE MADE A DEAL, FLASH! AURALON HAS AGREED TO HELP!
DEAL? WHAT KIND OF A DEAL?
I THINK WE'D BETTER GO INSIDE! AURALON IS WAITING!
AURALON HAS ISOLATED A TOTALLY SELF-GENERATING ORGANIC ENERGY SOURCE IN THE BODY ITSELF! IT WORKED--TOO WELL!
IT CREATES MASSIVE AMOUNTS OF UNSTABLE ENERGY AND DISCHARGES IT AS HARMFUL RADIATION!
I HAVE ONE CHANCE TO SAVE HER--BOMBARDMENT OF ISOTOPE PARTICLES!
WHICH MEANS I MUST CONSTRUCT MONGO'S FIRST SPECIALIZED PARTICLE ACCELERATOR!
BUT WE'LL NEED TIME, FLASH--TIME WE DON'T HAVE...
...UNLESS WE HAVE A WAY OF STOPPING MING!
END PART 1

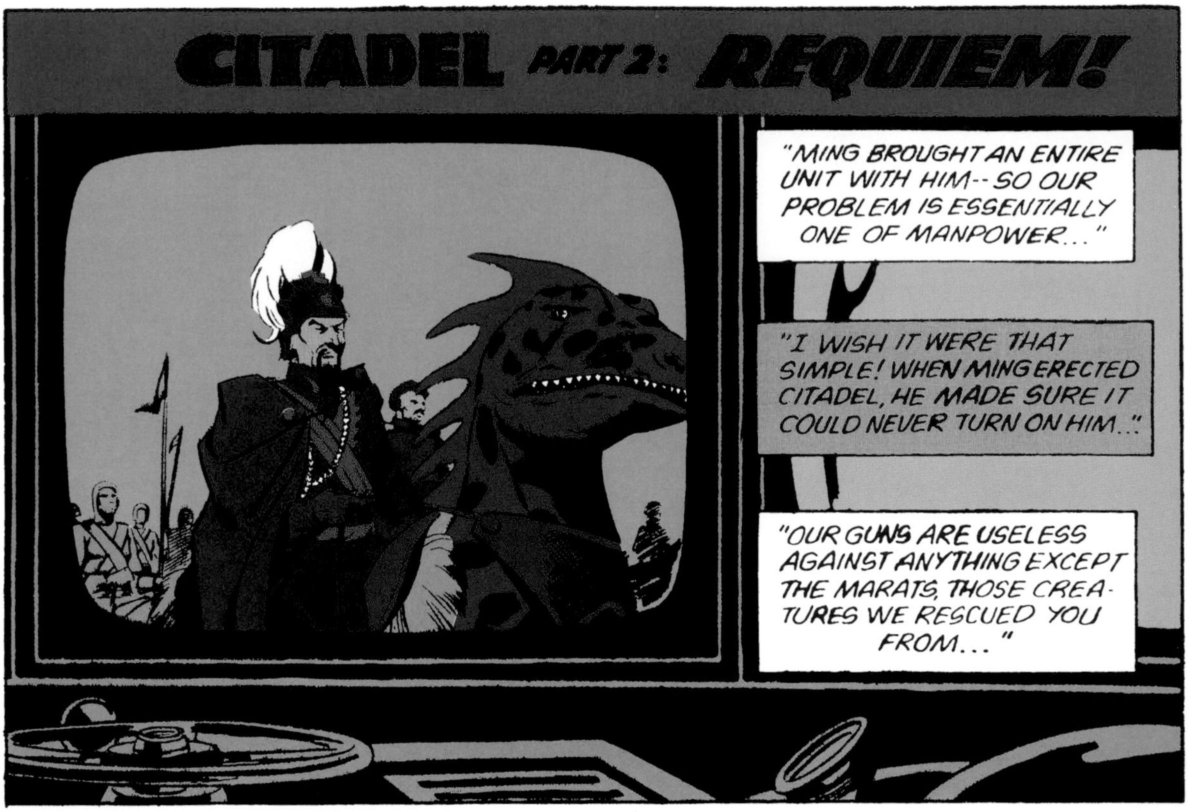
CITADEL PART 2: REQUIEM!
"MING BROUGHT AN ENTIRE UNIT WITH HIM-- SO OUR PROBLEM IS ESSENTIALLY ONE OF MANPOWER..."
"I WISH IT WERE THAT SIMPLE! WHEN MING ERECTED CITADEL, HE MADE SURE IT COULD NEVER TURN ON HIM..."
"OUR GUNS ARE USELESS AGAINST ANYTHING EXCEPT THE MARATS, THOSE CREATURES WE RESCUED YOU FROM..."

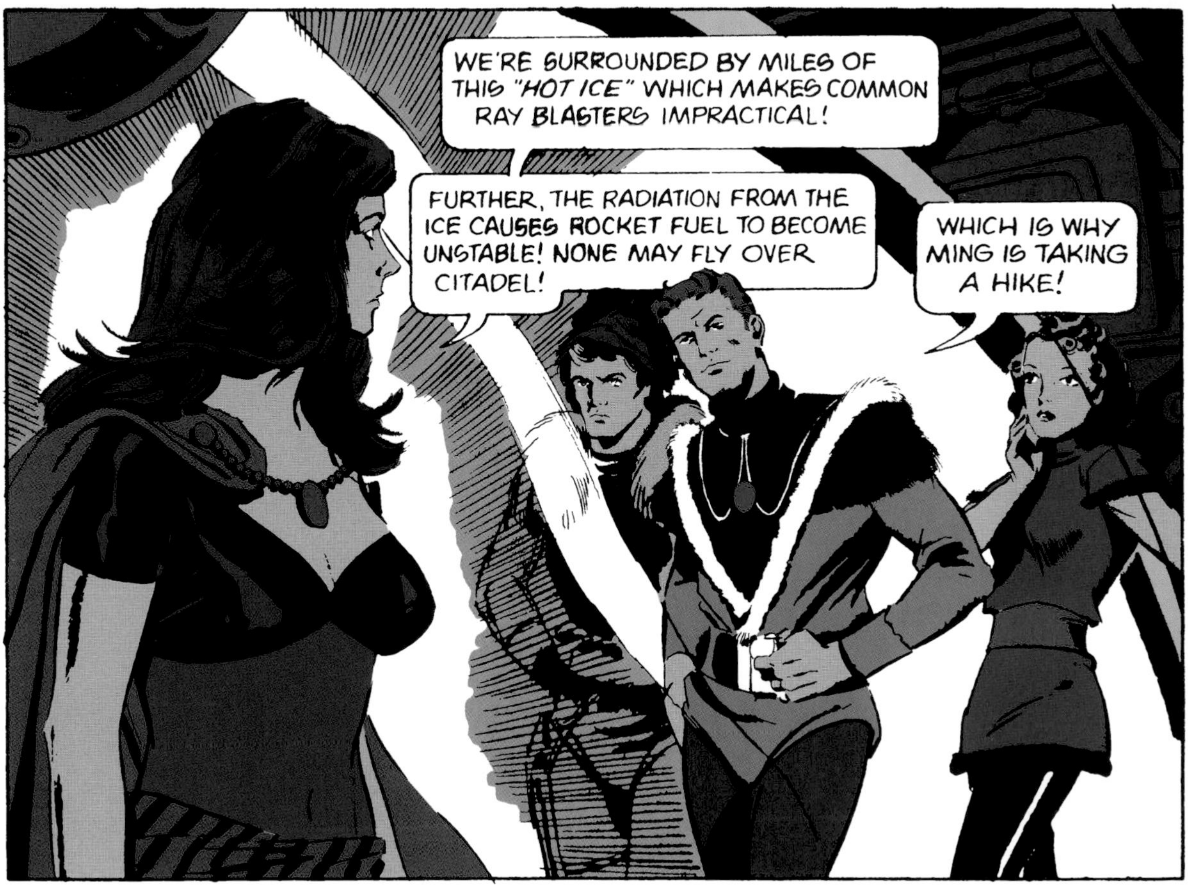
WE'RE SURROUNDED BY MILES OF THIS "HOT ICE" WHICH MAKES COMMON RAY BLASTERS IMPRACTICAL!
FURTHER, THE RADIATION FROM THE ICE CAUSES ROCKET FUEL TO BECOME UNSTABLE! NONE MAY FLY OVER CITADEL!
WHICH IS WHY MING IS TAKING A HIKE!

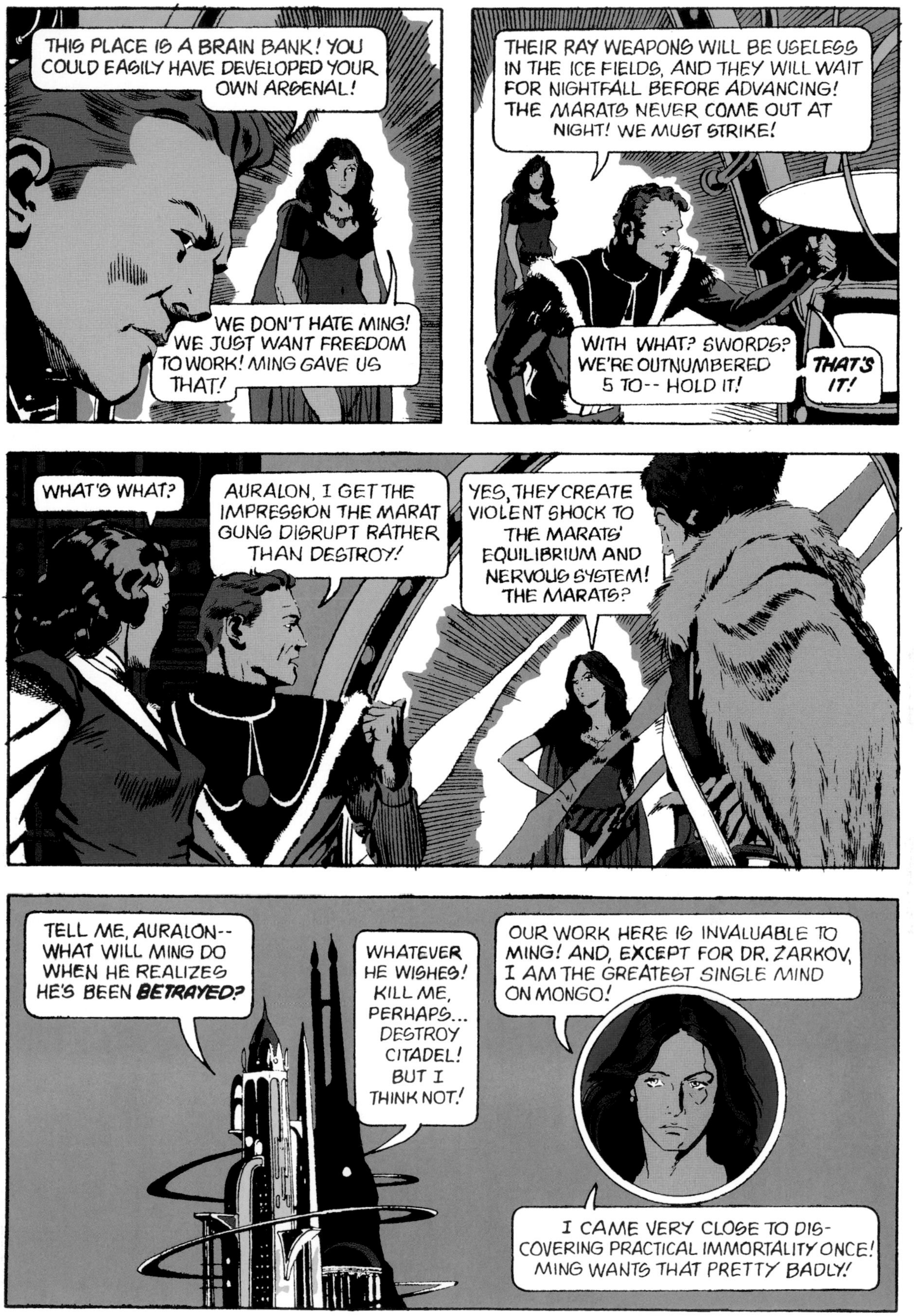

THIS PLACE IS A BRAIN BANK! YOU COULD EASILY HAVE DEVELOPED YOUR OWN ARSENAL!
WE DON'T HATE MING! WE JUST WANT FREEDOM TO WORK! MING GAVE US THAT!
THEIR RAY WEAPONS WILL BE USELESS IN THE ICE FIELDS, AND THEY WILL WAIT FOR NIGHTFALL BEFORE ADVANCING! THE MARATS NEVER COME OUT AT NIGHT! WE MUST STRIKE!
WITH WHAT? SWORDS? WE'RE OUTNUMBERED 5 TO-- HOLD IT!
THAT'S IT!
WHAT'S WHAT?
AURALON, I GET THE IMPRESSION THE MARAT GUNS DISRUPT RATHER THAN DESTROY!
YES, THEY CREATE VIOLENT SHOCK TO THE MARATS' EQUILIBRIUM AND NERVOUS SYSTEM! THE MARATS?
TELL ME, AURALON-- WHAT WILL MING DO WHEN HE REALIZES HE'S BEEN BETRAYED?
WHATEVER HE WISHES! KILL ME, PERHAPS... DESTROY CITADEL! BUT I THINK NOT!
OUR WORK HERE IS INVALUABLE TO MING! AND, EXCEPT FOR DR. ZARKOV, I AM THE GREATEST SINGLE MIND ON MONGO!
I CAME VERY CLOSE TO DIS-COVERING PRACTICAL IMMORTALITY ONCE! MING WANTS THAT PRETTY BADLY!

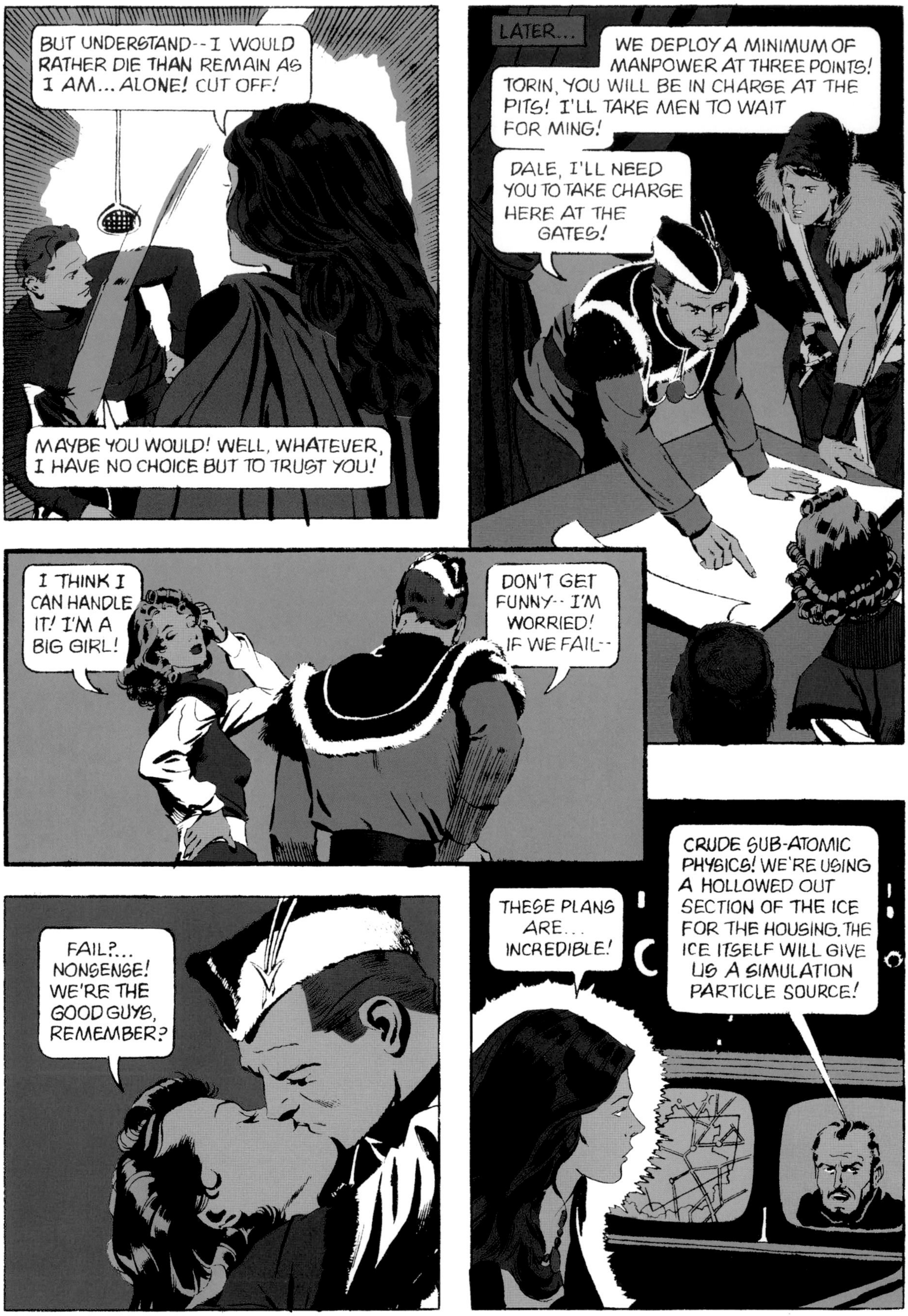
BUT UNDERSTAND--I WOULD RATHER DIE THAN REMAIN AS I AM... ALONE! CUT OFF!
MAYBE YOU WOULD! WELL, WHATEVER, I HAVE NO CHOICE BUT TO TRUST YOU!
LATER...
WE DEPLOY A MINIMUM OF MANPOWER AT THREE POINTS! TORIN, YOU WILL BE IN CHARGE AT THE PITS! I'LL TAKE MEN TO WAIT FOR MING!
DALE, I'LL NEED YOU TO TAKE CHARGE HERE AT THE GATES!
I THINK I CAN HANDLE IT! I'M A BIG GIRL!
DON'T GET FUNNY--I'M WORRIED! IF WE FAIL--
FAIL?... NONSENSE! WE'RE THE GOOD GUYS, REMEMBER?
THESE PLANS ARE... INCREDIBLE!
CRUDE SUB-ATOMIC PHYSICS! WE'RE USING A HOLLOWED OUT SECTION OF THE ICE FOR THE HOUSING. THE ICE ITSELF WILL GIVE US A SIMULATION PARTICLE SOURCE!

THIS AUXILIARY TUNNEL-- AN EMERGENCY EXIT?

UH, YES...WELL, THIS IS A DANGEROUS OPERATION!

BUT, OF COURSE! YOU ARE A MAN OF HONOR, DR. ZARKOV, AND I TRUST YOU! *I* HAVE NO CHOICE! I WILL MISS YOU WHEN YOU ARE GONE!

DUSK SETTLES LIKE FINE SILVER DUST OVER CITADEL, THREE MILES TO THE SOUTH...

OKAY! I GOT THE SPECTRO-FOOTAGE FOR COMP RECORDS!

ALL MEN AT READY--AND, BY TAO, HOLD YOUR COVER!

NOW!

SKAKK! SHRAK SCREEE

SCREEEEEE SPRAK! SKAKK

WE'VE GOT THEM ON THE MOVE!

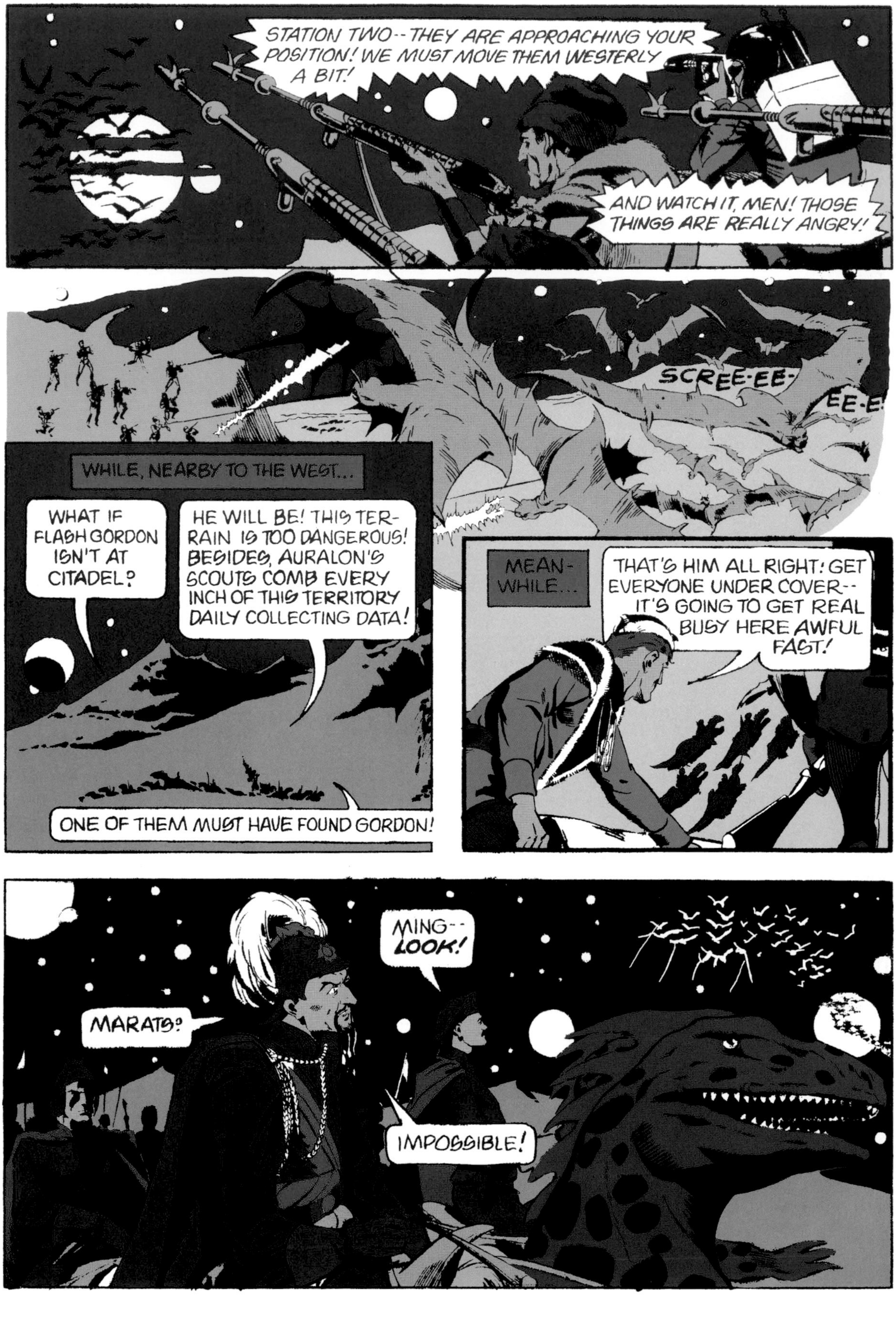

STATION TWO--THEY ARE APPROACHING YOUR POSITION! WE MUST MOVE THEM WESTERLY A BIT!
AND WATCH IT, MEN! THOSE THINGS ARE REALLY ANGRY!
SCREE-EE-EE-E!
WHILE, NEARBY TO THE WEST...
WHAT IF FLASH GORDON ISN'T AT CITADEL?
HE WILL BE! THIS TERRAIN IS TOO DANGEROUS! BESIDES, AURALON'S SCOUTS COMB EVERY INCH OF THIS TERRITORY DAILY COLLECTING DATA!
ONE OF THEM MUST HAVE FOUND GORDON!
MEAN-WHILE...
THAT'S HIM ALL RIGHT: GET EVERYONE UNDER COVER--IT'S GOING TO GET REAL BUSY HERE AWFUL FAST!
MING--LOOK!
MARATS?
IMPOSSIBLE!

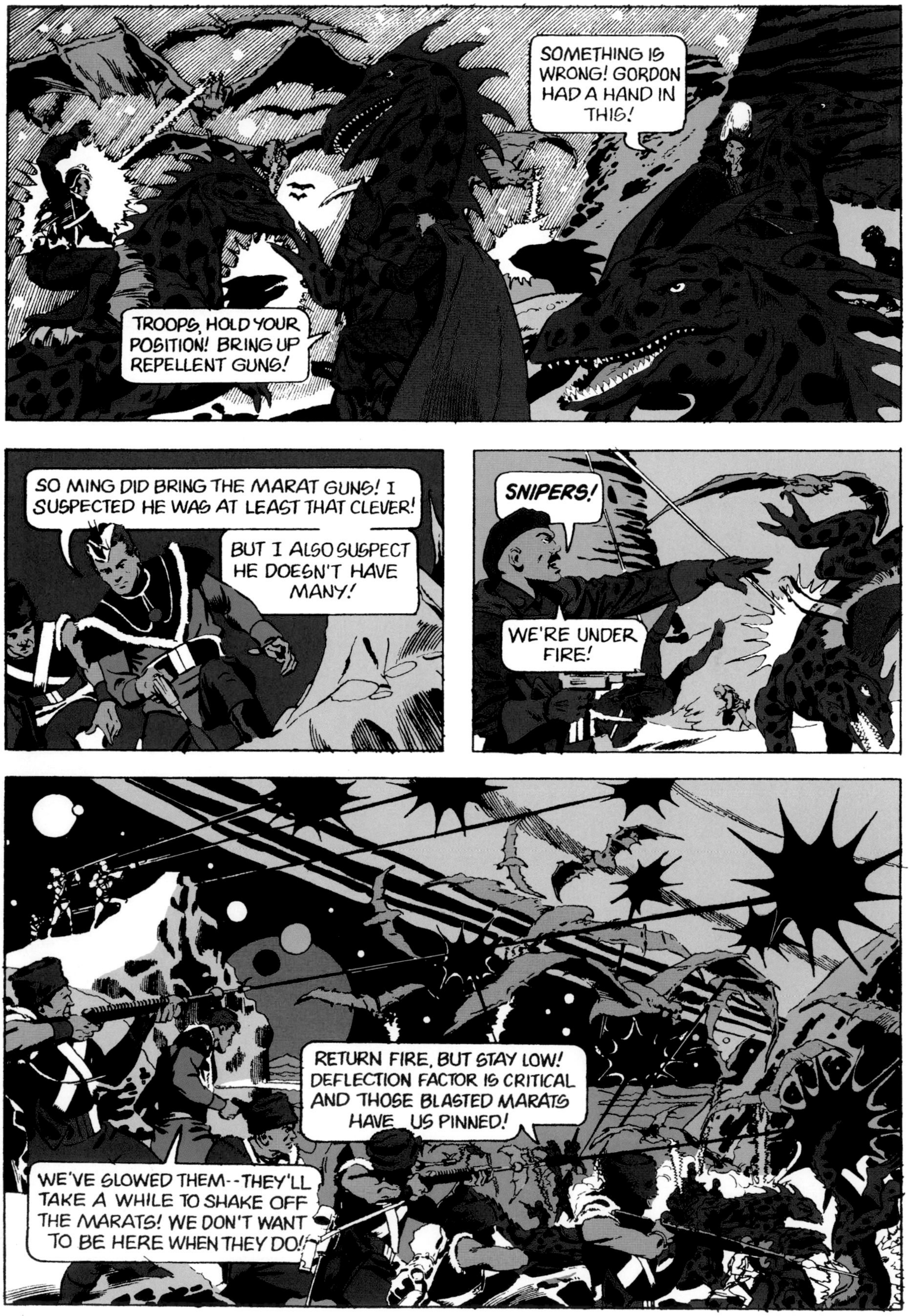
SOMETHING IS WRONG! GORDON HAD A HAND IN THIS!
TROOPS, HOLD YOUR POSITION! BRING UP REPELLENT GUNS!
SO MING DID BRING THE MARAT GUNS! I SUSPECTED HE WAS AT LEAST THAT CLEVER!
BUT I ALSO SUSPECT HE DOESN'T HAVE MANY!
SNIPERS!
WE'RE UNDER FIRE!
RETURN FIRE, BUT STAY LOW! DEFLECTION FACTOR IS CRITICAL AND THOSE BLASTED MARATS HAVE US PINNED!
WE'VE SLOWED THEM--THEY'LL TAKE A WHILE TO SHAKE OFF THE MARATS! WE DON'T WANT TO BE HERE WHEN THEY DO!

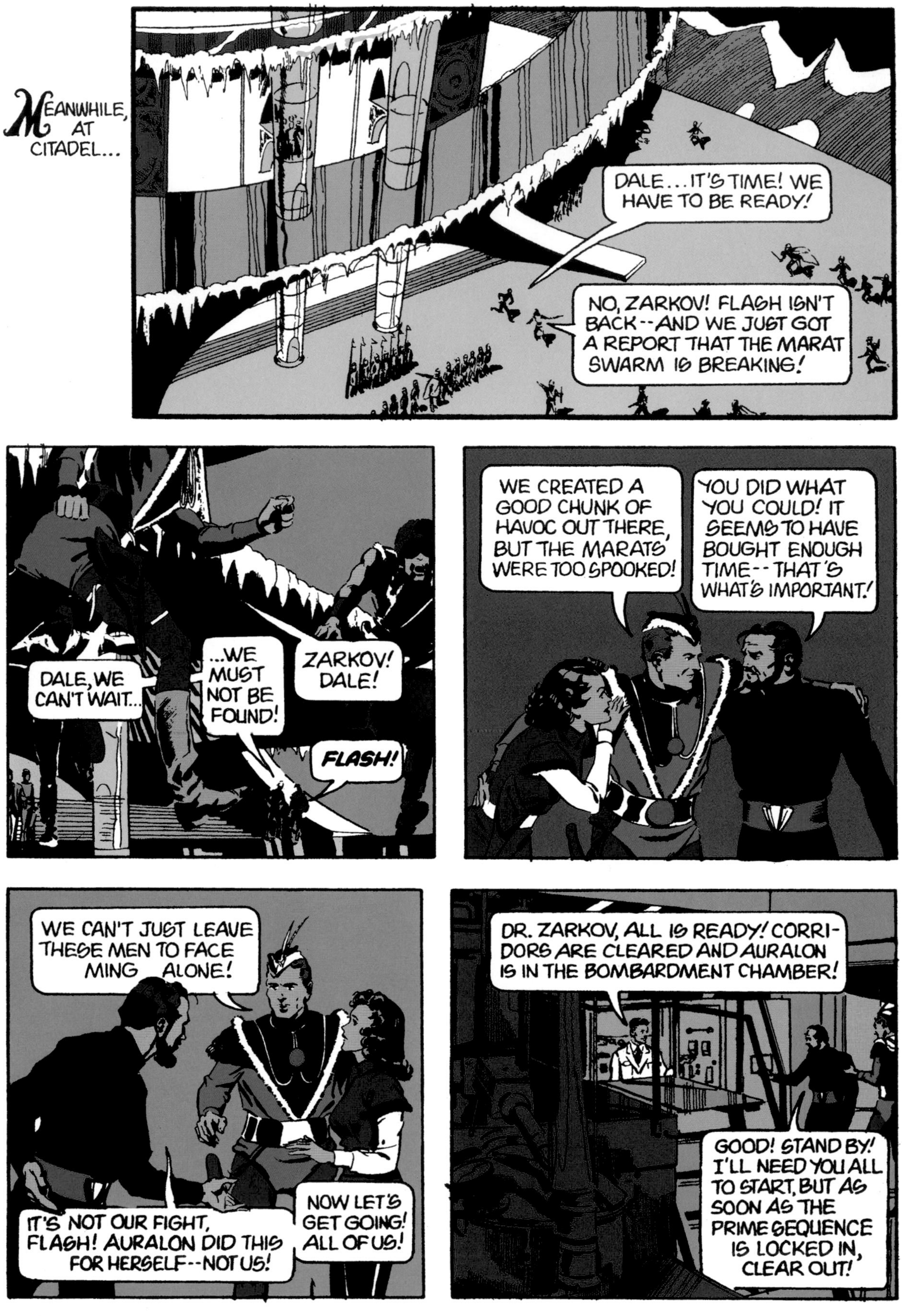
MEANWHILE, AT CITADEL...
DALE... IT'S TIME! WE HAVE TO BE READY!
NO, ZARKOV! FLASH ISN'T BACK--AND WE JUST GOT A REPORT THAT THE MARAT SWARM IS BREAKING!
DALE, WE CAN'T WAIT...
...WE MUST NOT BE FOUND!
ZARKOV! DALE!
FLASH!
WE CREATED A GOOD CHUNK OF HAVOC OUT THERE, BUT THE MARATS WERE TOO SPOOKED!
YOU DID WHAT YOU COULD! IT SEEMS TO HAVE BOUGHT ENOUGH TIME--THAT'S WHAT'S IMPORTANT!
WE CAN'T JUST LEAVE THESE MEN TO FACE MING ALONE!
IT'S NOT OUR FIGHT, FLASH! AURALON DID THIS FOR HERSELF--NOT US!
NOW LET'S GET GOING! ALL OF US!
DR. ZARKOV, ALL IS READY! CORRIDORS ARE CLEARED AND AURALON IS IN THE BOMBARDMENT CHAMBER!
GOOD! STAND BY! I'LL NEED YOU ALL TO START, BUT AS SOON AS THE PRIME SEQUENCE IS LOCKED IN, CLEAR OUT!

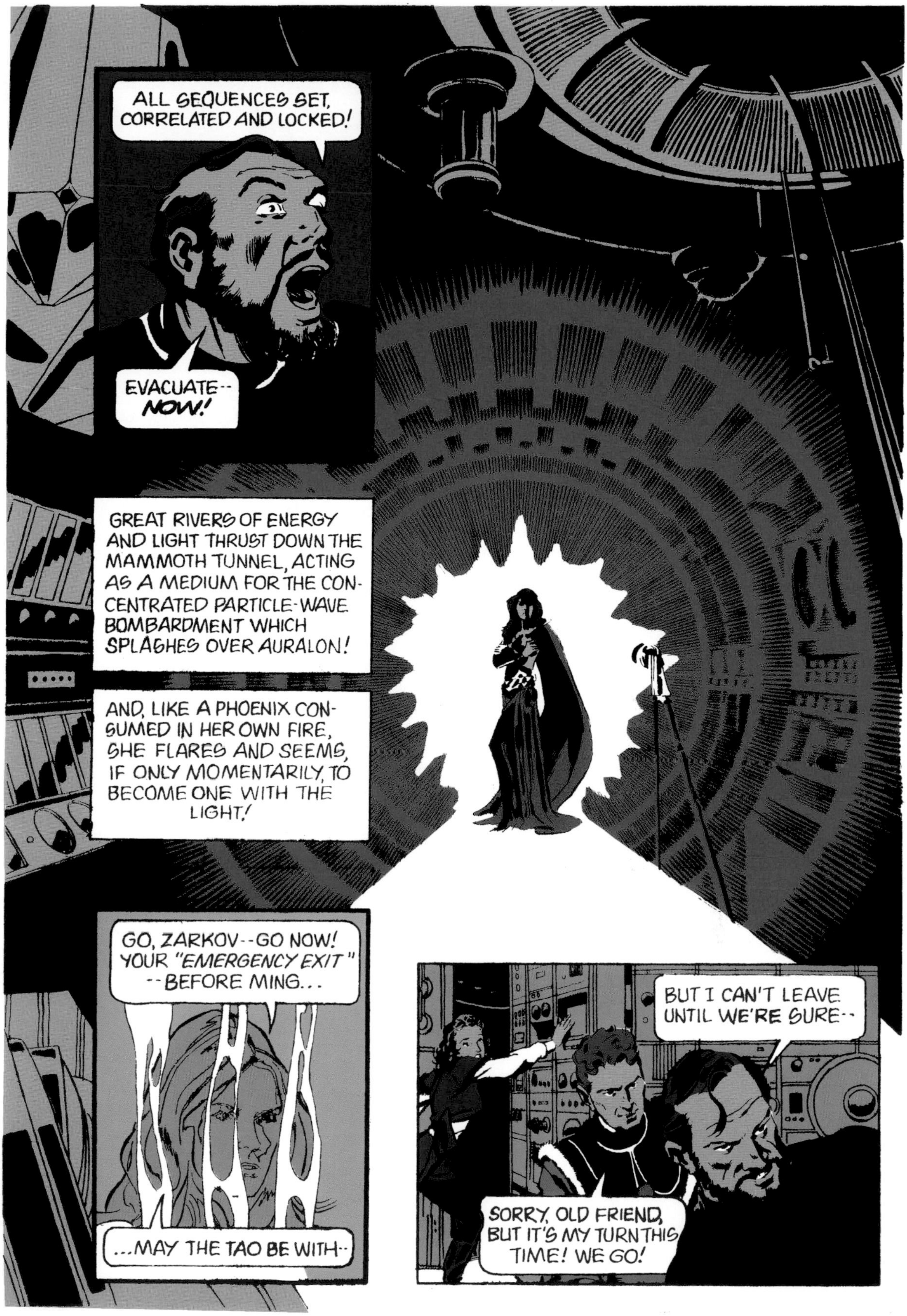

ALL SEQUENCES SET, CORRELATED AND LOCKED!
EVACUATE-- NOW!
GREAT RIVERS OF ENERGY AND LIGHT THRUST DOWN THE MAMMOTH TUNNEL, ACTING AS A MEDIUM FOR THE CON-CENTRATED PARTICLE-WAVE BOMBARDMENT WHICH SPLASHES OVER AURALON!
AND, LIKE A PHOENIX CON-SUMED IN HER OWN FIRE, SHE FLARES AND SEEMS, IF ONLY MOMENTARILY, TO BECOME ONE WITH THE LIGHT!
GO, ZARKOV--GO NOW! YOUR "EMERGENCY EXIT" --BEFORE MING...
...MAY THE TAO BE WITH--
BUT I CAN'T LEAVE UNTIL WE'RE SURE--
SORRY, OLD FRIEND, BUT IT'S MY TURN THIS TIME! WE GO!

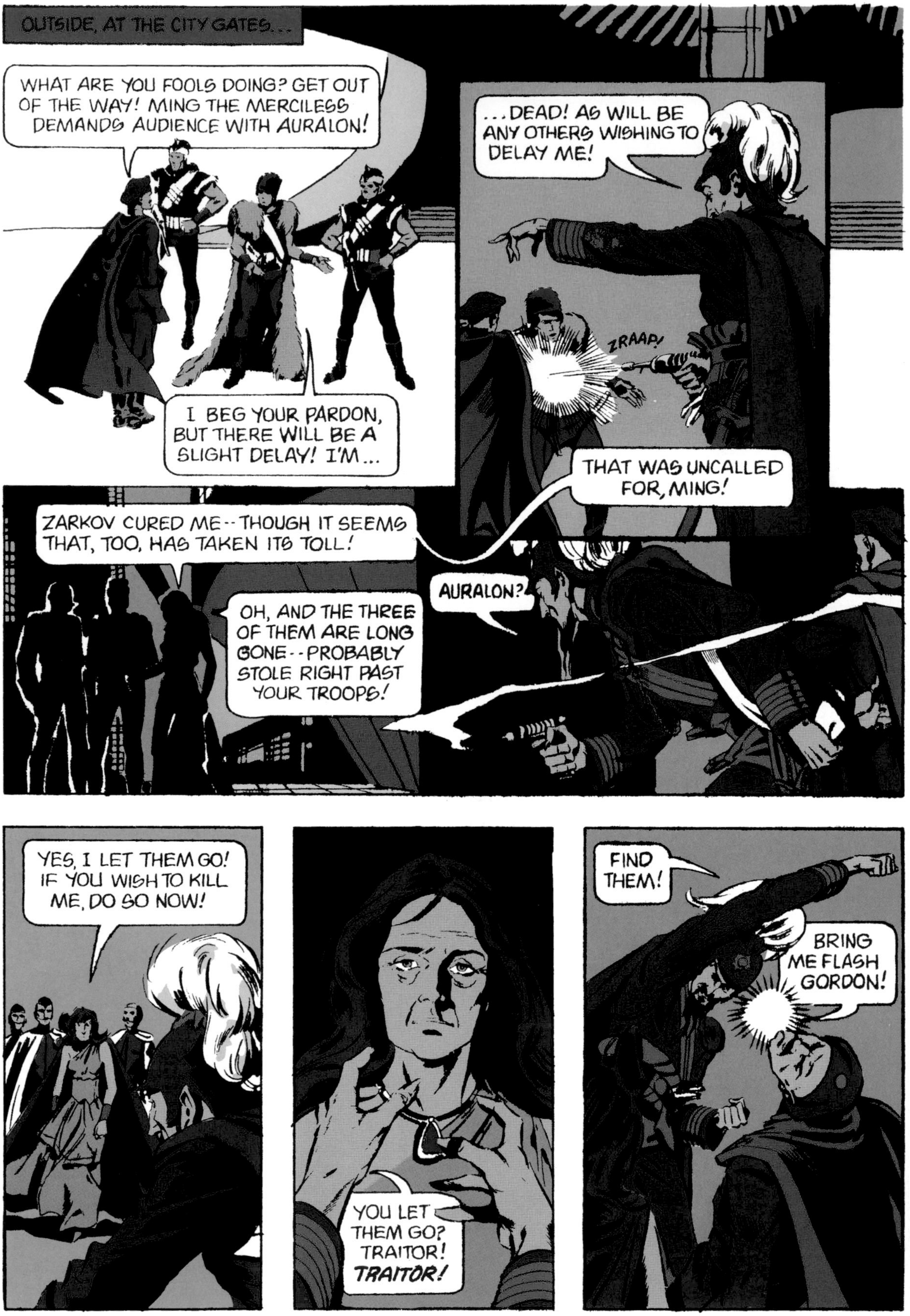
OUTSIDE, AT THE CITY GATES...
WHAT ARE YOU FOOLS DOING? GET OUT OF THE WAY! MING THE MERCILESS DEMANDS AUDIENCE WITH AURALON!
I BEG YOUR PARDON, BUT THERE WILL BE A SLIGHT DELAY! I'M...
...DEAD! AS WILL BE ANY OTHERS WISHING TO DELAY ME!
ZRAAP!
THAT WAS UNCALLED FOR, MING!
ZARKOV CURED ME--THOUGH IT SEEMS THAT, TOO, HAS TAKEN ITS TOLL!
AURALON?
OH, AND THE THREE OF THEM ARE LONG GONE--PROBABLY STOLE RIGHT PAST YOUR TROOPS!
YES, I LET THEM GO! IF YOU WISH TO KILL ME, DO SO NOW!
YOU LET THEM GO? TRAITOR! TRAITOR!
FIND THEM!
BRING ME FLASH GORDON!

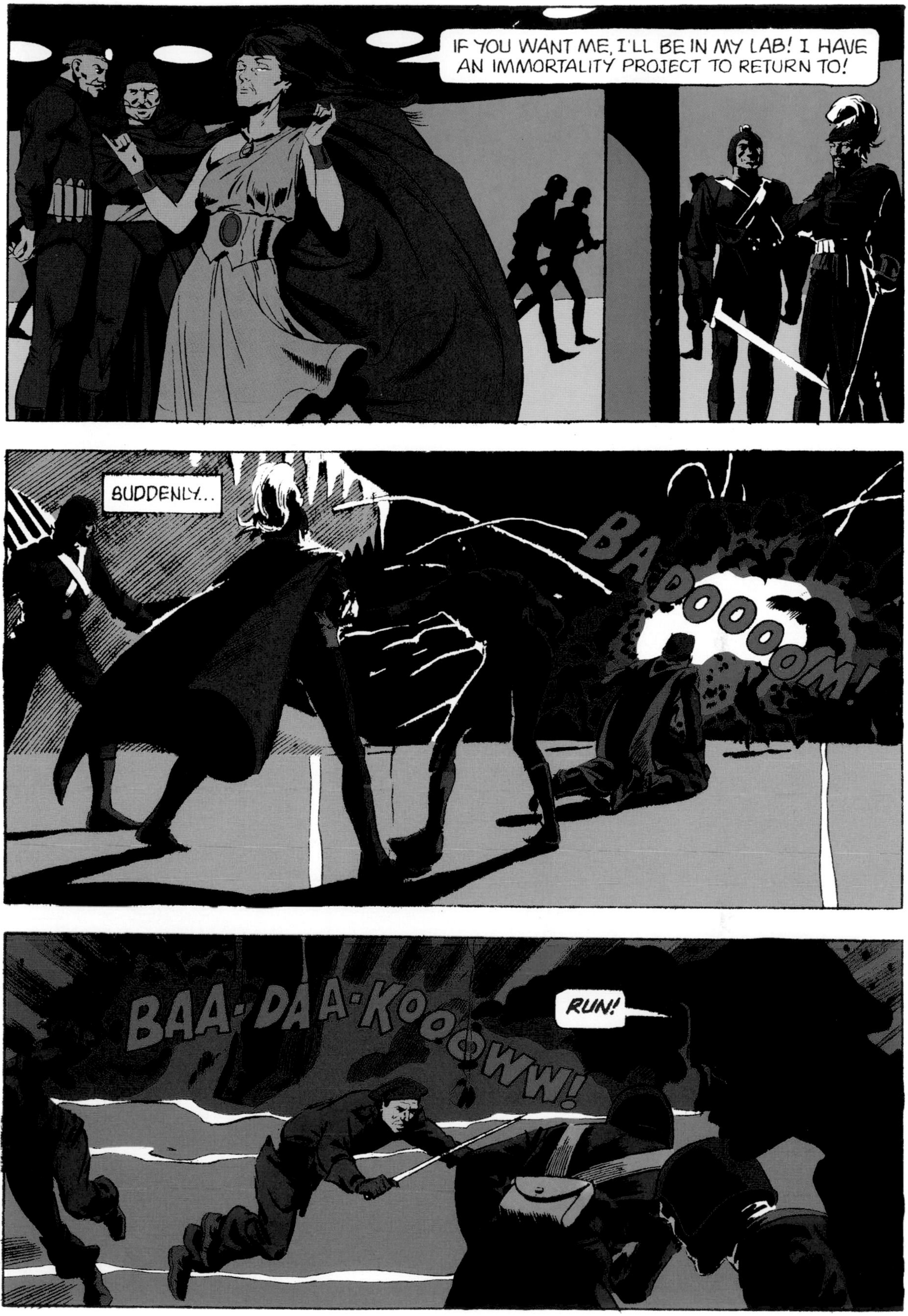
IF YOU WANT ME, I'LL BE IN MY LAB! I HAVE AN IMMORTALITY PROJECT TO RETURN TO!
SUDDENLY...
BADOOOOOM!
BAA-DAA-KOOOWW!
RUN!

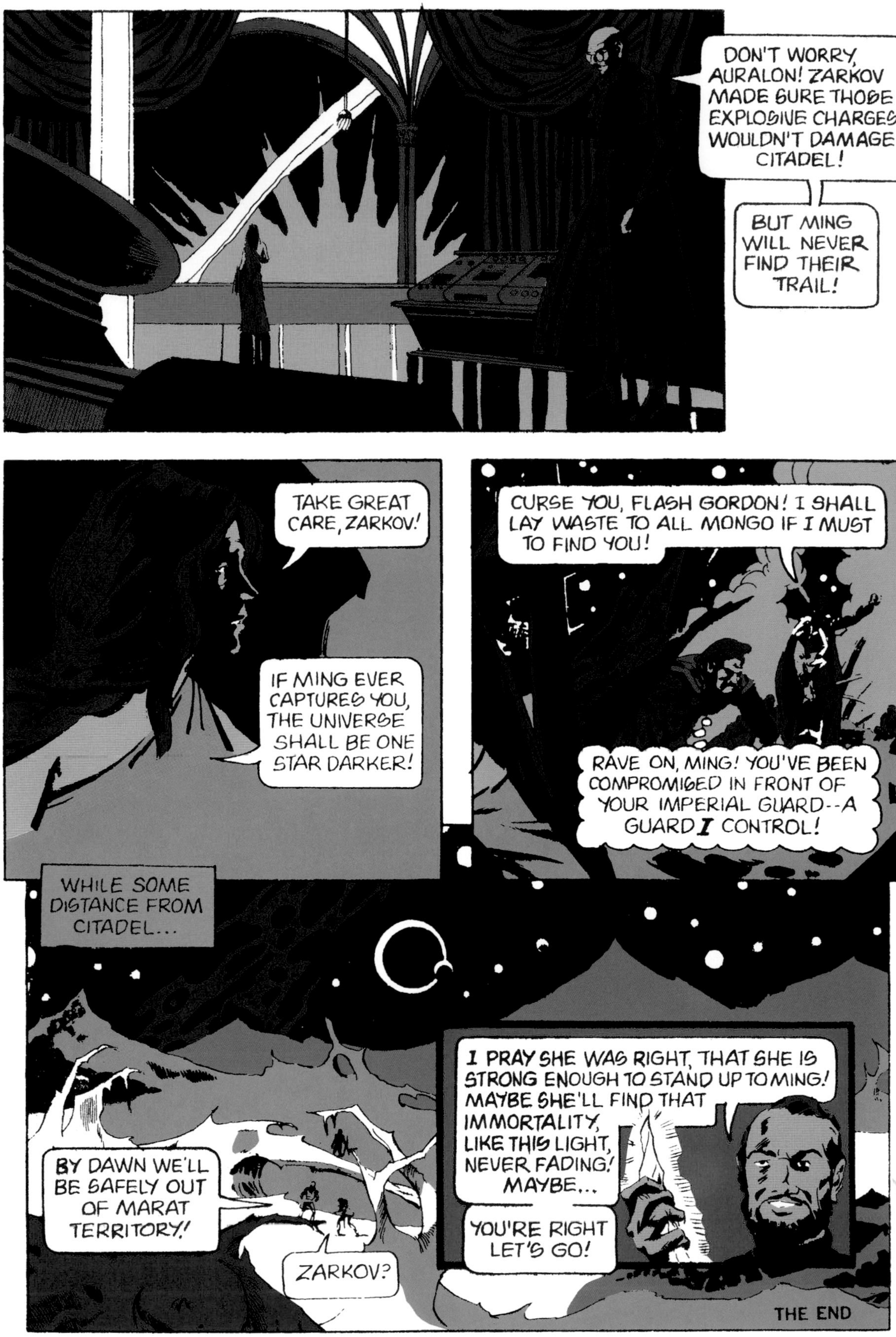
DON'T WORRY, AURALON! ZARKOV MADE SURE THOSE EXPLOSIVE CHARGES WOULDN'T DAMAGE CITADEL!
BUT MING WILL NEVER FIND THEIR TRAIL!
TAKE GREAT CARE, ZARKOV!
IF MING EVER CAPTURES YOU, THE UNIVERSE SHALL BE ONE STAR DARKER!
CURSE YOU, FLASH GORDON! I SHALL LAY WASTE TO ALL MONGO IF I MUST TO FIND YOU!
RAVE ON, MING! YOU'VE BEEN COMPROMISED IN FRONT OF YOUR IMPERIAL GUARD--A GUARD I CONTROL!
WHILE SOME DISTANCE FROM CITADEL...
I PRAY SHE WAS RIGHT, THAT SHE IS STRONG ENOUGH TO STAND UP TO MING! MAYBE SHE'LL FIND THAT IMMORTALITY, LIKE THIS LIGHT, NEVER FADING! MAYBE...
BY DAWN WE'LL BE SAFELY OUT OF MARAT TERRITORY!
ZARKOV?
YOU'RE RIGHT LET'S GO!
THE END

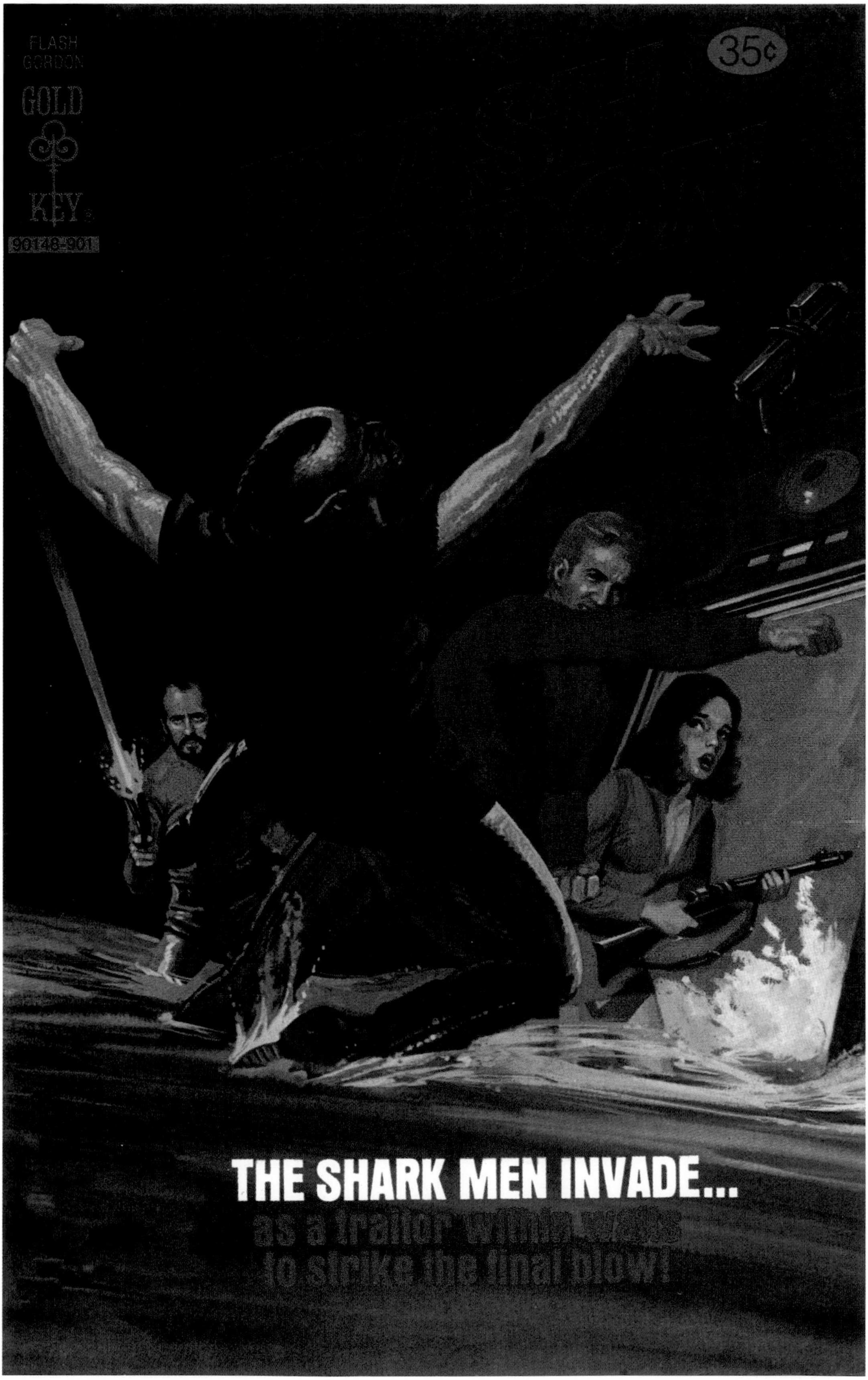
FLASH GORDON
GOLD KEY
90148-901
35¢
THE SHARK MEN INVADE...
as a traitor within waits
to strike the final blow!

Super Pocket Toy Values

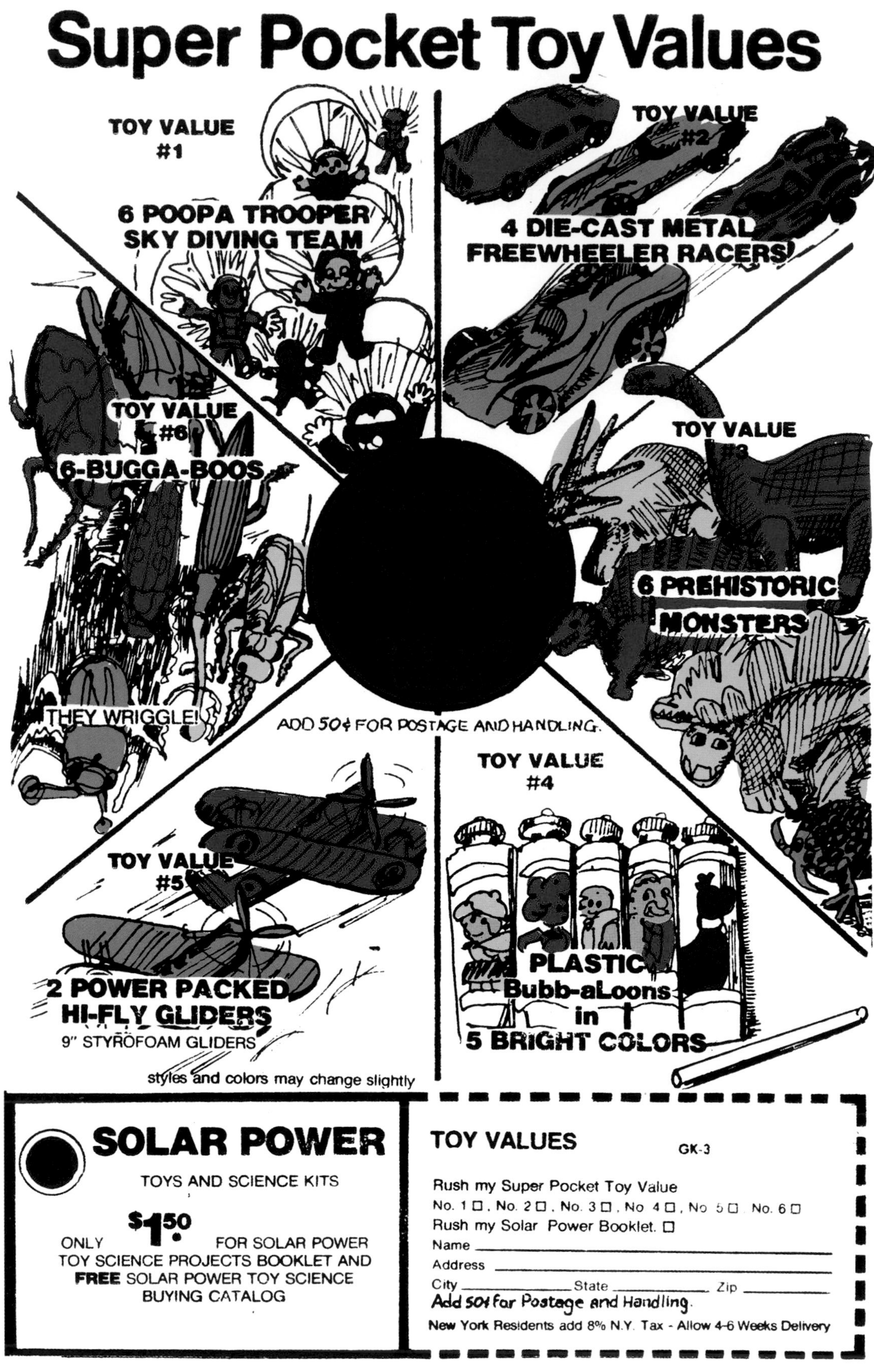

TOY VALUE #1
6 POOPA TROOPER SKY DIVING TEAM
TOY VALUE #2
4 DIE-CAST METAL FREEWHEELER RACERS
TOY VALUE #3
6 PREHISTORIC MONSTERS
TOY VALUE #6
6-BUGGA-BOOS
THEY WRIGGLE!
ADD 50¢ FOR POSTAGE AND HANDLING.
TOY VALUE #5
2 POWER PACKED HI-FLY GLIDERS
9" STYROFOAM GLIDERS
TOY VALUE #4
PLASTIC Bubb-aLoons in 5 BRIGHT COLORS

styles and colors may change slightly

SOLAR POWER

TOYS AND SCIENCE KITS

ONLY $1.50 FOR SOLAR POWER TOY SCIENCE PROJECTS BOOKLET AND **FREE** SOLAR POWER TOY SCIENCE BUYING CATALOG

TOY VALUES

GK-3

Rush my Super Pocket Toy Value

No. 1 ☐, No. 2 ☐, No. 3 ☐, No 4 ☐, No 5 ☐ No. 6 ☐

Rush my Solar Power Booklet. ☐

Name ____________________

Address ____________________

City __________ State __________ Zip __________

Add 50¢ for Postage and Handling.

New York Residents add 8% N.Y. Tax - Allow 4-6 Weeks Delivery

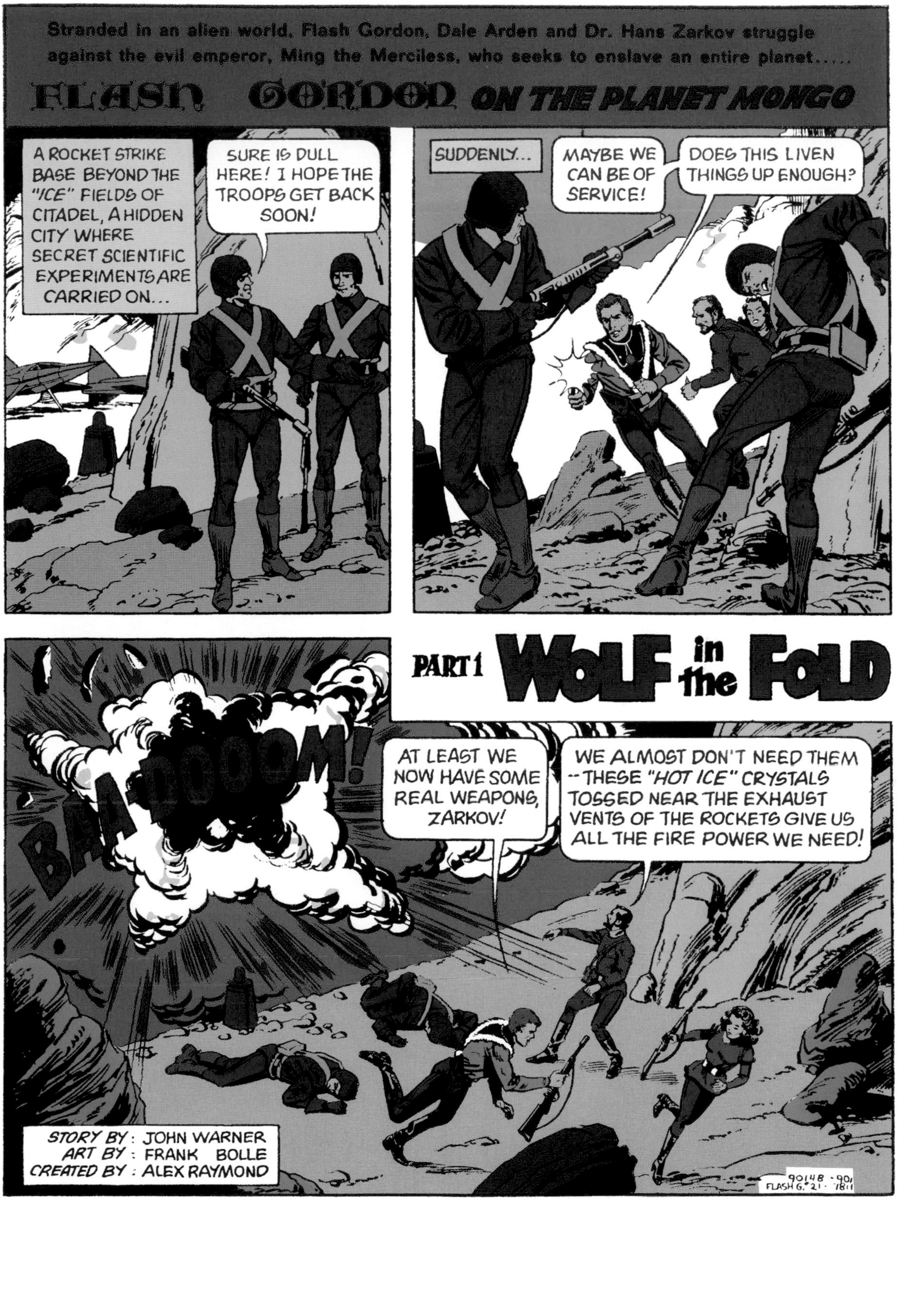
Stranded in an alien world, Flash Gordon, Dale Arden and Dr. Hans Zarkov struggle against the evil emperor, Ming the Merciless, who seeks to enslave an entire planet.....
FLASH GORDON ON THE PLANET MONGO
A ROCKET STRIKE BASE BEYOND THE "ICE" FIELDS OF CITADEL, A HIDDEN CITY WHERE SECRET SCIENTIFIC EXPERIMENTS ARE CARRIED ON...
SURE IS DULL HERE! I HOPE THE TROOPS GET BACK SOON!
SUDDENLY...
MAYBE WE CAN BE OF SERVICE!
DOES THIS LIVEN THINGS UP ENOUGH?
PART 1 WOLF in the FOLD
BA-DOOOOM!
AT LEAST WE NOW HAVE SOME REAL WEAPONS, ZARKOV!
WE ALMOST DON'T NEED THEM -- THESE "HOT ICE" CRYSTALS TOSSED NEAR THE EXHAUST VENTS OF THE ROCKETS GIVE US ALL THE FIRE POWER WE NEED!
STORY BY: JOHN WARNER
ART BY: FRANK BOLLE
CREATED BY: ALEX RAYMOND

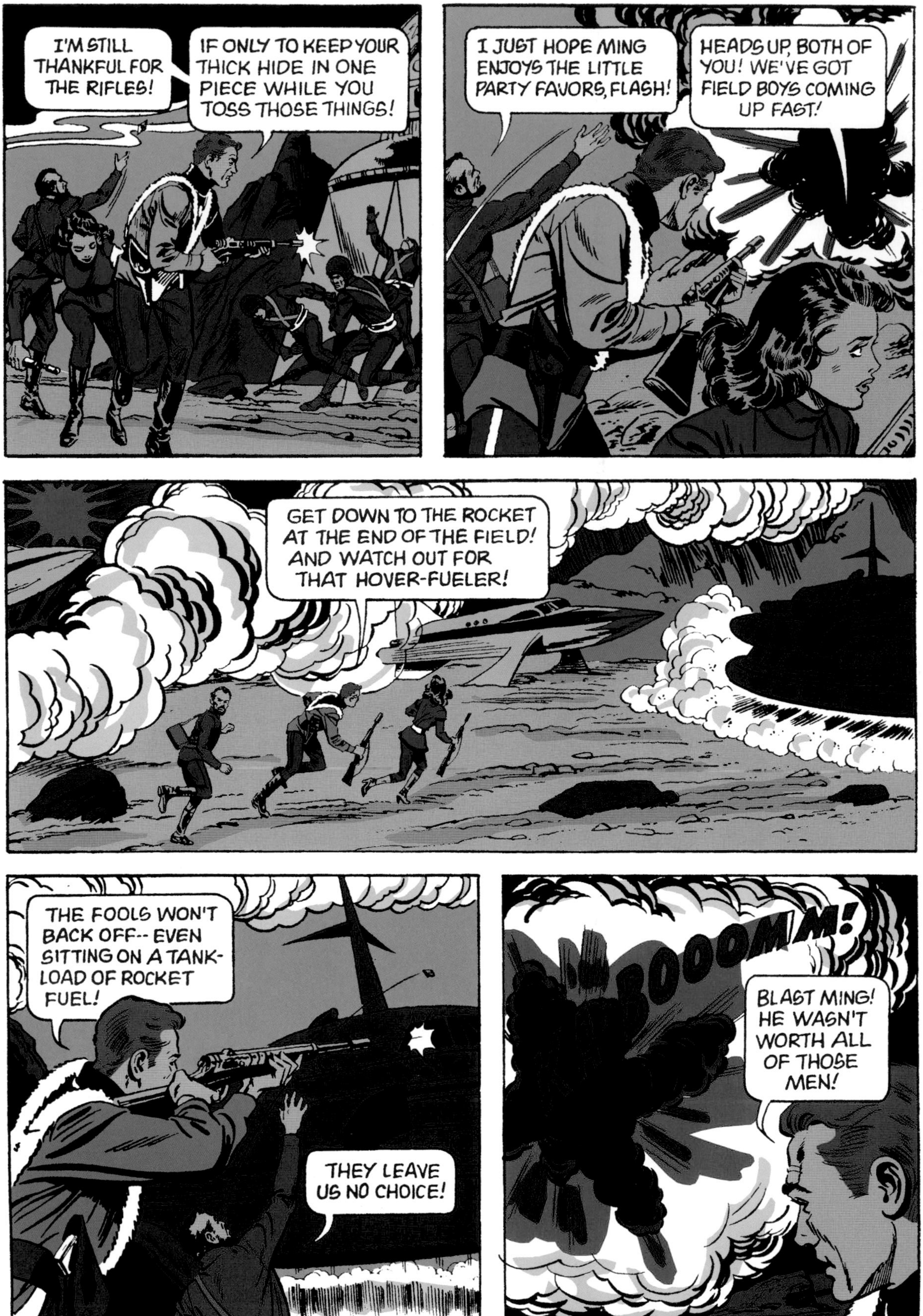
I'M STILL THANKFUL FOR THE RIFLES!
IF ONLY TO KEEP YOUR THICK HIDE IN ONE PIECE WHILE YOU TOSS THOSE THINGS!
I JUST HOPE MING ENJOYS THE LITTLE PARTY FAVORS, FLASH!
HEADS UP, BOTH OF YOU! WE'VE GOT FIELD BOYS COMING UP FAST!
GET DOWN TO THE ROCKET AT THE END OF THE FIELD! AND WATCH OUT FOR THAT HOVER-FUELER!
THE FOOLS WON'T BACK OFF-- EVEN SITTING ON A TANK-LOAD OF ROCKET FUEL!
THEY LEAVE US NO CHOICE!
BOOOOMMM!
BLAST MING! HE WASN'T WORTH ALL OF THOSE MEN!

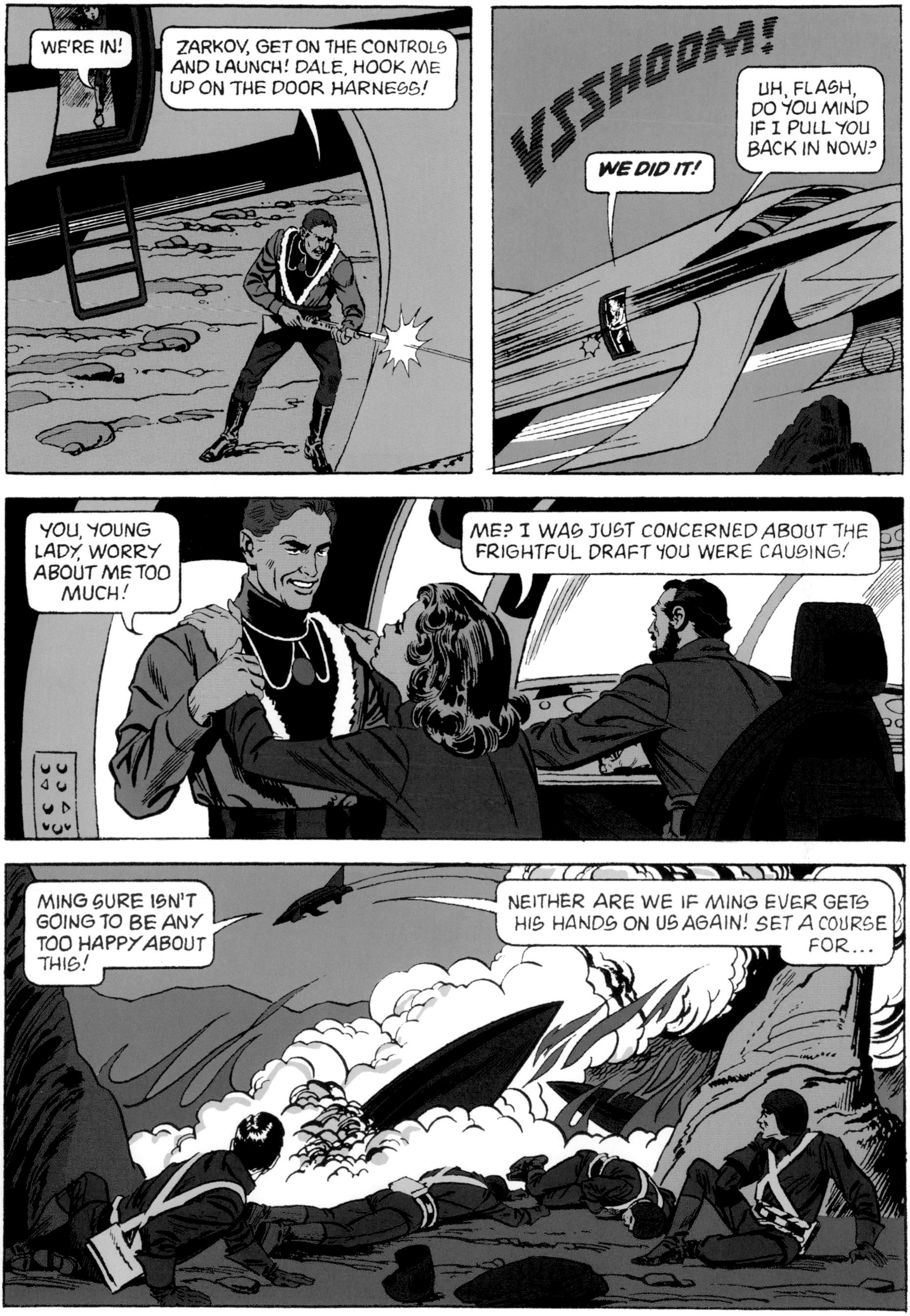
WE'RE IN!
ZARKOV, GET ON THE CONTROLS AND LAUNCH! DALE, HOOK ME UP ON THE DOOR HARNESS!
VSSHOOM!
WE DID IT!
UH, FLASH, DO YOU MIND IF I PULL YOU BACK IN NOW?
YOU, YOUNG LADY, WORRY ABOUT ME TOO MUCH!
ME? I WAS JUST CONCERNED ABOUT THE FRIGHTFUL DRAFT YOU WERE CAUSING!
MING SURE ISN'T GOING TO BE ANY TOO HAPPY ABOUT THIS!
NEITHER ARE WE IF MING EVER GETS HIS HANDS ON US AGAIN! SET A COURSE FOR...

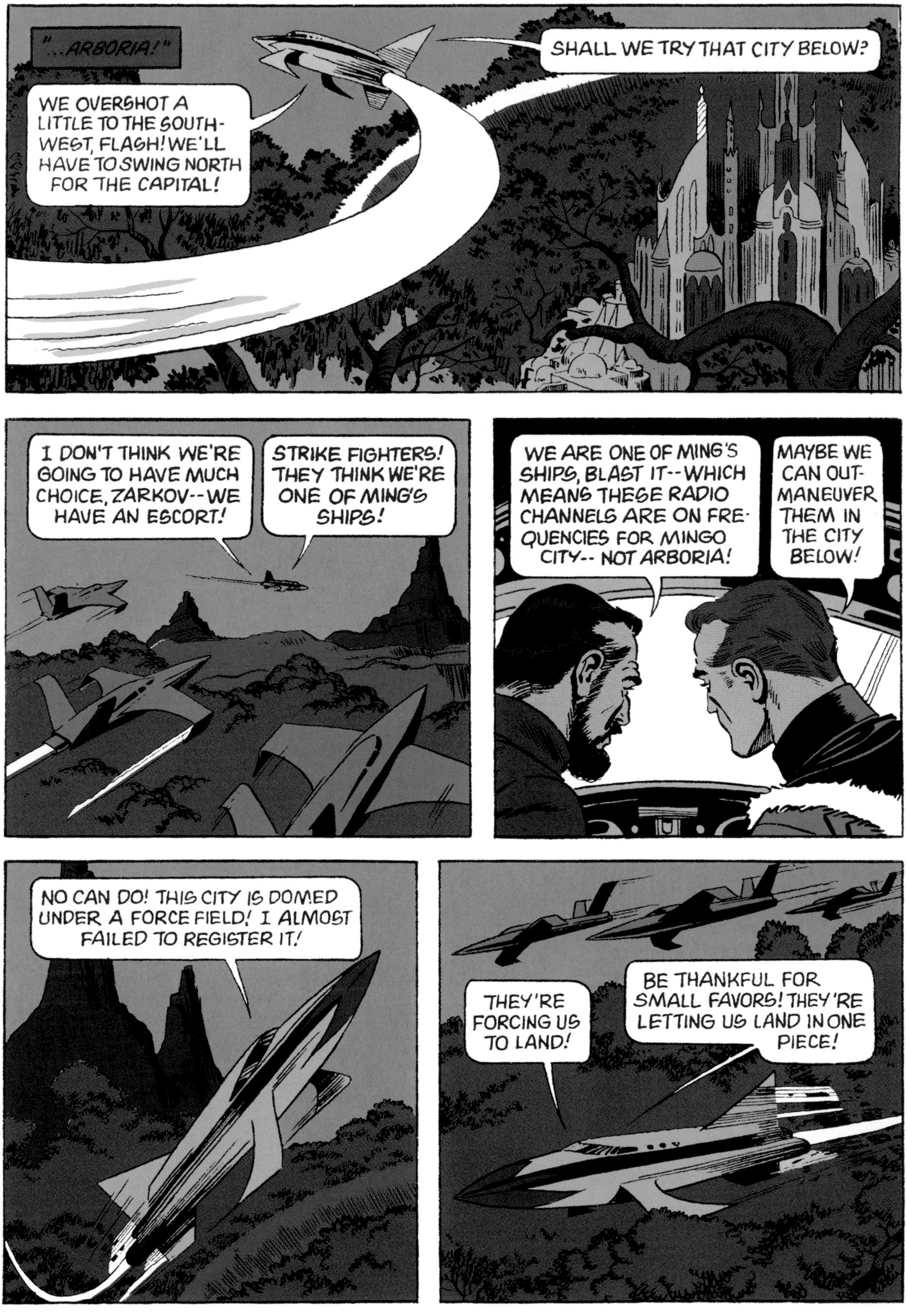
"...ARBORIA!"
WE OVERSHOT A LITTLE TO THE SOUTH-WEST, FLASH! WE'LL HAVE TO SWING NORTH FOR THE CAPITAL!
SHALL WE TRY THAT CITY BELOW?
I DON'T THINK WE'RE GOING TO HAVE MUCH CHOICE, ZARKOV--WE HAVE AN ESCORT!
STRIKE FIGHTERS! THEY THINK WE'RE ONE OF MING'S SHIPS!
WE ARE ONE OF MING'S SHIPS, BLAST IT--WHICH MEANS THESE RADIO CHANNELS ARE ON FRE-QUENCIES FOR MINGO CITY-- NOT ARBORIA!
MAYBE WE CAN OUT-MANEUVER THEM IN THE CITY BELOW!
NO CAN DO! THIS CITY IS DOMED UNDER A FORCE FIELD! I ALMOST FAILED TO REGISTER IT!
THEY'RE FORCING US TO LAND!
BE THANKFUL FOR SMALL FAVORS! THEY'RE LETTING US LAND IN ONE PIECE!

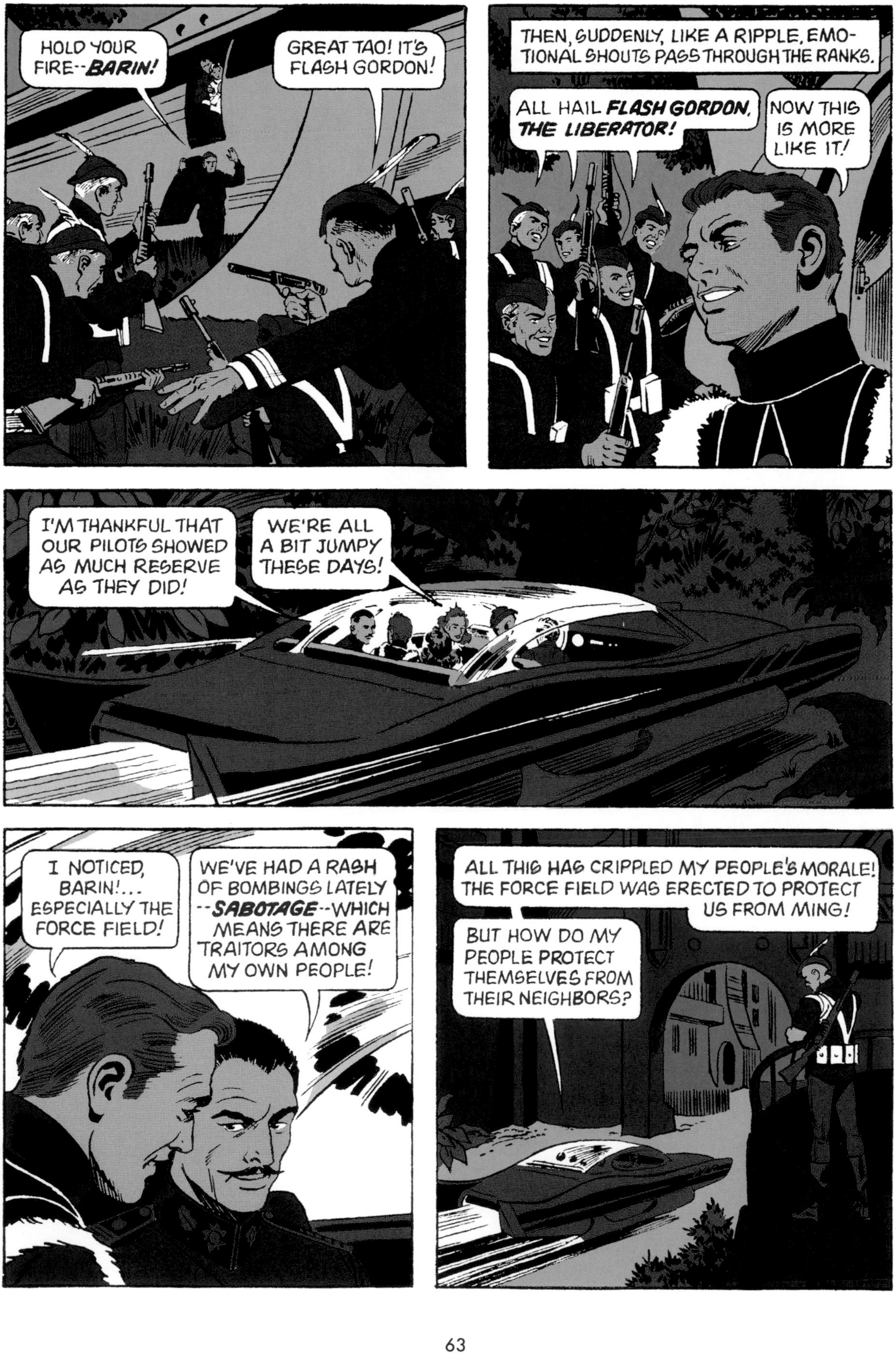
HOLD YOUR FIRE--BARIN!
GREAT TAO! IT'S FLASH GORDON!
THEN, SUDDENLY, LIKE A RIPPLE, EMOTIONAL SHOUTS PASS THROUGH THE RANKS.
ALL HAIL FLASH GORDON, THE LIBERATOR!
NOW THIS IS MORE LIKE IT!
I'M THANKFUL THAT OUR PILOTS SHOWED AS MUCH RESERVE AS THEY DID!
WE'RE ALL A BIT JUMPY THESE DAYS!
I NOTICED, BARIN!... ESPECIALLY THE FORCE FIELD!
WE'VE HAD A RASH OF BOMBINGS LATELY --SABOTAGE--WHICH MEANS THERE ARE TRAITORS AMONG MY OWN PEOPLE!
ALL THIS HAS CRIPPLED MY PEOPLE'S MORALE! THE FORCE FIELD WAS ERECTED TO PROTECT US FROM MING!
BUT HOW DO MY PEOPLE PROTECT THEMSELVES FROM THEIR NEIGHBORS?

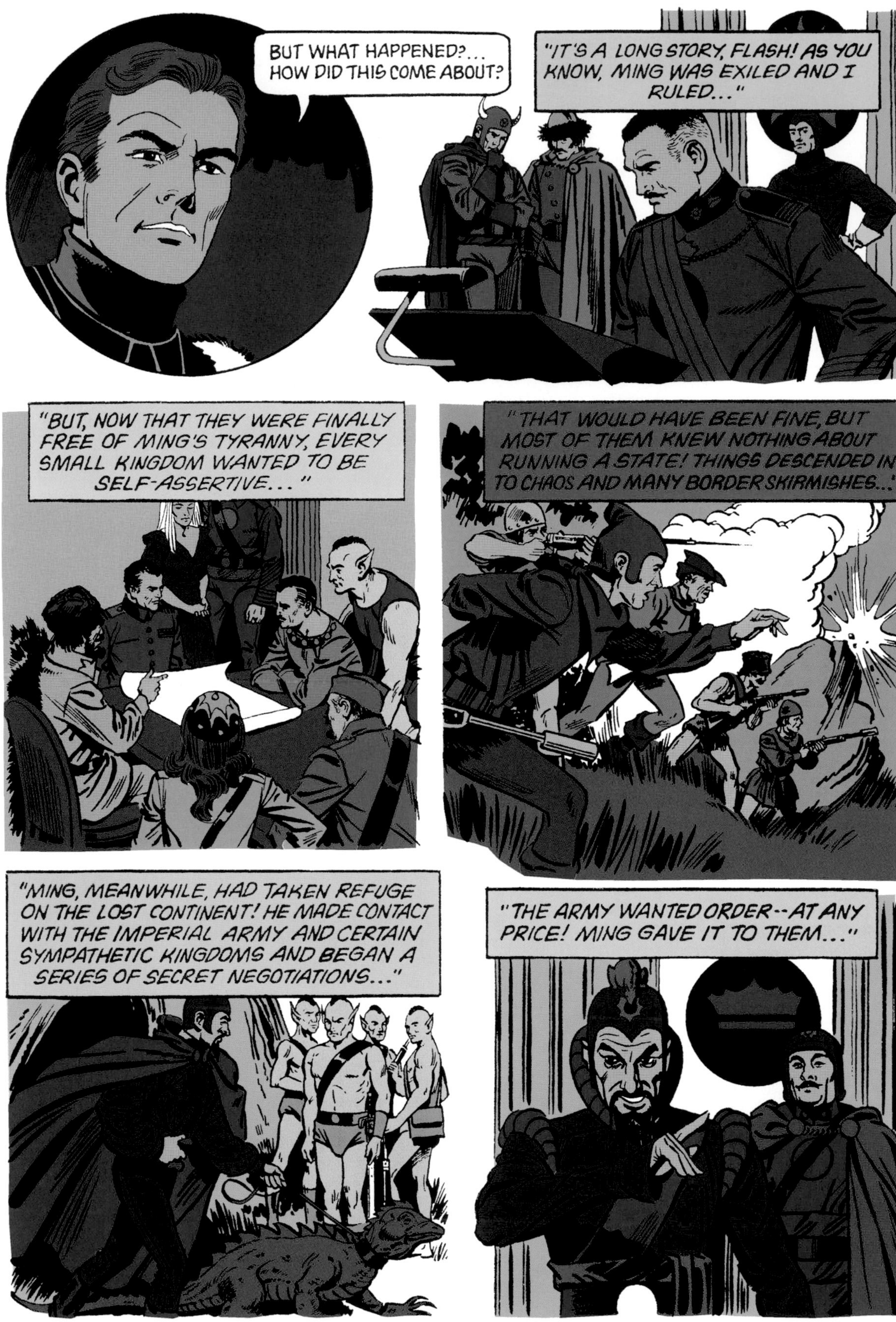
BUT WHAT HAPPENED?... HOW DID THIS COME ABOUT?
"IT'S A LONG STORY, FLASH! AS YOU KNOW, MING WAS EXILED AND I RULED..."
"BUT, NOW THAT THEY WERE FINALLY FREE OF MING'S TYRANNY, EVERY SMALL KINGDOM WANTED TO BE SELF-ASSERTIVE..."
"THAT WOULD HAVE BEEN FINE, BUT MOST OF THEM KNEW NOTHING ABOUT RUNNING A STATE! THINGS DESCENDED INTO CHAOS AND MANY BORDER SKIRMISHES..."
"MING, MEANWHILE, HAD TAKEN REFUGE ON THE LOST CONTINENT! HE MADE CONTACT WITH THE IMPERIAL ARMY AND CERTAIN SYMPATHETIC KINGDOMS AND BEGAN A SERIES OF SECRET NEGOTIATIONS..."
"THE ARMY WANTED ORDER--AT ANY PRICE! MING GAVE IT TO THEM..."

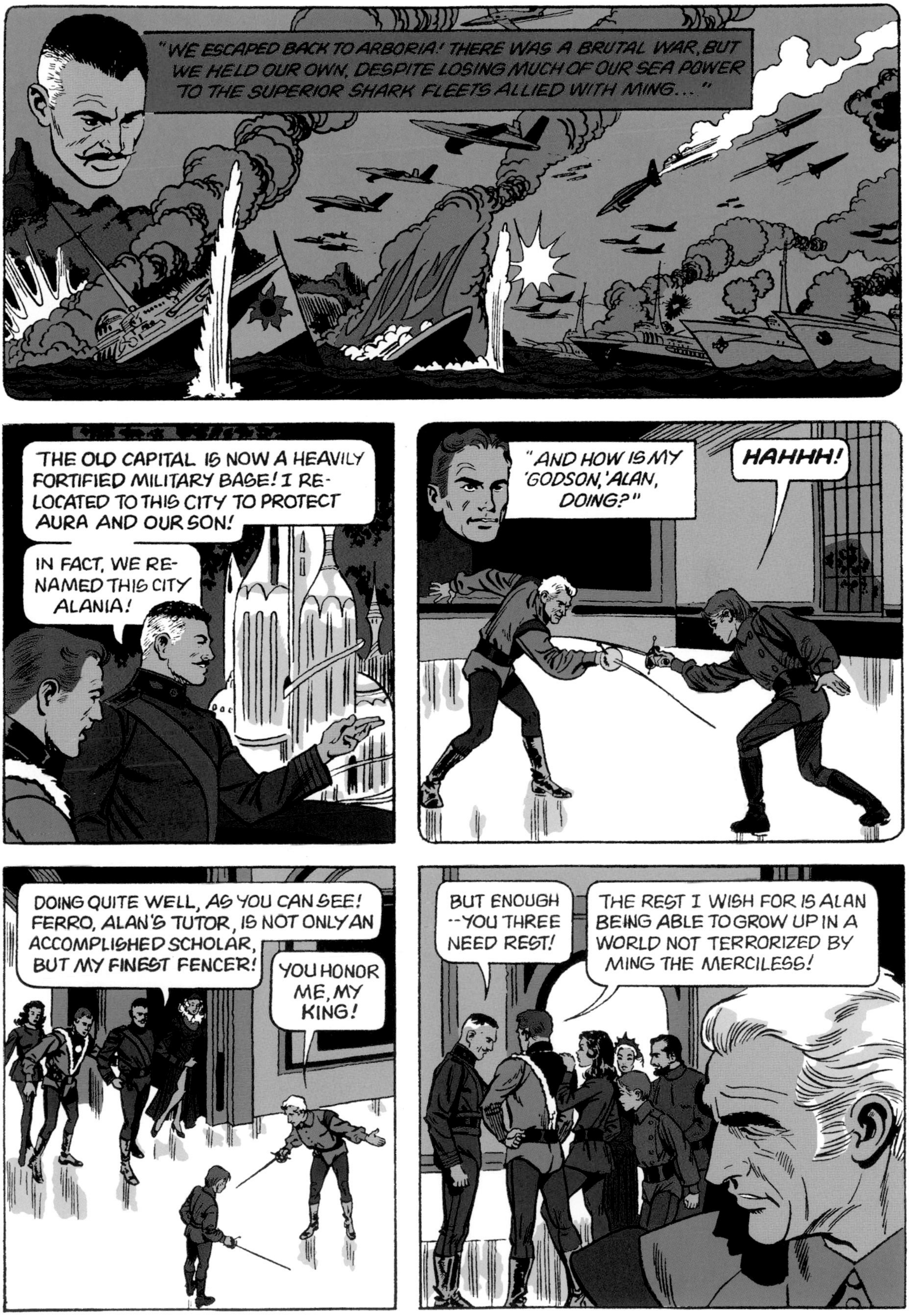
"WE ESCAPED BACK TO ARBORIA! THERE WAS A BRUTAL WAR, BUT WE HELD OUR OWN, DESPITE LOSING MUCH OF OUR SEA POWER TO THE SUPERIOR SHARK FLEETS ALLIED WITH MING..."
THE OLD CAPITAL IS NOW A HEAVILY FORTIFIED MILITARY BASE! I RE-LOCATED TO THIS CITY TO PROTECT AURA AND OUR SON!
IN FACT, WE RE-NAMED THIS CITY ALANIA!
"AND HOW IS MY 'GODSON,' ALAN, DOING?"
HAHHH!
DOING QUITE WELL, AS YOU CAN SEE! FERRO, ALAN'S TUTOR, IS NOT ONLY AN ACCOMPLISHED SCHOLAR, BUT MY FINEST FENCER!
YOU HONOR ME, MY KING!
BUT ENOUGH --YOU THREE NEED REST!
THE REST I WISH FOR IS ALAN BEING ABLE TO GROW UP IN A WORLD NOT TERRORIZED BY MING THE MERCILESS!

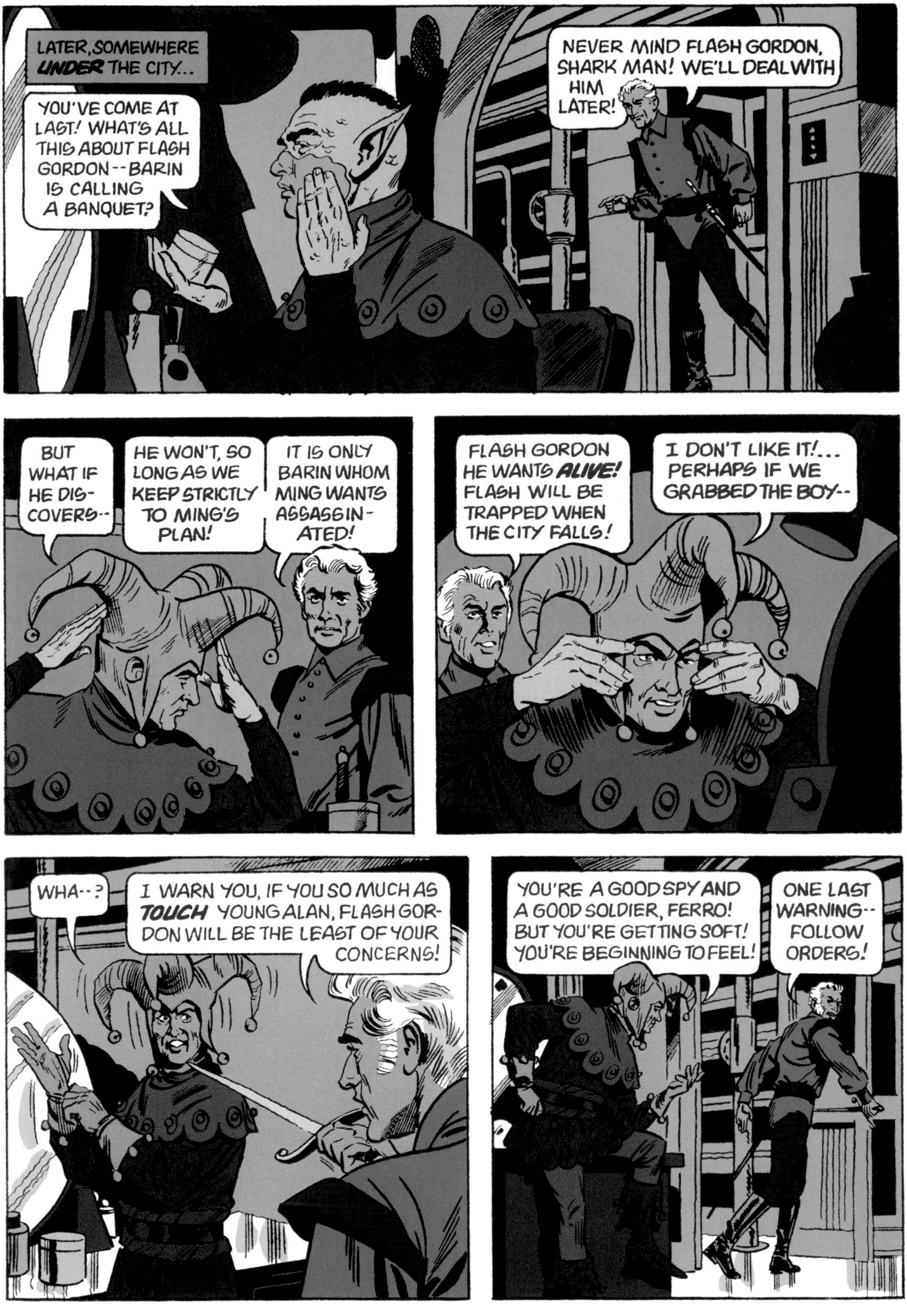
LATER, SOMEWHERE UNDER THE CITY...
YOU'VE COME AT LAST! WHAT'S ALL THIS ABOUT FLASH GORDON -- BARIN IS CALLING A BANQUET?
NEVER MIND FLASH GORDON, SHARK MAN! WE'LL DEAL WITH HIM LATER!
BUT WHAT IF HE DISCOVERS--
HE WON'T, SO LONG AS WE KEEP STRICTLY TO MING'S PLAN!
IT IS ONLY BARIN WHOM MING WANTS ASSASSINATED!
FLASH GORDON HE WANTS ALIVE! FLASH WILL BE TRAPPED WHEN THE CITY FALLS!
I DON'T LIKE IT!... PERHAPS IF WE GRABBED THE BOY--
WHA--?
I WARN YOU, IF YOU SO MUCH AS TOUCH YOUNG ALAN, FLASH GORDON WILL BE THE LEAST OF YOUR CONCERNS!
YOU'RE A GOOD SPY AND A GOOD SOLDIER, FERRO! BUT YOU'RE GETTING SOFT! YOU'RE BEGINNING TO FEEL!
ONE LAST WARNING-- FOLLOW ORDERS!

EVENING! THE ROYAL PALACE FILLS WITH LIGHT AND THE SOUNDS OF CELEBRATION...

FLASH, WILL YOU LOOK AT THIS! IT'S LIKE SOMETHING OUT OF THE ARABIAN NIGHTS!

BEHOLD, FLASH GORDON -- WHILE YOU SLEPT, MY PEOPLE GATHERED TOGETHER TO PAY YOU YOUR DUE HOMAGE!

COME ON, FLASH! STOP LOOKING SO GRIM!

I'M SORRY, DALE! I KNOW I'M BEING RUDE AFTER ALL THE TROUBLE BARIN HAS GONE TO! I CAN'T HELP IT!

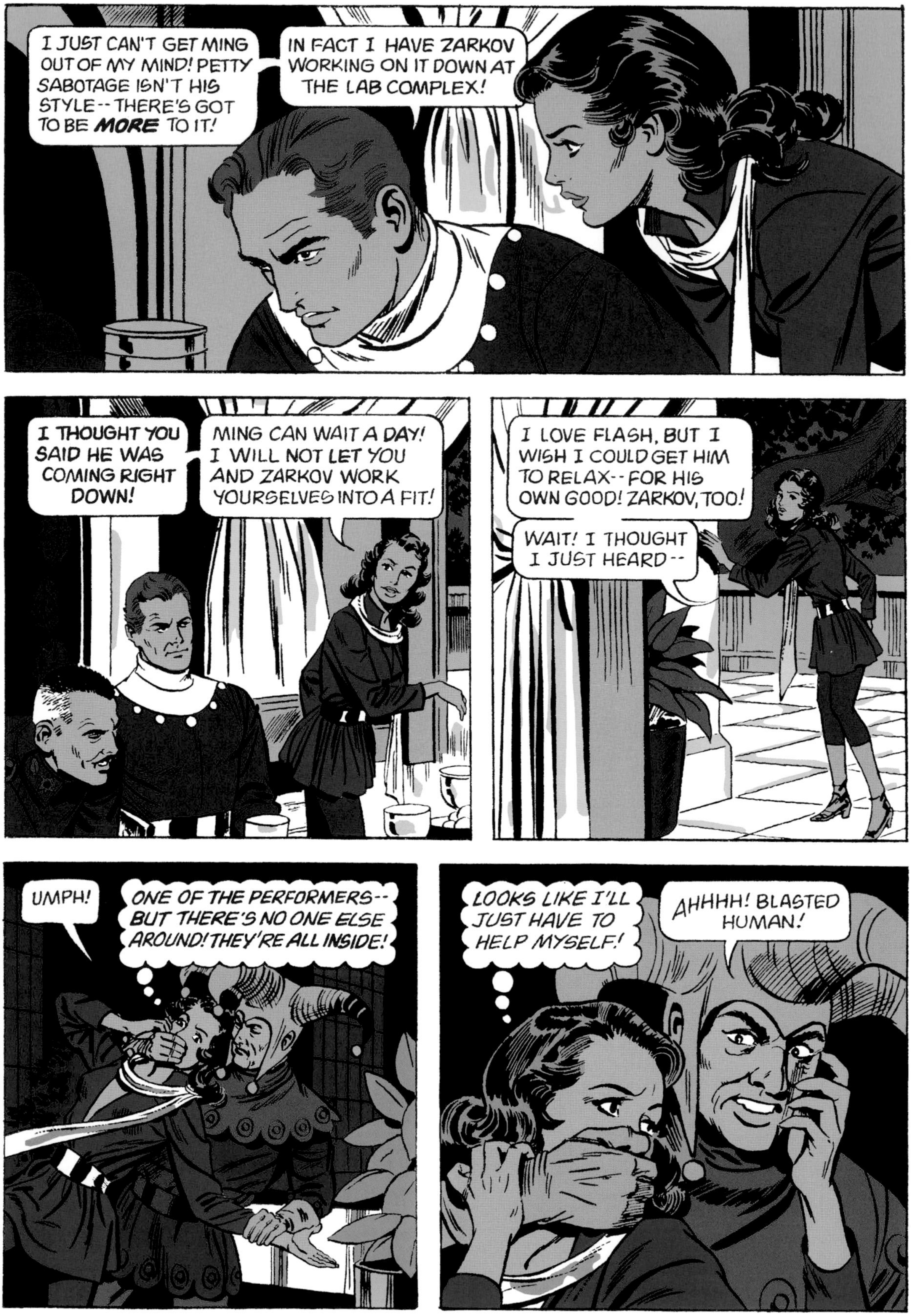
I JUST CAN'T GET MING OUT OF MY MIND! PETTY SABOTAGE ISN'T HIS STYLE -- THERE'S GOT TO BE MORE TO IT!
IN FACT I HAVE ZARKOV WORKING ON IT DOWN AT THE LAB COMPLEX!
I THOUGHT YOU SAID HE WAS COMING RIGHT DOWN!
MING CAN WAIT A DAY! I WILL NOT LET YOU AND ZARKOV WORK YOURSELVES INTO A FIT!
I LOVE FLASH, BUT I WISH I COULD GET HIM TO RELAX -- FOR HIS OWN GOOD! ZARKOV, TOO!
WAIT! I THOUGHT I JUST HEARD --
UMPH!
ONE OF THE PERFORMERS -- BUT THERE'S NO ONE ELSE AROUND! THEY'RE ALL INSIDE!
LOOKS LIKE I'LL JUST HAVE TO HELP MYSELF!
AHHHH! BLASTED HUMAN!

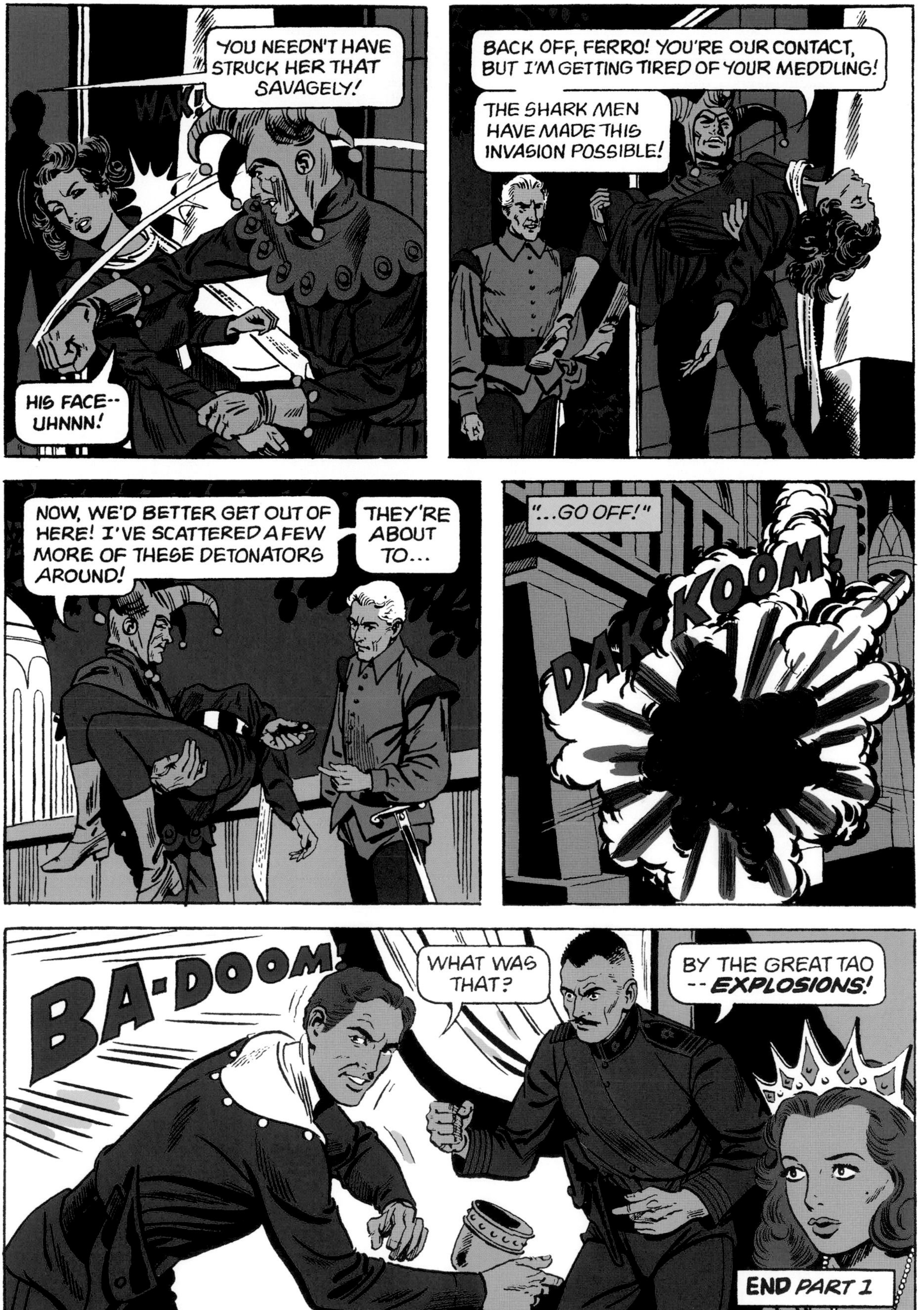
WAK!
YOU NEEDN'T HAVE STRUCK HER THAT SAVAGELY!
HIS FACE-- UHNNN!
BACK OFF, FERRO! YOU'RE OUR CONTACT, BUT I'M GETTING TIRED OF YOUR MEDDLING!
THE SHARK MEN HAVE MADE THIS INVASION POSSIBLE!
NOW, WE'D BETTER GET OUT OF HERE! I'VE SCATTERED A FEW MORE OF THESE DETONATORS AROUND!
THEY'RE ABOUT TO...
"...GO OFF!"
DAK-KOOM!
BA-DOOM!
WHAT WAS THAT?
BY THE GREAT TAO -- ***EXPLOSIONS!***
END *PART 1*

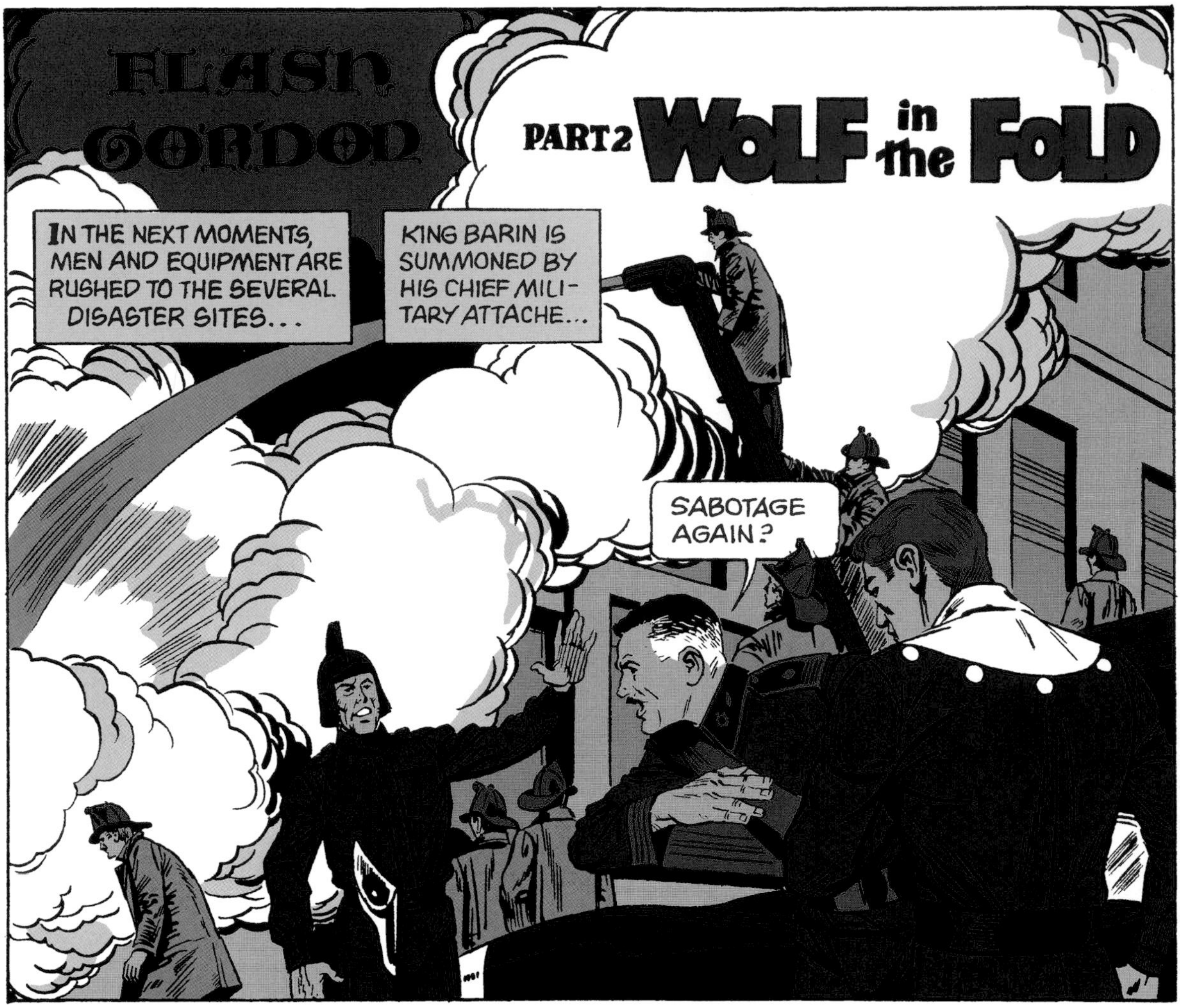
FLASH GORDON
PART 2 WOLF in the FOLD
IN THE NEXT MOMENTS, MEN AND EQUIPMENT ARE RUSHED TO THE SEVERAL DISASTER SITES...
KING BARIN IS SUMMONED BY HIS CHIEF MILITARY ATTACHE...
SABOTAGE AGAIN?

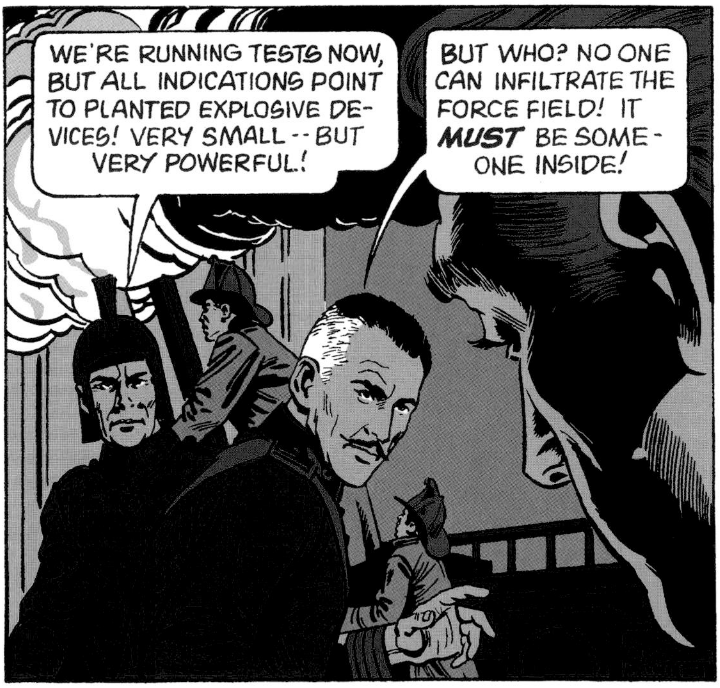
WE'RE RUNNING TESTS NOW, BUT ALL INDICATIONS POINT TO PLANTED EXPLOSIVE DEVICES! VERY SMALL -- BUT VERY POWERFUL!
BUT WHO? NO ONE CAN INFILTRATE THE FORCE FIELD! IT MUST BE SOMEONE INSIDE!

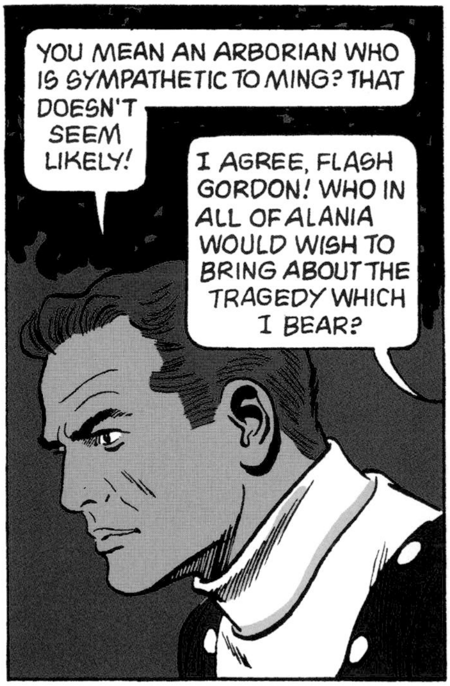
YOU MEAN AN ARBORIAN WHO IS SYMPATHETIC TO MING? THAT DOESN'T SEEM LIKELY!
I AGREE, FLASH GORDON! WHO IN ALL OF ALANIA WOULD WISH TO BRING ABOUT THE TRAGEDY WHICH I BEAR?

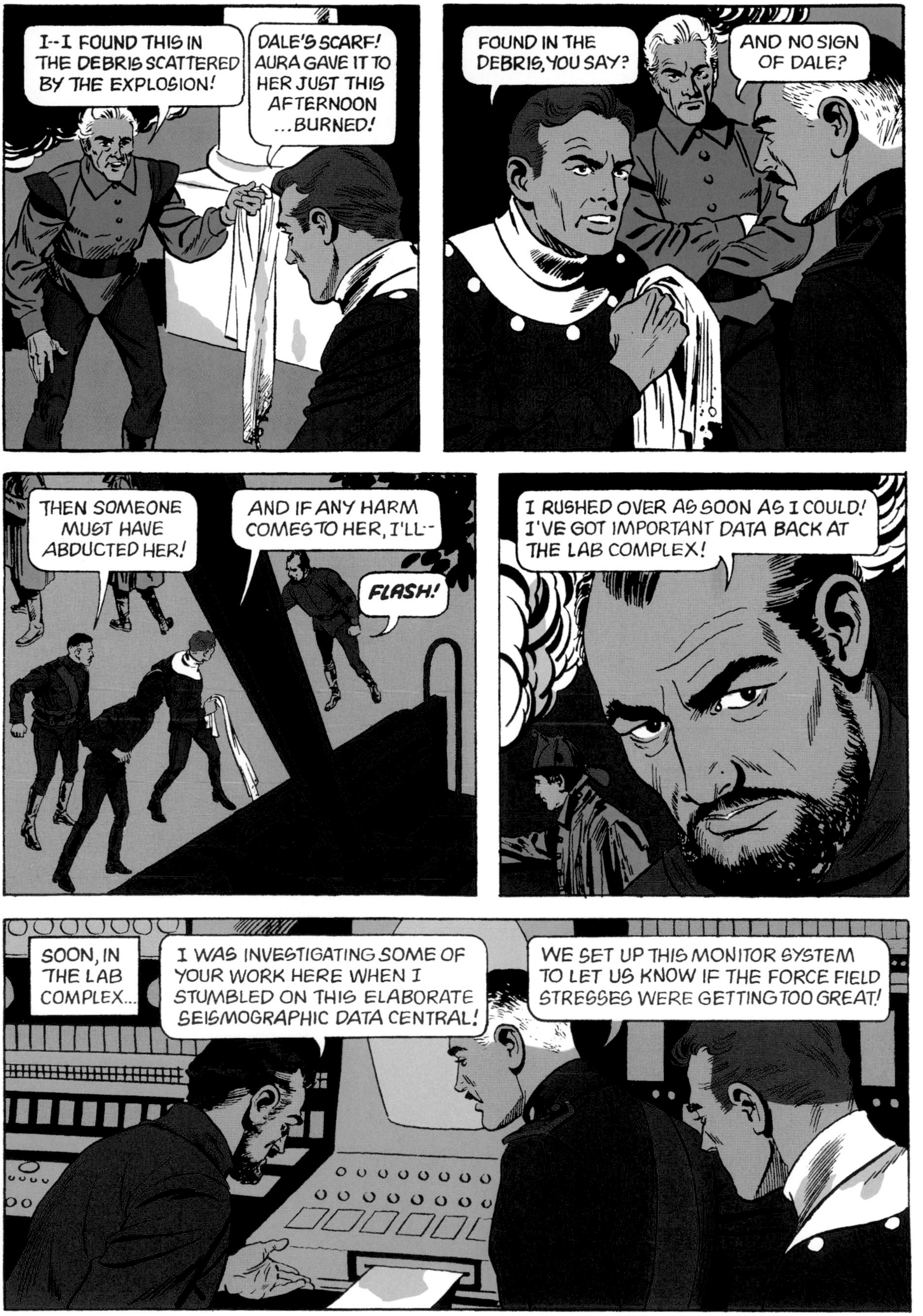
I--I FOUND THIS IN THE DEBRIS SCATTERED BY THE EXPLOSION!
DALE'S SCARF! AURA GAVE IT TO HER JUST THIS AFTERNOON ...BURNED!
FOUND IN THE DEBRIS, YOU SAY?
AND NO SIGN OF DALE?
THEN SOMEONE MUST HAVE ABDUCTED HER!
AND IF ANY HARM COMES TO HER, I'LL-
FLASH!
I RUSHED OVER AS SOON AS I COULD! I'VE GOT IMPORTANT DATA BACK AT THE LAB COMPLEX!
SOON, IN THE LAB COMPLEX...
I WAS INVESTIGATING SOME OF YOUR WORK HERE WHEN I STUMBLED ON THIS ELABORATE SEISMOGRAPHIC DATA CENTRAL!
WE SET UP THIS MONITOR SYSTEM TO LET US KNOW IF THE FORCE FIELD STRESSES WERE GETTING TOO GREAT!

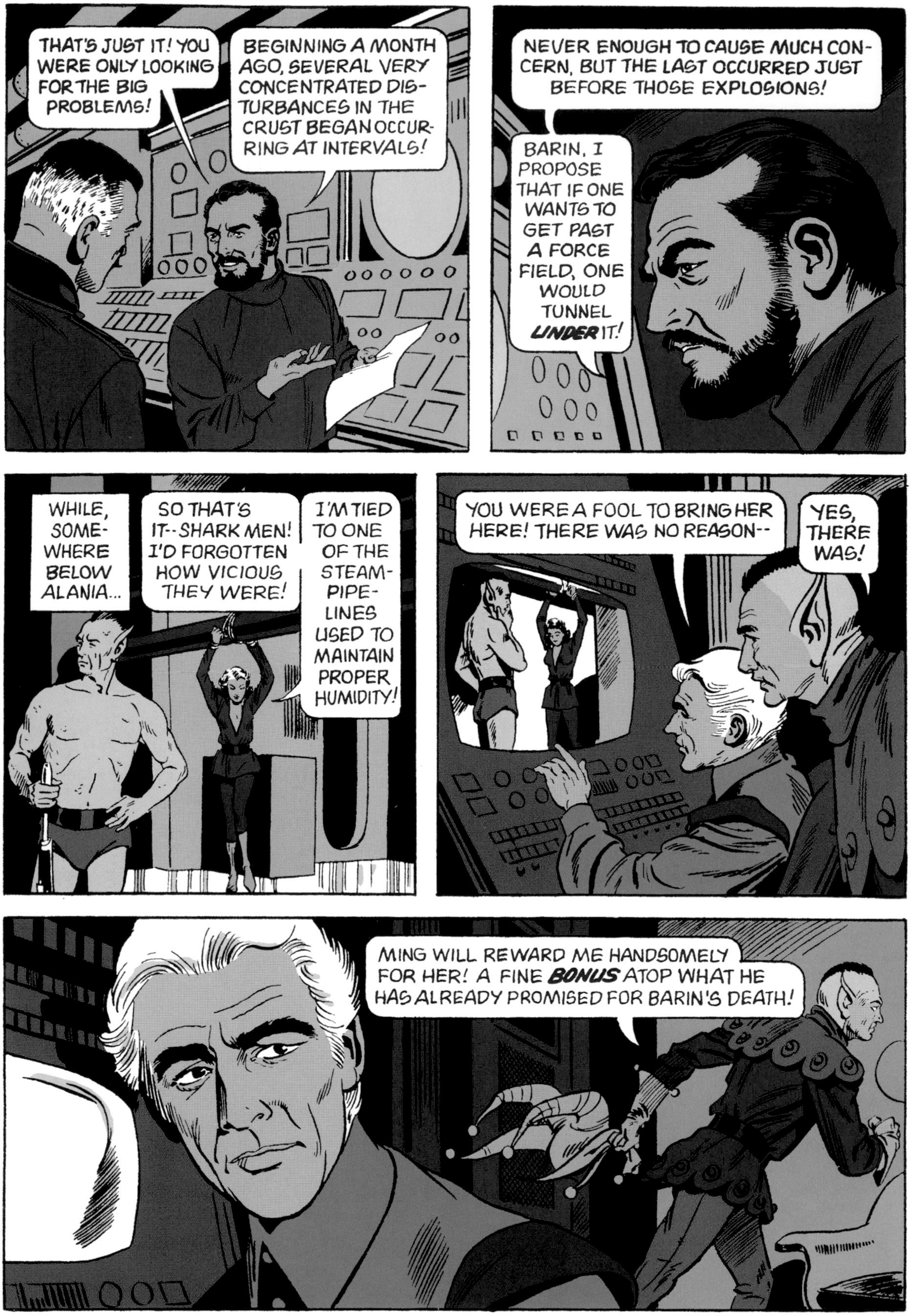

THAT'S JUST IT! YOU WERE ONLY LOOKING FOR THE BIG PROBLEMS!
BEGINNING A MONTH AGO, SEVERAL VERY CONCENTRATED DISTURBANCES IN THE CRUST BEGAN OCCURRING AT INTERVALS!
NEVER ENOUGH TO CAUSE MUCH CONCERN, BUT THE LAST OCCURRED JUST BEFORE THOSE EXPLOSIONS!
BARIN, I PROPOSE THAT IF ONE WANTS TO GET PAST A FORCE FIELD, ONE WOULD TUNNEL *UNDER* IT!
WHILE, SOMEWHERE BELOW ALANIA...
SO THAT'S IT--SHARK MEN! I'D FORGOTTEN HOW VICIOUS THEY WERE!
I'M TIED TO ONE OF THE STEAM-PIPE-LINES USED TO MAINTAIN PROPER HUMIDITY!
YOU WERE A FOOL TO BRING HER HERE! THERE WAS NO REASON--
YES, THERE WAS!
MING WILL REWARD ME HANDSOMELY FOR HER! A FINE *BONUS* ATOP WHAT HE HAS ALREADY PROMISED FOR BARIN'S DEATH!

BACK IN THE LAB COMPLEX...

THERE -- I THINK I HAVE SOMETHING -- THE NORTHWEST QUADRANT!

WHAT ARE YOU TALKING ABOUT?

I'VE MAPPED OUT ALL THE SITES OF THE RECENT SABOTAGE AND THEY NEARLY FORM A CIRCLE WITH ITS CENTER IN THE NORTH-WEST QUADRANT!

GREAT TAO! I JUST REALIZED WHAT'S AT THAT CENTER...

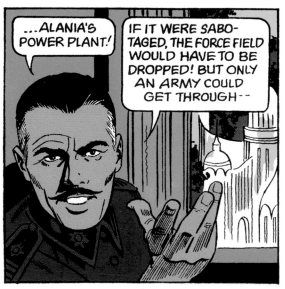

...ALANIA'S POWER PLANT!

IF IT WERE SABO-TAGED, THE FORCE FIELD WOULD HAVE TO BE DROPPED! BUT ONLY AN ARMY COULD GET THROUGH --

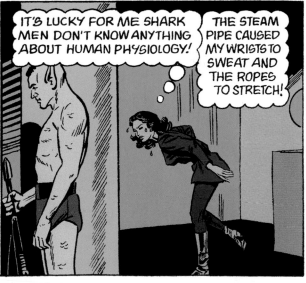

IT'S LUCKY FOR ME SHARK MEN DON'T KNOW ANYTHING ABOUT HUMAN PHYSIOLOGY!

THE STEAM PIPE CAUSED MY WRISTS TO SWEAT AND THE ROPES TO STRETCH!

...AND IT'S GOOD I KNOW WHERE SHARK MEN ARE VULNERABLE!

THOKK!

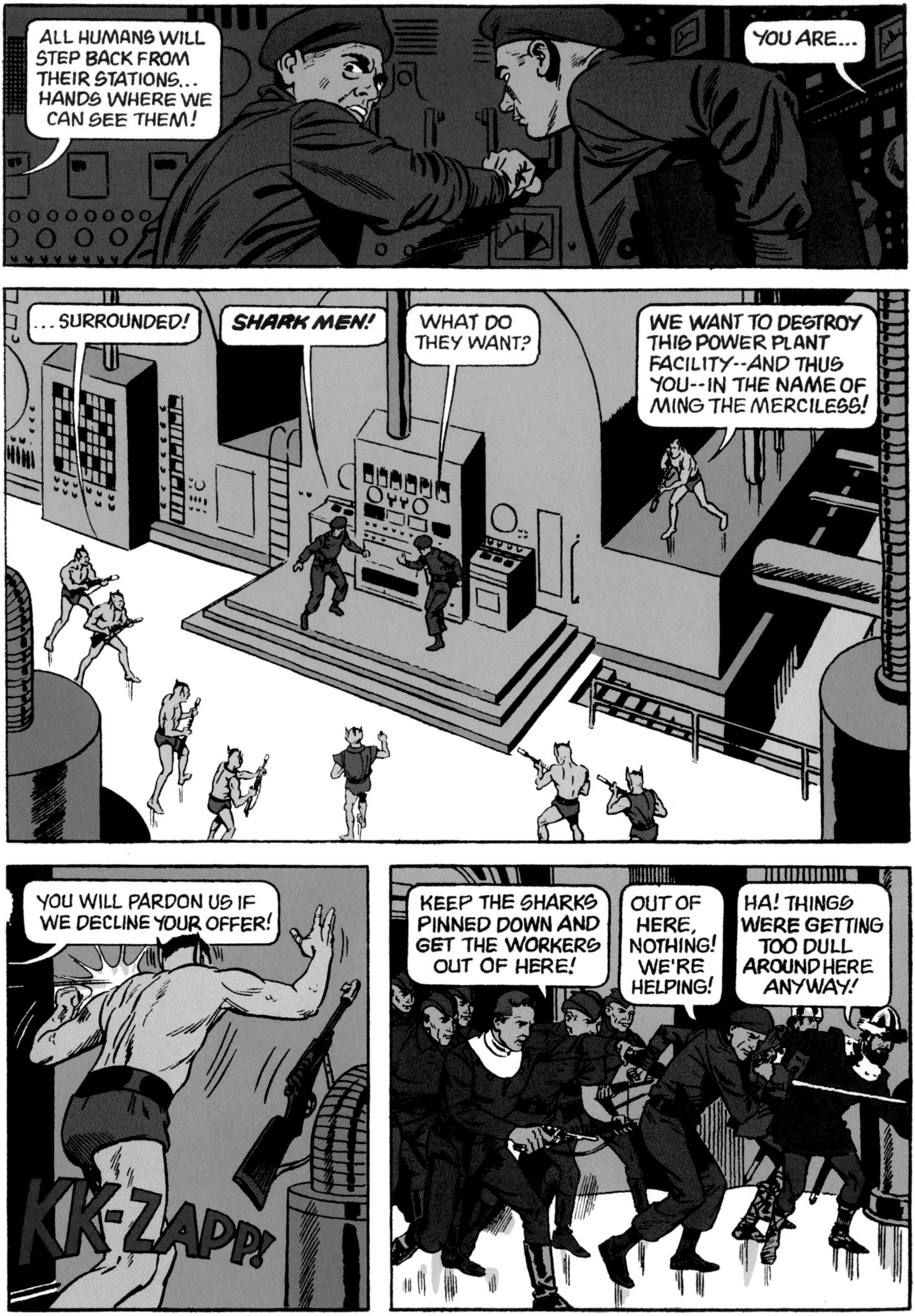
ALL HUMANS WILL STEP BACK FROM THEIR STATIONS... HANDS WHERE WE CAN SEE THEM!
YOU ARE...
...SURROUNDED!
SHARK MEN!
WHAT DO THEY WANT?
WE WANT TO DESTROY THIS POWER PLANT FACILITY--AND THUS YOU--IN THE NAME OF MING THE MERCILESS!
YOU WILL PARDON US IF WE DECLINE YOUR OFFER!
KK-ZAPP!
KEEP THE SHARKS PINNED DOWN AND GET THE WORKERS OUT OF HERE!
OUT OF HERE, NOTHING! WE'RE HELPING!
HA! THINGS WERE GETTING TOO DULL AROUND HERE ANYWAY!

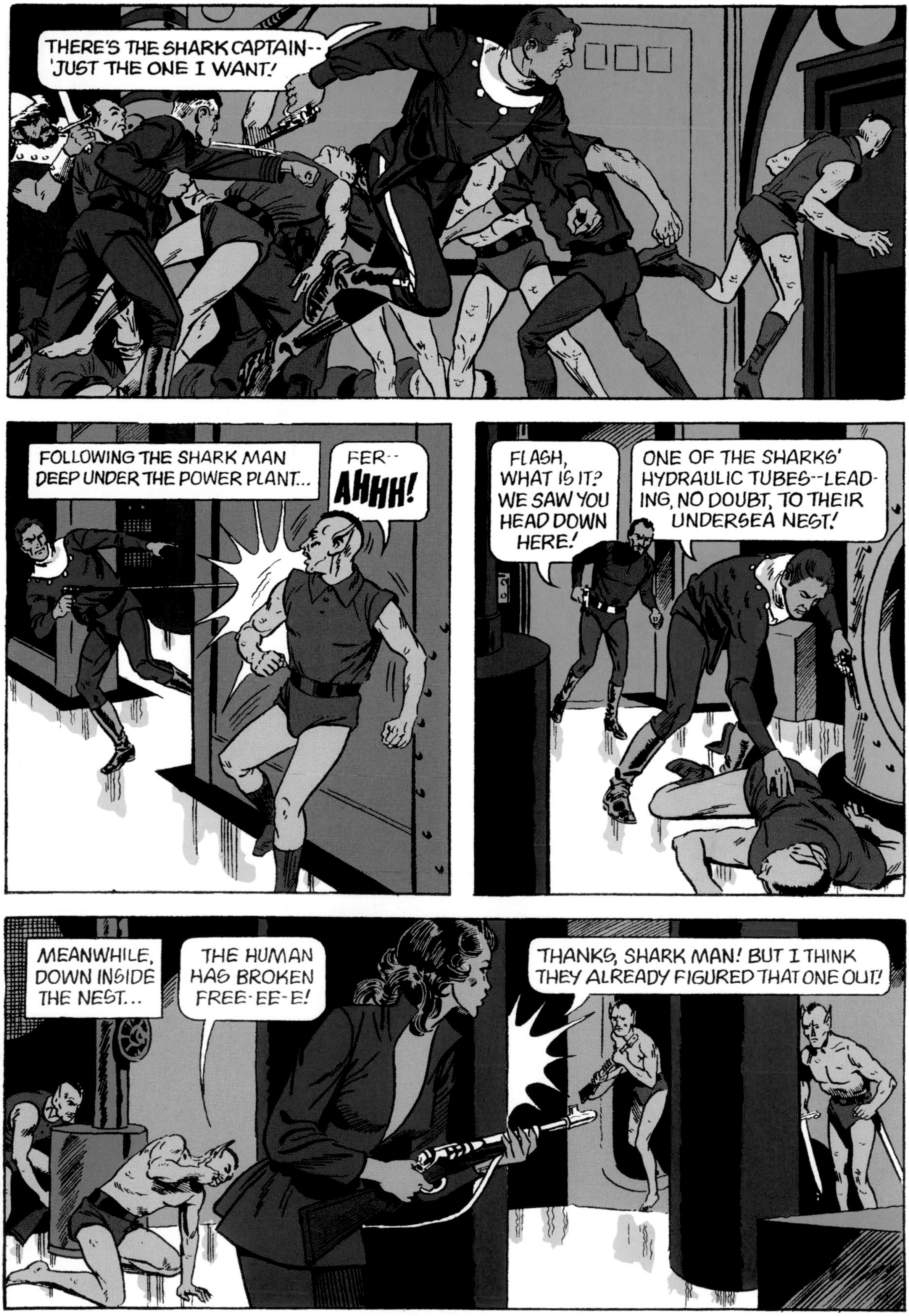
THERE'S THE SHARK CAPTAIN-- JUST THE ONE I WANT!
FOLLOWING THE SHARK MAN DEEP UNDER THE POWER PLANT...
FER-- AHHH!
FLASH, WHAT IS IT? WE SAW YOU HEAD DOWN HERE!
ONE OF THE SHARKS' HYDRAULIC TUBES--LEADING, NO DOUBT, TO THEIR UNDERSEA NEST!
MEANWHILE, DOWN INSIDE THE NEST...
THE HUMAN HAS BROKEN FREE-EE-E!
THANKS, SHARK MAN! BUT I THINK THEY ALREADY FIGURED THAT ONE OUT!

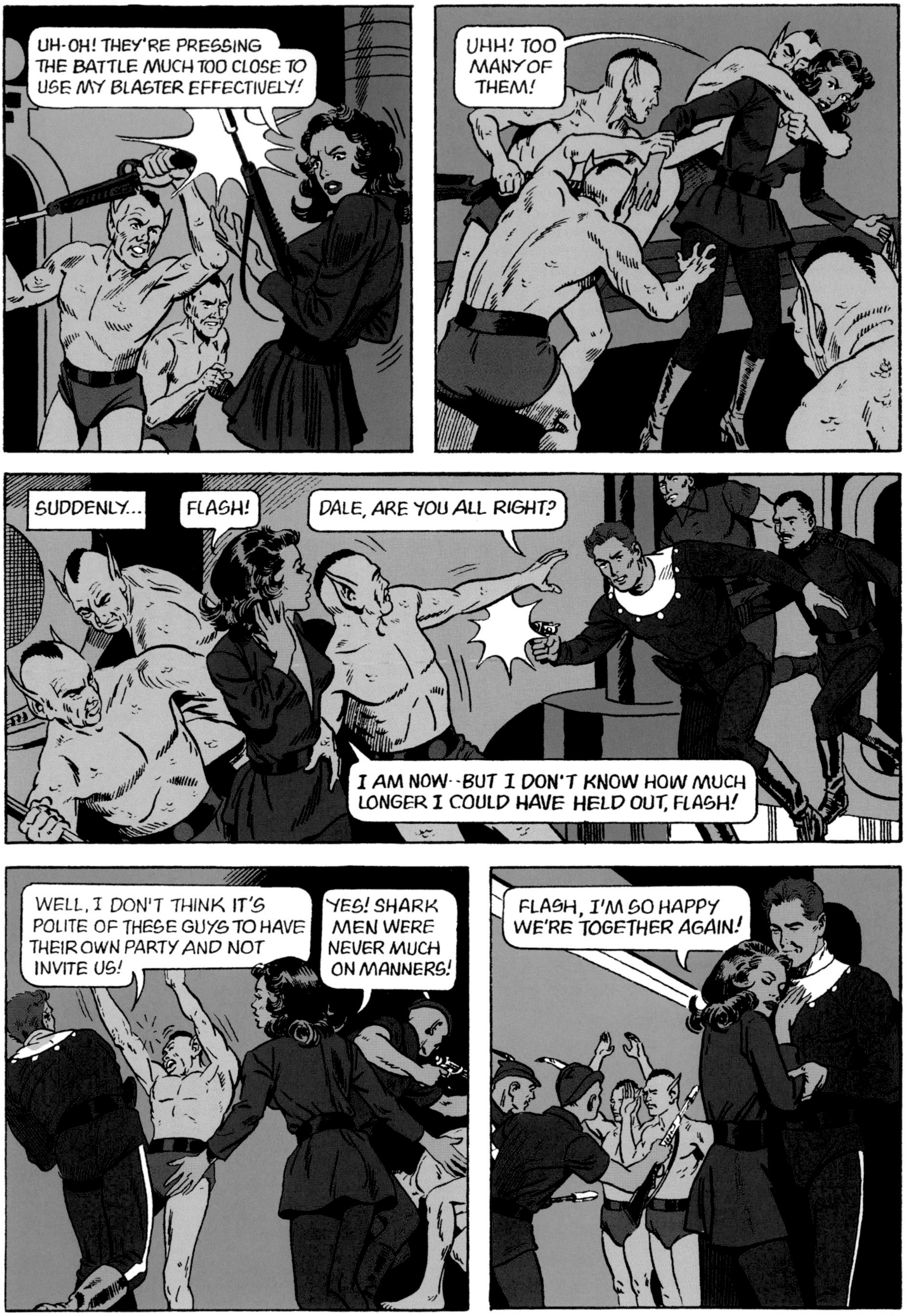
UH-OH! THEY'RE PRESSING THE BATTLE MUCH TOO CLOSE TO USE MY BLASTER EFFECTIVELY!
UHH! TOO MANY OF THEM!
SUDDENLY...
FLASH!
DALE, ARE YOU ALL RIGHT?
I AM NOW--BUT I DON'T KNOW HOW MUCH LONGER I COULD HAVE HELD OUT, FLASH!
WELL, I DON'T THINK IT'S POLITE OF THESE GUYS TO HAVE THEIR OWN PARTY AND NOT INVITE US!
YES! SHARK MEN WERE NEVER MUCH ON MANNERS!
FLASH, I'M SO HAPPY WE'RE TOGETHER AGAIN!

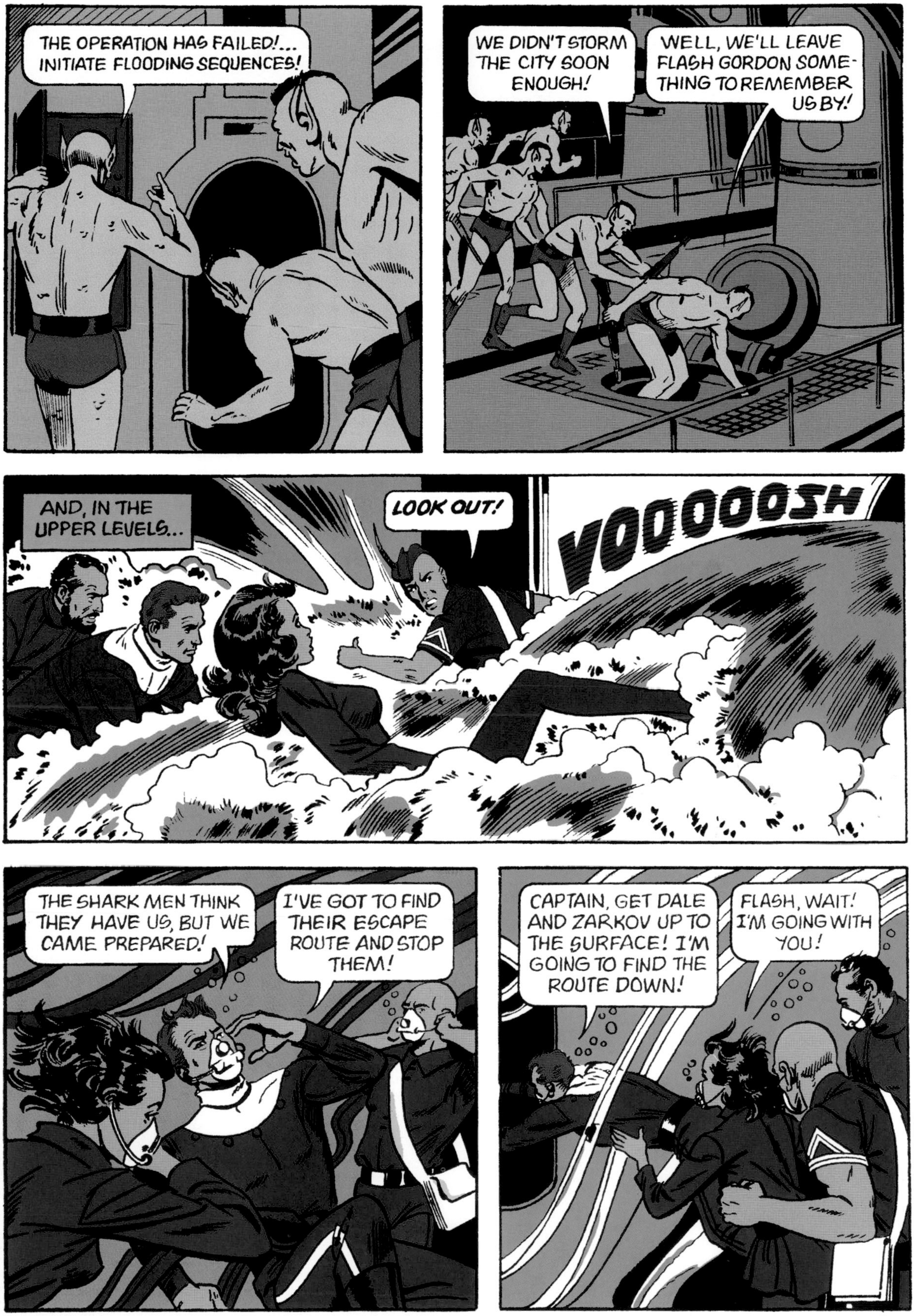
THE OPERATION HAS FAILED!... INITIATE FLOODING SEQUENCES!
WE DIDN'T STORM THE CITY SOON ENOUGH!
WELL, WE'LL LEAVE FLASH GORDON SOMETHING TO REMEMBER US BY!
AND, IN THE UPPER LEVELS...
LOOK OUT!
VOOOOOSH
THE SHARK MEN THINK THEY HAVE US, BUT WE CAME PREPARED!
I'VE GOT TO FIND THEIR ESCAPE ROUTE AND STOP THEM!
CAPTAIN, GET DALE AND ZARKOV UP TO THE SURFACE! I'M GOING TO FIND THE ROUTE DOWN!
FLASH, WAIT! I'M GOING WITH YOU!

COME BACK! I--

IT'S NO USE--SHE'S MADE UP HER MIND! AND IT WON'T HELP TO SEND ANY MORE DOWN! LET'S GO!

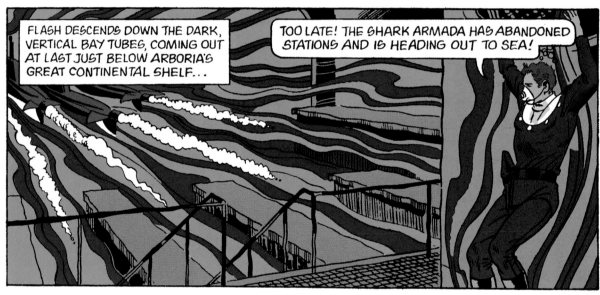

FLASH DESCENDS DOWN THE DARK, VERTICAL BAY TUBES, COMING OUT AT LAST JUST BELOW ARBORIA'S GREAT CONTINENTAL SHELF...

TOO LATE! THE SHARK ARMADA HAS ABANDONED STATIONS AND IS HEADING OUT TO SEA!

THEY'LL CONNECT SOMEWHERE WITH MING, NO DOUBT!

LET THEM GO! NOW THAT WE KNOW ABOUT THESE TUBES...

...THEY CAN'T USE THEM TO INVADE!

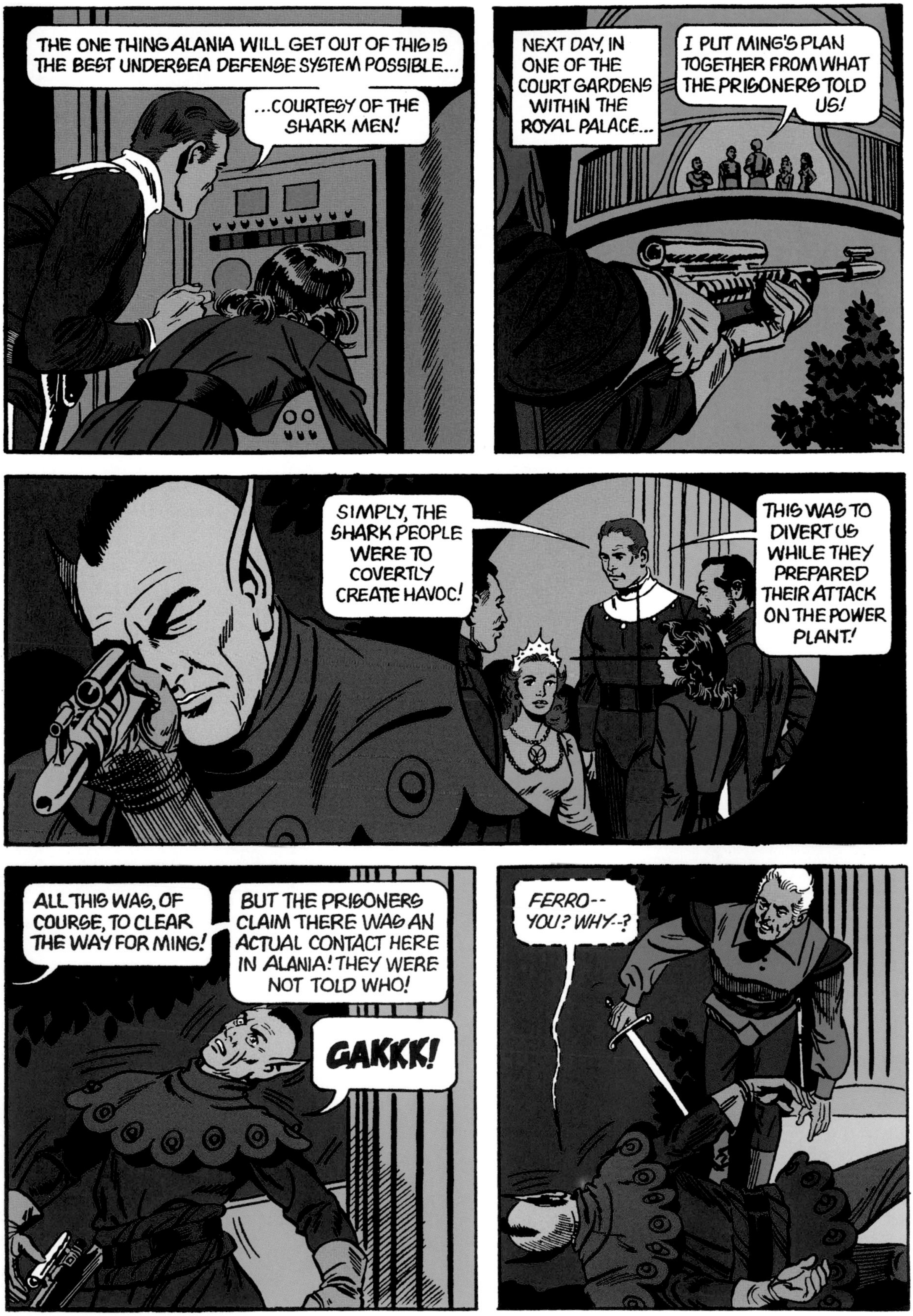
THE ONE THING ALANIA WILL GET OUT OF THIS IS THE BEST UNDERSEA DEFENSE SYSTEM POSSIBLE...
...COURTESY OF THE SHARK MEN!
NEXT DAY, IN ONE OF THE COURT GARDENS WITHIN THE ROYAL PALACE...
I PUT MING'S PLAN TOGETHER FROM WHAT THE PRISONERS TOLD US!
SIMPLY, THE SHARK PEOPLE WERE TO COVERTLY CREATE HAVOC!
THIS WAS TO DIVERT US WHILE THEY PREPARED THEIR ATTACK ON THE POWER PLANT!
ALL THIS WAS, OF COURSE, TO CLEAR THE WAY FOR MING!
BUT THE PRISONERS CLAIM THERE WAS AN ACTUAL CONTACT HERE IN ALANIA! THEY WERE NOT TOLD WHO!
GAKKK!
FERRO-- YOU? WHY--?

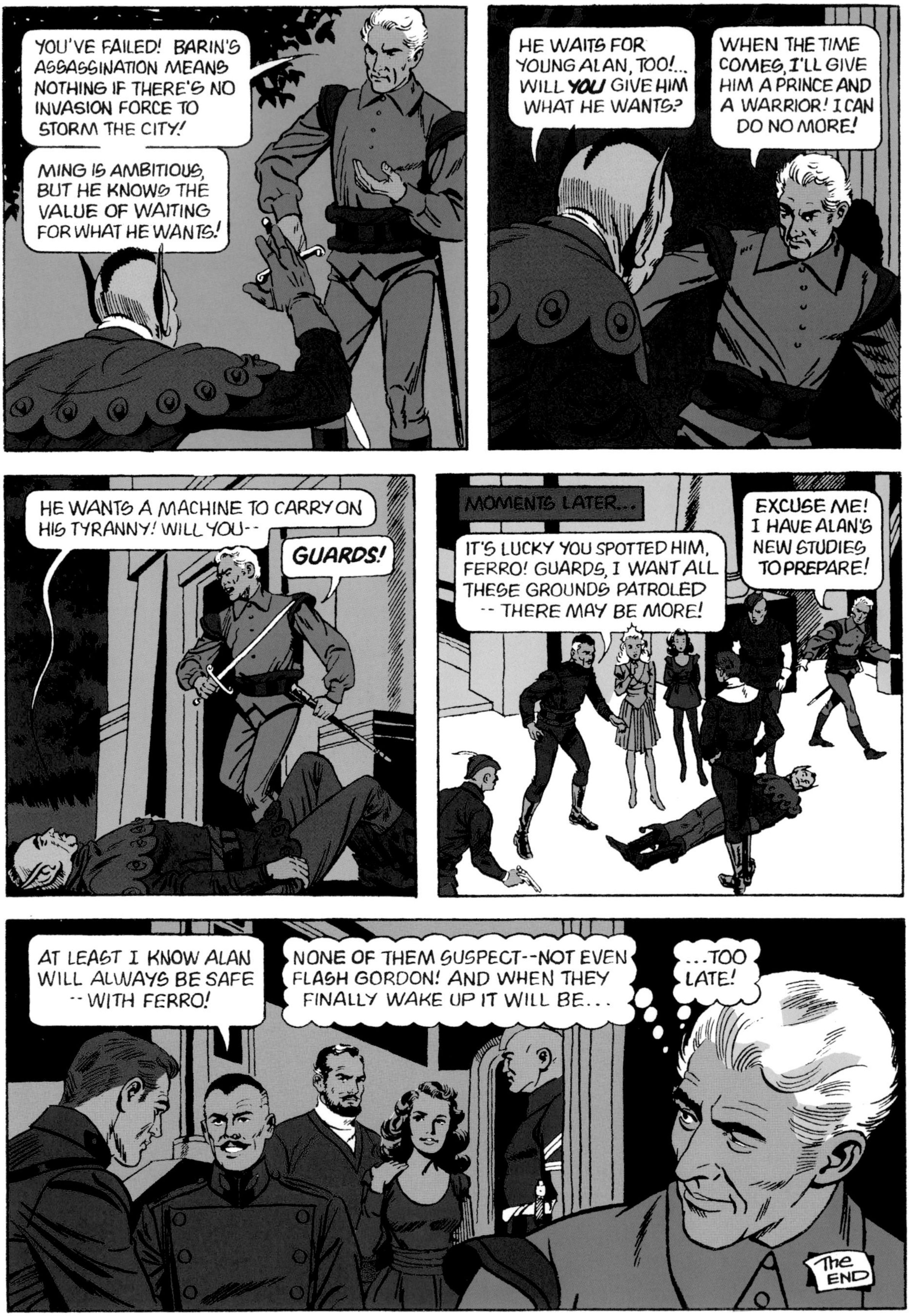
YOU'VE FAILED! BARIN'S ASSASSINATION MEANS NOTHING IF THERE'S NO INVASION FORCE TO STORM THE CITY!
MING IS AMBITIOUS, BUT HE KNOWS THE VALUE OF WAITING FOR WHAT HE WANTS!
HE WAITS FOR YOUNG ALAN, TOO!... WILL YOU GIVE HIM WHAT HE WANTS?
WHEN THE TIME COMES, I'LL GIVE HIM A PRINCE AND A WARRIOR! I CAN DO NO MORE!
HE WANTS A MACHINE TO CARRY ON HIS TYRANNY! WILL YOU--
GUARDS!
MOMENTS LATER...
IT'S LUCKY YOU SPOTTED HIM, FERRO! GUARDS, I WANT ALL THESE GROUNDS PATROLED -- THERE MAY BE MORE!
EXCUSE ME! I HAVE ALAN'S NEW STUDIES TO PREPARE!
AT LEAST I KNOW ALAN WILL ALWAYS BE SAFE -- WITH FERRO!
NONE OF THEM SUSPECT--NOT EVEN FLASH GORDON! AND WHEN THEY FINALLY WAKE UP IT WILL BE...
...TOO LATE!
The END

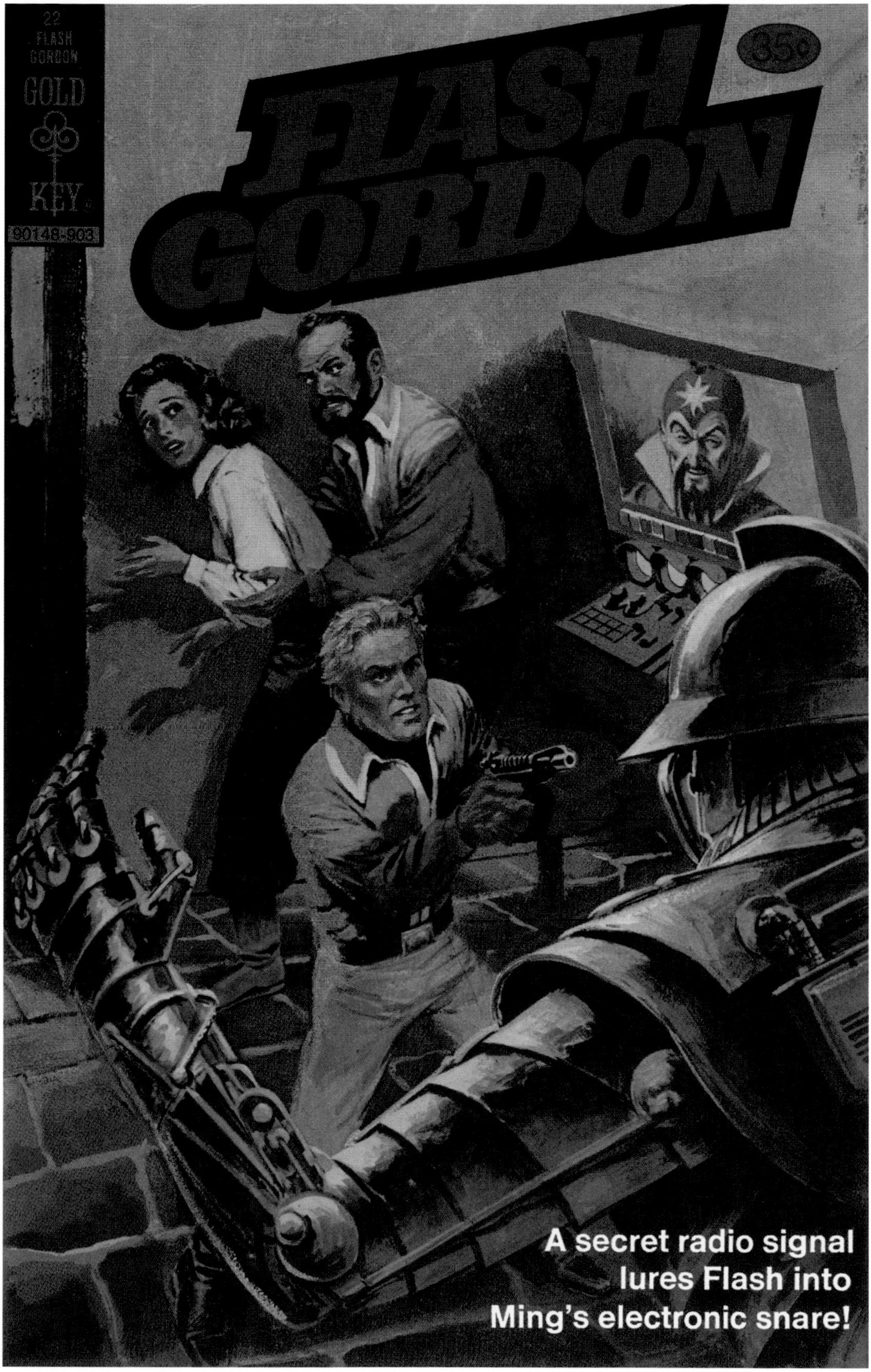
22
FLASH
GORDON
GOLD
KEY
90148-903
35¢
FLASH GORDON
A secret radio signal
lures Flash into
Ming's electronic snare!

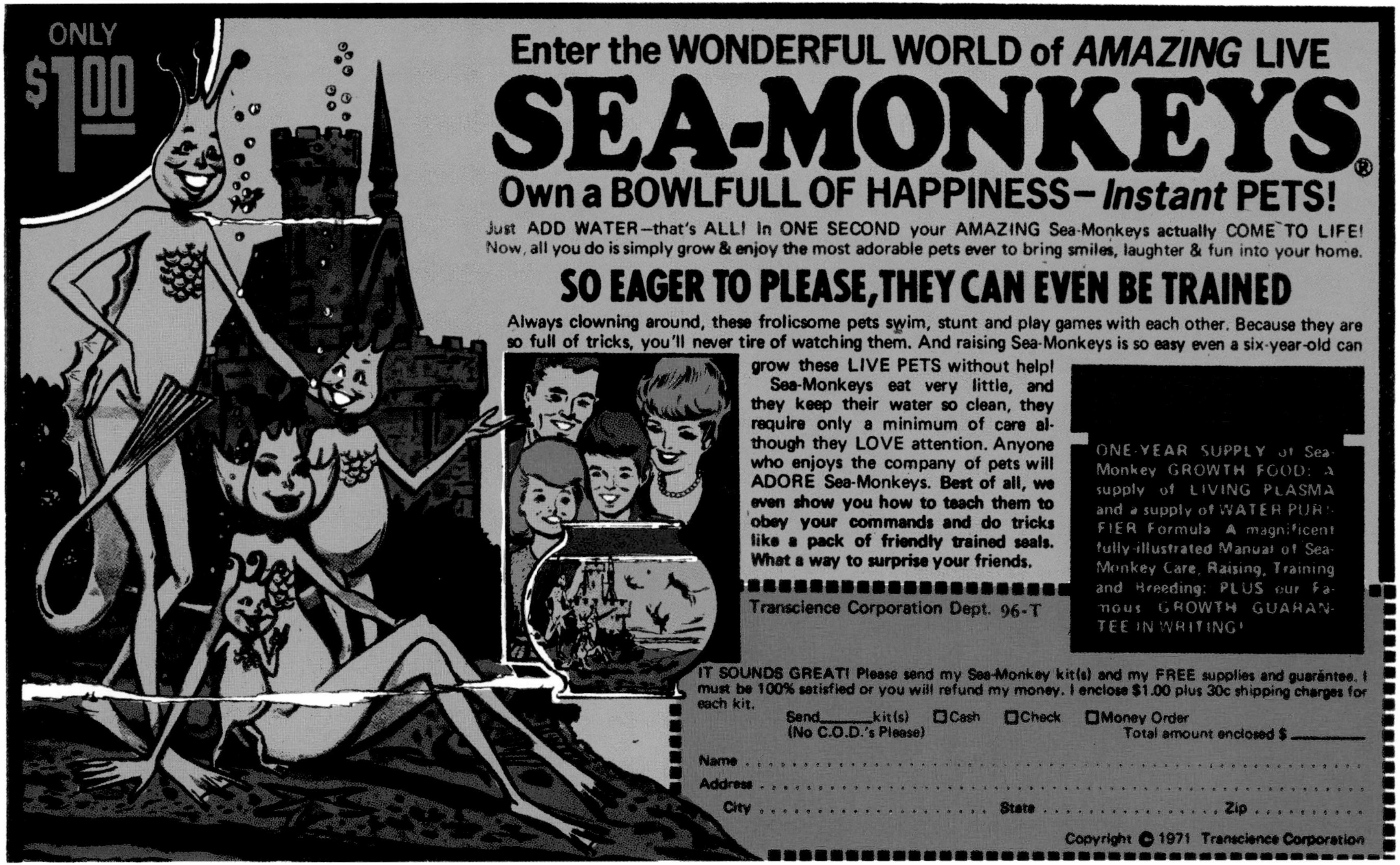
ONLY $1.00
Enter the WONDERFUL WORLD of AMAZING LIVE
SEA-MONKEYS®
Own a BOWLFULL OF HAPPINESS—Instant PETS!
Just ADD WATER—that's ALL! In ONE SECOND your AMAZING Sea-Monkeys actually COME TO LIFE! Now, all you do is simply grow & enjoy the most adorable pets ever to bring smiles, laughter & fun into your home.
SO EAGER TO PLEASE, THEY CAN EVEN BE TRAINED
Always clowning around, these frolicsome pets swim, stunt and play games with each other. Because they are so full of tricks, you'll never tire of watching them. And raising Sea-Monkeys is so easy even a six-year-old can grow these LIVE PETS without help!
Sea-Monkeys eat very little, and they keep their water so clean, they require only a minimum of care although they LOVE attention. Anyone who enjoys the company of pets will ADORE Sea-Monkeys. Best of all, we even show you how to teach them to obey your commands and do tricks like a pack of friendly trained seals. What a way to surprise your friends.
ONE-YEAR SUPPLY of Sea-Monkey GROWTH FOOD: A supply of LIVING PLASMA and a supply of WATER PURIFIER Formula. A magnificent fully-illustrated Manual of Sea-Monkey Care, Raising, Training and Breeding: PLUS our Famous GROWTH GUARANTEE IN WRITING!
Transcience Corporation Dept. 96-T
IT SOUNDS GREAT! Please send my Sea-Monkey kit(s) and my FREE supplies and guarantee. I must be 100% satisfied or you will refund my money. I enclose $1.00 plus 30c shipping charges for each kit.
Send______kit(s) (No C.O.D.'s Please) ☐Cash ☐Check ☐Money Order
Total amount enclosed $ ______
Name
Address
City State Zip
Copyright © 1971 Transcience Corporation

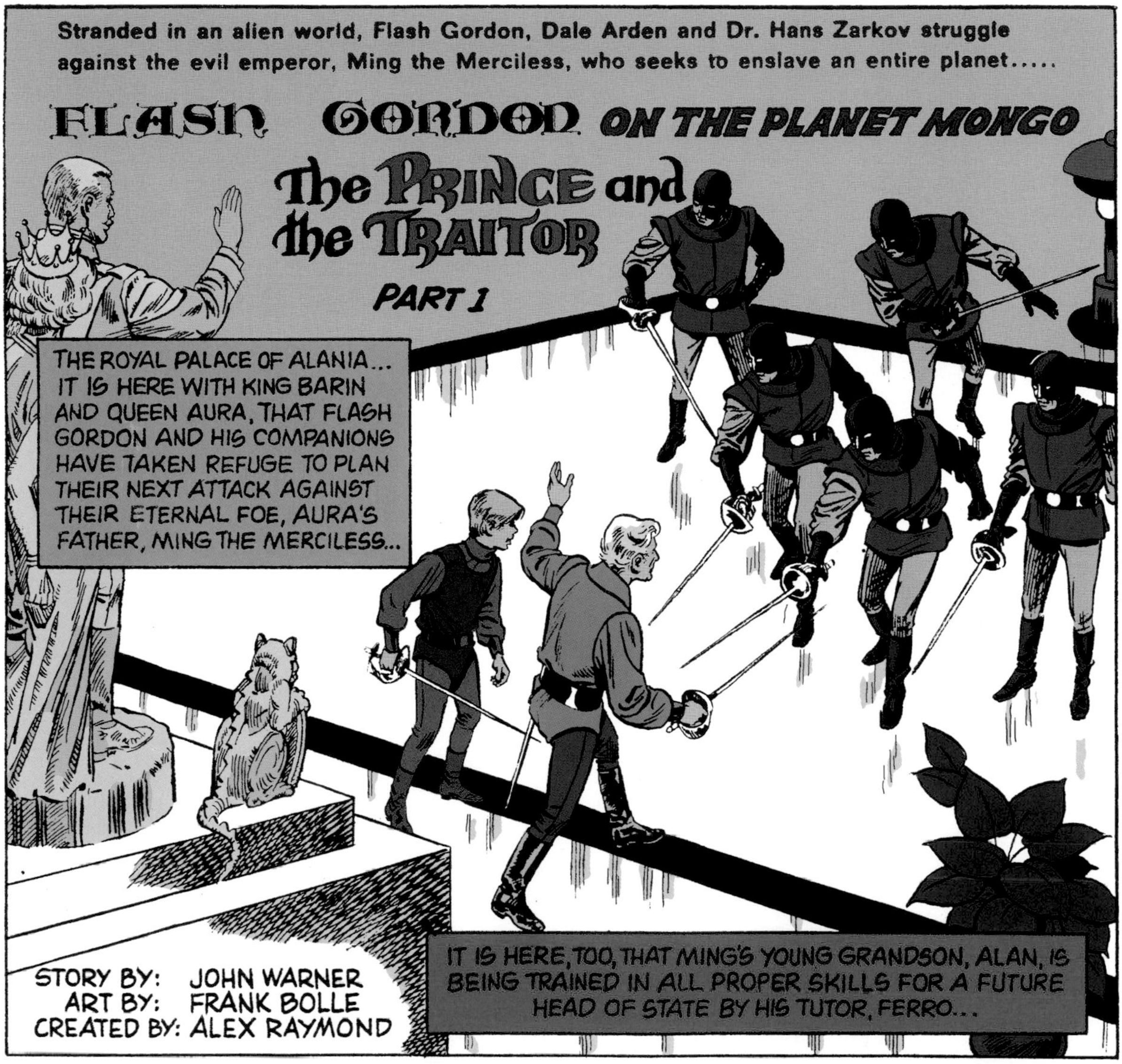
Stranded in an alien world, Flash Gordon, Dale Arden and Dr. Hans Zarkov struggle against the evil emperor, Ming the Merciless, who seeks to enslave an entire planet.....
FLASH GORDON ON THE PLANET MONGO
The PRINCE and the TRAITOR
PART 1
THE ROYAL PALACE OF ALANIA... IT IS HERE WITH KING BARIN AND QUEEN AURA, THAT FLASH GORDON AND HIS COMPANIONS HAVE TAKEN REFUGE TO PLAN THEIR NEXT ATTACK AGAINST THEIR ETERNAL FOE, AURA'S FATHER, MING THE MERCILESS...
STORY BY: JOHN WARNER
ART BY: FRANK BOLLE
CREATED BY: ALEX RAYMOND
IT IS HERE, TOO, THAT MING'S YOUNG GRANDSON, ALAN, IS BEING TRAINED IN ALL PROPER SKILLS FOR A FUTURE HEAD OF STATE BY HIS TUTOR, FERRO...

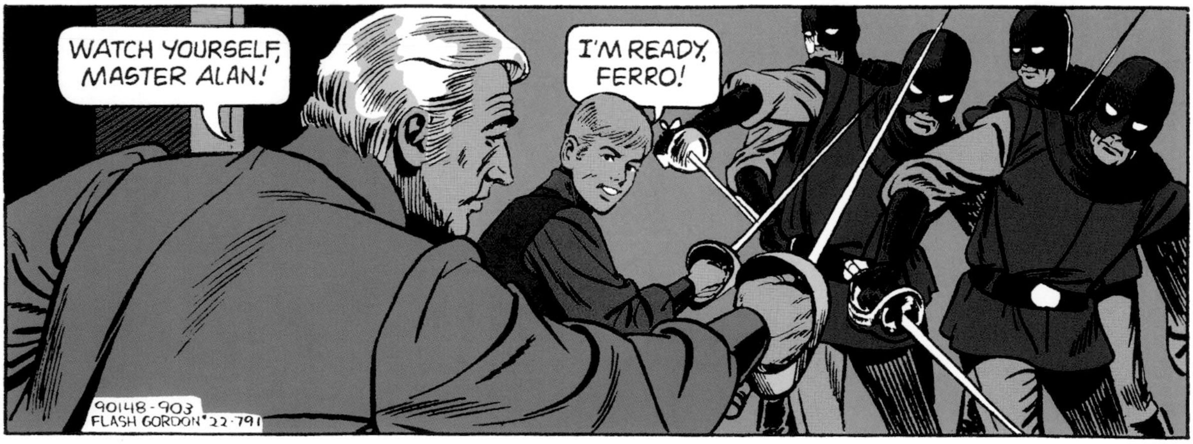
WATCH YOURSELF, MASTER ALAN!
I'M READY, FERRO!
90148-903
FLASH GORDON 22-791

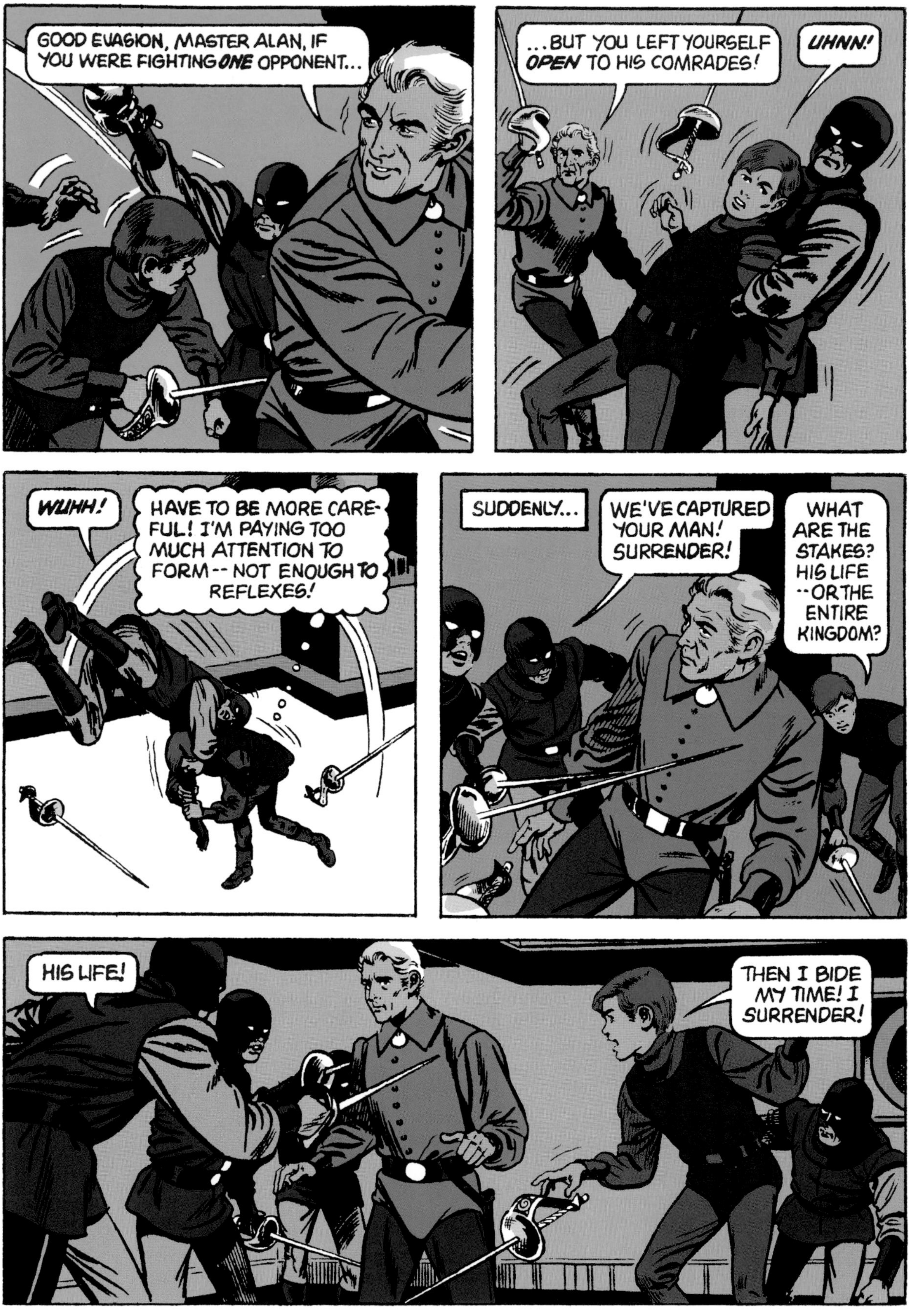
GOOD EVASION, MASTER ALAN, IF YOU WERE FIGHTING ONE OPPONENT...
...BUT YOU LEFT YOURSELF OPEN TO HIS COMRADES!
UHNN!
WUHH!
HAVE TO BE MORE CAREFUL! I'M PAYING TOO MUCH ATTENTION TO FORM -- NOT ENOUGH TO REFLEXES!
SUDDENLY...
WE'VE CAPTURED YOUR MAN! SURRENDER!
WHAT ARE THE STAKES? HIS LIFE -- OR THE ENTIRE KINGDOM?
HIS LIFE!
THEN I BIDE MY TIME! I SURRENDER!

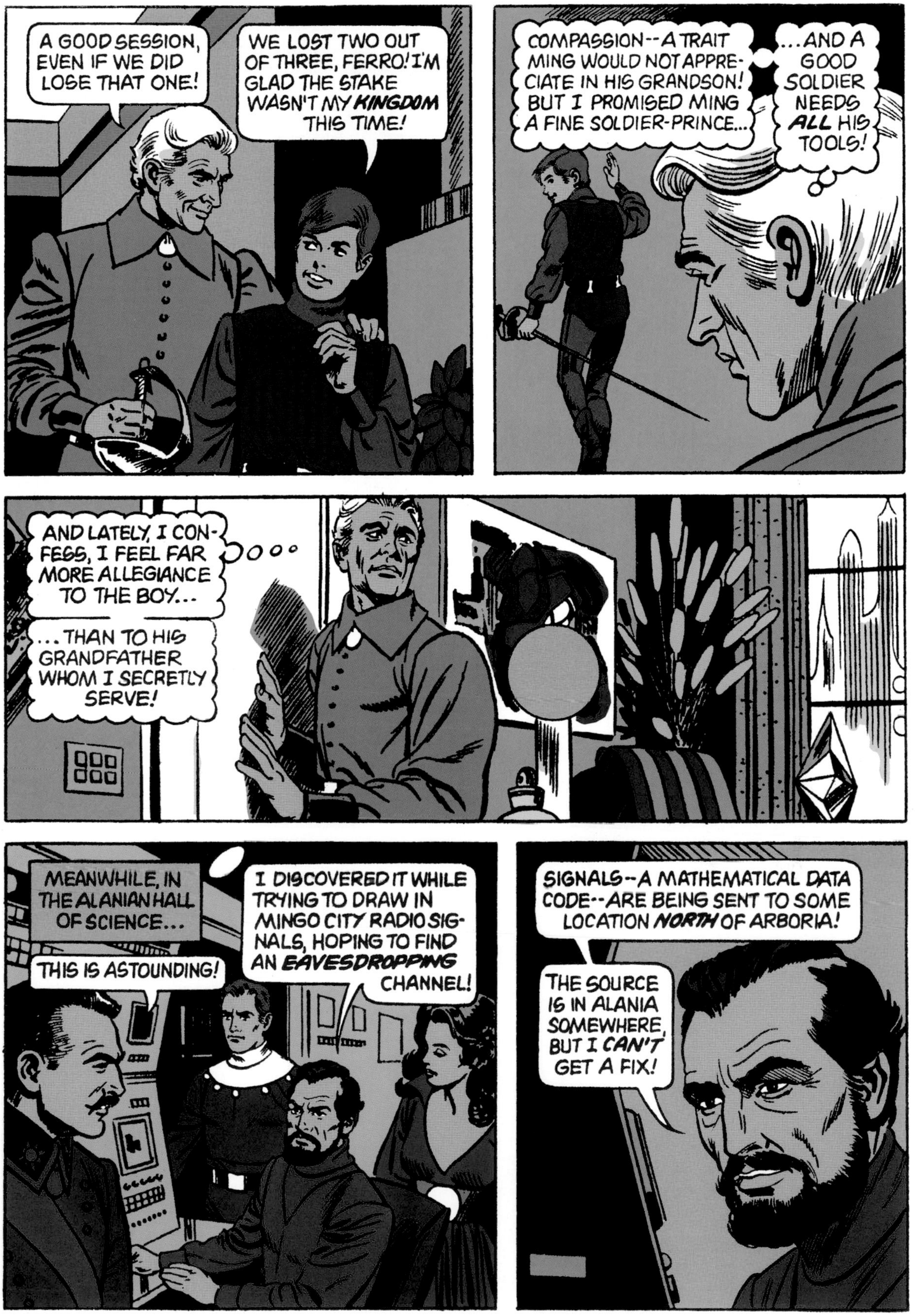
A GOOD SESSION, EVEN IF WE DID LOSE THAT ONE!
WE LOST TWO OUT OF THREE, FERRO! I'M GLAD THE STAKE WASN'T MY KINGDOM THIS TIME!
COMPASSION--A TRAIT MING WOULD NOT APPRECIATE IN HIS GRANDSON! BUT I PROMISED MING A FINE SOLDIER-PRINCE...
...AND A GOOD SOLDIER NEEDS ALL HIS TOOLS!
AND LATELY, I CONFESS, I FEEL FAR MORE ALLEGIANCE TO THE BOY...
...THAN TO HIS GRANDFATHER WHOM I SECRETLY SERVE!
MEANWHILE, IN THE ALANIAN HALL OF SCIENCE...
THIS IS ASTOUNDING!
I DISCOVERED IT WHILE TRYING TO DRAW IN MINGO CITY RADIO SIGNALS, HOPING TO FIND AN EAVESDROPPING CHANNEL!
SIGNALS--A MATHEMATICAL DATA CODE--ARE BEING SENT TO SOME LOCATION NORTH OF ARBORIA!
THE SOURCE IS IN ALANIA SOMEWHERE, BUT I CAN'T GET A FIX!

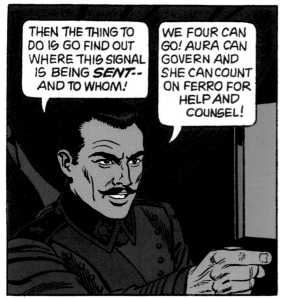

THEN THE THING TO DO IS GO FIND OUT WHERE THIS SIGNAL IS BEING *SENT*-- AND TO WHOM!

WE FOUR CAN GO! AURA CAN GOVERN AND SHE CAN COUNT ON FERRO FOR HELP AND COUNSEL!

SHORTLY...

YOU SENT FOR ME, SIRE?

YES, FERRO, WE'VE DISCOVERED A COMMUNICATIONS CHANNEL THAT WE CAN'T ACCOUNT FOR!

OUTWARDLY, FERRO REMAINS CALM, BUT INWARDLY...

ZARKOV! ONLY *HE* COULD HAVE DISCOVERED MY PATCH FREQUENCY TO MING! BUT DO THEY KNOW ABOUT *ME*?

WE WILL INVESTIGATE WHERE THE SIGNAL IS BEING SENT TO! I WANT YOU TO STAY AND TAKE CARE OF SECURITY OPERATIONS HERE!

YOU CAN DEPEND ON ME, YOUR MAJESTY! YOUR MISSION WILL BE KEPT *TOP SECRET!*

IT COULDN'T HAVE WORKED OUT BETTER IF I HAD PLANNED IT THIS WAY!

MING'S FOUR GREATEST ENEMIES DELIVERING THEMSELVES RIGHT INTO HIS *DEADLY GRASP!*

I JUST WANT TO QUICKLY CHECK ON MASTER ALAN, YOUR HIGHNESS! I'M AT YOUR SERVICE WHEN YOU *NEED* ME!

FERRO IS SUCH A HELP--AND HE'S SO GOOD AND ATTENTIVE WITH ALAN! I SOMETIMES WONDER HOW WE'D GET BY WITHOUT HIM!

BUT SOON, IN FERRO'S SECRET CHAMBER...

THIS IS PERFECT! NO ONE WILL BE MONITORING KING BARIN'S PRIVATE FREQUENCY...

BLACK CLOUD TO STORM--PLEASE ACKNOWLEDGE! THIS IS PRIORITY CODE RED!

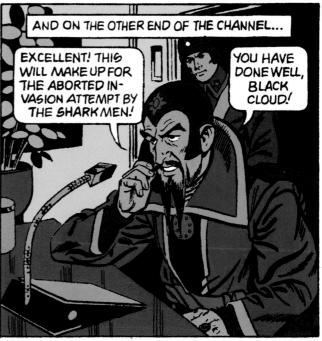

AND ON THE OTHER END OF THE CHANNEL...

EXCELLENT! THIS WILL MAKE UP FOR THE ABORTED IN-VASION ATTEMPT BY THE SHARK MEN!

YOU HAVE DONE WELL, BLACK CLOUD!

AWAIT FURTHER INSTRUCTIONS-- *CLICK!*

YES! EVER THE EFFICIENT SOLDIER! I SHOULD BE HAPPY!

I'VE JUST SET IN *MOTION* EVENTS THAT WILL ASSURE VICTORY OVER AR-BORIA FOR MY EMPEROR, MING THE MERCILESS...

...SO WHY DO I FEEL-- SADDENED?

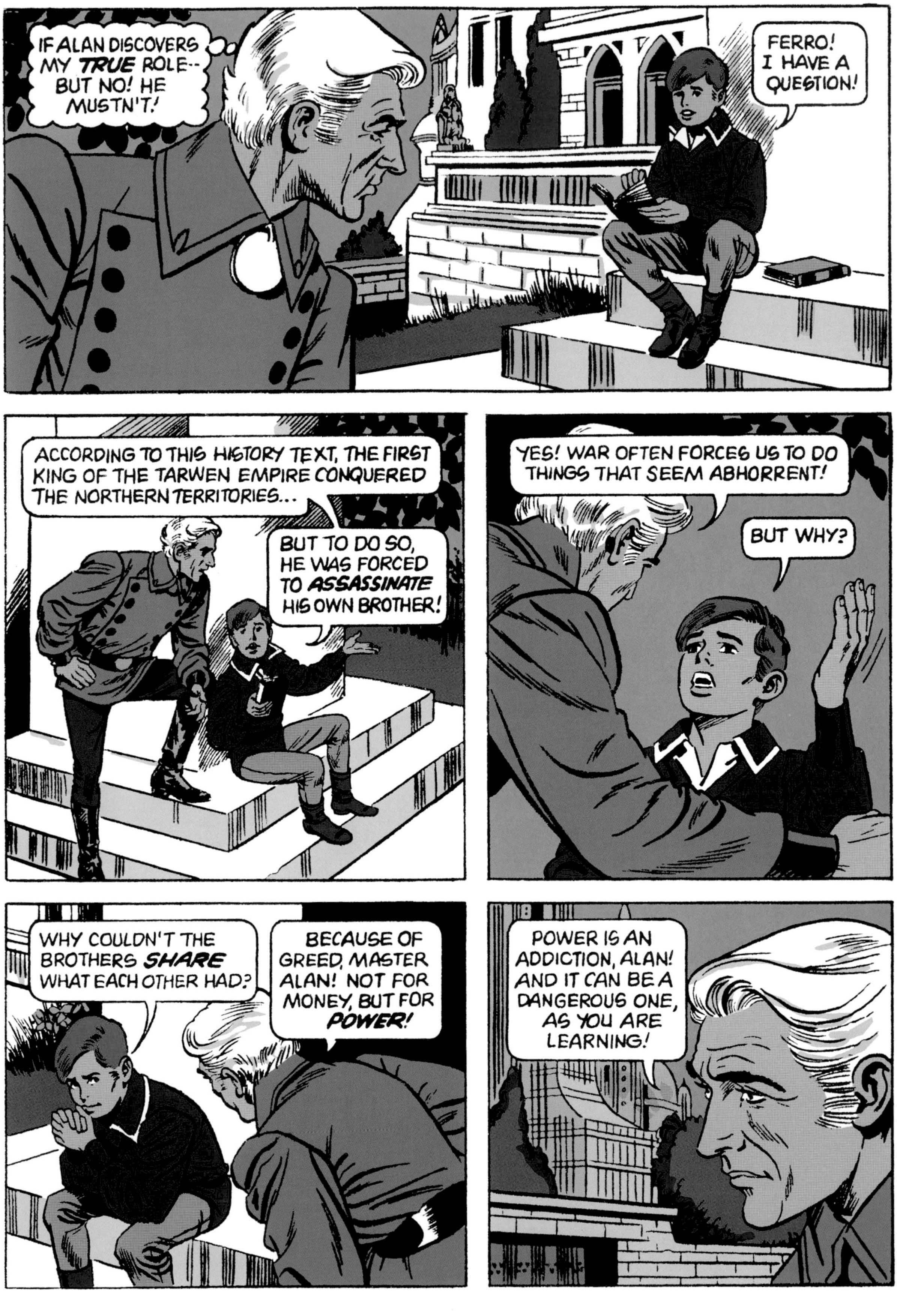
IF ALAN DISCOVERS MY TRUE ROLE-- BUT NO! HE MUSTN'T!
FERRO! I HAVE A QUESTION!
ACCORDING TO THIS HISTORY TEXT, THE FIRST KING OF THE TARWEN EMPIRE CONQUERED THE NORTHERN TERRITORIES...
BUT TO DO SO, HE WAS FORCED TO ASSASSINATE HIS OWN BROTHER!
YES! WAR OFTEN FORCES US TO DO THINGS THAT SEEM ABHORRENT!
BUT WHY?
WHY COULDN'T THE BROTHERS SHARE WHAT EACH OTHER HAD?
BECAUSE OF GREED, MASTER ALAN! NOT FOR MONEY, BUT FOR POWER!
POWER IS AN ADDICTION, ALAN! AND IT CAN BE A DANGEROUS ONE, AS YOU ARE LEARNING!

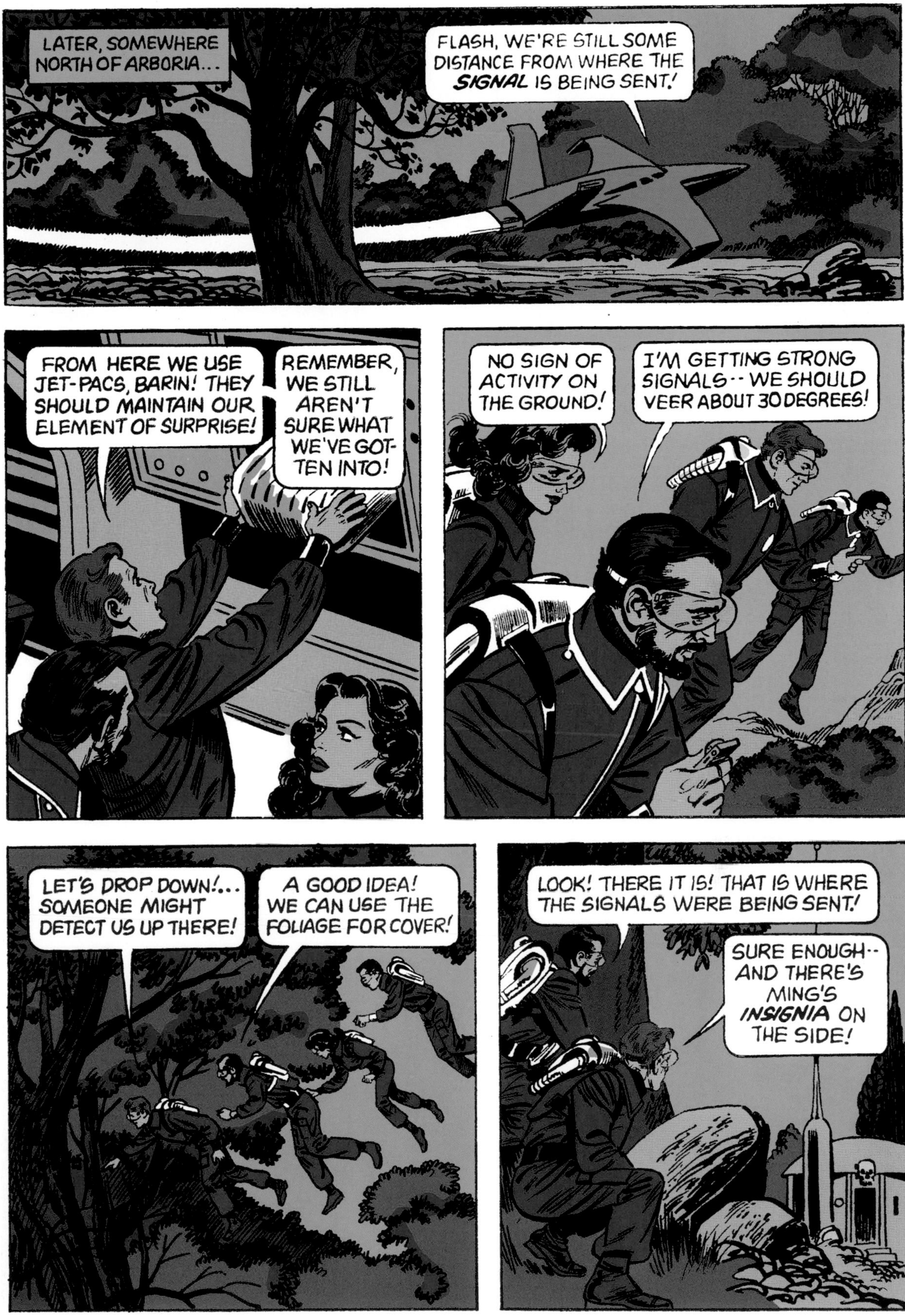
LATER, SOMEWHERE NORTH OF ARBORIA...
FLASH, WE'RE STILL SOME DISTANCE FROM WHERE THE SIGNAL IS BEING SENT!
FROM HERE WE USE JET-PACS, BARIN! THEY SHOULD MAINTAIN OUR ELEMENT OF SURPRISE!
REMEMBER, WE STILL AREN'T SURE WHAT WE'VE GOTTEN INTO!
NO SIGN OF ACTIVITY ON THE GROUND!
I'M GETTING STRONG SIGNALS-- WE SHOULD VEER ABOUT 30 DEGREES!
LET'S DROP DOWN!... SOMEONE MIGHT DETECT US UP THERE!
A GOOD IDEA! WE CAN USE THE FOLIAGE FOR COVER!
LOOK! THERE IT IS! THAT IS WHERE THE SIGNALS WERE BEING SENT!
SURE ENOUGH-- AND THERE'S MING'S INSIGNIA ON THE SIDE!

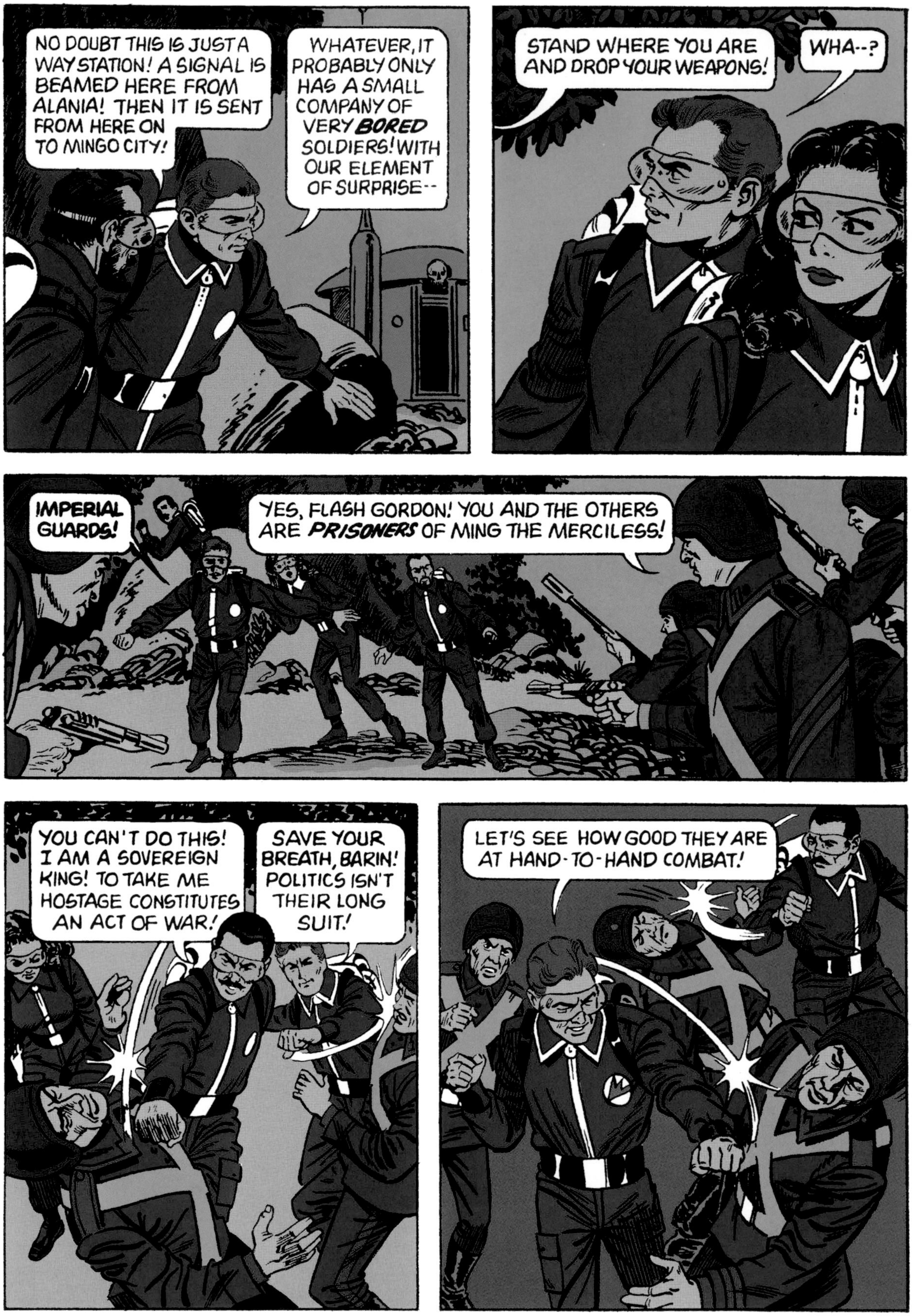
NO DOUBT THIS IS JUST A WAY STATION! A SIGNAL IS BEAMED HERE FROM ALANIA! THEN IT IS SENT FROM HERE ON TO MINGO CITY!
WHATEVER, IT PROBABLY ONLY HAS A SMALL COMPANY OF VERY BORED SOLDIERS! WITH OUR ELEMENT OF SURPRISE--
STAND WHERE YOU ARE AND DROP YOUR WEAPONS!
WHA--?
IMPERIAL GUARDS!
YES, FLASH GORDON! YOU AND THE OTHERS ARE PRISONERS OF MING THE MERCILESS!
YOU CAN'T DO THIS! I AM A SOVEREIGN KING! TO TAKE ME HOSTAGE CONSTITUTES AN ACT OF WAR!
SAVE YOUR BREATH, BARIN! POLITICS ISN'T THEIR LONG SUIT!
LET'S SEE HOW GOOD THEY ARE AT HAND-TO-HAND COMBAT!

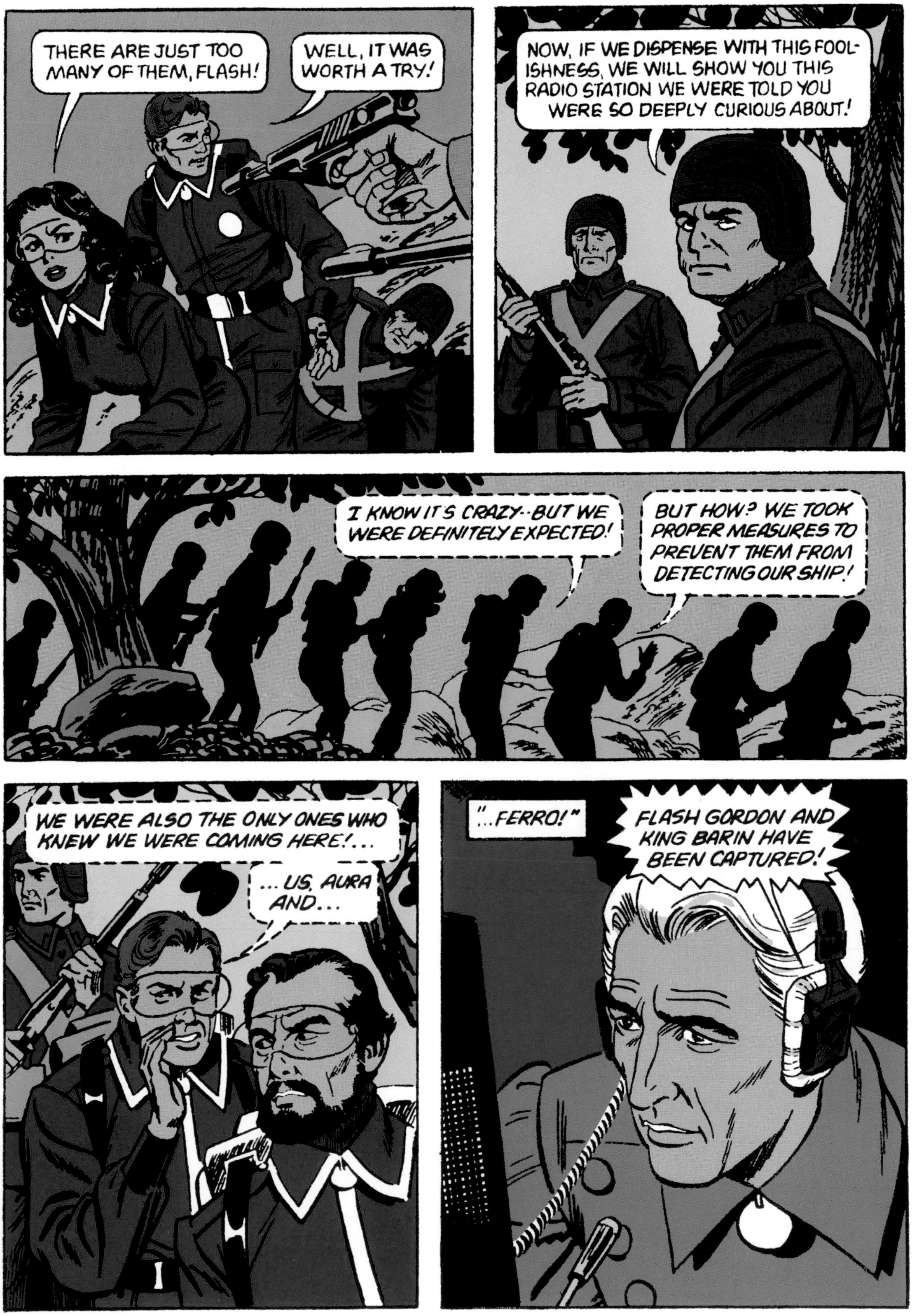

THERE ARE JUST TOO MANY OF THEM, FLASH!
WELL, IT WAS WORTH A TRY!
NOW, IF WE DISPENSE WITH THIS FOOL-ISHNESS, WE WILL SHOW YOU THIS RADIO STATION WE WERE TOLD YOU WERE SO DEEPLY CURIOUS ABOUT!
I KNOW IT'S CRAZY.. BUT WE WERE DEFINITELY EXPECTED!
BUT HOW? WE TOOK PROPER MEASURES TO PREVENT THEM FROM DETECTING OUR SHIP!
WE WERE ALSO THE ONLY ONES WHO KNEW WE WERE COMING HERE!...
...US, AURA AND...
"...FERRO!"
FLASH GORDON AND KING BARIN HAVE BEEN CAPTURED!

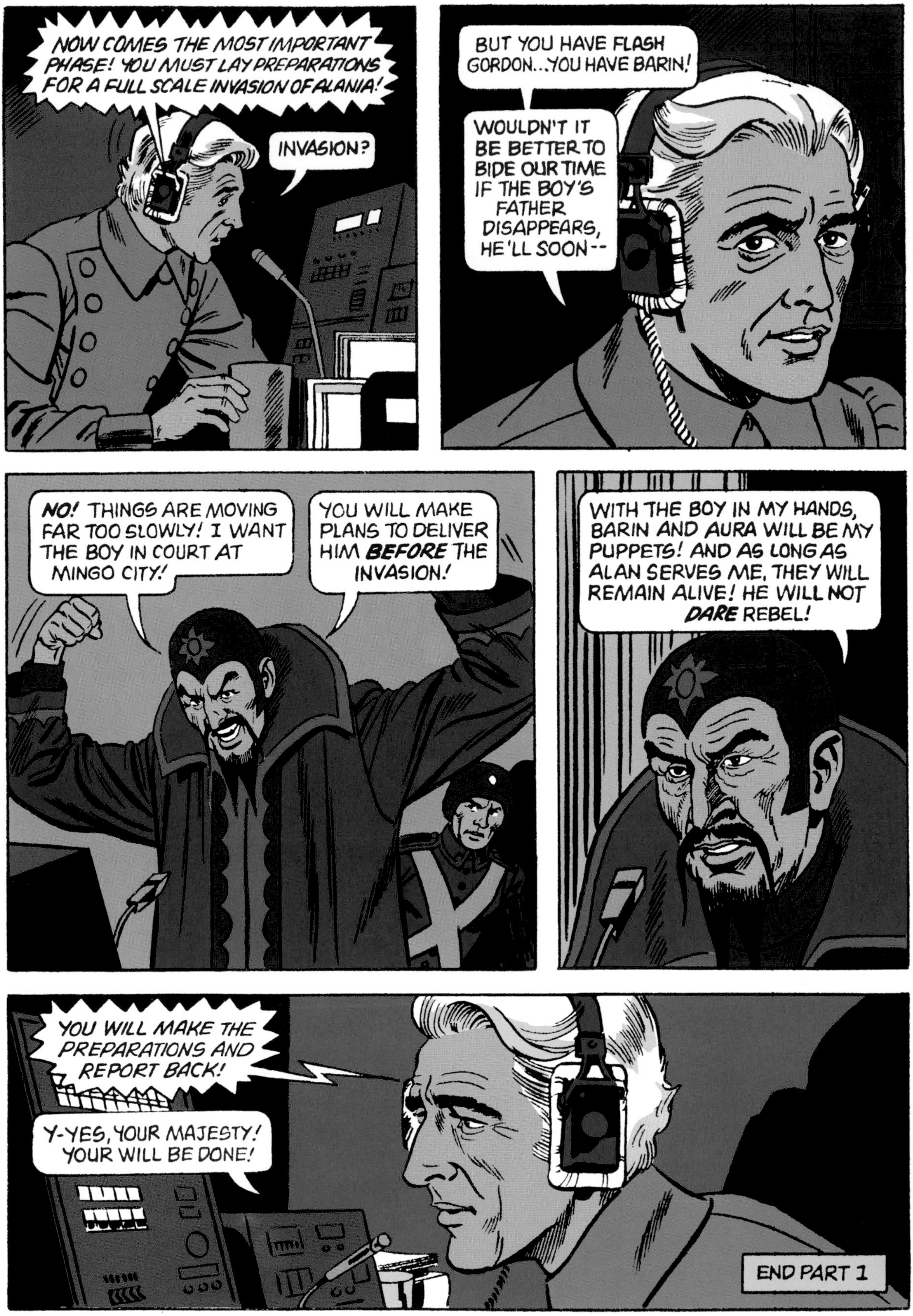
NOW COMES THE MOST IMPORTANT PHASE! YOU MUST LAY PREPARATIONS FOR A FULL SCALE INVASION OF ALANIA!
INVASION?
BUT YOU HAVE FLASH GORDON...YOU HAVE BARIN!
WOULDN'T IT BE BETTER TO BIDE OUR TIME IF THE BOY'S FATHER DISAPPEARS, HE'LL SOON--
NO! THINGS ARE MOVING FAR TOO SLOWLY! I WANT THE BOY IN COURT AT MINGO CITY!
YOU WILL MAKE PLANS TO DELIVER HIM BEFORE THE INVASION!
WITH THE BOY IN MY HANDS, BARIN AND AURA WILL BE MY PUPPETS! AND AS LONG AS ALAN SERVES ME, THEY WILL REMAIN ALIVE! HE WILL NOT DARE REBEL!
YOU WILL MAKE THE PREPARATIONS AND REPORT BACK!
Y-YES, YOUR MAJESTY! YOUR WILL BE DONE!
END PART 1

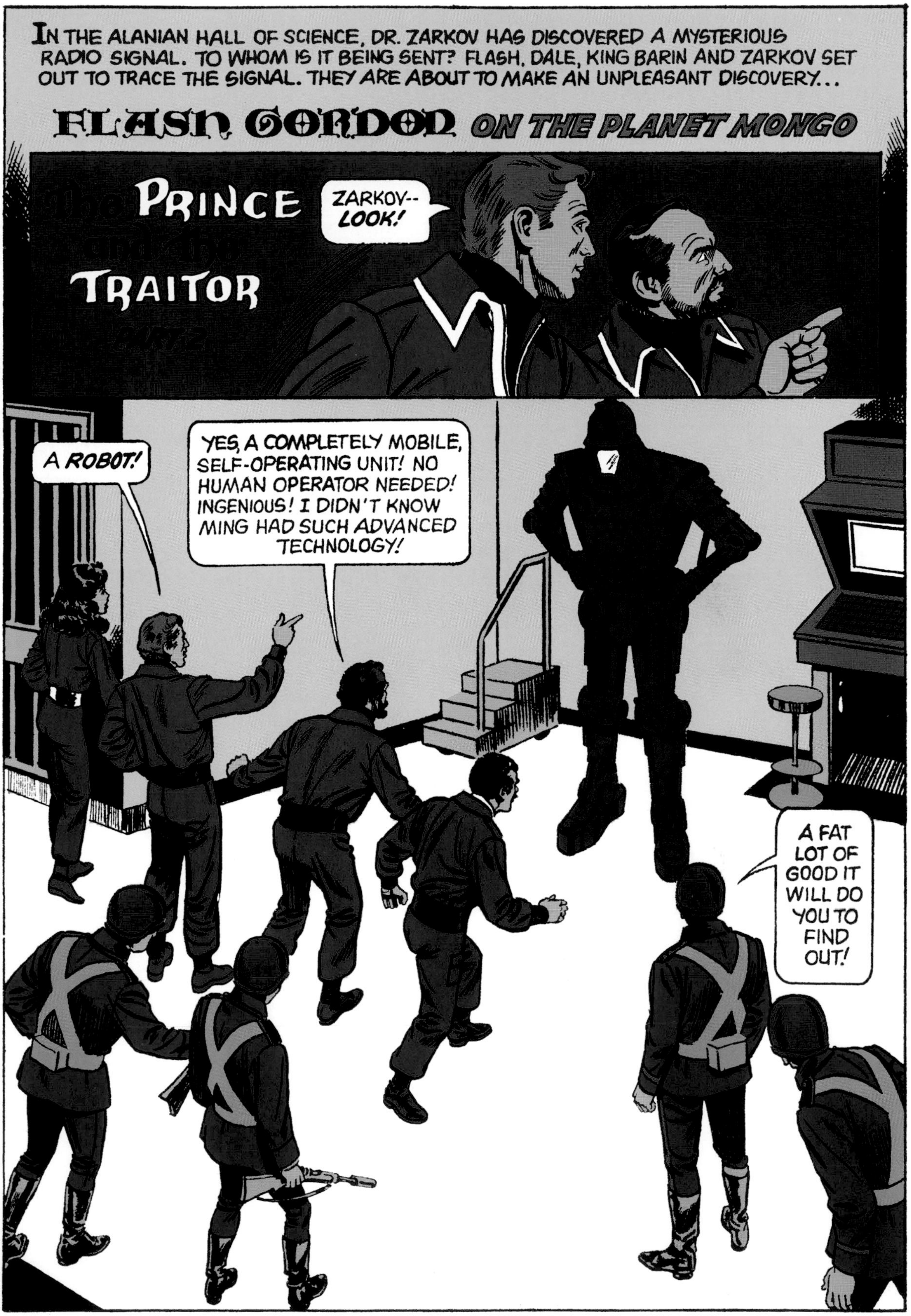

IN THE ALANIAN HALL OF SCIENCE, DR. ZARKOV HAS DISCOVERED A MYSTERIOUS RADIO SIGNAL. TO WHOM IS IT BEING SENT? FLASH, DALE, KING BARIN AND ZARKOV SET OUT TO TRACE THE SIGNAL. THEY ARE ABOUT TO MAKE AN UNPLEASANT DISCOVERY...
FLASH GORDON ON THE PLANET MONGO
PRINCE
TRAITOR
ZARKOV-- LOOK!
A ROBOT!
YES, A COMPLETELY MOBILE, SELF-OPERATING UNIT! NO HUMAN OPERATOR NEEDED! INGENIOUS! I DIDN'T KNOW MING HAD SUCH ADVANCED TECHNOLOGY!
A FAT LOT OF GOOD IT WILL DO YOU TO FIND OUT!

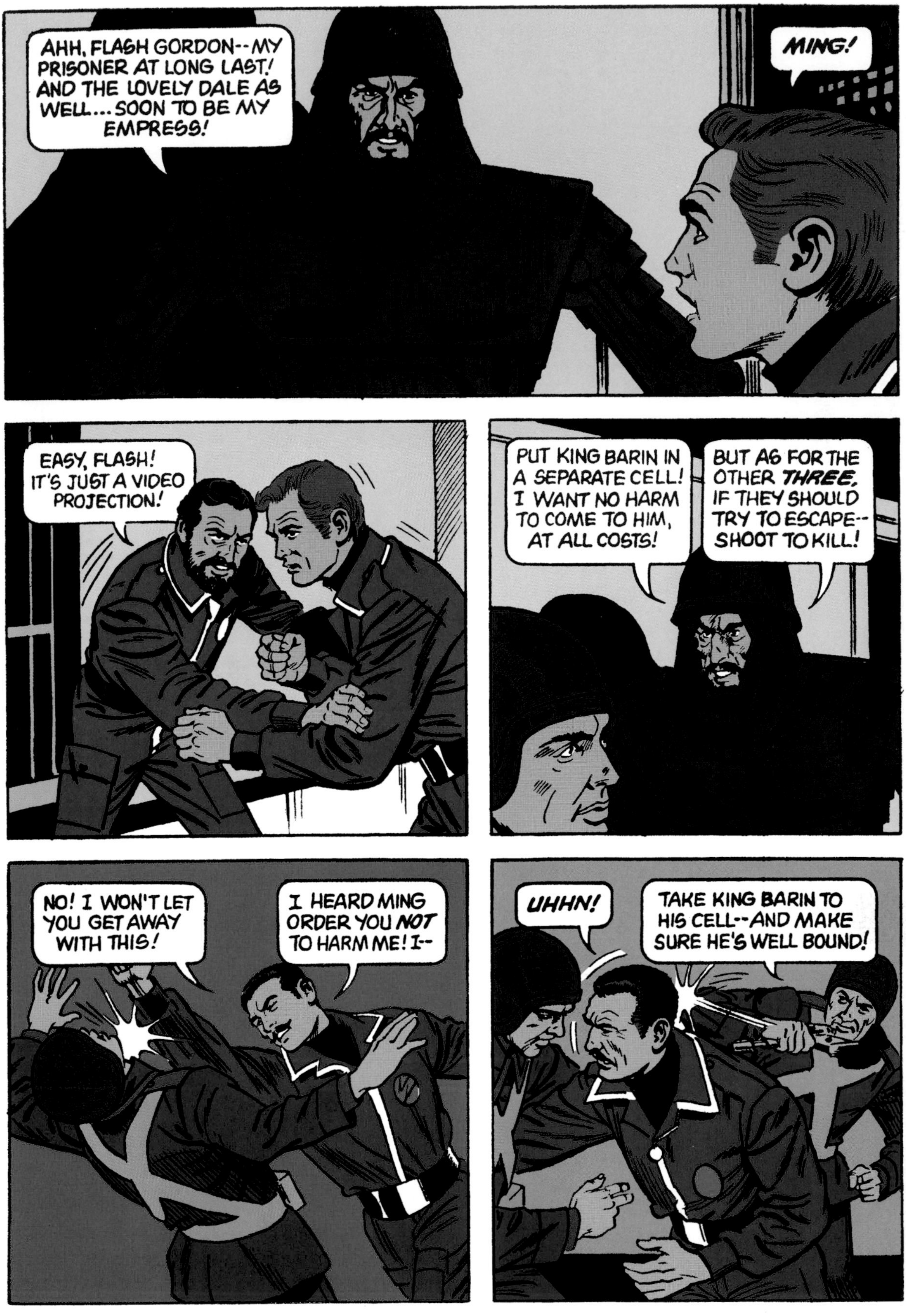
AHH, FLASH GORDON--MY PRISONER AT LONG LAST! AND THE LOVELY DALE AS WELL...SOON TO BE MY EMPRESS!
MING!
EASY, FLASH! IT'S JUST A VIDEO PROJECTION!
PUT KING BARIN IN A SEPARATE CELL! I WANT NO HARM TO COME TO HIM, AT ALL COSTS!
BUT AS FOR THE OTHER THREE, IF THEY SHOULD TRY TO ESCAPE--SHOOT TO KILL!
NO! I WON'T LET YOU GET AWAY WITH THIS!
I HEARD MING ORDER YOU NOT TO HARM ME! I--
UHHN!
TAKE KING BARIN TO HIS CELL--AND MAKE SURE HE'S WELL BOUND!

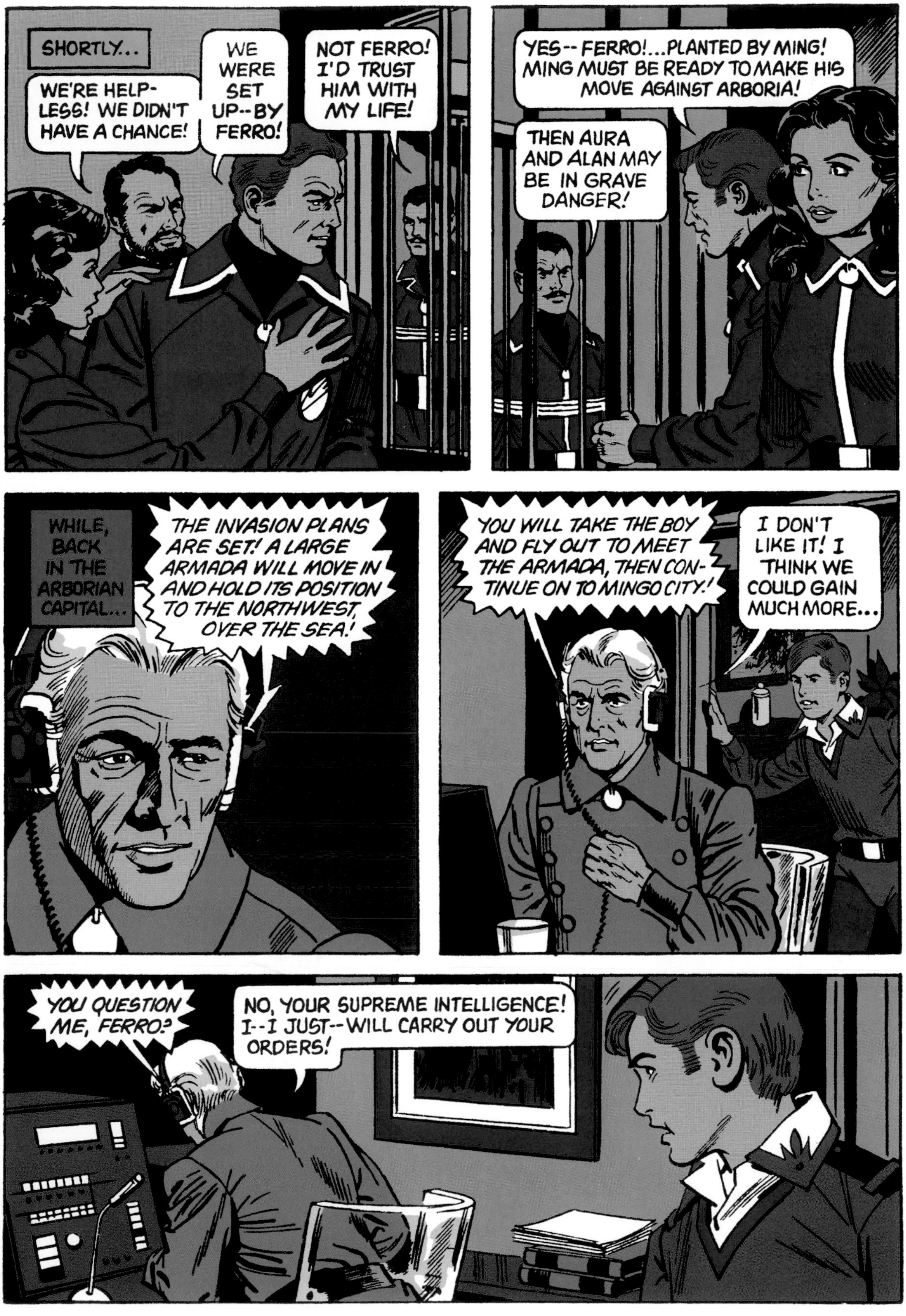
SHORTLY...
WE'RE HELPLESS! WE DIDN'T HAVE A CHANCE!
WE WERE SET UP--BY FERRO!
NOT FERRO! I'D TRUST HIM WITH MY LIFE!
YES--FERRO!...PLANTED BY MING! MING MUST BE READY TO MAKE HIS MOVE AGAINST ARBORIA!
THEN AURA AND ALAN MAY BE IN GRAVE DANGER!
WHILE, BACK IN THE ARBORIAN CAPITAL...
THE INVASION PLANS ARE SET! A LARGE ARMADA WILL MOVE IN AND HOLD ITS POSITION TO THE NORTHWEST, OVER THE SEA!
YOU WILL TAKE THE BOY AND FLY OUT TO MEET THE ARMADA, THEN CONTINUE ON TO MINGO CITY!
I DON'T LIKE IT! I THINK WE COULD GAIN MUCH MORE...
YOU QUESTION ME, FERRO?
NO, YOUR SUPREME INTELLIGENCE! I--I JUST--WILL CARRY OUT YOUR ORDERS!

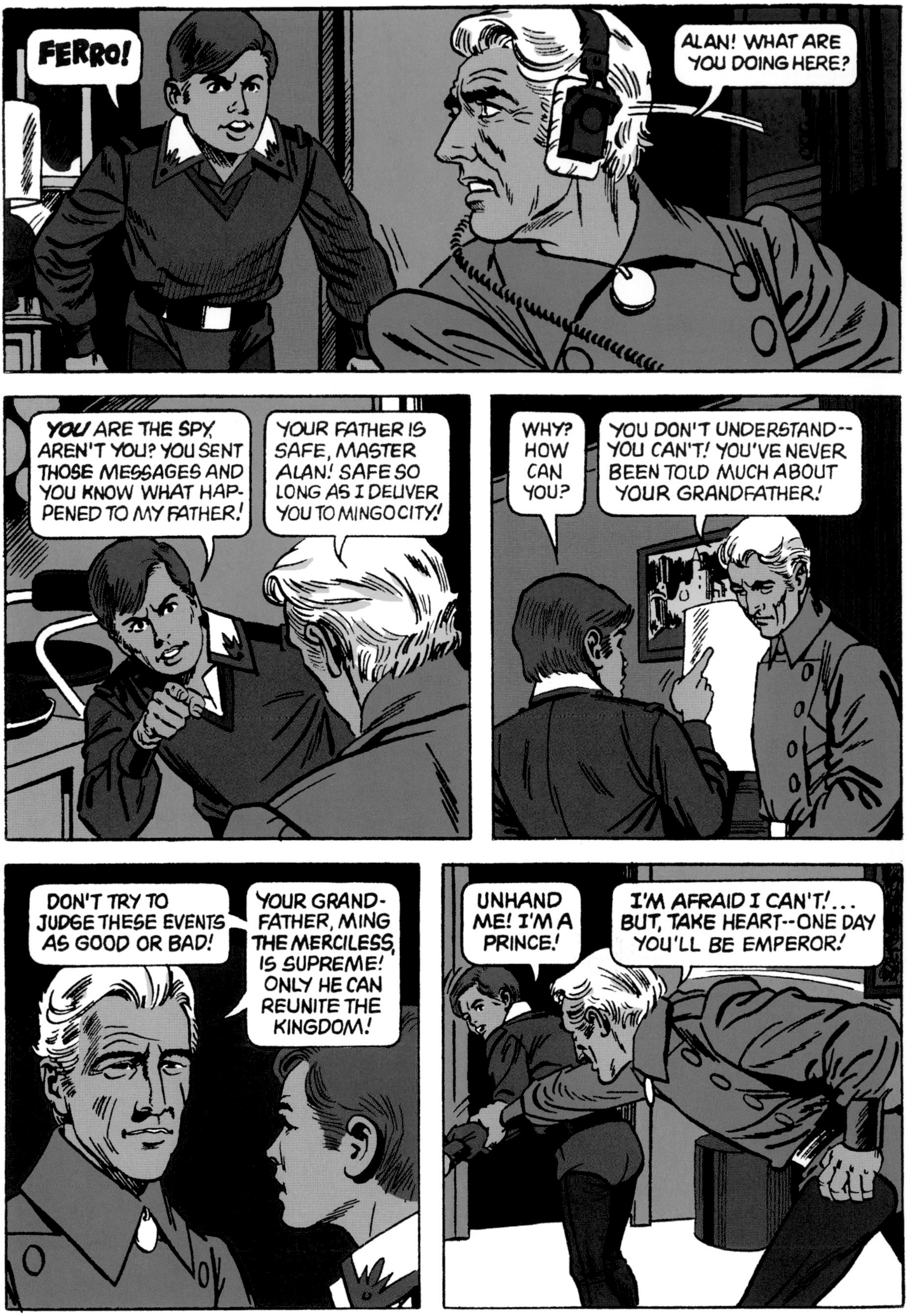
FERRO!
ALAN! WHAT ARE YOU DOING HERE?
YOU ARE THE SPY, AREN'T YOU? YOU SENT THOSE MESSAGES AND YOU KNOW WHAT HAPPENED TO MY FATHER!
YOUR FATHER IS SAFE, MASTER ALAN! SAFE SO LONG AS I DELIVER YOU TO MINGO CITY!
WHY? HOW CAN YOU?
YOU DON'T UNDERSTAND-- YOU CAN'T! YOU'VE NEVER BEEN TOLD MUCH ABOUT YOUR GRANDFATHER!
DON'T TRY TO JUDGE THESE EVENTS AS GOOD OR BAD!
YOUR GRANDFATHER, MING THE MERCILESS, IS SUPREME! ONLY HE CAN REUNITE THE KINGDOM!
UNHAND ME! I'M A PRINCE!
I'M AFRAID I CAN'T!... BUT, TAKE HEART--ONE DAY YOU'LL BE EMPEROR!

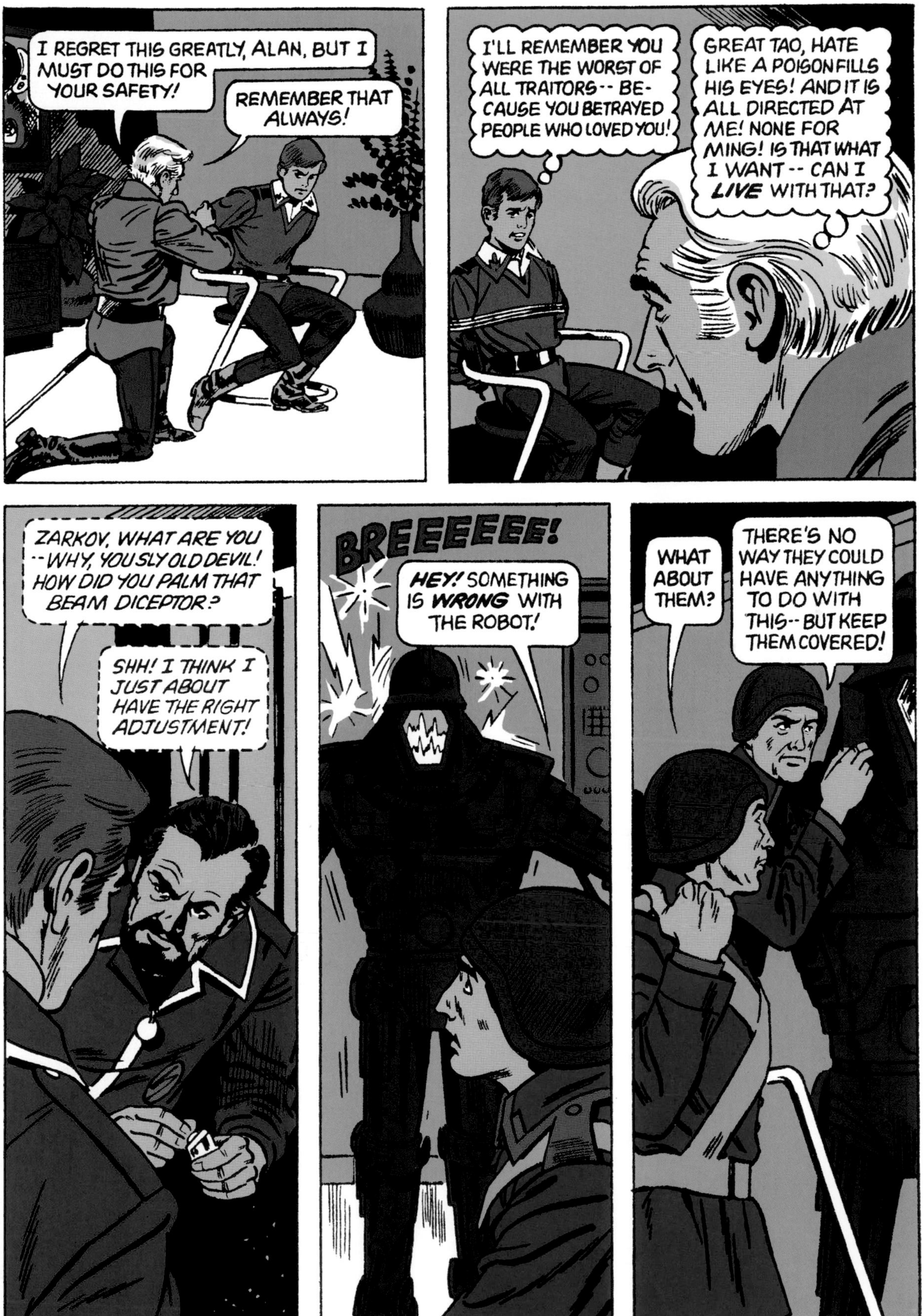
I REGRET THIS GREATLY, ALAN, BUT I MUST DO THIS FOR YOUR SAFETY!
REMEMBER THAT ALWAYS!
I'LL REMEMBER YOU WERE THE WORST OF ALL TRAITORS -- BE-CAUSE YOU BETRAYED PEOPLE WHO LOVED YOU!
GREAT TAO, HATE LIKE A POISON FILLS HIS EYES! AND IT IS ALL DIRECTED AT ME! NONE FOR MING! IS THAT WHAT I WANT -- CAN I LIVE WITH THAT?
ZARKOV, WHAT ARE YOU -- WHY, YOU SLY OLD DEVIL! HOW DID YOU PALM THAT BEAM DICEPTOR?
SHH! I THINK I JUST ABOUT HAVE THE RIGHT ADJUSTMENT!
BREEEEEEE!
HEY! SOMETHING IS WRONG WITH THE ROBOT!
WHAT ABOUT THEM?
THERE'S NO WAY THEY COULD HAVE ANYTHING TO DO WITH THIS -- BUT KEEP THEM COVERED!

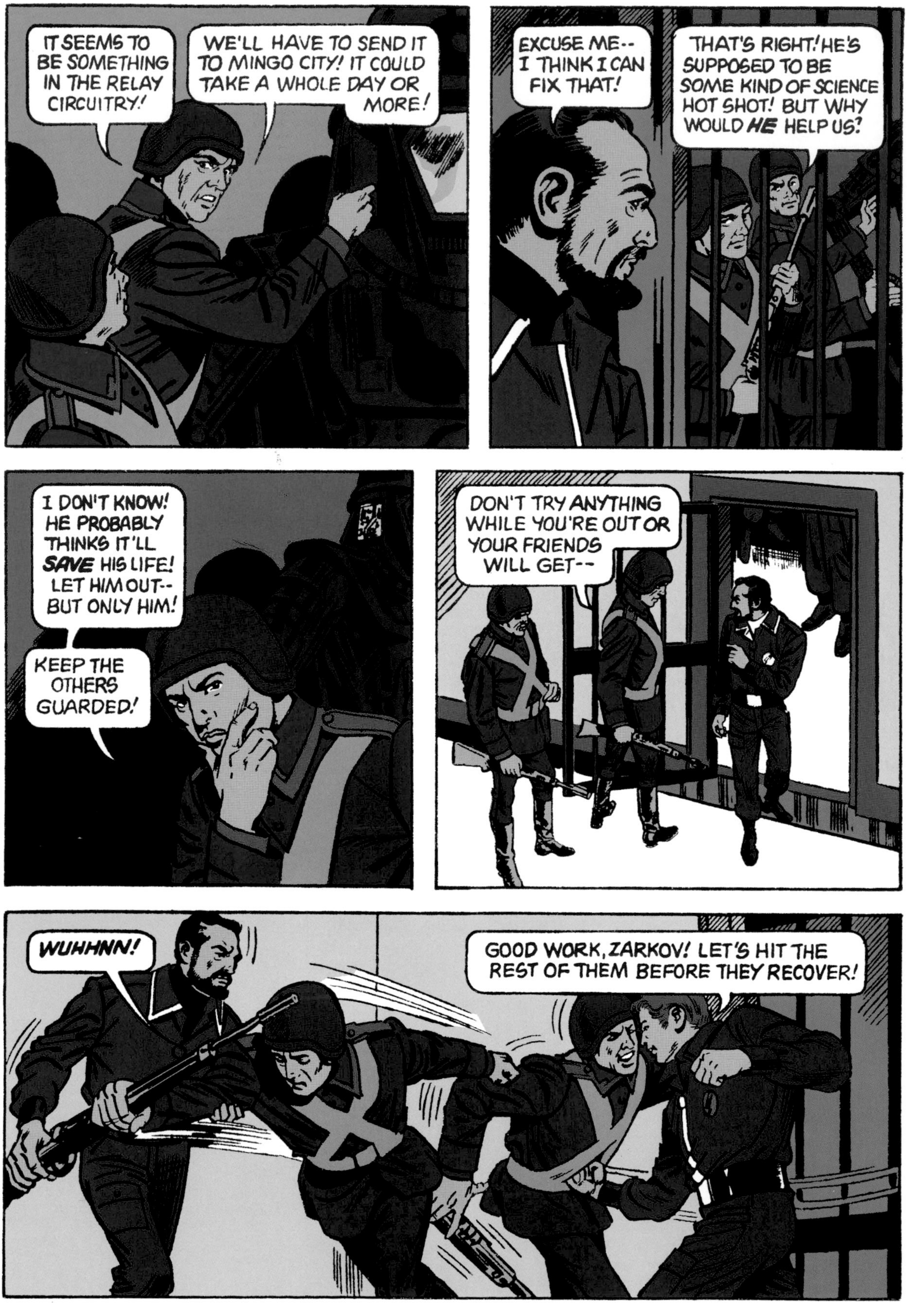
IT SEEMS TO BE SOMETHING IN THE RELAY CIRCUITRY!
WE'LL HAVE TO SEND IT TO MINGO CITY! IT COULD TAKE A WHOLE DAY OR MORE!
EXCUSE ME-- I THINK I CAN FIX THAT!
THAT'S RIGHT! HE'S SUPPOSED TO BE SOME KIND OF SCIENCE HOT SHOT! BUT WHY WOULD HE HELP US?
I DON'T KNOW! HE PROBABLY THINKS IT'LL SAVE HIS LIFE! LET HIM OUT-- BUT ONLY HIM!
KEEP THE OTHERS GUARDED!
DON'T TRY ANYTHING WHILE YOU'RE OUT OR YOUR FRIENDS WILL GET--
WUHHNN!
GOOD WORK, ZARKOV! LET'S HIT THE REST OF THEM BEFORE THEY RECOVER!

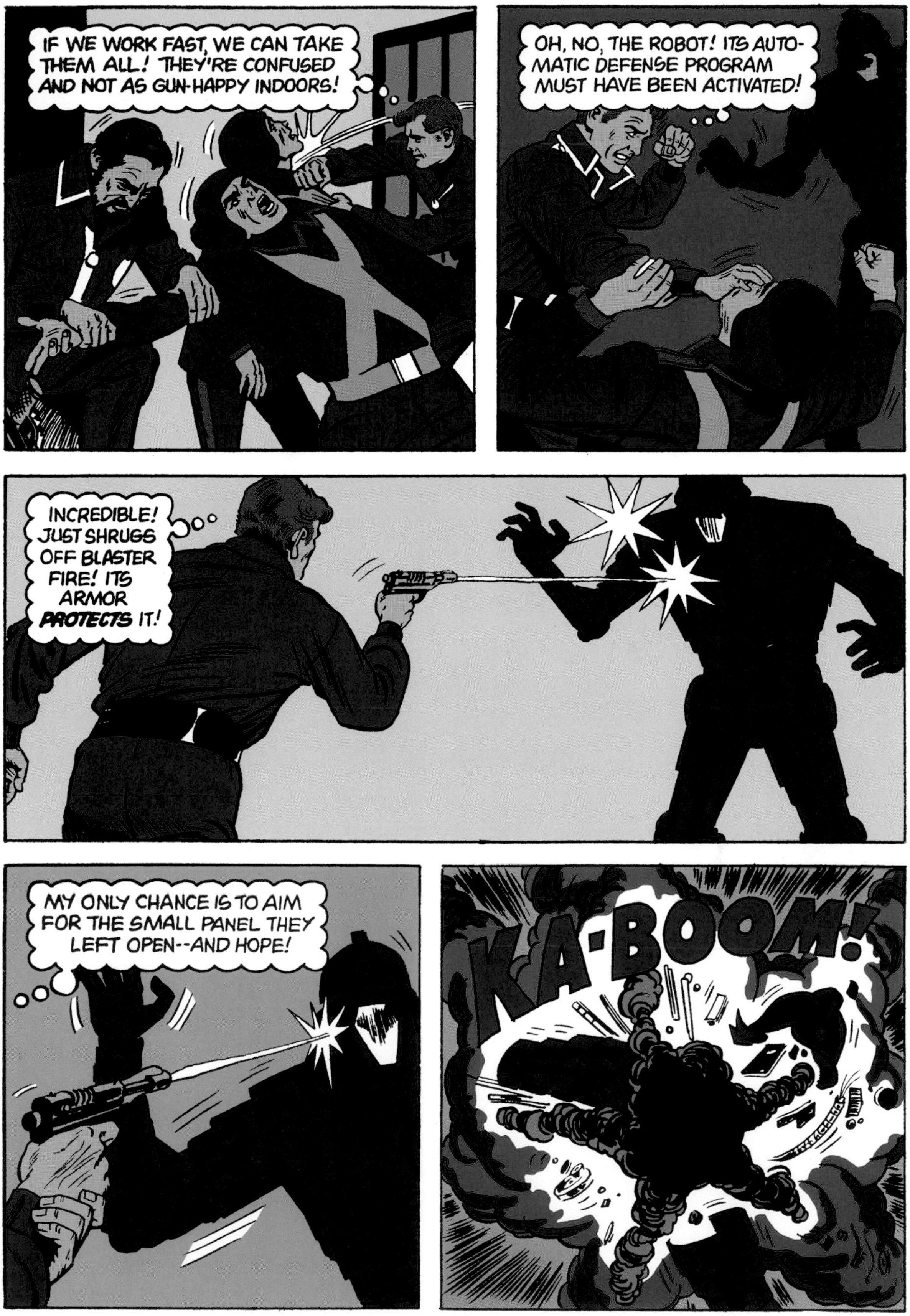
IF WE WORK FAST, WE CAN TAKE THEM ALL! THEY'RE CONFUSED AND NOT AS GUN-HAPPY INDOORS!
OH, NO, THE ROBOT! ITS AUTO-MATIC DEFENSE PROGRAM MUST HAVE BEEN ACTIVATED!
INCREDIBLE! JUST SHRUGS OFF BLASTER FIRE! ITS ARMOR PROTECTS IT!
MY ONLY CHANCE IS TO AIM FOR THE SMALL PANEL THEY LEFT OPEN--AND HOPE!
KA-BOOM!

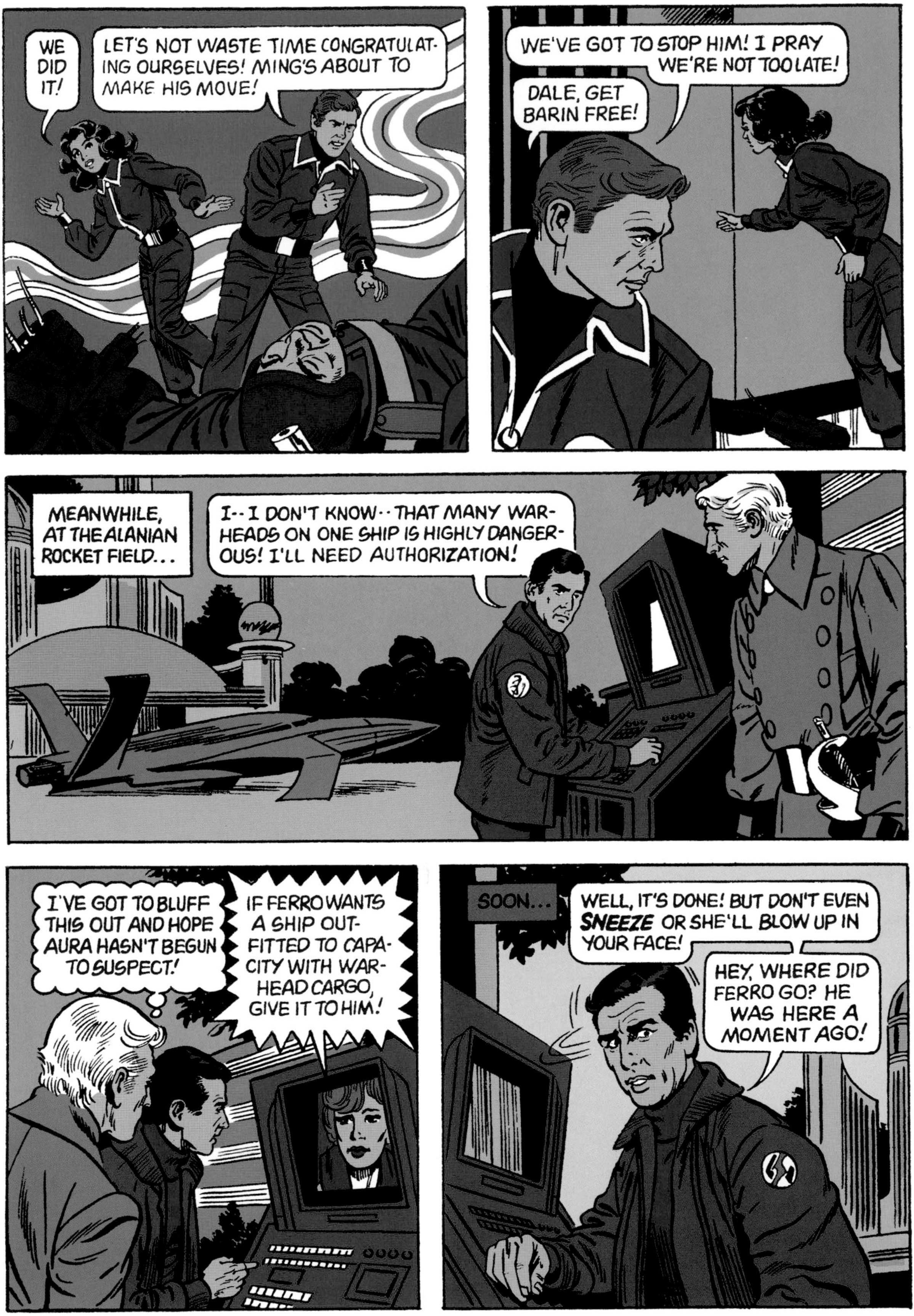
WE DID IT!
LET'S NOT WASTE TIME CONGRATULATING OURSELVES! MING'S ABOUT TO MAKE HIS MOVE!
WE'VE GOT TO STOP HIM! I PRAY WE'RE NOT TOO LATE!
DALE, GET BARIN FREE!
MEANWHILE, AT THE ALANIAN ROCKET FIELD...
I-- I DON'T KNOW-- THAT MANY WARHEADS ON ONE SHIP IS HIGHLY DANGEROUS! I'LL NEED AUTHORIZATION!
I'VE GOT TO BLUFF THIS OUT AND HOPE AURA HASN'T BEGUN TO SUSPECT!
IF FERRO WANTS A SHIP OUTFITTED TO CAPACITY WITH WARHEAD CARGO, GIVE IT TO HIM!
SOON...
WELL, IT'S DONE! BUT DON'T EVEN SNEEZE OR SHE'LL BLOW UP IN YOUR FACE!
HEY, WHERE DID FERRO GO? HE WAS HERE A MOMENT AGO!

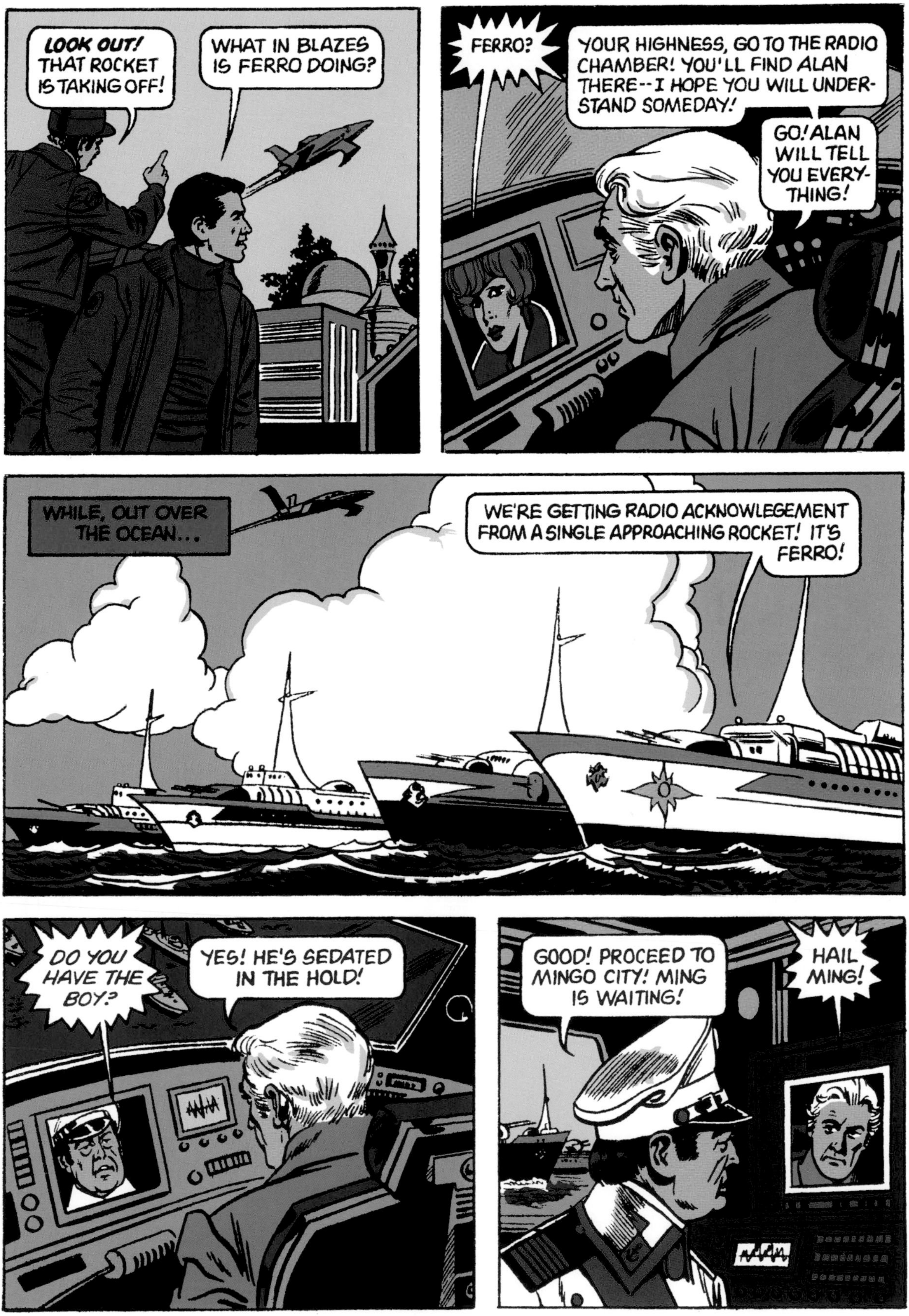
LOOK OUT! THAT ROCKET IS TAKING OFF!
WHAT IN BLAZES IS FERRO DOING?
FERRO?
YOUR HIGHNESS, GO TO THE RADIO CHAMBER! YOU'LL FIND ALAN THERE--I HOPE YOU WILL UNDERSTAND SOMEDAY!
GO! ALAN WILL TELL YOU EVERYTHING!
WHILE, OUT OVER THE OCEAN...
WE'RE GETTING RADIO ACKNOWLEGEMENT FROM A SINGLE APPROACHING ROCKET! IT'S FERRO!
DO YOU HAVE THE BOY?
YES! HE'S SEDATED IN THE HOLD!
GOOD! PROCEED TO MINGO CITY! MING IS WAITING!
HAIL MING!

ONWARD! FOR THE GLORY OF THE EMPIRE! THIS WILL BE OUR GREATEST VICTORY!

FAREWELL, ALAN! THIS IS FOR YOU, FOR YOUR FUTURE! IT'S LIKE THAT GAME OF STAKES-- THIS TIME IT'S YOUR KINGDOM!

MY LIFE IS THE *PRICE* TO BE PAID!

DESTRUCT SEQUENCE ACTIVATED

DA-KOOOM!

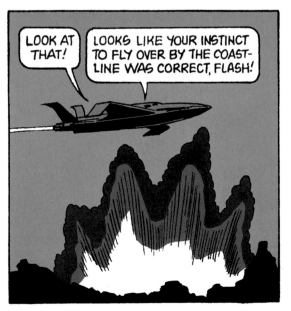

LOOK AT THAT!

LOOKS LIKE YOUR INSTINCT TO FLY OVER BY THE COASTLINE WAS CORRECT, FLASH!

I FIGURED IF MING WERE SENDING IN WARSHIPS, THIS WOULD BE THEIR APPROACH-- AND THERE THEY ARE!

ONLY SOMEBODY ALREADY *GOT* TO THEM!

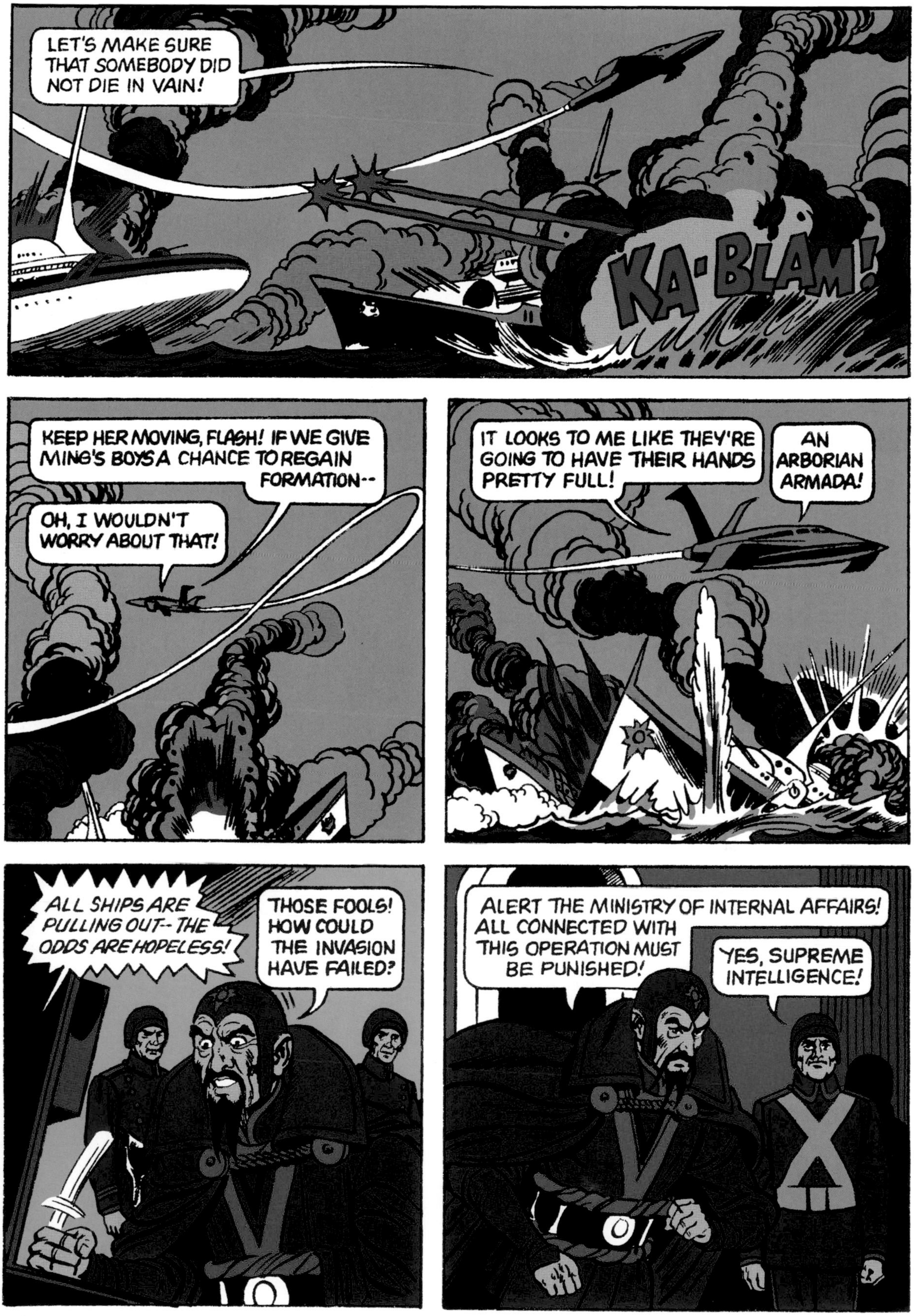
LET'S MAKE SURE THAT SOMEBODY DID NOT DIE IN VAIN!
KA-BLAM!
KEEP HER MOVING, FLASH! IF WE GIVE MING'S BOYS A CHANCE TO REGAIN FORMATION--
OH, I WOULDN'T WORRY ABOUT THAT!
IT LOOKS TO ME LIKE THEY'RE GOING TO HAVE THEIR HANDS PRETTY FULL!
AN ARBORIAN ARMADA!
ALL SHIPS ARE PULLING OUT-- THE ODDS ARE HOPELESS!
THOSE FOOLS! HOW COULD THE INVASION HAVE FAILED?
ALERT THE MINISTRY OF INTERNAL AFFAIRS! ALL CONNECTED WITH THIS OPERATION MUST BE PUNISHED!
YES, SUPREME INTELLIGENCE!

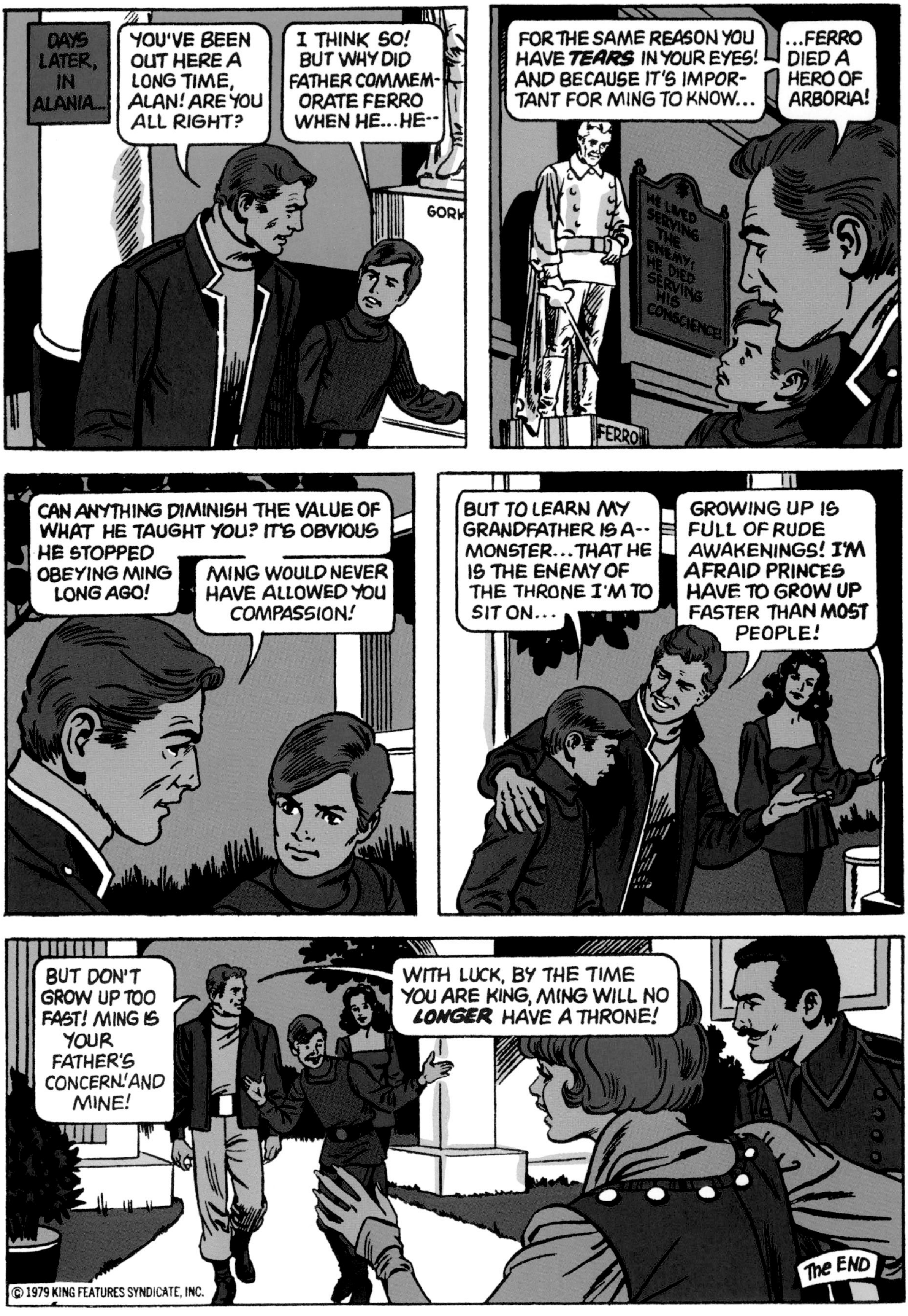
DAYS LATER, IN ALANIA...
YOU'VE BEEN OUT HERE A LONG TIME, ALAN! ARE YOU ALL RIGHT?
I THINK SO! BUT WHY DID FATHER COMMEMORATE FERRO WHEN HE... HE--
GORK
FOR THE SAME REASON YOU HAVE TEARS IN YOUR EYES! AND BECAUSE IT'S IMPORTANT FOR MING TO KNOW...
...FERRO DIED A HERO OF ARBORIA!
HE LIVED SERVING THE ENEMY; HE DIED SERVING HIS CONSCIENCE!
FERRO
CAN ANYTHING DIMINISH THE VALUE OF WHAT HE TAUGHT YOU? IT'S OBVIOUS HE STOPPED OBEYING MING LONG AGO!
MING WOULD NEVER HAVE ALLOWED YOU COMPASSION!
BUT TO LEARN MY GRANDFATHER IS A-- MONSTER... THAT HE IS THE ENEMY OF THE THRONE I'M TO SIT ON...
GROWING UP IS FULL OF RUDE AWAKENINGS! I'M AFRAID PRINCES HAVE TO GROW UP FASTER THAN MOST PEOPLE!
BUT DON'T GROW UP TOO FAST! MING IS YOUR FATHER'S CONCERN! AND MINE!
WITH LUCK, BY THE TIME YOU ARE KING, MING WILL NO LONGER HAVE A THRONE!
The END
© 1979 KING FEATURES SYNDICATE, INC.

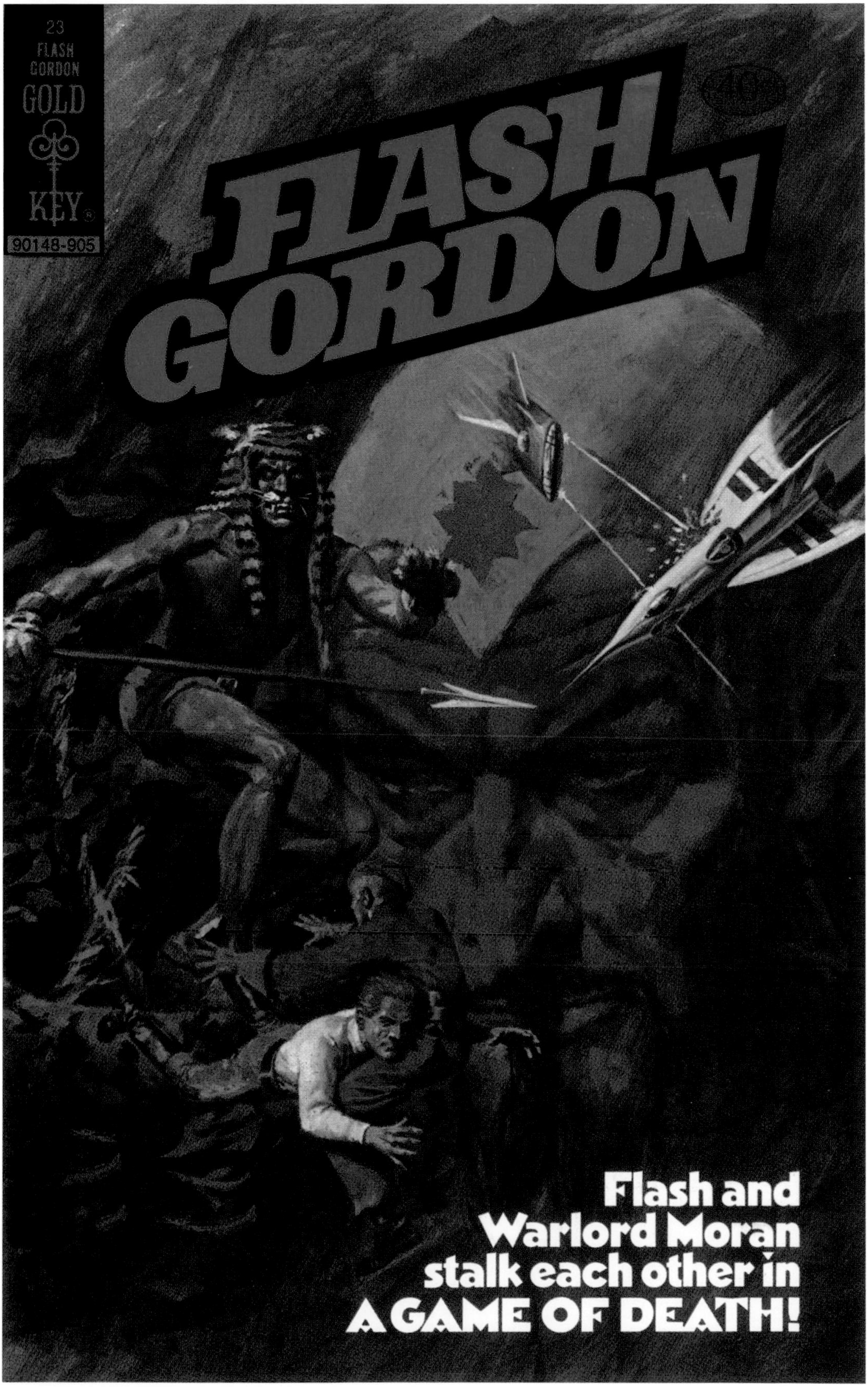
23
FLASH
GORDON
GOLD
KEY
90148-905
FLASH GORDON
Flash and
Warlord Moran
stalk each other in
A GAME OF DEATH!

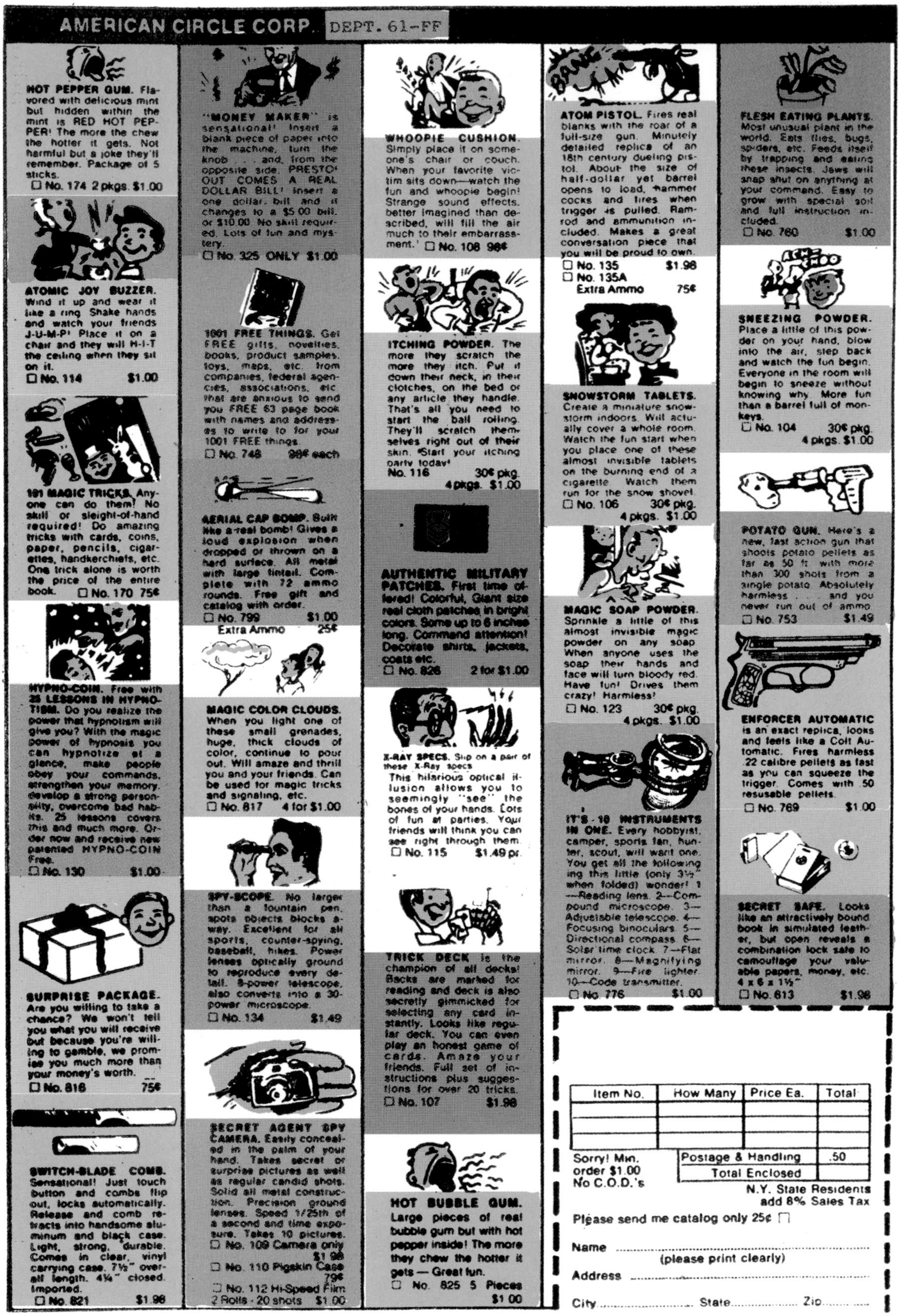

AMERICAN CIRCLE CORP. DEPT. 61-FF
HOT PEPPER GUM. Flavored with delicious mint but hidden within the mint is RED HOT PEPPER! The more the chew the hotter it gets. Not harmful but a joke they'll remember. Package of 5 sticks.
☐ No. 174 2 pkgs. $1.00
ATOMIC JOY BUZZER. Wind it up and wear it like a ring. Shake hands and watch your friends J-U-M-P! Place it on a chair and they will H-I-T the ceiling when they sit on it.
☐ No. 114 $1.00
101 MAGIC TRICKS. Anyone can do them! No skill or sleight-of-hand required! Do amazing tricks with cards, coins, paper, pencils, cigarettes, handkerchiefs, etc. One trick alone is worth the price of the entire book. ☐ No. 170 75¢
HYPNO-COIN. Free with 25 LESSONS IN HYPNOTISM. Do you realize the power that hypnotism will give you? With the magic power of hypnosis you can hypnotize at a glance, make people obey your commands, strengthen your memory, develop a strong personality, overcome bad habits. 25 lessons covers this and much more. Order now and receive new patented HYPNO-COIN Free.
☐ No. 130 $1.00
SURPRISE PACKAGE. Are you willing to take a chance? We won't tell you what you will receive but because you're willing to gamble, we promise you much more than your money's worth.
☐ No. 818 75¢
SWITCH-BLADE COMB. Sensational! Just touch button and combs flip out, locks automatically. Release and comb retracts into handsome aluminum and black case. Light, strong, durable. Comes in clear, vinyl carrying case. 7½" overall length. 4¾" closed. Imported.
☐ No. 821 $1.98
"MONEY MAKER" is sensational! Insert a blank piece of paper into the machine, turn the knob . . . and, from the opposite side, PRESTO! OUT COMES A REAL DOLLAR BILL! Insert a one dollar bill and it changes to a $5.00 bill, or $10.00. No skill required. Lots of fun and mystery.
☐ No. 325 ONLY $1.00
1001 FREE THINGS. Get FREE gifts, novelties, books, product samples, toys, maps, etc. from companies, federal agencies, associations, etc. that are anxious to send you FREE 63 page book with names and addresses to write to for your 1001 FREE things.
☐ No. 748 98¢ each
AERIAL CAP BOMB. Built like a real bomb! Gives a loud explosion when dropped or thrown on a hard surface. All metal with large tinteil. Complete with 72 ammo rounds. Free gift and catalog with order.
☐ No. 799 $1.00
Extra Ammo 25¢
MAGIC COLOR CLOUDS. When you light one of these small grenades, huge, thick clouds of color, continue to pour out. Will amaze and thrill you and your friends. Can be used for magic tricks and signaling, etc.
☐ No. 817 4 for $1.00
SPY-SCOPE. No larger than a fountain pen, spots objects blocks away. Excellent for all sports, counter-spying, baseball, hikes. Power lenses optically ground to reproduce every detail. 8-power telescope, also converts into a 30-power microscope.
☐ No. 134 $1.49
SECRET AGENT SPY CAMERA. Easily concealed in the palm of your hand. Takes secret or surprise pictures as well as regular candid shots. Solid all metal construction. Precision ground lenses. Speed 1/25th of a second and time exposure. Takes 10 pictures.
☐ No. 109 Camera only $1.98
☐ No. 110 Pigskin Case 79¢
☐ No. 112 Hi-Speed Film 2 Rolls - 20 shots $1.00
WHOOPIE CUSHION. Simply place it on someone's chair or couch. When your favorite victim sits down—watch the fun and whoopie begin! Strange sound effects, better imagined than described, will fill the air much to their embarrassment.' ☐ No. 108 98¢
ITCHING POWDER. The more they scratch the more they itch. Put it down their neck, in their clotches, on the bed or any article they handle. That's all you need to start the ball rolling. They'll scratch themselves right out of their skin. *Start your itching party today*
No. 116 30¢ pkg. 4 pkgs. $1.00
AUTHENTIC MILITARY PATCHES. First time offered! Colorful, Giant size real cloth patches in bright colors. Some up to 6 inches long. Command attention! Decorate shirts, jackets, coats etc.
☐ No. 826 2 for $1.00
X-RAY SPECS. Slip on a pair of these X-Ray specs This hilarious optical illusion allows you to seemingly "see" the bones of your hands. Lots of fun at parties. Your friends will think you can see right through them.
☐ No. 115 $1.49 pr.
TRICK DECK is the champion of all decks! Backs are marked for reading and deck is also secretly gimmicked for selecting any card instantly. Looks like regular deck. You can even play an honest game of cards. Amaze your friends. Full set of instructions plus suggestions for over 20 tricks.
☐ No. 107 $1.98
HOT BUBBLE GUM. Large pieces of real bubble gum but with hot pepper inside! The more they chew the hotter it gets — Great fun.
☐ No. 825 5 Pieces $1.00
BANG
ATOM PISTOL. Fires real blanks with the roar of a full-size gun. Minutely detailed replica of an 18th century dueling pistol. About the size of half-dollar yet barrel opens to load, hammer cocks and fires when trigger is pulled. Ramrod and ammunition included. Makes a great conversation piece that you will be proud to own.
☐ No. 135 $1.98
☐ No. 135A Extra Ammo 75¢
SNOWSTORM TABLETS. Create a miniature snowstorm indoors. Will actually cover a whole room. Watch the fun start when you place one of these almost invisible tablets on the burning end of a cigarette. Watch them run for the snow shovel.
☐ No. 106 30¢ pkg. 4 pkgs. $1.00
MAGIC SOAP POWDER. Sprinkle a little of this almost invisible magic powder on any soap. When anyone uses the soap their hands and face will turn bloody red. Have fun! Drives them crazy! Harmless!
☐ No. 123 30¢ pkg. 4 pkgs. $1.00
IT'S 10 INSTRUMENTS IN ONE. Every hobbyist, camper, sports fan, hunter, scout, will want one. You get all the following ing this little (only 3½" when folded) wonder! 1—Reading lens. 2—Compound microscope. 3—Adjustable telescope. 4—Focusing binoculars. 5—Directional compass. 6—Solar time clock. 7—Flat mirror. 8—Magnifying mirror. 9—Fire lighter. 10—Code transmitter.
☐ No. 776 $1.00
FLESH EATING PLANTS. Most unusual plant in the world. Eats flies, bugs, spiders, etc. Feeds itself by trapping and eating these insects. Jaws will snap shut on anything at your command. Easy to grow with special soil and full instruction included.
☐ No. 760 $1.00
ACH-CHOO
SNEEZING POWDER. Place a little of this powder on your hand, blow into the air, step back and watch the fun begin. Everyone in the room will begin to sneeze without knowing why. More fun than a barrel full of monkeys.
☐ No. 104 30¢ pkg. 4 pkgs. $1.00
POTATO GUN. Here's a new, fast action gun that shoots potato pellets as far as 50 ft. with more than 300 shots from a single potato. Absolutely harmless . . . and you never run out of ammo.
☐ No. 753 $1.49
ENFORCER AUTOMATIC is an exact replica, looks and feels like a Colt Automatic. Fires harmless .22 calibre pellets as fast as you can squeeze the trigger. Comes with 50 resusable pellets.
☐ No. 769 $1.00
SECRET SAFE. Looks like an attractively bound book in simulated leather, but open reveals a combination lock safe to camouflage your valuable papers, money, etc. 4 x 6 x 1½"
☐ No. 813 $1.98
Item No. | How Many | Price Ea. | Total
Sorry! Min. order $1.00 No C.O.D.'s
Postage & Handling .50
Total Enclosed
N.Y. State Residents add 8% Sales Tax
Please send me catalog only 25¢ ☐
Name ....
(please print clearly)
Address ....
City .... State .... Zip ....

Stranded in an alien world, Flash Gordon, Dale Arden and Dr. Hans Zarkov struggle against the evil emperor, Ming the Merciless, who seeks to enslave an entire planet.....

FLASH GORDON ON THE PLANET MONGO

THE GAME OF DEATH

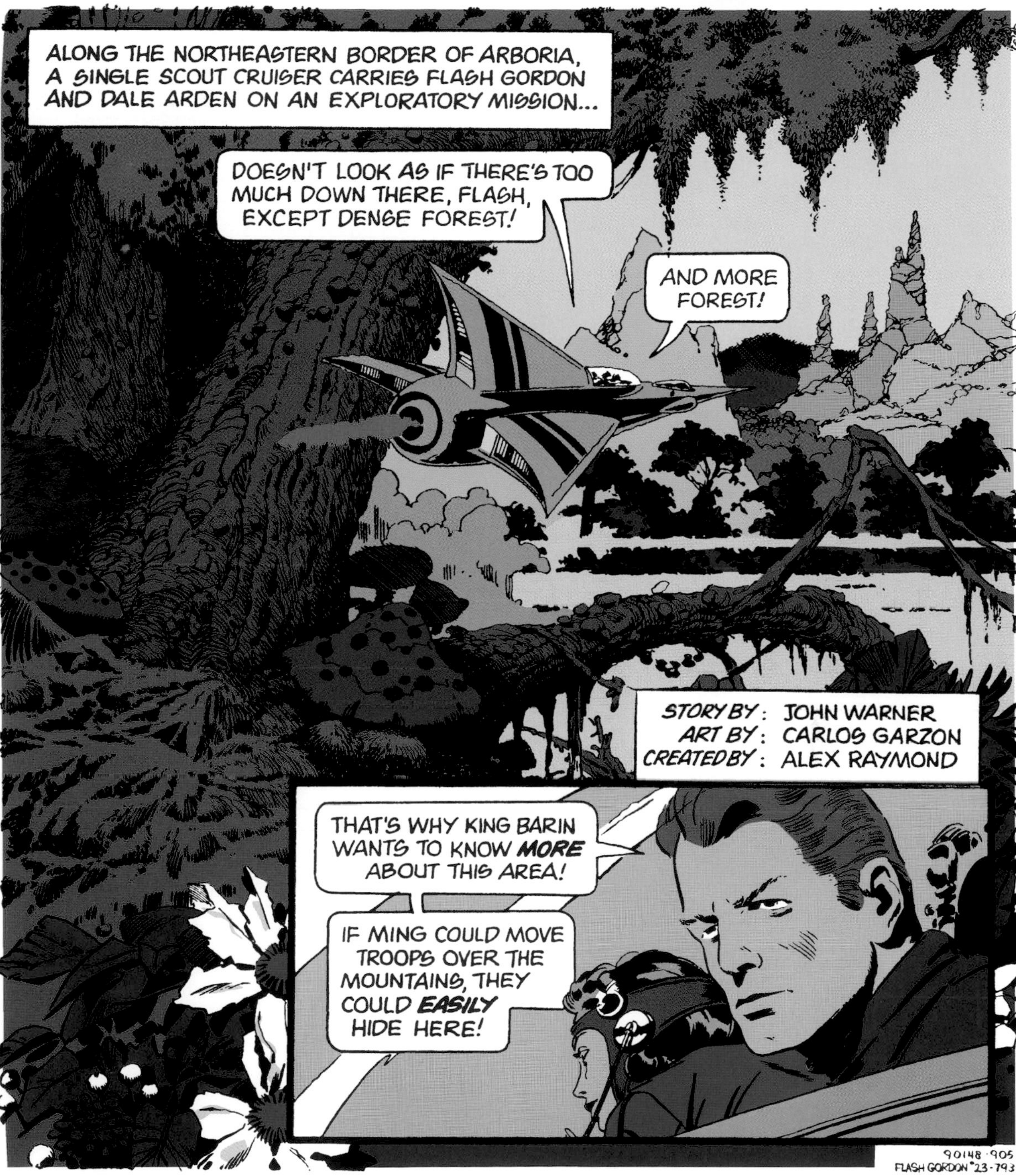
ALONG THE NORTHEASTERN BORDER OF ARBORIA, A SINGLE SCOUT CRUISER CARRIES FLASH GORDON AND DALE ARDEN ON AN EXPLORATORY MISSION...
DOESN'T LOOK AS IF THERE'S TOO MUCH DOWN THERE, FLASH, EXCEPT DENSE FOREST!
AND MORE FOREST!
STORY BY: JOHN WARNER
ART BY: CARLOS GARZON
CREATED BY: ALEX RAYMOND
THAT'S WHY KING BARIN WANTS TO KNOW MORE ABOUT THIS AREA!
IF MING COULD MOVE TROOPS OVER THE MOUNTAINS, THEY COULD EASILY HIDE HERE!

90148-905
FLASH GORDON® 23-793

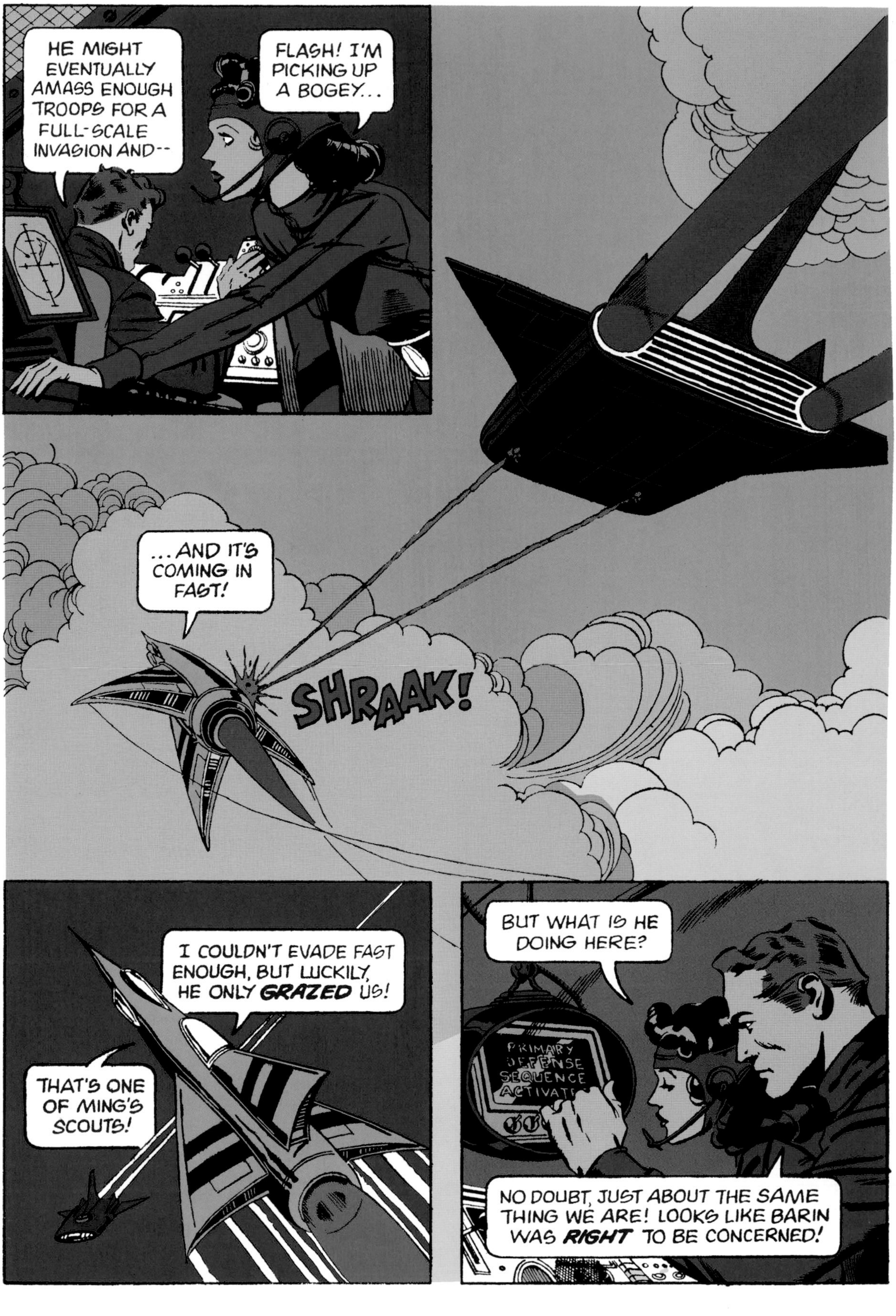

HE MIGHT EVENTUALLY AMASS ENOUGH TROOPS FOR A FULL-SCALE INVASION AND--
FLASH! I'M PICKING UP A BOGEY...
...AND IT'S COMING IN FAST!
SHRAAK!
I COULDN'T EVADE FAST ENOUGH, BUT LUCKILY, HE ONLY **GRAZED** US!
THAT'S ONE OF MING'S SCOUTS!
BUT WHAT IS HE DOING HERE?
PRIMARY DEFENSE SEQUENCE
NO DOUBT, JUST ABOUT THE SAME THING WE ARE! LOOKS LIKE BARIN WAS **RIGHT** TO BE CONCERNED!

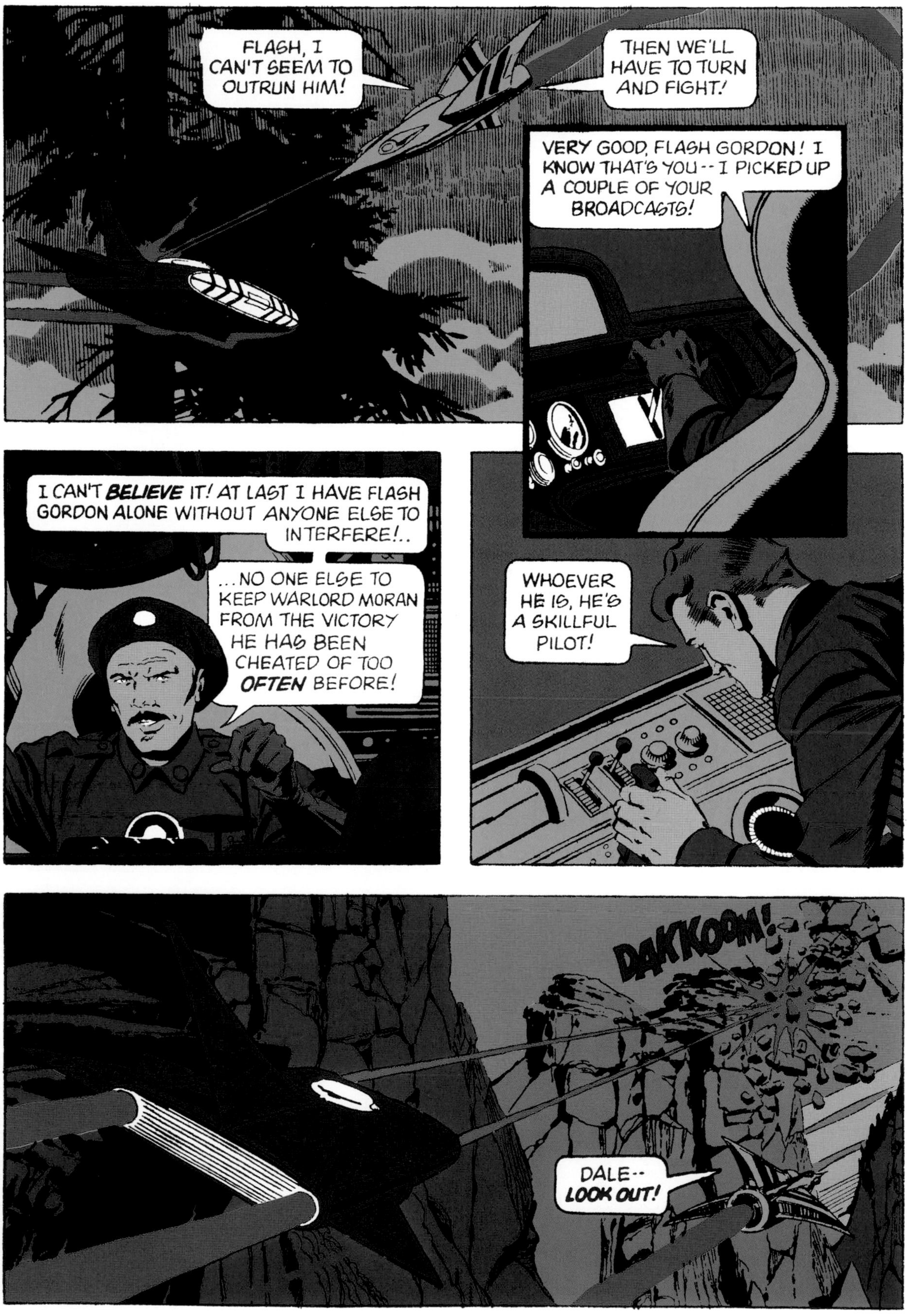
FLASH, I CAN'T SEEM TO OUTRUN HIM!
THEN WE'LL HAVE TO TURN AND FIGHT!
VERY GOOD, FLASH GORDON! I KNOW THAT'S YOU -- I PICKED UP A COUPLE OF YOUR BROADCASTS!
I CAN'T BELIEVE IT! AT LAST I HAVE FLASH GORDON ALONE WITHOUT ANYONE ELSE TO INTERFERE!..
...NO ONE ELSE TO KEEP WARLORD MORAN FROM THE VICTORY HE HAS BEEN CHEATED OF TOO OFTEN BEFORE!
WHOEVER HE IS, HE'S A SKILLFUL PILOT!
DAKKOOM!
DALE-- LOOK OUT!

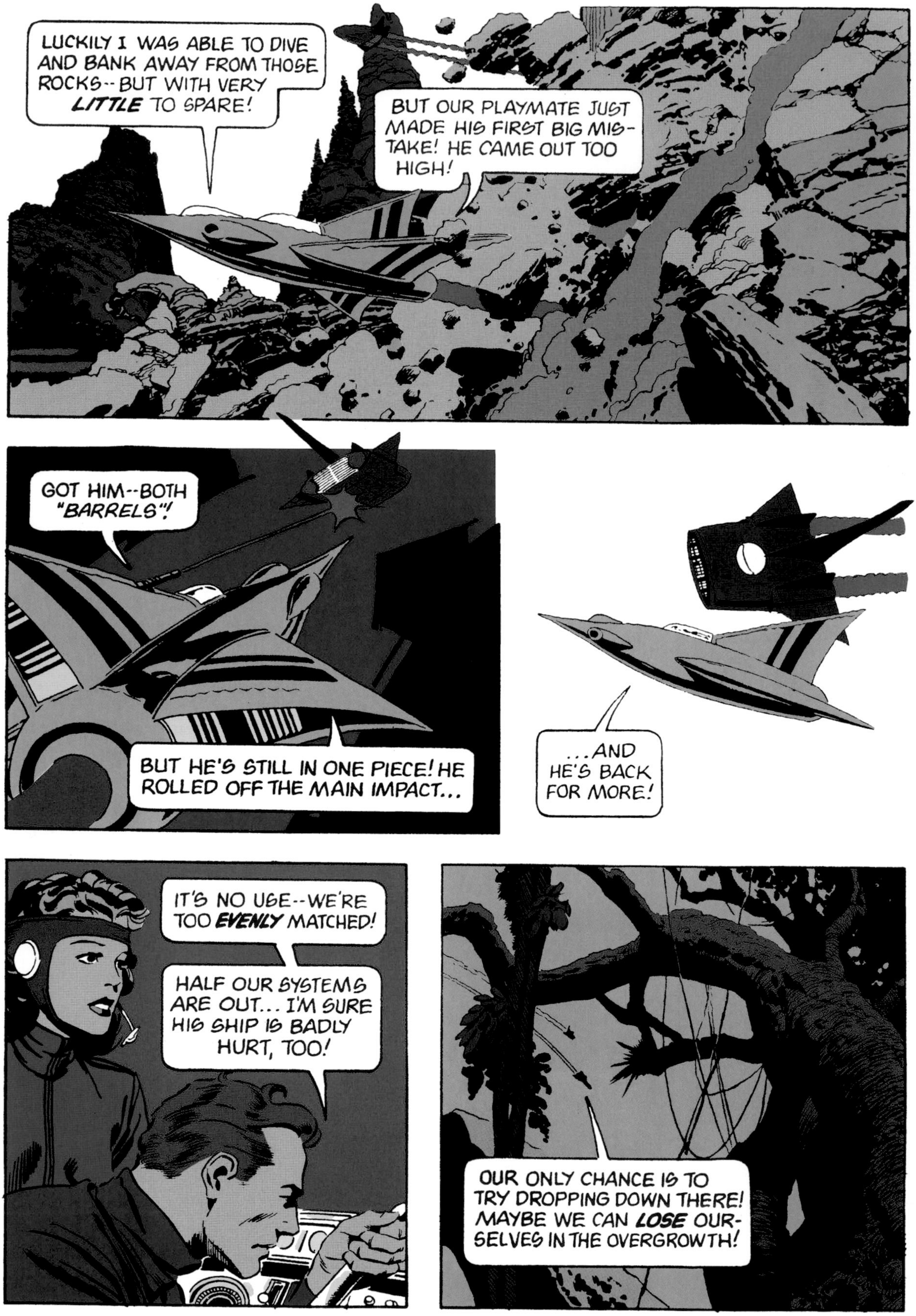
LUCKILY I WAS ABLE TO DIVE AND BANK AWAY FROM THOSE ROCKS--BUT WITH VERY LITTLE TO SPARE!
BUT OUR PLAYMATE JUST MADE HIS FIRST BIG MISTAKE! HE CAME OUT TOO HIGH!
GOT HIM--BOTH "BARRELS"!
BUT HE'S STILL IN ONE PIECE! HE ROLLED OFF THE MAIN IMPACT...
...AND HE'S BACK FOR MORE!
IT'S NO USE--WE'RE TOO EVENLY MATCHED!
HALF OUR SYSTEMS ARE OUT... I'M SURE HIS SHIP IS BADLY HURT, TOO!
OUR ONLY CHANCE IS TO TRY DROPPING DOWN THERE! MAYBE WE CAN LOSE OURSELVES IN THE OVERGROWTH!

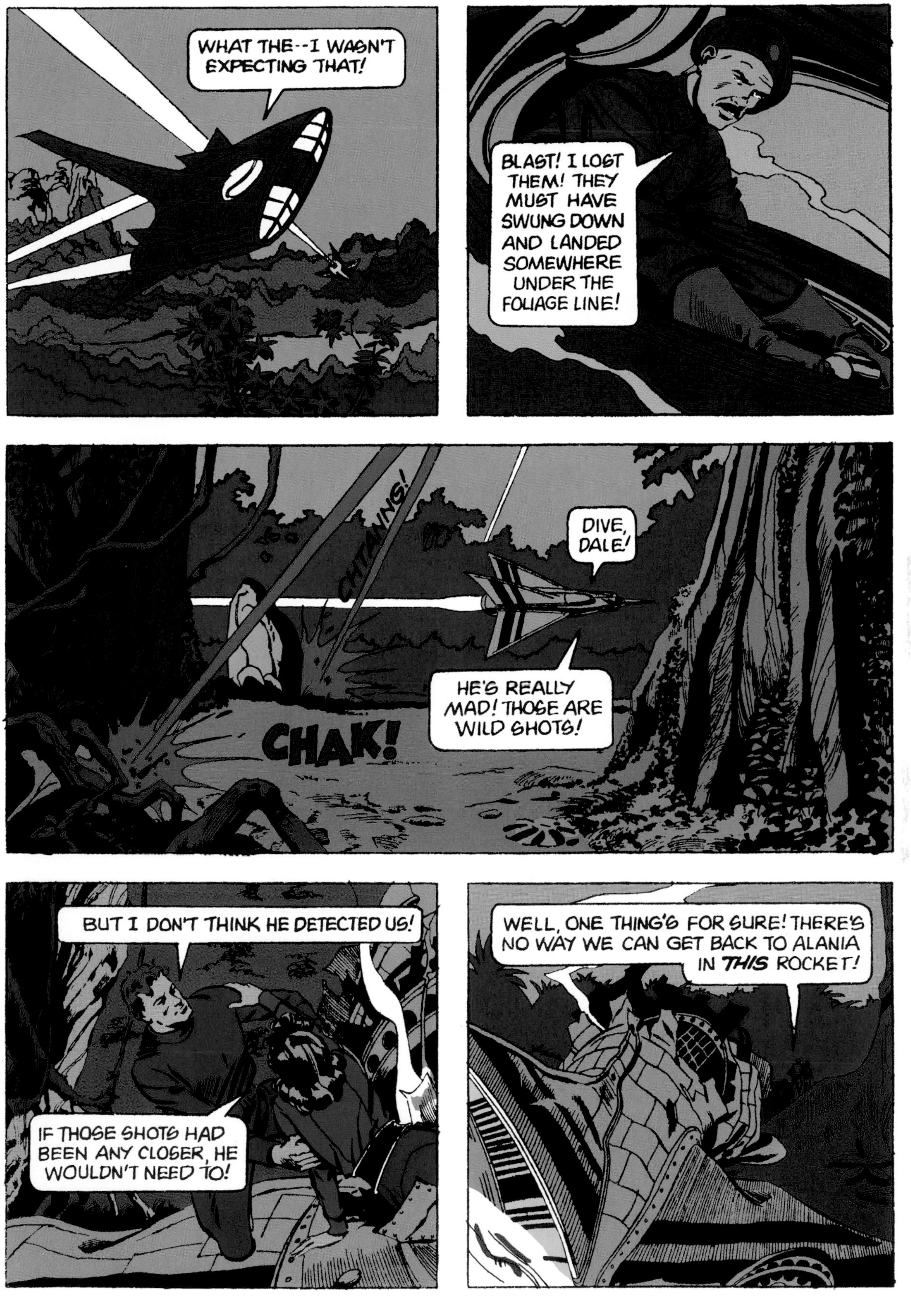
WHAT THE--I WASN'T EXPECTING THAT!
BLAST! I LOST THEM! THEY MUST HAVE SWUNG DOWN AND LANDED SOMEWHERE UNDER THE FOLIAGE LINE!
CHTANNG!
DIVE, DALE!
CHAK!
HE'S REALLY MAD! THOSE ARE WILD SHOTS!
BUT I DON'T THINK HE DETECTED US!
IF THOSE SHOTS HAD BEEN ANY CLOSER, HE WOULDN'T NEED TO!
WELL, ONE THING'S FOR SURE! THERE'S NO WAY WE CAN GET BACK TO ALANIA IN *THIS* ROCKET!

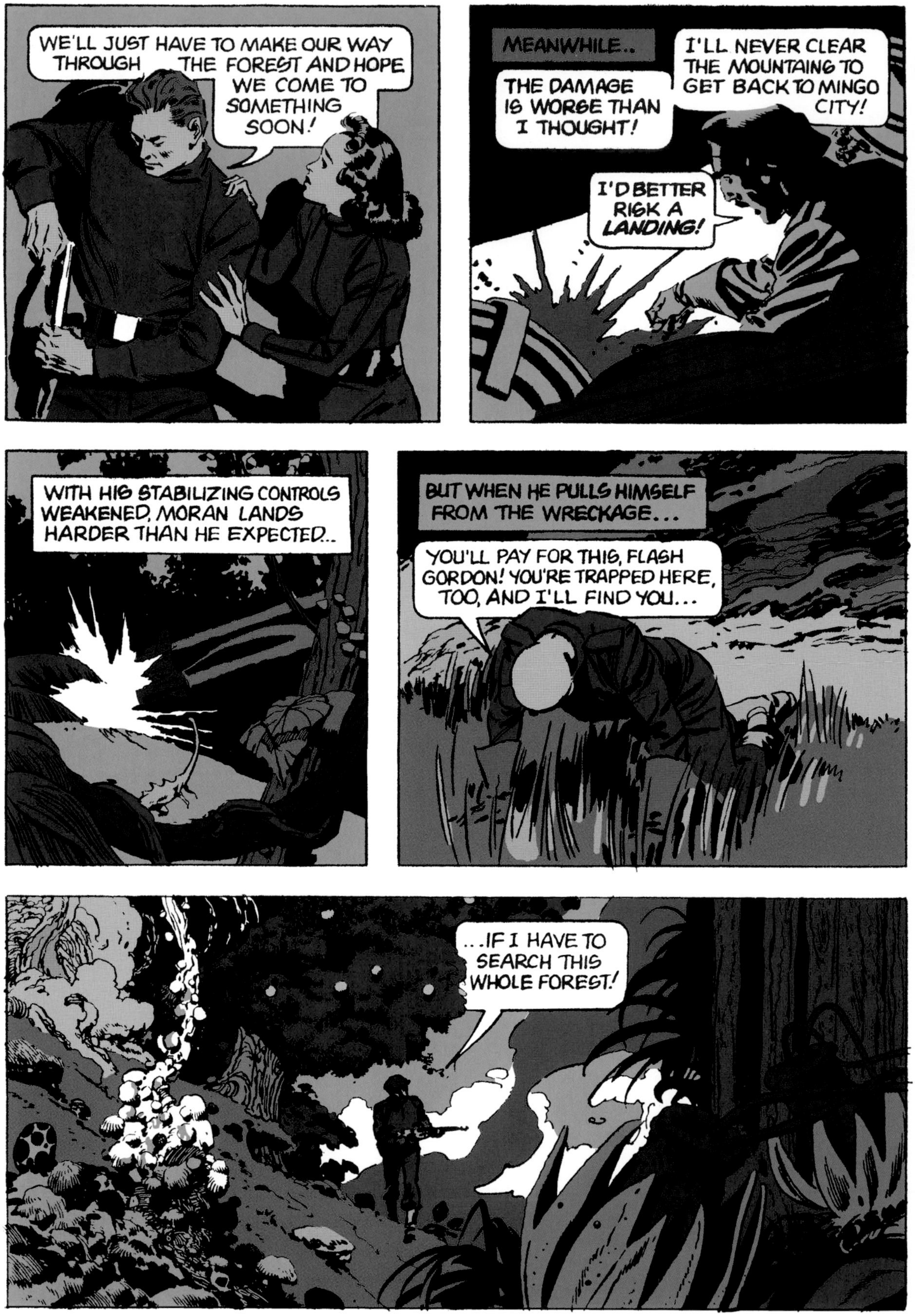
WE'LL JUST HAVE TO MAKE OUR WAY THROUGH THE FOREST AND HOPE WE COME TO SOMETHING SOON!
MEANWHILE..
THE DAMAGE IS WORSE THAN I THOUGHT!
I'LL NEVER CLEAR THE MOUNTAINS TO GET BACK TO MINGO CITY!
I'D BETTER RISK A LANDING!
WITH HIS STABILIZING CONTROLS WEAKENED, MORAN LANDS HARDER THAN HE EXPECTED..
BUT WHEN HE PULLS HIMSELF FROM THE WRECKAGE...
YOU'LL PAY FOR THIS, FLASH GORDON! YOU'RE TRAPPED HERE, TOO, AND I'LL FIND YOU...
...IF I HAVE TO SEARCH THIS WHOLE FOREST!

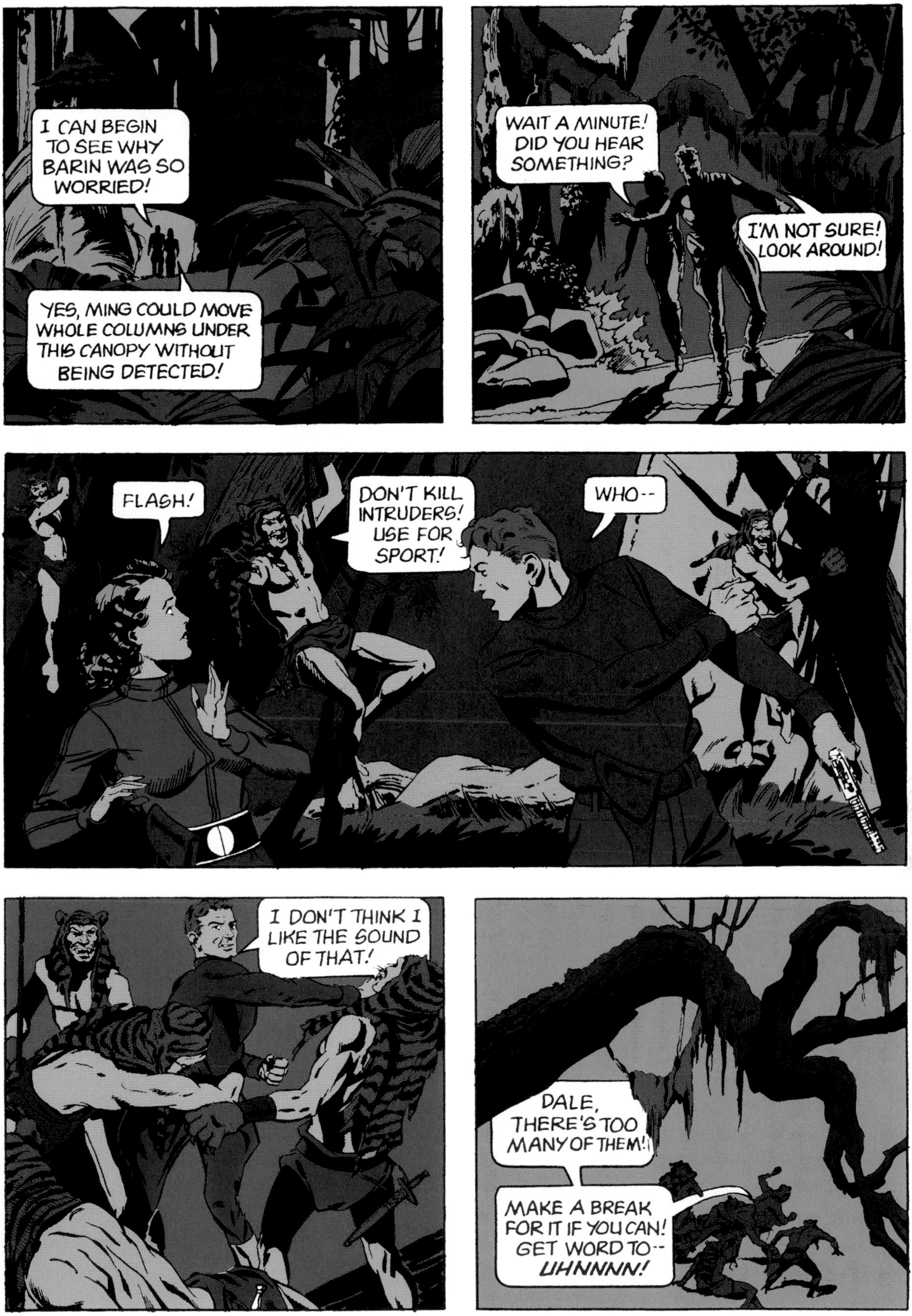
I CAN BEGIN TO SEE WHY BARIN WAS SO WORRIED!
YES, MING COULD MOVE WHOLE COLUMNS UNDER THIS CANOPY WITHOUT BEING DETECTED!
WAIT A MINUTE! DID YOU HEAR SOMETHING?
I'M NOT SURE! LOOK AROUND!
FLASH!
DON'T KILL INTRUDERS! USE FOR SPORT!
WHO--
I DON'T THINK I LIKE THE SOUND OF THAT!
DALE, THERE'S TOO MANY OF THEM!
MAKE A BREAK FOR IT IF YOU CAN! GET WORD TO-- *UHNNNN!*

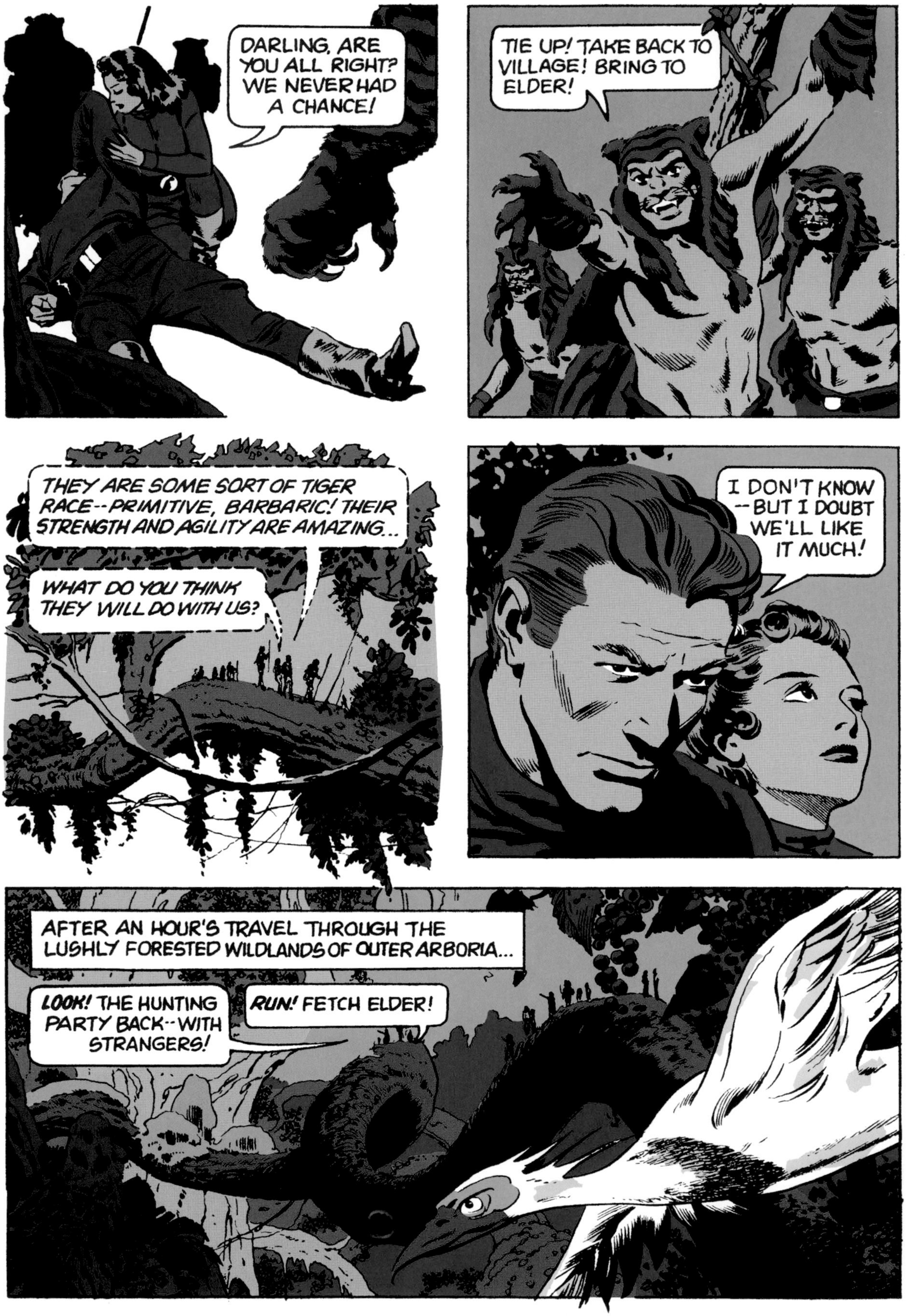
DARLING, ARE YOU ALL RIGHT? WE NEVER HAD A CHANCE!
TIE UP! TAKE BACK TO VILLAGE! BRING TO ELDER!
THEY ARE SOME SORT OF TIGER RACE--PRIMITIVE, BARBARIC! THEIR STRENGTH AND AGILITY ARE AMAZING...
WHAT DO YOU THINK THEY WILL DO WITH US?
I DON'T KNOW --BUT I DOUBT WE'LL LIKE IT MUCH!
AFTER AN HOUR'S TRAVEL THROUGH THE LUSHLY FORESTED WILDLANDS OF OUTER ARBORIA...
LOOK! THE HUNTING PARTY BACK--WITH STRANGERS!
RUN! FETCH ELDER!

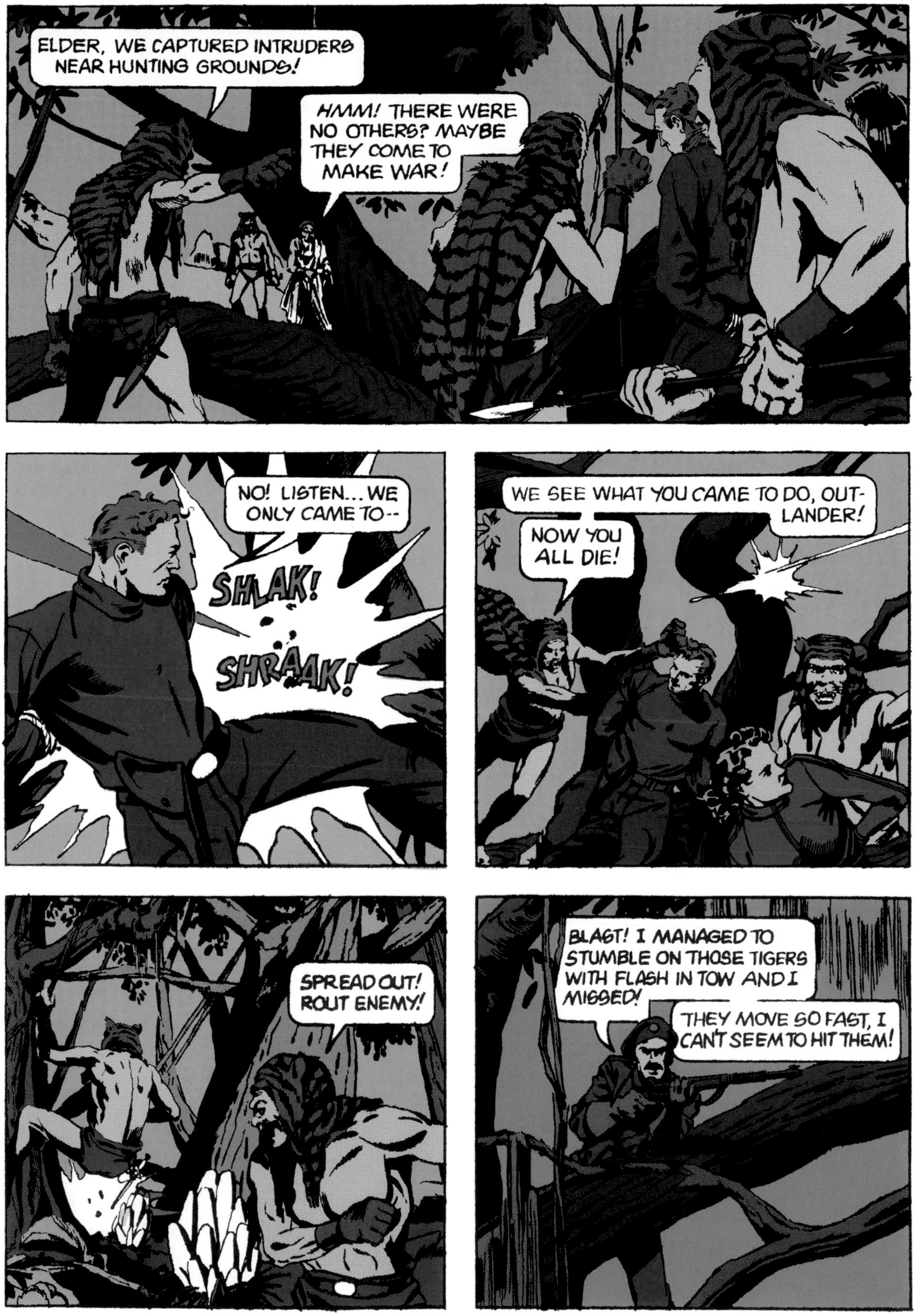
ELDER, WE CAPTURED INTRUDERS NEAR HUNTING GROUNDS!
HMM! THERE WERE NO OTHERS? MAYBE THEY COME TO MAKE WAR!
NO! LISTEN... WE ONLY CAME TO--
SHLAK!
SHRAAK!
WE SEE WHAT YOU CAME TO DO, OUT-LANDER!
NOW YOU ALL DIE!
SPREAD OUT! ROUT ENEMY!
BLAST! I MANAGED TO STUMBLE ON THOSE TIGERS WITH FLASH IN TOW AND I MISSED!
THEY MOVE SO FAST, I CAN'T SEEM TO HIT THEM!

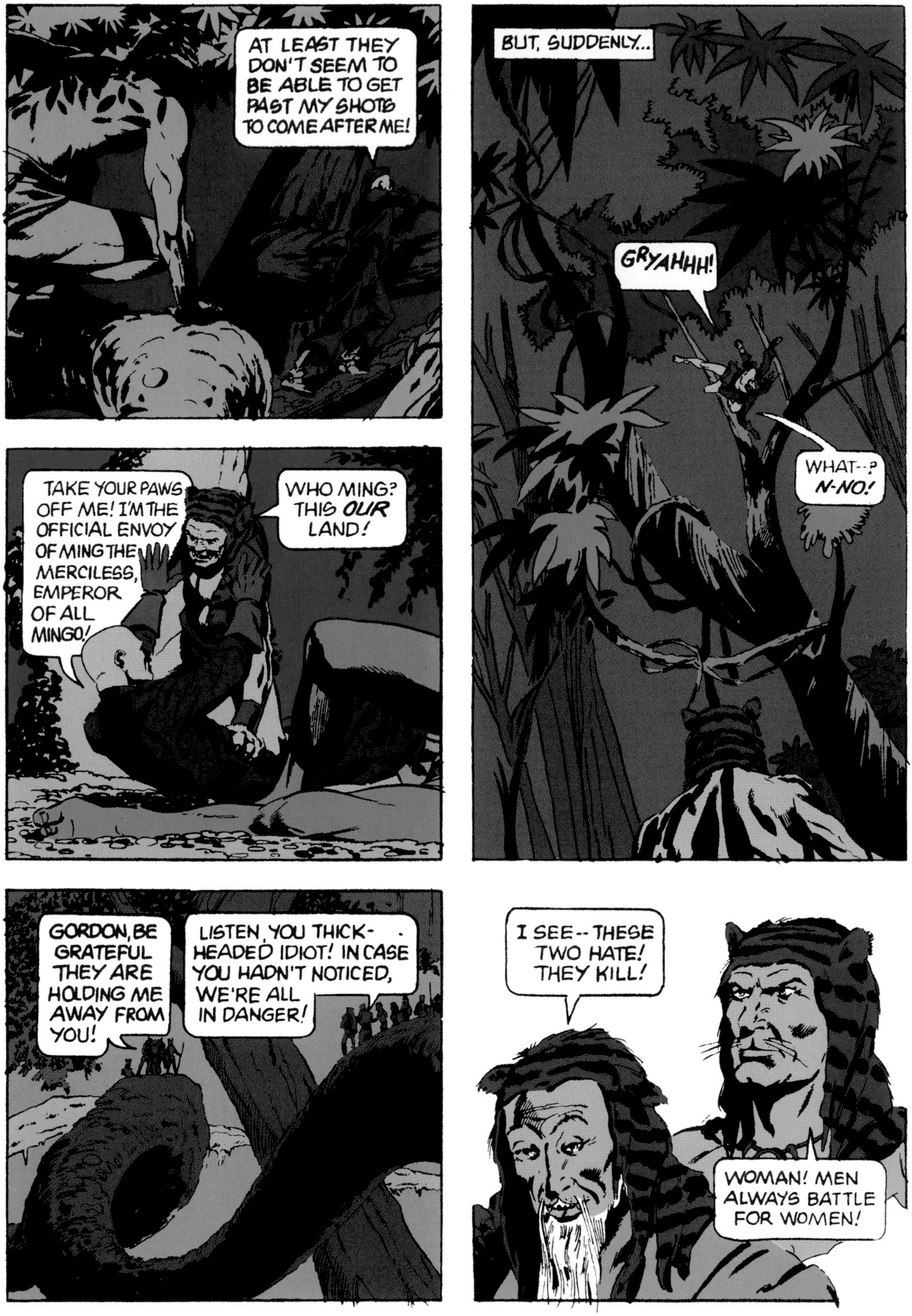
AT LEAST THEY DON'T SEEM TO BE ABLE TO GET PAST MY SHOTS TO COME AFTER ME!
TAKE YOUR PAWS OFF ME! I'M THE OFFICIAL ENVOY OF MING THE MERCILESS, EMPEROR OF ALL MINGO!
WHO MING? THIS *OUR* LAND!
BUT, SUDDENLY...
GRYAHHH!
WHAT--? *N-NO!*
GORDON, BE GRATEFUL THEY ARE HOLDING ME AWAY FROM YOU!
LISTEN, YOU THICK-HEADED IDIOT! IN CASE YOU HADN'T NOTICED, WE'RE ALL IN DANGER!
I SEE--THESE TWO HATE! THEY KILL!
WOMAN! MEN ALWAYS BATTLE FOR WOMEN!

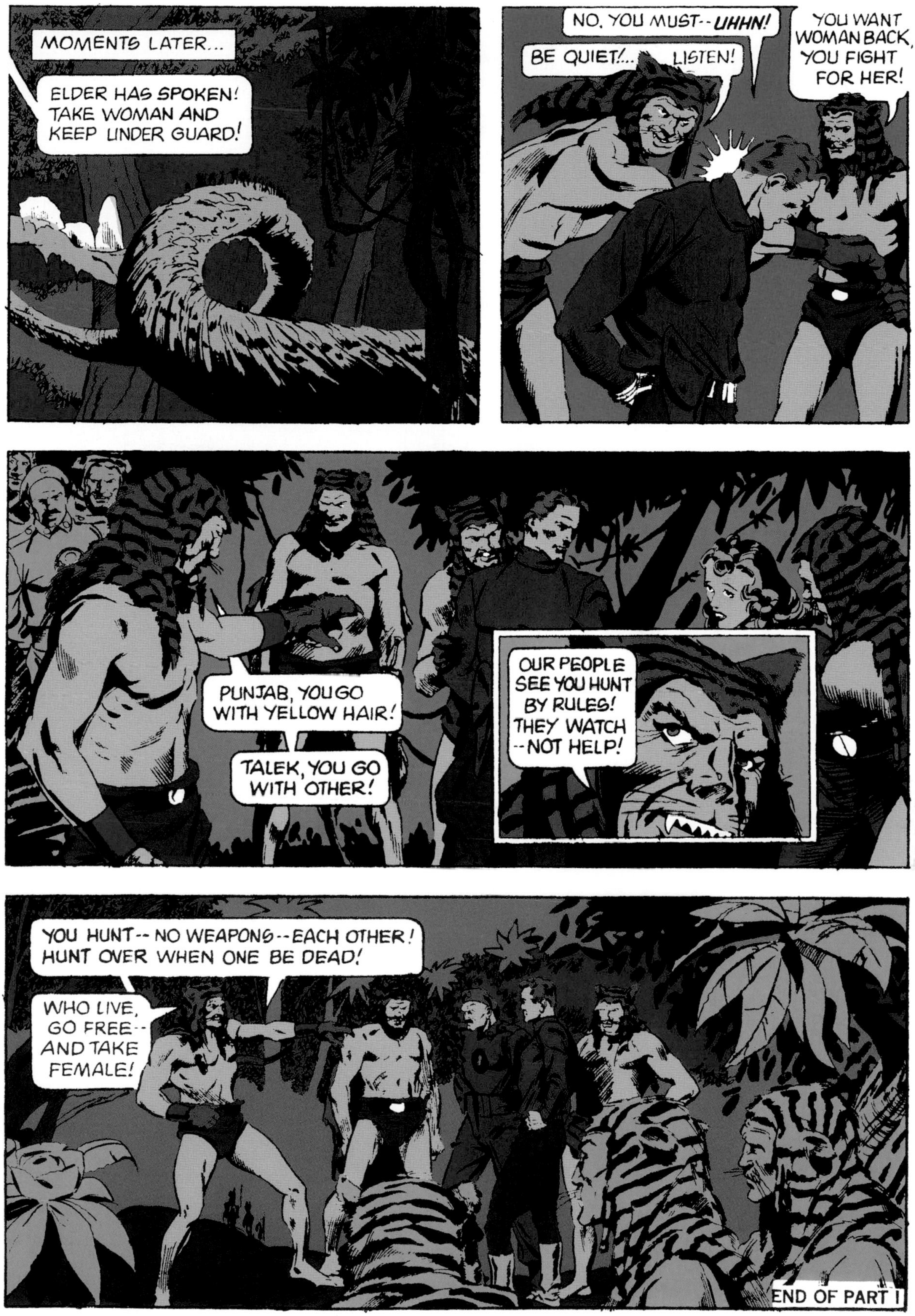
MOMENTS LATER...
ELDER HAS SPOKEN! TAKE WOMAN AND KEEP UNDER GUARD!
NO. YOU MUST--UHHN!
BE QUIET!... LISTEN!
YOU WANT WOMAN BACK, YOU FIGHT FOR HER!
PUNJAB, YOU GO WITH YELLOW HAIR!
TALEK, YOU GO WITH OTHER!
OUR PEOPLE SEE YOU HUNT BY RULES! THEY WATCH --NOT HELP!
YOU HUNT-- NO WEAPONS--EACH OTHER! HUNT OVER WHEN ONE BE DEAD!
WHO LIVE, GO FREE-- AND TAKE FEMALE!
END OF PART I

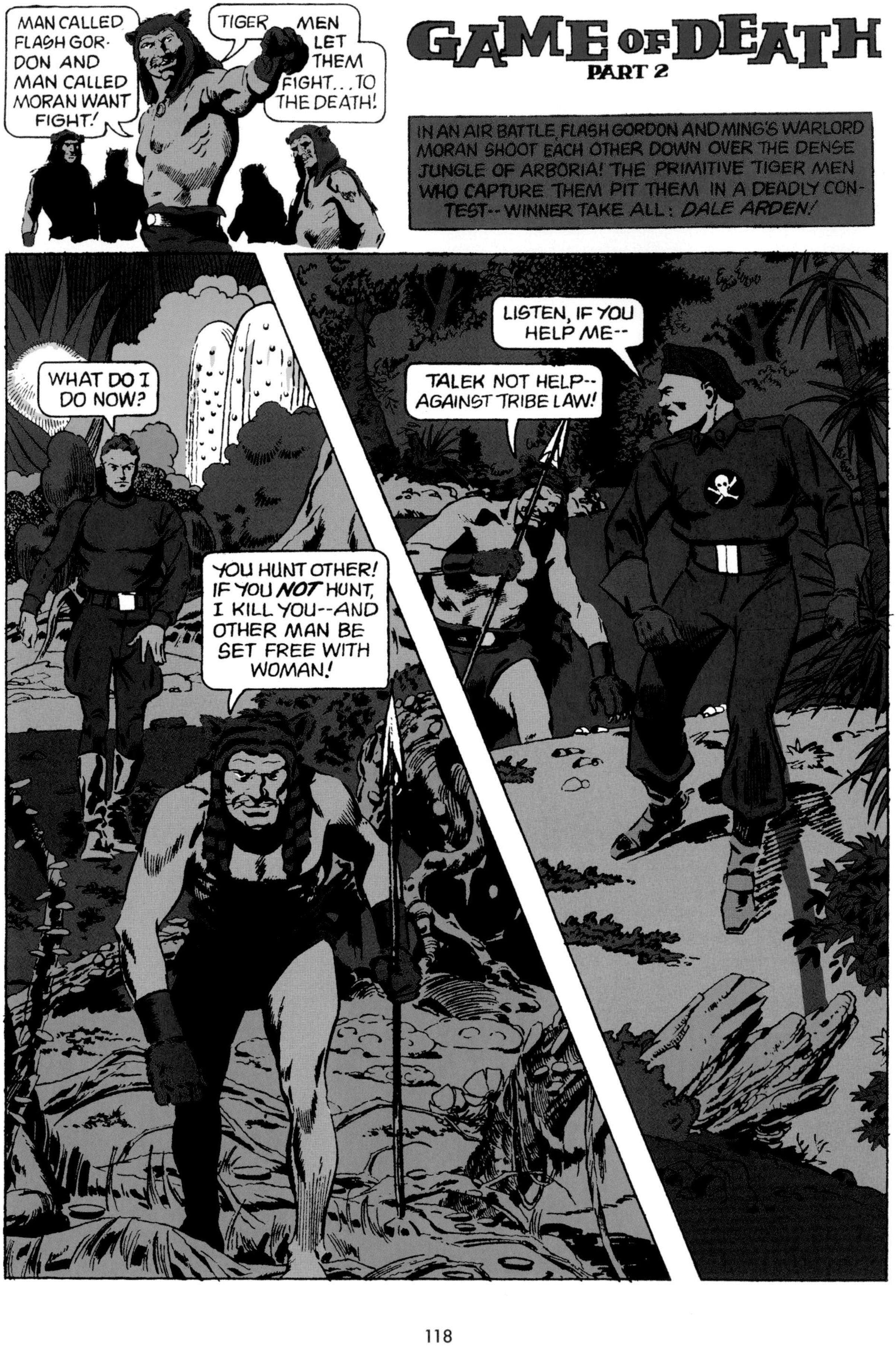
MAN CALLED FLASH GOR-DON AND MAN CALLED MORAN WANT FIGHT!
TIGER MEN LET THEM FIGHT. . . TO THE DEATH!
GAME OF DEATH
PART 2
IN AN AIR BATTLE, FLASH GORDON AND MING'S WARLORD MORAN SHOOT EACH OTHER DOWN OVER THE DENSE JUNGLE OF ARBORIA! THE PRIMITIVE TIGER MEN WHO CAPTURE THEM PIT THEM IN A DEADLY CON-TEST-- WINNER TAKE ALL: DALE ARDEN!
WHAT DO I DO NOW?
YOU HUNT OTHER! IF YOU NOT HUNT, I KILL YOU--AND OTHER MAN BE SET FREE WITH WOMAN!
LISTEN, IF YOU HELP ME--
TALEK NOT HELP-- AGAINST TRIBE LAW!

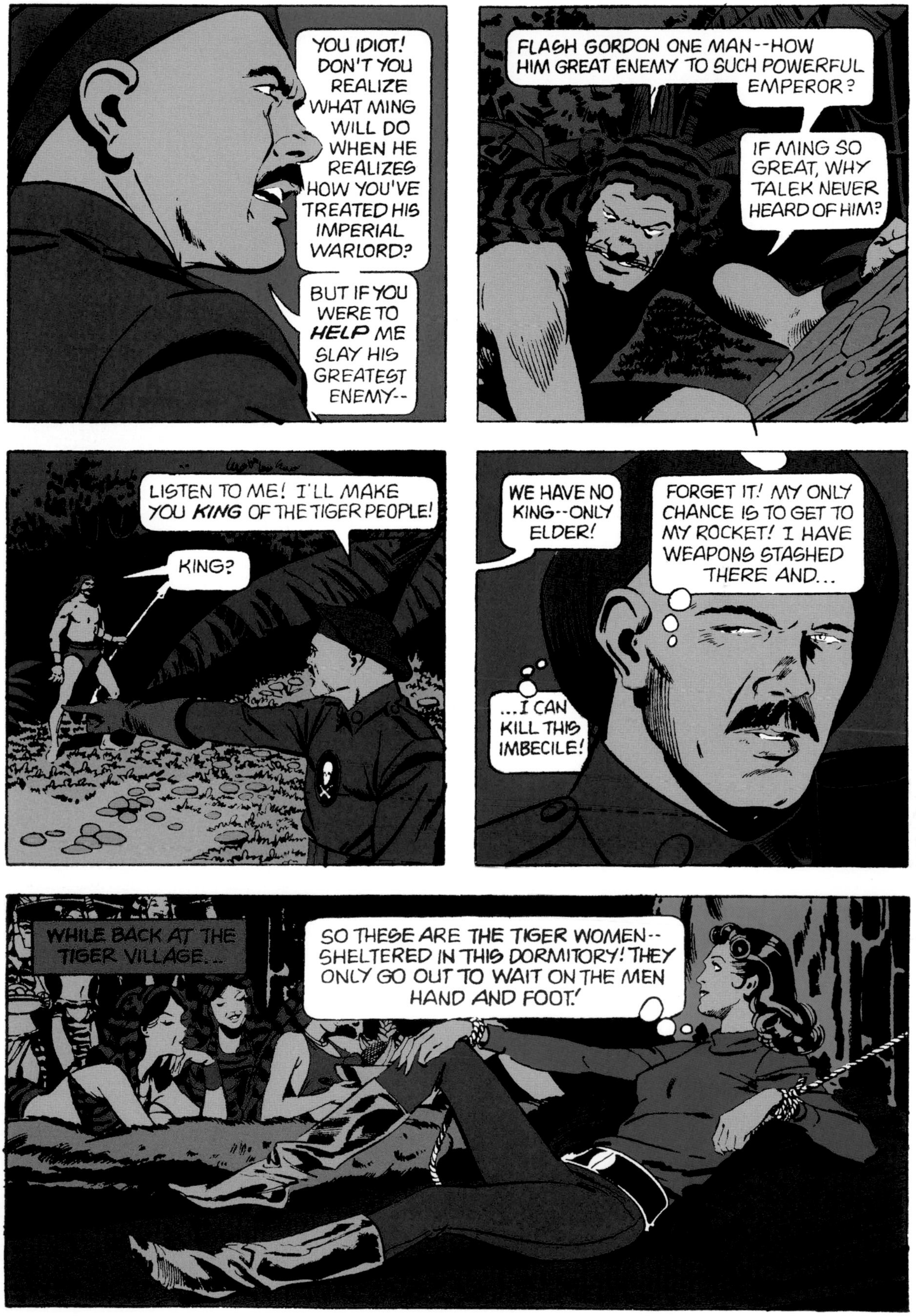
YOU IDIOT! DON'T YOU REALIZE WHAT MING WILL DO WHEN HE REALIZES HOW YOU'VE TREATED HIS IMPERIAL WARLORD?
BUT IF YOU WERE TO HELP ME SLAY HIS GREATEST ENEMY--
FLASH GORDON ONE MAN--HOW HIM GREAT ENEMY TO SUCH POWERFUL EMPEROR?
IF MING SO GREAT, WHY TALEK NEVER HEARD OF HIM?
LISTEN TO ME! I'LL MAKE YOU KING OF THE TIGER PEOPLE!
KING?
WE HAVE NO KING--ONLY ELDER!
FORGET IT! MY ONLY CHANCE IS TO GET TO MY ROCKET! I HAVE WEAPONS STASHED THERE AND...
...I CAN KILL THIS IMBECILE!
WHILE BACK AT THE TIGER VILLAGE...
SO THESE ARE THE TIGER WOMEN--SHELTERED IN THIS DORMITORY! THEY ONLY GO OUT TO WAIT ON THE MEN HAND AND FOOT!

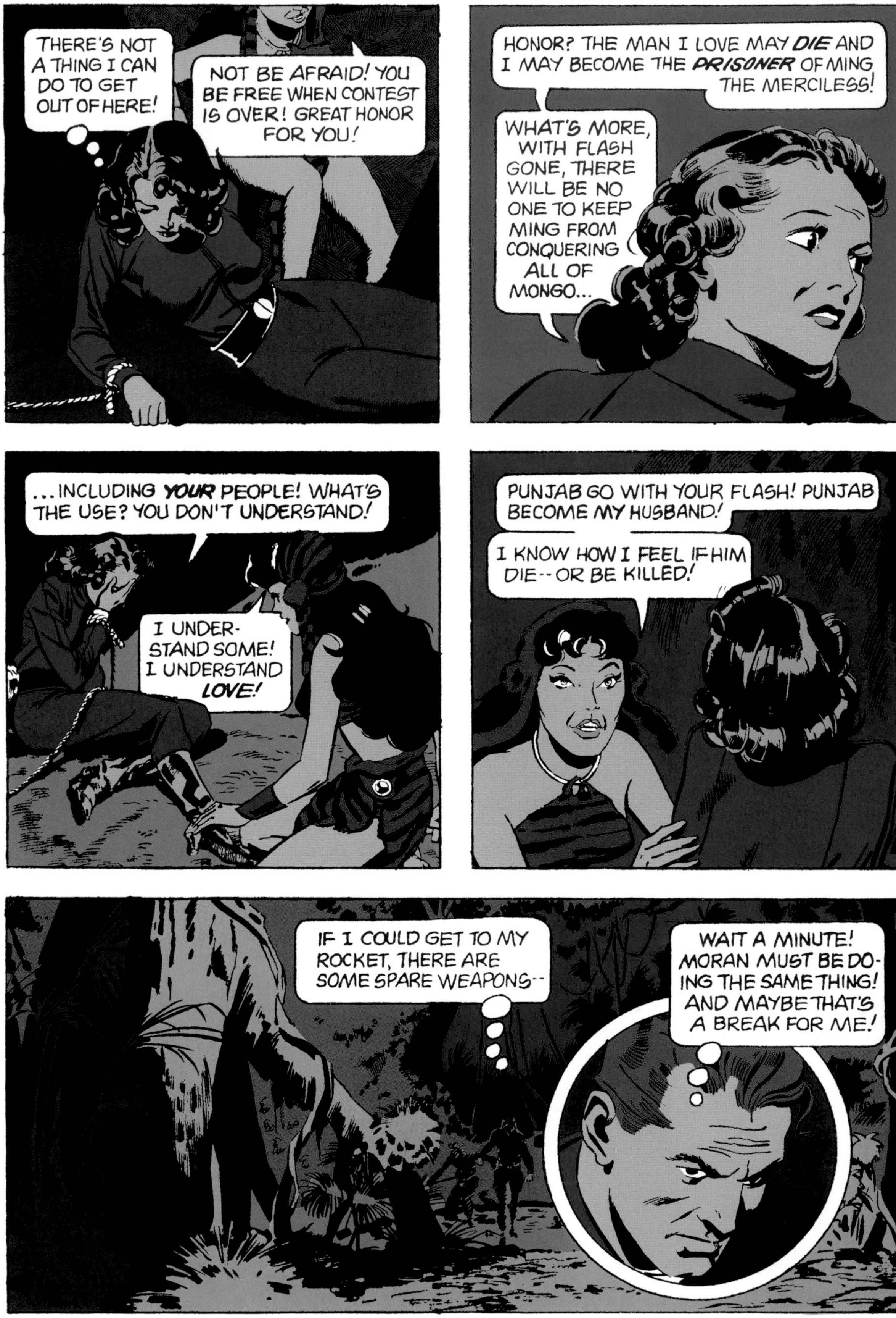
THERE'S NOT A THING I CAN DO TO GET OUT OF HERE!
NOT BE AFRAID! YOU BE FREE WHEN CONTEST IS OVER! GREAT HONOR FOR YOU!
HONOR? THE MAN I LOVE MAY **DIE** AND I MAY BECOME THE **PRISONER** OF MING THE MERCILESS!
WHAT'S MORE, WITH FLASH GONE, THERE WILL BE NO ONE TO KEEP MING FROM CONQUERING ALL OF MONGO...
...INCLUDING **YOUR** PEOPLE! WHAT'S THE USE? YOU DON'T UNDERSTAND!
I UNDERSTAND SOME! I UNDERSTAND **LOVE!**
PUNJAB GO WITH YOUR FLASH! PUNJAB BECOME **MY** HUSBAND!
I KNOW HOW I FEEL IF HIM DIE--OR BE KILLED!
IF I COULD GET TO MY ROCKET, THERE ARE SOME SPARE WEAPONS--
WAIT A MINUTE! MORAN MUST BE DOING THE SAME THING! AND MAYBE THAT'S A BREAK FOR ME!

IF I COULD FIND OUT WHERE MORAN'S SHIP IS AND TRACK HIM THERE, I COULD GAIN A VALUABLE ELEMENT OF SURPRISE!

DO YOU KNOW WHERE MORAN'S ROCKET CRASHED?

YES, BUT NOT ALLOWED TO HELP YOU!

MUST FIND YOURSELF!

RIGHT, PUNJAB-- BUT I THINK I JUST GOT AN ANGLE!

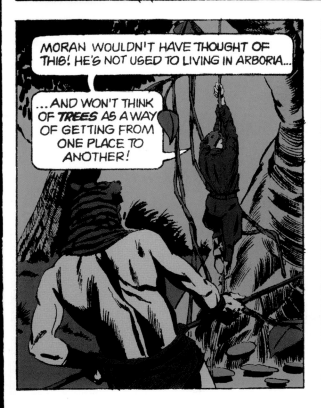

MORAN WOULDN'T HAVE THOUGHT OF THIS! HE'S NOT USED TO LIVING IN ARBORIA...

...AND WON'T THINK OF *TREES* AS A WAY OF GETTING FROM ONE PLACE TO ANOTHER!

YOU CLEVER-- FOR HUMAN! BUT WHY YOU GO SO HIGH?

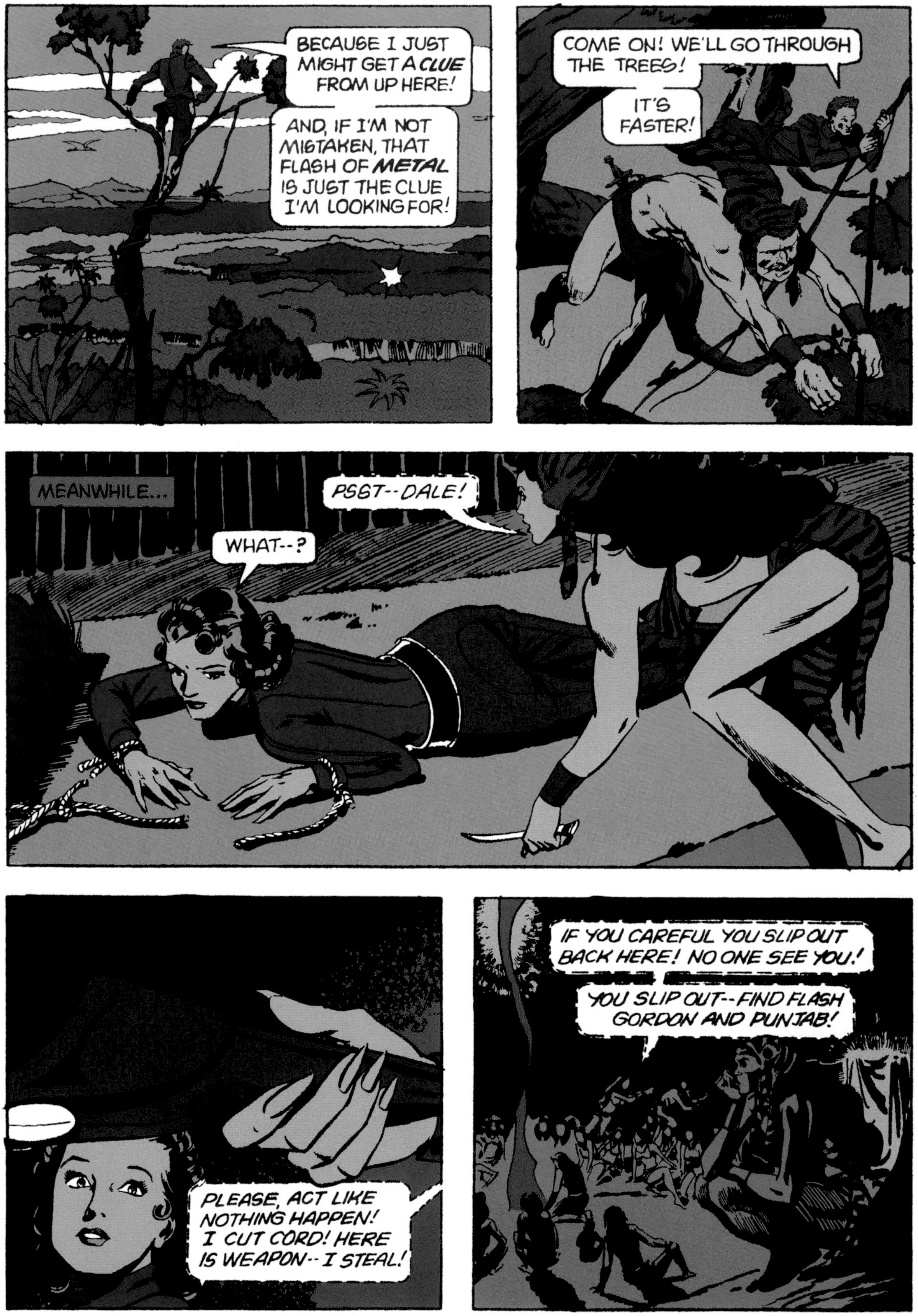
BECAUSE I JUST MIGHT GET A CLUE FROM UP HERE!
AND, IF I'M NOT MISTAKEN, THAT FLASH OF METAL IS JUST THE CLUE I'M LOOKING FOR!
COME ON! WE'LL GO THROUGH THE TREES!
IT'S FASTER!
MEANWHILE...
PSST--DALE!
WHAT--?
PLEASE, ACT LIKE NOTHING HAPPEN! I CUT CORD! HERE IS WEAPON--I STEAL!
IF YOU CAREFUL YOU SLIP OUT BACK HERE! NO ONE SEE YOU!
YOU SLIP OUT--FIND FLASH GORDON AND PUNJAB!

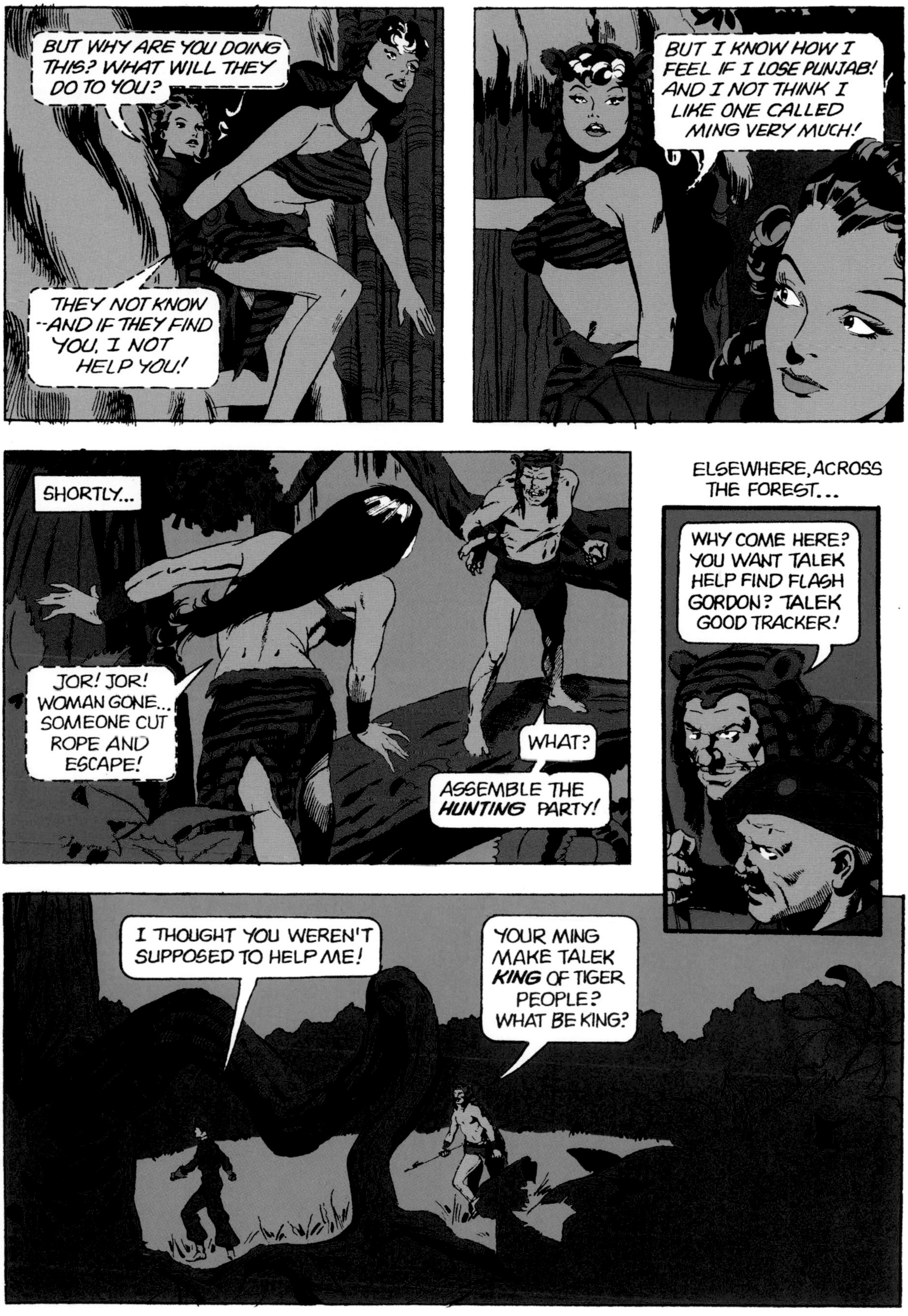
BUT WHY ARE YOU DOING THIS? WHAT WILL THEY DO TO YOU?
THEY NOT KNOW --AND IF THEY FIND YOU, I NOT HELP YOU!
BUT I KNOW HOW I FEEL IF I LOSE PUNJAB! AND I NOT THINK I LIKE ONE CALLED MING VERY MUCH!
SHORTLY...
JOR! JOR! WOMAN GONE... SOMEONE CUT ROPE AND ESCAPE!
WHAT?
ASSEMBLE THE HUNTING PARTY!
ELSEWHERE, ACROSS THE FOREST...
WHY COME HERE? YOU WANT TALEK HELP FIND FLASH GORDON? TALEK GOOD TRACKER!
I THOUGHT YOU WEREN'T SUPPOSED TO HELP ME!
YOUR MING MAKE TALEK KING OF TIGER PEOPLE? WHAT BE KING?

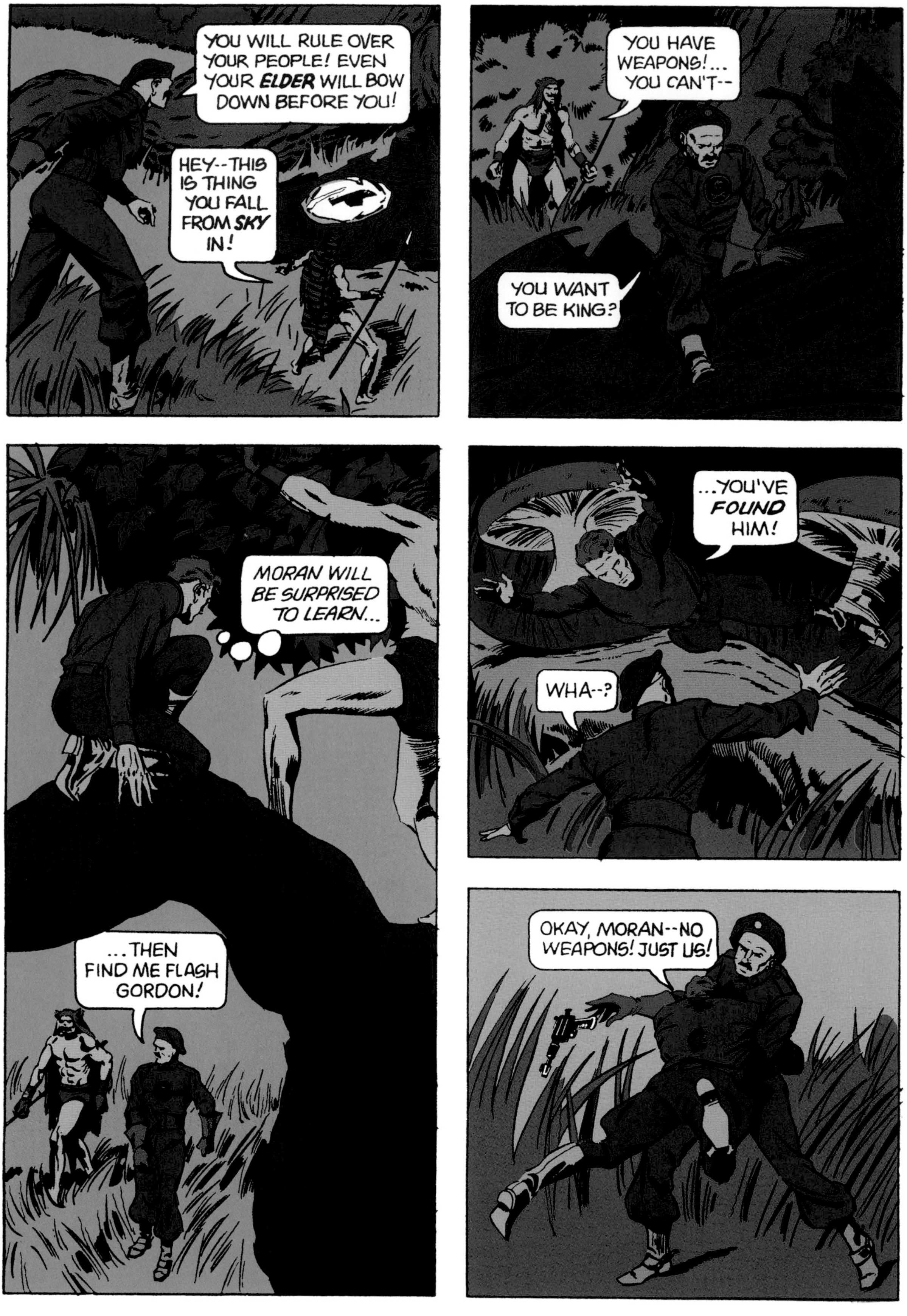
YOU WILL RULE OVER YOUR PEOPLE! EVEN YOUR ELDER WILL BOW DOWN BEFORE YOU!
HEY--THIS IS THING YOU FALL FROM SKY IN!
YOU HAVE WEAPONS!... YOU CAN'T--
YOU WANT TO BE KING?
MORAN WILL BE SURPRISED TO LEARN...
...THEN FIND ME FLASH GORDON!
...YOU'VE FOUND HIM!
WHA--?
OKAY, MORAN--NO WEAPONS! JUST US!

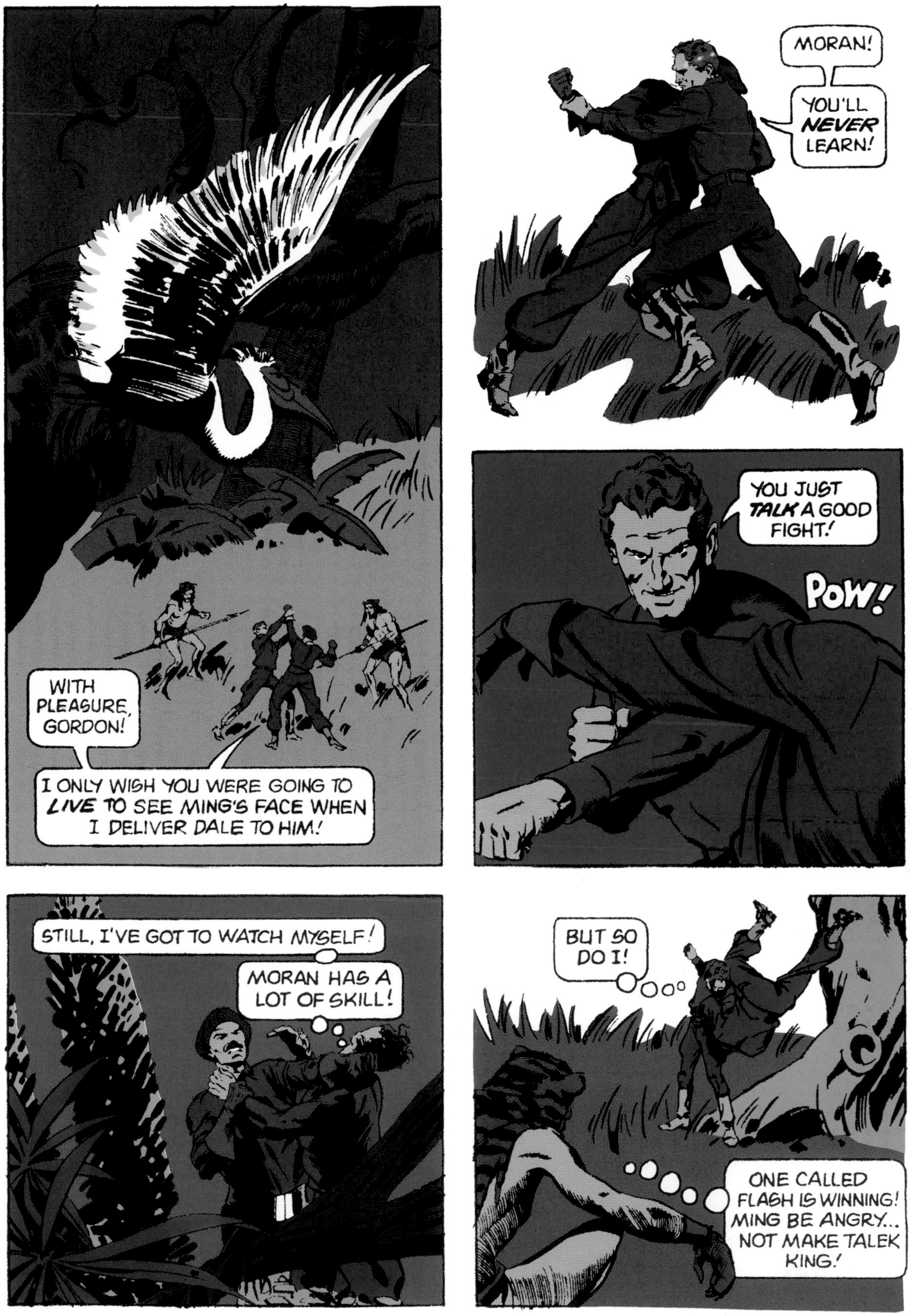
WITH PLEASURE, GORDON!
I ONLY WISH YOU WERE GOING TO LIVE TO SEE MING'S FACE WHEN I DELIVER DALE TO HIM!
MORAN!
YOU'LL NEVER LEARN!
YOU JUST TALK A GOOD FIGHT!
POW!
STILL, I'VE GOT TO WATCH MYSELF!
MORAN HAS A LOT OF SKILL!
BUT SO DO I!
ONE CALLED FLASH IS WINNING! MING BE ANGRY... NOT MAKE TALEK KING!

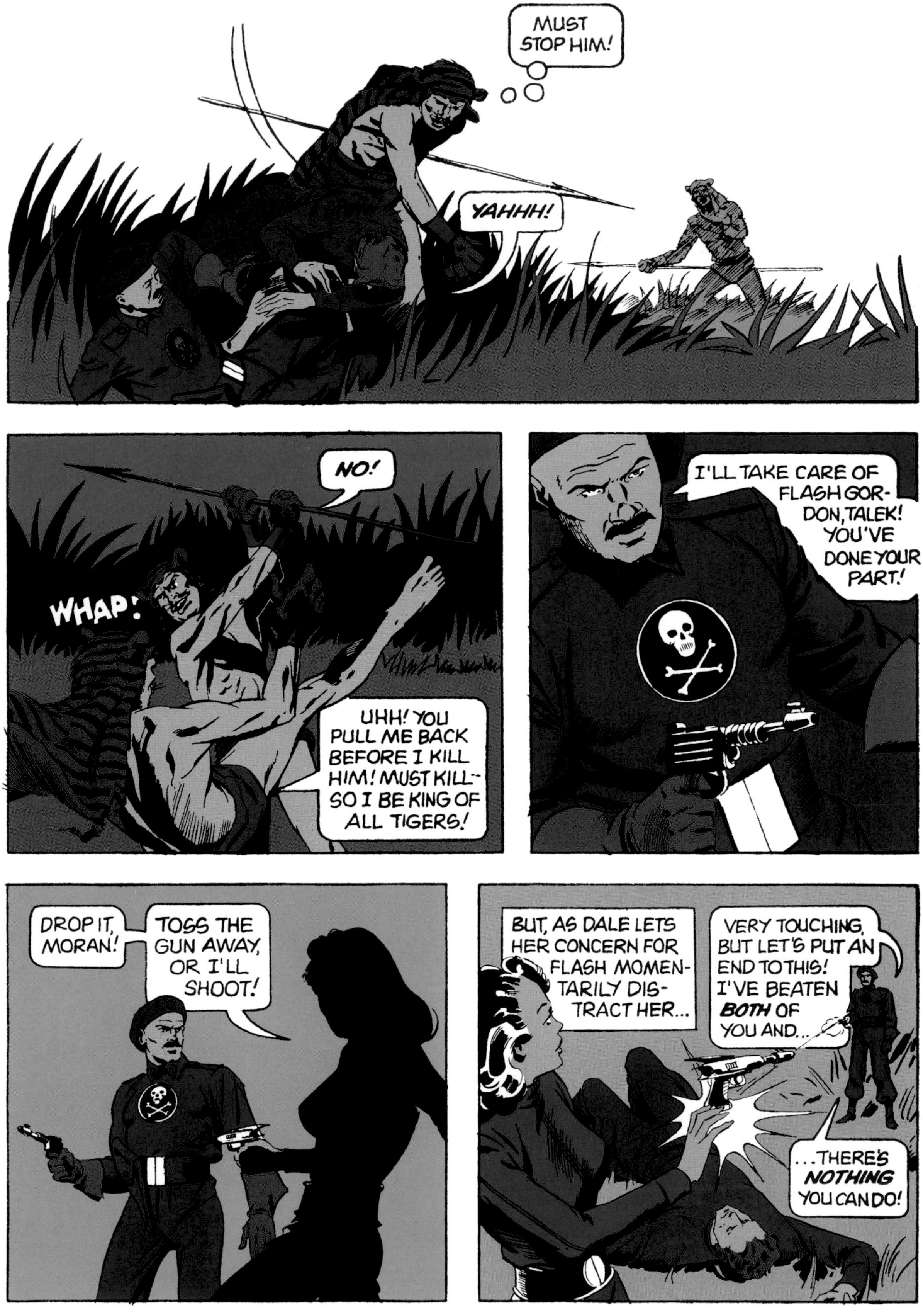
MUST STOP HIM!
YAHHH!
NO!
WHAP!
UHH! YOU PULL ME BACK BEFORE I KILL HIM! MUST KILL-- SO I BE KING OF ALL TIGERS!
I'LL TAKE CARE OF FLASH GORDON, TALEK! YOU'VE DONE YOUR PART!
DROP IT, MORAN!
TOSS THE GUN AWAY, OR I'LL SHOOT!
BUT, AS DALE LETS HER CONCERN FOR FLASH MOMENTARILY DISTRACT HER...
VERY TOUCHING, BUT LET'S PUT AN END TO THIS! I'VE BEATEN BOTH OF YOU AND...
...THERE'S NOTHING YOU CAN DO!

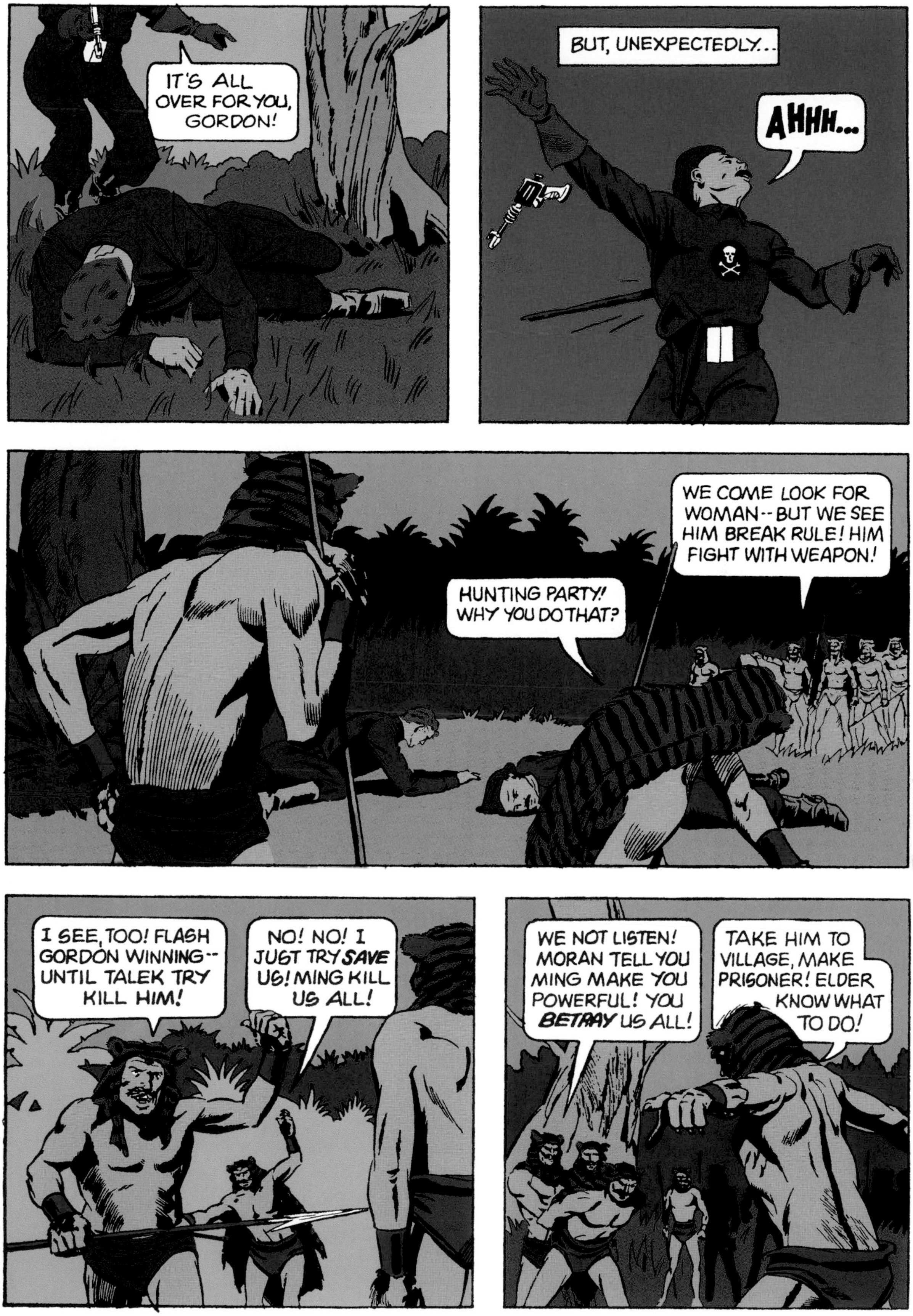
IT'S ALL OVER FOR YOU, GORDON!
BUT, UNEXPECTEDLY...
AHHH...
HUNTING PARTY! WHY YOU DO THAT?
WE COME LOOK FOR WOMAN -- BUT WE SEE HIM BREAK RULE! HIM FIGHT WITH WEAPON!
I SEE, TOO! FLASH GORDON WINNING -- UNTIL TALEK TRY KILL HIM!
NO! NO! I JUST TRY SAVE US! MING KILL US ALL!
WE NOT LISTEN! MORAN TELL YOU MING MAKE YOU POWERFUL! YOU BETRAY US ALL!
TAKE HIM TO VILLAGE, MAKE PRISONER! ELDER KNOW WHAT TO DO!

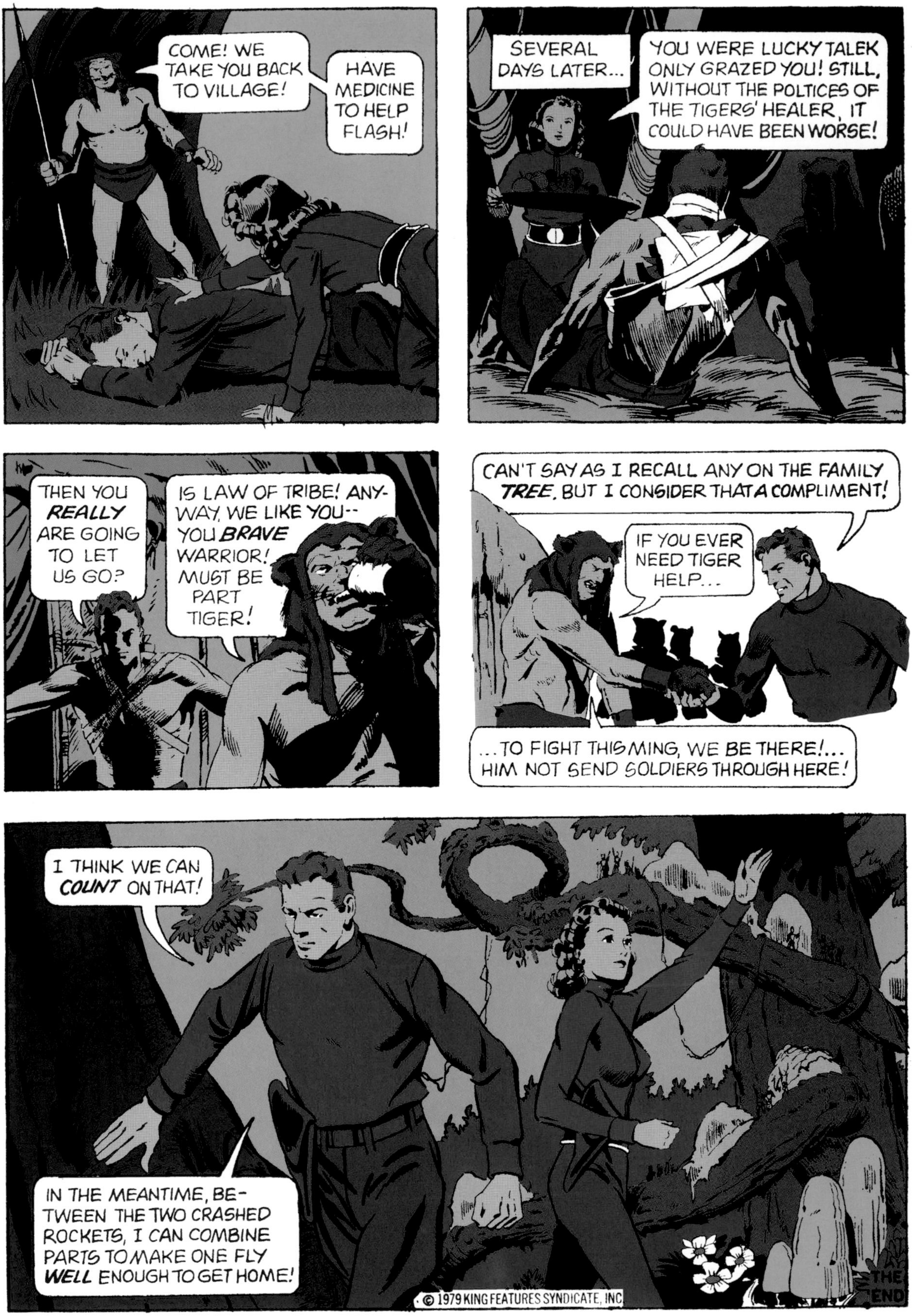
COME! WE TAKE YOU BACK TO VILLAGE!
HAVE MEDICINE TO HELP FLASH!
SEVERAL DAYS LATER...
YOU WERE LUCKY TALEK ONLY GRAZED YOU! STILL, WITHOUT THE POLTICES OF THE TIGERS' HEALER, IT COULD HAVE BEEN WORSE!
THEN YOU REALLY ARE GOING TO LET US GO?
IS LAW OF TRIBE! ANYWAY, WE LIKE YOU-- YOU BRAVE WARRIOR! MUST BE PART TIGER!
CAN'T SAY AS I RECALL ANY ON THE FAMILY TREE, BUT I CONSIDER THAT A COMPLIMENT!
IF YOU EVER NEED TIGER HELP...
...TO FIGHT THIS MING, WE BE THERE!... HIM NOT SEND SOLDIERS THROUGH HERE!
I THINK WE CAN COUNT ON THAT!
IN THE MEANTIME, BETWEEN THE TWO CRASHED ROCKETS, I CAN COMBINE PARTS TO MAKE ONE FLY WELL ENOUGH TO GET HOME!
© 1979 KING FEATURES SYNDICATE, INC
THE END

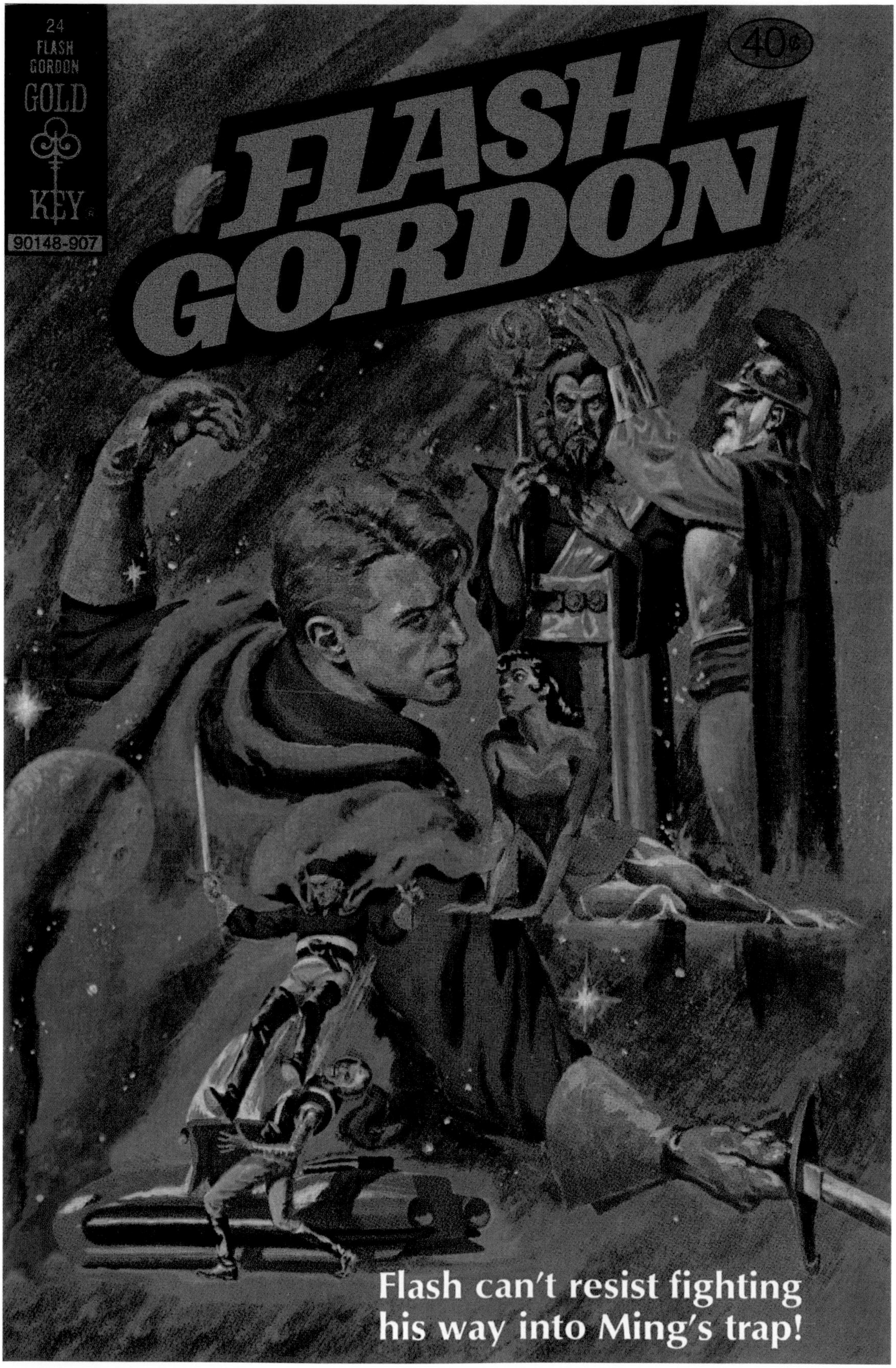
24
FLASH
GORDON
GOLD
KEY
90148-907
40¢
FLASH GORDON
Flash can't resist fighting
his way into Ming's trap!

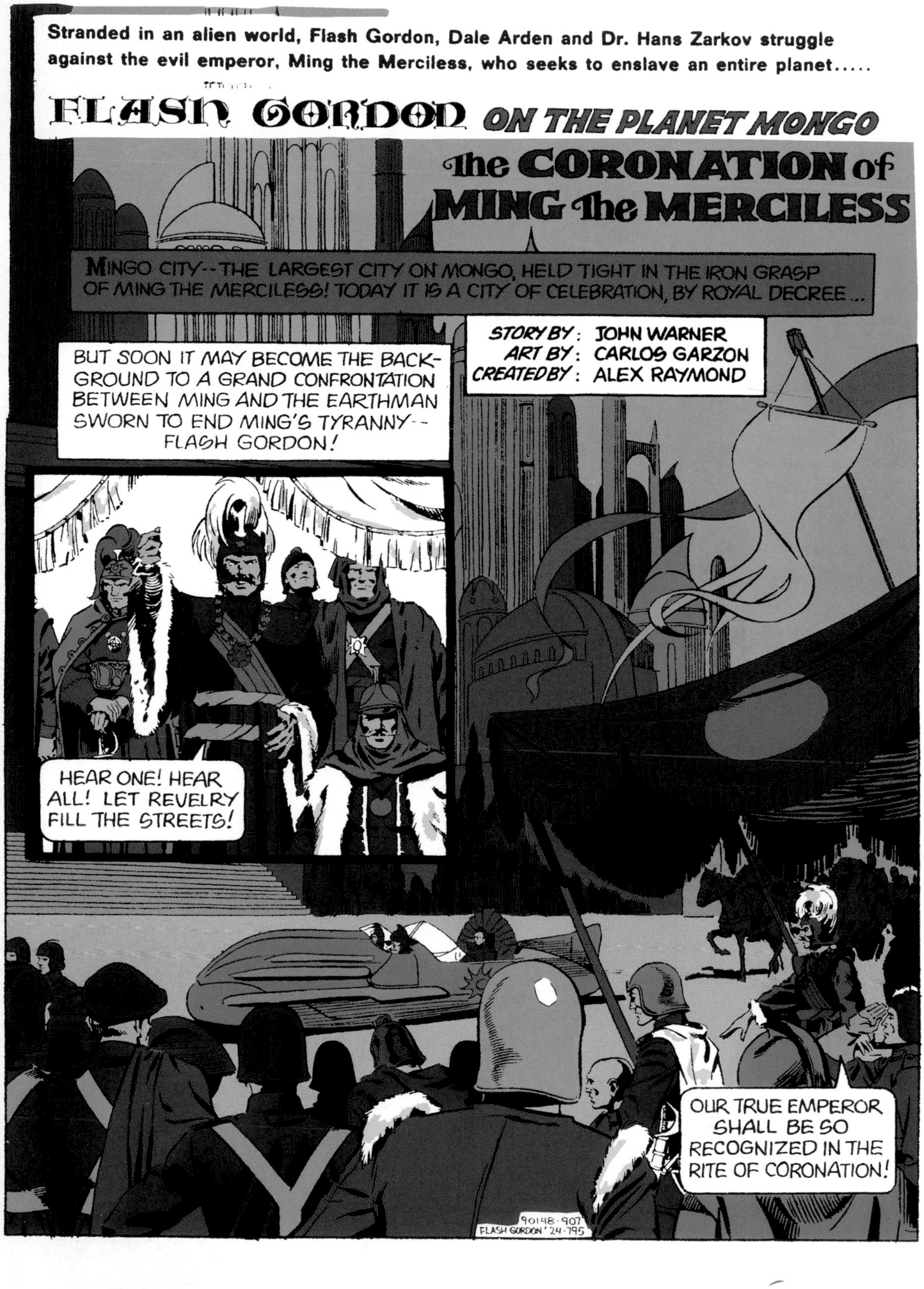
Stranded in an alien world, Flash Gordon, Dale Arden and Dr. Hans Zarkov struggle against the evil emperor, Ming the Merciless, who seeks to enslave an entire planet.....
FLASH GORDON ON THE PLANET MONGO
The CORONATION of MING the MERCILESS
MINGO CITY--THE LARGEST CITY ON MONGO, HELD TIGHT IN THE IRON GRASP OF MING THE MERCILESS! TODAY IT IS A CITY OF CELEBRATION, BY ROYAL DECREE...
STORY BY: JOHN WARNER
ART BY: CARLOS GARZON
CREATED BY: ALEX RAYMOND
BUT SOON IT MAY BECOME THE BACKGROUND TO A GRAND CONFRONTATION BETWEEN MING AND THE EARTHMAN SWORN TO END MING'S TYRANNY--FLASH GORDON!
HEAR ONE! HEAR ALL! LET REVELRY FILL THE STREETS!
OUR TRUE EMPEROR SHALL BE SO RECOGNIZED IN THE RITE OF CORONATION!
90148-907 FLASH GORDON '24-795

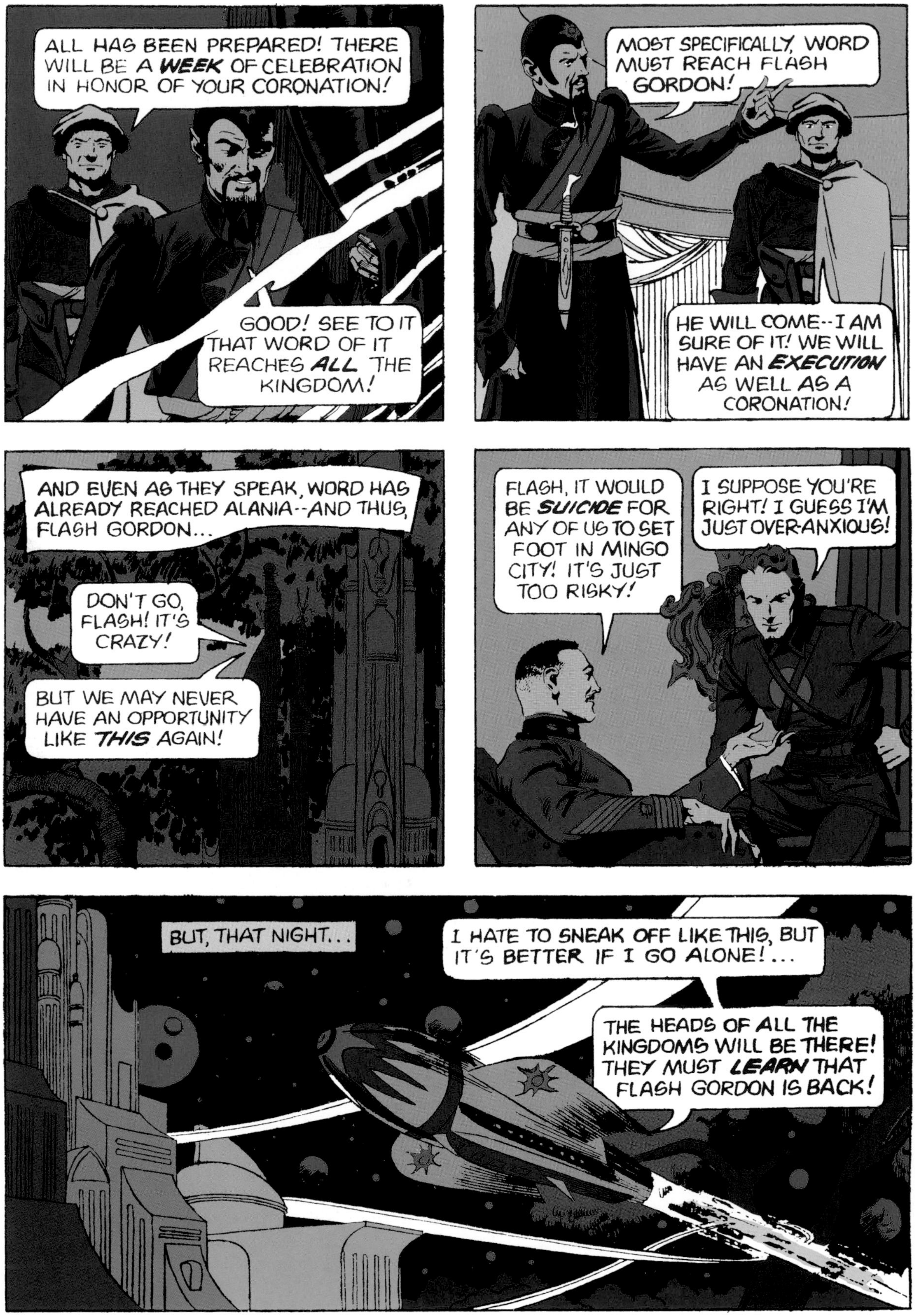
ALL HAS BEEN PREPARED! THERE WILL BE A WEEK OF CELEBRATION IN HONOR OF YOUR CORONATION!
GOOD! SEE TO IT THAT WORD OF IT REACHES ALL THE KINGDOM!
MOST SPECIFICALLY, WORD MUST REACH FLASH GORDON!
HE WILL COME--I AM SURE OF IT! WE WILL HAVE AN EXECUTION AS WELL AS A CORONATION!
AND EVEN AS THEY SPEAK, WORD HAS ALREADY REACHED ALANIA--AND THUS, FLASH GORDON...
DON'T GO, FLASH! IT'S CRAZY!
BUT WE MAY NEVER HAVE AN OPPORTUNITY LIKE THIS AGAIN!
FLASH, IT WOULD BE SUICIDE FOR ANY OF US TO SET FOOT IN MINGO CITY! IT'S JUST TOO RISKY!
I SUPPOSE YOU'RE RIGHT! I GUESS I'M JUST OVER-ANXIOUS!
BUT, THAT NIGHT...
I HATE TO SNEAK OFF LIKE THIS, BUT IT'S BETTER IF I GO ALONE!...
THE HEADS OF ALL THE KINGDOMS WILL BE THERE! THEY MUST LEARN THAT FLASH GORDON IS BACK!

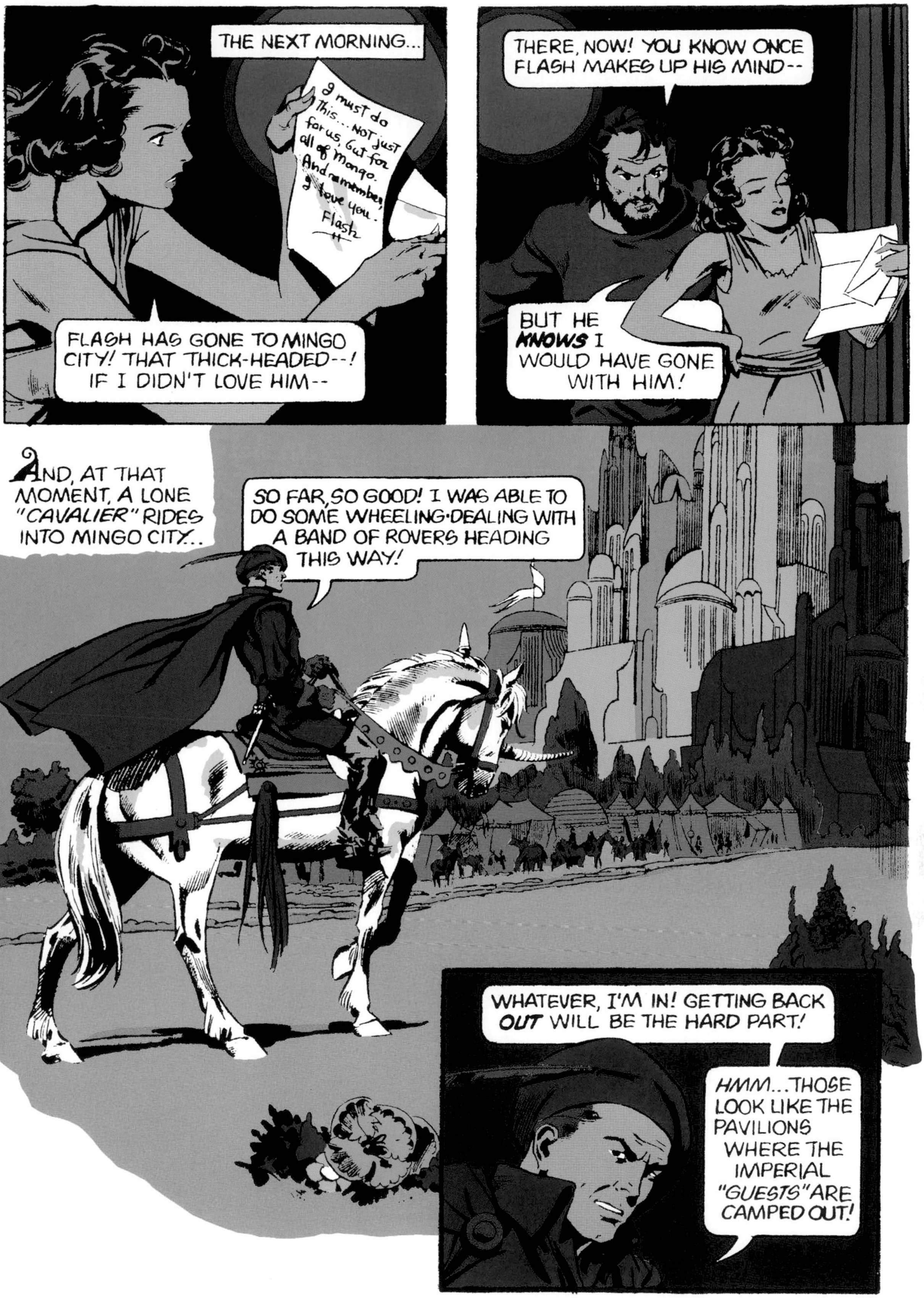
THE NEXT MORNING...
I must do This... NOT just for us but for all of Mongo. And remember, I love you. Flash
FLASH HAS GONE TO MINGO CITY! THAT THICK-HEADED--! IF I DIDN'T LOVE HIM--
THERE, NOW! YOU KNOW ONCE FLASH MAKES UP HIS MIND--
BUT HE KNOWS I WOULD HAVE GONE WITH HIM!
AND, AT THAT MOMENT, A LONE "CAVALIER" RIDES INTO MINGO CITY...
SO FAR, SO GOOD! I WAS ABLE TO DO SOME WHEELING-DEALING WITH A BAND OF ROVERS HEADING THIS WAY!
WHATEVER, I'M IN! GETTING BACK OUT WILL BE THE HARD PART!
HMM... THOSE LOOK LIKE THE PAVILIONS WHERE THE IMPERIAL "GUESTS" ARE CAMPED OUT!

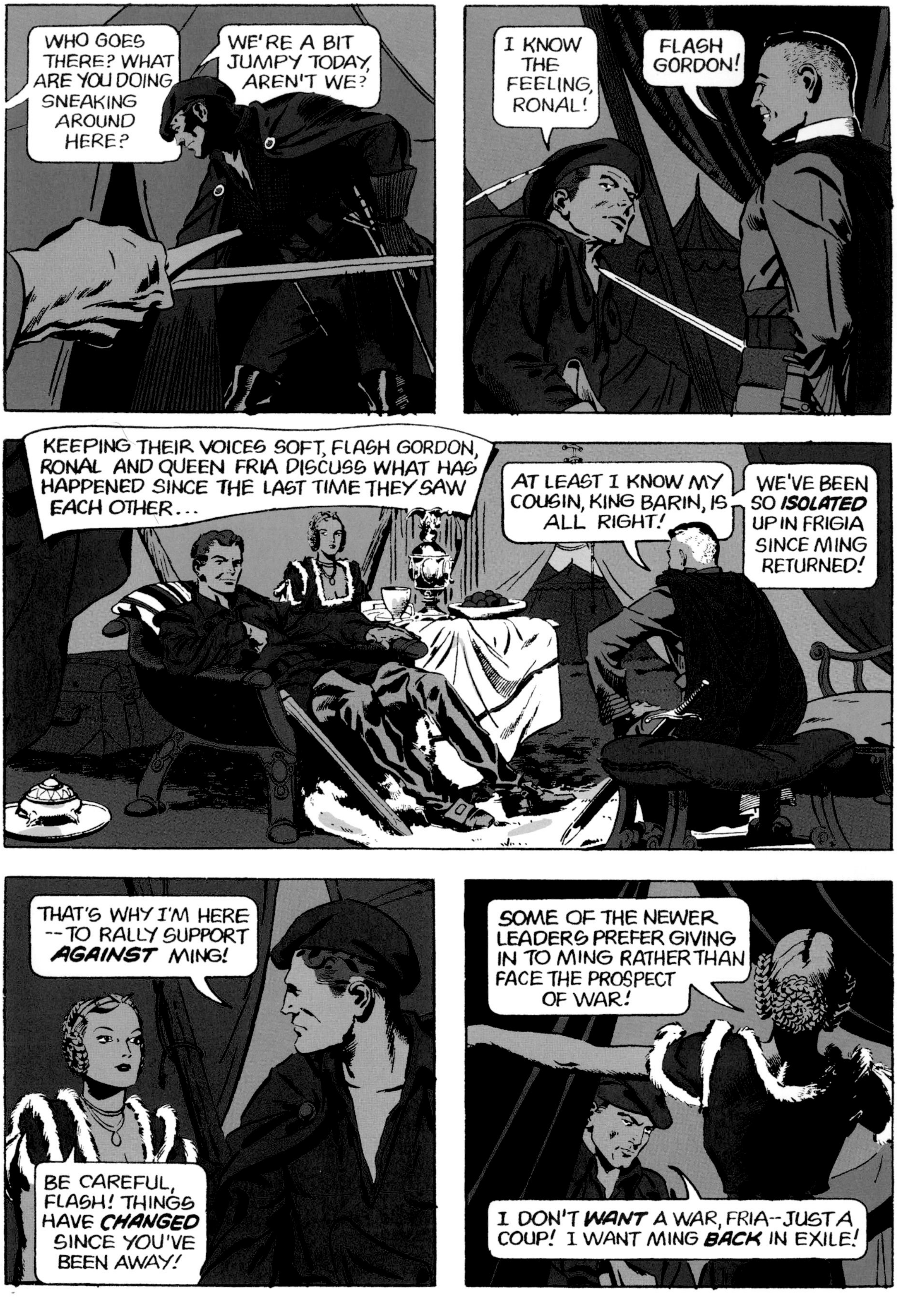
WHO GOES THERE? WHAT ARE YOU DOING SNEAKING AROUND HERE?
WE'RE A BIT JUMPY TODAY, AREN'T WE?
I KNOW THE FEELING, RONAL!
FLASH GORDON!
KEEPING THEIR VOICES SOFT, FLASH GORDON, RONAL AND QUEEN FRIA DISCUSS WHAT HAS HAPPENED SINCE THE LAST TIME THEY SAW EACH OTHER...
AT LEAST I KNOW MY COUSIN, KING BARIN, IS ALL RIGHT!
WE'VE BEEN SO ISOLATED UP IN FRIGIA SINCE MING RETURNED!
THAT'S WHY I'M HERE --TO RALLY SUPPORT AGAINST MING!
BE CAREFUL, FLASH! THINGS HAVE CHANGED SINCE YOU'VE BEEN AWAY!
SOME OF THE NEWER LEADERS PREFER GIVING IN TO MING RATHER THAN FACE THE PROSPECT OF WAR!
I DON'T WANT A WAR, FRIA--JUST A COUP! I WANT MING BACK IN EXILE!

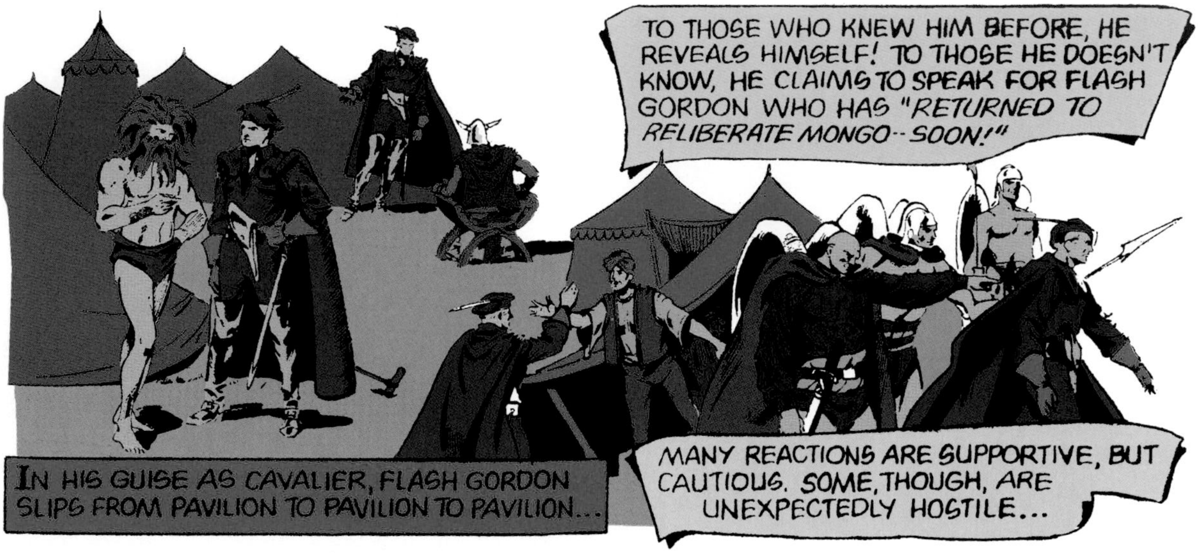
TO THOSE WHO KNEW HIM BEFORE, HE REVEALS HIMSELF! TO THOSE HE DOESN'T KNOW, HE CLAIMS TO SPEAK FOR FLASH GORDON WHO HAS "RETURNED TO RELIBERATE MONGO--SOON!"
IN HIS GUISE AS CAVALIER, FLASH GORDON SLIPS FROM PAVILION TO PAVILION TO PAVILION...
MANY REACTIONS ARE SUPPORTIVE, BUT CAUTIOUS. SOME, THOUGH, ARE UNEXPECTEDLY HOSTILE...

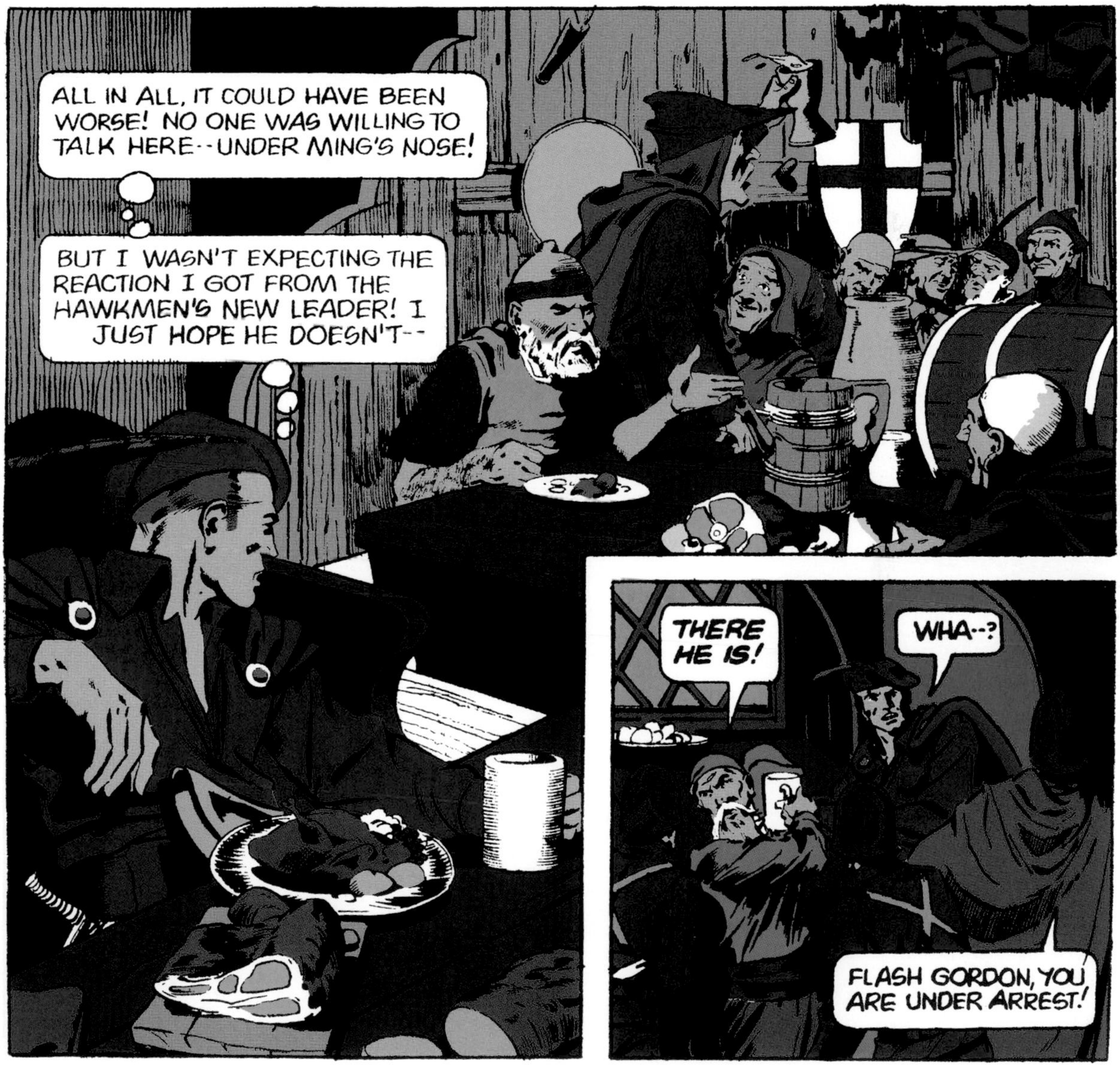
ALL IN ALL, IT COULD HAVE BEEN WORSE! NO ONE WAS WILLING TO TALK HERE--UNDER MING'S NOSE!
BUT I WASN'T EXPECTING THE REACTION I GOT FROM THE HAWKMEN'S NEW LEADER! I JUST HOPE HE DOESN'T--
THERE HE IS!
WHA--?
FLASH GORDON, YOU ARE UNDER ARREST!

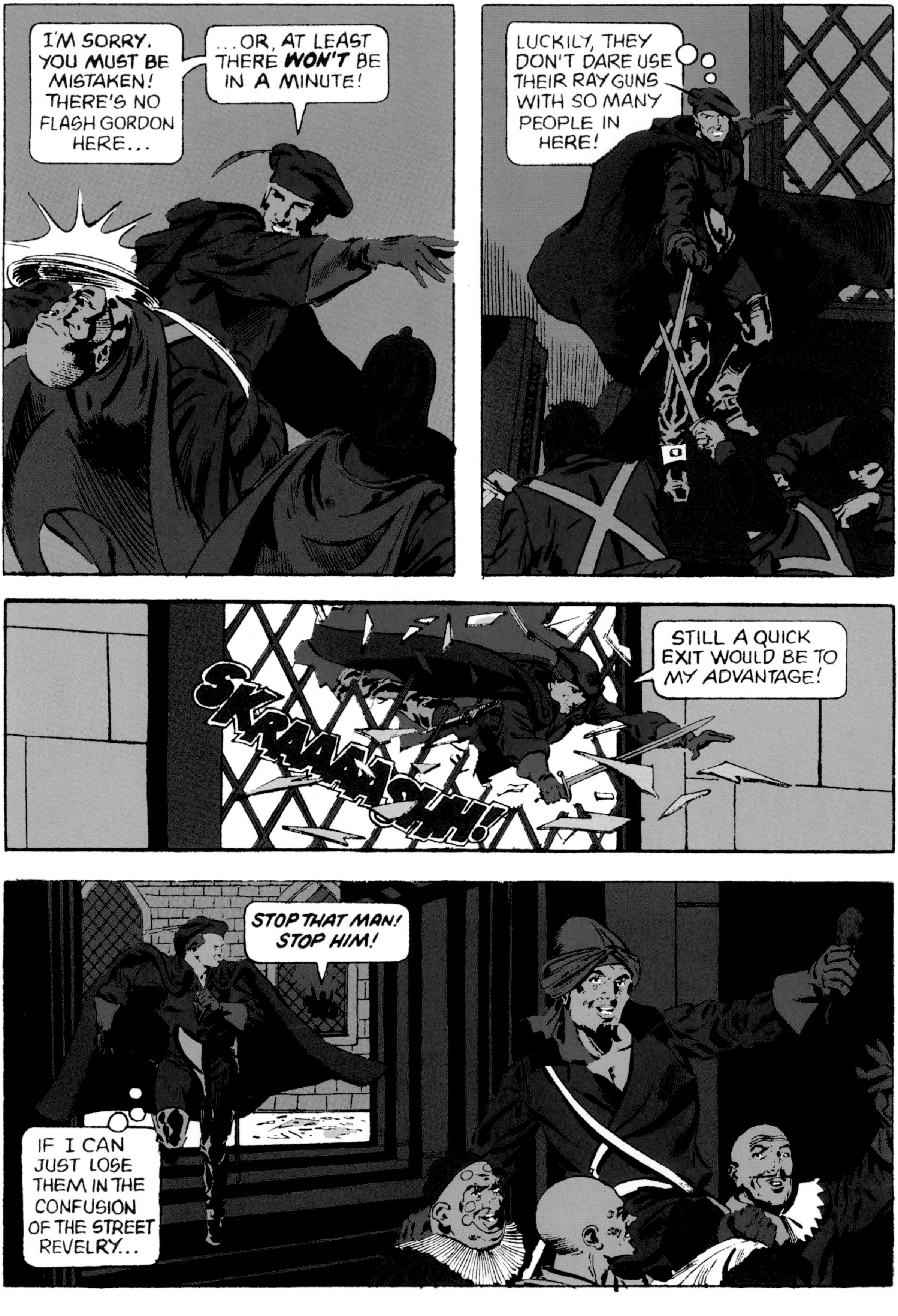
I'M SORRY. YOU MUST BE MISTAKEN! THERE'S NO FLASH GORDON HERE...
...OR, AT LEAST THERE WON'T BE IN A MINUTE!
LUCKILY, THEY DON'T DARE USE THEIR RAY GUNS WITH SO MANY PEOPLE IN HERE!
SKRAAAASHH!
STILL A QUICK EXIT WOULD BE TO MY ADVANTAGE!
STOP THAT MAN! STOP HIM!
IF I CAN JUST LOSE THEM IN THE CONFUSION OF THE STREET REVELRY...

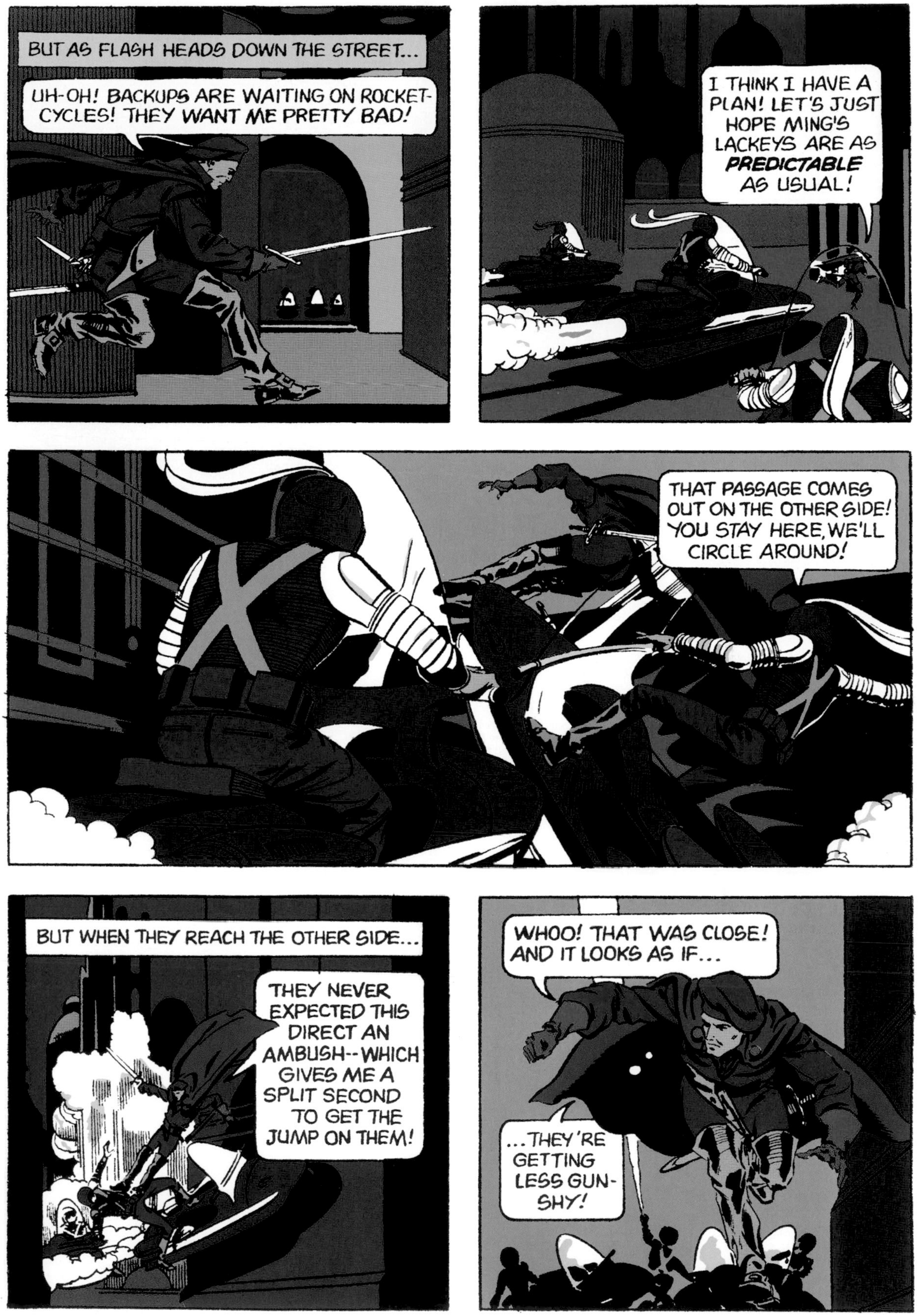
BUT AS FLASH HEADS DOWN THE STREET...
UH-OH! BACKUPS ARE WAITING ON ROCKET-CYCLES! THEY WANT ME PRETTY BAD!
I THINK I HAVE A PLAN! LET'S JUST HOPE MING'S LACKEYS ARE AS PREDICTABLE AS USUAL!
THAT PASSAGE COMES OUT ON THE OTHER SIDE! YOU STAY HERE, WE'LL CIRCLE AROUND!
BUT WHEN THEY REACH THE OTHER SIDE...
THEY NEVER EXPECTED THIS DIRECT AN AMBUSH--WHICH GIVES ME A SPLIT SECOND TO GET THE JUMP ON THEM!
WHOO! THAT WAS CLOSE! AND IT LOOKS AS IF...
...THEY'RE GETTING LESS GUN-SHY!

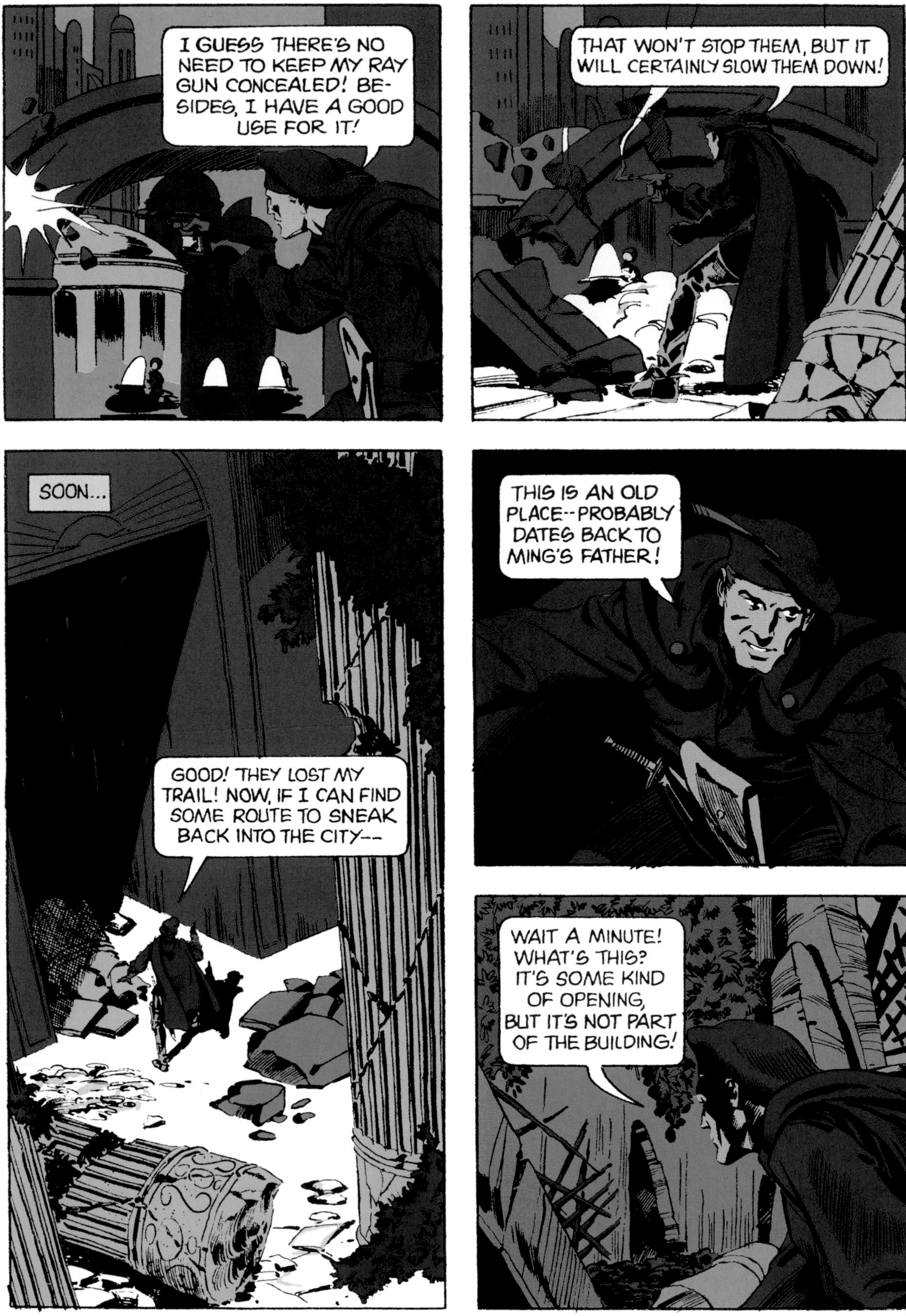
I GUESS THERE'S NO NEED TO KEEP MY RAY GUN CONCEALED! BESIDES, I HAVE A GOOD USE FOR IT!
THAT WON'T STOP THEM, BUT IT WILL CERTAINLY SLOW THEM DOWN!
SOON...
GOOD! THEY LOST MY TRAIL! NOW, IF I CAN FIND SOME ROUTE TO SNEAK BACK INTO THE CITY--
THIS IS AN OLD PLACE--PROBABLY DATES BACK TO MING'S FATHER!
WAIT A MINUTE! WHAT'S THIS? IT'S SOME KIND OF OPENING, BUT IT'S NOT PART OF THE BUILDING!

FLASH USES HIS RAY GUN TO MAKE A TORCH...

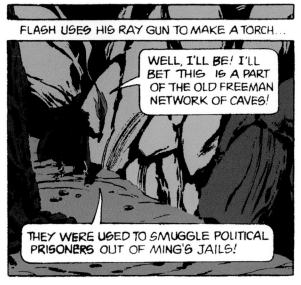

WELL, I'LL BE! I'LL BET THIS IS A PART OF THE OLD FREEMAN NETWORK OF CAVES!

THEY WERE USED TO SMUGGLE POLITICAL PRISONERS OUT OF MING'S JAILS!

SNEK!

EH? DID I HEAR SOMETHING?

THAT YOU MOST CERTAINLY DID!

I HAVE NO EMPEROR! I AM A FREE MAN!

I SHOULD LIKE TO KNOW *WHO* IS TRESPASSING--AND WHETHER HE SERVES OUR EMPEROR, MING!

COME DOWN, IF YOU THINK YOU CAN TAKE ME, AND I'LL SHOW YOU HOW A FREE MAN FIGHTS!

HO! HO! WITH PLEASURE!

CLANNG!

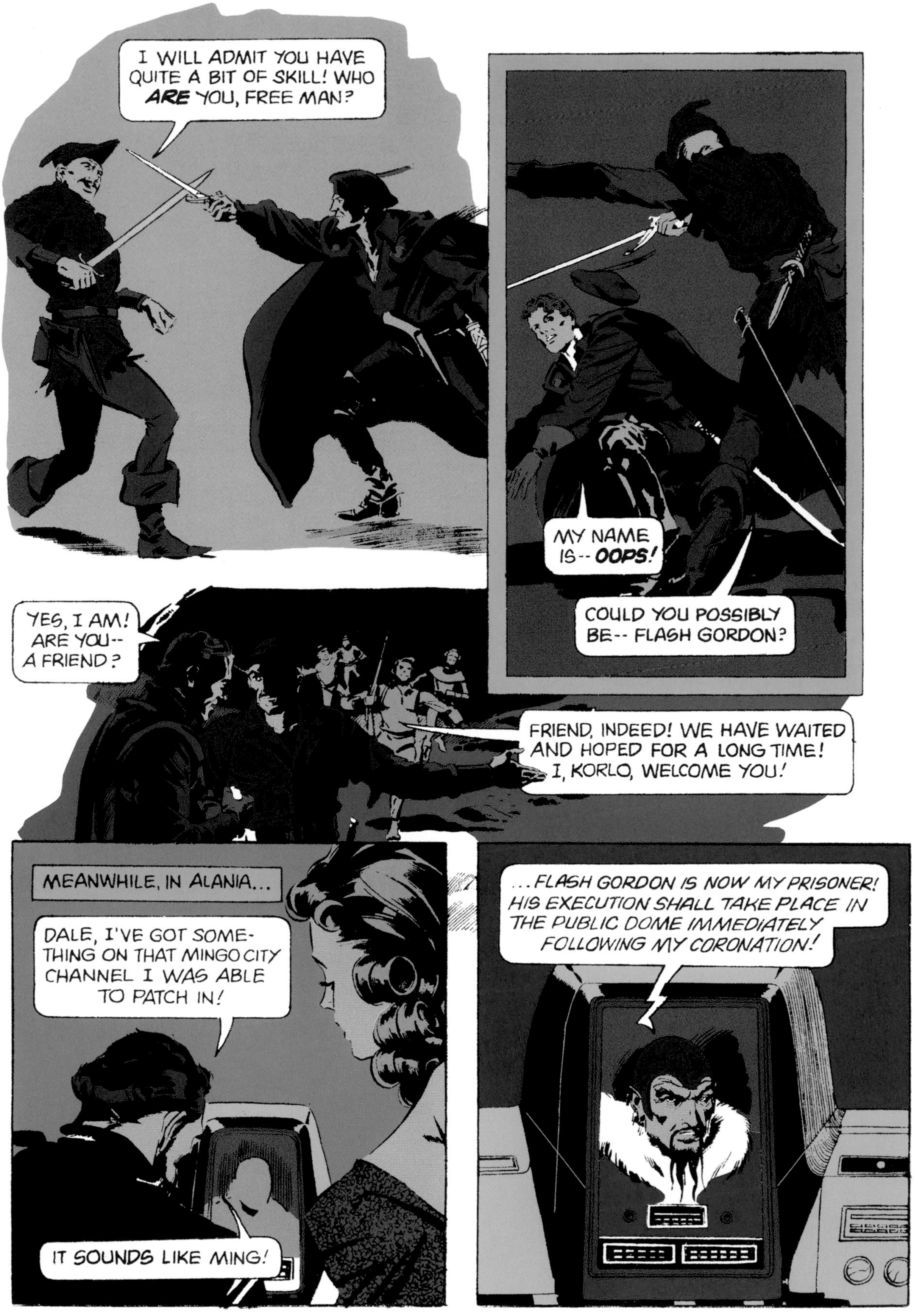
I WILL ADMIT YOU HAVE QUITE A BIT OF SKILL! WHO ARE YOU, FREE MAN?
MY NAME IS-- OOPS!
COULD YOU POSSIBLY BE-- FLASH GORDON?
YES, I AM! ARE YOU-- A FRIEND?
FRIEND, INDEED! WE HAVE WAITED AND HOPED FOR A LONG TIME! I, KORLO, WELCOME YOU!
MEANWHILE, IN ALANIA...
DALE, I'VE GOT SOMETHING ON THAT MINGO CITY CHANNEL I WAS ABLE TO PATCH IN!
IT SOUNDS LIKE MING!
...FLASH GORDON IS NOW MY PRISONER! HIS EXECUTION SHALL TAKE PLACE IN THE PUBLIC DOME IMMEDIATELY FOLLOWING MY CORONATION!

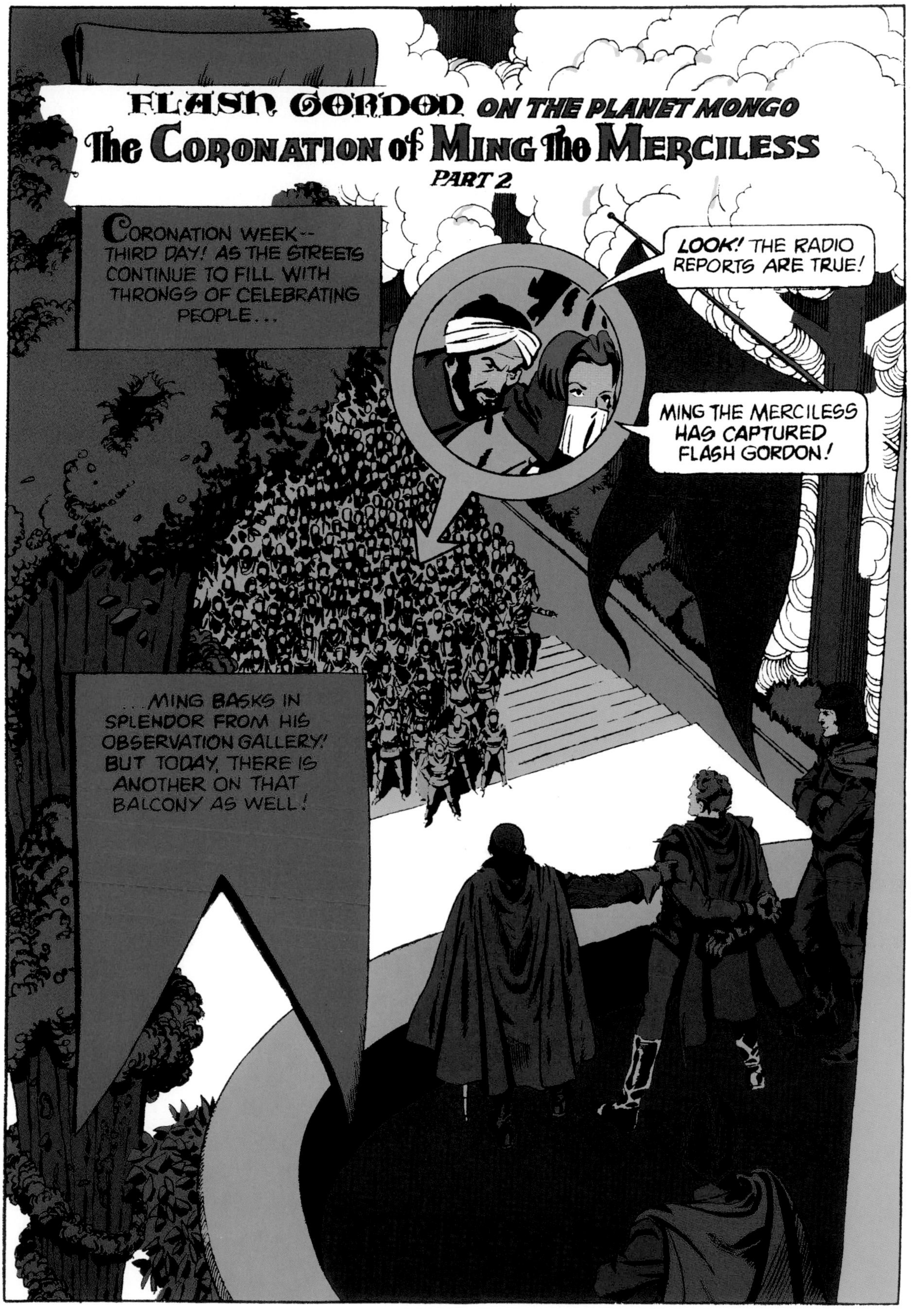
FLASH GORDON ON THE PLANET MONGO
The Coronation of Ming the Merciless
PART 2
CORONATION WEEK-- THIRD DAY! AS THE STREETS CONTINUE TO FILL WITH THRONGS OF CELEBRATING PEOPLE...
LOOK! THE RADIO REPORTS ARE TRUE!
MING THE MERCILESS HAS CAPTURED FLASH GORDON!
...MING BASKS IN SPLENDOR FROM HIS OBSERVATION GALLERY! BUT TODAY, THERE IS ANOTHER ON THAT BALCONY AS WELL!

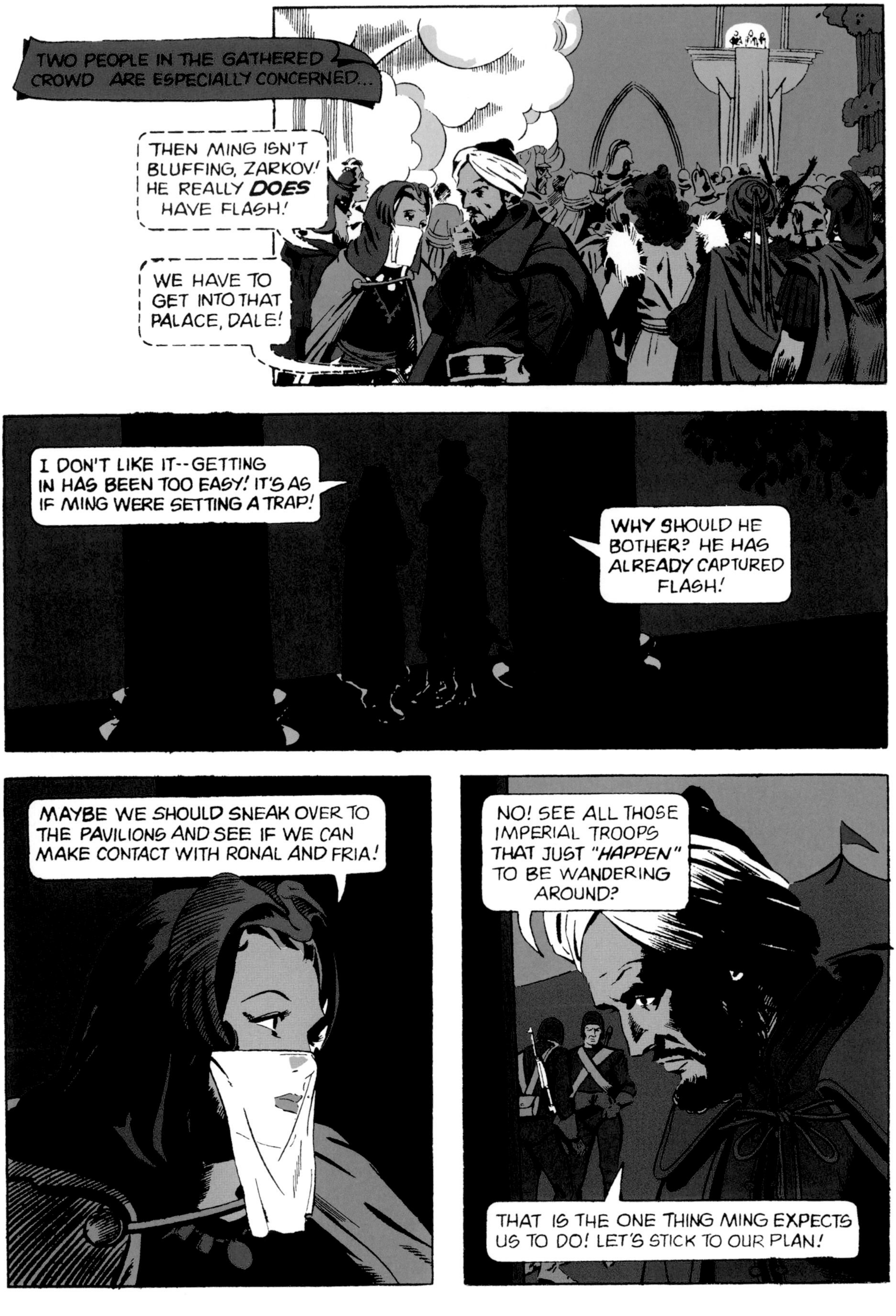
TWO PEOPLE IN THE GATHERED CROWD ARE ESPECIALLY CONCERNED...
THEN MING ISN'T BLUFFING, ZARKOV! HE REALLY DOES HAVE FLASH!
WE HAVE TO GET INTO THAT PALACE, DALE!
I DON'T LIKE IT--GETTING IN HAS BEEN TOO EASY! IT'S AS IF MING WERE SETTING A TRAP!
WHY SHOULD HE BOTHER? HE HAS ALREADY CAPTURED FLASH!
MAYBE WE SHOULD SNEAK OVER TO THE PAVILIONS AND SEE IF WE CAN MAKE CONTACT WITH RONAL AND FRIA!
NO! SEE ALL THOSE IMPERIAL TROOPS THAT JUST "HAPPEN" TO BE WANDERING AROUND?
THAT IS THE ONE THING MING EXPECTS US TO DO! LET'S STICK TO OUR PLAN!

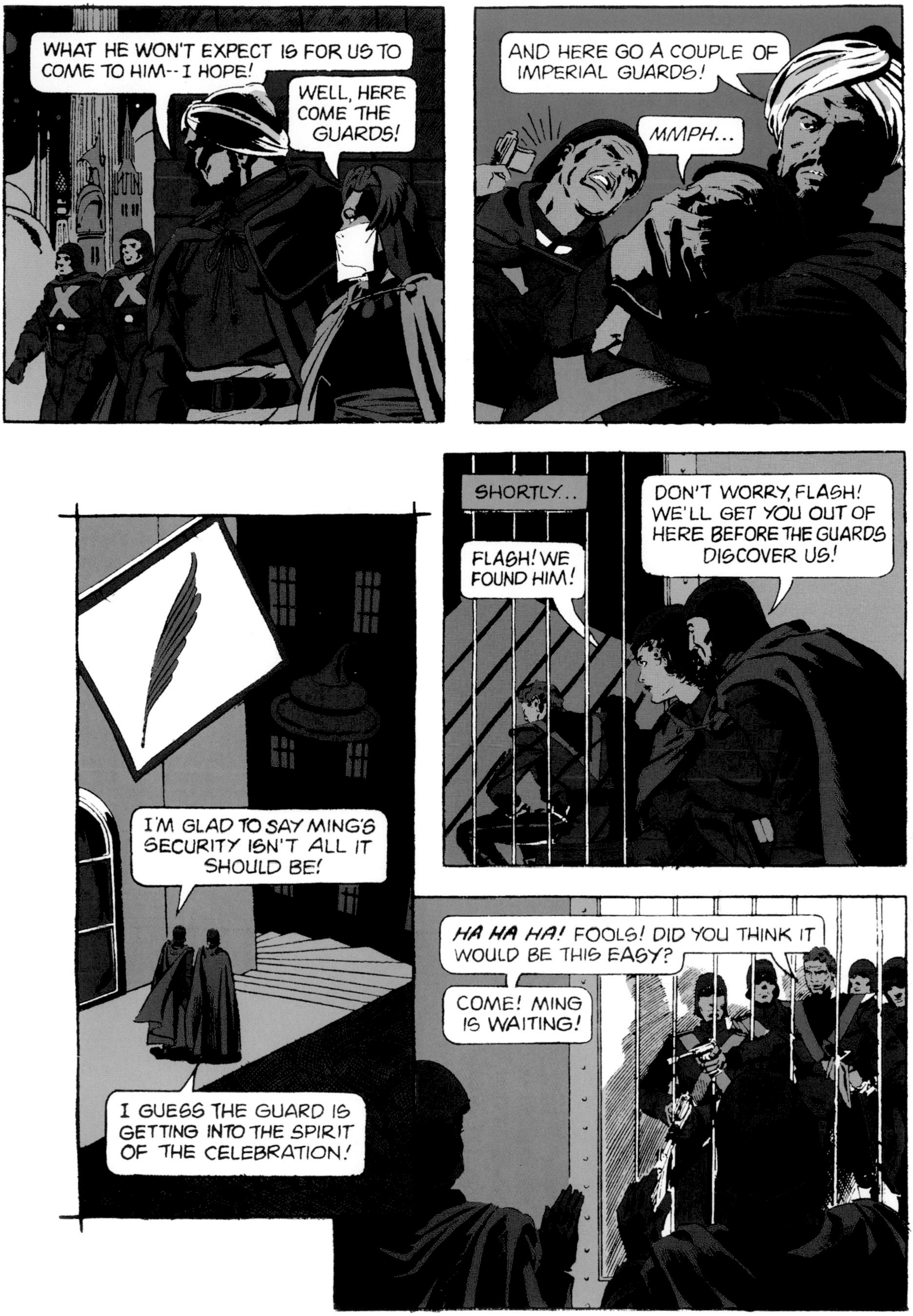
WHAT HE WON'T EXPECT IS FOR US TO COME TO HIM-- I HOPE!
WELL, HERE COME THE GUARDS!
AND HERE GO A COUPLE OF IMPERIAL GUARDS!
MMPH...
I'M GLAD TO SAY MING'S SECURITY ISN'T ALL IT SHOULD BE!
I GUESS THE GUARD IS GETTING INTO THE SPIRIT OF THE CELEBRATION!
SHORTLY...
FLASH! WE FOUND HIM!
DON'T WORRY, FLASH! WE'LL GET YOU OUT OF HERE BEFORE THE GUARDS DISCOVER US!
HA HA HA! FOOLS! DID YOU THINK IT WOULD BE THIS EASY?
COME! MING IS WAITING!

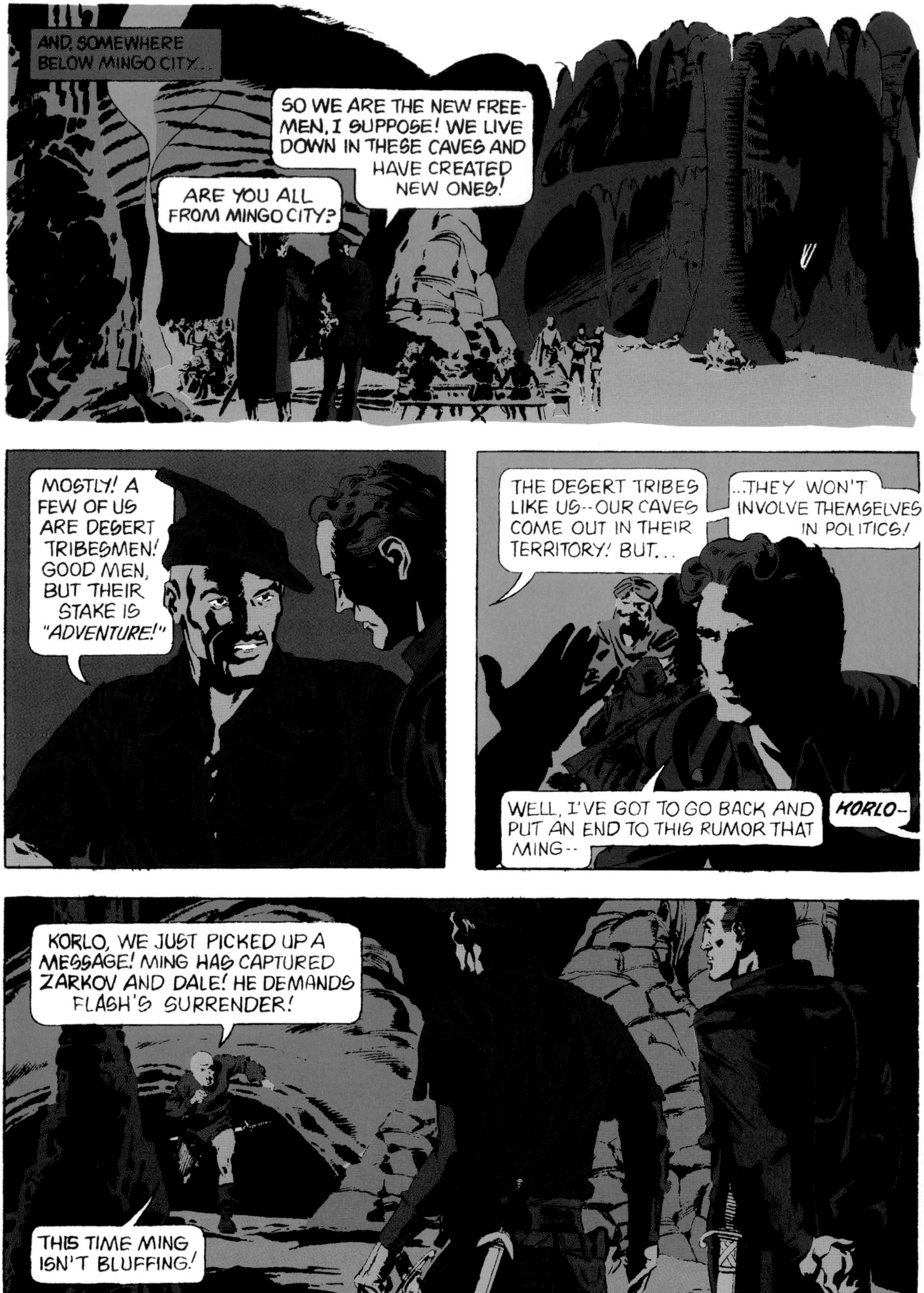
AND, SOMEWHERE BELOW MINGO CITY...
ARE YOU ALL FROM MINGO CITY?
SO WE ARE THE NEW FREE-MEN, I SUPPOSE! WE LIVE DOWN IN THESE CAVES AND HAVE CREATED NEW ONES!
MOSTLY! A FEW OF US ARE DESERT TRIBESMEN! GOOD MEN, BUT THEIR STAKE IS "ADVENTURE!"
THE DESERT TRIBES LIKE US--OUR CAVES COME OUT IN THEIR TERRITORY! BUT...
...THEY WON'T INVOLVE THEMSELVES IN POLITICS!
WELL, I'VE GOT TO GO BACK AND PUT AN END TO THIS RUMOR THAT MING--
KORLO--
KORLO, WE JUST PICKED UP A MESSAGE! MING HAS CAPTURED ZARKOV AND DALE! HE DEMANDS FLASH'S SURRENDER!
THIS TIME MING ISN'T BLUFFING!

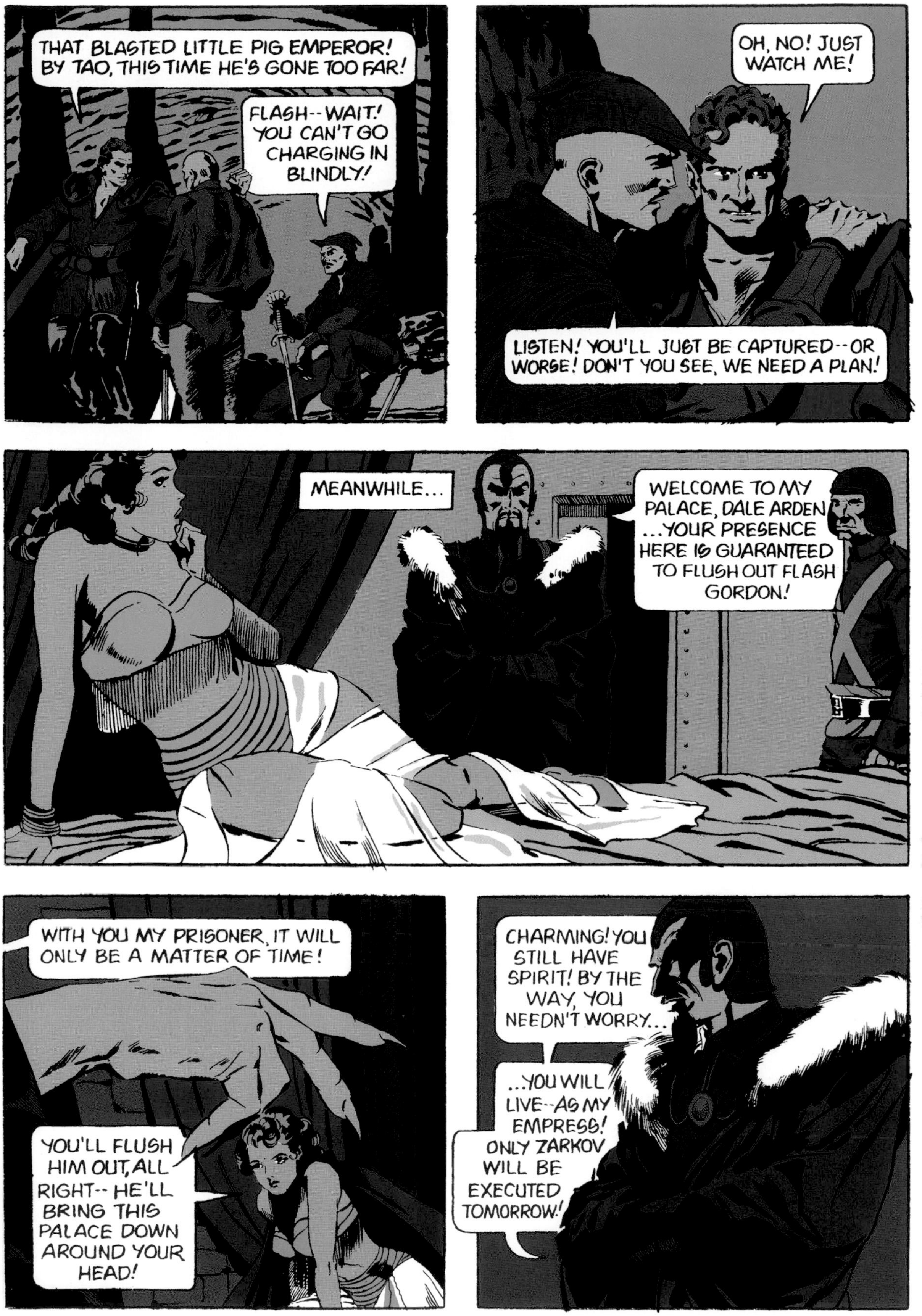
THAT BLASTED LITTLE PIG EMPEROR! BY TAO, THIS TIME HE'S GONE TOO FAR!
FLASH--WAIT! YOU CAN'T GO CHARGING IN BLINDLY!
OH, NO! JUST WATCH ME!
LISTEN! YOU'LL JUST BE CAPTURED--OR WORSE! DON'T YOU SEE, WE NEED A PLAN!
MEANWHILE...
WELCOME TO MY PALACE, DALE ARDEN ...YOUR PRESENCE HERE IS GUARANTEED TO FLUSH OUT FLASH GORDON!
WITH YOU MY PRISONER, IT WILL ONLY BE A MATTER OF TIME!
YOU'LL FLUSH HIM OUT, ALL RIGHT-- HE'LL BRING THIS PALACE DOWN AROUND YOUR HEAD!
CHARMING! YOU STILL HAVE SPIRIT! BY THE WAY, YOU NEEDN'T WORRY...
...YOU WILL LIVE--AS MY EMPRESS! ONLY ZARKOV WILL BE EXECUTED TOMORROW!

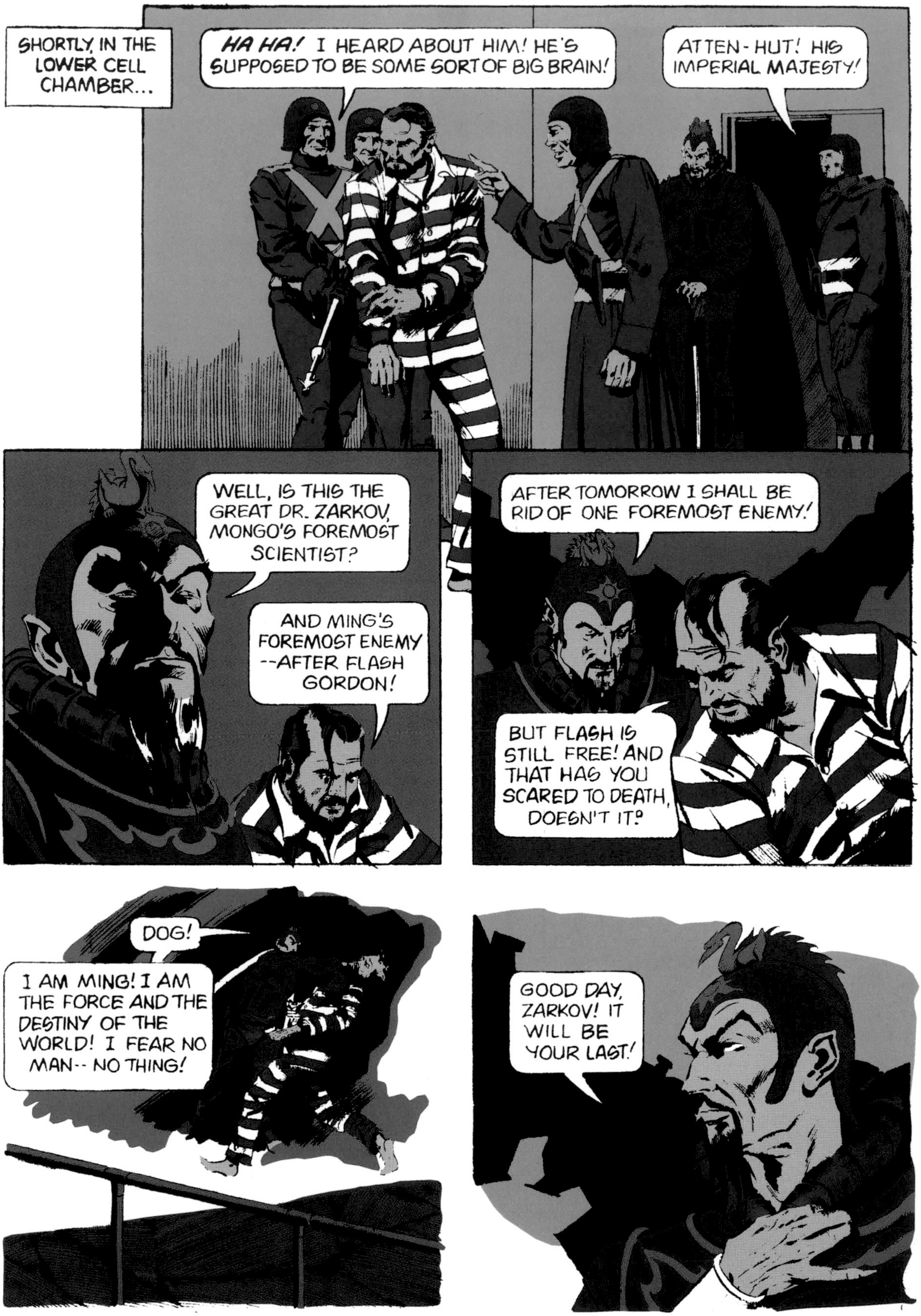
SHORTLY, IN THE LOWER CELL CHAMBER...
HA HA! I HEARD ABOUT HIM! HE'S SUPPOSED TO BE SOME SORT OF BIG BRAIN!
ATTEN-HUT! HIS IMPERIAL MAJESTY!
WELL, IS THIS THE GREAT DR. ZARKOV, MONGO'S FOREMOST SCIENTIST?
AND MING'S FOREMOST ENEMY --AFTER FLASH GORDON!
AFTER TOMORROW I SHALL BE RID OF ONE FOREMOST ENEMY!
BUT FLASH IS STILL FREE! AND THAT HAS YOU SCARED TO DEATH, DOESN'T IT?
DOG!
I AM MING! I AM THE FORCE AND THE DESTINY OF THE WORLD! I FEAR NO MAN-- NO THING!
GOOD DAY, ZARKOV! IT WILL BE YOUR LAST!

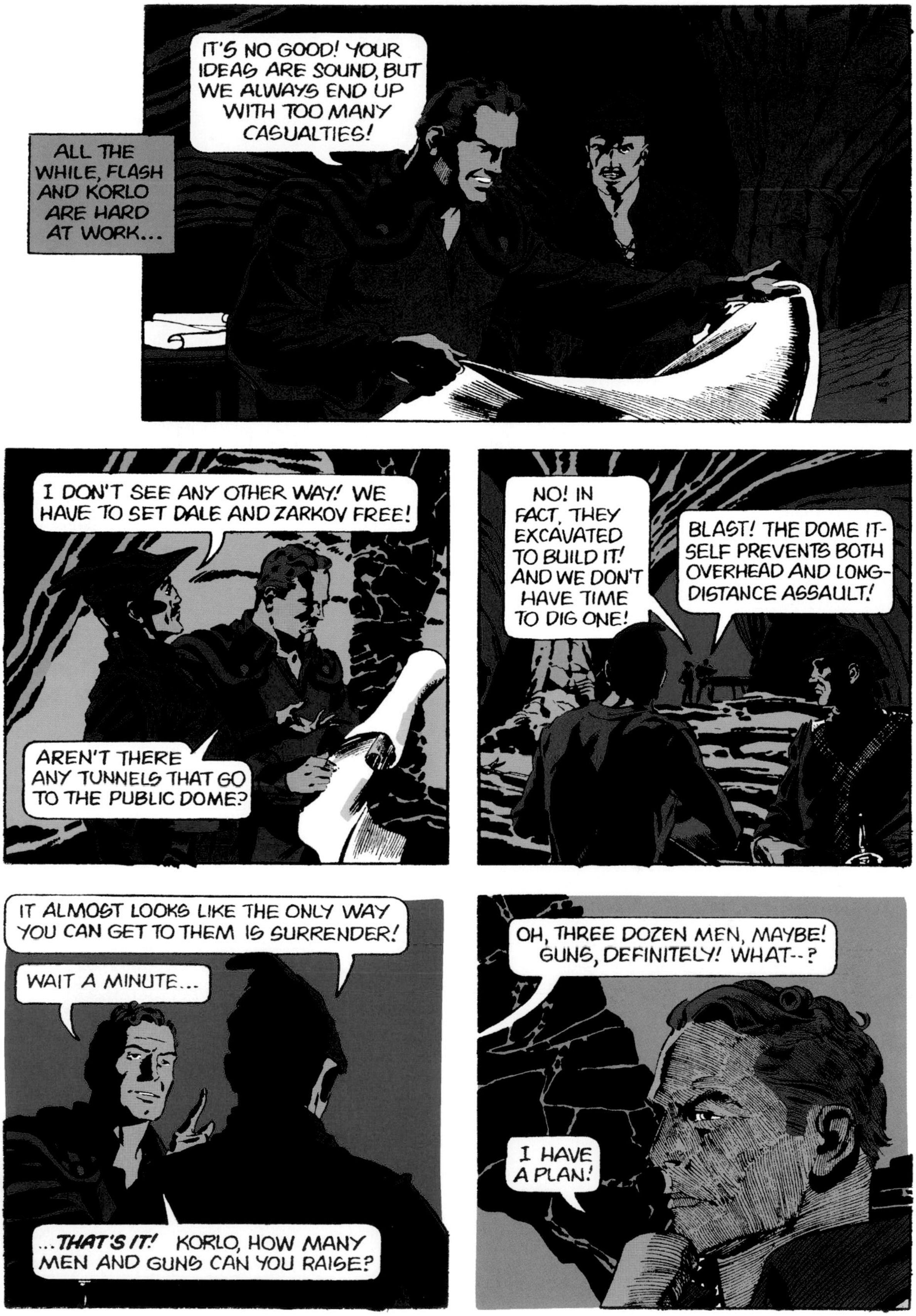
ALL THE WHILE, FLASH AND KORLO ARE HARD AT WORK...
IT'S NO GOOD! YOUR IDEAS ARE SOUND, BUT WE ALWAYS END UP WITH TOO MANY CASUALTIES!
I DON'T SEE ANY OTHER WAY! WE HAVE TO SET DALE AND ZARKOV FREE!
AREN'T THERE ANY TUNNELS THAT GO TO THE PUBLIC DOME?
NO! IN FACT, THEY EXCAVATED TO BUILD IT! AND WE DON'T HAVE TIME TO DIG ONE!
BLAST! THE DOME IT-SELF PREVENTS BOTH OVERHEAD AND LONG-DISTANCE ASSAULT!
IT ALMOST LOOKS LIKE THE ONLY WAY YOU CAN GET TO THEM IS SURRENDER!
WAIT A MINUTE...
...THAT'S IT! KORLO, HOW MANY MEN AND GUNS CAN YOU RAISE?
OH, THREE DOZEN MEN, MAYBE! GUNS, DEFINITELY! WHAT--?
I HAVE A PLAN!

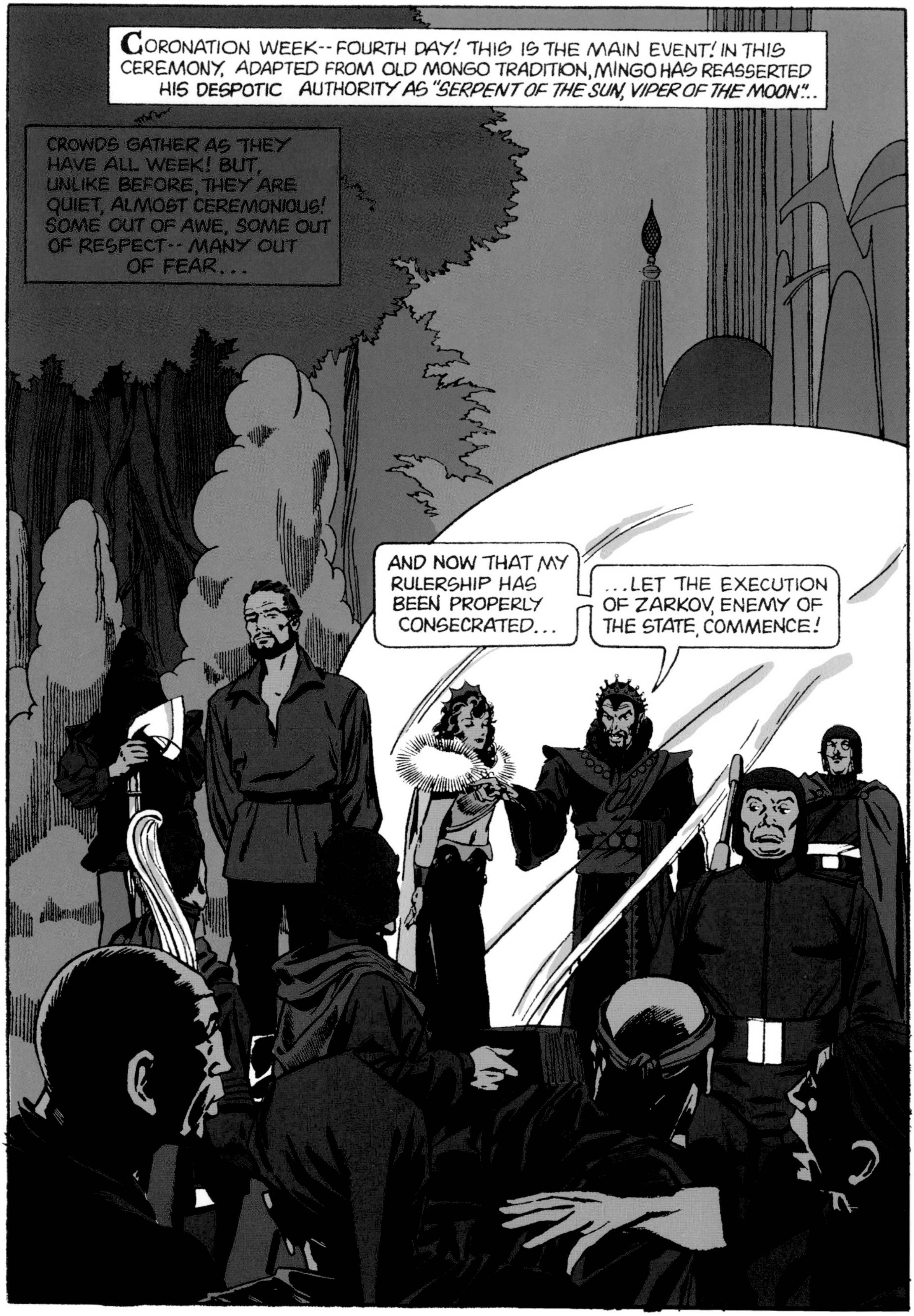
CORONATION WEEK--FOURTH DAY! THIS IS THE MAIN EVENT! IN THIS CEREMONY, ADAPTED FROM OLD MONGO TRADITION, MINGO HAS REASSERTED HIS DESPOTIC AUTHORITY AS "SERPENT OF THE SUN, VIPER OF THE MOON"..
CROWDS GATHER AS THEY HAVE ALL WEEK! BUT, UNLIKE BEFORE, THEY ARE QUIET, ALMOST CEREMONIOUS! SOME OUT OF AWE, SOME OUT OF RESPECT-- MANY OUT OF FEAR...
AND NOW THAT MY RULERSHIP HAS BEEN PROPERLY CONSECRATED...
...LET THE EXECUTION OF ZARKOV, ENEMY OF THE STATE, COMMENCE!

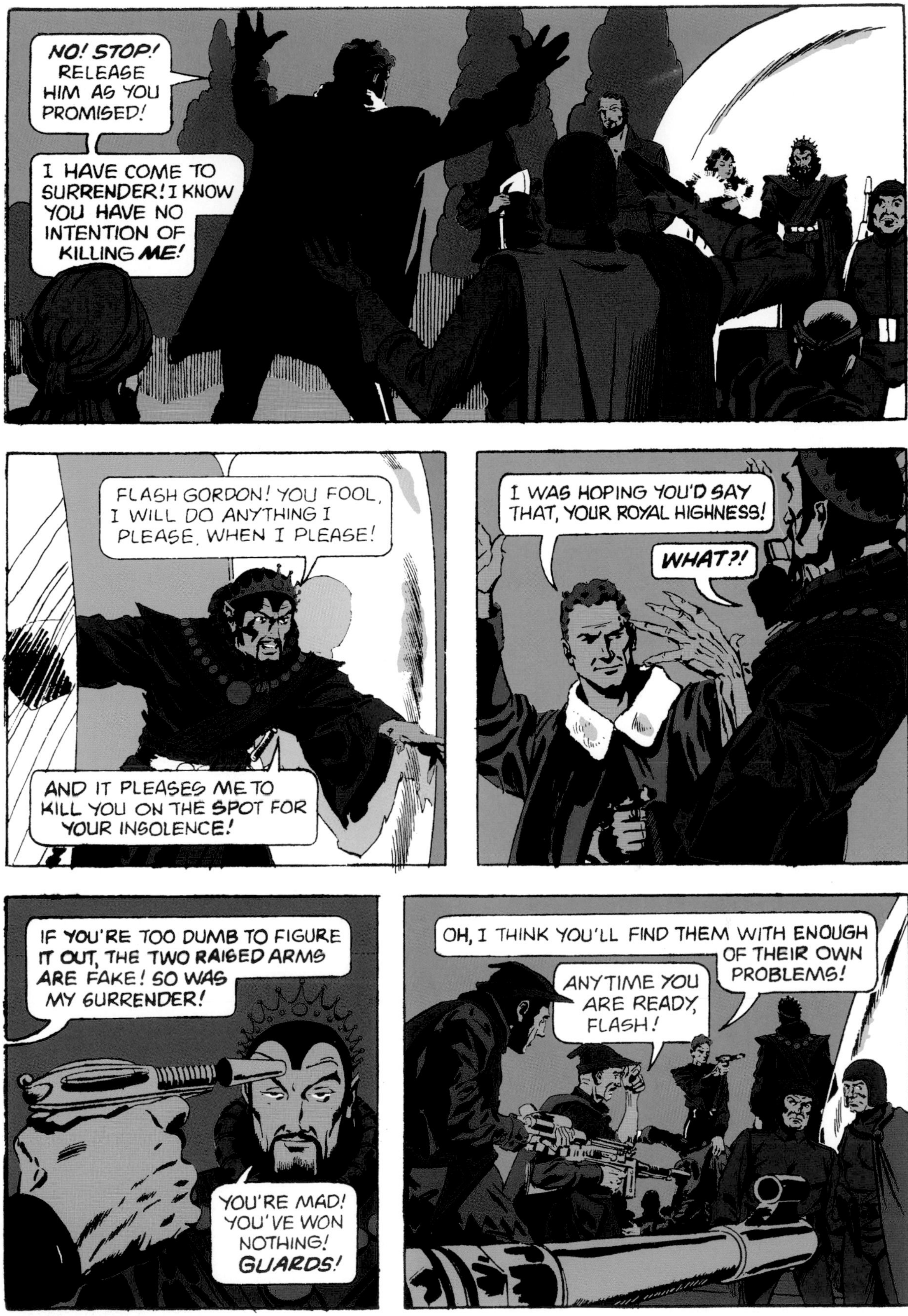
NO! STOP! RELEASE HIM AS YOU PROMISED!
I HAVE COME TO SURRENDER! I KNOW YOU HAVE NO INTENTION OF KILLING ME!
FLASH GORDON! YOU FOOL, I WILL DO ANYTHING I PLEASE, WHEN I PLEASE!
AND IT PLEASES ME TO KILL YOU ON THE SPOT FOR YOUR INSOLENCE!
I WAS HOPING YOU'D SAY THAT, YOUR ROYAL HIGHNESS!
WHAT?!
IF YOU'RE TOO DUMB TO FIGURE IT OUT, THE TWO RAISED ARMS ARE FAKE! SO WAS MY SURRENDER!
YOU'RE MAD! YOU'VE WON NOTHING! GUARDS!
OH, I THINK YOU'LL FIND THEM WITH ENOUGH OF THEIR OWN PROBLEMS!
ANYTIME YOU ARE READY, FLASH!

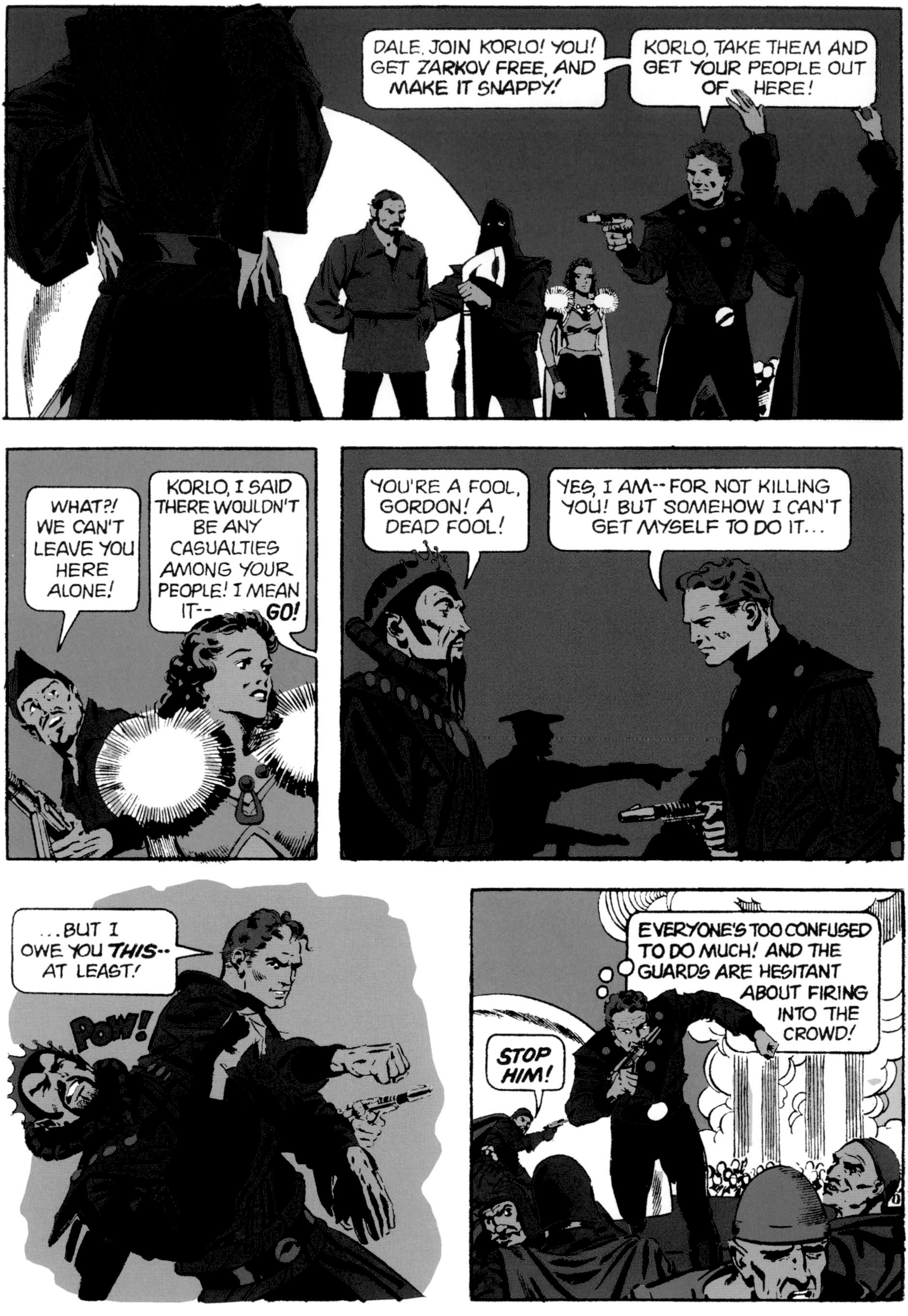
DALE, JOIN KORLO! YOU! GET ZARKOV FREE, AND MAKE IT SNAPPY!
KORLO, TAKE THEM AND GET YOUR PEOPLE OUT OF HERE!
WHAT?! WE CAN'T LEAVE YOU HERE ALONE!
KORLO, I SAID THERE WOULDN'T BE ANY CASUALTIES AMONG YOUR PEOPLE! I MEAN IT-- GO!
YOU'RE A FOOL, GORDON! A DEAD FOOL!
YES, I AM--FOR NOT KILLING YOU! BUT SOMEHOW I CAN'T GET MYSELF TO DO IT...
...BUT I OWE YOU THIS-- AT LEAST!
POW!
EVERYONE'S TOO CONFUSED TO DO MUCH! AND THE GUARDS ARE HESITANT ABOUT FIRING INTO THE CROWD!
STOP HIM!

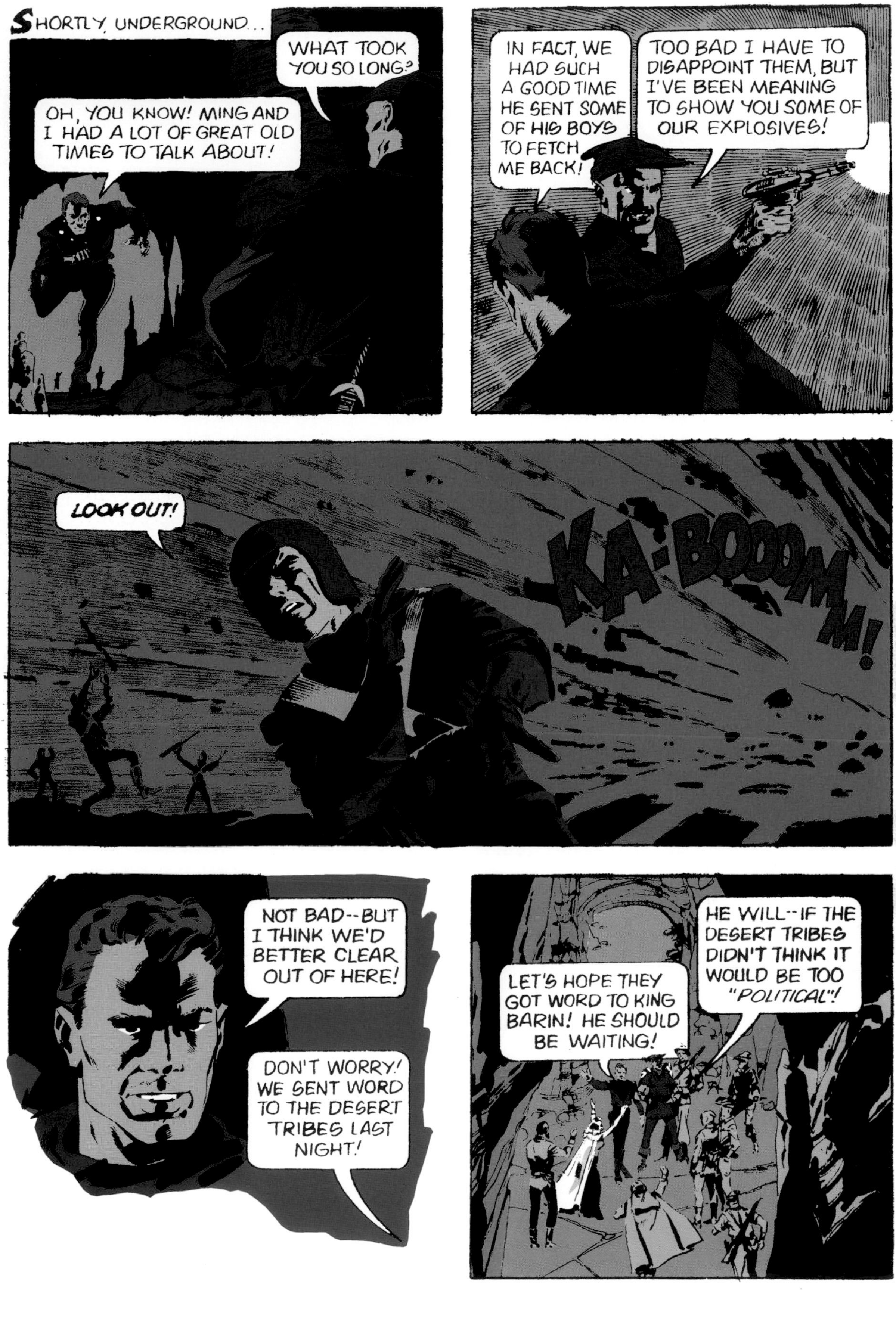
SHORTLY, UNDERGROUND...
WHAT TOOK YOU SO LONG?
OH, YOU KNOW! MING AND I HAD A LOT OF GREAT OLD TIMES TO TALK ABOUT!
IN FACT, WE HAD SUCH A GOOD TIME HE SENT SOME OF HIS BOYS TO FETCH ME BACK!
TOO BAD I HAVE TO DISAPPOINT THEM, BUT I'VE BEEN MEANING TO SHOW YOU SOME OF OUR EXPLOSIVES!
LOOK OUT!
KA-BOOOMMM!
NOT BAD--BUT I THINK WE'D BETTER CLEAR OUT OF HERE!
DON'T WORRY! WE SENT WORD TO THE DESERT TRIBES LAST NIGHT!
LET'S HOPE THEY GOT WORD TO KING BARIN! HE SHOULD BE WAITING!
HE WILL--IF THE DESERT TRIBES DIDN'T THINK IT WOULD BE TOO "POLITICAL"!

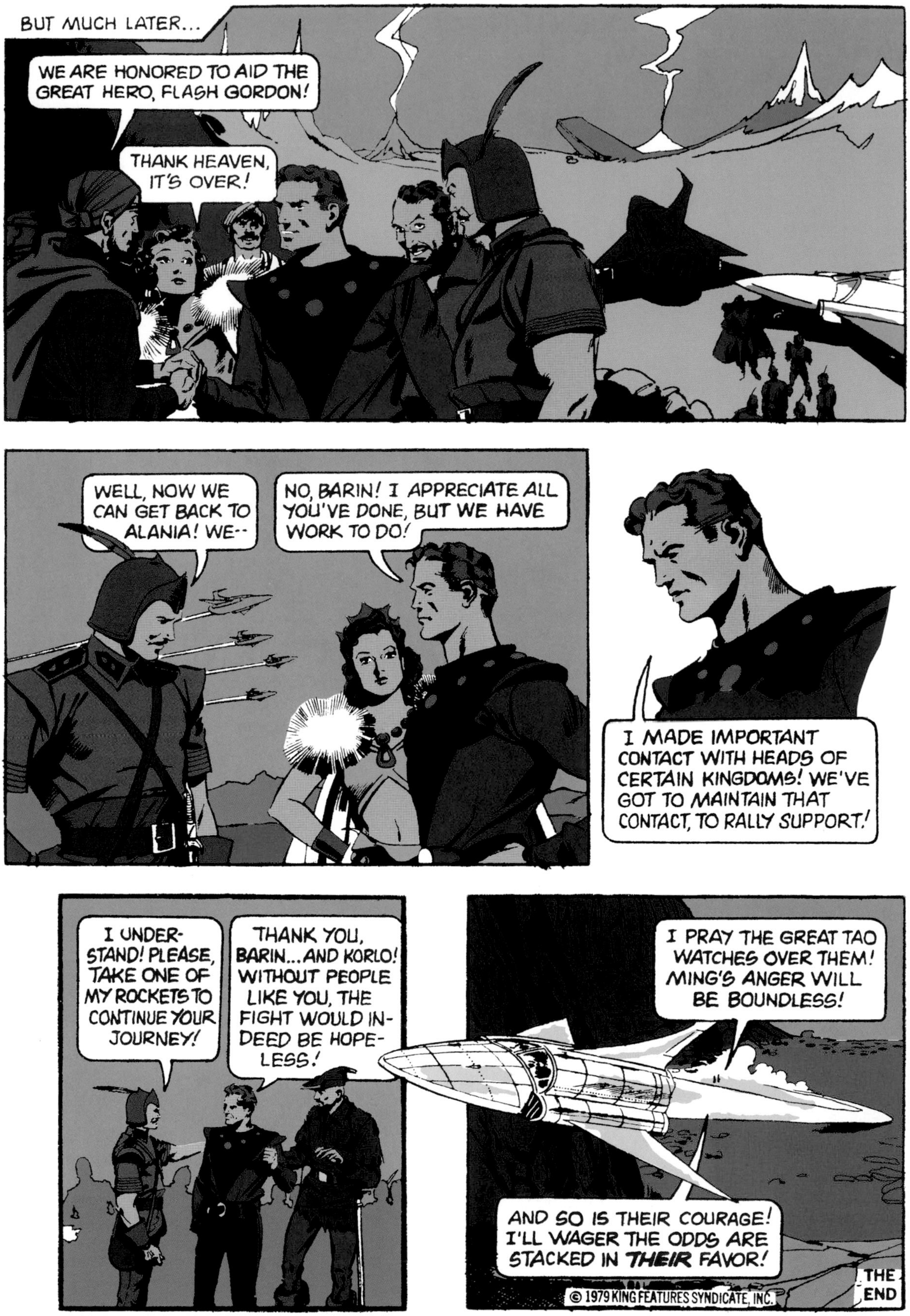
BUT MUCH LATER...
WE ARE HONORED TO AID THE GREAT HERO, FLASH GORDON!
THANK HEAVEN, IT'S OVER!
WELL, NOW WE CAN GET BACK TO ALANIA! WE--
NO, BARIN! I APPRECIATE ALL YOU'VE DONE, BUT WE HAVE WORK TO DO!
I MADE IMPORTANT CONTACT WITH HEADS OF CERTAIN KINGDOMS! WE'VE GOT TO MAINTAIN THAT CONTACT, TO RALLY SUPPORT!
I UNDER-STAND! PLEASE, TAKE ONE OF MY ROCKETS TO CONTINUE YOUR JOURNEY!
THANK YOU, BARIN... AND KORLO! WITHOUT PEOPLE LIKE YOU, THE FIGHT WOULD IN-DEED BE HOPE-LESS!
I PRAY THE GREAT TAO WATCHES OVER THEM! MING'S ANGER WILL BE BOUNDLESS!
AND SO IS THEIR COURAGE! I'LL WAGER THE ODDS ARE STACKED IN THEIR FAVOR!
THE END
© 1979 KING FEATURES SYNDICATE, INC.

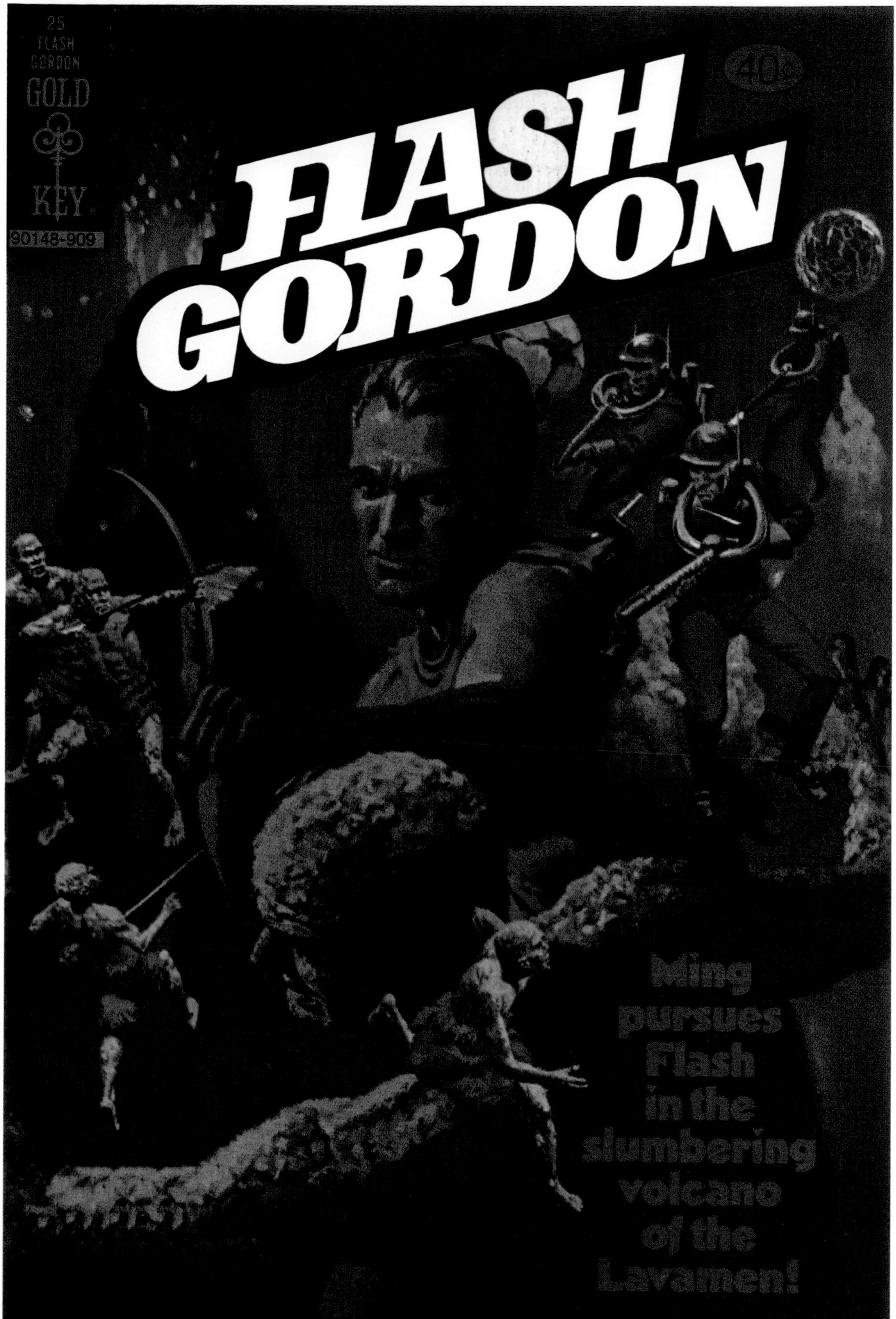
25
FLASH
GORDON
GOLD
KEY
90148-909
40¢
FLASH GORDON
Ming pursues Flash in the slumbering volcano of the Lavamen!

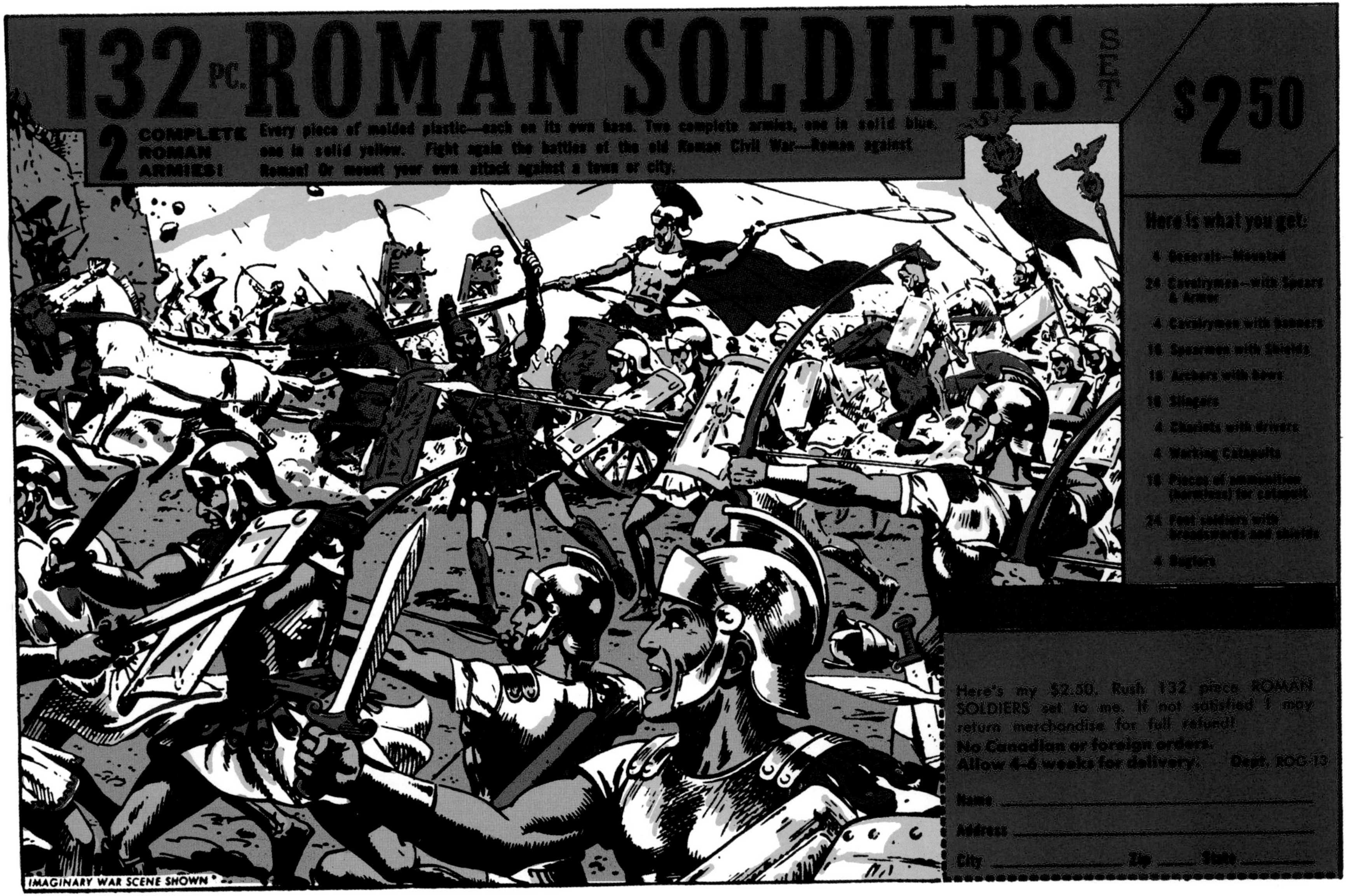

132 PC. ROMAN SOLDIERS SET
$2.50
2 COMPLETE ROMAN ARMIES!
Every piece of molded plastic—each on its own base. Two complete armies, one in solid blue, one in solid yellow. Fight again the battles of the old Roman Civil War—Roman against Roman! Or mount your own attack against a town or city.
Here is what you get:
4 Generals—Mounted
24 Cavalrymen—with Spears & Armor
4 Cavalrymen with Banners
16 Spearmen with Shields
16 Archers with bows
16 Slingers
4 Chariots with drivers
4 Working Catapults
16 Pieces of ammunition (boulders) for catapult
24 Foot soldiers with broadswords and shields
4 Buglers
Here's my $2.50. Rush 132 piece ROMAN SOLDIERS set to me. If not satisfied I may return merchandise for full refund!
No Canadian or foreign orders.
Allow 4-6 weeks for delivery.
Dept. ROG-13
Name
Address
City
Zip
State
IMAGINARY WAR SCENE SHOWN

Stranded in an alien world, Flash Gordon, Dale Arden and Dr. Hans Zarkov struggle against the evil emperor, Ming the Merciless, who seeks to enslave an entire planet.....

FLASH GORDON ON THE PLANET MONGO

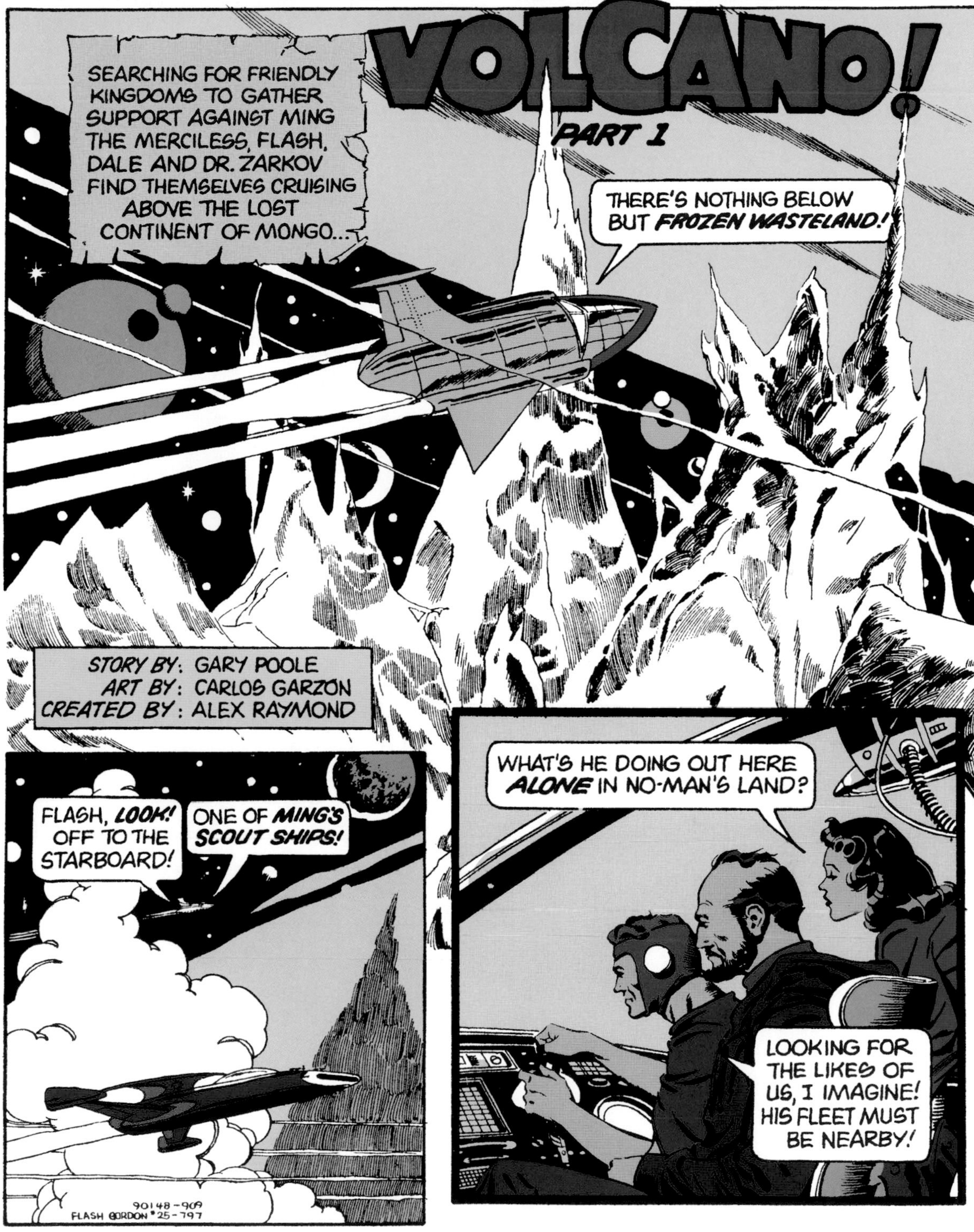

VOLCANO!
PART 1
SEARCHING FOR FRIENDLY KINGDOMS TO GATHER SUPPORT AGAINST MING THE MERCILESS, FLASH, DALE AND DR. ZARKOV FIND THEMSELVES CRUISING ABOVE THE LOST CONTINENT OF MONGO...
THERE'S NOTHING BELOW BUT FROZEN WASTELAND!
STORY BY: GARY POOLE
ART BY: CARLOS GARZON
CREATED BY: ALEX RAYMOND
FLASH, LOOK! OFF TO THE STARBOARD!
ONE OF MING'S SCOUT SHIPS!
90148-909
FLASH GORDON #25-797
WHAT'S HE DOING OUT HERE ALONE IN NO-MAN'S LAND?
LOOKING FOR THE LIKES OF US, I IMAGINE! HIS FLEET MUST BE NEARBY!

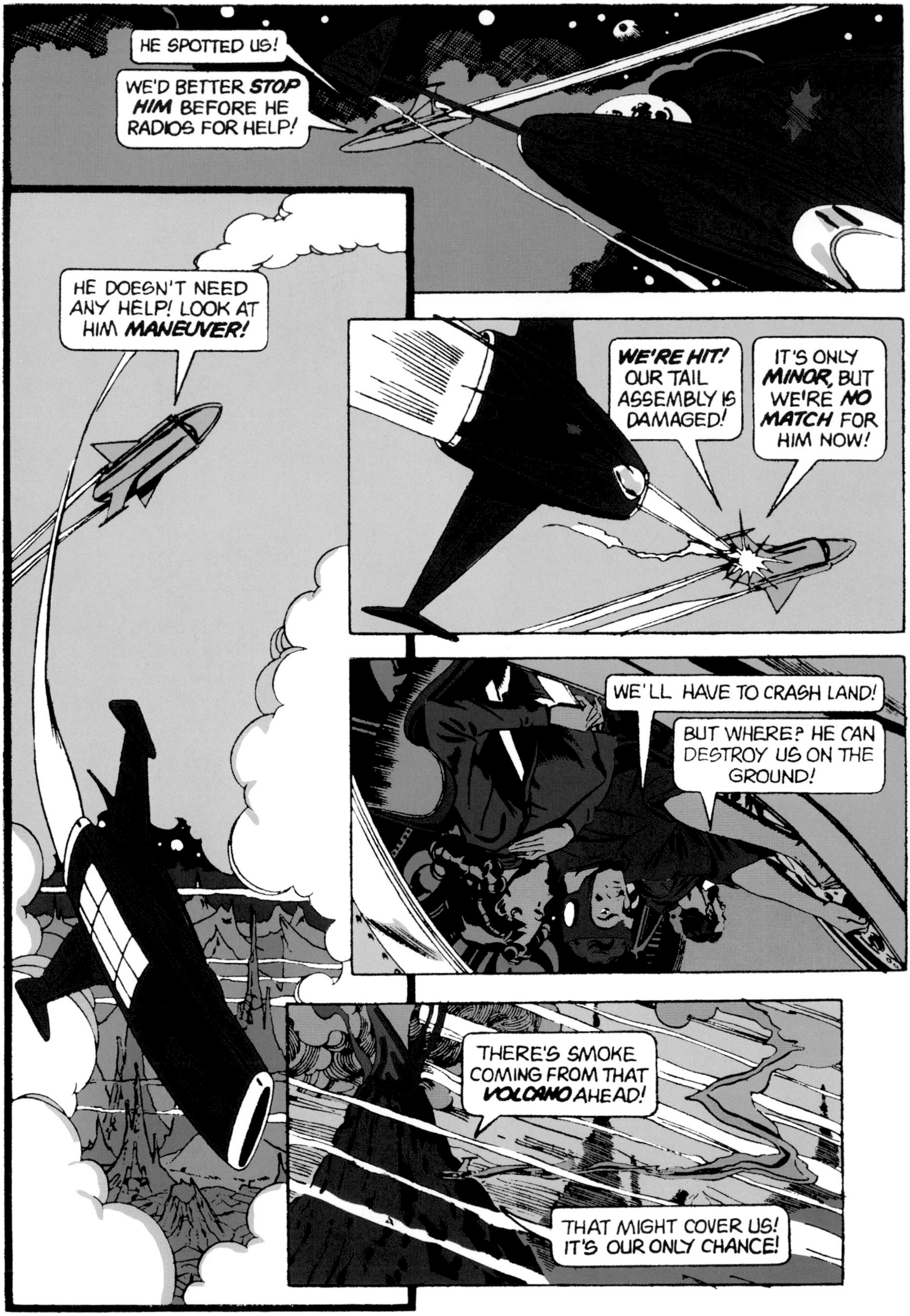
HE SPOTTED US!
WE'D BETTER STOP HIM BEFORE HE RADIOS FOR HELP!
HE DOESN'T NEED ANY HELP! LOOK AT HIM MANEUVER!
WE'RE HIT! OUR TAIL ASSEMBLY IS DAMAGED!
IT'S ONLY MINOR, BUT WE'RE NO MATCH FOR HIM NOW!
WE'LL HAVE TO CRASH LAND!
BUT WHERE? HE CAN DESTROY US ON THE GROUND!
THERE'S SMOKE COMING FROM THAT VOLCANO AHEAD!
THAT MIGHT COVER US! IT'S OUR ONLY CHANCE!

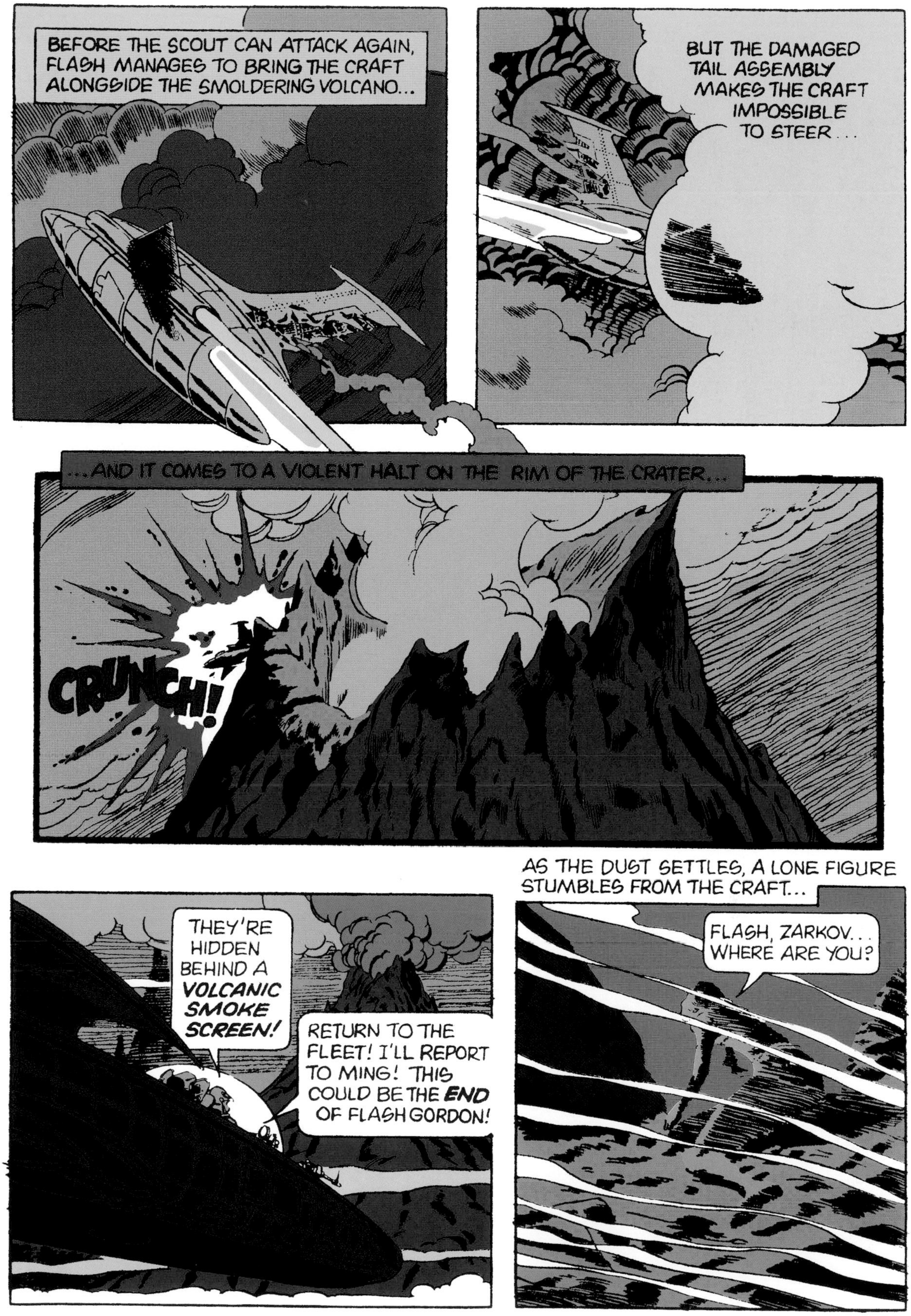
BEFORE THE SCOUT CAN ATTACK AGAIN, FLASH MANAGES TO BRING THE CRAFT ALONGSIDE THE SMOLDERING VOLCANO...
BUT THE DAMAGED TAIL ASSEMBLY MAKES THE CRAFT IMPOSSIBLE TO STEER...
...AND IT COMES TO A VIOLENT HALT ON THE RIM OF THE CRATER...
CRUNCH!
THEY'RE HIDDEN BEHIND A VOLCANIC SMOKE SCREEN!
RETURN TO THE FLEET! I'LL REPORT TO MING! THIS COULD BE THE END OF FLASH GORDON!
AS THE DUST SETTLES, A LONE FIGURE STUMBLES FROM THE CRAFT...
FLASH, ZARKOV... WHERE ARE YOU?

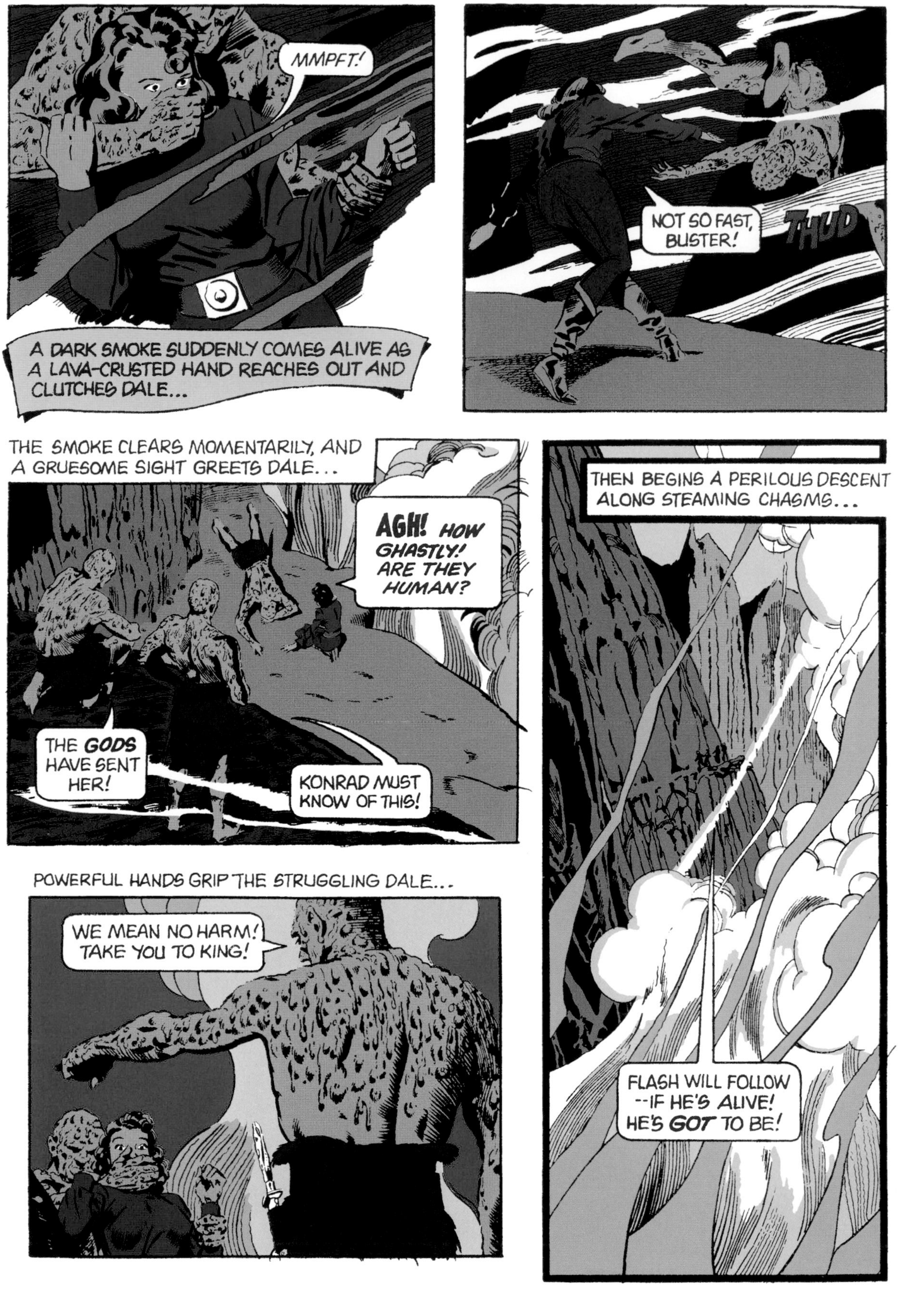
MMPFT!
A DARK SMOKE SUDDENLY COMES ALIVE AS A LAVA-CRUSTED HAND REACHES OUT AND CLUTCHES DALE...
NOT SO FAST, BUSTER!
THUD
THE SMOKE CLEARS MOMENTARILY, AND A GRUESOME SIGHT GREETS DALE...
AGH! HOW GHASTLY! ARE THEY HUMAN?
THE GODS HAVE SENT HER!
KONRAD MUST KNOW OF THIS!
POWERFUL HANDS GRIP THE STRUGGLING DALE...
WE MEAN NO HARM! TAKE YOU TO KING!
THEN BEGINS A PERILOUS DESCENT ALONG STEAMING CHASMS...
FLASH WILL FOLLOW --IF HE'S ALIVE! HE'S GOT TO BE!

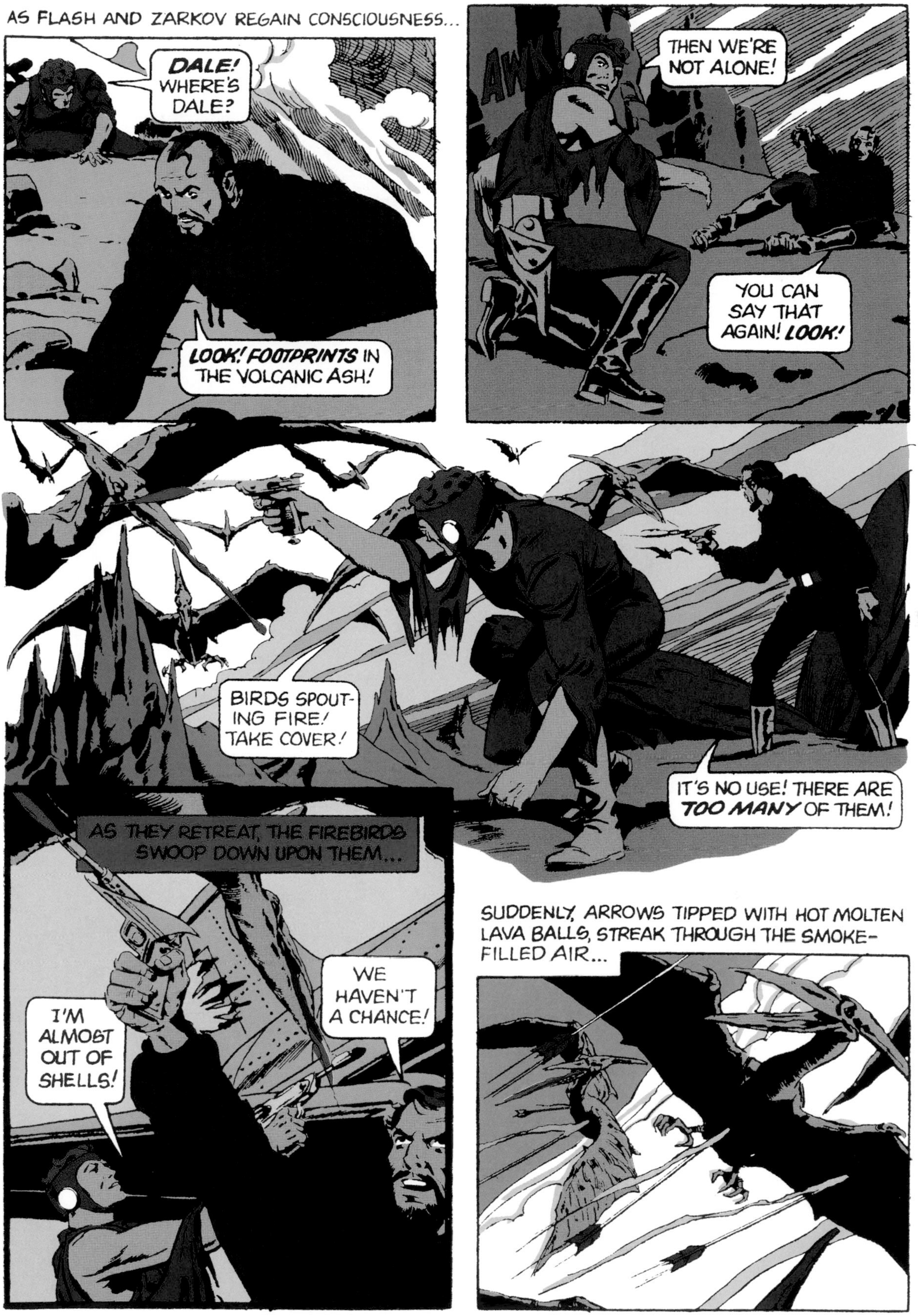
AS FLASH AND ZARKOV REGAIN CONSCIOUSNESS...
DALE! WHERE'S DALE?
LOOK! FOOTPRINTS IN THE VOLCANIC ASH!
THEN WE'RE NOT ALONE!
YOU CAN SAY THAT AGAIN! LOOK!
BIRDS SPOUTING FIRE! TAKE COVER!
IT'S NO USE! THERE ARE TOO MANY OF THEM!
AS THEY RETREAT, THE FIREBIRDS SWOOP DOWN UPON THEM...
WE HAVEN'T A CHANCE!
I'M ALMOST OUT OF SHELLS!
SUDDENLY, ARROWS TIPPED WITH HOT MOLTEN LAVA BALLS, STREAK THROUGH THE SMOKE-FILLED AIR...

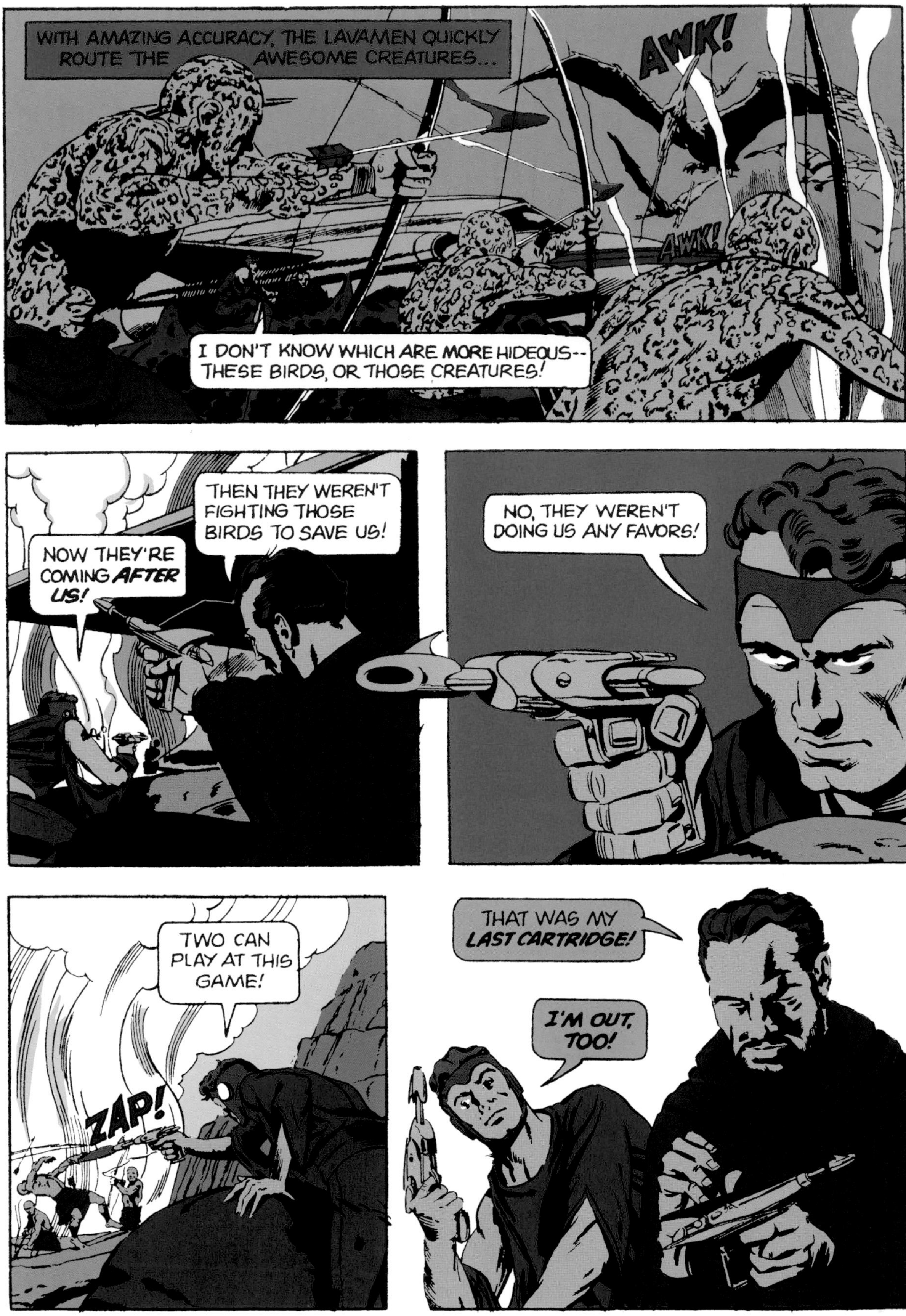

WITH AMAZING ACCURACY, THE LAVAMEN QUICKLY ROUTE THE AWESOME CREATURES...
AWK!
AWK!
I DON'T KNOW WHICH ARE MORE HIDEOUS-- THESE BIRDS, OR THOSE CREATURES!
THEN THEY WEREN'T FIGHTING THOSE BIRDS TO SAVE US!
NOW THEY'RE COMING AFTER US!
NO, THEY WEREN'T DOING US ANY FAVORS!
TWO CAN PLAY AT THIS GAME!
ZAP!
THAT WAS MY LAST CARTRIDGE!
I'M OUT, TOO!

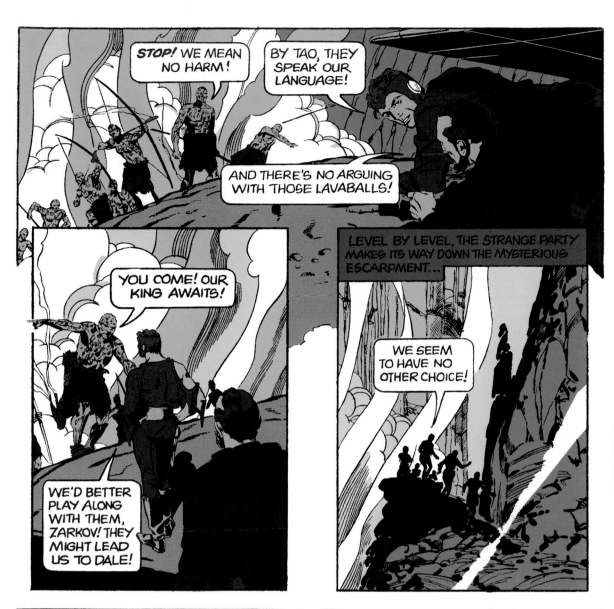

STOP! WE MEAN NO HARM!

BY TAO, THEY SPEAK OUR LANGUAGE!

AND THERE'S NO ARGUING WITH THOSE LAVABALLS!

YOU COME! OUR KING AWAITS!

WE'D BETTER PLAY ALONG WITH THEM, ZARKOV! THEY MIGHT LEAD US TO DALE!

LEVEL BY LEVEL, THE STRANGE PARTY MAKES ITS WAY DOWN THE MYSTERIOUS ESCARPMENT...

WE SEEM TO HAVE NO OTHER CHOICE!

MEANWHILE, MING RECEIVES THE NEWS...

CRASH LANDED, EH? BUT I MUST KNOW FOR CERTAIN THAT FLASH GORDON IS DEAD!

YES, O GREAT MING!

IF, BY TAO, DALE ARDEN SURVIVED, YOU WILL BRING HER TO ME!

REST ASSURED, O SUPREME ONE!

I WILL LEAD THE COMMANDO TEAM MYSELF!

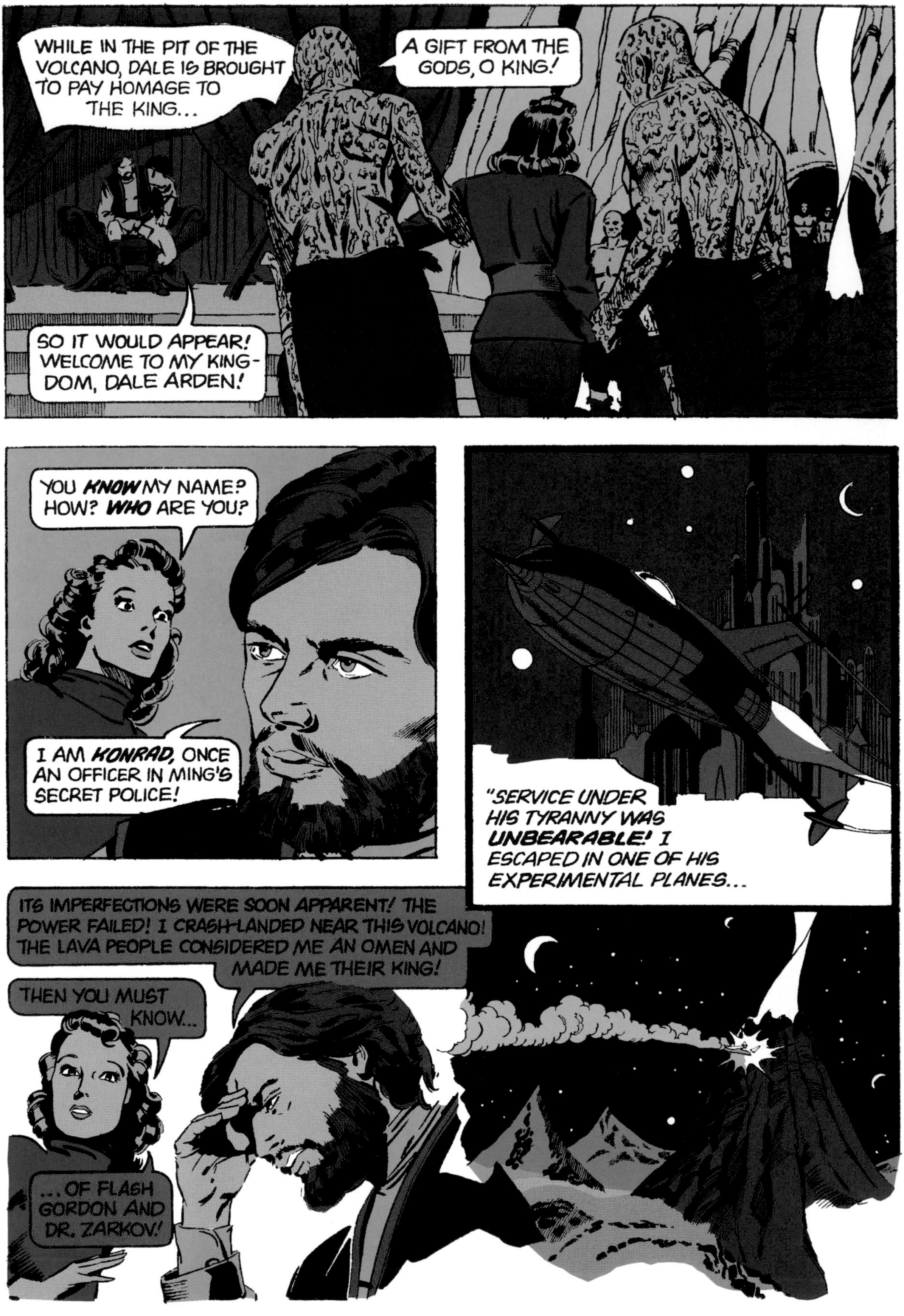
WHILE IN THE PIT OF THE VOLCANO, DALE IS BROUGHT TO PAY HOMAGE TO THE KING...
A GIFT FROM THE GODS, O KING!
SO IT WOULD APPEAR! WELCOME TO MY KING-DOM, DALE ARDEN!
YOU **KNOW** MY NAME? HOW? **WHO** ARE YOU?
I AM **KONRAD,** ONCE AN OFFICER IN MING'S SECRET POLICE!
"SERVICE UNDER HIS TYRANNY WAS **UNBEARABLE!** I ESCAPED IN ONE OF HIS EXPERIMENTAL PLANES...
ITS IMPERFECTIONS WERE SOON APPARENT! THE POWER FAILED! I CRASH-LANDED NEAR THIS VOLCANO! THE LAVA PEOPLE CONSIDERED ME AN OMEN AND MADE ME THEIR KING!
THEN YOU MUST KNOW...
...OF FLASH GORDON AND DR. ZARKOV!

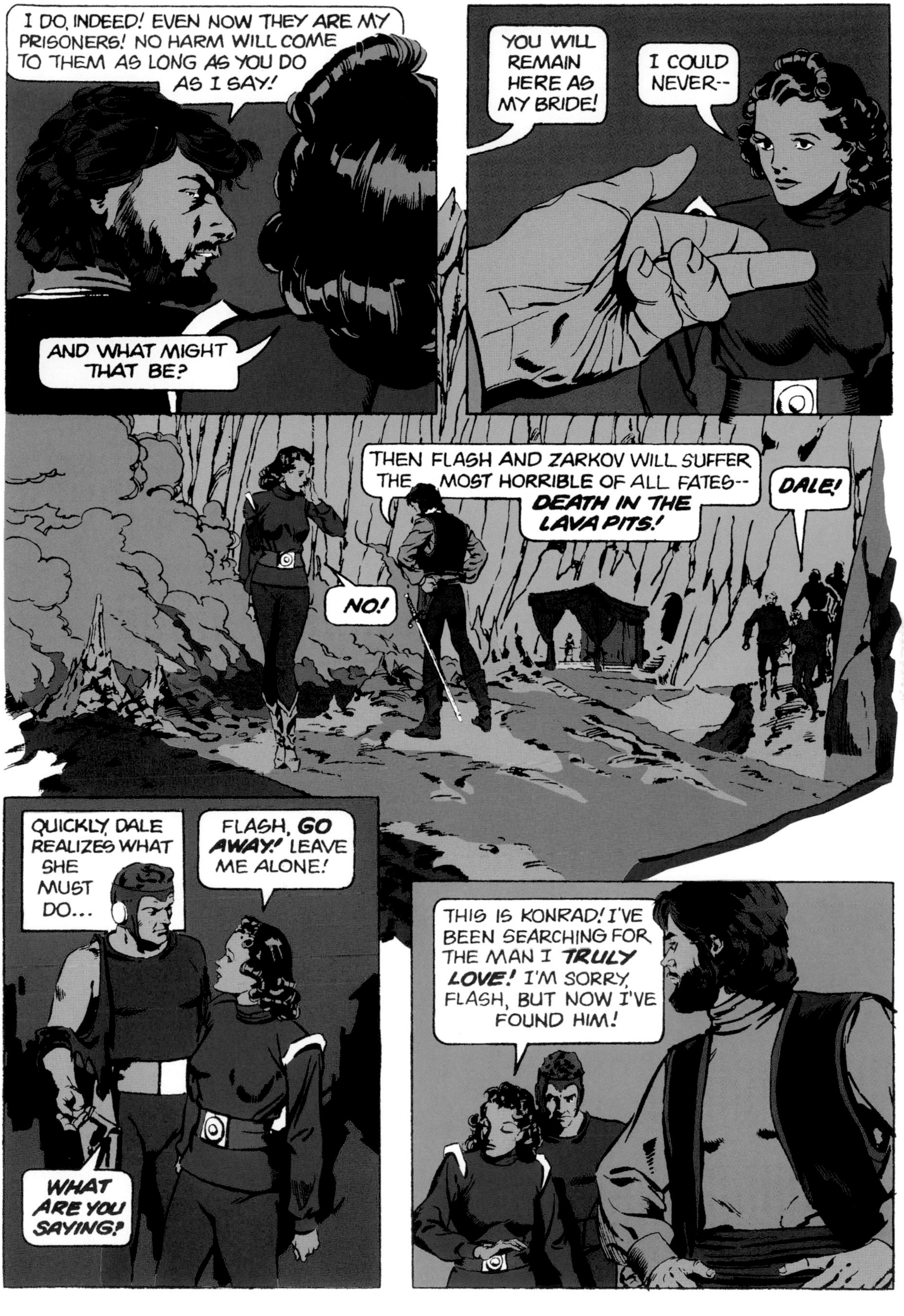

I DO, INDEED! EVEN NOW THEY ARE MY PRISONERS! NO HARM WILL COME TO THEM AS LONG AS YOU DO AS I SAY!
AND WHAT MIGHT THAT BE?
YOU WILL REMAIN HERE AS MY BRIDE!
I COULD NEVER--
THEN FLASH AND ZARKOV WILL SUFFER THE MOST HORRIBLE OF ALL FATES-- DEATH IN THE LAVA PITS!
NO!
DALE!
QUICKLY, DALE REALIZES WHAT SHE MUST DO...
FLASH, GO AWAY! LEAVE ME ALONE!
WHAT ARE YOU SAYING?
THIS IS KONRAD! I'VE BEEN SEARCHING FOR THE MAN I TRULY LOVE! I'M SORRY, FLASH, BUT NOW I'VE FOUND HIM!

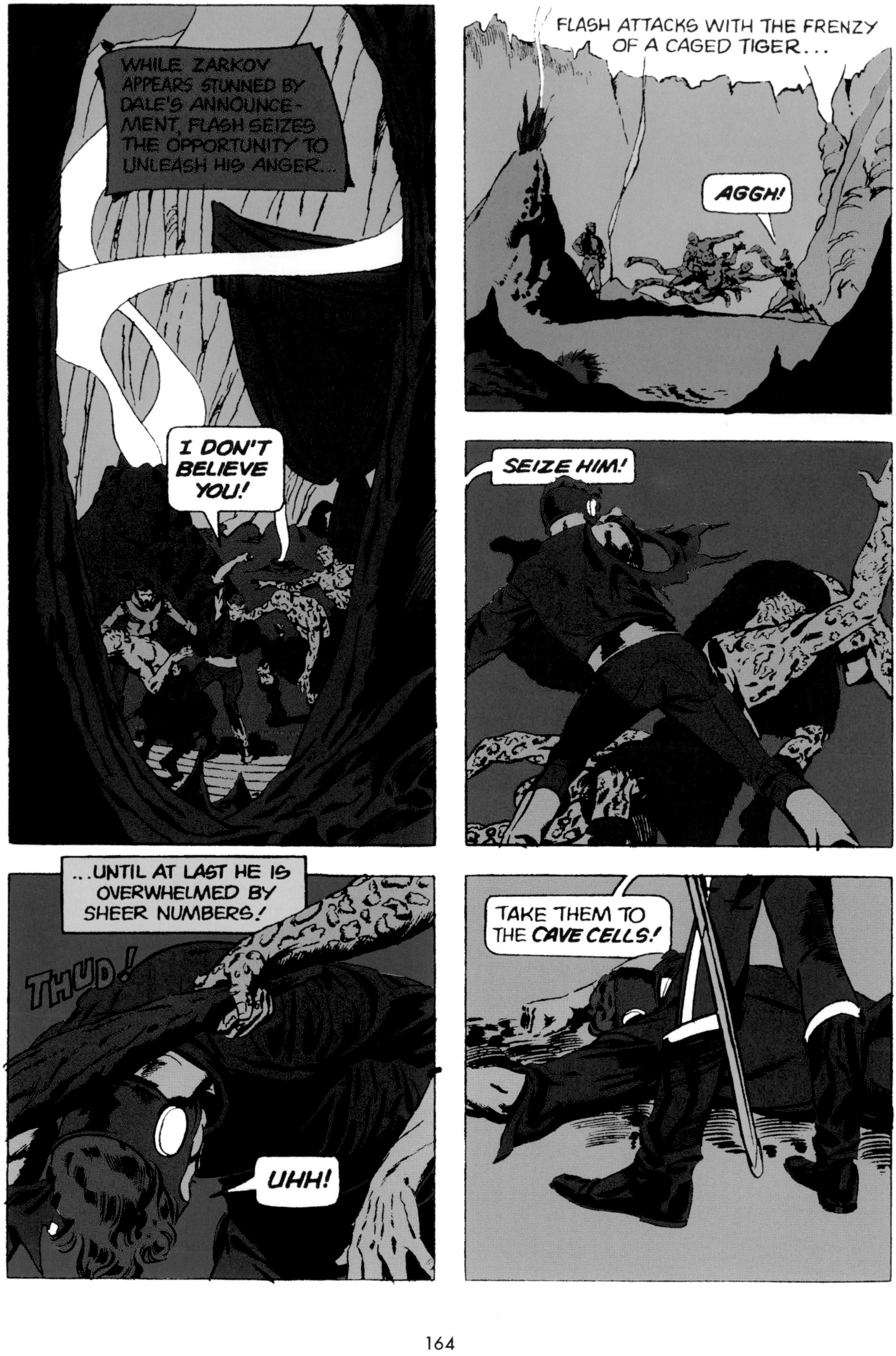
WHILE ZARKOV APPEARS STUNNED BY DALE'S ANNOUNCE-MENT, FLASH SEIZES THE OPPORTUNITY TO UNLEASH HIS ANGER...
I DON'T BELIEVE YOU!
FLASH ATTACKS WITH THE FRENZY OF A CAGED TIGER...
AGGH!
SEIZE HIM!
...UNTIL AT LAST HE IS OVERWHELMED BY SHEER NUMBERS!
THUD!
UHH!
TAKE THEM TO THE CAVE CELLS!

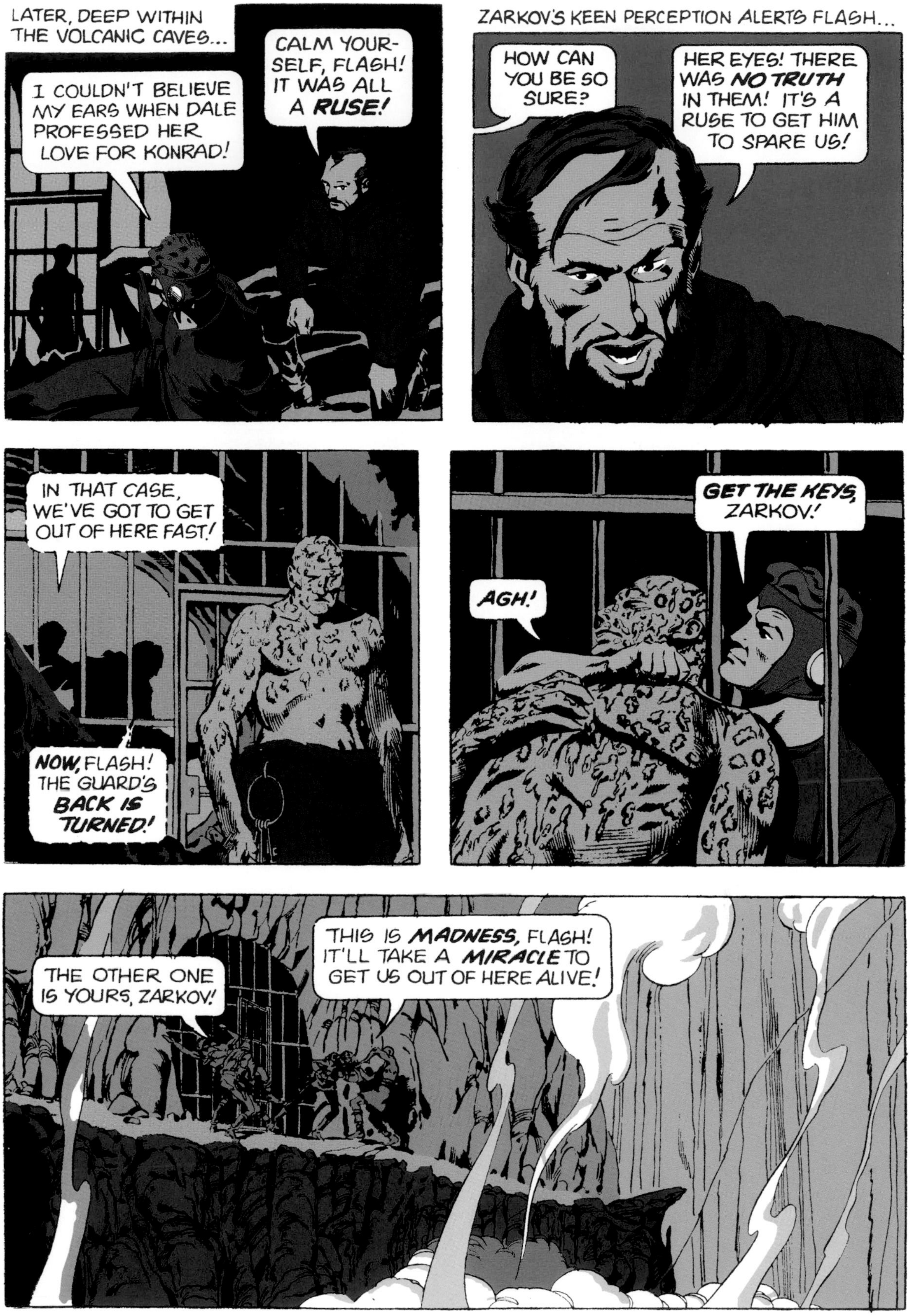
LATER, DEEP WITHIN THE VOLCANIC CAVES...
I COULDN'T BELIEVE MY EARS WHEN DALE PROFESSED HER LOVE FOR KONRAD!
CALM YOURSELF, FLASH! IT WAS ALL A RUSE!
ZARKOV'S KEEN PERCEPTION ALERTS FLASH...
HOW CAN YOU BE SO SURE?
HER EYES! THERE WAS NO TRUTH IN THEM! IT'S A RUSE TO GET HIM TO SPARE US!
IN THAT CASE, WE'VE GOT TO GET OUT OF HERE FAST!
NOW, FLASH! THE GUARD'S BACK IS TURNED!
GET THE KEYS, ZARKOV!
AGH!
THE OTHER ONE IS YOURS, ZARKOV!
THIS IS MADNESS, FLASH! IT'LL TAKE A MIRACLE TO GET US OUT OF HERE ALIVE!

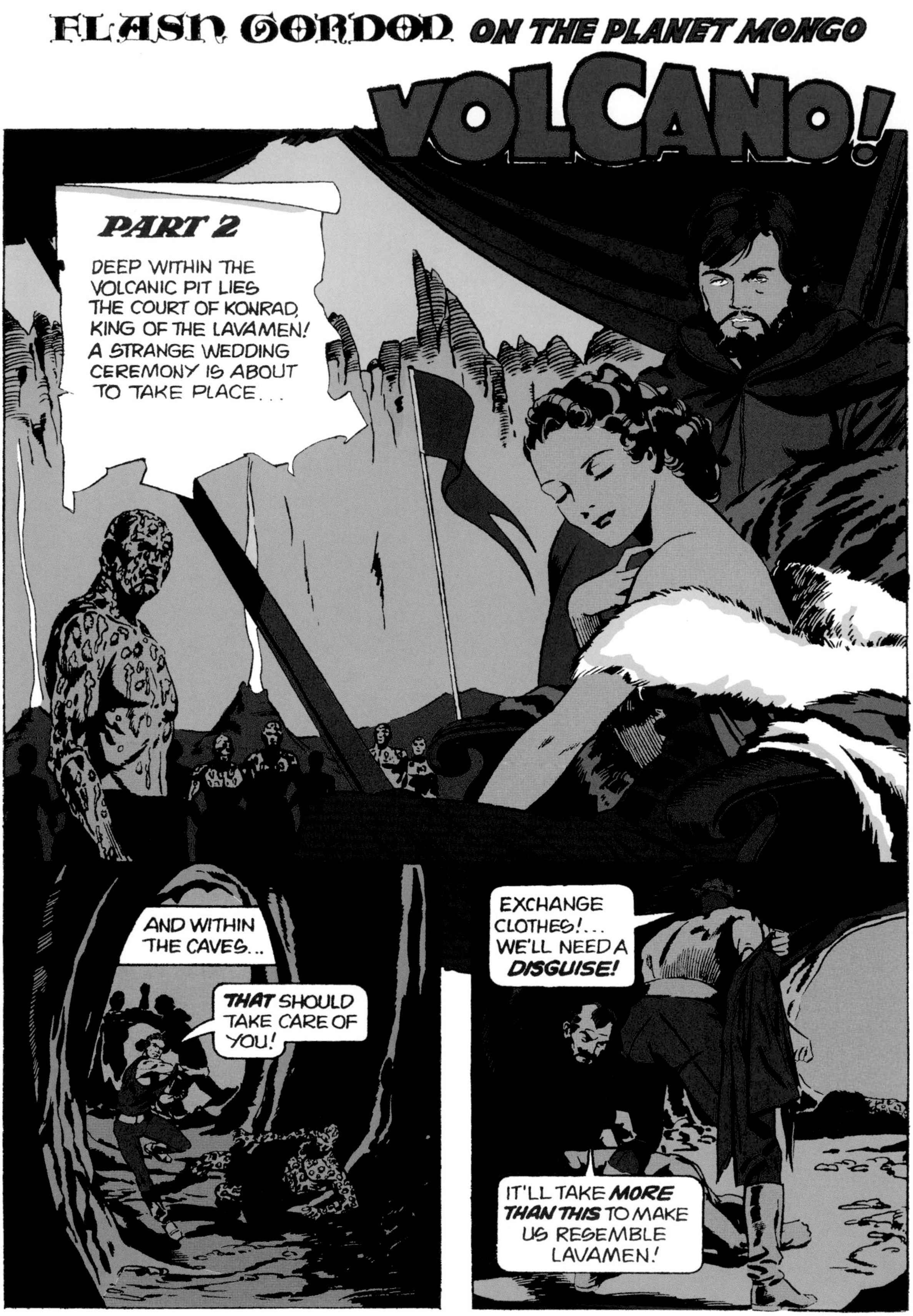
FLASH GORDON ON THE PLANET MONGO
VOLCANO!
PART 2
DEEP WITHIN THE VOLCANIC PIT LIES THE COURT OF KONRAD, KING OF THE LAVAMEN! A STRANGE WEDDING CEREMONY IS ABOUT TO TAKE PLACE...
AND WITHIN THE CAVES...
THAT SHOULD TAKE CARE OF YOU!
EXCHANGE CLOTHES!... WE'LL NEED A DISGUISE!
IT'LL TAKE MORE THAN THIS TO MAKE US RESEMBLE LAVAMEN!

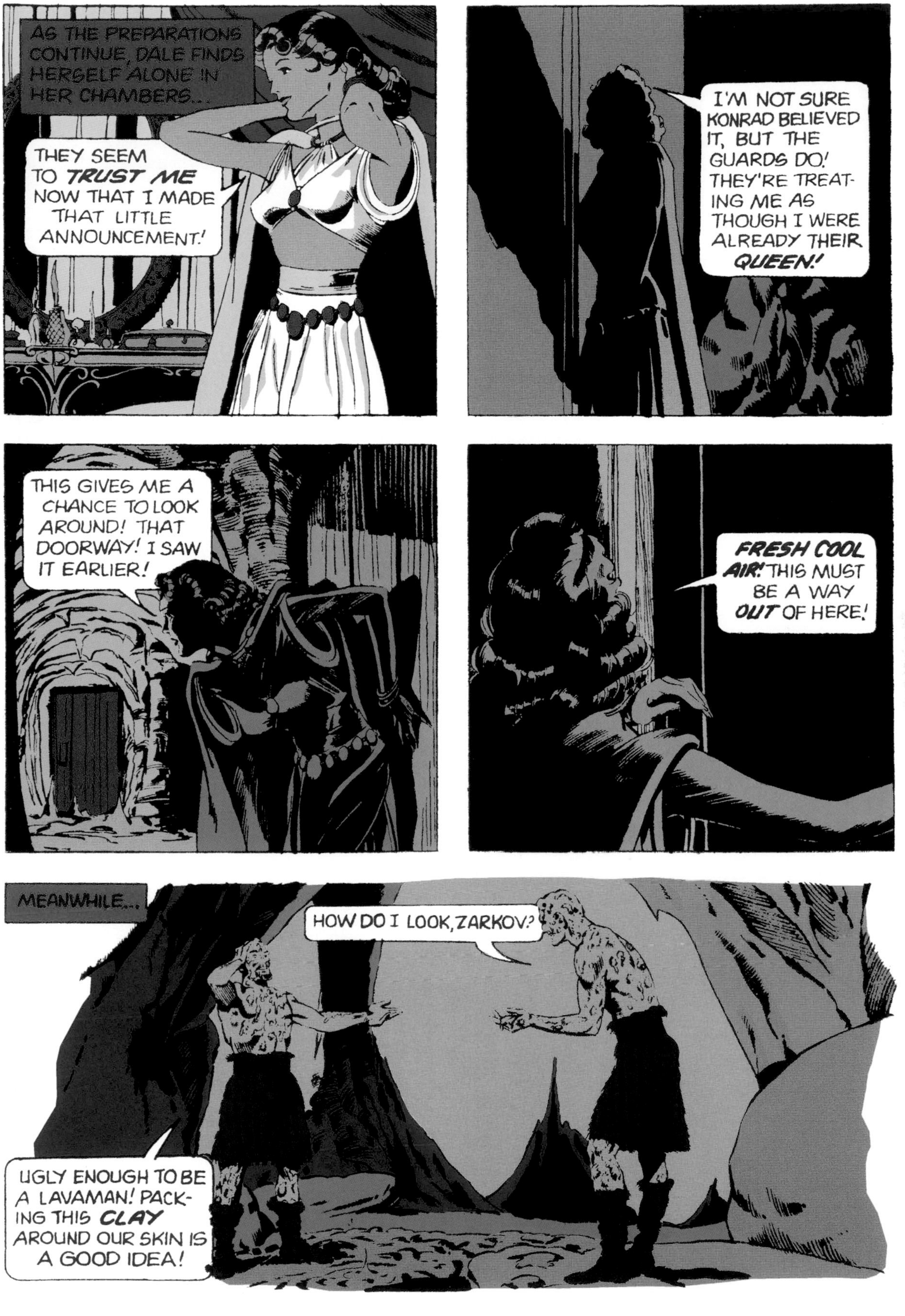
AS THE PREPARATIONS CONTINUE, DALE FINDS HERSELF ALONE IN HER CHAMBERS...
THEY SEEM TO TRUST ME NOW THAT I MADE THAT LITTLE ANNOUNCEMENT!
I'M NOT SURE KONRAD BELIEVED IT, BUT THE GUARDS DO! THEY'RE TREATING ME AS THOUGH I WERE ALREADY THEIR QUEEN!
THIS GIVES ME A CHANCE TO LOOK AROUND! THAT DOORWAY! I SAW IT EARLIER!
FRESH COOL AIR! THIS MUST BE A WAY OUT OF HERE!
MEANWHILE...
HOW DO I LOOK, ZARKOV?
UGLY ENOUGH TO BE A LAVAMAN! PACKING THIS CLAY AROUND OUR SKIN IS A GOOD IDEA!

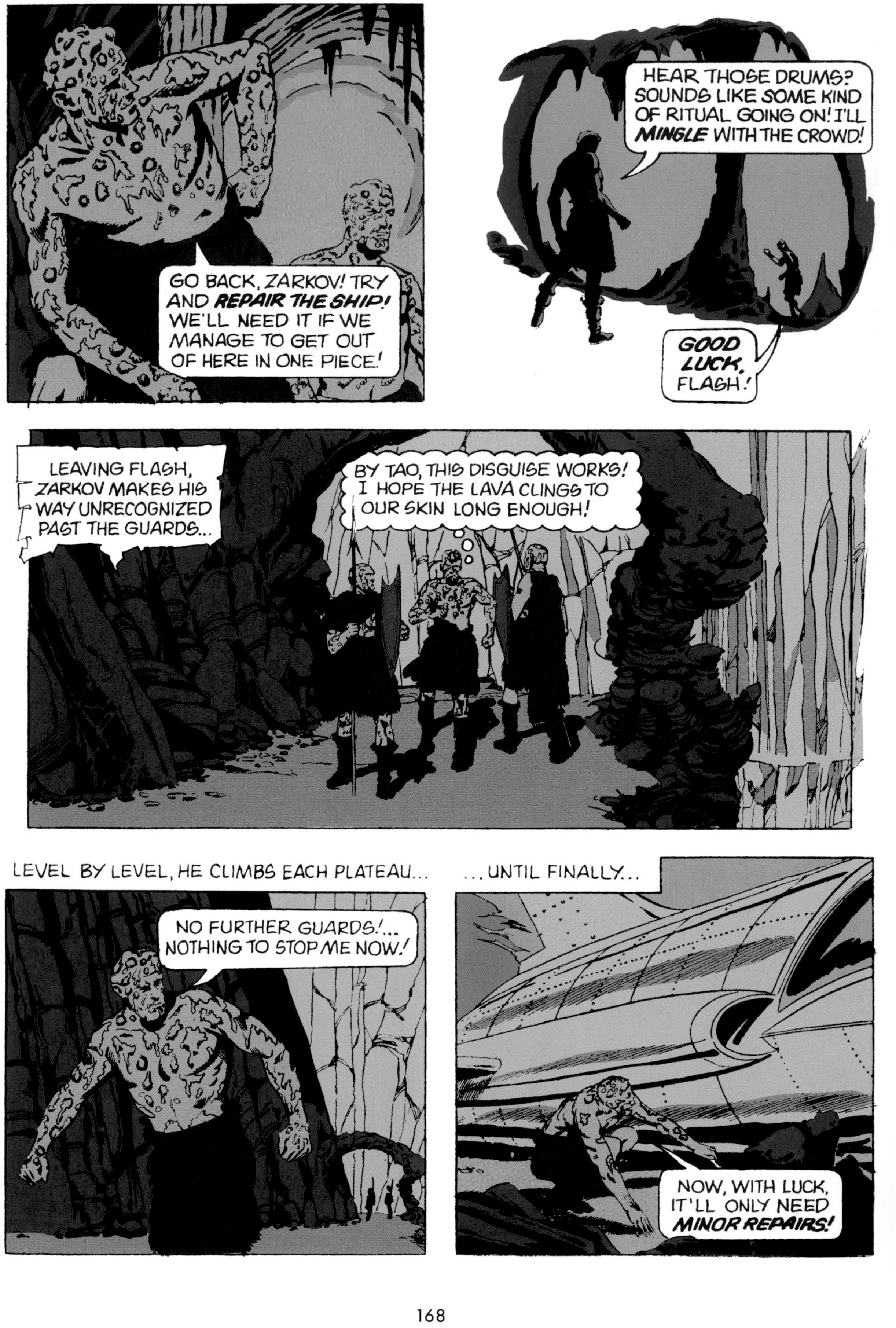
GO BACK, ZARKOV! TRY AND REPAIR THE SHIP! WE'LL NEED IT IF WE MANAGE TO GET OUT OF HERE IN ONE PIECE!
HEAR THOSE DRUMS? SOUNDS LIKE SOME KIND OF RITUAL GOING ON! I'LL MINGLE WITH THE CROWD!
GOOD LUCK, FLASH!
LEAVING FLASH, ZARKOV MAKES HIS WAY UNRECOGNIZED PAST THE GUARDS...
BY TAO, THIS DISGUISE WORKS! I HOPE THE LAVA CLINGS TO OUR SKIN LONG ENOUGH!
LEVEL BY LEVEL, HE CLIMBS EACH PLATEAU...
NO FURTHER GUARDS!... NOTHING TO STOP ME NOW!
...UNTIL FINALLY...
NOW, WITH LUCK, IT'LL ONLY NEED MINOR REPAIRS!

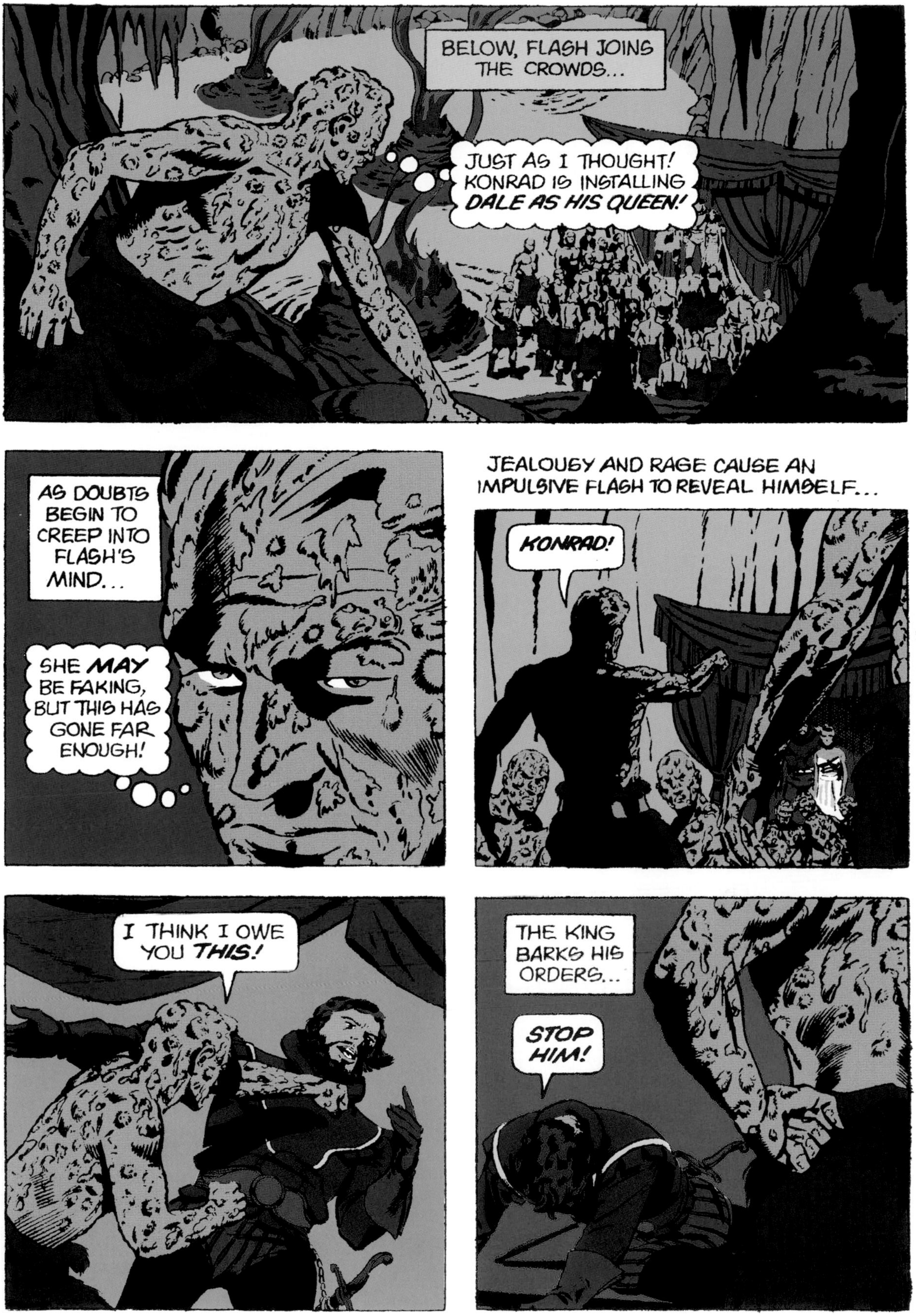
BELOW, FLASH JOINS THE CROWDS...
JUST AS I THOUGHT! KONRAD IS INSTALLING DALE AS HIS QUEEN!
AS DOUBTS BEGIN TO CREEP INTO FLASH'S MIND...
SHE MAY BE FAKING, BUT THIS HAS GONE FAR ENOUGH!
JEALOUSY AND RAGE CAUSE AN IMPULSIVE FLASH TO REVEAL HIMSELF...
KONRAD!
I THINK I OWE YOU THIS!
THE KING BARKS HIS ORDERS...
STOP HIM!

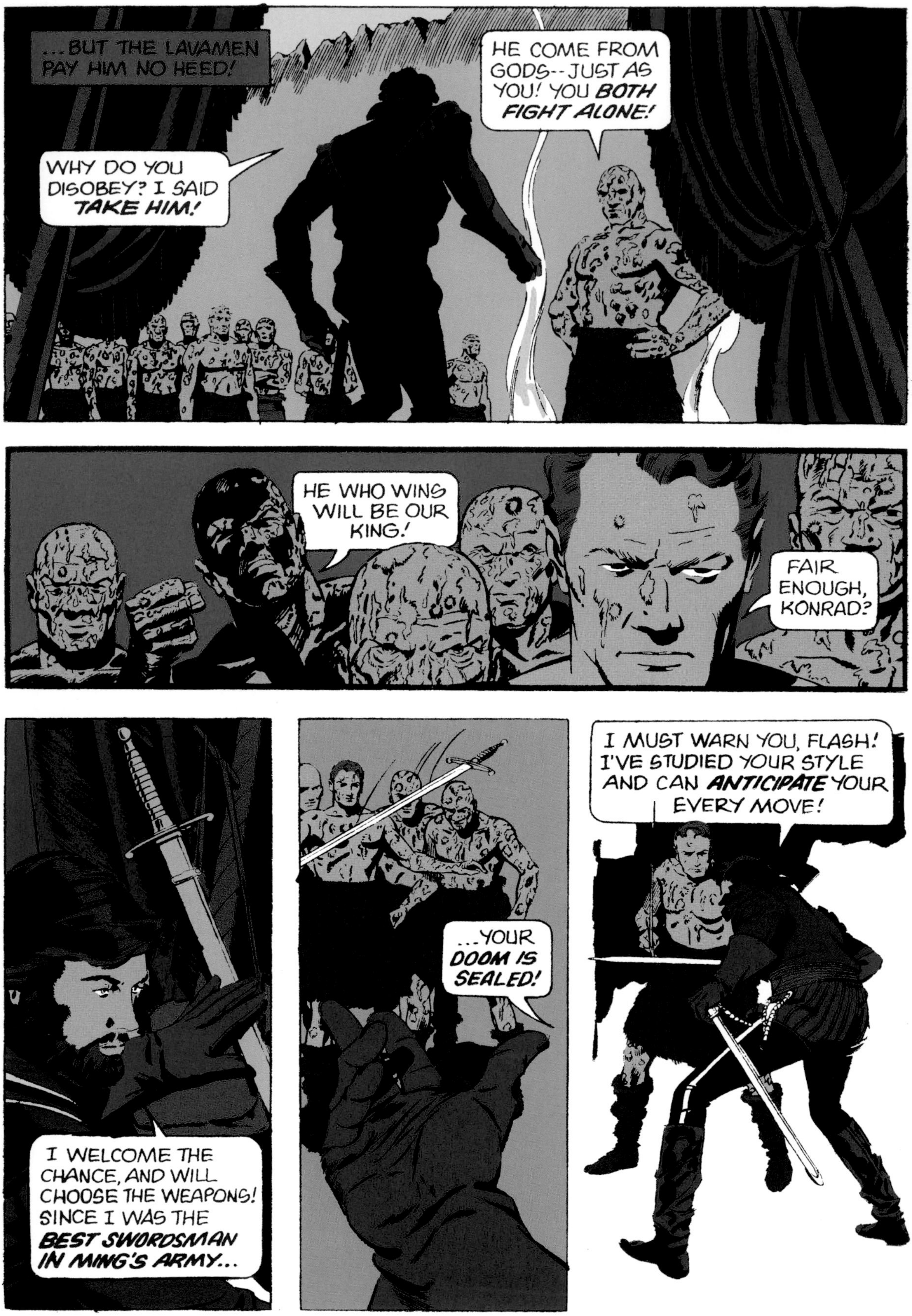
...BUT THE LAVAMEN PAY HIM NO HEED!
WHY DO YOU DISOBEY? I SAID TAKE HIM!
HE COME FROM GODS--JUST AS YOU! YOU BOTH FIGHT ALONE!
HE WHO WINS WILL BE OUR KING!
FAIR ENOUGH, KONRAD?
I WELCOME THE CHANCE, AND WILL CHOOSE THE WEAPONS! SINCE I WAS THE BEST SWORDSMAN IN MING'S ARMY...
...YOUR DOOM IS SEALED!
I MUST WARN YOU, FLASH! I'VE STUDIED YOUR STYLE AND CAN ANTICIPATE YOUR EVERY MOVE!

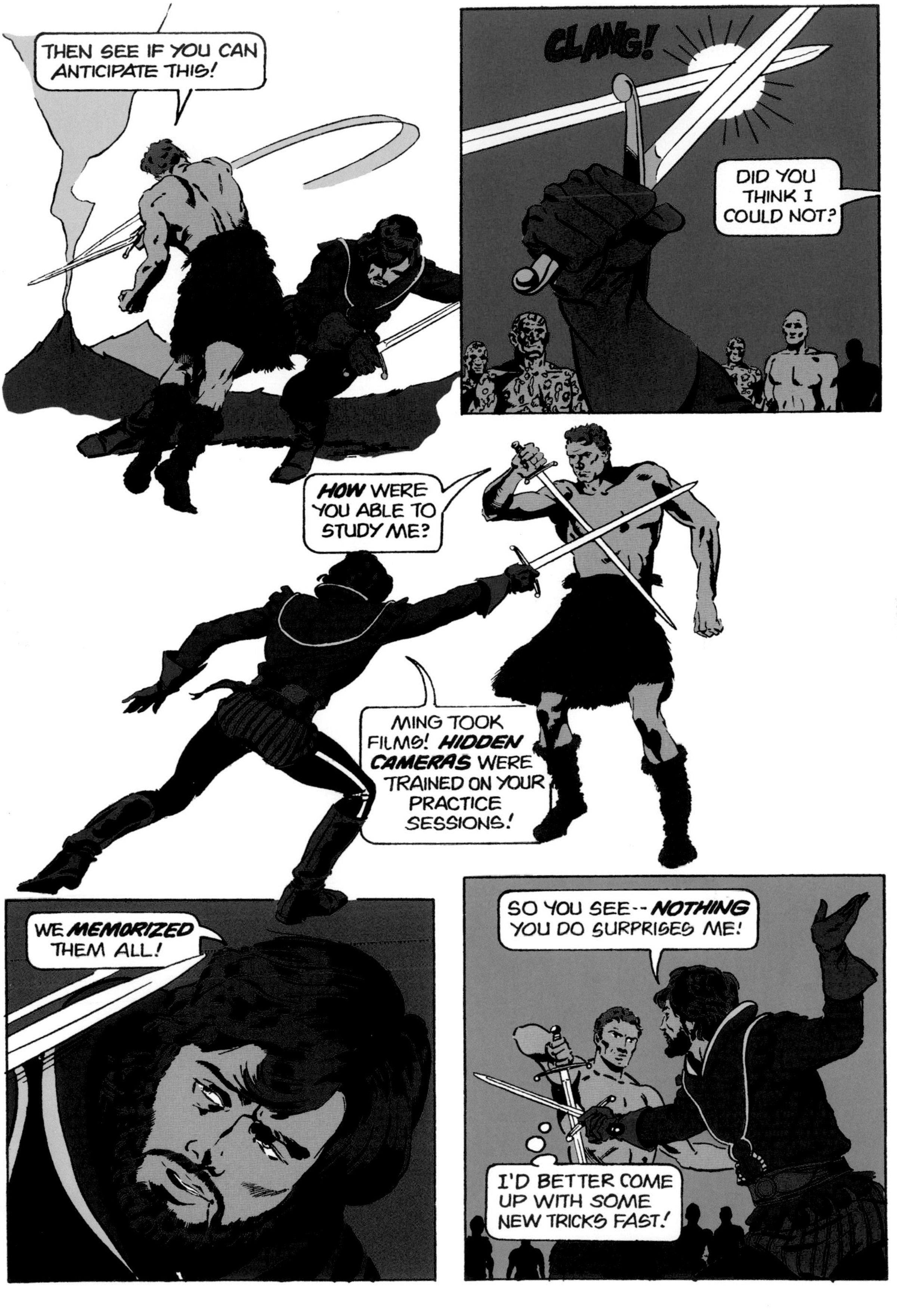
THEN SEE IF YOU CAN ANTICIPATE THIS!
CLANG!
DID YOU THINK I COULD NOT?
HOW WERE YOU ABLE TO STUDY ME?
MING TOOK FILMS! HIDDEN CAMERAS WERE TRAINED ON YOUR PRACTICE SESSIONS!
WE MEMORIZED THEM ALL!
SO YOU SEE-- NOTHING YOU DO SURPRISES ME!
I'D BETTER COME UP WITH SOME NEW TRICKS FAST!

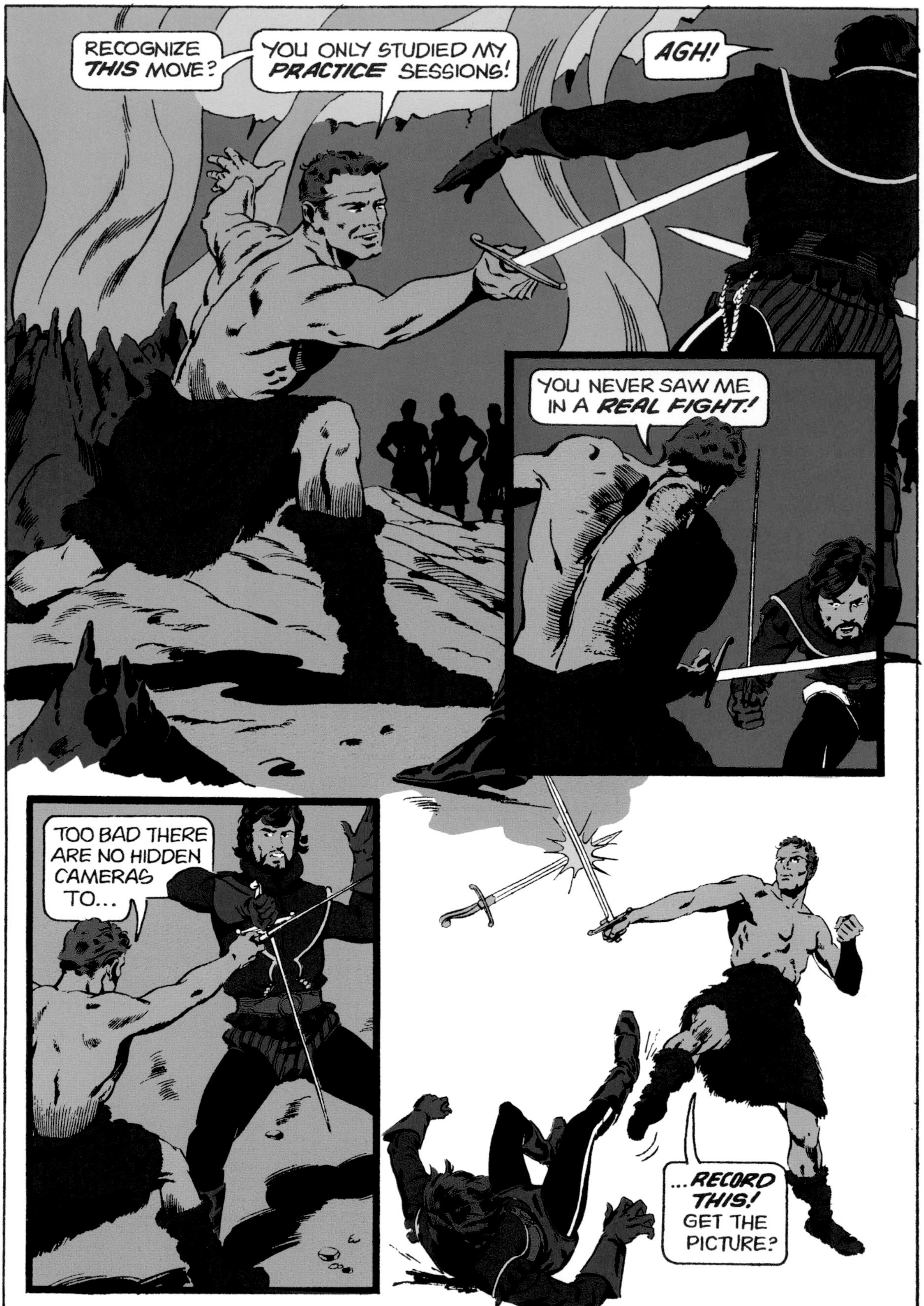
RECOGNIZE THIS MOVE?
YOU ONLY STUDIED MY PRACTICE SESSIONS!
AGH!
YOU NEVER SAW ME IN A REAL FIGHT!
TOO BAD THERE ARE NO HIDDEN CAMERAS TO...
...RECORD THIS! GET THE PICTURE?

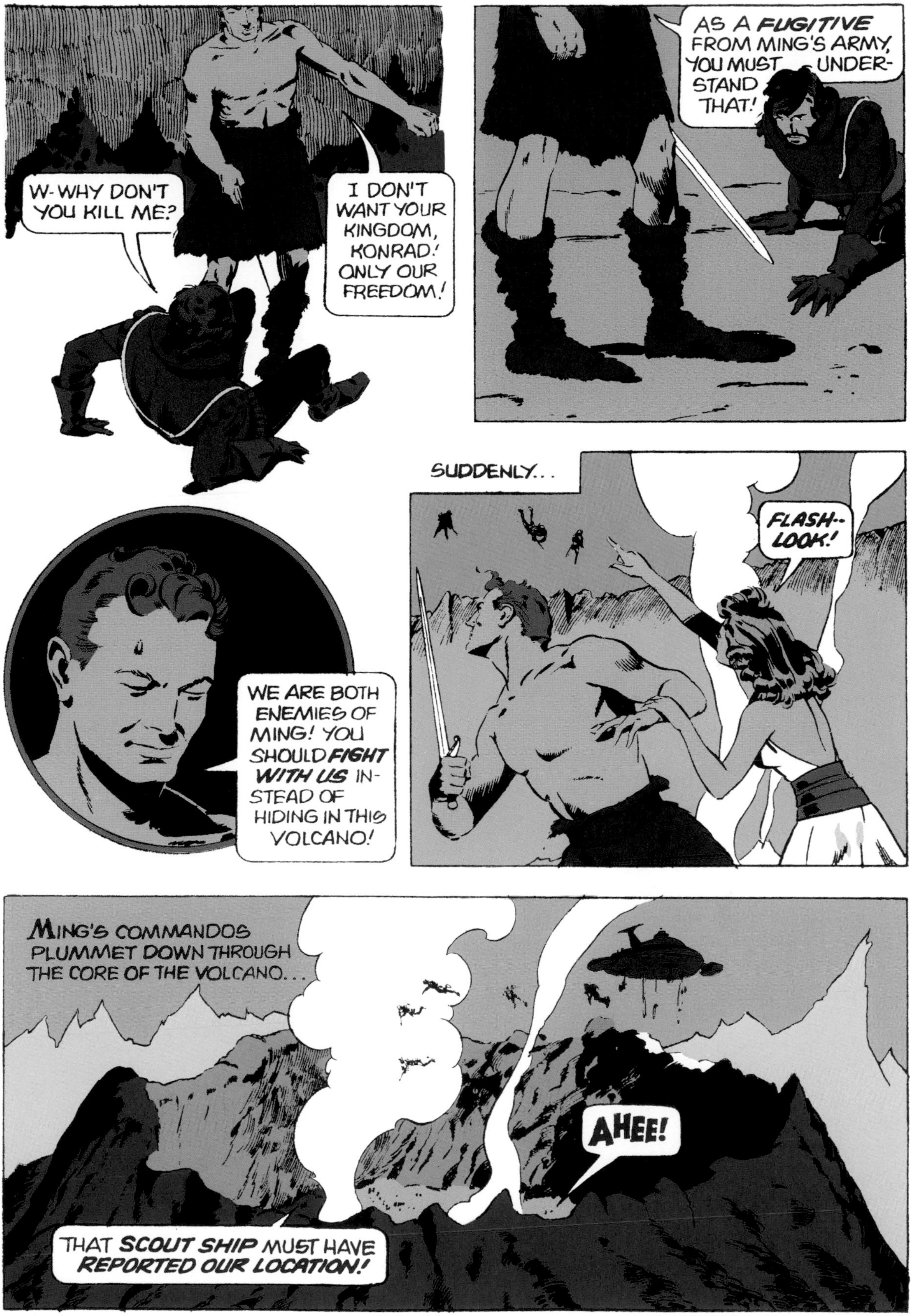
W-WHY DON'T YOU KILL ME?
I DON'T WANT YOUR KINGDOM, KONRAD! ONLY OUR FREEDOM!
AS A FUGITIVE FROM MING'S ARMY, YOU MUST UNDER-STAND THAT!
WE ARE BOTH ENEMIES OF MING! YOU SHOULD FIGHT WITH US IN-STEAD OF HIDING IN THIS VOLCANO!
SUDDENLY...
FLASH-- LOOK!
MING'S COMMANDOS PLUMMET DOWN THROUGH THE CORE OF THE VOLCANO...
AHEE!
THAT SCOUT SHIP MUST HAVE REPORTED OUR LOCATION!

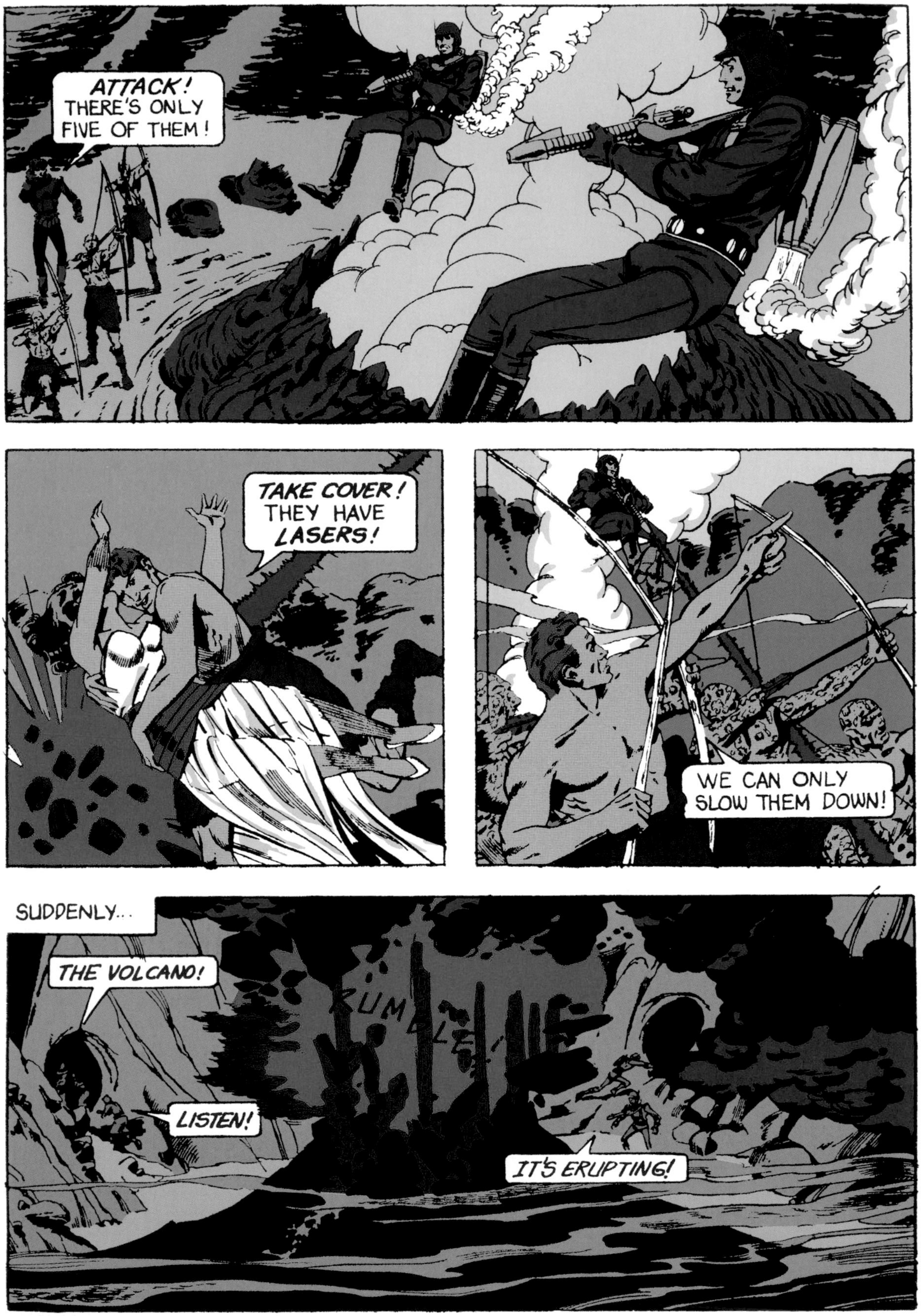
ATTACK! THERE'S ONLY FIVE OF THEM!
TAKE COVER! THEY HAVE LASERS!
WE CAN ONLY SLOW THEM DOWN!
SUDDENLY...
THE VOLCANO!
RUMBLE
LISTEN!
IT'S ERUPTING!

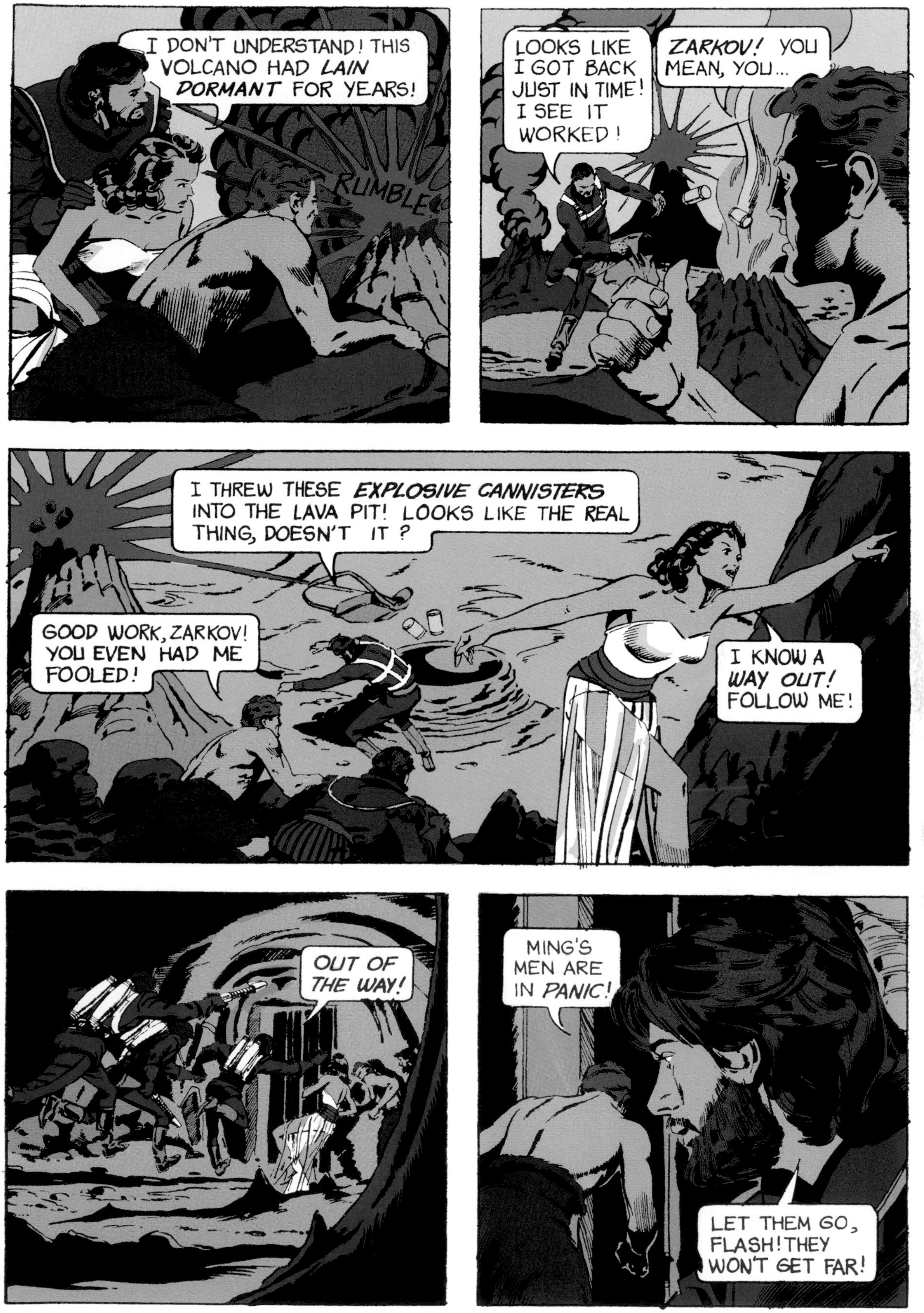
I DON'T UNDERSTAND! THIS VOLCANO HAD LAIN DORMANT FOR YEARS!
RUMBLE
LOOKS LIKE I GOT BACK JUST IN TIME! I SEE IT WORKED!
ZARKOV! YOU MEAN, YOU...
I THREW THESE EXPLOSIVE CANNISTERS INTO THE LAVA PIT! LOOKS LIKE THE REAL THING, DOESN'T IT ?
GOOD WORK, ZARKOV! YOU EVEN HAD ME FOOLED!
I KNOW A WAY OUT! FOLLOW ME!
OUT OF THE WAY!
MING'S MEN ARE IN PANIC!
LET THEM GO, FLASH! THEY WON'T GET FAR!

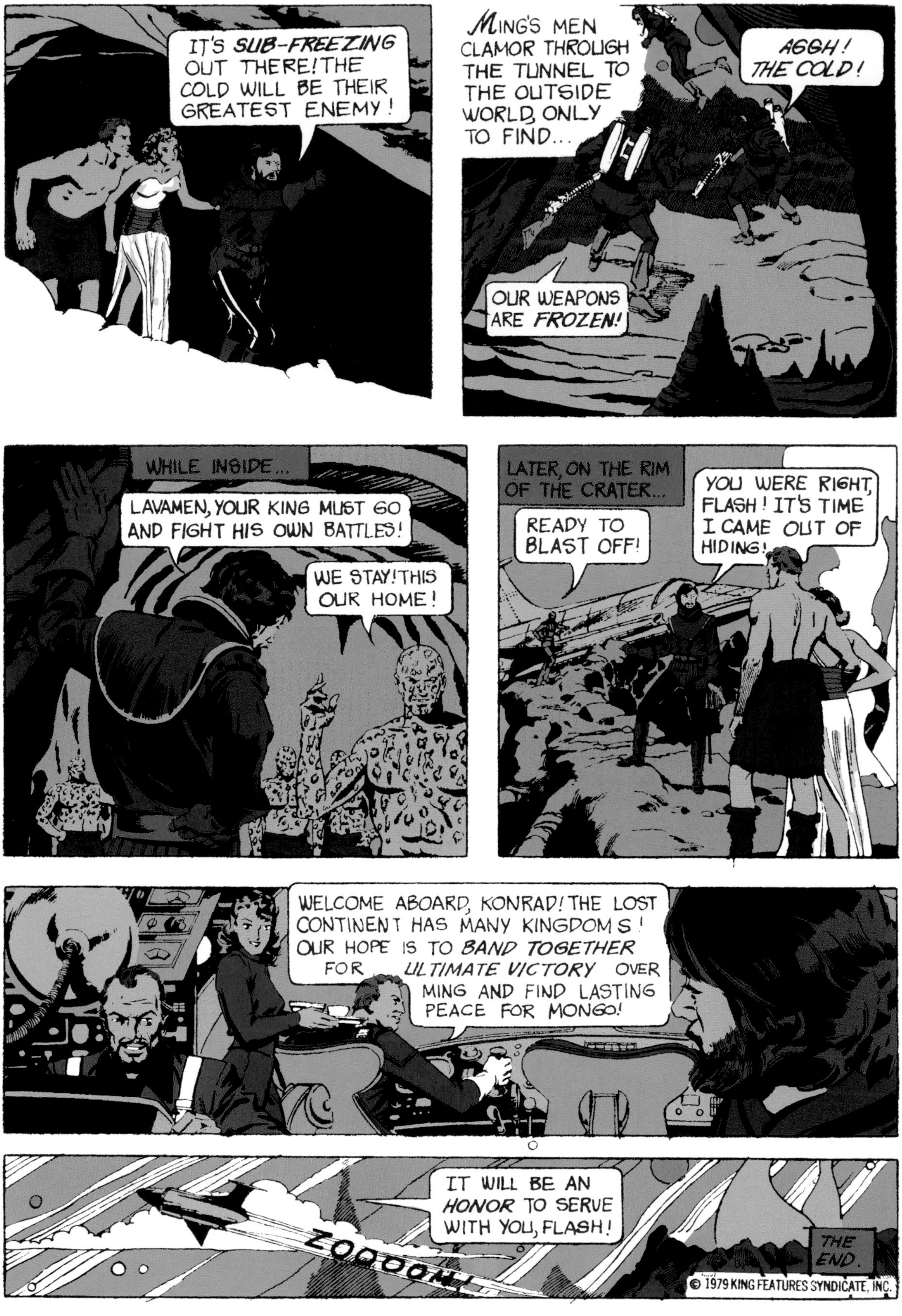

IT'S SUB-FREEZING OUT THERE! THE COLD WILL BE THEIR GREATEST ENEMY!
MING'S MEN CLAMOR THROUGH THE TUNNEL TO THE OUTSIDE WORLD, ONLY TO FIND...
AGGH! THE COLD!
OUR WEAPONS ARE FROZEN!
WHILE INSIDE...
LAVAMEN, YOUR KING MUST GO AND FIGHT HIS OWN BATTLES!
WE STAY! THIS OUR HOME!
LATER, ON THE RIM OF THE CRATER...
READY TO BLAST OFF!
YOU WERE RIGHT, FLASH! IT'S TIME I CAME OUT OF HIDING!
WELCOME ABOARD, KONRAD! THE LOST CONTINENT HAS MANY KINGDOMS! OUR HOPE IS TO BAND TOGETHER FOR ULTIMATE VICTORY OVER MING AND FIND LASTING PEACE FOR MONGO!
IT WILL BE AN HONOR TO SERVE WITH YOU, FLASH!
ZOOOOON!
THE END.
© 1979 KING FEATURES SYNDICATE, INC.

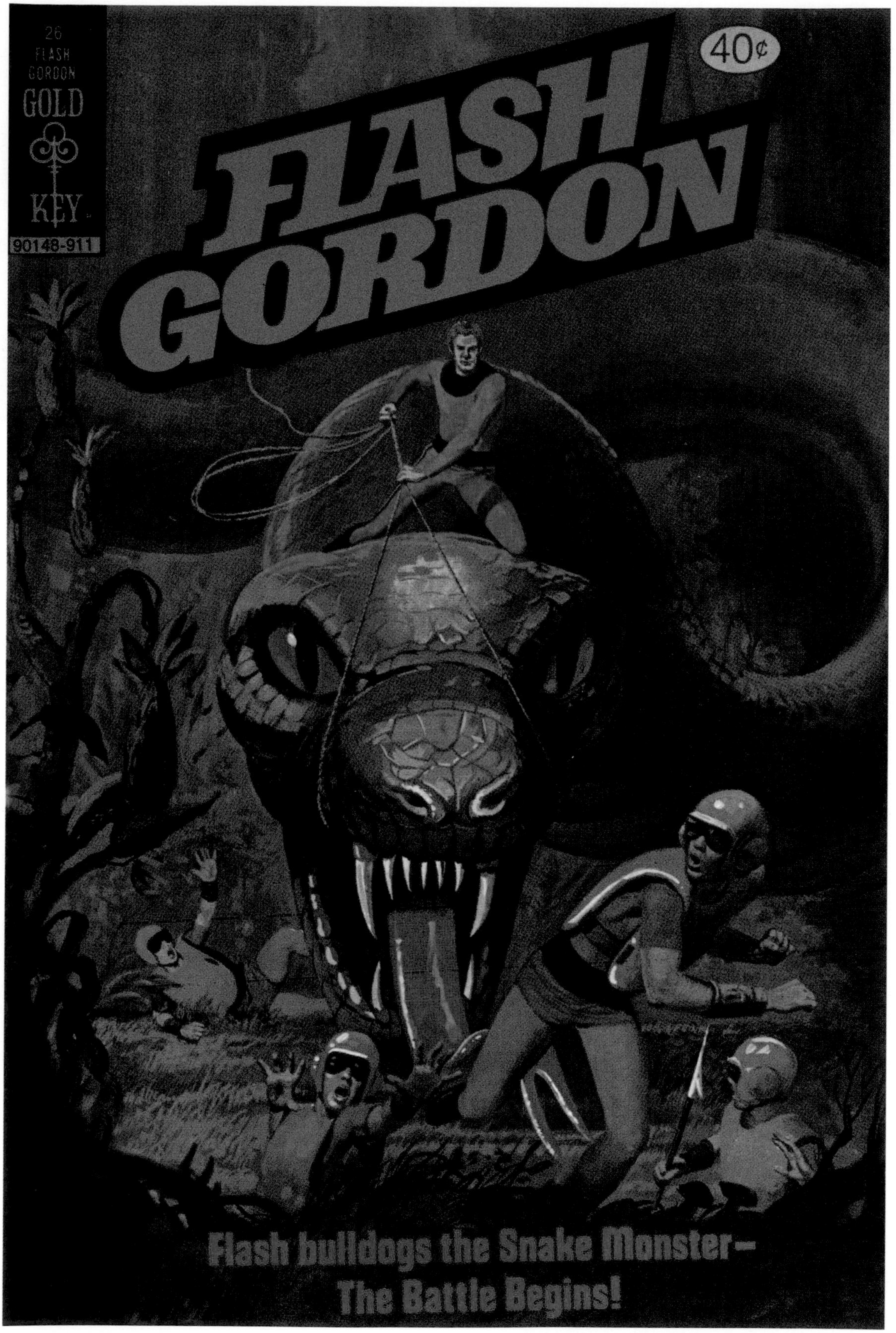
26
FLASH
GORDON
GOLD
KEY
90148-911
FLASH GORDON
40¢
Flash bulldogs the Snake Monster–
The Battle Begins!

Stranded in an alien world, Flash Gordon, Dale Arden and Dr. Hans Zarkov struggle against the evil emperor, Ming the Merciless, who seeks to enslave an entire planet.....

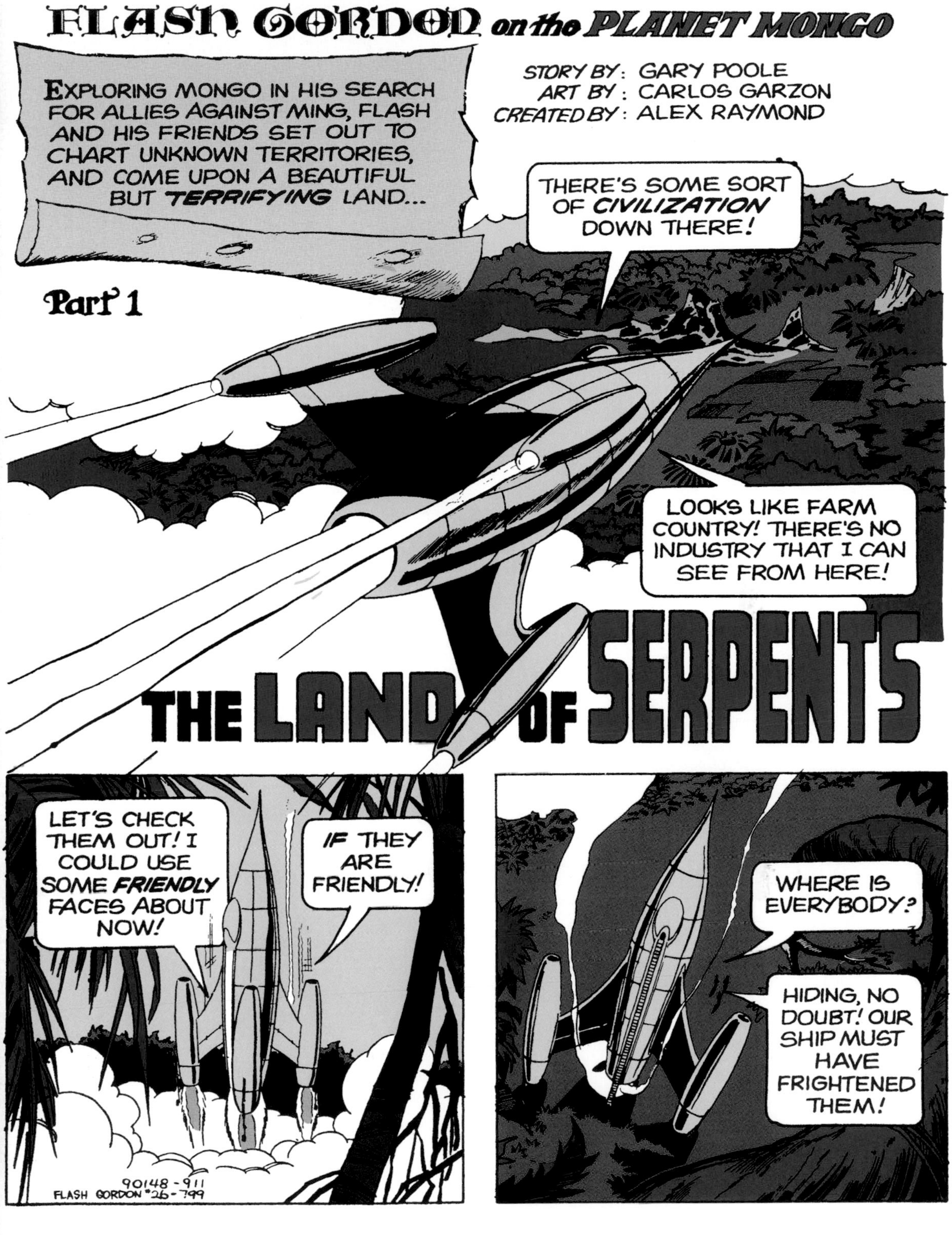
FLASH GORDON on the PLANET MONGO
EXPLORING MONGO IN HIS SEARCH FOR ALLIES AGAINST MING, FLASH AND HIS FRIENDS SET OUT TO CHART UNKNOWN TERRITORIES, AND COME UPON A BEAUTIFUL BUT TERRIFYING LAND...
STORY BY: GARY POOLE
ART BY: CARLOS GARZON
CREATED BY: ALEX RAYMOND
Part 1
THERE'S SOME SORT OF CIVILIZATION DOWN THERE!
LOOKS LIKE FARM COUNTRY! THERE'S NO INDUSTRY THAT I CAN SEE FROM HERE!
THE LAND OF SERPENTS
LET'S CHECK THEM OUT! I COULD USE SOME FRIENDLY FACES ABOUT NOW!
IF THEY ARE FRIENDLY!
90148-911
FLASH GORDON #26-799
WHERE IS EVERYBODY?
HIDING, NO DOUBT! OUR SHIP MUST HAVE FRIGHTENED THEM!

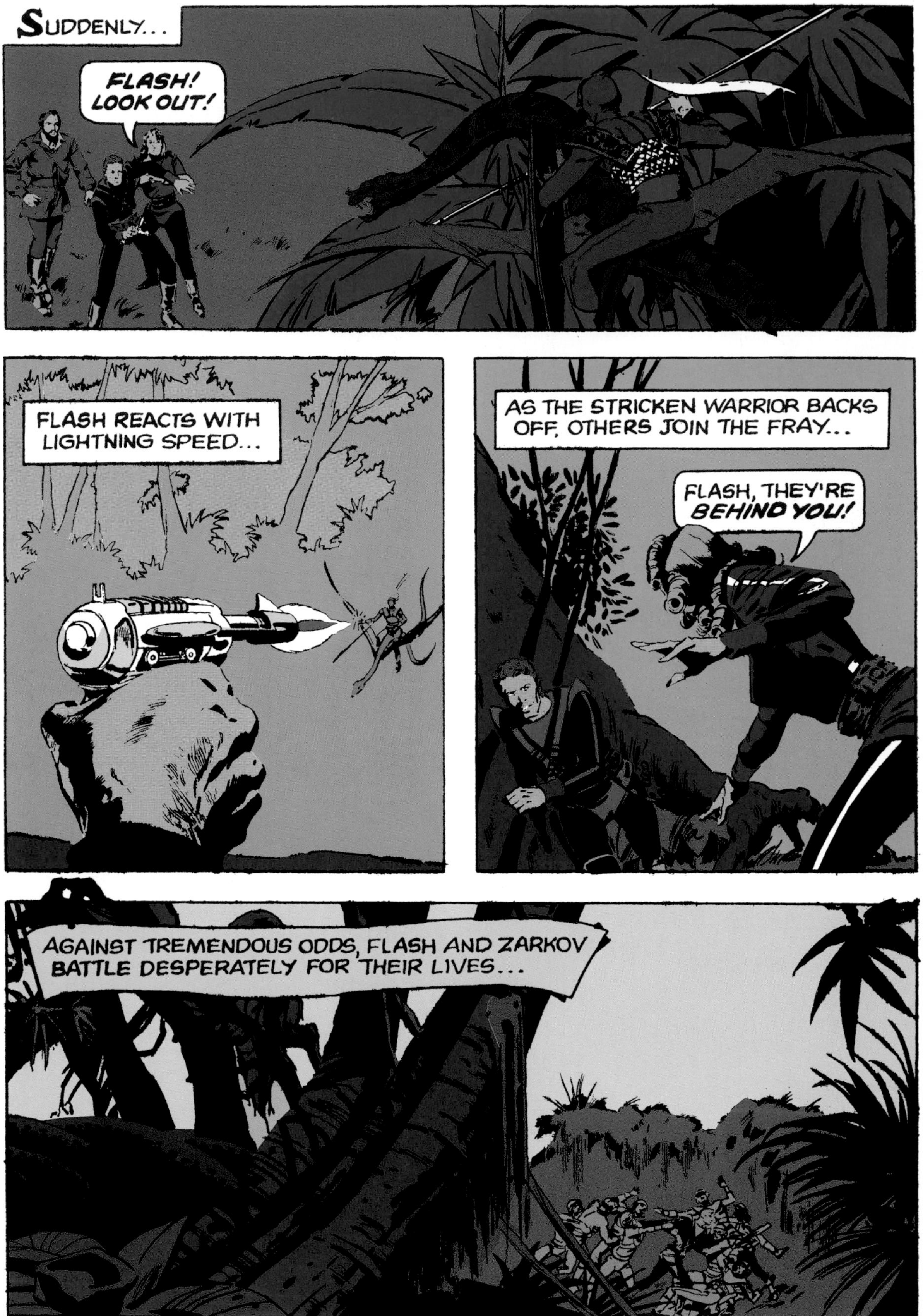
SUDDENLY...
FLASH! LOOK OUT!
FLASH REACTS WITH LIGHTNING SPEED...
AS THE STRICKEN WARRIOR BACKS OFF, OTHERS JOIN THE FRAY...
FLASH, THEY'RE *BEHIND YOU!*
AGAINST TREMENDOUS ODDS, FLASH AND ZARKOV BATTLE DESPERATELY FOR THEIR LIVES...

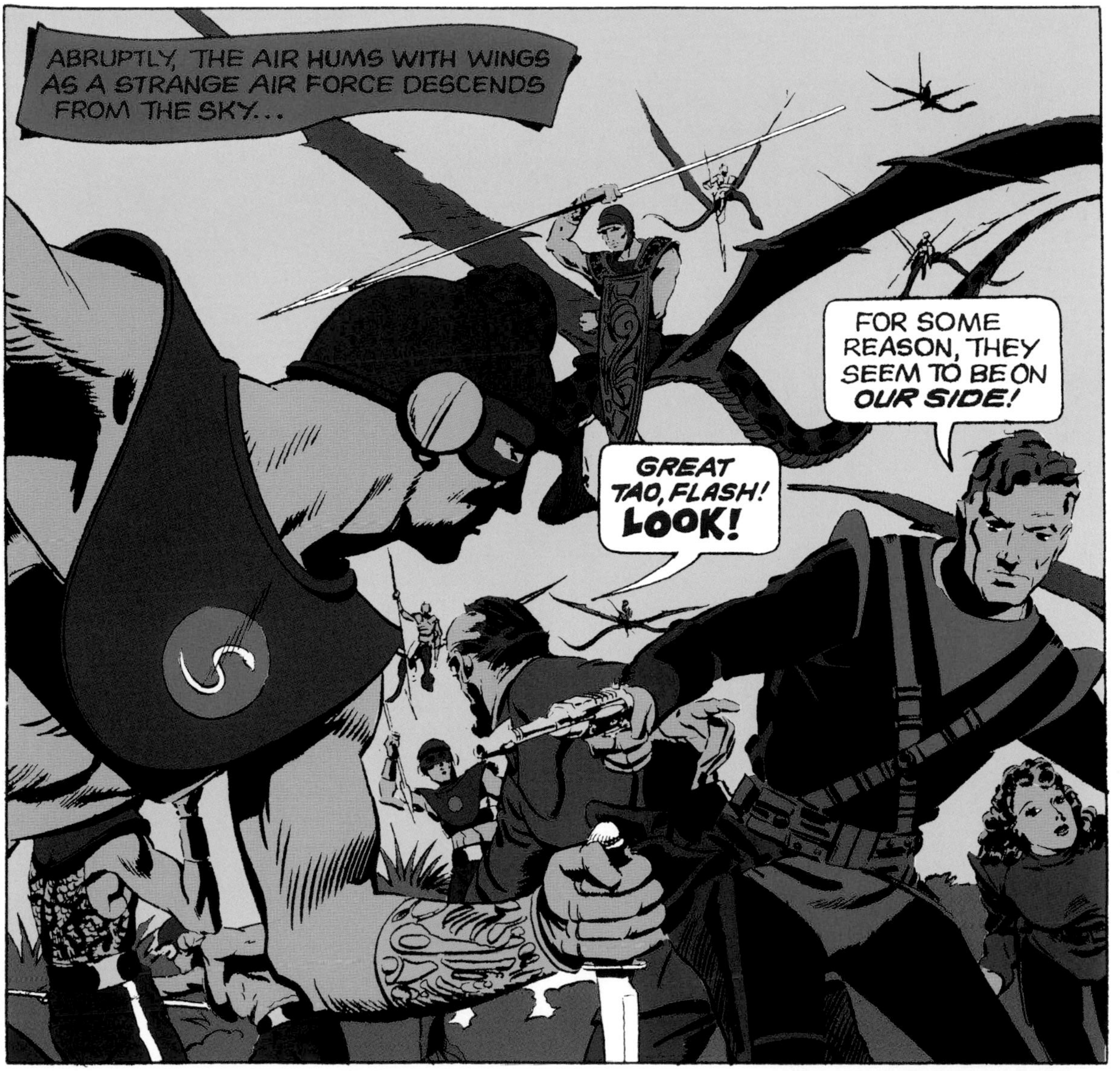
ABRUPTLY, THE AIR HUMS WITH WINGS AS A STRANGE AIR FORCE DESCENDS FROM THE SKY...
FOR SOME REASON, THEY SEEM TO BE ON OUR SIDE!
GREAT TAO, FLASH! LOOK!

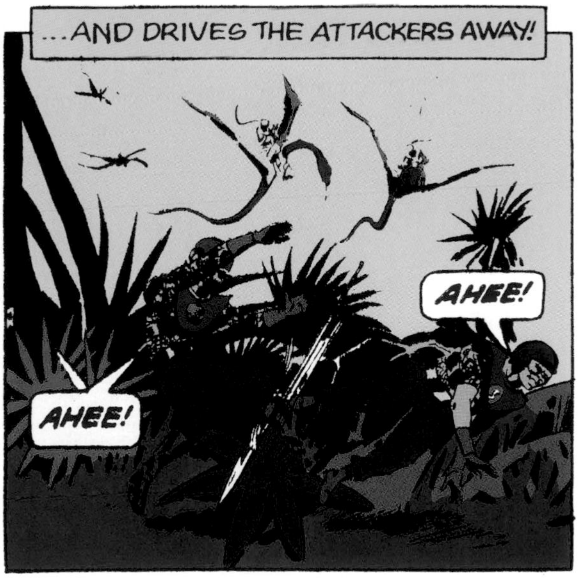
...AND DRIVES THE ATTACKERS AWAY!
AHEE!
AHEE!

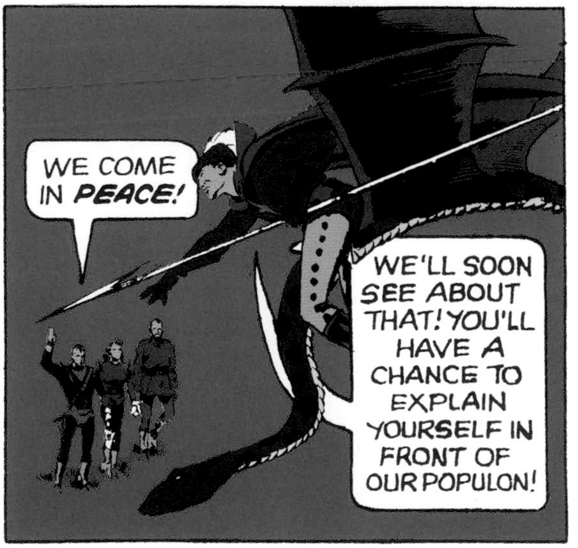
WE COME IN PEACE!
WE'LL SOON SEE ABOUT THAT! YOU'LL HAVE A CHANCE TO EXPLAIN YOURSELF IN FRONT OF OUR POPULON!

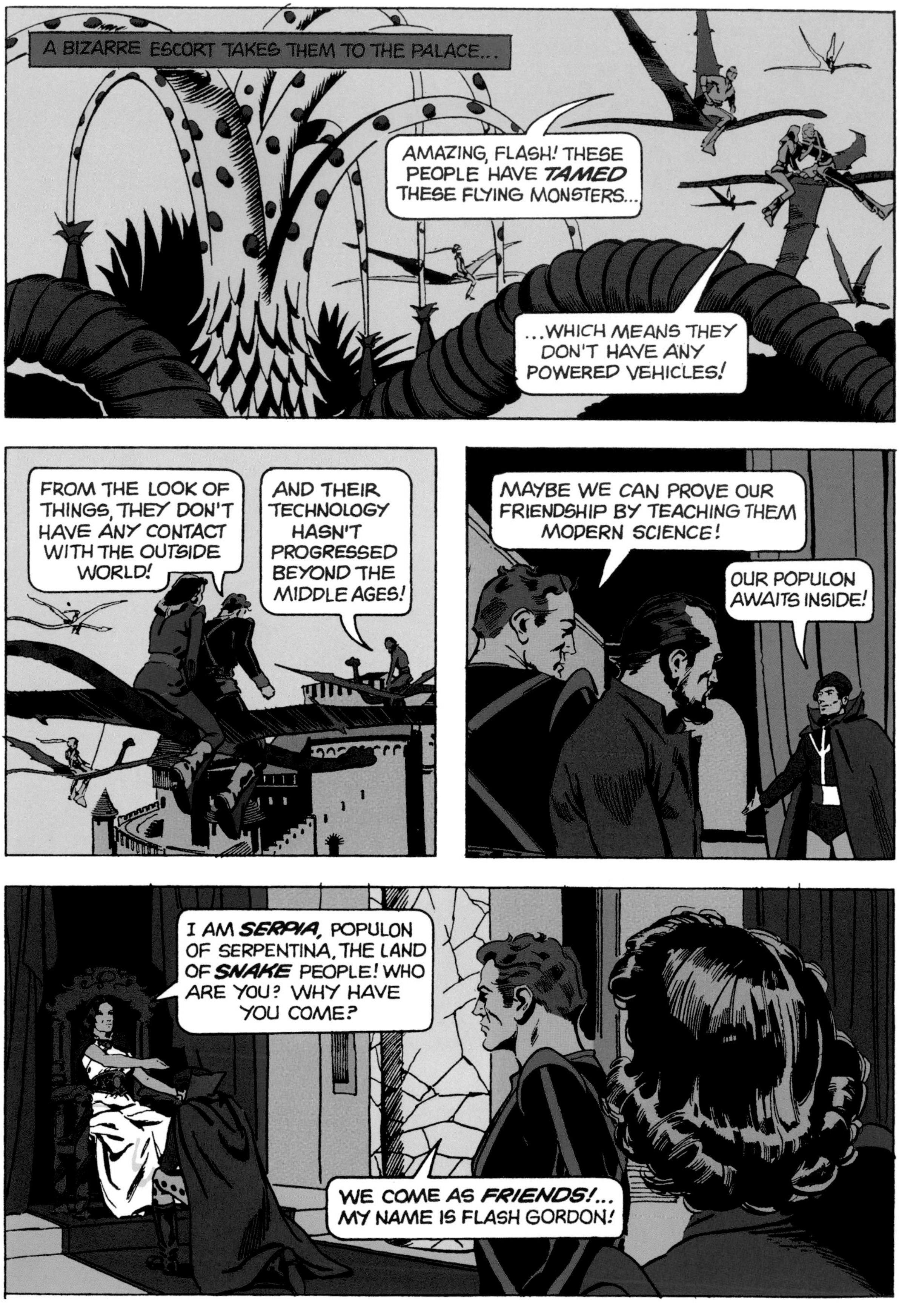
A BIZARRE ESCORT TAKES THEM TO THE PALACE...
AMAZING, FLASH! THESE PEOPLE HAVE TAMED THESE FLYING MONSTERS...
...WHICH MEANS THEY DON'T HAVE ANY POWERED VEHICLES!
FROM THE LOOK OF THINGS, THEY DON'T HAVE ANY CONTACT WITH THE OUTSIDE WORLD!
AND THEIR TECHNOLOGY HASN'T PROGRESSED BEYOND THE MIDDLE AGES!
MAYBE WE CAN PROVE OUR FRIENDSHIP BY TEACHING THEM MODERN SCIENCE!
OUR POPULON AWAITS INSIDE!
I AM SERPIA, POPULON OF SERPENTINA, THE LAND OF SNAKE PEOPLE! WHO ARE YOU? WHY HAVE YOU COME?
WE COME AS FRIENDS!... MY NAME IS FLASH GORDON!

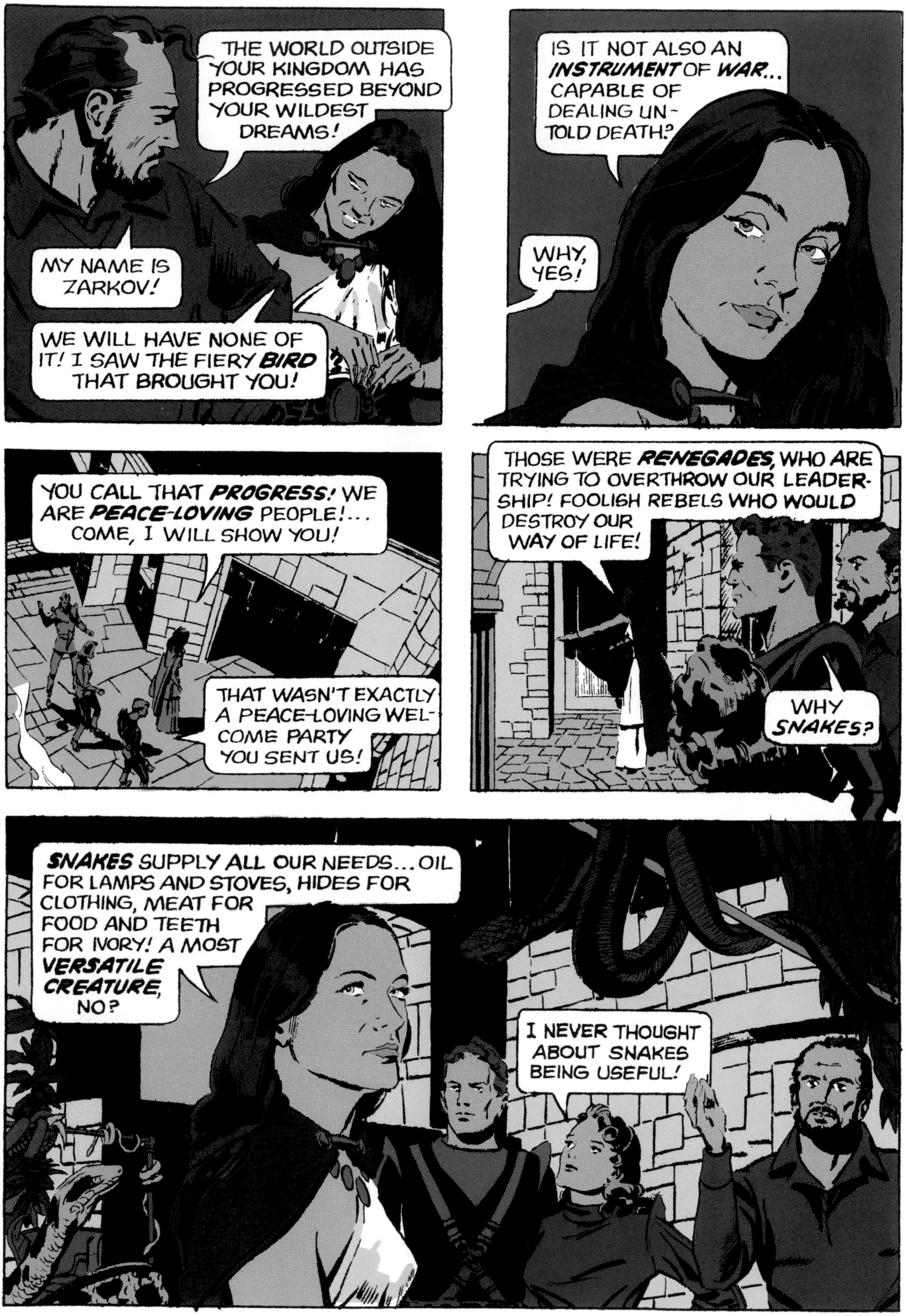
THE WORLD OUTSIDE YOUR KINGDOM HAS PROGRESSED BEYOND YOUR WILDEST DREAMS!
MY NAME IS ZARKOV!
WE WILL HAVE NONE OF IT! I SAW THE FIERY BIRD THAT BROUGHT YOU!
IS IT NOT ALSO AN INSTRUMENT OF WAR... CAPABLE OF DEALING UN-TOLD DEATH?
WHY, YES!
YOU CALL THAT PROGRESS! WE ARE PEACE-LOVING PEOPLE!... COME, I WILL SHOW YOU!
THAT WASN'T EXACTLY A PEACE-LOVING WEL-COME PARTY YOU SENT US!
THOSE WERE RENEGADES, WHO ARE TRYING TO OVERTHROW OUR LEADER-SHIP! FOOLISH REBELS WHO WOULD DESTROY OUR WAY OF LIFE!
WHY SNAKES?
SNAKES SUPPLY ALL OUR NEEDS... OIL FOR LAMPS AND STOVES, HIDES FOR CLOTHING, MEAT FOR FOOD AND TEETH FOR IVORY! A MOST VERSATILE CREATURE, NO?
I NEVER THOUGHT ABOUT SNAKES BEING USEFUL!

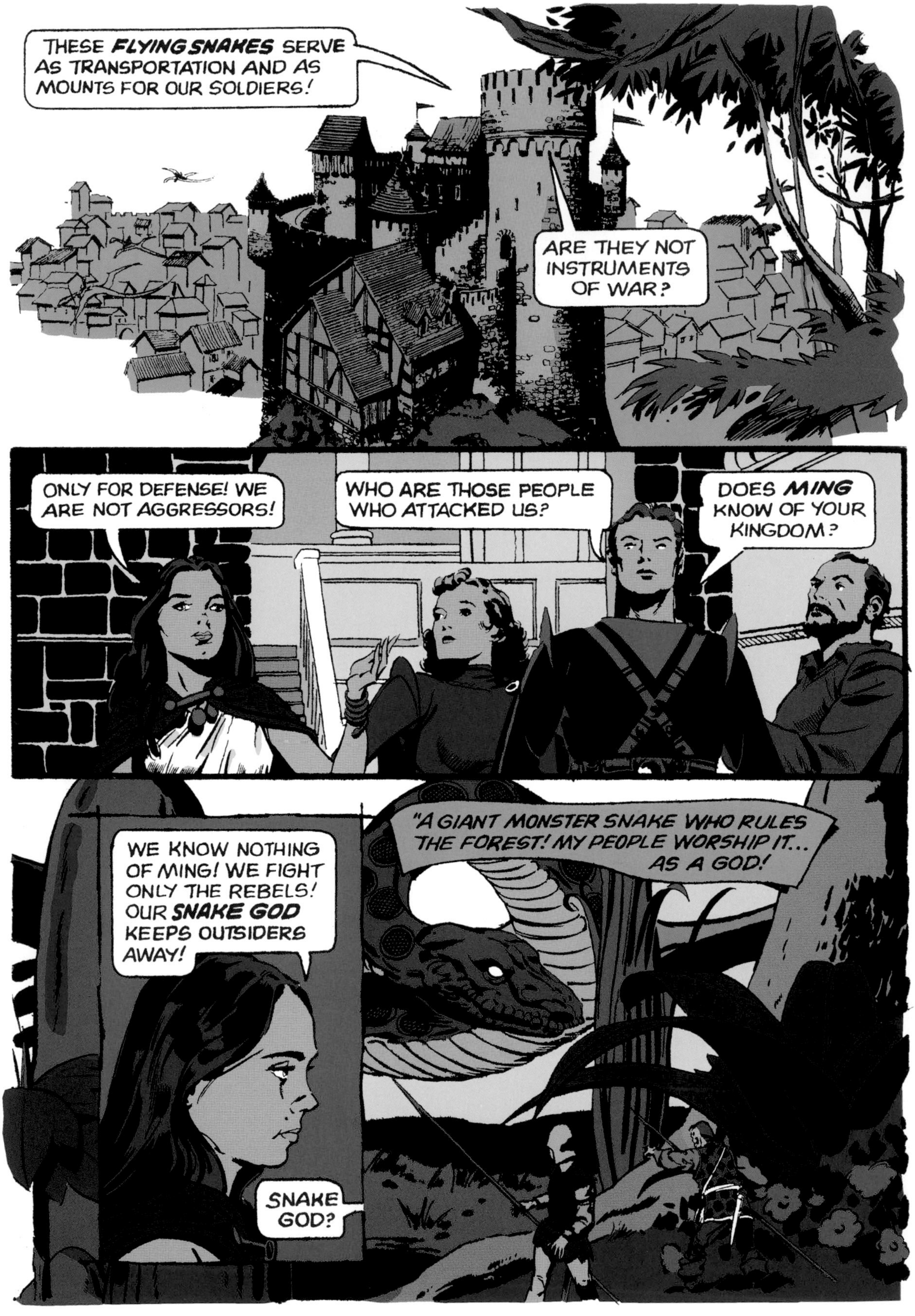
THESE FLYING SNAKES SERVE AS TRANSPORTATION AND AS MOUNTS FOR OUR SOLDIERS!
ARE THEY NOT INSTRUMENTS OF WAR?
ONLY FOR DEFENSE! WE ARE NOT AGGRESSORS!
WHO ARE THOSE PEOPLE WHO ATTACKED US?
DOES MING KNOW OF YOUR KINGDOM?
WE KNOW NOTHING OF MING! WE FIGHT ONLY THE REBELS! OUR SNAKE GOD KEEPS OUTSIDERS AWAY!
SNAKE GOD?
"A GIANT MONSTER SNAKE WHO RULES THE FOREST! MY PEOPLE WORSHIP IT... AS A GOD!

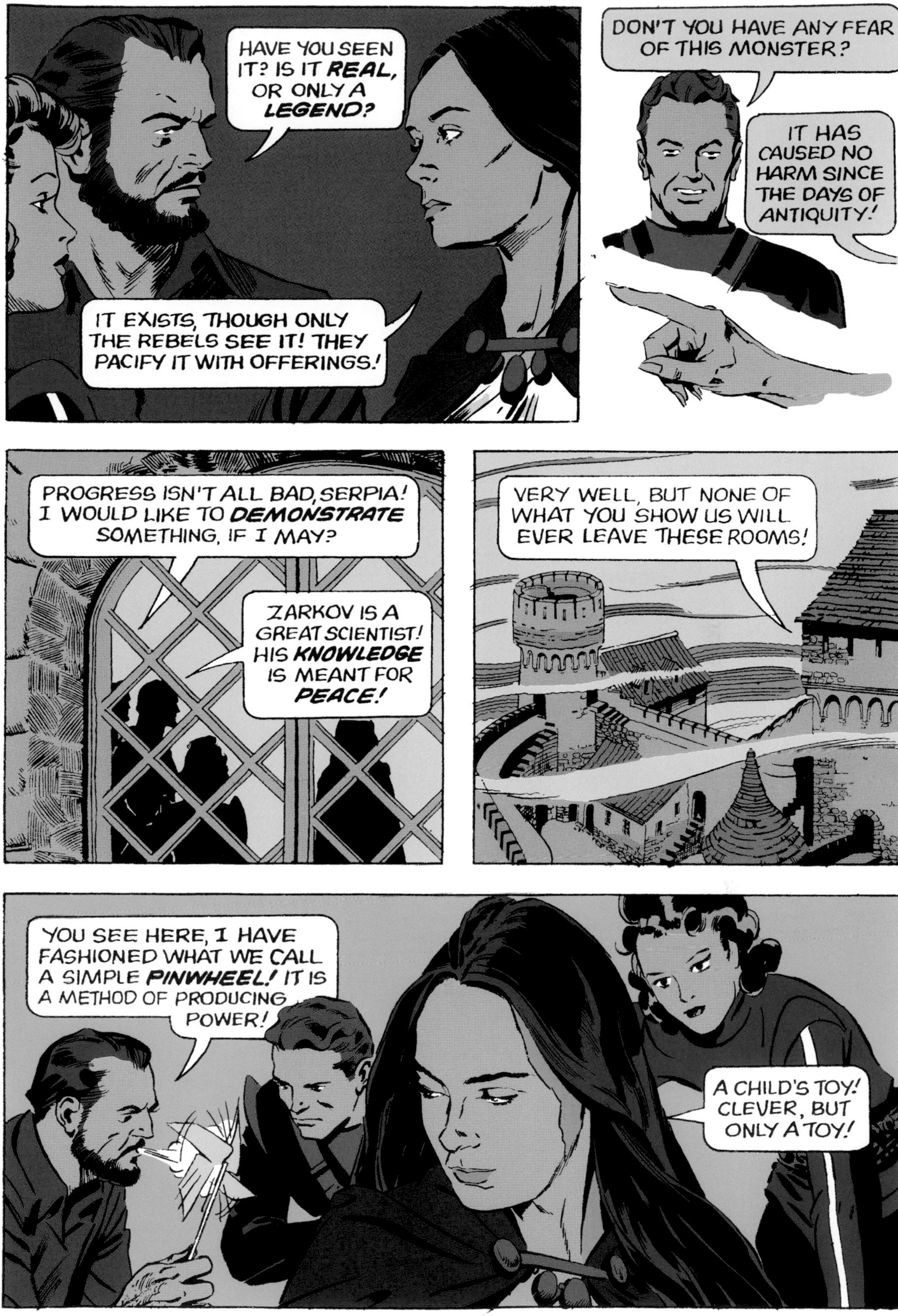
HAVE YOU SEEN IT? IS IT REAL, OR ONLY A LEGEND?
IT EXISTS, THOUGH ONLY THE REBELS SEE IT! THEY PACIFY IT WITH OFFERINGS!
DON'T YOU HAVE ANY FEAR OF THIS MONSTER?
IT HAS CAUSED NO HARM SINCE THE DAYS OF ANTIQUITY!
PROGRESS ISN'T ALL BAD, SERPIA! I WOULD LIKE TO DEMONSTRATE SOMETHING, IF I MAY?
ZARKOV IS A GREAT SCIENTIST! HIS KNOWLEDGE IS MEANT FOR PEACE!
VERY WELL, BUT NONE OF WHAT YOU SHOW US WILL EVER LEAVE THESE ROOMS!
YOU SEE HERE, I HAVE FASHIONED WHAT WE CALL A SIMPLE PINWHEEL! IT IS A METHOD OF PRODUCING POWER!
A CHILD'S TOY! CLEVER, BUT ONLY A TOY!

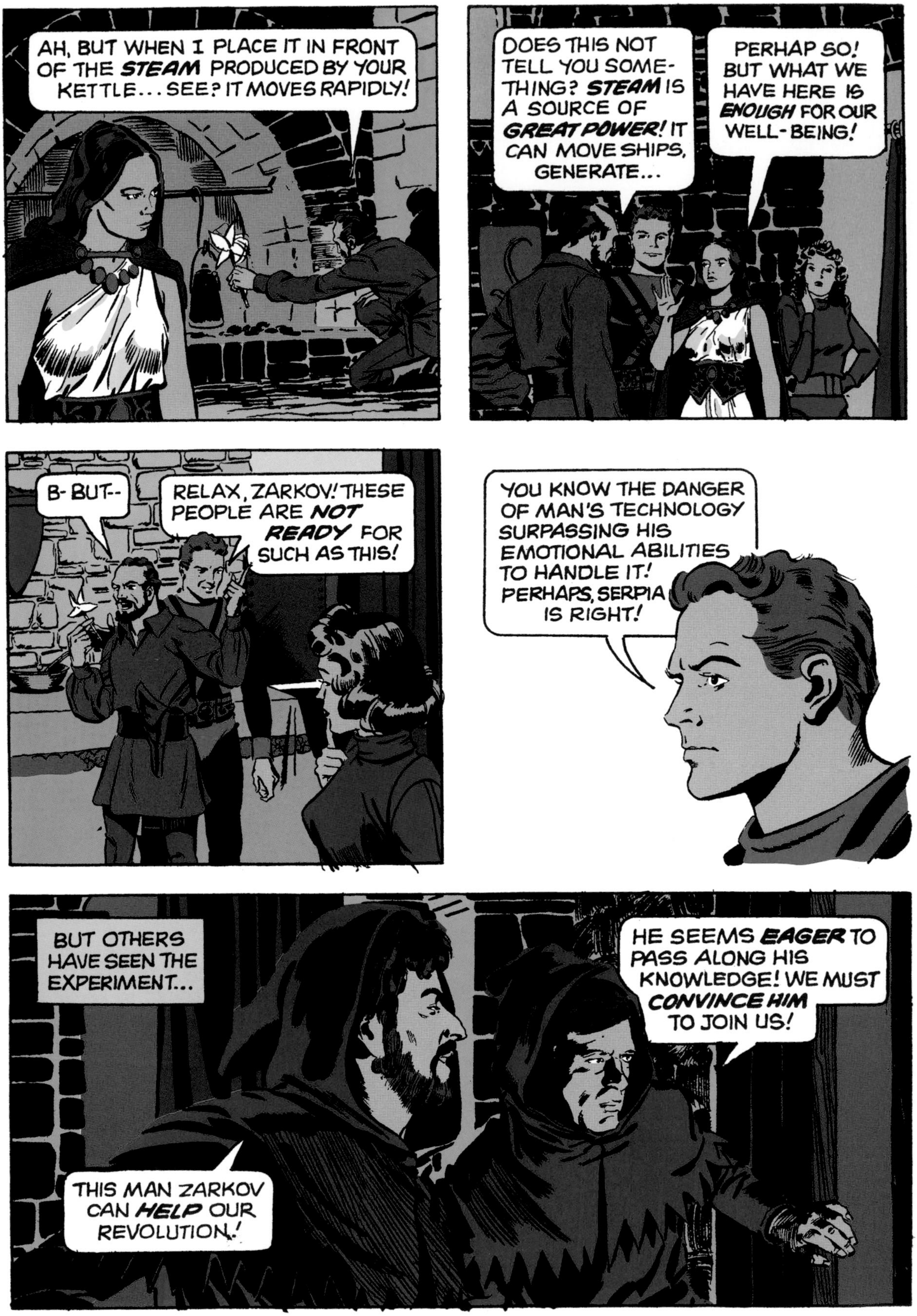
AH, BUT WHEN I PLACE IT IN FRONT OF THE STEAM PRODUCED BY YOUR KETTLE... SEE? IT MOVES RAPIDLY!
DOES THIS NOT TELL YOU SOME-THING? STEAM IS A SOURCE OF GREAT POWER! IT CAN MOVE SHIPS, GENERATE...
PERHAP SO! BUT WHAT WE HAVE HERE IS ENOUGH FOR OUR WELL-BEING!
B-BUT--
RELAX, ZARKOV! THESE PEOPLE ARE NOT READY FOR SUCH AS THIS!
YOU KNOW THE DANGER OF MAN'S TECHNOLOGY SURPASSING HIS EMOTIONAL ABILITIES TO HANDLE IT! PERHAPS, SERPIA IS RIGHT!
BUT OTHERS HAVE SEEN THE EXPERIMENT...
HE SEEMS EAGER TO PASS ALONG HIS KNOWLEDGE! WE MUST CONVINCE HIM TO JOIN US!
THIS MAN ZARKOV CAN HELP OUR REVOLUTION!

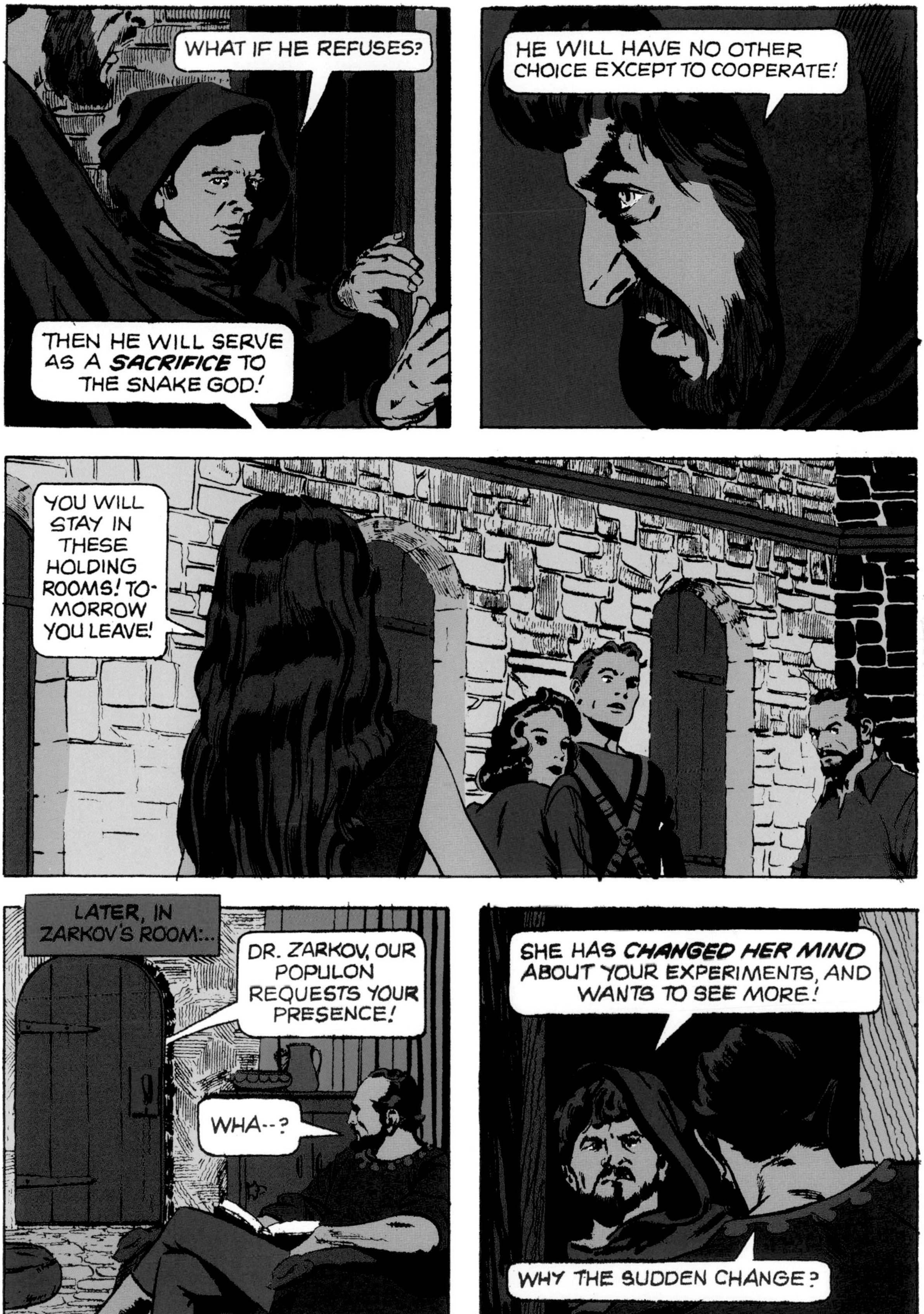
WHAT IF HE REFUSES?
THEN HE WILL SERVE AS A SACRIFICE TO THE SNAKE GOD!
HE WILL HAVE NO OTHER CHOICE EXCEPT TO COOPERATE!
YOU WILL STAY IN THESE HOLDING ROOMS! TO-MORROW YOU LEAVE!
LATER, IN ZARKOV'S ROOM:..
DR. ZARKOV, OUR POPULON REQUESTS YOUR PRESENCE!
WHA--?
SHE HAS CHANGED HER MIND ABOUT YOUR EXPERIMENTS, AND WANTS TO SEE MORE!
WHY THE SUDDEN CHANGE?

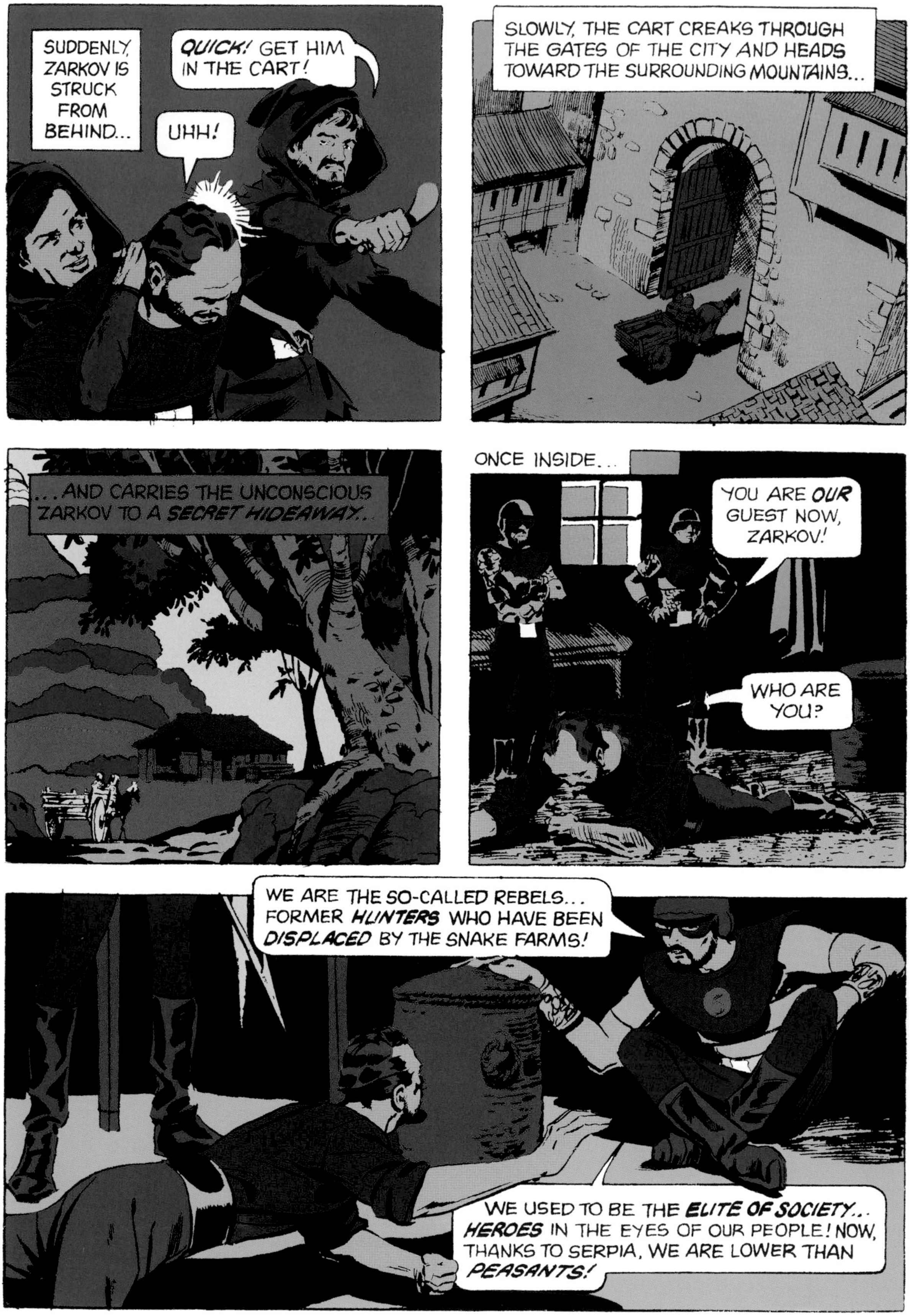
SUDDENLY, ZARKOV IS STRUCK FROM BEHIND...
QUICK! GET HIM IN THE CART!
UHH!
SLOWLY, THE CART CREAKS THROUGH THE GATES OF THE CITY AND HEADS TOWARD THE SURROUNDING MOUNTAINS...
...AND CARRIES THE UNCONSCIOUS ZARKOV TO A SECRET HIDEAWAY...
ONCE INSIDE...
YOU ARE OUR GUEST NOW, ZARKOV!
WHO ARE YOU?
WE ARE THE SO-CALLED REBELS... FORMER HUNTERS WHO HAVE BEEN DISPLACED BY THE SNAKE FARMS!
WE USED TO BE THE ELITE OF SOCIETY... HEROES IN THE EYES OF OUR PEOPLE! NOW, THANKS TO SERPIA, WE ARE LOWER THAN PEASANTS!

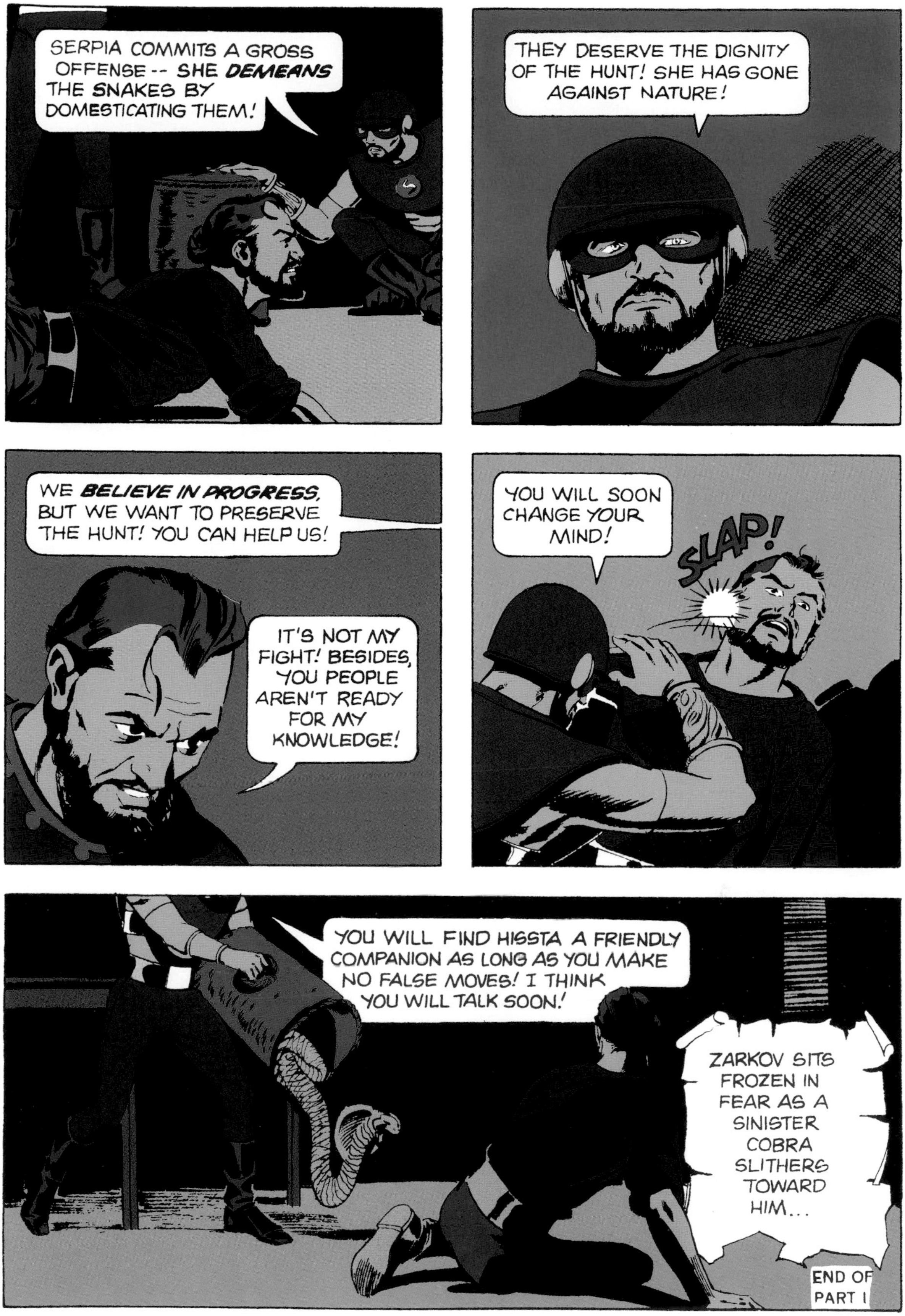
SERPIA COMMITS A GROSS OFFENSE -- SHE DEMEANS THE SNAKES BY DOMESTICATING THEM!
THEY DESERVE THE DIGNITY OF THE HUNT! SHE HAS GONE AGAINST NATURE!
WE BELIEVE IN PROGRESS, BUT WE WANT TO PRESERVE THE HUNT! YOU CAN HELP US!
IT'S NOT MY FIGHT! BESIDES, YOU PEOPLE AREN'T READY FOR MY KNOWLEDGE!
YOU WILL SOON CHANGE YOUR MIND!
SLAP!
YOU WILL FIND HISSTA A FRIENDLY COMPANION AS LONG AS YOU MAKE NO FALSE MOVES! I THINK YOU WILL TALK SOON!
ZARKOV SITS FROZEN IN FEAR AS A SINISTER COBRA SLITHERS TOWARD HIM...
END OF PART I

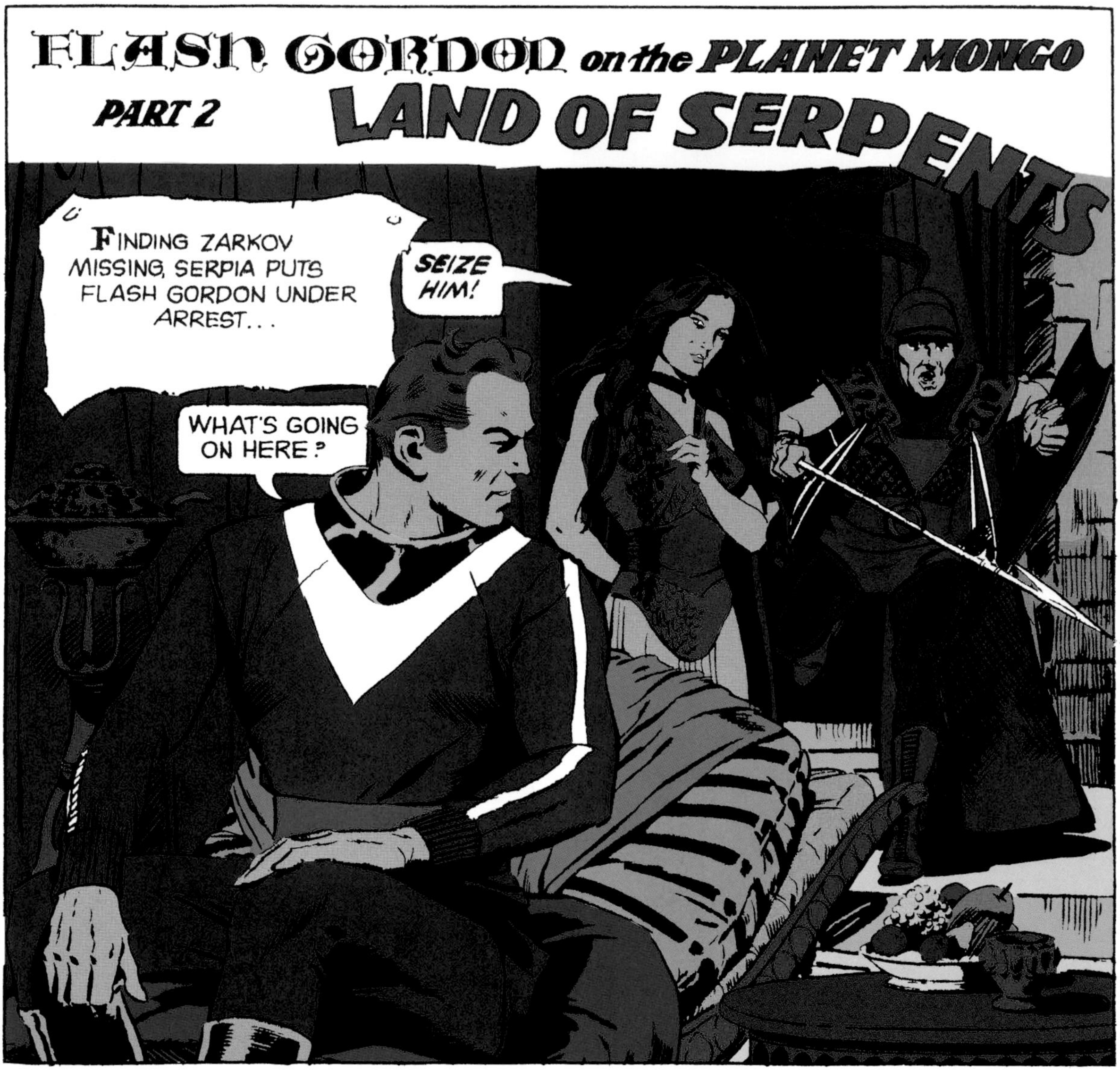
FLASH GORDON on the PLANET MONGO
PART 2
LAND OF SERPENTS
FINDING ZARKOV MISSING, SERPIA PUTS FLASH GORDON UNDER ARREST...
SEIZE HIM!
WHAT'S GOING ON HERE?

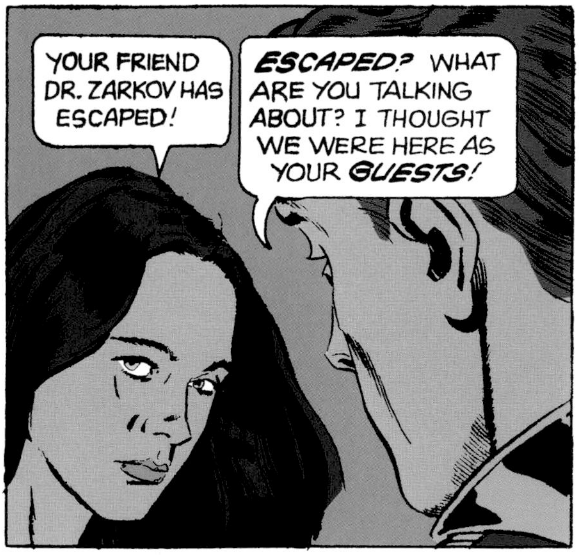
YOUR FRIEND DR. ZARKOV HAS ESCAPED!
ESCAPED? WHAT ARE YOU TALKING ABOUT? I THOUGHT WE WERE HERE AS YOUR GUESTS!

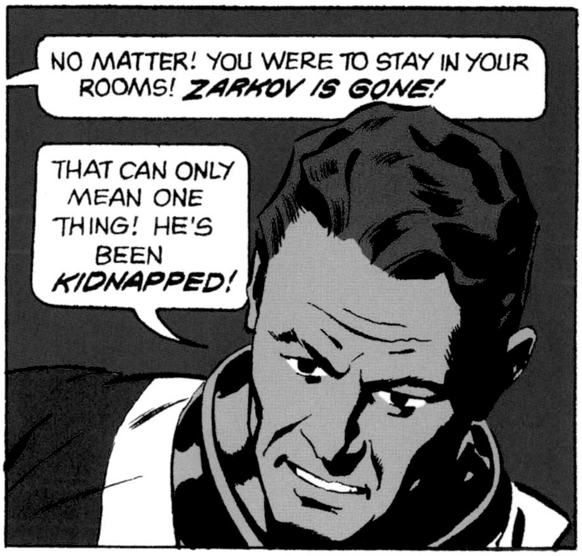
NO MATTER! YOU WERE TO STAY IN YOUR ROOMS! ZARKOV IS GONE!
THAT CAN ONLY MEAN ONE THING! HE'S BEEN KIDNAPPED!

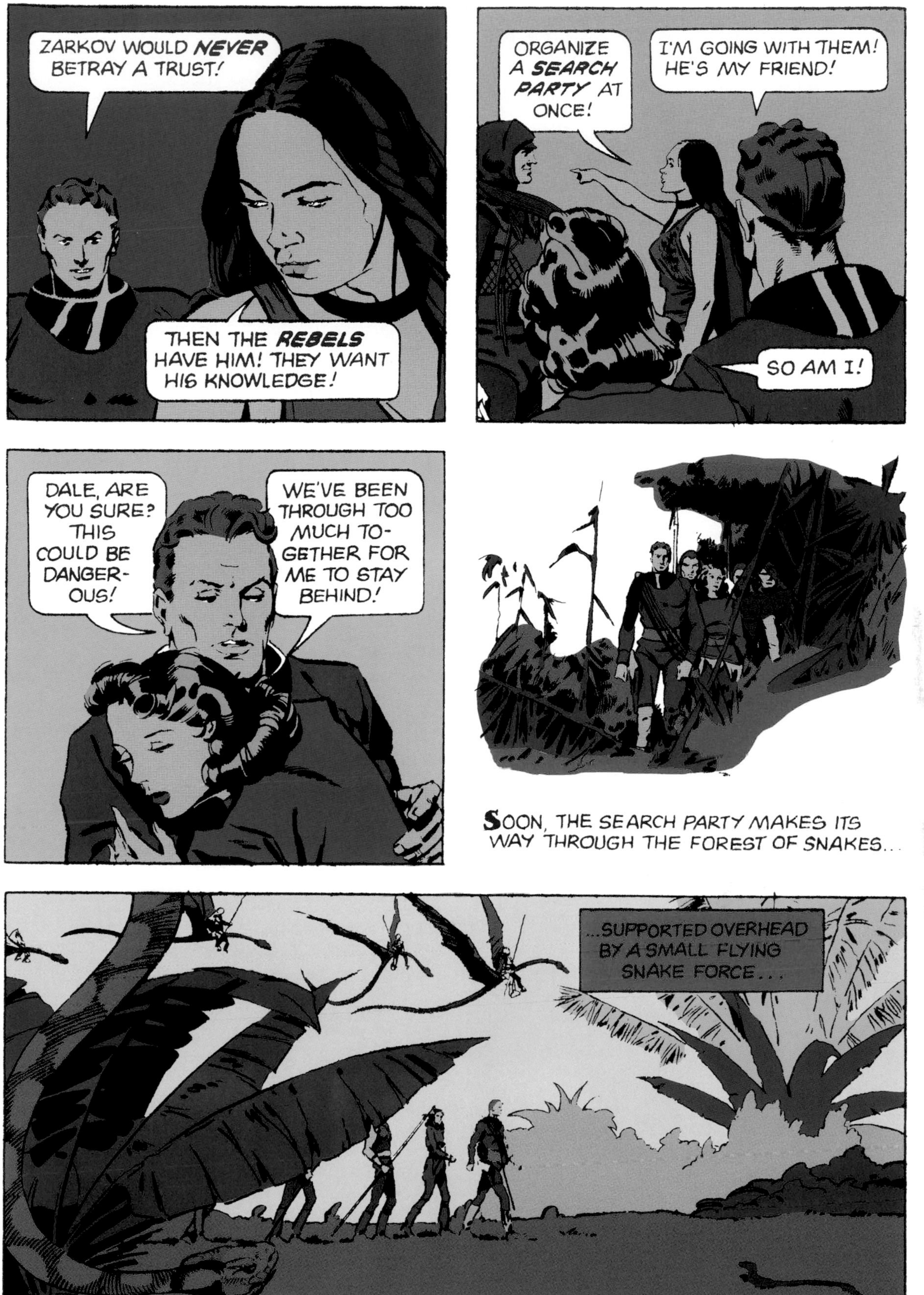
ZARKOV WOULD NEVER BETRAY A TRUST!
THEN THE REBELS HAVE HIM! THEY WANT HIS KNOWLEDGE!
ORGANIZE A SEARCH PARTY AT ONCE!
I'M GOING WITH THEM! HE'S MY FRIEND!
SO AM I!
DALE, ARE YOU SURE? THIS COULD BE DANGER-OUS!
WE'VE BEEN THROUGH TOO MUCH TO-GETHER FOR ME TO STAY BEHIND!
SOON, THE SEARCH PARTY MAKES ITS WAY THROUGH THE FOREST OF SNAKES...
...SUPPORTED OVERHEAD BY A SMALL FLYING SNAKE FORCE...

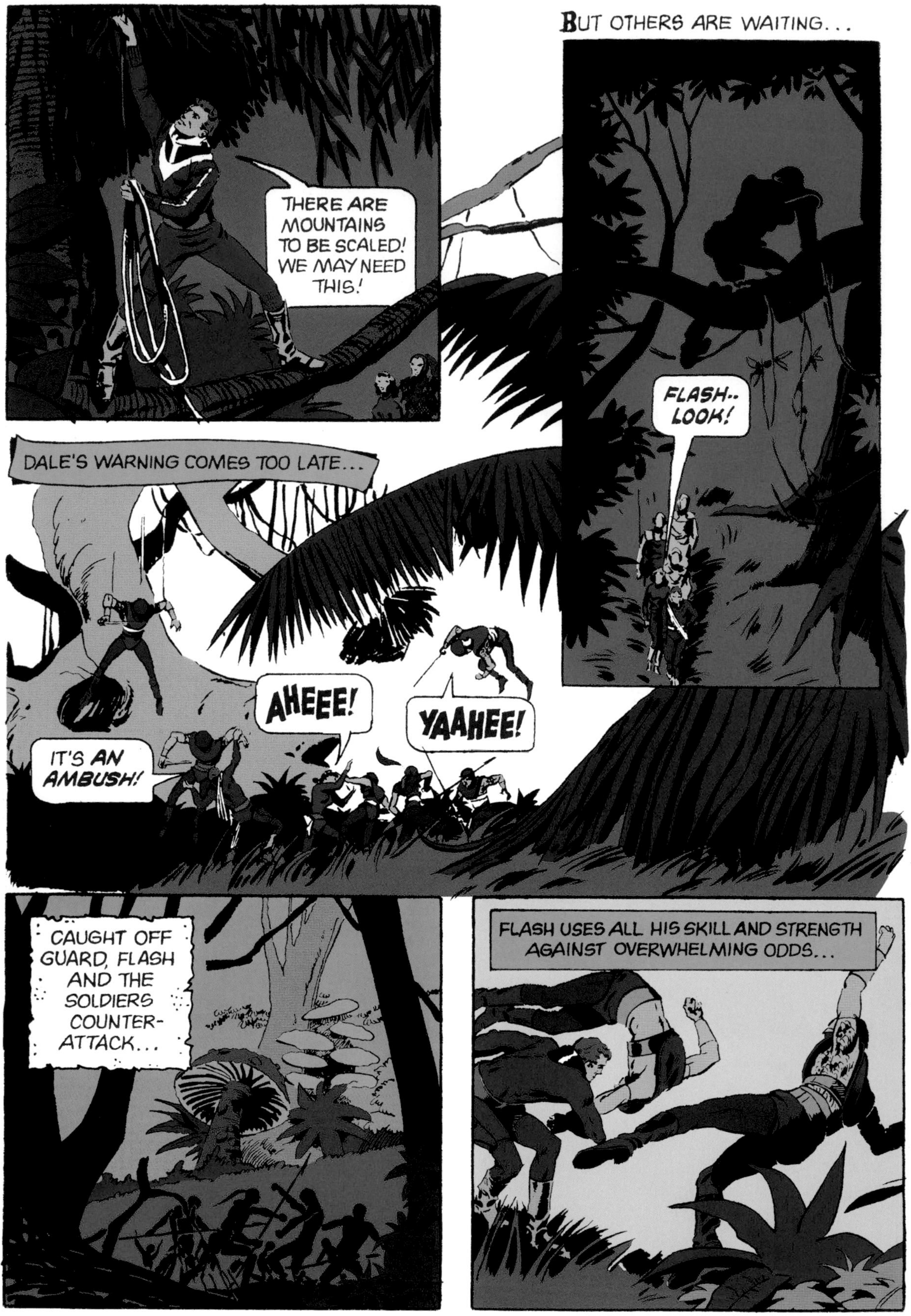
THERE ARE MOUNTAINS TO BE SCALED! WE MAY NEED THIS!
BUT OTHERS ARE WAITING...
FLASH.. LOOK!
DALE'S WARNING COMES TOO LATE...
IT'S AN AMBUSH!
AHEEE!
YAAHEE!
CAUGHT OFF GUARD, FLASH AND THE SOLDIERS COUNTER-ATTACK...
FLASH USES ALL HIS SKILL AND STRENGTH AGAINST OVERWHELMING ODDS...

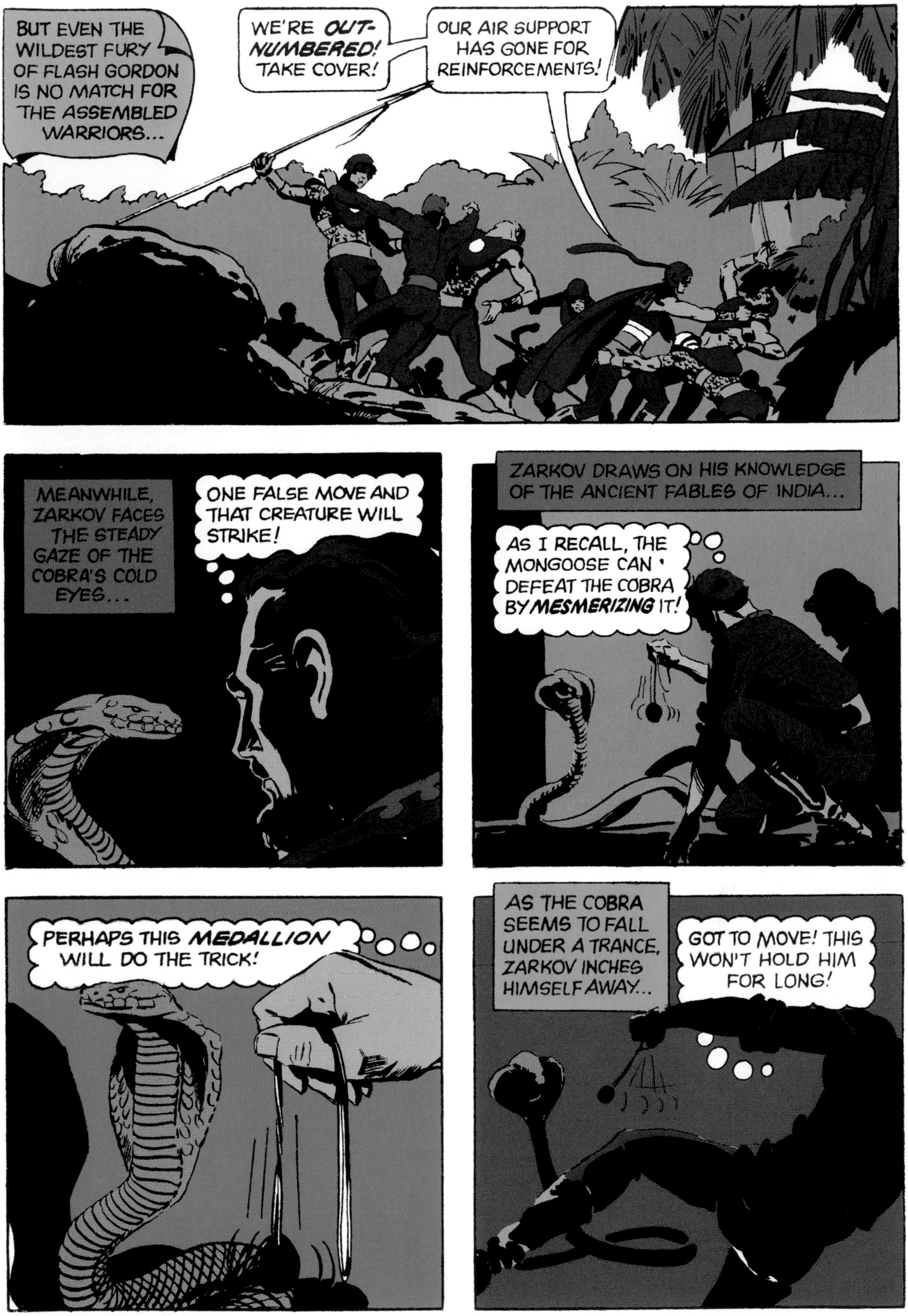
BUT EVEN THE WILDEST FURY OF FLASH GORDON IS NO MATCH FOR THE ASSEMBLED WARRIORS...
WE'RE OUT-NUMBERED! TAKE COVER!
OUR AIR SUPPORT HAS GONE FOR REINFORCEMENTS!
MEANWHILE, ZARKOV FACES THE STEADY GAZE OF THE COBRA'S COLD EYES...
ONE FALSE MOVE AND THAT CREATURE WILL STRIKE!
ZARKOV DRAWS ON HIS KNOWLEDGE OF THE ANCIENT FABLES OF INDIA...
AS I RECALL, THE MONGOOSE CAN DEFEAT THE COBRA BY MESMERIZING IT!
PERHAPS THIS MEDALLION WILL DO THE TRICK!
AS THE COBRA SEEMS TO FALL UNDER A TRANCE, ZARKOV INCHES HIMSELF AWAY...
GOT TO MOVE! THIS WON'T HOLD HIM FOR LONG!

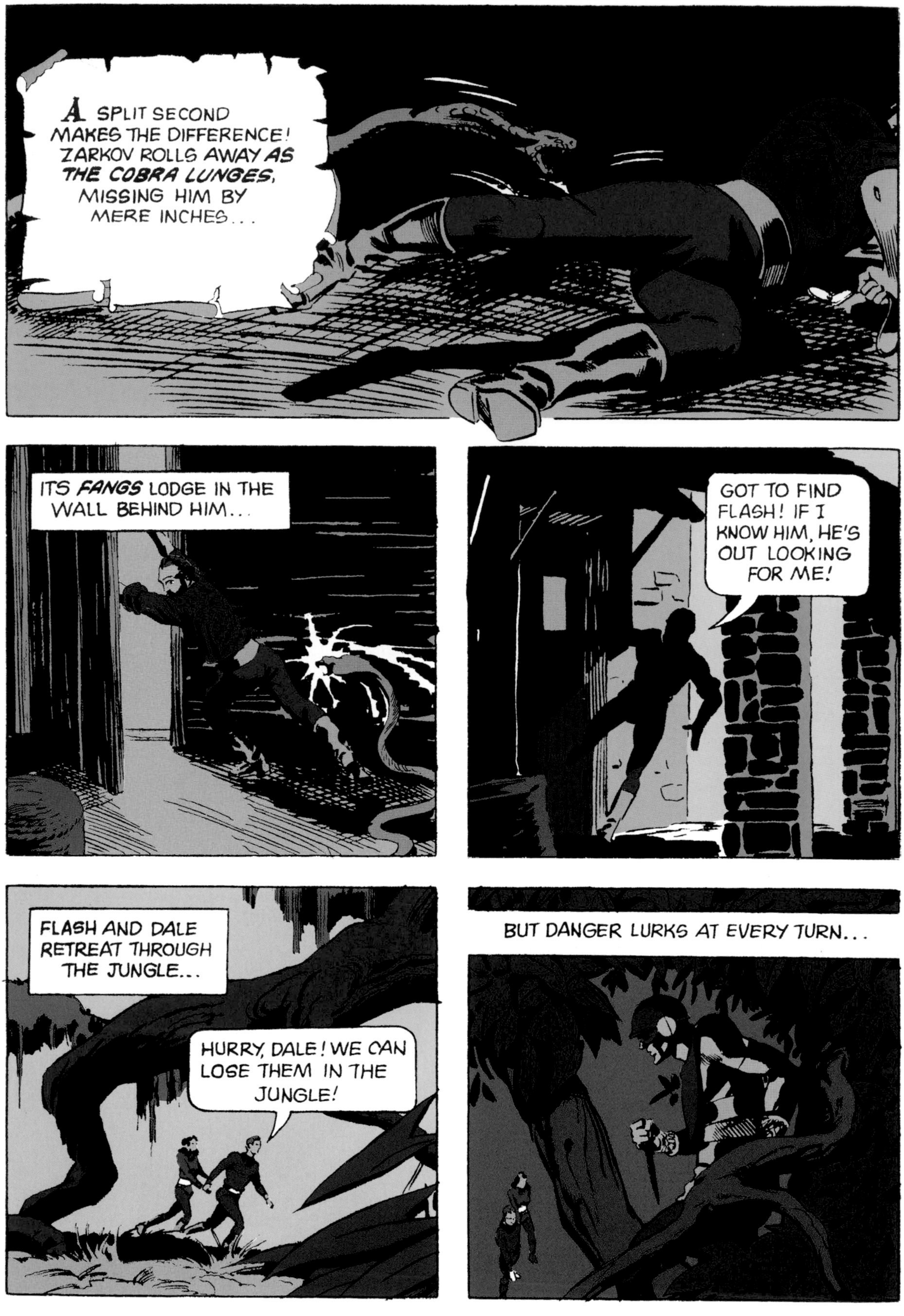
A SPLIT SECOND MAKES THE DIFFERENCE! ZARKOV ROLLS AWAY AS THE COBRA LUNGES, MISSING HIM BY MERE INCHES...
ITS FANGS LODGE IN THE WALL BEHIND HIM...
GOT TO FIND FLASH! IF I KNOW HIM, HE'S OUT LOOKING FOR ME!
FLASH AND DALE RETREAT THROUGH THE JUNGLE...
HURRY, DALE! WE CAN LOSE THEM IN THE JUNGLE!
BUT DANGER LURKS AT EVERY TURN...

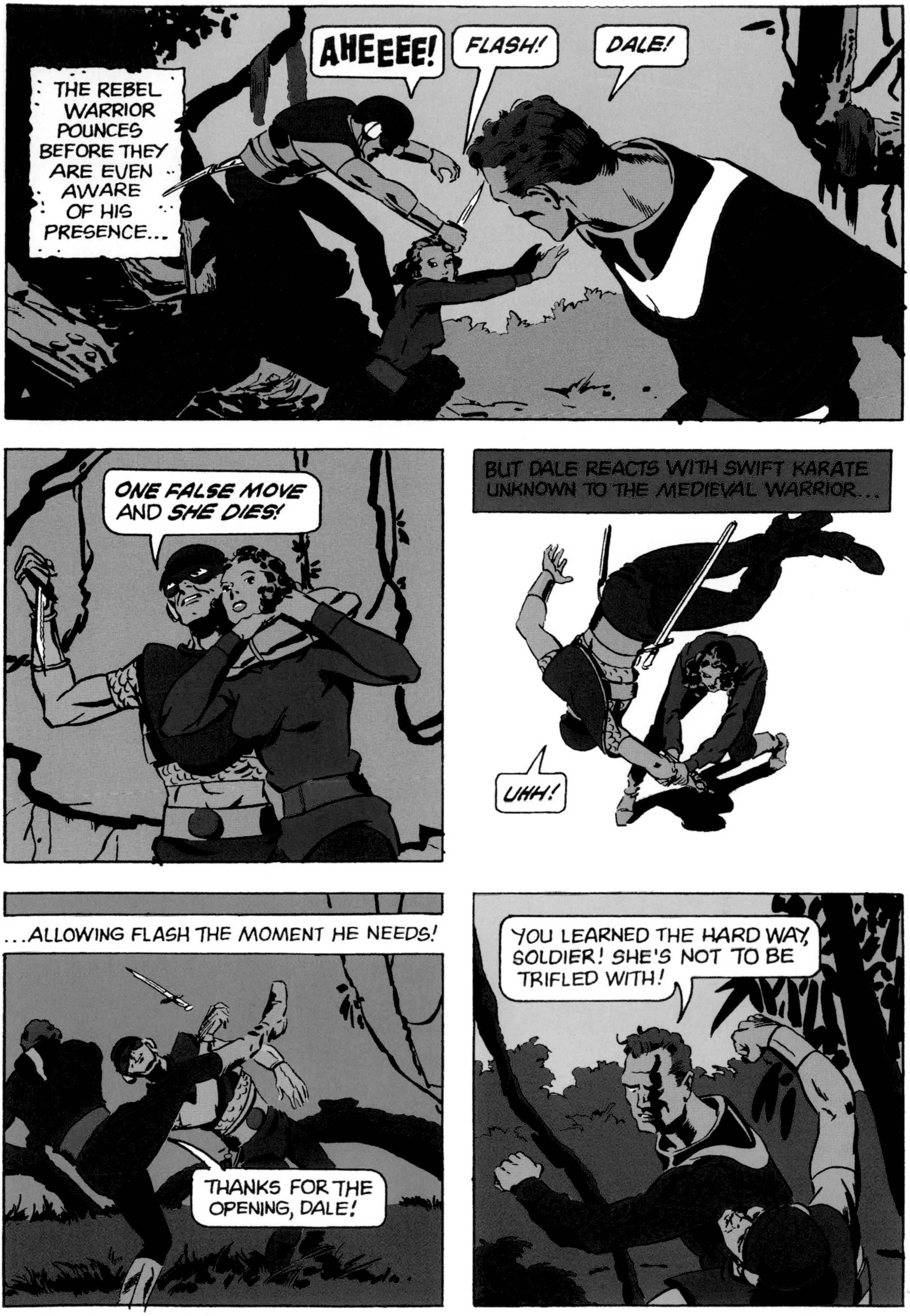
THE REBEL WARRIOR POUNCES BEFORE THEY ARE EVEN AWARE OF HIS PRESENCE...
AHEEEE!
FLASH!
DALE!
ONE FALSE MOVE AND SHE DIES!
BUT DALE REACTS WITH SWIFT KARATE UNKNOWN TO THE MEDIEVAL WARRIOR...
UHH!
...ALLOWING FLASH THE MOMENT HE NEEDS!
THANKS FOR THE OPENING, DALE!
YOU LEARNED THE HARD WAY, SOLDIER! SHE'S NOT TO BE TRIFLED WITH!

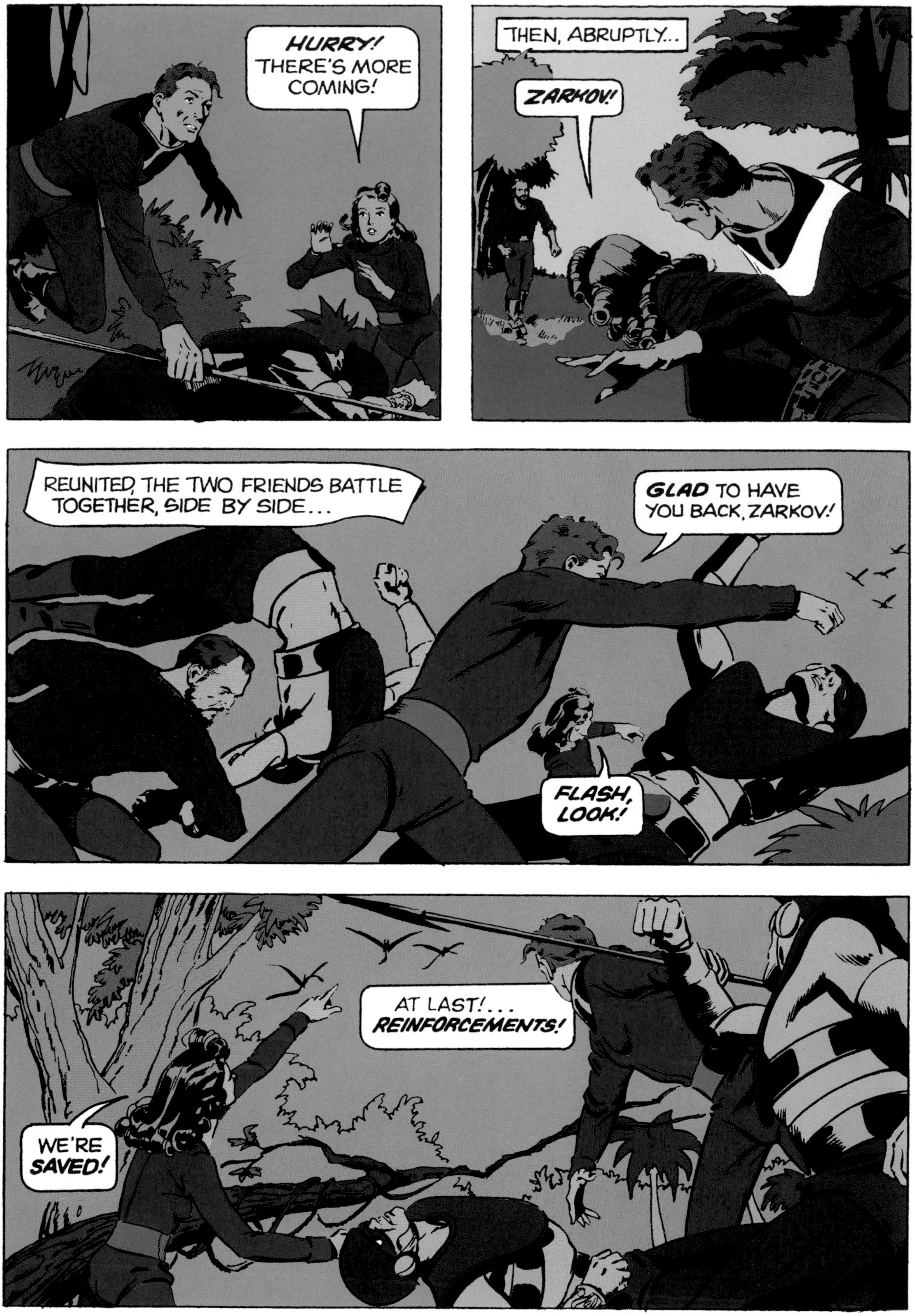
HURRY! THERE'S MORE COMING!
THEN, ABRUPTLY...
ZARKOV!
REUNITED, THE TWO FRIENDS BATTLE TOGETHER, SIDE BY SIDE...
GLAD TO HAVE YOU BACK, ZARKOV!
FLASH, LOOK!
AT LAST!... REINFORCEMENTS!
WE'RE SAVED!

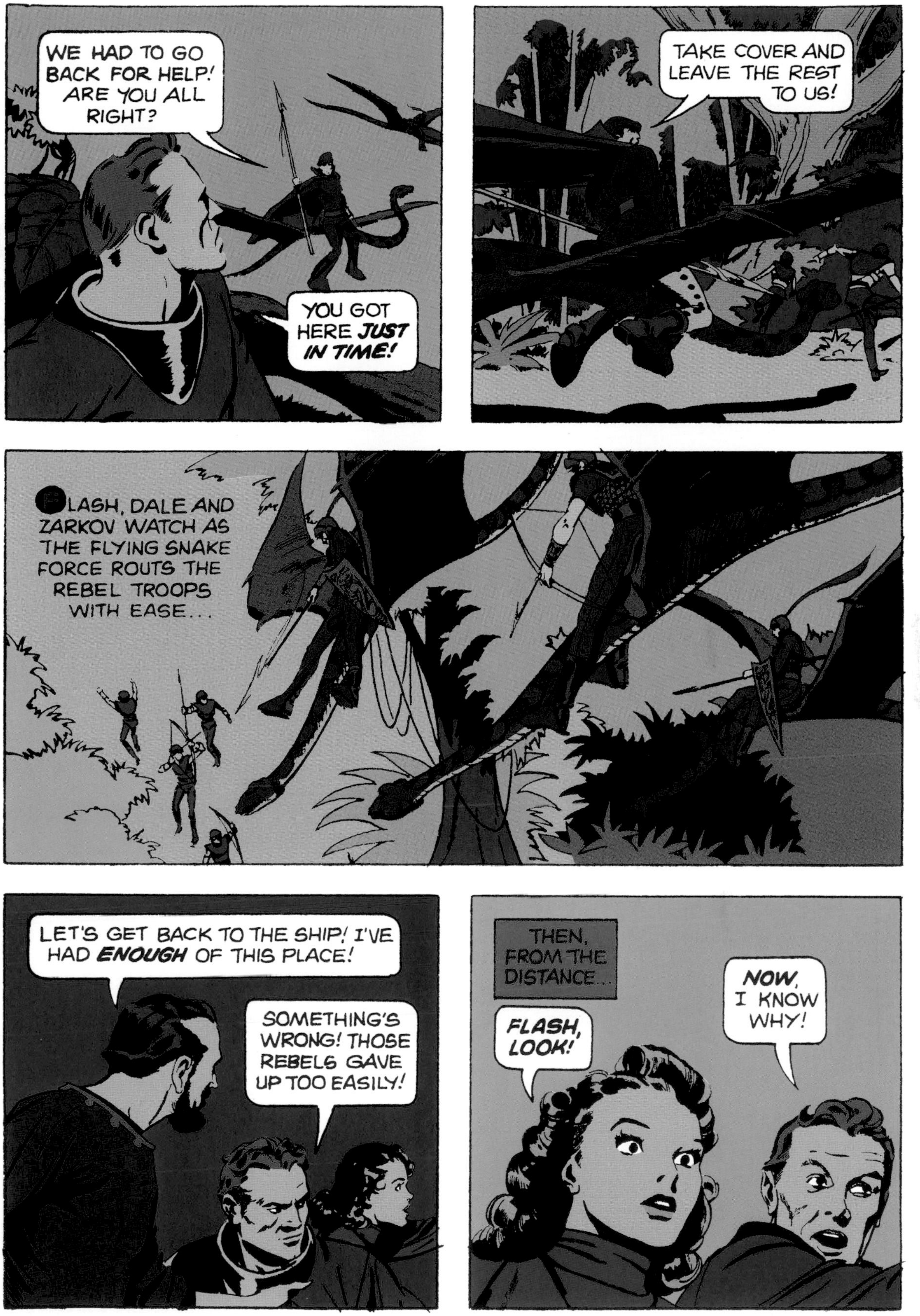
WE HAD TO GO BACK FOR HELP! ARE YOU ALL RIGHT?
YOU GOT HERE **JUST IN TIME!**
TAKE COVER AND LEAVE THE REST TO US!
FLASH, DALE AND ZARKOV WATCH AS THE FLYING SNAKE FORCE ROUTS THE REBEL TROOPS WITH EASE...
LET'S GET BACK TO THE SHIP! I'VE HAD **ENOUGH** OF THIS PLACE!
SOMETHING'S WRONG! THOSE REBELS GAVE UP TOO EASILY!
THEN, FROM THE DISTANCE...
FLASH, LOOK!
NOW, I KNOW WHY!

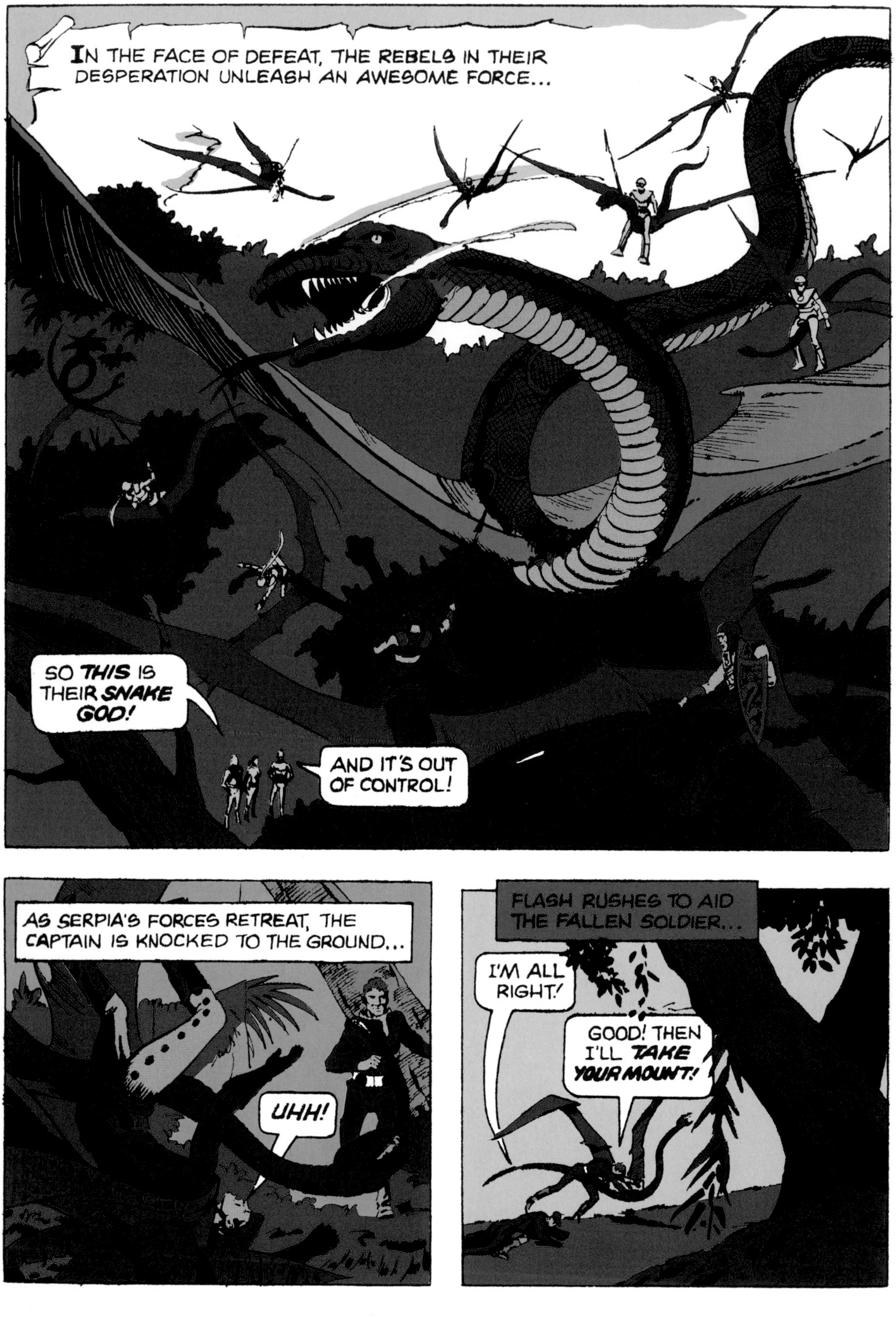
IN THE FACE OF DEFEAT, THE REBELS IN THEIR DESPERATION UNLEASH AN AWESOME FORCE...
SO THIS IS THEIR SNAKE GOD!
AND IT'S OUT OF CONTROL!
AS SERPIA'S FORCES RETREAT, THE CAPTAIN IS KNOCKED TO THE GROUND...
UHH!
FLASH RUSHES TO AID THE FALLEN SOLDIER...
I'M ALL RIGHT!
GOOD! THEN I'LL TAKE YOUR MOUNT!

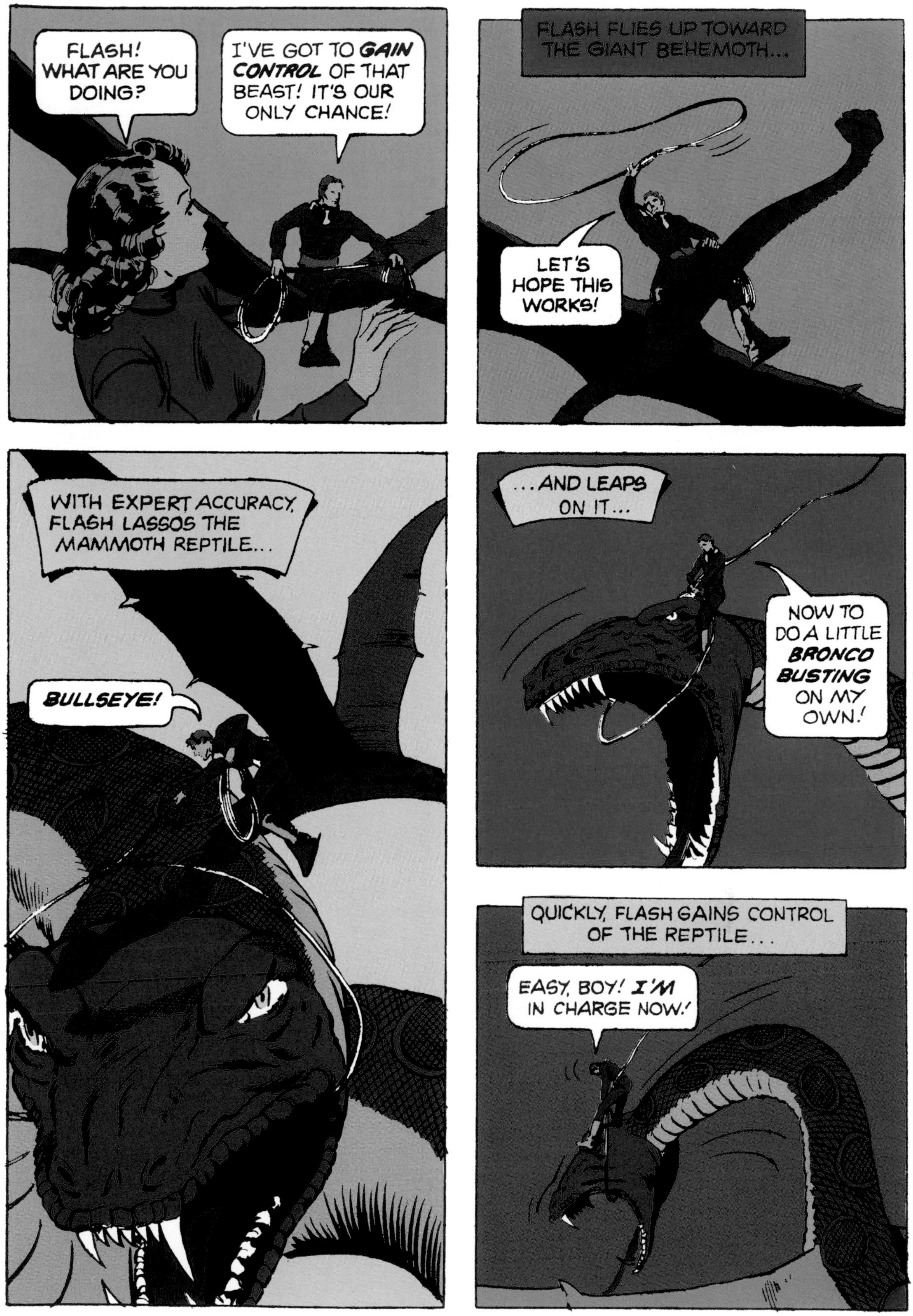
FLASH! WHAT ARE YOU DOING?
I'VE GOT TO GAIN CONTROL OF THAT BEAST! IT'S OUR ONLY CHANCE!
FLASH FLIES UP TOWARD THE GIANT BEHEMOTH...
LET'S HOPE THIS WORKS!
WITH EXPERT ACCURACY, FLASH LASSOS THE MAMMOTH REPTILE...
BULLSEYE!
...AND LEAPS ON IT...
NOW TO DO A LITTLE BRONCO BUSTING ON MY OWN!
QUICKLY, FLASH GAINS CONTROL OF THE REPTILE...
EASY, BOY! I'M IN CHARGE NOW!

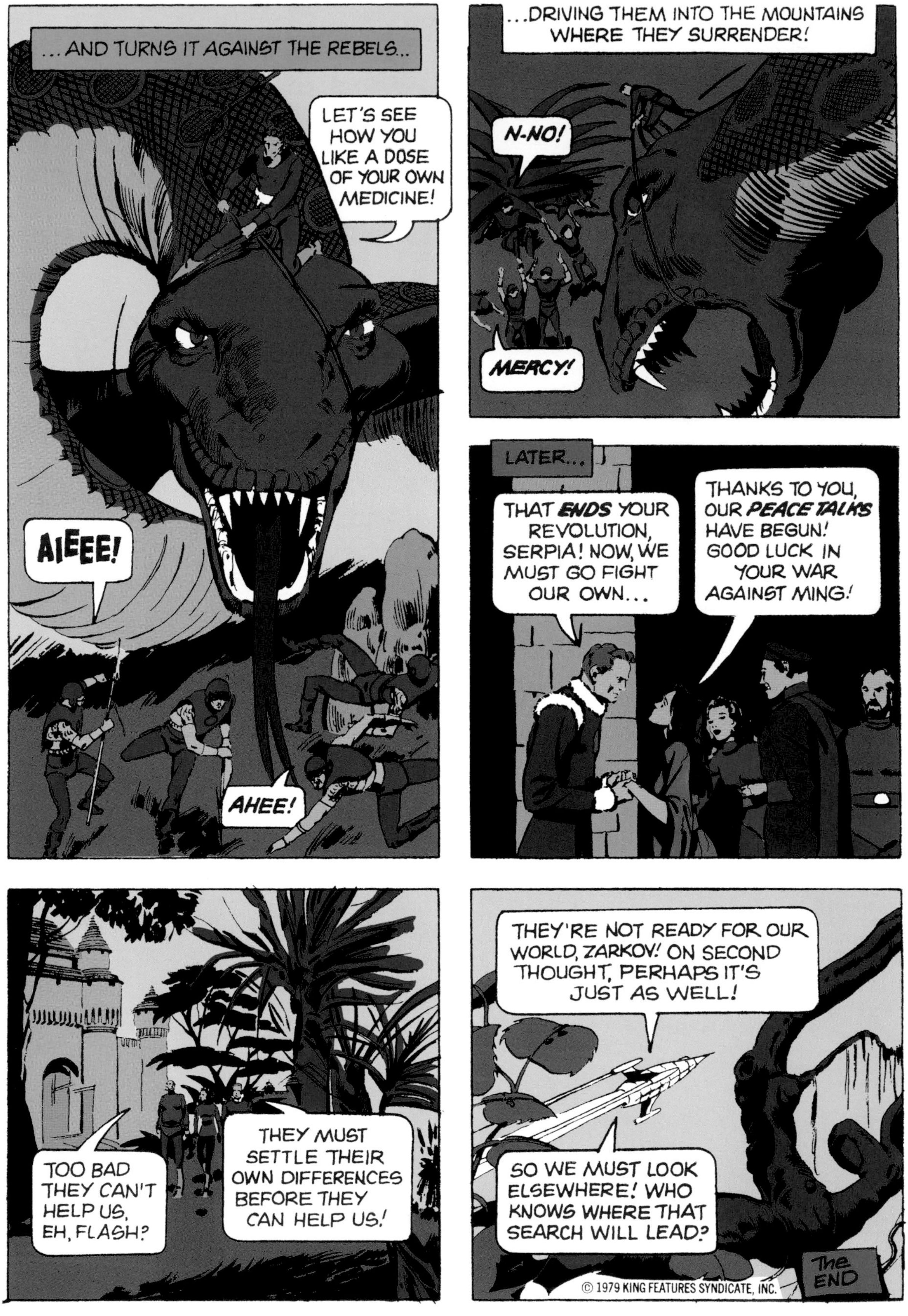
...AND TURNS IT AGAINST THE REBELS...
LET'S SEE HOW YOU LIKE A DOSE OF YOUR OWN MEDICINE!
AIEEE!
AHEE!
...DRIVING THEM INTO THE MOUNTAINS WHERE THEY SURRENDER!
N-NO!
MERCY!
LATER...
THAT ENDS YOUR REVOLUTION, SERPIA! NOW, WE MUST GO FIGHT OUR OWN...
THANKS TO YOU, OUR PEACE TALKS HAVE BEGUN! GOOD LUCK IN YOUR WAR AGAINST MING!
TOO BAD THEY CAN'T HELP US, EH, FLASH?
THEY MUST SETTLE THEIR OWN DIFFERENCES BEFORE THEY CAN HELP US!
THEY'RE NOT READY FOR OUR WORLD, ZARKOV! ON SECOND THOUGHT, PERHAPS IT'S JUST AS WELL!
SO WE MUST LOOK ELSEWHERE! WHO KNOWS WHERE THAT SEARCH WILL LEAD?
The END
© 1979 KING FEATURES SYNDICATE, INC.

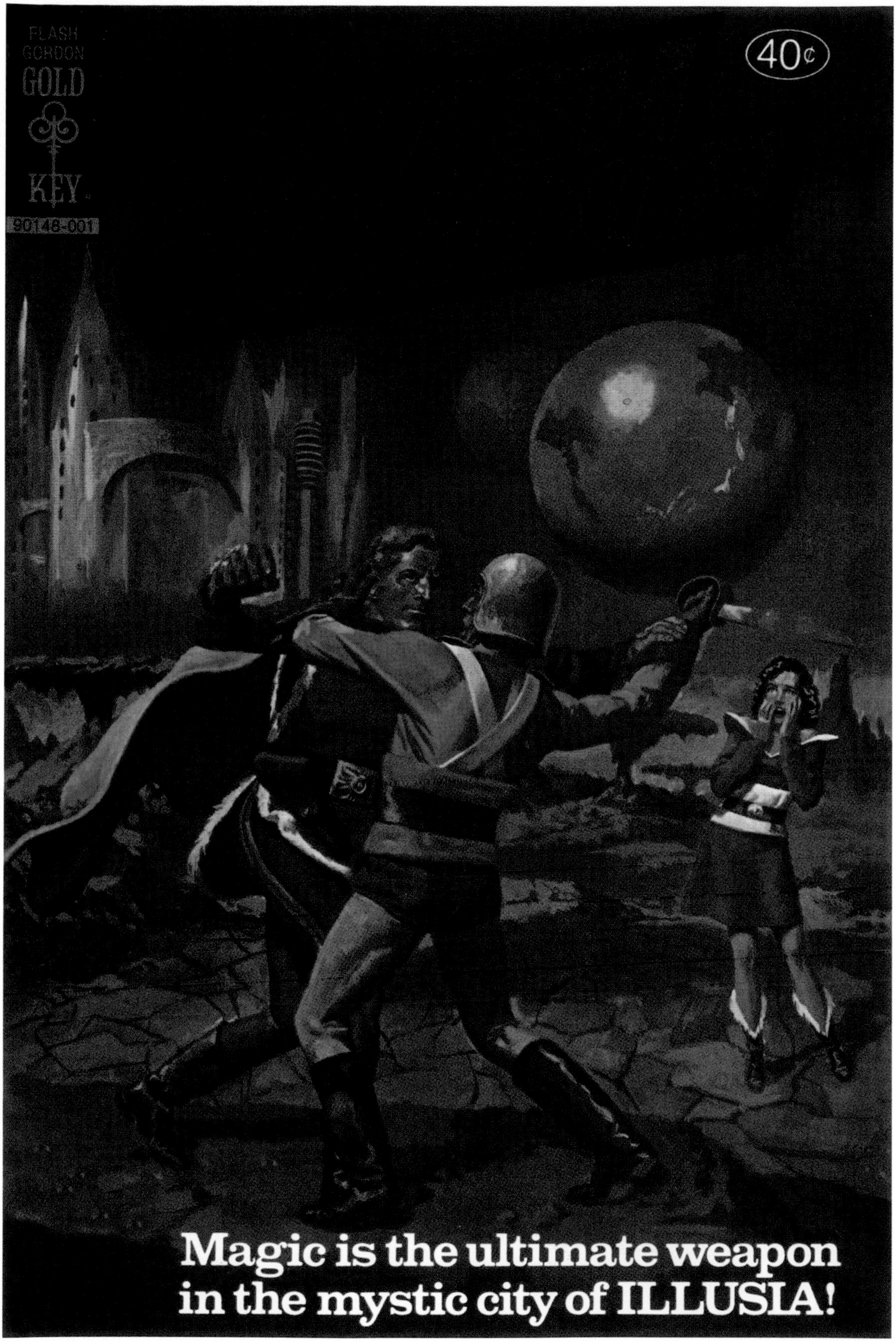
FLASH GORDON
GOLD KEY
90148-001
40¢
Magic is the ultimate weapon in the mystic city of ILLUSIA!

Stranded in an alien world, Flash Gordon, Dale Arden and Dr. Hans Zarkov struggle against the evil emperor, Ming the Merciless, who seeks to enslave an entire planet.....

FLASH GORDON on the PLANET MONGO
THE ENCHANTED CITY PART 1

EXPLORING THE FAR REACHES OF MONGO, FLASH GORDON AND HIS COMPANIONS SPOT A ROVING ENEMY SHIP STREAKING THROUGH THE DISTANT SKY...

STORY BY: CARY POOLE
ART BY: CARLOS GARZON
CREATED BY: ALEX RAYMOND

IT LOOKS LIKE ONE OF MING'S SHIPS!

APPARENTLY, THEY HAVEN'T SEEN US YET!

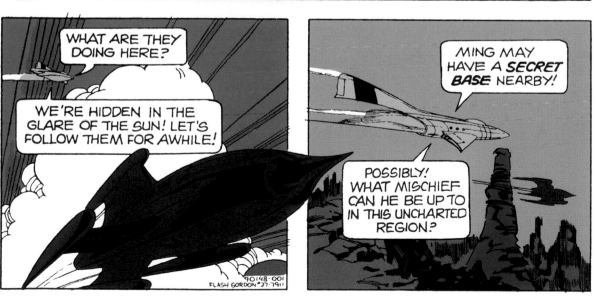

WHAT ARE THEY DOING HERE?

WE'RE HIDDEN IN THE GLARE OF THE SUN! LET'S FOLLOW THEM FOR AWHILE!

90148-001
FLASH GORDON #27-7911

MING MAY HAVE A SECRET BASE NEARBY!

POSSIBLY! WHAT MISCHIEF CAN HE BE UP TO IN THIS UNCHARTED REGION?

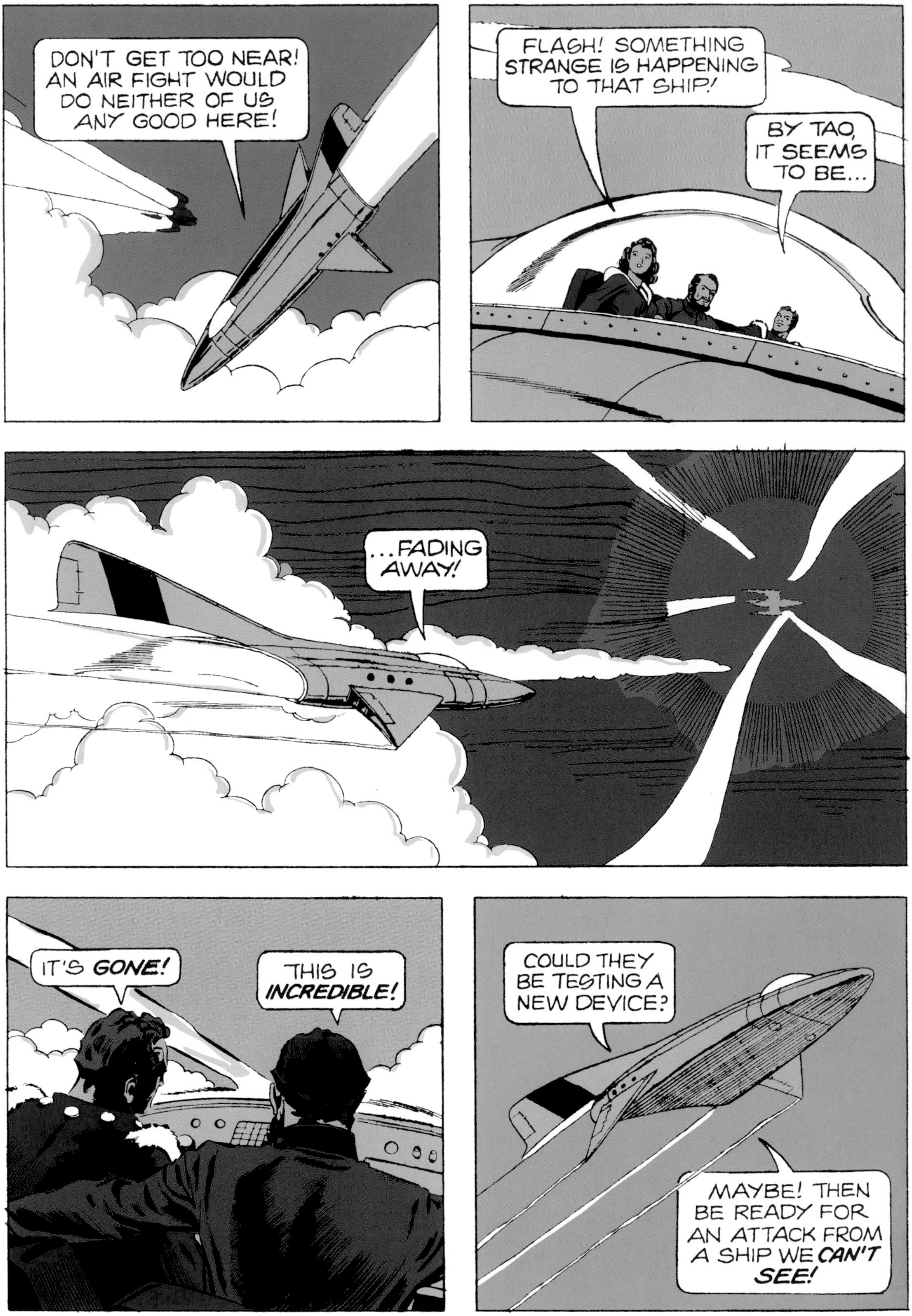
DON'T GET TOO NEAR! AN AIR FIGHT WOULD DO NEITHER OF US ANY GOOD HERE!
FLASH! SOMETHING STRANGE IS HAPPENING TO THAT SHIP!
BY TAO, IT SEEMS TO BE...
...FADING AWAY!
IT'S GONE!
THIS IS INCREDIBLE!
COULD THEY BE TESTING A NEW DEVICE?
MAYBE! THEN BE READY FOR AN ATTACK FROM A SHIP WE CAN'T SEE!

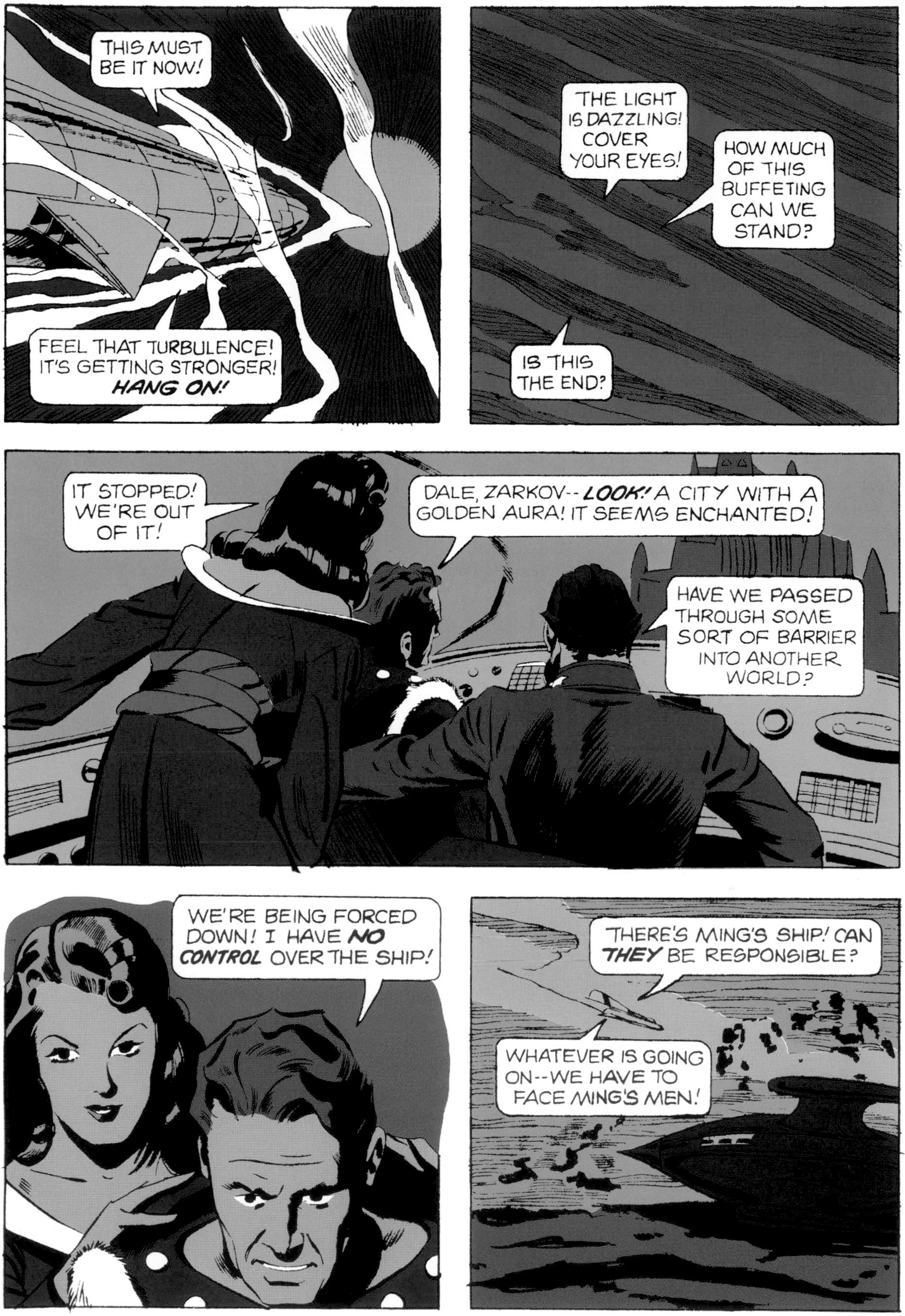
THIS MUST BE IT NOW!
FEEL THAT TURBULENCE! IT'S GETTING STRONGER! HANG ON!
THE LIGHT IS DAZZLING! COVER YOUR EYES!
HOW MUCH OF THIS BUFFETING CAN WE STAND?
IS THIS THE END?
IT STOPPED! WE'RE OUT OF IT!
DALE, ZARKOV--LOOK! A CITY WITH A GOLDEN AURA! IT SEEMS ENCHANTED!
HAVE WE PASSED THROUGH SOME SORT OF BARRIER INTO ANOTHER WORLD?
WE'RE BEING FORCED DOWN! I HAVE NO CONTROL OVER THE SHIP!
THERE'S MING'S SHIP! CAN THEY BE RESPONSIBLE?
WHATEVER IS GOING ON--WE HAVE TO FACE MING'S MEN!

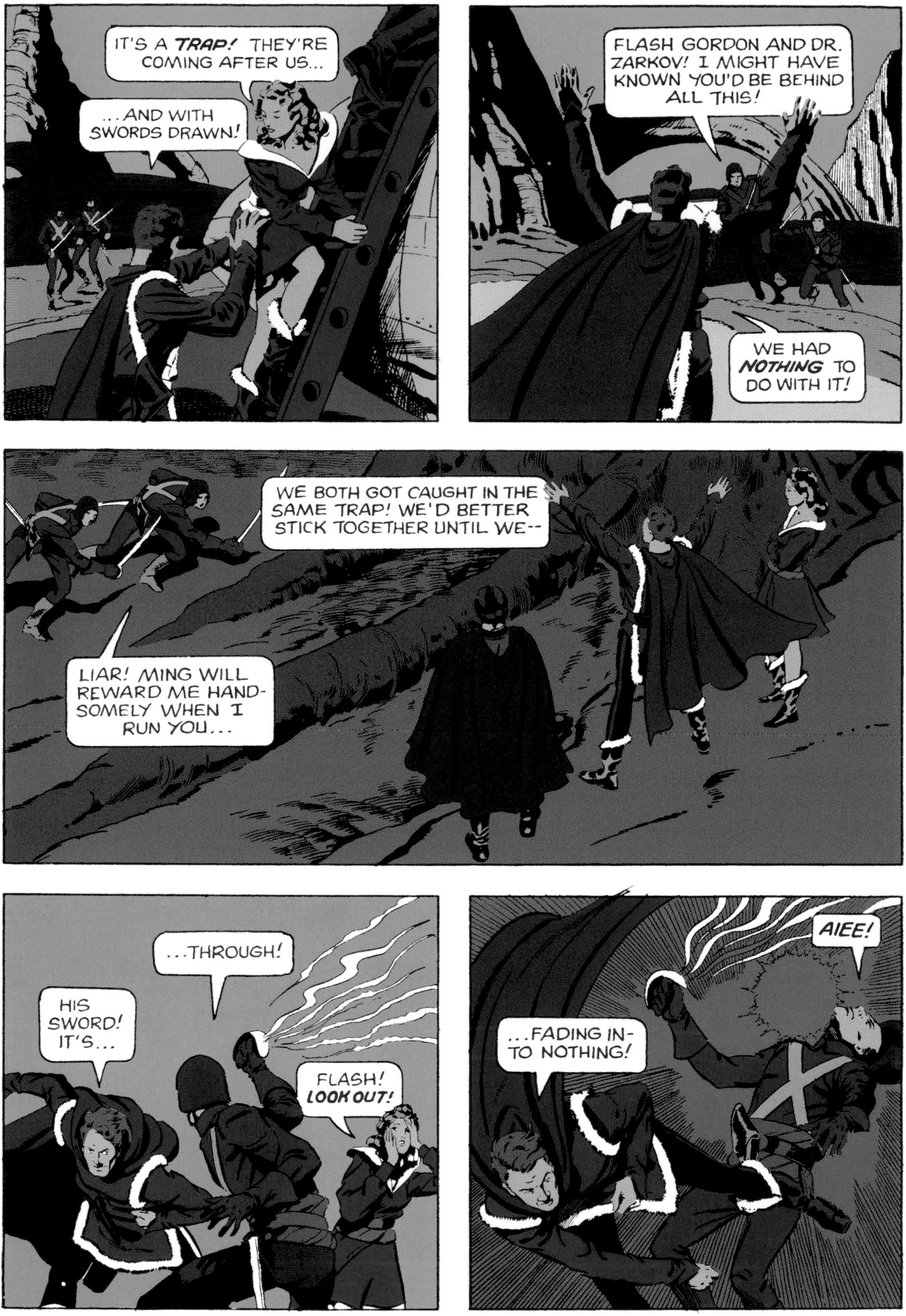

IT'S A TRAP! THEY'RE COMING AFTER US...
...AND WITH SWORDS DRAWN!
FLASH GORDON AND DR. ZARKOV! I MIGHT HAVE KNOWN YOU'D BE BEHIND ALL THIS!
WE HAD NOTHING TO DO WITH IT!
WE BOTH GOT CAUGHT IN THE SAME TRAP! WE'D BETTER STICK TOGETHER UNTIL WE--
LIAR! MING WILL REWARD ME HANDSOMELY WHEN I RUN YOU...
...THROUGH!
HIS SWORD! IT'S...
FLASH! LOOK OUT!
AIEE!
...FADING INTO NOTHING!

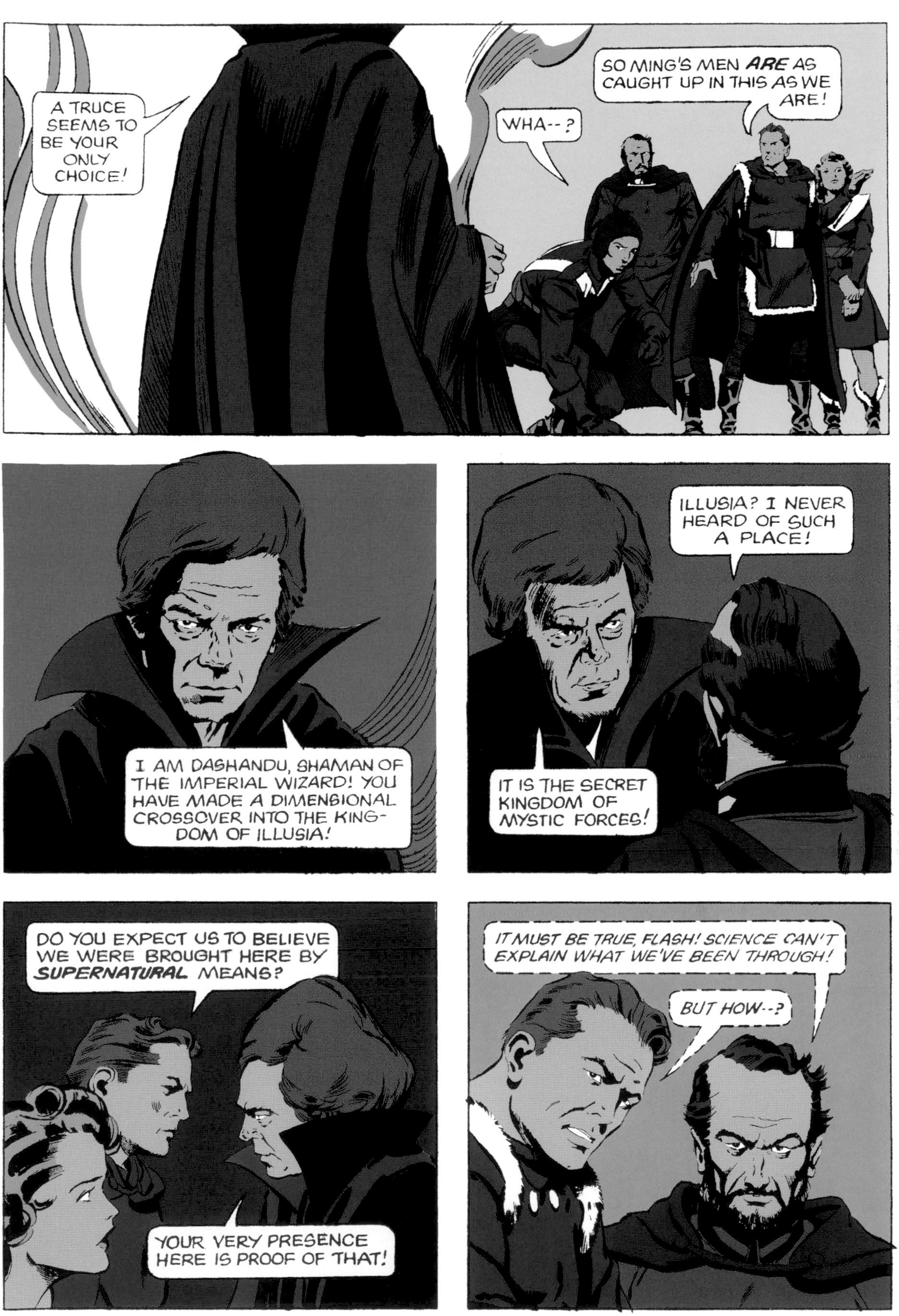
A TRUCE SEEMS TO BE YOUR ONLY CHOICE!
WHA--?
SO MING'S MEN ARE AS CAUGHT UP IN THIS AS WE ARE!
I AM DASHANDU, SHAMAN OF THE IMPERIAL WIZARD! YOU HAVE MADE A DIMENSIONAL CROSSOVER INTO THE KINGDOM OF ILLUSIA!
ILLUSIA? I NEVER HEARD OF SUCH A PLACE!
IT IS THE SECRET KINGDOM OF MYSTIC FORCES!
DO YOU EXPECT US TO BELIEVE WE WERE BROUGHT HERE BY SUPERNATURAL MEANS?
YOUR VERY PRESENCE HERE IS PROOF OF THAT!
IT MUST BE TRUE, FLASH! SCIENCE CAN'T EXPLAIN WHAT WE'VE BEEN THROUGH!
BUT HOW--?

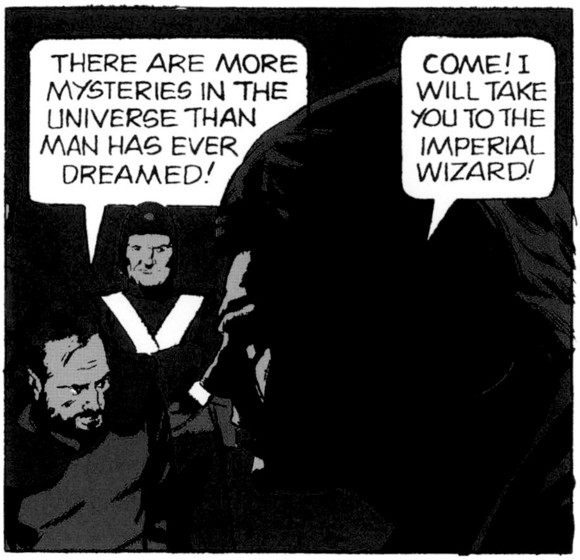
THERE ARE MORE MYSTERIES IN THE UNIVERSE THAN MAN HAS EVER DREAMED!
COME! I WILL TAKE YOU TO THE IMPERIAL WIZARD!

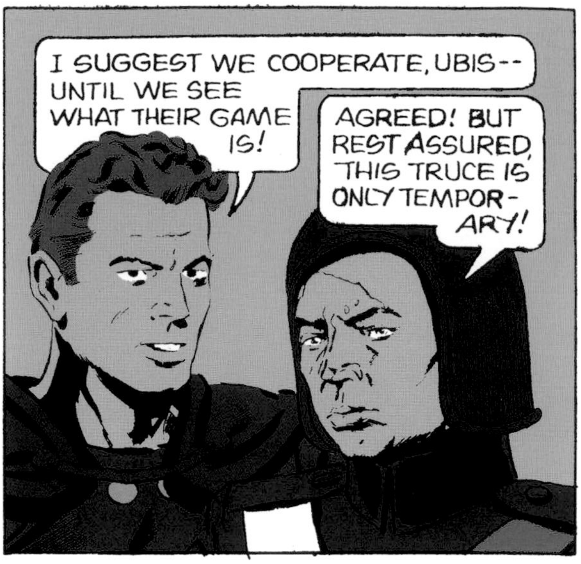
I SUGGEST WE COOPERATE, UBIS-- UNTIL WE SEE WHAT THEIR GAME IS!
AGREED! BUT REST ASSURED, THIS TRUCE IS ONLY TEMPORARY!

SOON, THEY ENTER A WONDROUS ENCHANTED KINGDOM...

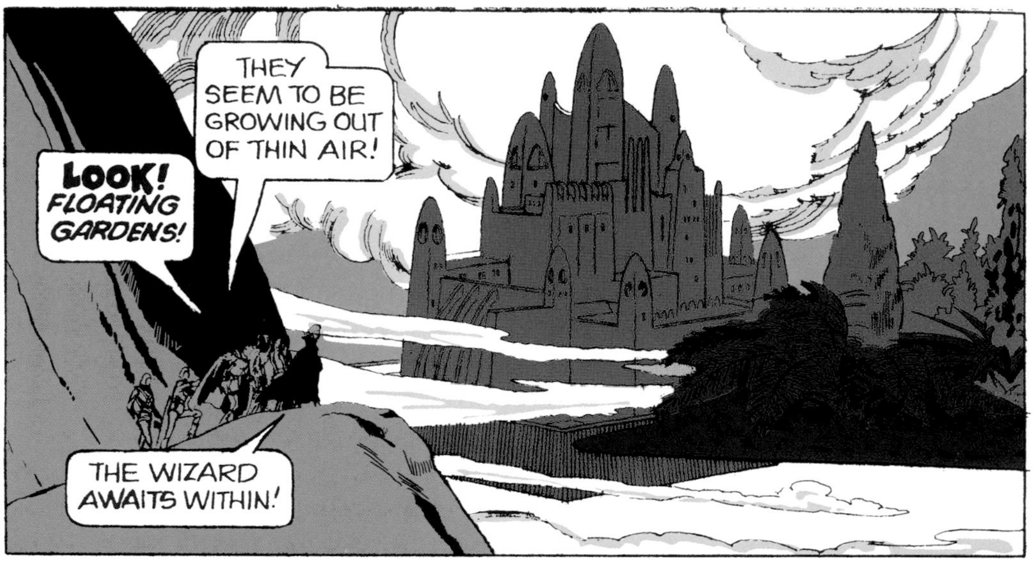
LOOK! FLOATING GARDENS!
THEY SEEM TO BE GROWING OUT OF THIN AIR!
THE WIZARD AWAITS WITHIN!

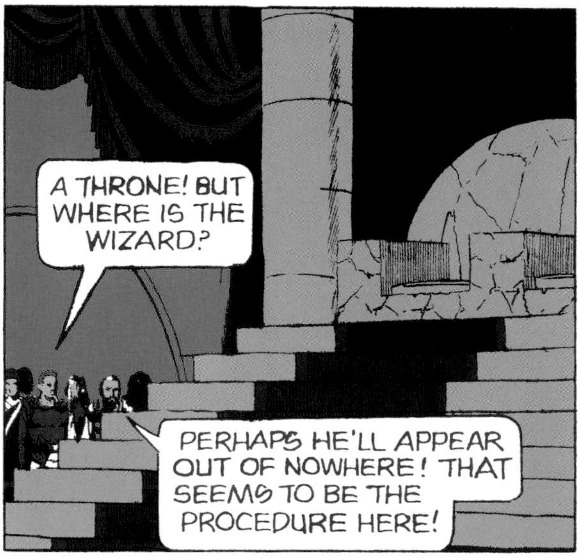
A THRONE! BUT WHERE IS THE WIZARD?
PERHAPS HE'LL APPEAR OUT OF NOWHERE! THAT SEEMS TO BE THE PROCEDURE HERE!

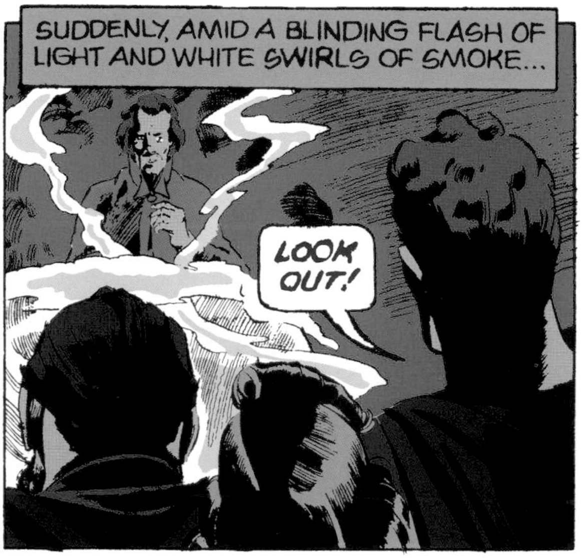
SUDDENLY, AMID A BLINDING FLASH OF LIGHT AND WHITE SWIRLS OF SMOKE...
LOOK OUT!

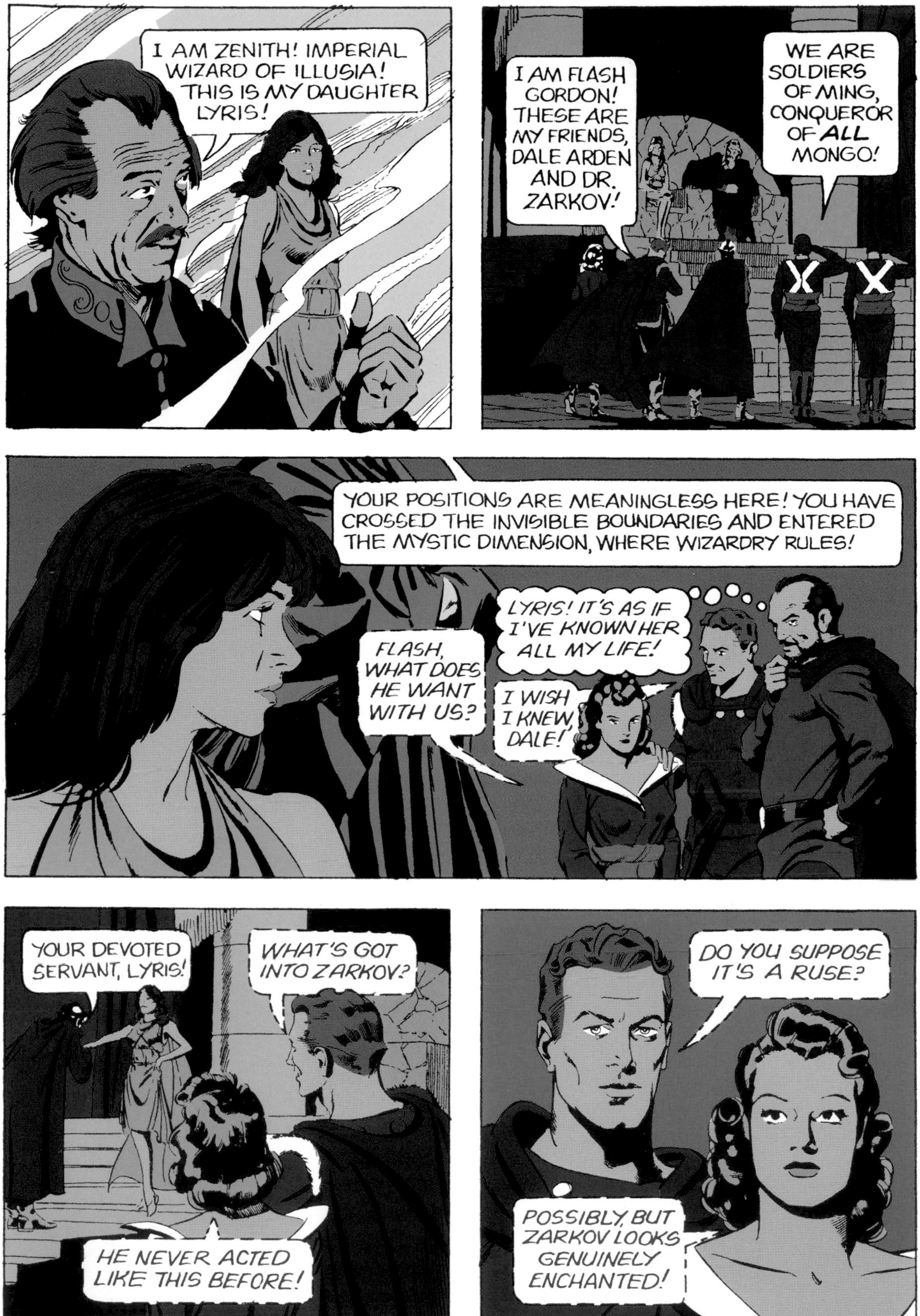
I AM ZENITH! IMPERIAL WIZARD OF ILLUSIA! THIS IS MY DAUGHTER LYRIS!
I AM FLASH GORDON! THESE ARE MY FRIENDS, DALE ARDEN AND DR. ZARKOV!
WE ARE SOLDIERS OF MING, CONQUEROR OF ALL MONGO!
YOUR POSITIONS ARE MEANINGLESS HERE! YOU HAVE CROSSED THE INVISIBLE BOUNDARIES AND ENTERED THE MYSTIC DIMENSION, WHERE WIZARDRY RULES!
LYRIS! IT'S AS IF I'VE KNOWN HER ALL MY LIFE!
FLASH, WHAT DOES HE WANT WITH US?
I WISH I KNEW, DALE!
YOUR DEVOTED SERVANT, LYRIS!
WHAT'S GOT INTO ZARKOV?
HE NEVER ACTED LIKE THIS BEFORE!
DO YOU SUPPOSE IT'S A RUSE?
POSSIBLY, BUT ZARKOV LOOKS GENUINELY ENCHANTED!

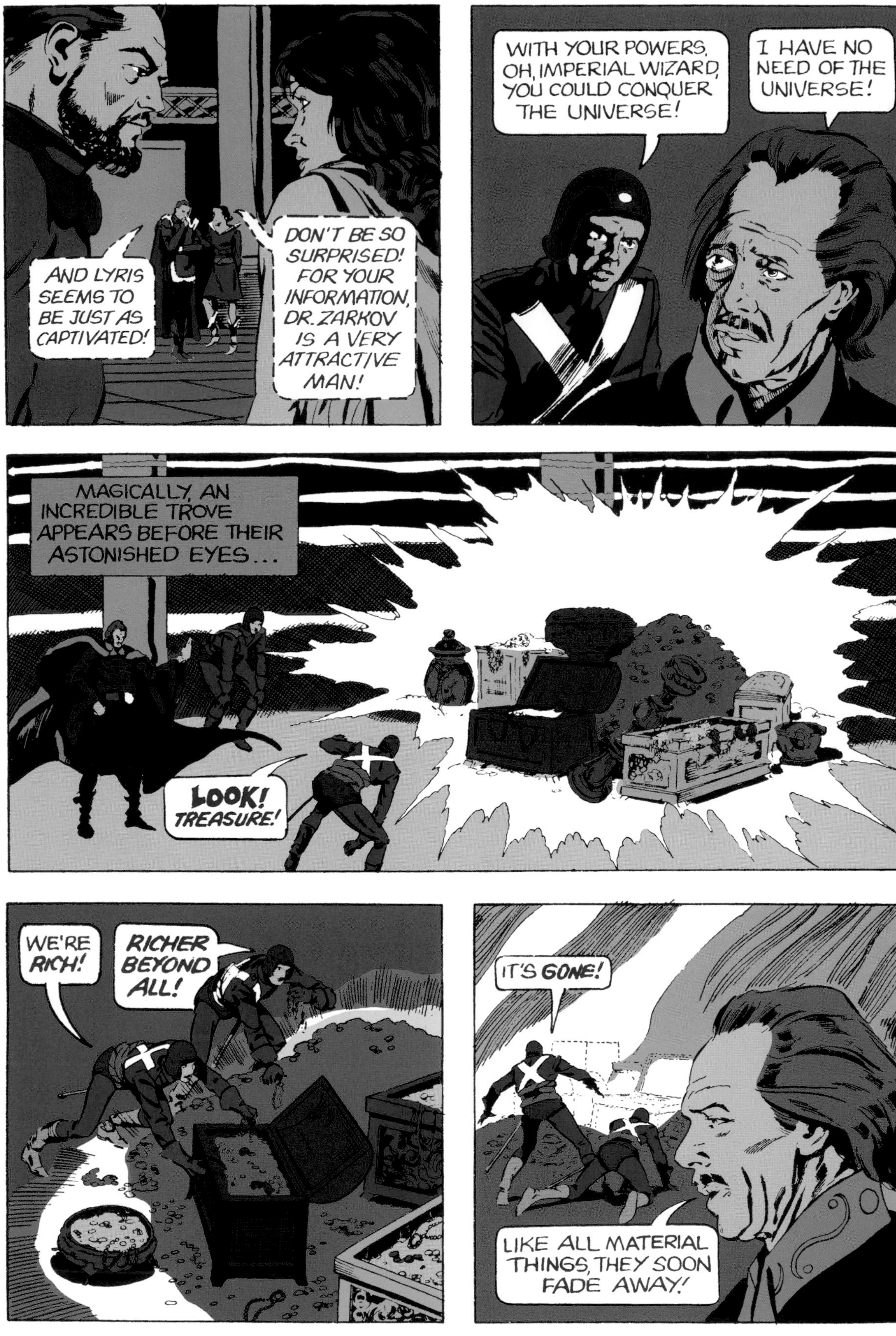

AND LYRIS SEEMS TO BE JUST AS CAPTIVATED!
DON'T BE SO SURPRISED! FOR YOUR INFORMATION, DR. ZARKOV IS A VERY ATTRACTIVE MAN!
WITH YOUR POWERS, OH, IMPERIAL WIZARD, YOU COULD CONQUER THE UNIVERSE!
I HAVE NO NEED OF THE UNIVERSE!
MAGICALLY, AN INCREDIBLE TROVE APPEARS BEFORE THEIR ASTONISHED EYES...
LOOK! TREASURE!
WE'RE RICH!
RICHER BEYOND ALL!
IT'S GONE!
LIKE ALL MATERIAL THINGS, THEY SOON FADE AWAY!

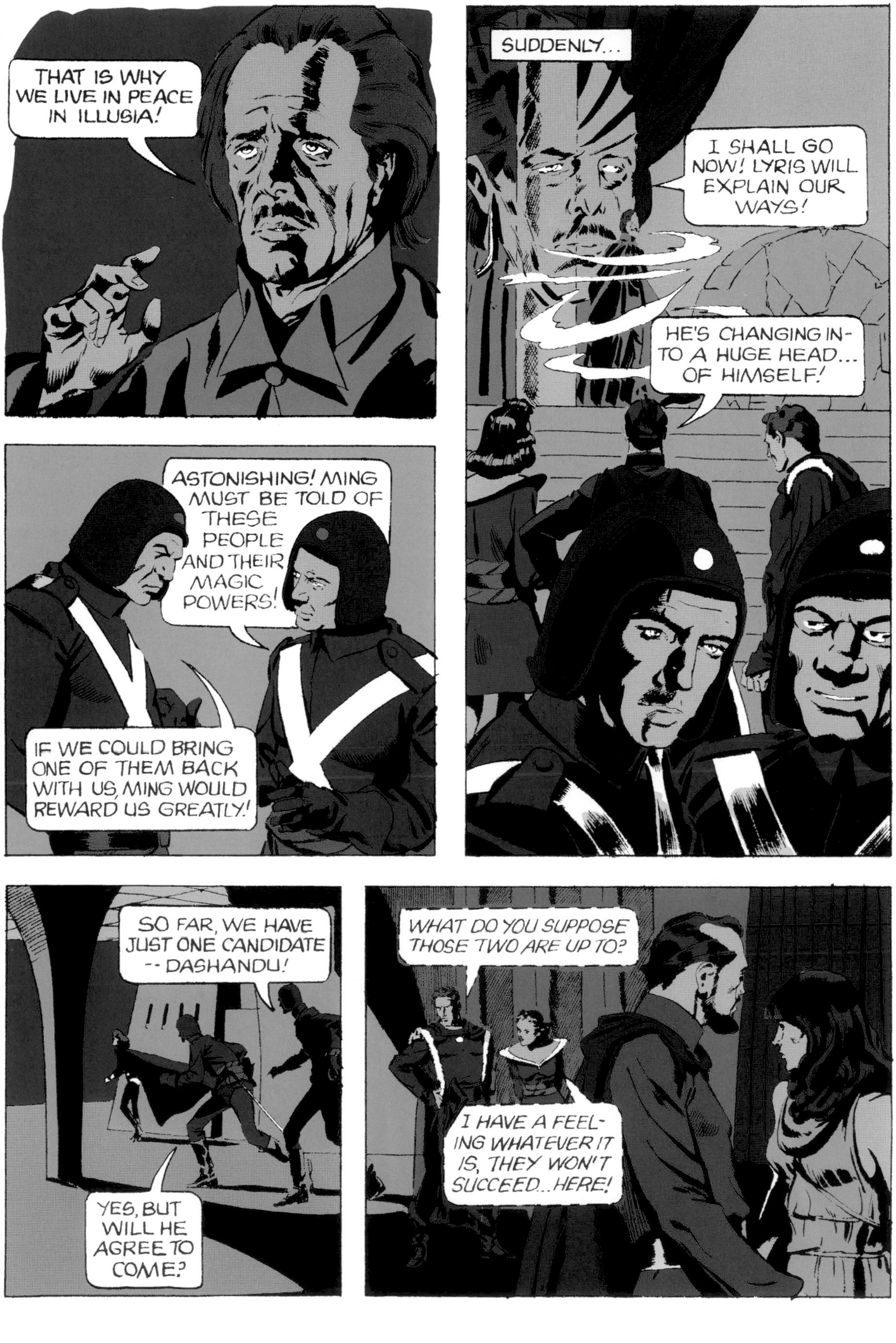
THAT IS WHY WE LIVE IN PEACE IN ILLUSIA!
SUDDENLY...
I SHALL GO NOW! LYRIS WILL EXPLAIN OUR WAYS!
HE'S CHANGING INTO A HUGE HEAD... OF HIMSELF!
ASTONISHING! MING MUST BE TOLD OF THESE PEOPLE AND THEIR MAGIC POWERS!
IF WE COULD BRING ONE OF THEM BACK WITH US, MING WOULD REWARD US GREATLY!
SO FAR, WE HAVE JUST ONE CANDIDATE -- DASHANDU!
YES, BUT WILL HE AGREE TO COME?
WHAT DO YOU SUPPOSE THOSE TWO ARE UP TO?
I HAVE A FEELING WHATEVER IT IS, THEY WON'T SUCCEED...HERE!

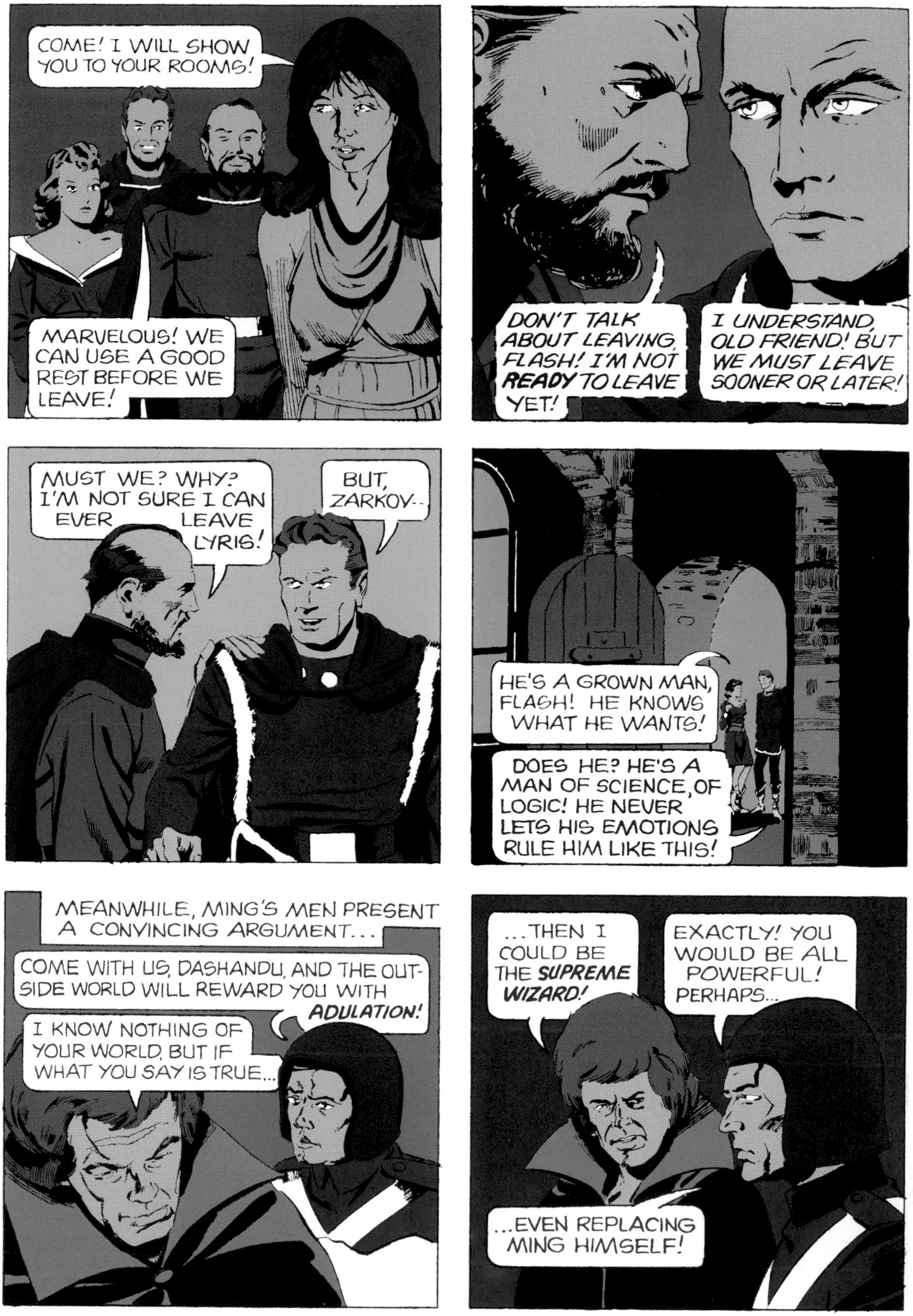
COME! I WILL SHOW YOU TO YOUR ROOMS!
MARVELOUS! WE CAN USE A GOOD REST BEFORE WE LEAVE!
DON'T TALK ABOUT LEAVING, FLASH! I'M NOT READY TO LEAVE YET!
I UNDERSTAND, OLD FRIEND! BUT WE MUST LEAVE SOONER OR LATER!
MUST WE? WHY? I'M NOT SURE I CAN EVER LEAVE LYRIS!
BUT, ZARKOV--
HE'S A GROWN MAN, FLASH! HE KNOWS WHAT HE WANTS!
DOES HE? HE'S A MAN OF SCIENCE, OF LOGIC! HE NEVER LETS HIS EMOTIONS RULE HIM LIKE THIS!
MEANWHILE, MING'S MEN PRESENT A CONVINCING ARGUMENT...
COME WITH US, DASHANDU, AND THE OUTSIDE WORLD WILL REWARD YOU WITH ADULATION!
I KNOW NOTHING OF YOUR WORLD, BUT IF WHAT YOU SAY IS TRUE...
...THEN I COULD BE THE SUPREME WIZARD!
EXACTLY! YOU WOULD BE ALL POWERFUL! PERHAPS...
...EVEN REPLACING MING HIMSELF!

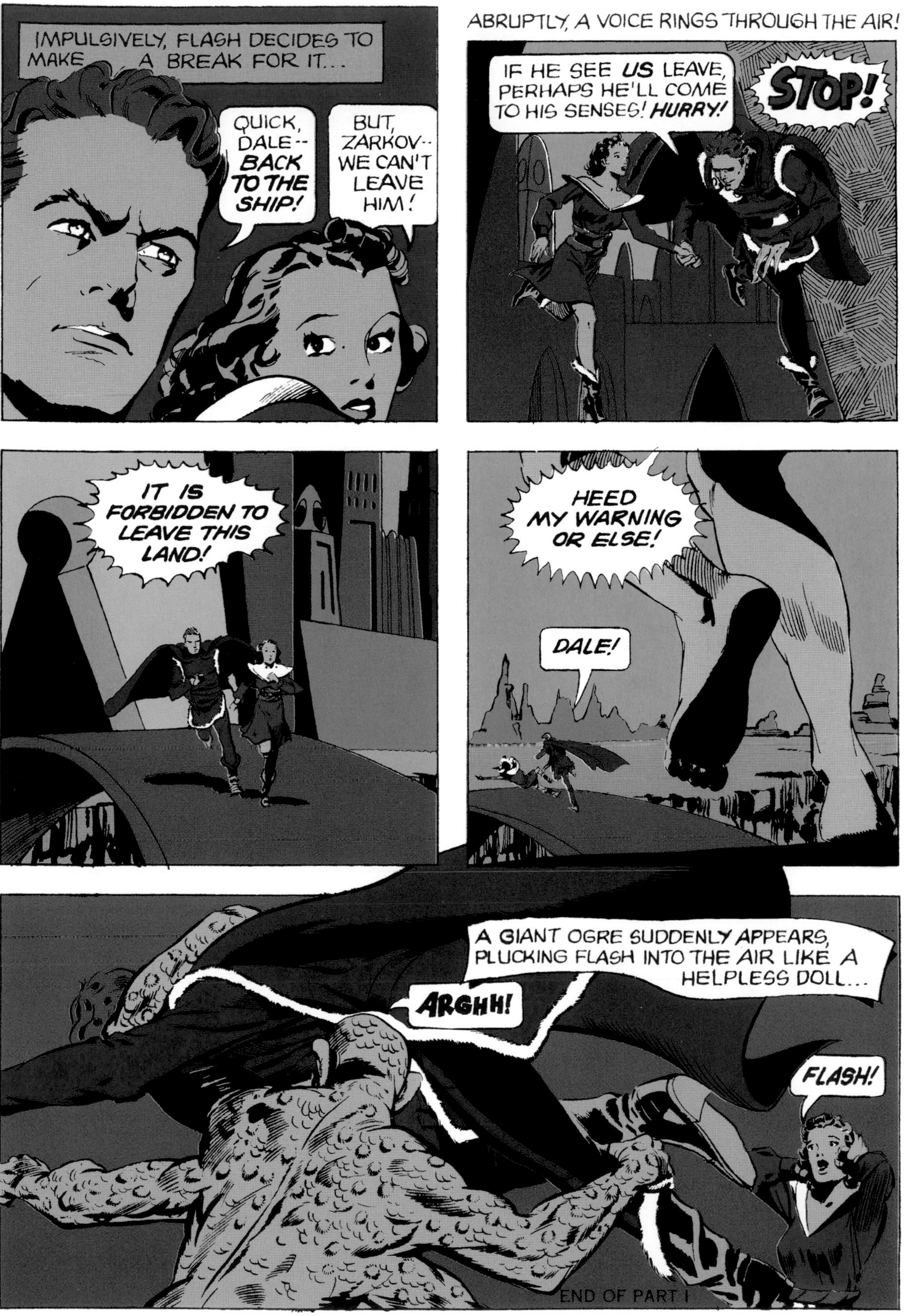
IMPULSIVELY, FLASH DECIDES TO MAKE A BREAK FOR IT...
QUICK, DALE-- BACK TO THE SHIP!
BUT, ZARKOV-- WE CAN'T LEAVE HIM!
ABRUPTLY, A VOICE RINGS THROUGH THE AIR!
IF HE SEE US LEAVE, PERHAPS HE'LL COME TO HIS SENSES! HURRY!
STOP!
IT IS FORBIDDEN TO LEAVE THIS LAND!
HEED MY WARNING OR ELSE!
DALE!
A GIANT OGRE SUDDENLY APPEARS, PLUCKING FLASH INTO THE AIR LIKE A HELPLESS DOLL...
ARGHH!
FLASH!
END OF PART I

FLASH GORDON on the PLANET MONGO

THE ENCHANTED CITY PART 2

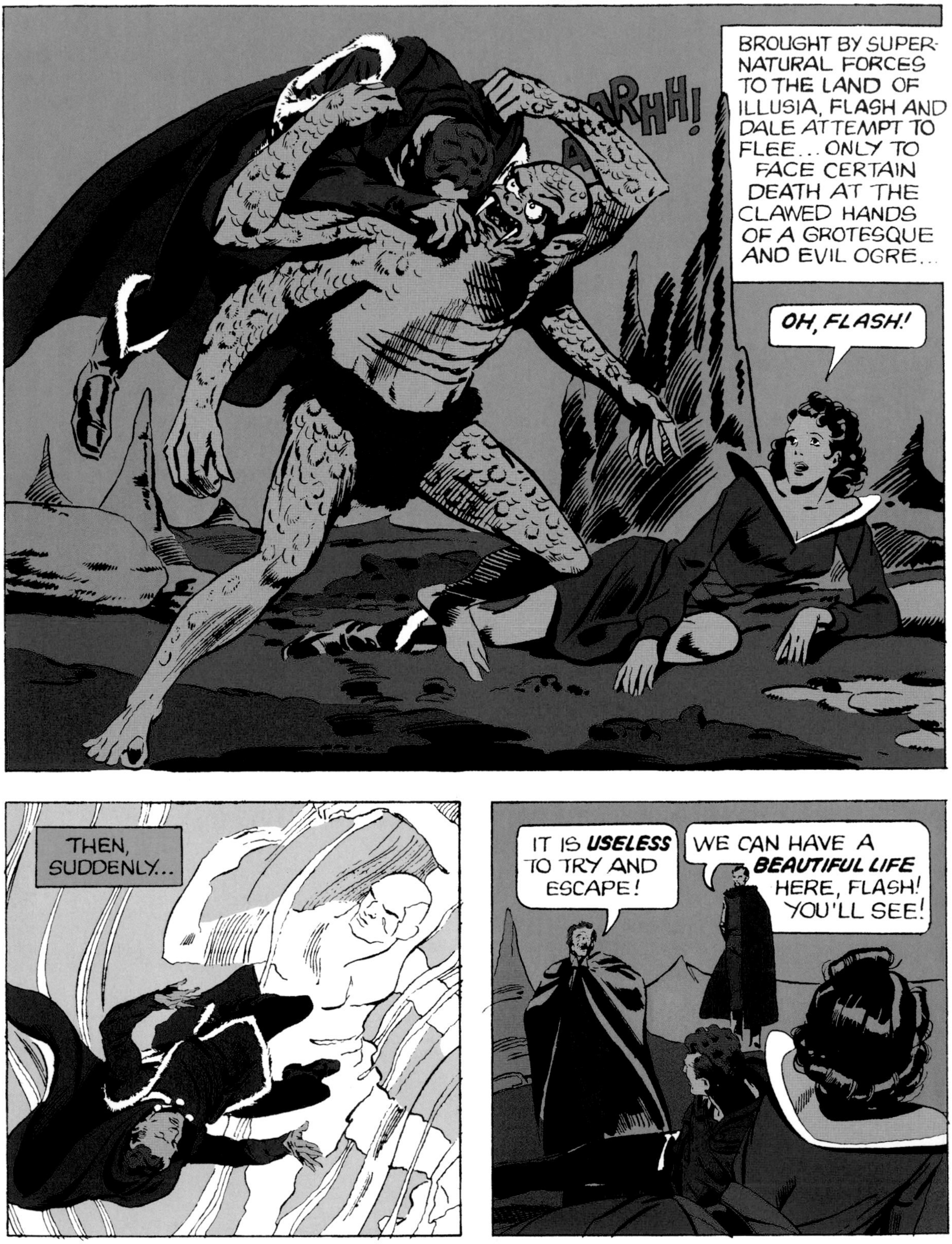
BROUGHT BY SUPERNATURAL FORCES TO THE LAND OF ILLUSIA, FLASH AND DALE ATTEMPT TO FLEE... ONLY TO FACE CERTAIN DEATH AT THE CLAWED HANDS OF A GROTESQUE AND EVIL OGRE...
AARHHH!
OH, FLASH!
THEN, SUDDENLY...
IT IS USELESS TO TRY AND ESCAPE!
WE CAN HAVE A BEAUTIFUL LIFE HERE, FLASH! YOU'LL SEE!

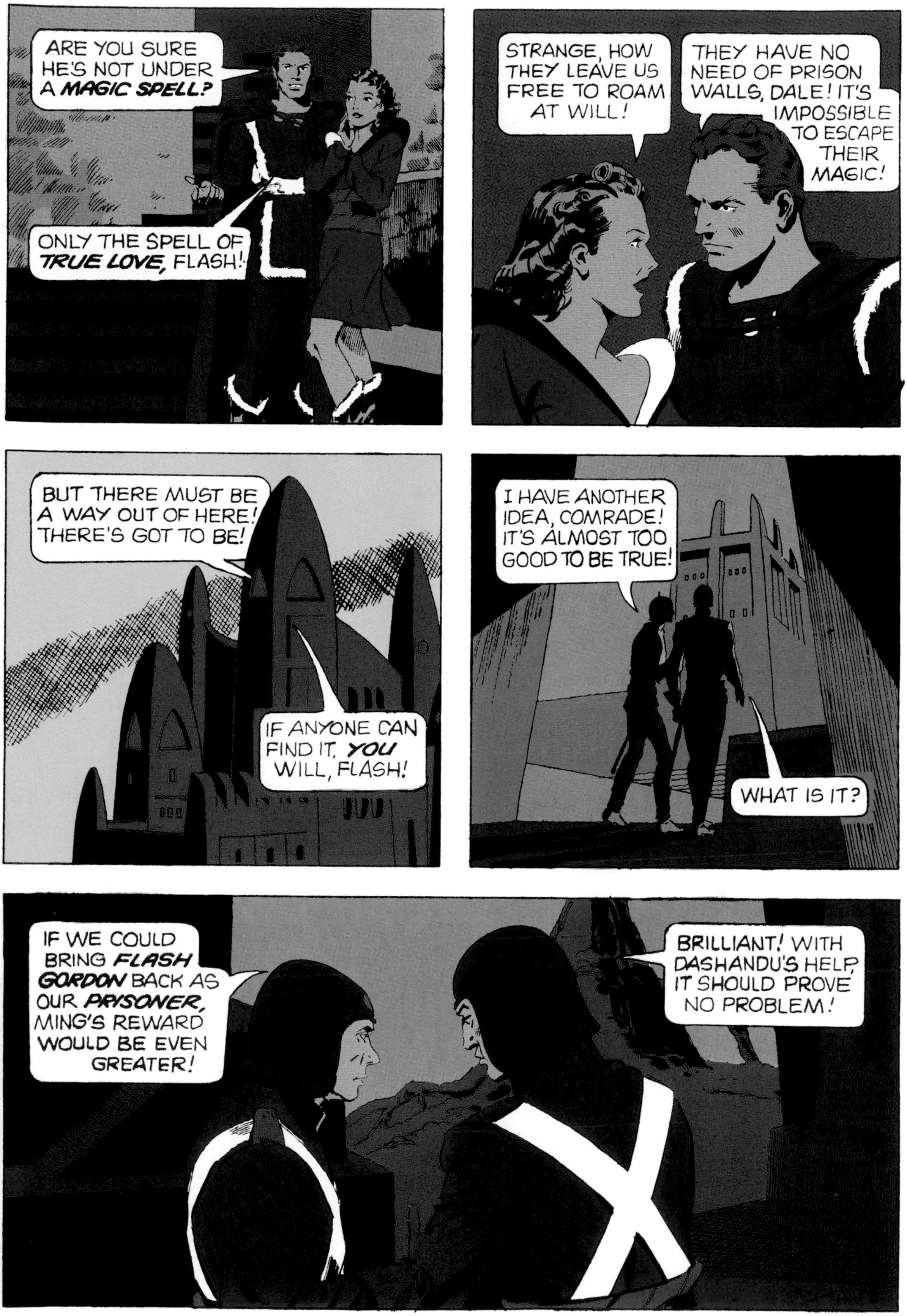
ARE YOU SURE HE'S NOT UNDER A MAGIC SPELL?
ONLY THE SPELL OF TRUE LOVE, FLASH!
STRANGE, HOW THEY LEAVE US FREE TO ROAM AT WILL!
THEY HAVE NO NEED OF PRISON WALLS, DALE! IT'S IMPOSSIBLE TO ESCAPE THEIR MAGIC!
BUT THERE MUST BE A WAY OUT OF HERE! THERE'S GOT TO BE!
IF ANYONE CAN FIND IT, YOU WILL, FLASH!
I HAVE ANOTHER IDEA, COMRADE! IT'S ALMOST TOO GOOD TO BE TRUE!
WHAT IS IT?
IF WE COULD BRING FLASH GORDON BACK AS OUR PRISONER, MING'S REWARD WOULD BE EVEN GREATER!
BRILLIANT! WITH DASHANDU'S HELP, IT SHOULD PROVE NO PROBLEM!

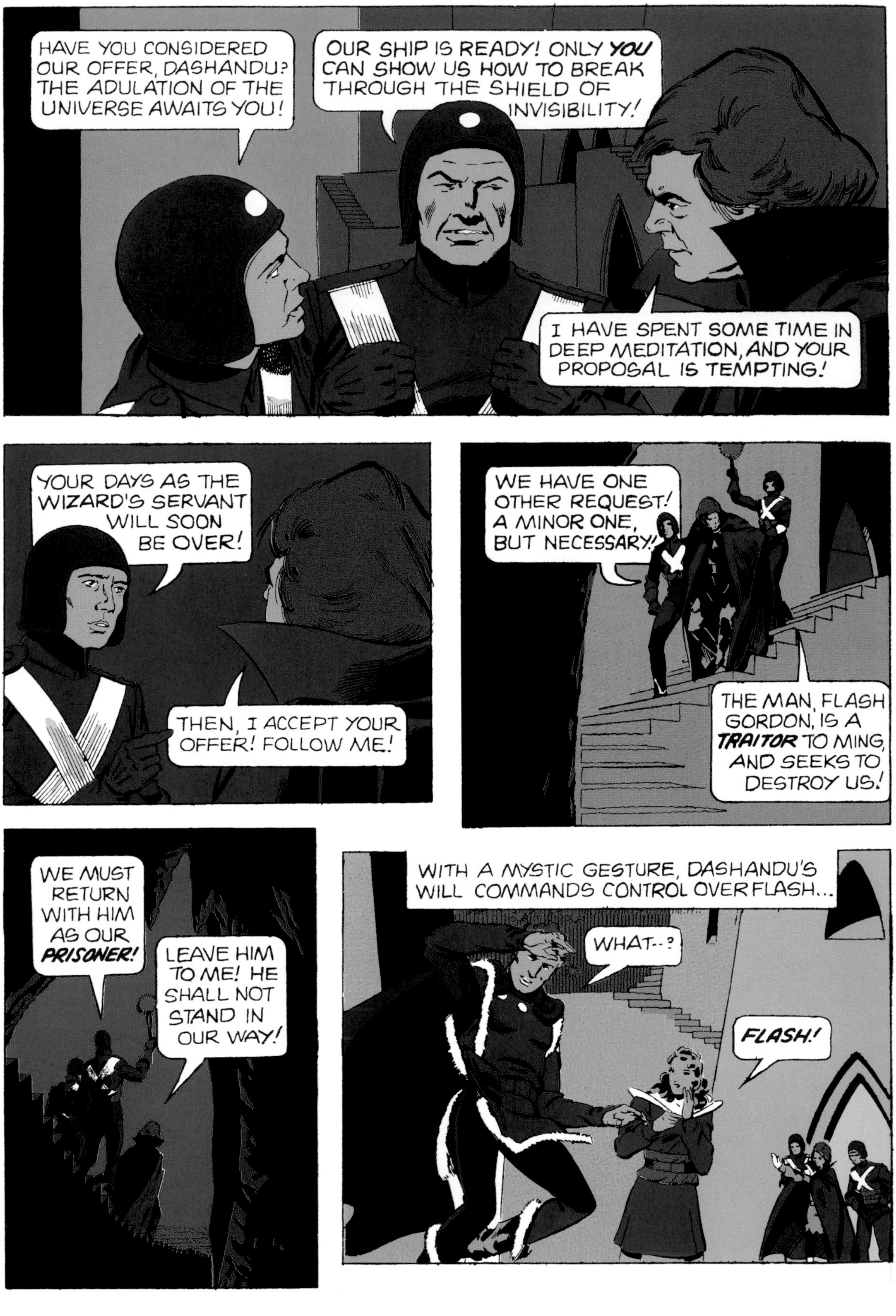
HAVE YOU CONSIDERED OUR OFFER, DASHANDU? THE ADULATION OF THE UNIVERSE AWAITS YOU!
OUR SHIP IS READY! ONLY YOU CAN SHOW US HOW TO BREAK THROUGH THE SHIELD OF INVISIBILITY!
I HAVE SPENT SOME TIME IN DEEP MEDITATION, AND YOUR PROPOSAL IS TEMPTING!
YOUR DAYS AS THE WIZARD'S SERVANT WILL SOON BE OVER!
THEN, I ACCEPT YOUR OFFER! FOLLOW ME!
WE HAVE ONE OTHER REQUEST! A MINOR ONE, BUT NECESSARY!
THE MAN, FLASH GORDON, IS A TRAITOR TO MING, AND SEEKS TO DESTROY US!
WE MUST RETURN WITH HIM AS OUR PRISONER!
LEAVE HIM TO ME! HE SHALL NOT STAND IN OUR WAY!
WITH A MYSTIC GESTURE, DASHANDU'S WILL COMMANDS CONTROL OVER FLASH...
WHAT--?
FLASH!

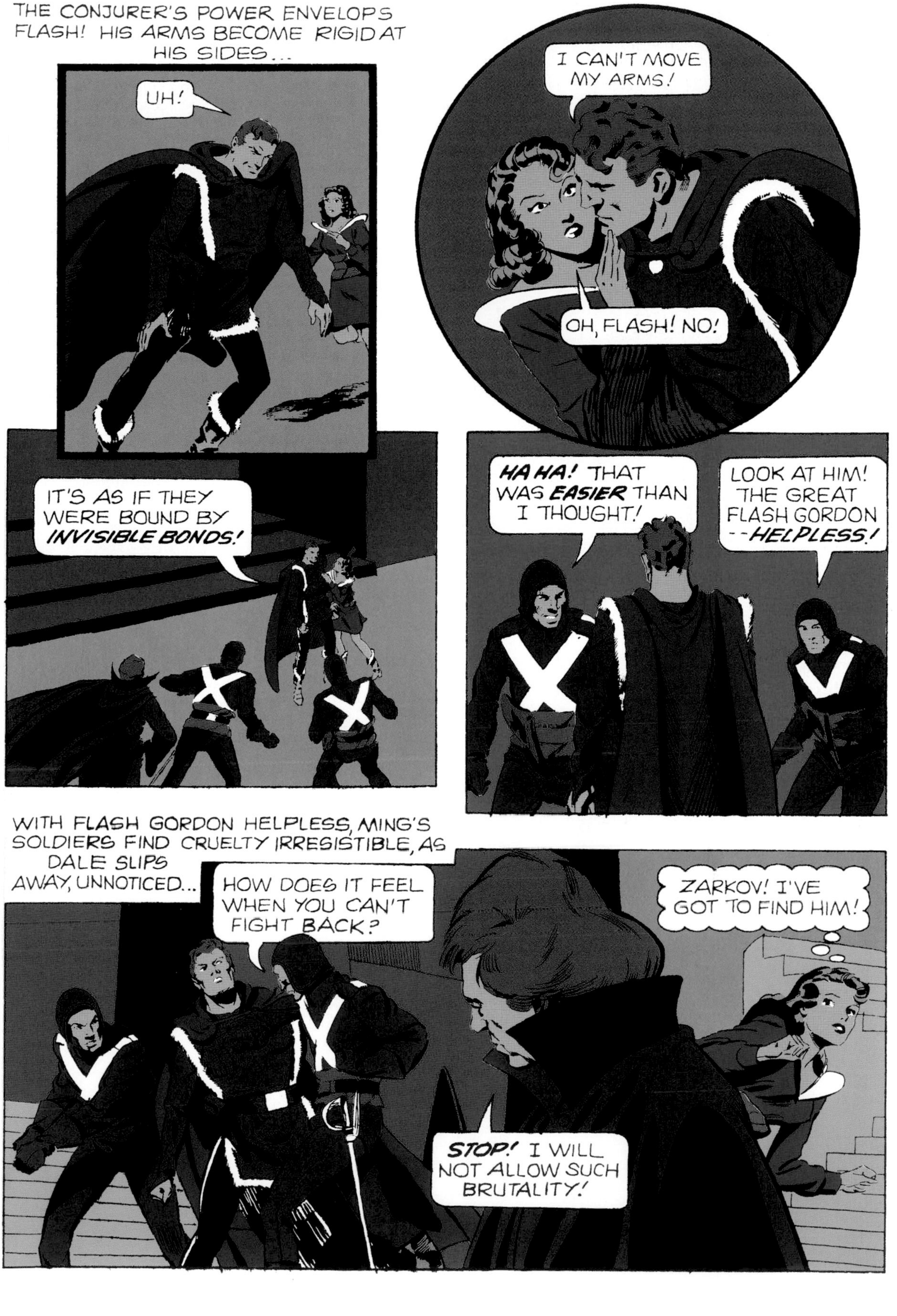
THE CONJURER'S POWER ENVELOPS FLASH! HIS ARMS BECOME RIGID AT HIS SIDES...
UH!
I CAN'T MOVE MY ARMS!
OH, FLASH! NO!
IT'S AS IF THEY WERE BOUND BY INVISIBLE BONDS!
HA HA! THAT WAS EASIER THAN I THOUGHT!
LOOK AT HIM! THE GREAT FLASH GORDON --HELPLESS!
WITH FLASH GORDON HELPLESS, MING'S SOLDIERS FIND CRUELTY IRRESISTIBLE, AS DALE SLIPS AWAY, UNNOTICED...
HOW DOES IT FEEL WHEN YOU CAN'T FIGHT BACK?
ZARKOV! I'VE GOT TO FIND HIM!
STOP! I WILL NOT ALLOW SUCH BRUTALITY!

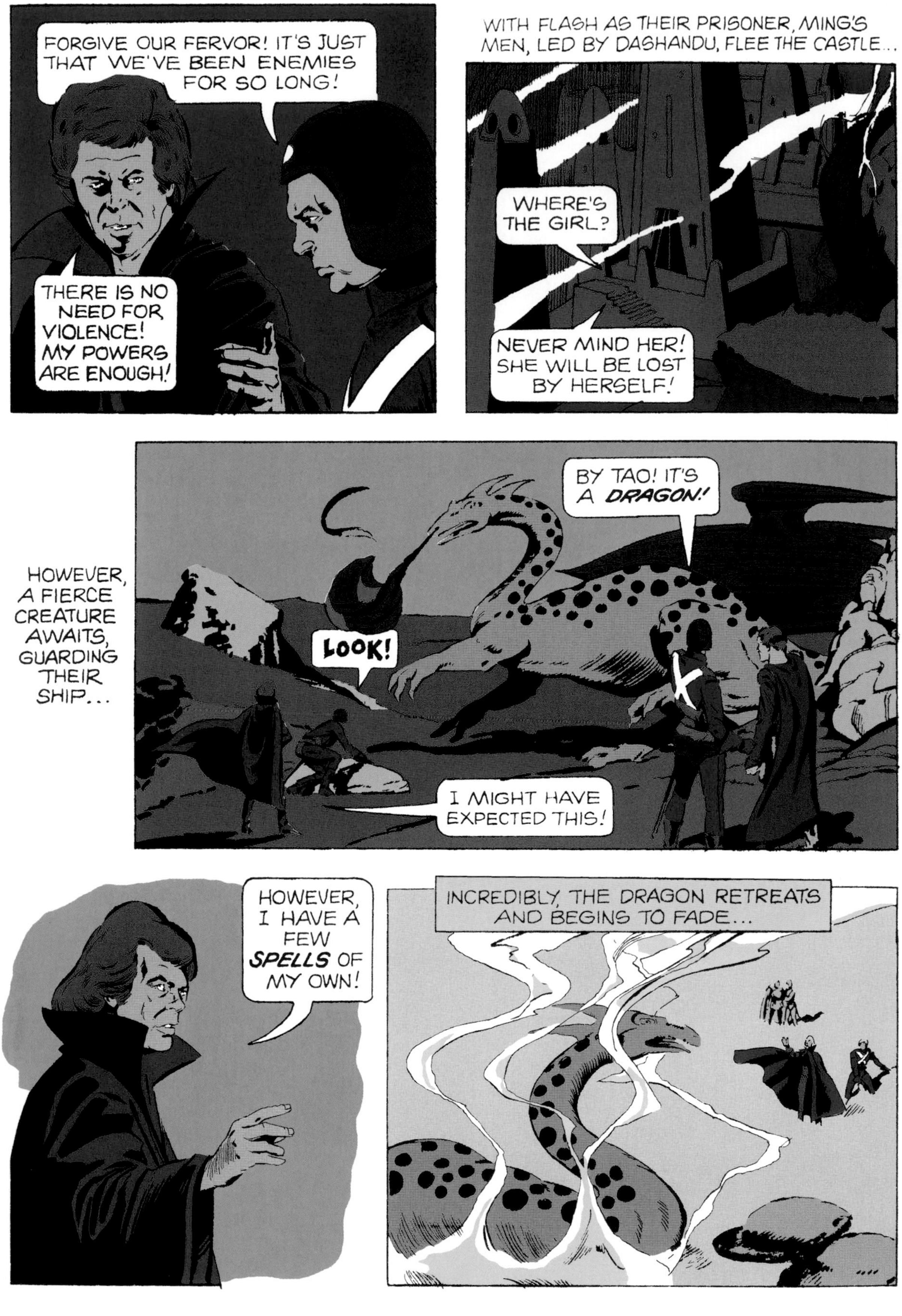
FORGIVE OUR FERVOR! IT'S JUST THAT WE'VE BEEN ENEMIES FOR SO LONG!
THERE IS NO NEED FOR VIOLENCE! MY POWERS ARE ENOUGH!
WITH FLASH AS THEIR PRISONER, MING'S MEN, LED BY DASHANDU, FLEE THE CASTLE...
WHERE'S THE GIRL?
NEVER MIND HER! SHE WILL BE LOST BY HERSELF!
HOWEVER, A FIERCE CREATURE AWAITS, GUARDING THEIR SHIP...
BY TAO! IT'S A DRAGON!
LOOK!
I MIGHT HAVE EXPECTED THIS!
HOWEVER, I HAVE A FEW SPELLS OF MY OWN!
INCREDIBLY, THE DRAGON RETREATS AND BEGINS TO FADE...

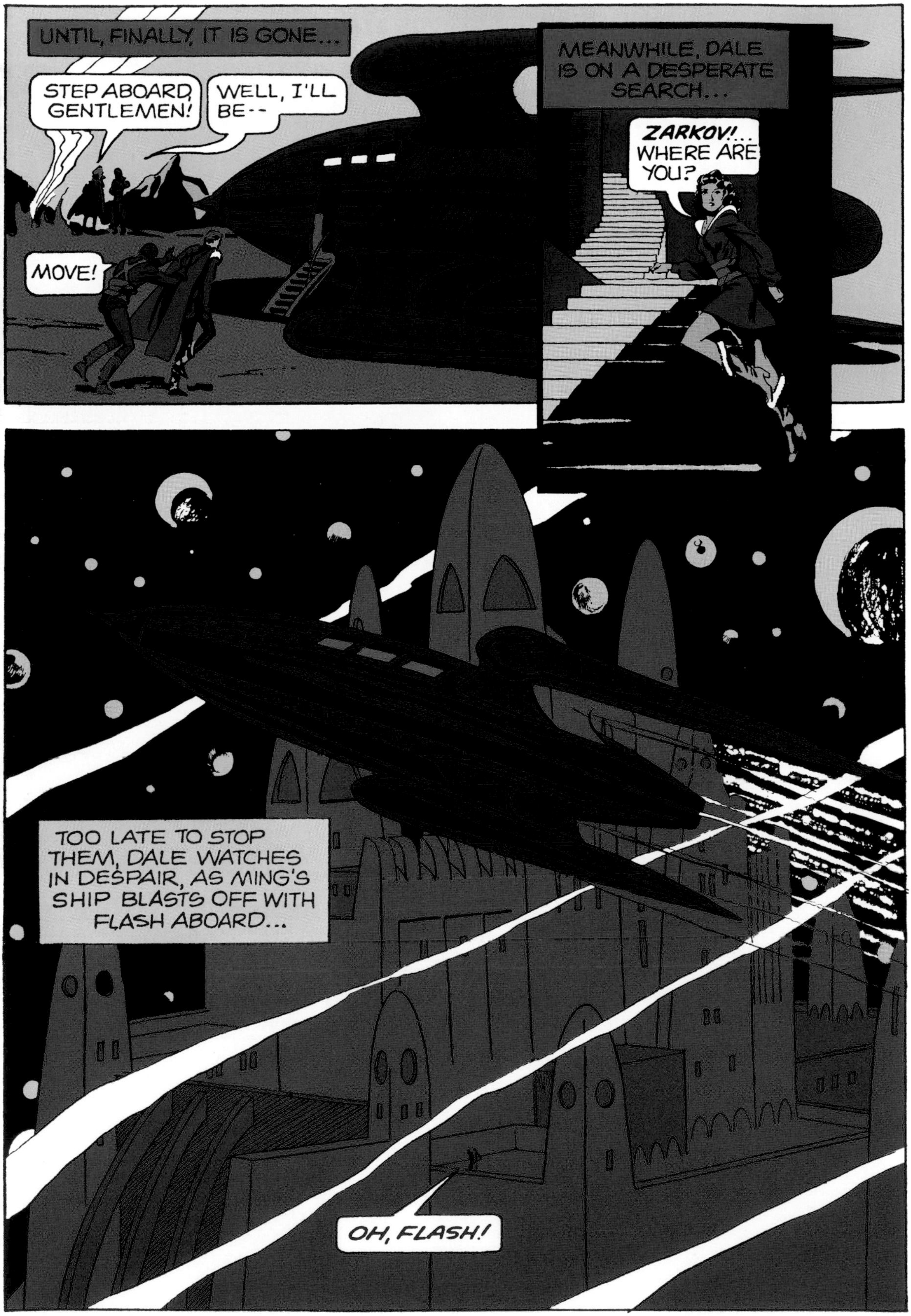
UNTIL, FINALLY, IT IS GONE...
STEP ABOARD, GENTLEMEN!
WELL, I'LL BE--
MOVE!
MEANWHILE, DALE IS ON A DESPERATE SEARCH...
ZARKOV!... WHERE ARE YOU?
TOO LATE TO STOP THEM, DALE WATCHES IN DESPAIR, AS MING'S SHIP BLASTS OFF WITH FLASH ABOARD...
OH, FLASH!

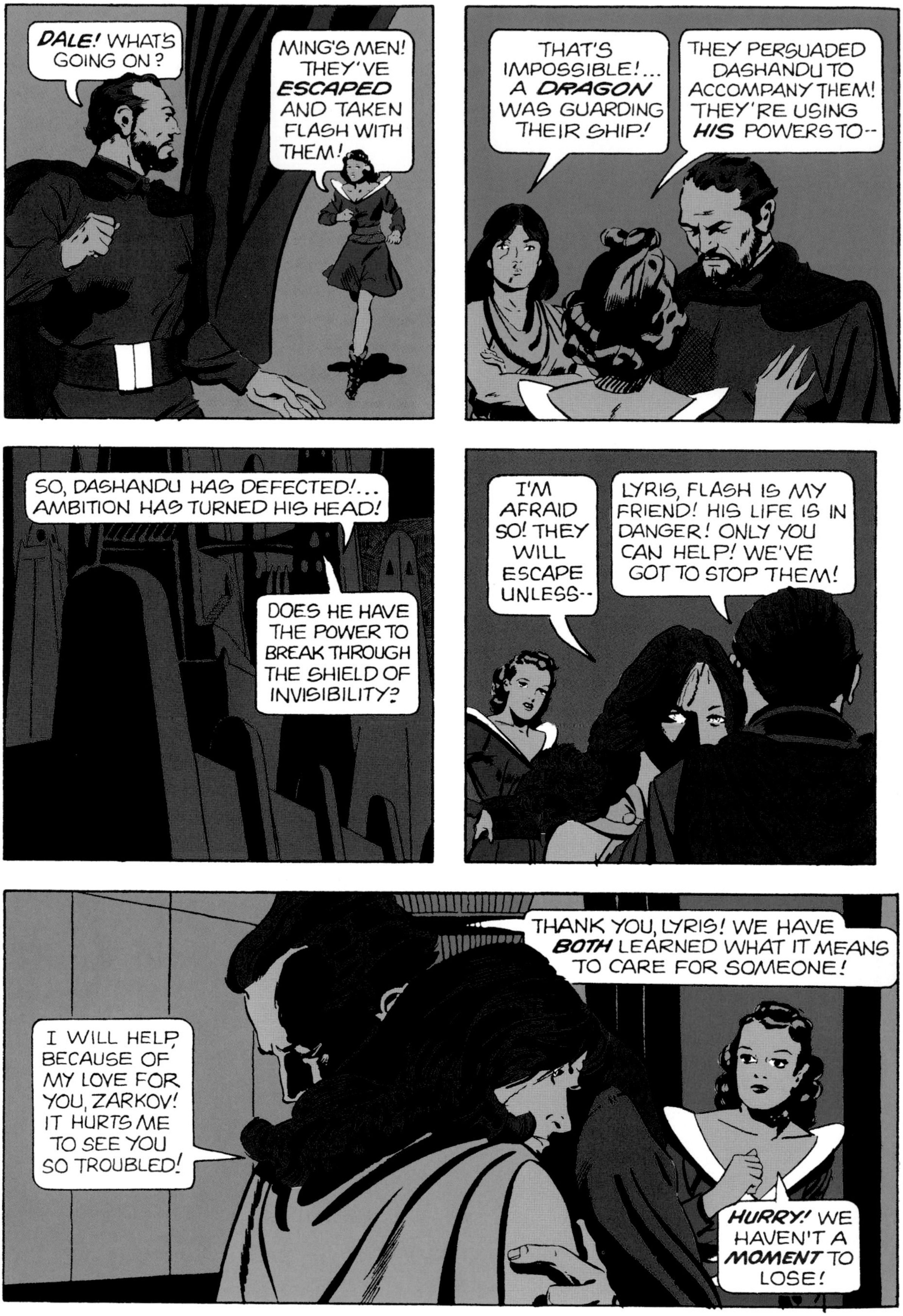
DALE! WHAT'S GOING ON?
MING'S MEN! THEY'VE ESCAPED AND TAKEN FLASH WITH THEM!
THAT'S IMPOSSIBLE!... A DRAGON WAS GUARDING THEIR SHIP!
THEY PERSUADED DASHANDU TO ACCOMPANY THEM! THEY'RE USING HIS POWERS TO--
SO, DASHANDU HAS DEFECTED!... AMBITION HAS TURNED HIS HEAD!
DOES HE HAVE THE POWER TO BREAK THROUGH THE SHIELD OF INVISIBILITY?
I'M AFRAID SO! THEY WILL ESCAPE UNLESS--
LYRIS, FLASH IS MY FRIEND! HIS LIFE IS IN DANGER! ONLY YOU CAN HELP! WE'VE GOT TO STOP THEM!
I WILL HELP, BECAUSE OF MY LOVE FOR YOU, ZARKOV! IT HURTS ME TO SEE YOU SO TROUBLED!
THANK YOU, LYRIS! WE HAVE BOTH LEARNED WHAT IT MEANS TO CARE FOR SOMEONE!
HURRY! WE HAVEN'T A MOMENT TO LOSE!

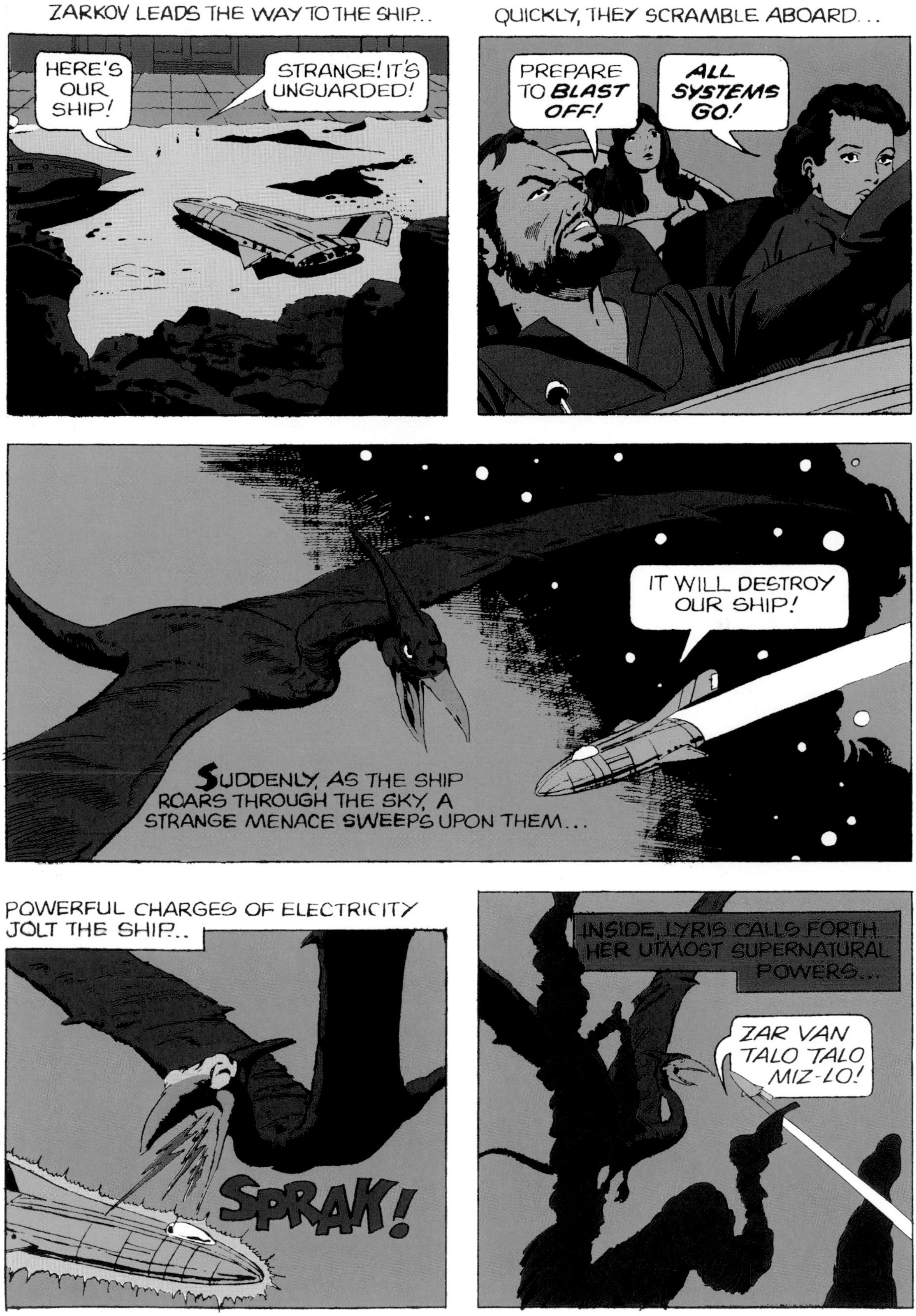
ZARKOV LEADS THE WAY TO THE SHIP. . .
HERE'S OUR SHIP!
STRANGE! IT'S UNGUARDED!
QUICKLY, THEY SCRAMBLE ABOARD. . .
PREPARE TO BLAST OFF!
ALL SYSTEMS GO!
IT WILL DESTROY OUR SHIP!
SUDDENLY, AS THE SHIP ROARS THROUGH THE SKY, A STRANGE MENACE SWEEPS UPON THEM. . .
POWERFUL CHARGES OF ELECTRICITY JOLT THE SHIP. . .
SPRAK!
INSIDE, LYRIS CALLS FORTH HER UTMOST SUPERNATURAL POWERS. . .
ZAR VAN TALO TALO MIZ-LO!

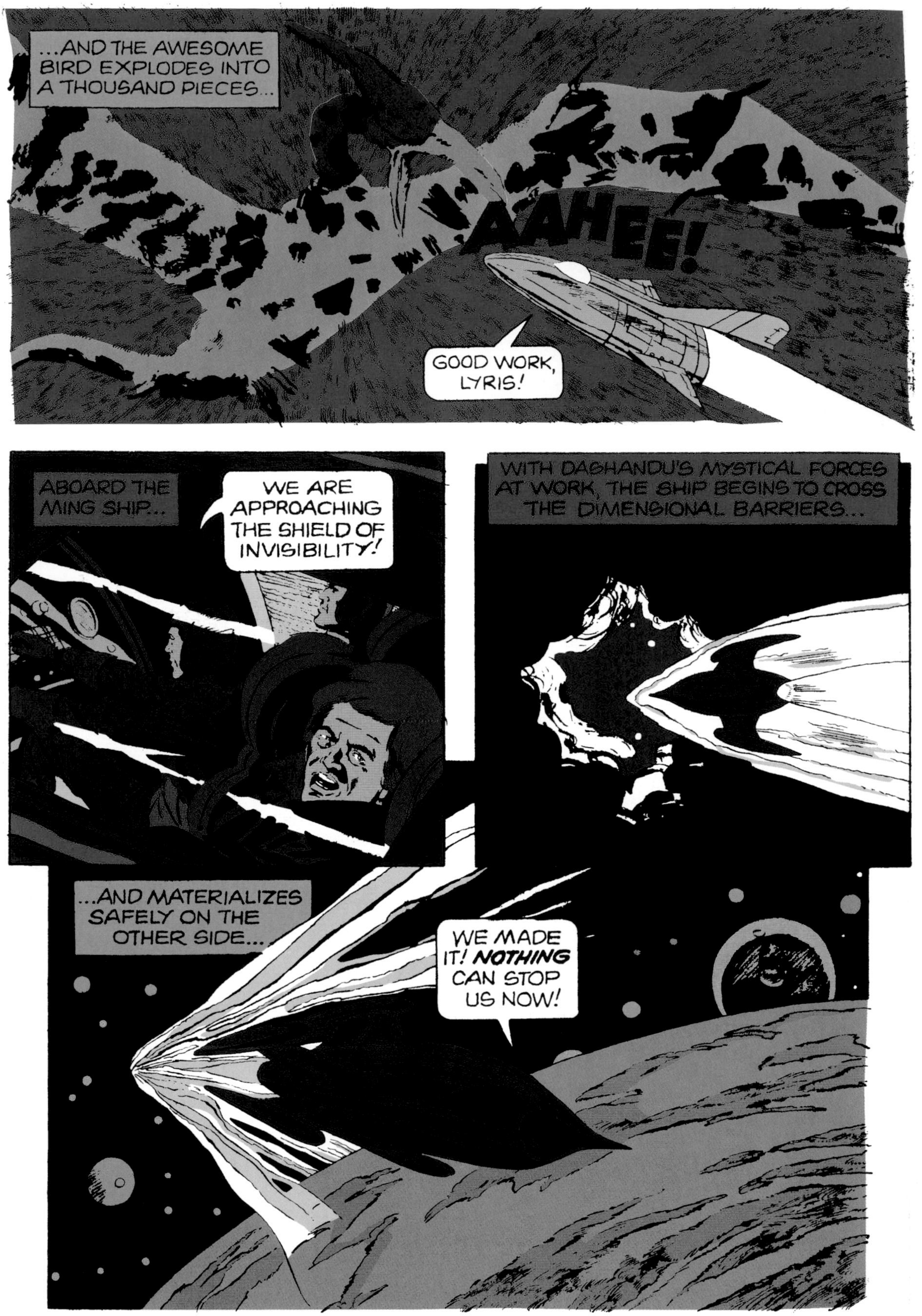
...AND THE AWESOME BIRD EXPLODES INTO A THOUSAND PIECES...
AAHEE!
GOOD WORK, LYRIS!
ABOARD THE MING SHIP...
WE ARE APPROACHING THE SHIELD OF INVISIBILITY!
WITH DAGHANDU'S MYSTICAL FORCES AT WORK, THE SHIP BEGINS TO CROSS THE DIMENSIONAL BARRIERS...
...AND MATERIALIZES SAFELY ON THE OTHER SIDE...
WE MADE IT! NOTHING CAN STOP US NOW!

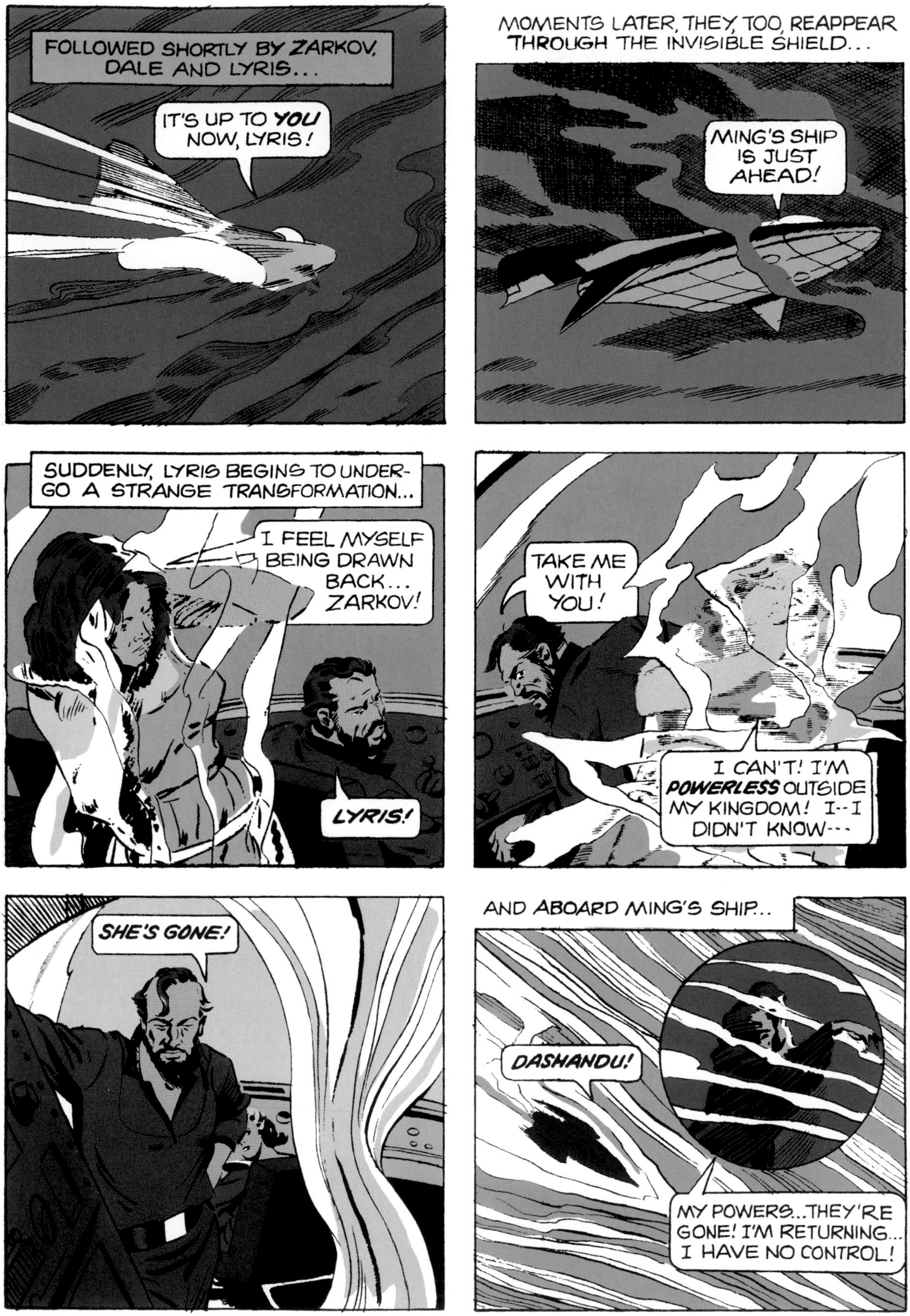
FOLLOWED SHORTLY BY ZARKOV, DALE AND LYRIS...
IT'S UP TO YOU NOW, LYRIS!
MOMENTS LATER, THEY, TOO, REAPPEAR THROUGH THE INVISIBLE SHIELD...
MING'S SHIP IS JUST AHEAD!
SUDDENLY, LYRIS BEGINS TO UNDERGO A STRANGE TRANSFORMATION...
I FEEL MYSELF BEING DRAWN BACK... ZARKOV!
LYRIS!
TAKE ME WITH YOU!
I CAN'T! I'M POWERLESS OUTSIDE MY KINGDOM! I-- I DIDN'T KNOW---
SHE'S GONE!
AND ABOARD MING'S SHIP...
DASHANDU!
MY POWERS...THEY'RE GONE! I'M RETURNING... I HAVE NO CONTROL!

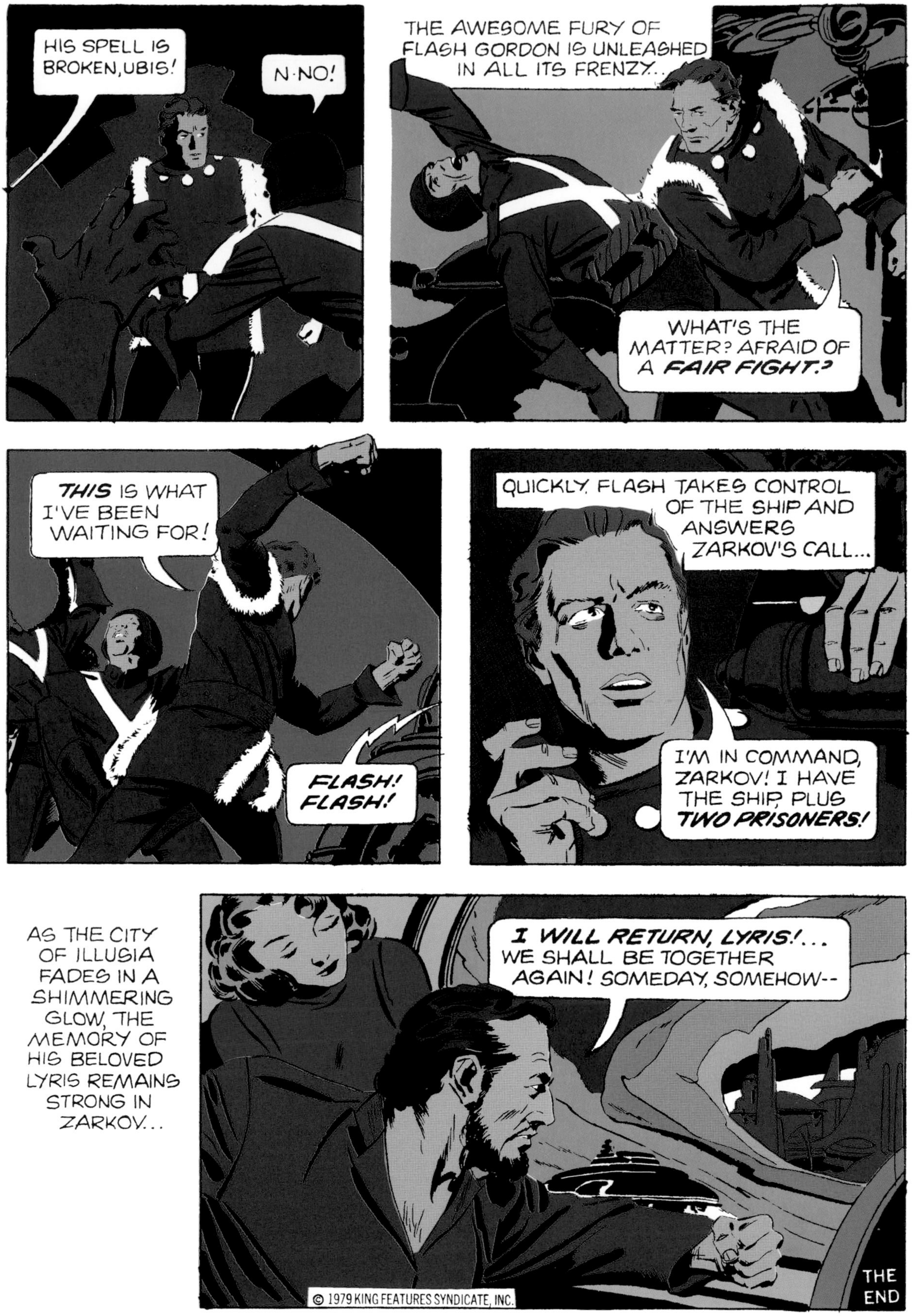
HIS SPELL IS BROKEN, UBIS!
N-NO!
THE AWESOME FURY OF FLASH GORDON IS UNLEASHED IN ALL ITS FRENZY...
WHAT'S THE MATTER? AFRAID OF A FAIR FIGHT?
THIS IS WHAT I'VE BEEN WAITING FOR!
FLASH! FLASH!
QUICKLY, FLASH TAKES CONTROL OF THE SHIP AND ANSWERS ZARKOV'S CALL...
I'M IN COMMAND, ZARKOV! I HAVE THE SHIP, PLUS TWO PRISONERS!
AS THE CITY OF ILLUSIA FADES IN A SHIMMERING GLOW, THE MEMORY OF HIS BELOVED LYRIS REMAINS STRONG IN ZARKOV...
I WILL RETURN, LYRIS!... WE SHALL BE TOGETHER AGAIN! SOMEDAY, SOMEHOW--
© 1979 KING FEATURES SYNDICATE, INC.
THE END

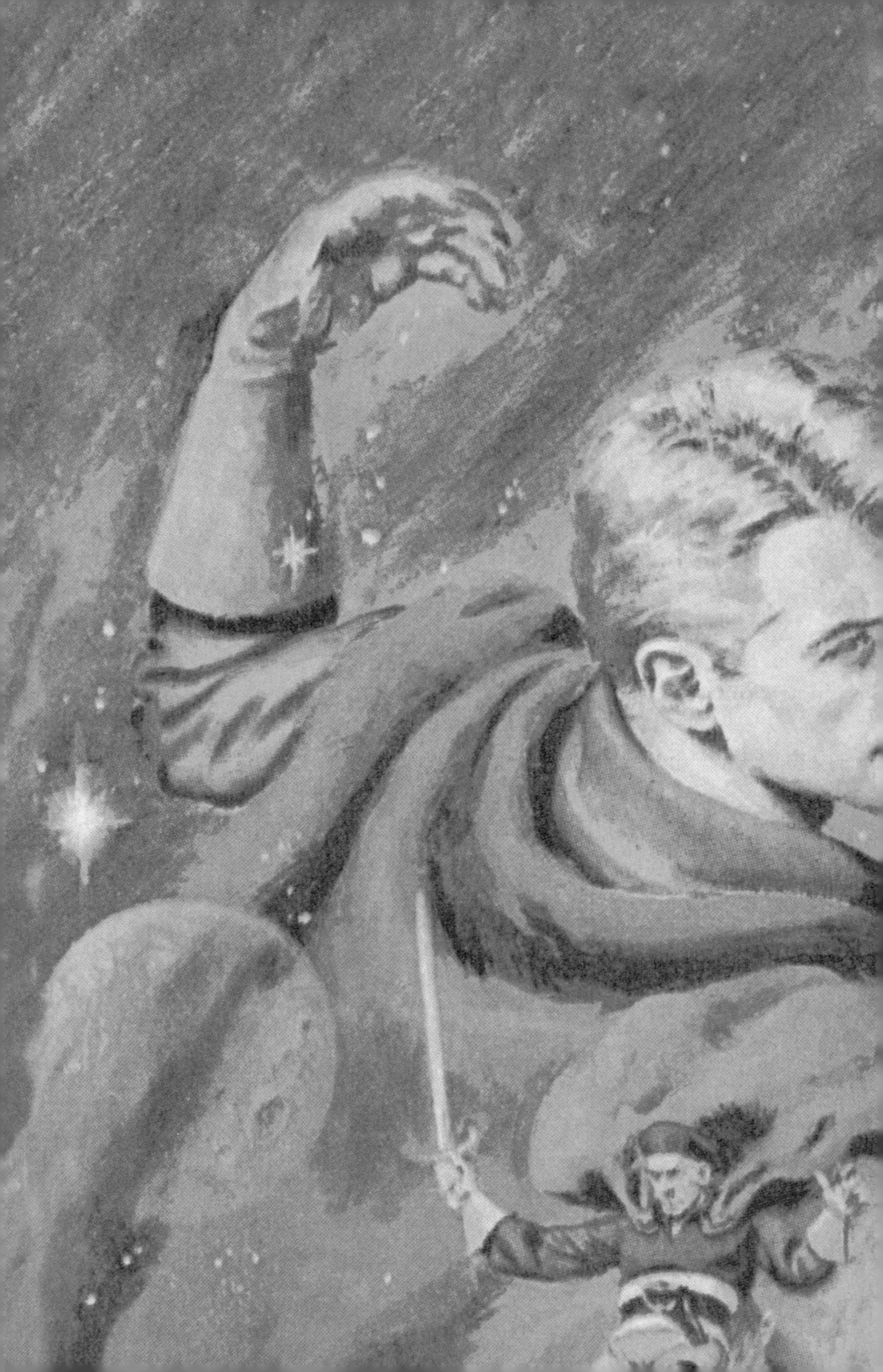